DATE DUE FOR RETURN

25

The Rocks and Sticks of Words

Cross / Cultures

Readings in the Post/Colonial Literatures in English

5

Series Editors:

Gordon	Hena	Geoffrey
Collier	Maes-Jelinek	Davis
(Giessen)	(Liège)	(Aachen)

The Rocks and Sticks of Words

*Style, Discourse and Narrative Structure
in the Fiction of Patrick White*

Gordon Collier

Amsterdam - Atlanta, GA 1992

Typography and layout: the author

CIP-GEGEVENS KONINKLIJKE BIBLIOTHEEK, DEN HAAG

Collier, Gordon

The rocks and sticks of words : style, discourse and
narrative structure in the fiction of Patrick White /
Gordon Collier. — Amsterdam - Atlanta, GA 1992 : Rodopi. -
(Cross/cultures, ISSN 0924-1426 ; 5)
ISBN: 90-5183-393-8
Trefw.: White, Patrick (werken) ; tekstanalyse /
Australische letterkunde.

©Editions Rodopi B.V., Amsterdam - Atlanta, GA 1992
Printed in The Netherlands

TABLE OF CONTENTS

v

vi

vii

LIST OF TABLES

Preface and Acknowledgements

The present work is an abridgement of a doctoral dissertation accepted by the Justus Liebig University, Giessen, in 1984. Wherever possible, I have aimed at reducing technicality of reference and density of exemplification, particularly when the latter was originally linguistic and statistical. In the dissertation, which was essentially my systematized reaction to what I saw as fundamental misreadings of White, I took the opportunity of giving free rein to my disagreement with past criticism; traces of this *via negativa* can still be glimpsed in places.

For the provision of ideal working conditions during the original project, and for his constant support, I should like to express my thanks to Herbert Grabes. An important stage of restructuring benefitted from Richard Humphrey's fine eye for disjunctions in the longer lines of argument, while the stoical patience and astute textual criticisms of my wife, Heather, were indispensable at all times. My gratitude to these—and to other, secret readers (who know who they are and what they have had to put up with).

I am grateful to The Viking Press Inc. (Viking Penguin Inc.) and to Jonathan Cape Ltd. for permission to quote copyright material from Patrick White's works. The following copyrights apply to the extracts from Patrick White's works in the United States, reprinted by permission of the Viking Press (Viking Penguin Inc.): *The Tree of Man*, Copyright 1955; *Voss*, Copyright 1957; *Riders in the Chariot*, Copyright 1961; *The Solid Mandala*, Copyright 1966; *The Twyborn Affair*, Copyright 1979; *Flaws in the Glass*, Copyright 1981.

PREFACE AND ACKNOWLEDGEMENTS

1

IN DEFENCE OF A STYLE

This is a study of the techniques used by Patrick White in building the edifice of one of his novels *(The Solid Mandala)* with "the rocks and sticks of words" (White 1958:158). When White used this metaphor to characterize the completely new form he was struggling to create in his fiction, he meant that his raw material was not only words but also "the rocks and sticks of the burnt-up landscape" of such novels as *Voss* (White 1982:[4]). It is the often resistantly elemental nature of this material, whose *Urform* is retained in the finished artefact, that has fascinated and disturbed his readers. My own fascination with White dates from my dream-time in the 1960s; I was spellbound by him, as I already had been by Faulkner. The vocabulary of the black arts is meant more than half-seriously here. There was something thrillingly uncanny about the reading-experience, some recurrent *frisson* of discovery. The novels *Voss* and *The Tree of Man* left such an indelible impression on me that I knew Australia in the marrow of my bones long before my actual encounter with that continent. In *The Solid Mandala*, White's sleepy suburban hollow of Sarsaparilla resembled, on the surface of it, the innocuous New Zealand town I grew up in, But I wasn't prepared for the intense subterranean pathology of everyday life down Terminus Road. It was less easy to accommodate oneself to the psychical violence residing in what one had thought was familiar, than to similar phenomena as they might occur in a geographically and culturally much more distant fictive landscape, such as Faulkner's Yoknapatawpha County.

There was one thing I luxuriated in whenever I read White: the almost palpable density and enigmatic *ductus* of the language. It was the language, too—the sheer individuality of the "voice"—that enthralled me most in Faulkner, though the experience (of fatalistic, hypnotic, "oral" mediation of the past's intercalations with the present) was not the same as with White. The primacy of this personal response to the texture of language has never entirely disappeared, despite the increasing familiarity of that texture. It was the indrawing power of White's language that granted me access to his main strength, which is his understanding of human psychology. With writers who do not evince this density of language, who do not pull me in on the short, taut tether of a commanding style, I tend even today to feel somewhat short-changed. All this, then, by way of confessing myself to be a biassed witness for the defence.

The defence of whom?—of White. In the early 1970s, the unpleasant realization grew on me that a war—or, rather, a one-sided campaign of tank manoeuvres with blank ammunition—had been in progress all through my years of dreaming delight. The first jolt came when I belatedly came across a brutal and supercilious hatchet-job (1956) on White's *The Tree of Man* by the Australian academic, poet and critic A.D. Hope, who, while praising the author as a "born writer" (and, later, for his "serious depth and impressive creative energy", 1963:15), characterized his prose as "pretentious and illiterate verbal sludge", complaining that his narrative technique was one of "irritating and persistent omniscience". There are slightly more specific criticisms, too—the "devices of poetry" to be found in White's prose look "absurd and pretentious"; the fault of the syntax is that "we have detached phrases masquerading as sentences or even as paragraphs". Himself an accomplished neo-Augustan poet of considerable power, Hope falls victim to an aesthetic fallacy born of his formalist dogmatism: "The novelist needs a plain style, a clear easy stride, a good open texture of language to carry him to the end of his path"; and White evidently had none of this. I saw that I would have to come to terms with the fact that not everybody loved White's style the way I did, or at all. And there was something else I began to notice: critics who mentioned style simply—*mentioned* it. Nowhere could I find any commentary on White's language that allowed me a response—the shock of recognition—commensurate with my own response to the novels. Nor were these mentions of "style" concrete enough to allow a detailed defence of White's style, either. A composite, elusive opponent, I thought, if I were put to the test of defending my faith in White.

This study is in good part a defence of that faith. Even now, years after closing my files with their in-gatherings of other people's comments on White's language, it would still seem a necessary defence and (perhaps unfortunately) not a mopping-up operation. There have been many critics who have issued statements stressing the desirability of investigating White's style but who are evidently reluctant to take any steps in that direction themselves. One of the earliest of such statements was made by McLaren:

we have the gabble about his style and his exploration of the mythopoetical regions of experience, comment which is largely remarkable for its failure to tell us just how his style operates, or what new regions he has defined through it. [McLaren 1963:237]

Or there is John Holloway, who follows up a generalization on White's "close, detailed mastery of style" with the recommendation:

an important article could be written on Patrick White's fiction which discussed nothing on a larger scale than the construction of individual sentences or the handling of dialogue and of the continuing movement of narrative or description. [Holloway 1983:162]

There are, too, critics who regard style as something one absorbs analytically and critically on the way to Higher Things; this would seem to be part of the attitude of Adrian Mitchell, who is oblivious of the fact that there is actually a dearth of useful published comment on White's style:

Nobody would argue with the proposition that White's novels are most immediately arresting for their use of language. Much of the critical work which has been done on White relies on a close, meticulous study of the words; and from that, the most elaborate patterns of significance have been developed. And we feel justified in doing this, we feel we *can* safely take up the exercise of accounting for all the ramifications of his style, because we have confidence in

White's remarkable use of language. The effects are all planned, all deliberate, we feel. [Mitchell 1978:5]

Considerable constraints are placed on a defence, or even elucidation, of a particular author's style. White's style cannot be adequately dealt with on the basis of citing random examples drawn from this or that novel or story. Furthermore, it is impossible to consider White's style except in close connection with specific narrative contexts and with due regard for the function of that style as the load-bearing structure of the narrational method (tone, mood, perspective). In other words, general principles can be established only by examining a large number of instances; individual instances are thereby rendered consistently comprehensible—but will always require a large amount of contextual elucidation if the principle cannot be assumed to be familiar.

There is another, related problem. One of the stumbling-blocks with White is not so much the poetic density of his fiction as the fact that this density is combined with length, breadth or sheer quantity. It has been suggested that White is the Last Outlaw in the mainstream of nineteenth-century fiction: his novels possess "amplitude" in the sense in which we might apply this term to Tolstoy, Dostoevsky or Flaubert. If the poetic in White cannot be considered in isolation from the modes of narrative discourse, nor can the question of breadth (of vision and of fictive action) be completely uncoupled from the question of style. For one thing, the bigness of White's novels makes it difficult to get a proper hand-hold on his style—one reason, perhaps, why critics have so signally failed to present a rounded picture of White's stylistic resources. For another, control of scale involves control of structure: and the concept of structure (the ultimate of form) is indispensable to the study of both style and narrative discourse. What is more, we are left with the unmistakable impression, on reading the critics, that many sense a yawning gap between stylistic originality and conventionality of action (both frequently unpalatable to them), while others respond positively to the epic scale of White's vision yet sceptically towards the means whereby White forms and specifies this epic vision. Among later views, that of John Holloway is representative of the dangers of reductionism. After isolating various "narrative sophistications" in the structure, he suggests that a concentration on the study of "local technique" is unlikely to pay off (1983:148-49). This is reminiscent of Brian Kiernan's argument against analyzing White's "poetic texture":

[White's novels] are "poems" in the sense that they are extremely complex, ambiguous and ironic linguistic constructs. Paradoxically, by attempting to respond fully to the poetic texture by close analysis of it there is the danger that such detailed examination will fail to establish anything that is convincingly true of the whole dramatic context and will come to seem an attempt ... to cut down to a critically manageable size an imagination too rich, subtle and original for conventional critical demands. [Kiernan 1971:103, repeated 1980:138]

True enough in what Kiernan says is the danger of reducing White—but the danger does not reside in the kind of reduction based on "close analysis" of his "linguistic structures". Rather, it is reduction through the bland formulae of certain of White's busier critics that does most to block access to the novelist's true magnitude. Admittedly, numerous investigations of White's "poetic style" (or "imagery") have also helped deflect attention away from the productive functions of his craft and back onto "message" or "theme". "Imagery" is used as fodder for critics of Big Meaning (the "gushers": see White 1982:[4]) to ruminate on, usually without due regard for the connotative complexity of White's "poetry".[1]

The de-emphasizing of "textural" analysis can be dictated by the critic's methodological interests. These, in the case of Holloway, are very much vested in the reductive typological sort of structuralist analysis of narrative performed by Propp and Greimas. Little is gained when Holloway applies to White the generic label of the "life-history" novelist. As soon as one tries to approach White's novels by concentrating on the configuration of external action, one runs the risk of losing sight of what is the true centre of his fiction: the exploratory operation of consciousness upon itself and upon the environment that has helped shape or shatter it. And, immediately, we quit the territory of Thanatos (linear, historical time as demarcated by physical, "life-history" mortality) and enter the territory of Hypnos (the intercalations of non-linear dream-time or memory, as demarcated by the psyche's myth-making power). Fictive representation of this "country of the mind" (Alvarez 1961:653, quoting *Voss*) is quintessentially a matter of process, of detail, of incrementation, of "local technique". A good

---

[1] Heseltine (1963b) devotes most of his discussion of "style" to a patchy listing of "imagery". St. Pierre (1978) takes time-expressions and associated metaphor as representing "the very peculiarity of the style". Cotter (1978:17–18) announces that he intends to "examine White's style as an embodiment of meaning"—"style" as all verbal-expressive means, one would assume—and proceeds to discuss "imagery". He is concerned only with "the presentative aspect of prose", and thinks of "images as linguistic structures which have a metaphoric quality"—thus ignoring connotative and polysemantic phenomena that are not primarily metaphoric, such as ambiguity, certain features of irony, punning, and syntactic structuring. Cotter is more interested in "structural and thematic functions" of imagery than in "style". To this extent, he does not differ in his approach from earlier critics, devoting most of his attention to "central images" as they take on the function of symbol (including character and whole narratives). He is not writing about "style" but about one area of sense-constitution characteristic of White. An essay by George Lyon (1990) starts off with a two-page summary of critical reaction to White's "style" and "effects" before launching into what is essentially an intelligent and rewarding analysis of the *theme* of (written) language in *Voss*. The best writing on White's poetic metaphoricity (Beatson 1976 and 1987, Tacey 1976, Gingell-Beckman 1982, Whaley 1983) gravitates strongly towards pivotal, archetypal symbols and actional analogues. The rest shuttles indifferently between the vague polarities of "imagery"—in its proper sense, a non-transferential phenomenon—and symbolism: Gzell 1964; Phillips 1965; McLaren 1966; Herring 1965:14–18; Mackenzie 1966; Watson 1971; Morley 1972; Schermbrucker 1973; Docker 1973/74; Smith 1975; Mackenzie 1977; Myers 1978 *passim*; Durix 1979; Kiernan 1980:27–28; McCulloch 1983:78–81 and *passim;* Sharrad 1984; Hansson 1984; Tacey 1988. The title of Rodney Edgecombe's book-length study (1989) proclaims that White's "vision and style" will be discussed. Apart from a couple of non-elucidatory mentions of language (such as "fragmentary syntax ... used ... with meaning"), Edgecombe *transfers* the notion of "style" into White's handling of thematic continuities, allegorical relationships and the like. Even more astonishingly, reviewers of Edgecombe's (otherwise spirited and well-directed) study have not even *noticed* this absence of a "normal" understanding of the term "style" (cf, for example, Kim 1989).

number of critics claim that White's plots are classic or conventional, but their structure complex.[2] Others see mainly a vigorous structural design, including intricacy of plot.[3] Yet others are drawn to the temporal configuration of White's fiction, though it has never been the subject of structural analysis.[4] For Zulfikar Ghose (1979:262), only the sheer quality of White's prose allows him to transcend the clichéd old-fashionedness of his subject-matter or plots and structure or "form".

Alongside this dissenting, dualistic view I would place that of John Beston (1982:85–86), who questions the author's authority—specifically, White's own listing of his "three best novels": *The Solid Mandala, The Aunt's Story,* and *The Twyborn Affair* (see *Flaws in the Glass:* 145). Critics have been chary about risking their necks on absolute ratings of White's novels; but when Beston admits, of White's three, only *The Aunt's Story,* he is on safe ground.[5] Beston's own evaluation is based on his moral reaction to the novels' "content" or action; he disqualifies White's own judgement by suggesting that the novelist is myth-making—choosing experimental works with a complex structure (most of the novels being structurally weak and traditionalist). I would defend White's own choice. His three "best" represent his most consistent, daring, and unified essays into the nature of human identity (particularly the quest for psychical and sexual wholeness). I would also suggest that all of White's fiction is bound up with the reconciliation, in fruitful tension, of the experimental and the traditional. It is wellnigh unthinkable, anyway, to find individual manifestations of experimental narrative that do *not* contain within themselves—like traces of a "primitive" form in evolutionarily advanced organisms—elements of some tradition or other. And, finally: I would maintain that White is not "weak at structure" if, by "structure", one understands all verbal means intrinsic to establishing a fictive order appropriate to the novelist's vision. A negative judgement on "structure" is possible only if one ignores the subtle specificity of White's language and reduces the narrative action to an abstract thought-schema, to pure thematics or the static typologizing of character. Few novels would survive such reduction.

Structure in the broader sense aside, the only study so far that has managed to account for the specific nature of White's language, style and narrative method is that of Hilary Heltay (1983). That she has managed to demonstrate the interdependence of these three aspects or elements by investigating *one* linguistic marker only (the articles) is all to her credit. Heltay studies one style-feature as it occurs throughout White's fiction; I propose to study those salient features of

---

[2] Hope 1956; Green 1956; McLaren 1963:241; Rundall 1964; Rosenthal 1970:536; Beer 1976; Berger 1970.

[3] Southron 1940; Donaldson 1962; Beatson 1976; Dutton 1971:28; Kramer 1974:269; Mitchell 1978:13; *TLS* 1973.

[4] For example, Core 1974:8/1977:768 and Lawson 1979:292, who view the structures as being fragmented through the agency of memory. Beatson 1976 discusses time from an archetypal and holistic angle, not in terms of the tectonics of narrative.

[5] It is White's "most perfect", "most experimental", or finest book: Hadgraft 1977, Kiernan 1980:23, Brissenden 1969:15.

style that manifest themselves in one novel by White: *The Solid Mandala*. This novel is used as a test-case for measuring the adequacy of stylistic interpretation as applied to White's other fiction. It is thus not a study of all possible—or even all salient—style-features in White's fiction. *The Solid Mandala* was chosen in full cognizance of the fact that some critics see in it a dilution of that density of language and metaphoricity which they associate with such earlier novels as *Voss* or *Riders in the Chariot*.[6] Among other things, I have endeavoured to show that this is not the case—that the essential features of White's style, discourse and structure can be found in equal plenitude in *The Solid Mandala*. This has afforded an opportunity to find solutions to more general questions of interpretation relating to that novel. I am primarily concerned to study the style and discourse (or discoursal style) of *The Solid Mandala;* to the extent that this has entailed an examination of formal structure, I have also corrected frequent misreadings of actional detail. The present study, however, is not intended to provide a tidy interpretation of the novel in terms of comprehensive thematic categories.

In order to establish not only the objective configurations of style but also its specific conditioning by the exigencies of character-representation, I have occasionally had to take a long run-up to "style" proper. Much attention is devoted to an investigation of "point of view", chiefly in order to cast serious doubt on the existence of "intrusion", auctorial or otherwise, and on conventional conceptions of the "unreliable narrator". This has enabled me to argue for a radical perspectival determination of the stylistic constants—to explain, in effect, why readers should be disturbed by White's prose. As, however, the narrative perspective in White's fiction is psychologically encoded, as it were,[7] rather than being at every point open to local formal analysis, I have been obliged to unmask mood and perspective by an analysis of narrative structure.[8] In the remainder of this introduction (here, and ch. 2), I present a survey of reactions to White's style. In the light of such evidence, it should gradually become clear to the reader

---

[6] The one critic I have found who wholeheartedly endorses *The Solid Mandala* does so on almost non-aesthetic grounds: David Tacey (1988:121) finds the book "the most significant of all White's novels" for its presentation of a "central myth", its "new style of psychological existence", and its sensitive depiction of "an individuation crisis". Cf also Seymour-Smith 1990: *The Solid Mandala* is "to my own mind his most finished and powerful work".

[7] White-criticism seldom adverts to this fact. In the earlier novels, it has been noted, "the syntax is ... an instrument for grappling with particular states of consciousness" (Heseltine 1963a); the style is the "direct transcription", often "wilfully subjective", of psychic energy (Mather 1963:93/101) or provides "access to the whole of a character's mind" (*TLS* 1962); White shows stylistic subtlety in rendering "moments of self-awareness" (Wilson 1976:281; cf also *TLS* 1941, Kiernan 1974:81–82). But, along with the lip-service paid to stream-of-consciousness techniques and to the "psychological novel" (A.D. Hope standing almost alone in the latter generic classification), such comments remain undeveloped and unspecified.

[8] *The Solid Mandala* deserves exemplary status in contemporary narrative theory, by virtue of its mode of "twice-telling". Narrative theorists have not, however, submitted the novel to any degree of analysis in order to determine its narrative complexities. The original stimulus for Rimmon-Kenan's passing note on *The Solid Mandala* (1983:120) was most probably Manfred Mackenzie's spirited study of the novel (1969).

progressing through this study that not all the style-features which critics have isolated as being "characteristic" of White can be found in *The Solid Mandala*. This should give pause for thought. It is, it would seem, a *prima facie* argument in favour of a highly restricted list of central features which might be regarded as evidence for a "mind-style" or an "authorial" style that is at the same time an expression of the mental universe or dynamics of the human actors in White's fictions. It would also suggest the desirability of compiling a more general list of peripheral features which are not constants of White's style but which fulfill expressive or significational purposes within specific novels.[9]

The original documentary basis of this study (apart from the works of White) was a selection, after scrutiny of over 400 reviews, essays and books, of some 200 items which revealed in one way or another some attitude towards White's style, language or narrative technique (it goes without saying that the material discarded made no reference at all to these matters). Some 30% of the items analyzed have no more than one or two sentences on "style"; about one-sixth of these touch on nothing but narrative perspective, structure, and "influences"— matters which are not specific to style in the usual senses, or which are not explicitly related to style by the critics concerned.

Many of the critical comments already cited clearly indicate that positive views on White's use of language are not lacking. Indeed, specifically with reference to his language, he has been termed a stylist of the first rank, a great novelist, "potentially greater than any other living novelist", "the most distinguished writer of English prose still working in a traditional mode", "one of the five novelists at present ... truly possessed of greatness" (and, from the same critic after White won the Nobel Prize: "the one novelist at present ... indisputably possessed of genius").[10] Evaluations can range from how exciting or delightful the style is to "psychological" characterizations: it is "edgy", or reveals a "tense, pervading watchfulness".[11] The style is "simple and effective" or even unostentatiously "gossamer thin", "sensitive but unrhetorical", showing "clarity", "lucidity", or "hard, analytical precision"; it is "dry, formal", or even

---

[9] Chapter 13 below includes a control-study of critical interpretations of passages from other novels by White, including a comparative stylistic analysis of *The Twyborn Affair*. The critical misreadings I discuss there can all be clarified by recourse to the stylistic paradigms established for *The Solid Mandala;* and analysis of the later novel also confirms these paradigms. I have explained both the central stylistic and discoursal features and the central critical misunderstandings of *The Solid Mandala* as being traceable to White's thoroughgoing "psychologizing" of the narrative and the narration. This corrective was felt to be necessary. Carolyn Bliss (1986:102/219–20) is the first to confirm my view of the presence of "indirect discourse". But her treatment of this feature in isolation from the remaining stylistic and narrative features is as alien to my approach as is her tendency to try and clarify White by making loose technical analogies with modernist writers. I would also maintain that "indirect discourse" is a far more pervasive technique in all of White's fiction than even Bliss can bring herself to credit.

[10] Blamires 1980:85; Thomson 1966:21; Mather 1963:101; Pilling 1978:89; King 1966/1973.

[11] *TLS* 1945, Basso 1948 or Osborne 1963:85; Hope 1964 and Hughes 1964:230.

"gnomic".[12] The language or style is rich, revealing great awareness of texture and detail;[13] it is disciplined, carefully deliberate, highly conscious, showing "a massive steady grasp", a virtuoso command, or total consonance with subject matter.[14] The conclusions that are drawn from such judgements can take one of a fairly restricted number of directions. White has been commended for being stylistically a risk-taker.[15] It is, however, more common for his prose to be classified as difficult and uncompromising. An anonymous reviewer of *The Aunt's Story* notes that "an effort of concentration is needed to get through" the novel (*TLS* 1948)—indeed, White himself remarked that borrowers of the book from the Mitchell Library seemed never to have read beyond the first quarter or so. The reviewers of the 1950s, especially, were unwilling to brook any challenge to conventional reading-habits: White's style is a "prose obstacle course".[16] Later critics often echo each other in stressing how the style "makes great demands on the reader",[17] sometimes suggesting that the active concentration exacted is somewhat unfair or even inhibits responsiveness.[18] That critics of White have had to struggle against their own conditioning to easy reading—no matter how liberal their professed evaluative stance—is revealed in reactions to *The Vivisector*, which was generally greeted with a sigh of relief as being "easier to read" than its predecessors.[19] That McLeod (1974:444) can judge the experiments with language in the same novel as being far more adventurous "than White had dared beforehand" would, however, suggest that there is room left for a discriminating analysis of White's prose-style, if opinions on simplicity and complexity, ease and difficulty, can differ so greatly.

The strain placed on the reader by White's style is sometimes traced to a profound distrust of, or dissatisfaction with, the very medium of verbal language (a view endorsed by White himself).[20] Or it is explained as the effect of having to deal with the dense poeticity of his prose. This notion of the poetic need not detain us long—it is undeniably central. White's view is clear enough: "The realistic novel is remote from art. A novel should heighten life ... it shouldn't set out what you know already" (White 1969:219). This applies, of course, to both "vision" and expression; in the words of McAuley (1958:5), "the very things that

---

[12] Southron 1940, Aurousseau 1962; Cooperman 1955; Donaldson 1962; *TLS* 1973; Rosenthal 1970:538; Scrutton 1956; Lawson 1979:292.

[13] Osborne 1963:85, Core 1974:15; Ross 1977:324, Kiernan 1980:17, Holloway 1983:147.

[14] Rundall 1964, McLaren 1963:238–39, Hough 1958:87 (but only of the "style" of the dialogue) and Mitchell 1962, Hughes 1964:230, *TLS* 1961, Binns 1961, or Boatwright 1955 and Colmer 1978b:136.

[15] Avant 1975 or Bail 1977:188.

[16] Campbell 1958; see also Stewart 1956:2, *New Yorker* 1957:158.

[17] Pringle 1961:68; Bergonzi 1961; Core 1977:771 and De Mott 1980:3; similarly Walsh 1976:8 and 1977:52, Lodge 1981, Johnson 1981:168; cf Salomon 1941.

[18] McAuley 1965:35, *TLS* 1966, Crowcroft 1974:50–51, Green 1974:309.

[19] McLaren 1970:38, Wall 1970, Herring 1971:3 (an untypically disappointed response, in being on the side of complexity), or Dutton 1971:39.

[20] Core 1974:15, for example, or Brissenden 1974:314; cf White 1973 *passim*.

White undertakes with such distinction are the things which have been the normal business of poetry". Some few commentators over-respectful of generic boundaries are hotly opposed to, or mutedly sceptical of, White's claim-jumping in this regard.[21] Amid a wealth of essentially positive responses to the poetic, and many instances where the notion of the "poetic" is a throwaway term that is submitted to no further examination in respect of textual detail, one feature persistently associated with the poeticity of White's prose is the almost hypnotic or "hallucinated" pull which results from the act of reading: an affective or reader-response "theory", as it were, designed to account subjectively for some quality in the writing which the critic has not managed to objectify.[22] The hypnotic appears to be restricted to characterizations of the mature style, rather than of the earlier novels with their (it is claimed) wholesale allegiance to a conventionally avant-garde, high-modernist mode of discourse.

The more ineffable critical responses to what is taken to be the poetically ineffable[23] shade off into a mixed bag of complaints, to the effect that White overwrites, is inflated and pretentious (or, at least, his prose is), and that his writing is portentous.[24] This view took quite some time to emerge, and is often inseparable from assertions that the prose is obscure, oblique or even mystical (the last two epithets being weighted negatively by some, neutrally or positively

---

[21] Particularly Hope 1956 and 1963:13, and Green 1974:309. There is considerable uneasiness to be sensed in the statements of even those critics who would profess to approach the more specific matter of White's poetic "imagery" in an impartial fashion: see, for example, Herring 1965:20 or Core 1974:11 and 1977:770. If Core writes unfavourably of "tangled" or "dense" metaphors and "overripe images", William Walsh's own metaphor for White's metaphoricity ("choking thickets of metaphors" or "choking thickets of imagery", 1976;8/30) betrays a fundamental lack of empathy with White's modality.

[22] Hughes 1964:230; McAuley 1965:35; *TLS* 1970 ("the awed numbness induced by a relentless black-jacking from the author's prose"); Kramer 1976:62 ("White's attentive deliberation induces a curious sense of lethargy"); Nye 1979; Ramsey 1980:93.

[23] Boatwright 1955; Burns 1975:179; Herd 1977:4; Driesen 1978:84; Colmer 1978c:5; Scheick 1979:141/144–45; Schermbrucker 1973 *passim*. This tendency has affinities with the frequent recourse of White's exegetes, whenever they encounter difficulty, to the claim that the author is struggling to speak the unsayable (see, for example, Deal 1957, McCulloch 1983:5 and *passim)*—a good ploy, this, as the theme of the unsayable is topicalized clearly and persistently in the thought and action of the novels.

[24] The accusation of over-writing or inflation: Hope 1956 and 1963:13; *Times* 1957; Buckley 1958:192–94 and 1964:422; Wilson 1961; *Times* 1964; Symons 1970; Coe 1970:527; Kiernan 1971:112; Bailey 1973; Core 1974:11; Kramer 1974:280; Steiner 1974:111–12; Edgar 1977:69; Walsh 1977:23; Colmer 1978a:73–75, 1978c:19–20 and 1982:194; Ross 1981:167. Striving for effect: *TLS* 1941; Mather 1963:96–97. Excess of significance: Brady 1977:139. Pretentiousness: *TLS* 1957; Buckley 1958:192–94 and 1964:421; Yaffe 1958; Martin 1959:55–56; Bergonzi 1961; Argyle 1967:13–14; Green 1974:309; McFarlane 1977:32; Heseltine 1982:107. Portentousness: Fuller 1961; McLaren 1963:239; Walters 1963:50; Tanner 1966:112; Kramer 1973:18 and 1976:62–63; Ratcliffe 1973; McFarlane 1977:33; Walsh 1977:62. What others see as portentousness—layers of meaning beneath the surface—Harries (1978:464–65) views as something positive, while Hilary Corke (1957) punningly thinks the language of *Voss* is "perhaps ... overwrought", with "the inverted significance of understatement".

by others).[25] Once again, criticism seldom goes beyond general opinion, unattached to specific instances. Where particular examples are referred to, it is fairly easy to show how inadequately the context has been construed. The critic's reading may have been impatient, closed to any dimension of signification beyond what can be adduced from a "simple", concrete actional surface and a narrational urge to abstraction. These two poles are never in isolation from each other in White; and both between them and *within* them is a dimension of protean nuances, created by the constant pressure on syntax, lexis and figuration from the novelist's fascination with psychological states and transitions. The result is not always obliquity or elusiveness—no more so, that is, than in a poem, where the accepted task of the reader is to resolve the the elusive into the richness of choices that are ultimately perceived for what they are: a sign system whose complexity of mediation serves epistemological exactitude.

There is more than a faint possibility that the talk about White's solipsistic, inflated mysticism is a species of displacement activity: a refusal to entertain the mythopoeic significance and authenticity of narrative action is subverted into a refusal to validate the process of signification itself. A fundamental withholding of acceptance from complex representations of characters' psychical involvement in the world can result in imputations of "allegory" to White's novels[26]—the allegory is imposed on the text by the critic, so that it can then be faulted. Or the novels are criticized for gesturing at meaning: "the vision splendid itself cannot be conveyed, only something of the rapt attention of the moment of heightened vision" (Mitchell 1978:12). This, were it the case, would be something a reader had to accept, as there is nothing morally, psychologically, or aesthetically indefensible about it. The fact is, that the "vision" is always *beyond* in White; all we get is a character's limited, all-too-human perspective on it—and the language is always scrupulously precise in conveying degrees of accessible vision. Even more extreme is Mitchell's thesis about White's "mysticism of words" (a radicalizing of Buckley's "mysticism of objects"): "White as well as his characters insists that you can understand what the words are about without understanding the words themselves" (1978:13). But the relationship between "word" and "object" is as problematical as the absence of any demonstration by Mitchell that (or *how*) "understanding" capitulates before the text; and what are the hermeneutic steps involved in determining this expressive inexpressibility? From another angle: a sense that there is a meaning (or a further meaning) beneath the "surface"—perhaps, concomitantly, that this meaning is about to be revealed (Harries 1978:464)—may as in poetry best be resolved by playing the reading-game according to the rules established by the prose texture itself.

---

[25] Obscurity: Prescott 1957; Mather 1963; Daniel 1964; *TLS* 1966; McFarlane 1977:32; Myers 1978:103. Mysticism associated positively by Americans with the bigness of Australia: Cooperman 1955, Balliett 1961:244; as something negative: Buckley 1964; Bailey 1973; Mitchell 1978:13; Sharrad 1984:212; mysticism interpreted positively: Crowcroft 1974:50.

[26] For example: Buckley 1964:424; Kiernan 1980:56; Kramer 1974; Edgecombe 1989.

2

THE CASE AGAINST WHITE

In the following, I want to consider in more detail and under thematic headings those particular areas of critical response to White which are most pertinent to the concerns of the present investigation: White's "mannerism"; his narrative technique (which is *extricably* linked with questions of style); and more specific comments, of a "linguistic" nature, on his style—as an outcome of which I draw up a basic working-list of style-features, before setting out, in conclusion, my views on the place of "style" in artistic expression.

I   Mannered prose

For most critics of White, the apparently "mannered" quality of his "poetic" style is a central, irritating feature. The notion of a "mannered" style first appears in the form of a negatively loaded substantive with an ostensibly broader and vaguer reference: as their epigone, White has "accepted both lessons and mannerisms" from his modernist masters (*Times* 1939), imposing an "always artificial" pattern (Muir 1939). The notion of "mannered" prose may be linked with the insinuation of "calculated" emotions to reinforce the notion that the former are inauthentic (*Times* 1957). A.D. Hope (1963:13/15) associates the "mannerisms of the poetic style" with selfconsciousness and heaviness of touch (the latter, however, is alien to any historically correct understanding of mannerist style). A reviewer may attempt to explain the "mannered" quality in terms of poeticity and the subjectivizing of objective detail (*Times* 1958), or uncomprehended syntactic devices may be labelled "the now familiar verbal mannerisms" (*Times* 1964). It is probably the same reviewer who, drawing attention to White's "elliptical" syntactic practice, opines that these "characteristic devices seem to recur because they have become a mannerism rather than because they have a specific function" (*TLS* 1964). A few years further on, the generalizing approach of the earliest reviewers can still be found: "It is characteristic of White to have no style, but rather a manner—an inflated manner" (*TLS* 1970).

"Mannerisms" seem to be construed as non-functional (ie, meaningless) tricks or devices, or as pervasive features of language which the reviewer has not managed to understand. This view amounts to a refusal to accept that such features might well impute intention: ie, meaningful function, a relationship of communicative decorum with the action. Such criticisms deny White a use of language which is genuinely characteristic of him ("style" should imply the latter). Other judgements on "manner" in its narrower sense are attached to a variety of Whitean phenomena. In drawing attention to "tricks of style", Alvarez (1961:653/56) clearly suggests something about White's writing that is imitable, as mannerisms (almost by definition) are. For Kiernan (1976:464), the "mannered modernist" mode in White is acceptably, if recognizably, derivative; in general, White is noted for "a characteristic idiom developed through stylistic mannerisms" (Kiernan 1971:96). Such a statement is, at best, unobtrusively tautologous.

One cluster of views related to "mannered" style has as its nexus the idea of parody. This takes numerous forms, one of which is reflected in competitions to "imitate the mannered idiom" of White (Harris 1971). Sidney J. Baker, one of the most acute documentarists of the Australian language, employs his own parody of *Voss* to expose the form/content dualism of White's most virulent critic, A.D. Hope, encoding the latter's thought rather than White's. What other, less wise parodists have imitated, however, is arguably inseparable from White's highly specific intentions regarding the nuanced representation of reality, theme, the mental processes of characters, or whatever. In which case, parody must fail (as it by and large does) if White's "idiom" is regarded as something so "mannered" that it can be crowbarred off the page and redisposed in unserious contexts. Parodies of White reflect populist-realist rejection of the novelist (cf Turner 1958:74), a mood which was widespread in Australia until the Nobel Prize award and which, subsiding into an intermittent twitch of resentment, has prevailed since. Indeed, the uncompromising nature of White's prose can tip it over into badness, argues Rosemary Dinnage (1980:25), and "he concentrates his style to the point of self-parody". We have moved here from White's style as the victim of parodists to White's style as its own victim. A third, acceptable view— "mannerism" as the conscious reappropriation of existing literary models—is tendered by Johnson (1978:97), who mentions "the elaborate narrative texture of his writing, with its parodies of styles and other modes of imaginative literature". But this non-extrinsic, historically accurate view of "manner" is rare in criticism of White.

When readers feel hit over the head by White's language, they tend to call it "a surprisingly mannered style", "a stylistic deliberateness" that is "mannerist if not precious", a "mannered style" that produces an "unreal and strained" effect, a "strangulated" or "peculiar" prose of "mannered inversions" that obtrudes between the reader and the story, or, more enthusiastically, a style which "daringly calls attention to itself".[1] William Schermbrucker (1973:18) percipiently notes the peculiar mode of vision—White, Lawrence and Faulkner present the reader "with a barrier of strangely mannered prose which draws attention first and foremost to a particular, idiosyncratic way of envisioning reality". But it is harmful to the coherence of Schermbrucker's argument that he should cleave as close as he does to categories of reader-response which attempt to give a positive valency to terms customarily weighed negatively by critics of

---

[1] Wyndham 1957; Brissenden 1969:21/25; Colmer 1978c:35 and *TLS* 1956; Duchêne 1966; Avant 1975; Beatson 1991:228 ("superbly mannered prose").

White. "Barrier" and "strangely" overstate the case for the initial inaccessibility of White's narratives and for the unsophistication or stolid conventionality of his worst readers. We might, however, tolerate the term "mannered" here as an imprecise token for the *neutral* notion (within the poetological system of Shklovsky, Jakobson et al.) of language which "draws attention" to *itself*. This aside, Adrian Mitchell (1981:151/53) would appear to sum up, in his comment on White's fiction in the 1970s, several of the hermeneutic assumptions mentioned above:

The word-consciousness is still a dominant feature [in *Voss*], the dialogue *stylized* and the narrative *deliberately* literary. His fiction continues to *call attention to itself* as a richly textured *construct*, to *insist on itself as self-conscious art, patterned* meaning .... *Voss* is the most *florid* of White's novels, and perhaps the most triumphant because of the *rhetorical excess*.[2] [my emphases]

The problem remains: what does Mitchell (or Graham Hough 1958:87) mean by dialogue that is "stylized"? Paul Sharrad (1984:209/11), who explains White's and Randolph Stow's "stylized prose" as a "conscious revolt against ... drab fifties realism", betrays his aesthetic ideology in his critical idiom: "consciously crafted prose that *made use of* ... imagery", "images ... *used as* emblems". This conscious *utilization* of superadded, "stylized" or "mannered" prose is inseparable from the notion of "excess". For Levin (1979), the prose is "jungle-lush"; for Scheick (1979: 144), "White's language is palpably present to the reader as it tends towards ponderousness frequently on the verge of excess". Whereas Scheick is fundamentally sympathetic towards White, almost glimpsing how the underlying "grace" of White's language resides in the controlling function of the syntax, Mitchell (1978:7-13 *passim*), is negatively disposed. The complexity of White's novels, he maintains, does not derive from the characters' discovery of self, but is "more an effect of language than anything else"; the language is "a kind of brilliant and engaging crust", a "mysticism of words", the structure "artificial". "White rather wastefully if splendidly heaps up enormous sets of details that ultimately don't signify .... The complexity is superadded". This is a devastating denial of the essence of White's artistic vision, a sophisticated and radical version of a dualistic (and ultimately utilitarian) aesthetic, with a divorcing of form from content. Mitchell is typical in treating as an ultimately discardable superficies what should arguably be taken as the *essentia* of White's fiction.

---

[2] Mitchell sees this style as being "in keeping with ... the overweening ambition" of Voss. Margaret Walters (1963:44-46), by contrast, does not see the "awkward and mannered poetry-in-prose" and the "hesitating structures" as "confined to the Laura-Voss relationship". Most of those critical of the language specific to *Voss* have not perceived its historicizing valency—Oliver (1958:49), Brissenden (1959:411) or Shrubb (1968:11) on supposed "lapses in style" or grammar, for example; Green (1974: 309), complaining about White's "relentlessly Germanic" narrative method; or Heltay (1983:15) and Stein (1983:87-88), who generalize from the presence of style-markers peculiar to *Voss*. This ignoring of the stylistic exigencies of individual narratives is to be found elsewhere as well (as when Harries laments the—designedly—"Victorian" writing of *A Fringe of Leaves;* 1978:467).

Several critics who are favourably disposed towards White exhibit a high degree of false consciousness or, more simply, aesthetic naivety in this regard. They fail to see that their praises are damning for any reader who seeks in style the communicative particularity of a given narrative. Harries (1978:470) can respond positively to "the embellishments of style" in White's novels. William Walsh, too, is a dualist, for whom style is baroque superaddition, despite his praise for White.[3] White's mature fictions have for him their "mannered phases" (Walsh 1977:3); for Christopher Ricks (1962, and 1974:20), White is a "dealer in words"—his best writing is "mannered" and self-conscious (though Ricks seems unaware that what he takes to be the less-good passages in White also evince, by the critic's own implicit definition, these same features). For other critics, White's style suits the matter of his fiction. "It is unnecessary", writes Colin Roderick (1962:76), "to multiply instances of the rightness of his style for the form and idea" of *Riders in the Chariot*. But Roderick offers *no* instances or analysis; nothing he says makes this novel any different in terms of "style" from the others, or demonstrates the style's specific tailoring to this one novel. Apart from which —and centrally—Roderick approves of White's style *because* it is "embellished with quaint ornaments of the author's predilection" (74). Roderick is a dualist: he uses the term "style", conceives of it essentially as decoration, and is really talking about thought or, at best, structure. Vincent Buckley, like Mitchell, regards "the famous style" as an excrescence; the more complex White's "material", "the more decorative" the prose (1958:193). Ricks sees White's "disparagement" of his characters as leading to arch mannerism; similarly, Buckley traces White's "prose mannerisms"—here, metaphoric conceits, supercilious authorial commentary—to a lack of authorial compassion (1964:421). But these things are "by themselves, ... no more than mannerisms, strains of the surface", as though they were mere mosquito-bites, quite irrelevant to the reader's understanding of the novel as a total body of meaning. Elsewhere in the same essay, however, Buckley sees what has "so often been taken for mere mannerism" to be "actually an inordinate (and perhaps defensive) insistence on *textures*" (1964:417)—once again, the emphasis is on excess and self-consciousness.

---

[3] White loves "the pure creative play or flourish, on occasion gravely to the detriment of his design" (Walsh 1976:21); he is "seldom able to keep within the limit of what is strictly necessary to his design. He loves the pure creative play or flourish"; White's bending of syntax "can seem clumsy and fabricated"—or "mannered"?; at other times, "when imaginatively controlled, it becomes an individual and functional skill which adds greatly to the armoury of the novelist" (Walsh 1977:43/128). There is no escaping the contradiction here between the "functional" or intrinsic character of language in respect of meaning, and a "skill" that can be (super)added to an "armoury" of detachable or extrinsic effects. Walsh is, too, evidently clearer in his mind than White about what is "strictly necessary" to the writer's "design". Dualism is also evident in nationalistic critics like John Barnes (1966:155/160), who—as a rhetorical pacifier—praises the medium but faults the message, and in reviewers like Bellette (1974:128), who—conversely—defends the integrity of White's fictions yet wishes "large parts rethought, rewritten, removed entirely".

Critics who use White as a punch-bag persist along similar lines. White's desire to be an important novelist leads him into "elaborate decoration ... mainly stylistic" and to "peculiar constructions" (Yaffe 1958:465–66, apropos *Voss*); he clings to "stylistic formulae" and dysfunctional "tricks of style" (Burgess 1961:50–51); his prose is "mannered", singlemindedly effect-seeking, full of "rococo ornamentation" and "meaningless flourishes"—for Rodney Mather (1970:34/38), all this goes hand in hand with "a cold, sometimes near-hysterical impersonality" and "an exquisite sharpness and variety of tone and sense of form". It is difficult to see how this last can be achieved in the presence of excrescence of language. Warm engagement with the ironic tonality of White's short fiction cannot prevent Myers (1978) from betraying a fundamental lack of sympathy for the integrating detail of language that *enables* the critic's judgements about theme and significance.[4]

My penultimate example of a judgement on "manner" comes from the novelist V.S. Naipaul (1964). Naipaul is no friend of "overt technique", which includes the "display of style"; he implicitly aligns himself with the "classical writer". He is hostile to a narrative mode, such as White's, which he takes to be lacking in that virtuous, self-effacing, Brahminical, scenic impersonality and bare "stylelessness" which are the hallmarks of his own style: Conrad without the subtly resonant discourse. Because Naipaul is unsympathetic towards late or high modernism, he tends to read with curmudgeonly stubbornness as though he were *expecting* White's prose to evince a Naipaulesque pellucidness. And, as a result of this, he misreads: "The manner, which has been described as stylish, cannot support the matter. And the stylishness ... comes over as pure embarrassment". Naipaul is clearly a dualist: style is an optional extra. The same question can be asked of him as of all dualists: how can he tell whether the "manner" "supports" (or not) "the matter", unless he disregards the crucial identity of manner and matter?

Finally, McAuley (1962:79) offers yet another view of what he calls White's "Mannerist style". Committing himself to art-historical categories, he specifies the following characteristics: "a keyed-up tautness, a continual shift of perspective, alteration of near and far focusing, interpenetration of planes of vision, or other dislocations of the syntax [*sic*] of reality." This is consonant with a definition of style only if style, for McAuley, is the same as what Wayne Booth calls the rhetoric of fiction: point of view, narrative discourse, focalization, *as well as* the structuring of narrative action in a broader sense (wherein the handling of temporality is the key factor). McAuley's appeal to an art-historical consensus about the meaning of "Mannerist"—the only attempt by any critic of White to define the concept—raises more problems than it resolves. Such categories are appropriate to White's fictions (or to some levels of reader-response to them), but are inapplicable to "style" unless the term is submitted to

---

4 "Sometimes the syntax seems unnecessarily mannered and disembodied" (13); the "expressions with which [White] represents his characters' search for grace" is "sometimes strained and mannered" (22); there is "a fastidious toying with ... mannered phrases" (30), a "precious style" (45), images which seem "artificial and forced, or irritatingly precious" (81).

clear demarcation: "style" as characteristic narrative mode, versus "style" as all mediating "devices" without which a narrative mode cannot be linguistically established. And I would reject McAuley's seemingly informed and specialized application of the term "Mannerist". The standard sources on the meaning of this elusive concept align themselves, even today, more closely with the common-or-garden variety of "manner" as employed by White's detractors—and this variety I reject as well.

One is essentially espousing a neoclassical aesthetic in postulating a discernible content which is somehow mediated "manneristically" through excess, decoration, or a clever show of craft for its own sake. If, however, one sees style as organic—as inseparable from meaning and even (in Leo Spitzer's view) as "almost a mode of apprehension" or vision (cf also Shklovsky, and Paul Ricoeur's views on the inherent metaphoricity of language)—then it is difficult to judge a style as excessive or "mannerist" with any implication that an independently valid semantic substrate has been somehow encrusted unnecessarily. A style could be called "peculiar" or "ingenious", certainly—but that which is accessible to stylistic analysis should not be called "mannerist", "excessive", "affected" or "ornamental", since what has been isolated is merely some part-aspect of a complex, intended or determinable meaning. This would hold true even more, were one to negate the primacy of single attainable meanings. Ernst Robert Curtius's historicist account of "Mannerism" (1973:ch. 15) reveals unmistakably the assumption that a writer is choosing deliberately the less usual of two courses of creative action (but that if he had chosen the more usual, the meaning would be no different). The stress is not on the will to the creative act as constitutive of meaning, but on the writer's reflexive understanding of means detachable from preconstituted meaning. In modern linguistic theory, of course, all *poiesis* involves some degree of deviance, foregrounding and defamiliarization: the "abnormal" is textually domesticated against the background of linguistic yet "extratextual" "normality". But modern theory, by its very nature, declines to accommodate the idea of "mannerism" as it is historically determined by Curtius. Shearman's exploration of the concept of mannerism (1967) draws on the parallels between theory and practice in literature and the visual arts. He suggests, most valuably, that "preciosity of style for its own sake" defines true Mannerism, which, since it is "extravagantly accomplished", "must have fed upon a previous period of supreme accomplishment" (35). What was historically a positive virtue has since become something negative. Critics who attempt to apply the term "mannered" or "mannerist" to White are hoist by their own petard. They can apply these epithets, in a resuscitation of a style-term applied to a closed phase of art-history, only with the implication that White is not his own man but rather epitomizes the peaking of prior developments in prose-writing. It is, in fact, a common critical ploy to downgrade the early works of novelists in terms which stress their derivativeness: what reviewers glorify is pure originality. This latter is a romantic doctrine in one of its chief manifestations.

My provisional conclusion on the topic of "mannerism" in White must be that the use of such a term is ultimately a form of shoddy impressionism, a catch-all for an omnium gatherum of syntactic, structural, textural and narrative characteristics of White's fiction. If there is a degree of linguistic and visionary extremism in White, it can be acknowledged; but it must be encountered on its own terms as intrinsic to signification, and not exploited for purposes of negative criticism whose ideological determinants are inapplicable aesthetic theories. Significantly, mannerism has been traditionally viewed as coldly calculating— hence the impression that Ricks, Buckley, Mather and others have of White's "cold impersonality" towards his characters. White is constantly being accused of being unsympathetic towards, or even disliking, his characters. It can be argued, conversely, that these accusations derive from misreadings of narrative perspective, and that the expectation of auctorial signals of warmth and sympathy is a naive one, irrelevant to White's concerns. These concerns—centered in the nuanced mediation of character-consciousness—can nevertheless involve an author's passionate commitment to the figures of his imagination.

II   The rhetoric of fiction

Reviewers of White devote considerable space to noting such features as authorial intrusion and indeterminacy of point of view. This is somewhat surprising, because the commentators seem so irritated at what they find that one might assume they were unacquainted with literary theory (let alone the range of narrative possibilities opened up both by the modernist novel and by its great nineteenth-century precursors), or were, conversely, conditioned by those branches of modernism *and* realism/naturalism that favoured (and still favour) "scenic" narration. The disinclination to accept the centrality of White's style (or language) to signification goes hand in hand with a persistent misclassification of White's narrative discourse (the attribution of point of view, etc) in conventional terms. Comment on White's style is fragmentary, negatively prescriptive, or puzzled; comment on White's narrative modes is, though often less fragmentary, equally an expression of disapproval or baffled impatience. I should stress that it is indicative of the separateness of White's style and narrative discourse from those of other novelists of his literary age that reviewers—and, in their wake, the academic critics—should feel compelled to mention these features, which go unremarked or undetailed in discussions of even the most lustrous luminaries of Anglo-American fiction.

INTRUSIVENESS

The critics' chief obsession is with **authorial intrusion.** At the simplest, least technical level, complaint centers on White's insistent instruction of the reader, his reluctance to let the novel "speak for itself".[5] Sometimes this authorial

---

[5] See, for example, *Times* 1958; Yaffe 1958:466; Pringle 1961:71; Davis 1970; Bailey 1973 (characters "slapped down with a firm authorial hand"); Green 1973a:402 and 1974:309;

presence, explicit commentary, or even "implied comment" is associated with a seldom accountable superciliousness.[6] Although intrusiveness is generally detected in White's fiction as a whole, a few critics seem surprisingly to locate it only selectively (eg, Oliver 1958:49; Brady 1977:139). Kramer (1974:271) reluctantly defends *some* of the "direct invasion of the narrative" in *The Tree of Man* because Stan Parker is for her an inarticulate protagonist. But the ubiquity of "intrusion" obliges her to broaden her terms of reference: "by the force of his intervention as narrator, White seeks the reader's assent"—which assent Kramer more than once withholds. If Kramer is not worried about the advisability of identifying narrator with author, nor are others slow to explain the effect of authorial presence in terms of irony—perhaps to accommodate themselves to the irritating impression that White is intrusive.[7] Irony undoubtedly abounds; but the route whereby irony is linked to White's "overriding point-of-view" (Myers 1978: 101-2) all too often turns out to be circuitous or tautological. The tonality of White's narrative discourse, it has been argued by Manly Johnson (1981:162.*n*4), could easily be misjudged; but there is no way of telling whether Johnson's remarks apply to the actual narrative voicing, and thus to "point of view". He cites Stephen Spender's observation to the effect that "any experience accurately and objectively described" can appear satiric, pointing out that the reader senses satire when obliged to confront what he usually "does not see". White, Johnson maintains, seems to be asking for a value judgement, but he is actually offering only "a report of what is observed": what is "observed", in fact, by the characters.

Like Kramer, critics who find the "visionary" nature of White's fictions their most conspicuous feature tend to justify "intrusion" by reference to the way in which the narrative rhetoric, under pressure from extratextual, cultural codes, seeks to impose an *entente* on the reader. Crowcroft (1974:51) sees White as intruding because he cannot assume basic "religious literacy" in his readers in a secular age; when it is the style (syntactic disruption) that intrudes, attention is successfully focused on the work itself, whereas Crowcroft is uncomfortable about White's argumentational intrusions. Indeed: this view can hardly have general aesthetic validity—consider, for example, the radical and unobtrusive solutions found by the Catholic novelist Flannery O'Connor for getting the Word across in a despiritualized age. What is interesting is the willingness of critics to see White himself—and not the age—as governed by a diffidence which he has

---

Core 1974:8 ("clumsy authorial intrusions") and 1977:770–71; Riemer 1974:249–50; Docker 1974:61; Kramer 1976:63; Mitchell 1978:12.

[6] Buckley 1964:414/421; Argyle 1967:14–15.

[7] Osborne 1964; Mather 1970:34; Delmonte 1974:37/42–43; Myers 1978: *passim*. Delmonte explains ironic intrusion as an urge to focus attention on broad spiritual issues, but seriously misjudges the tonality and perspective of the passages he uses as illustration. Because his concept of irony is often inflexibly limited, Myers similarly misreads point of view. In the chapter "Narrative Techniques in the Shorter Prose Fiction" (173–90), he talks about structure, epiphany and characterization but neglects to discuss narrative perspective, indirect auctorial commentary, or "White's many styles" (which range from "ridiculous mimicry" to the "startling power of his serious imagery").

eventually managed to shed. John Colmer (1978c:8) aligns the personal and psychological with the public and cultural: "If we are sometimes more conscious of the assertive tone of his prose than [of] its power to command imaginative assent, no doubt this uncertainty of touch [*sic*] springs from the insecurity of a visionary artist in an alien age". Such comments represent broad assumptions which are offered in the absence of textual analysis.[8]

APHORISTIC COMMENT

Aphoristic comment can be seen in statements which achieve salience in the narrative flow by appearing in the universalizing present tense. None of the many critics who have adverted to this phenomenon has taken the trouble to attempt any formal categorization, but those few instances in which sentences from White's works are actually quoted make this clear. Such assertive, interpretative comments are taken almost exclusively to be formulations of White's own thoughts, thus constituting a specific verbal form of intrusiveness. Like Kramer, a number of critics view *some* of this apparent interventionism as expressing either the unspoken thoughts of the characters or "the extraordinary that ordinary characters cannot think about".[9] Others restrict themselves to noting how "rich" and insightful this "aphoristic wisdom" is, with occasional reservations about its wilfulness of occurrence or precise applicability.[10] The feature is associated for some with "dogmatic judgment", didacticism or unashamedly "high level abstractions", or is seen as something laboured, "both elevated and curiously evasive", even gauchely obvious.[11]

Some few are responsive to the so-called "aphoristic" style in White. Johnson (1976:352) claims that it validates White's role as chorus or artist-witness—but this interpretation lacks general validity and is anyhow derived from misreadings of the perspective of specific passages. Lawson (1973a:349) attempts to defend White's aphorisms against critics who place "excessive interpretative reliance on the oracular statements" because of the general disorientation caused by "the constantly changing point-of-view". But the question remains: is the author the sole reference-point for such "oracular statements", and has their function in the text been rightly gauged? Is it just a matter of taste that one reader should find such comments "less subtle and less accurate", another "rich", while there is consensus on the persuasive power of the "imagery" and the "non-commentative" discourse? Can the elusive status of these comments be accounted for in terms of

---

[8] I can think of only one study that tries to come to terms properly with the "insecurity" and ambiguity inherent in White's fiction (Bliss 1986, with her investigation of the "paradox of fortunate failure"), but her examination of narrative stance is too impressionistic and miscellaneous to resolve the problem of whether or not White "intrudes".

[9] Argyle 1967:35-36; Colmer 1978c:6; Harries 1978:462; Mitchell 1978:10.

[10] Gannett 1957 ("epigrams" of "uneven effect"); Davis 1970; Mather 1970:37 (the "mannerist" argument appearing again in Mather's characterization of these "brilliant", "eminently quotable" aphorisms as unassimilated "arabesques").

[11] Heseltine 1962 and 1963a:212; McLeod 1974:440/443; Kramer 1974:273; Kiernan 1980:68.

some other narrational intention as yet unconsidered—something that might permit a reconciliation of the aesthetically illogical disjunction between the image of White as a soaring, balletic ironist and the image of White as an intrusive, earthbound dogmatist? It may well be that White's radicalism resides not in the "gauche" employment of a conventional technique of early novelistic narrative in a predominantly "modernist" discourse, but in his transformation of the contextual terms in which such a technique is to be understood—or in his subversion of it.

SHIFTS IN POINT OF VIEW

Although very few critics use the concept of stream of consciousness as a **general** benchmark for measuring White's narrative technique, most make vague reference to a dependence, particularly in the earlier novels, on this modernist technique. A very few commentators are specific enough to associate it with a shifting from one centre of consciousness or thought to another, or a mingling of these; the implicit assumption is usually that forms of interior monologue are involved. It was not until the 1970s that perspectival shifts beyond the customary range of modernist stream of consciousness became a topic of specific comment in relation to White. Observations are typically as inchoate about what is now termed "slipping" as they were about stream of consciousness. It is not simply that critics express difficulty in deciding on the perspectival status of shifts in point of view;[12] they seem to be surprised by the presence of such shifts, which have been detectable in the discourse of the novel from the days of Jane Austen at least. Myers (1978) gives the (mistaken?) impression that this normal phenomenon is new to him, and is something whose developed presence in modernist fiction cannot have trained the reader to cope with it: ""The shifting of the narrating person is ... confusing" (13–14); "There are so many delicate shifts in the narrative point of view that it is often difficult to decide ... whether the more sardonic passages are fragmented parts of ... interior monologue" (24). Alan Lawson, like others before him and since, proposes an area of research into White's style, while himself venturing only the most tentative of hunches:

Someday a critic will offer us a study of point-of-view in White's novels. It will reveal, I suspect, that the point-of-view is capable of changing within a single sentence, and often. Such changes of viewpoint enable us to see that characters regress almost as often as they progress. Herein lies one of the most important sources of White's difficulty. (1973a:347)

INDETERMINACY OF POINT OF VIEW

These admissions of difficulty in determining point of view reflect a central preoccupation of White's critics—once again, from the early 1970s onwards

---

12 "The viewpoint flickers—sometimes changing in mid-sentence—between objective and subjective observation" (Berger 1970); "points of view can be separated by slight modulations in one brief scene, even in one paragraph" (Avant 1975); "White's narrative stance shifts, and shifts unreliably too, even clumsily" (Mitchell 1978:12); White shifts with "mobility and speed" from sometimes "frankly omniscient" comment to description, "from one kind of narrative voice or tone to another" (Wilson 1976:281).

(though readers would have been experiencing difficulty long before the problem reached the stage of academic articulation). Sometimes the complaints, when examined in relation to the text-passages discussed, are clearly the result of inattentive reading. Argyle complains (1967:37) of *The Tree of Man* that it is not clear "whether the author or Stan Parker is responsible for this fragment of a synoptic view of the 'boundless garden'", but the passage he is referring to (p. 478) has in this case simply become the victim of his misreading: Stan, at any rate, cannot be "responsible", as he is already dead, and the "synoptic view" can be seen as located within the consciousness of Amy Parker, who has been left behind (see also pp. 424–30 below). Ratcliffe (1973) thinks that White, in *The Eye of the Storm,* "seems to attribute to Elizabeth Hunter's nurses an intellectuality of perception that clearly [*sic*] belongs to him", and he specifically cites the narrative voicing with "the Second Person Familiar" ("... you felt ...") in connection with the "essentially instinctive" Mary de Santis. If Argyle's misreading was of actional context, Ratcliffe's is of Mary's character. It is a fatal misjudgement to approach the narration with ready-made assumptions about conventional (and conventionally accessible) character-types, and to assume the validity of a principle of decorum that equates diction with authorial mindset when it cannot be equated with what a character would expectably *say*. Revealingly, Ratcliffe writes of Mary *saying* the "intellectual" words to which he takes exception, as though this verb were an appropriate transformation of "narrative voice". He is representative of the many readers who expect to find the syntax and lexis of personal verbal expression everywhere, when it should have been clear that other conventions also obtain in fiction—in the narrative articulation of preverbal thought, for instance. The critics' struggle to identify White's voicings can lead them to posit the presence of intentional ambiguity, an autobiographical lack of irony, the centrality of irony through the satirizing of the talkative characters' points of view, a balance of empathy and detachment, or a kind of confusion of identity.[13] George Core (1974:11) restates the general case fairly typically:

The intervention of the author [in *The Eye of the Storm]* can also be disabling: at certain moments the writer's godlike presence is almost as heavy-handed as Thackeray's. At such moments the post of observation has become indistinct: the perspectives of author and character are confused.

Core is drawing here on the views of Dorothy Green (1973a:402–403), who claims that "we can never be sure who is speaking or thinking, White or his character"; the characters "are presented already judged". Green *does*, then, seem to be ultimately "sure", at least, that all judgements are White's—with the logical conclusion, surely, that she attributes none of the thinking to the

---

[13] These views attributable in this order: Kramer 1973:17 and—somewhat disapprovingly— 1974:270; Smith 1972:177; Myers 1978:40; Mosley 1979; Taubman 1979. See also Johnson 1976:351, who, though making valid general observations about shifts in *The Eye of the Storm,* misreads contextual boundaries and crucial pronoun referentiality. Tout-Smith (1979:66–67) himself shifts confusingly in his comments on *The Twyborn Affair* between macrostructural shifts (narrative level) and problems of voicing (at the level of local narration).

characters. It is once again clear that the whole notion of "intrusive omniscience" is problematical, confusing, and often irrelevant in reading White's novels.

OTHER VIEWS

The structure of these subsections has had the intention of insinuating a dynamic of critical views. The least freighted or qualified view is that of critics who think that White is authorially intrusive. A subdivision of this view, and one which is at least more clearly demarcated in formal terms and by way of exemplification, is that of critics (not infrequently those of the first group) who try uneasily to come to terms with what they assume is aphoristic, authorial comment. A more balanced view of narrative is presented by those who recognize the interdependence of points of view (shifts, or slipping). This matter is complicated by the persistence with which readers feel that "authorial intrusion" ceases to be a clearly isolable technique and begins to colonize modal territories of discourse which are, at the same time, felt to be representations of the thought of the characters. This narrational indeterminacy is consistently discussed in tones of surprised pleasure or petulant puzzlement.

Other views can often be dovetailed into the preceding ones only with some difficulty—occasionally because the critics' terms of reference are as muddy as their bemusement.[14] It is very seldom that the borderline between narrative perspective and structure is discussed by critics of White. Core (1974:8–9) is deeply interested in the relationship between narration and temporality (memories rendered dramatically and directly through the "viewpoint character"'s consciousness rather than retrospectively), while Patricia Morley regards structural juxtaposition and selection of detail as more important means of controlling point of view than any occasional authorial presence in White.[15] Schermbrucker appears to accept the principle of intrusive narration in White and points to the unheralded shuttling between omniscience and character-subjectivity (1973:64/249), but he does not otherwise mention narrative perspective and the

---

[14] Brissenden (1969:12) writes of "a disembodied narrator", Shrubb (1968:8) of the "sleepwalking" *speech* of both characters and narrator, Myers (1978:29) of a "detached third-person narrator". Buckley (1964:414–15) criticizes the early novels for White's failure to "mime" his characters' thinking consistently and distinctively.

[15] Morley (1972), though she fails to demonstrate how point of view is "controlled" ("authorial control of point of view without actual commentary", 130; "an author's voice, without recourse to direct commentary, is still dominant through his handling of dialogue, patterns of imagery and symbol", etc., 126), attempts to struggle through—with her denial of "overt comment" and her stress on the "assumed mask"—to an acknowledgement that the "objective" or intrusive narratorial presence in the novels is less straightforward than most critics have supposed. Proceeding from Frye's fifth generic mode, irony, she goes beyond other critics' use of it as a means of resolving an impasse of understanding created by the narrative modality. Although she fails to elucidate the categories she employs in her concise paragraph on "viewpoint" (30), she does talk of "objective", Jamesian "indirect narration ... from the point of view of the fictional character". More problematically: "White's own viewpoint is fused with those of the fictional characters". The difficulties are not resolved, however, by using such conventional early-modernist categories.

ways in which this is mediated stylistically. The only potentially interesting observation—that White renders the theme of "alienating duality" "as *the form of the reader's experience*" (249)—is taken no further.

At one point Schermbrucker writes of Kate in Lawrence's *The Plumed Serpent* as thinking "directly" (92). In Continental parlance, this would have to be translated as *style indirect libre* or *erlebte Rede*, a half-century of research into which has hardly brushed the souls of White's critics, although it might have helped some out of more than one sticky attempt to pin down White's narrative technique. The first critic discerning enough to offer a formal explanation for the apparent indeterminacy of point of view in White was Heltay (1975). Although she still maintains that there is exaggerated narratorial omniscience in White, which is used for effects of tone and characterization, as is epigrammatic description, she also indicates cogently what a handful of previous critics could only guess at. The narrator, namely, may conceal his omniscience by assimilating the tone and syntax of his commentary to the speech of specific characters, in order to convey further information covertly: ie, through ungrammatical or idiolectal colouring. This constitutes a kind of "*erlebte Rede*" characteristic of White. Myers, too, makes reference to the *style indirect libre* in his study of the short fiction, but he never bothers to define what he means by the term, never feels under any obligation to provide analytical evidence for its presence (Myers 1978: 68/85/102). Too much perplexity, irritation, dissatisfaction and misplaced wonderment have been expressed by White's critics in the preceding decades for one to expect enlightenment to follow from the magical replacement of a miscellany of groping descriptions by such a lapidary concept. All in all, it has taken a long time—is still taking a long time—for critics to start analyzing White's apparent indeterminacy in terms of developed narrative theory. Holloway (1983:147–48), with all the advantages of his familiarity with such theory, misses a grand opportunity to account for the *constant* features of White's technique by restricting his comments to the early "modernist" novel, *The Living and the Dead*. Passages are marked for "free, indirect style", but that is all. It is precisely at the point where intensive analysis of free indirect style/speech/thought would have yielded up the hidden treasures of White's *particular* style that Holloway lapses into imprecise, subjective diction. If White's discourse is "almost", or "seems to speak", "a kind of" free indirect style, then what *exactly* is White's mode? There are, at least, a very few dissenting views which oppose conventional responses to White's narrative technique, or which take certain implications to their logical conclusion in an effort to absolve the novelist from accusations of having failed in his endeavour. Lawson (1979:286–87) denies that there is "authorial certitude" anywhere in White; this view (adopted and adapted by McCulloch 1983:79), however, does not fundamentally question the objective existence of a rhetoric of "intrusion", and tends to fall back on the Boothian terminology of "conjectural description". Johnson (1978: 97) sees White's fiction as aiming at "objectification" and "the elimination of authorial presence", but his not particularly novel notion of a consonance between author-psychology and character-psychology is a false snare. It cannot account for the specific mechanisms (if that is not too mechanistic a word) that might lead to the altogether persuasive conclusion that the "author" is not present in the narrative discourse. Only close, exploratory analysis can hope to prove or disprove such a contention.

III   'Linguistic' comment on style

Very little commentary has ventured to relate aspects of White's language or style to his modes of narrative discourse. There is a tendency to throw concepts like "symbolism", "expressionism", "impressionism" and "stream of consciousness" around with reckless abandon, in the hope that at least *something* familiar, tried and true will stick. Conversely, there are instances of critics faulting the syntax of White's sentences when the passages being pilloried actually do (as very occasionally happens in White) exhibit the oldest, most respectable techniques in the Joycean handbook of stream of consciousness.[16] As already indicated, most critics not only frown on White's style as being "mannered" (ie, separate from matter), but also comment on it separately from any other aspects they might be discussing. Reviewers especially show a concomitant tendency to go off the deep end about superficial matters that could easily be explained after a moment's reflection; it could well be that they have been profoundly unnerved by *other* features of White's style that are resistant to facile identification. Inasmuch as these views express or harbour reservations, their most striking features are: a relative absence of specific criticism turning on grammatical aspects of style; a high occurrence of one-off criticisms making much of minor (or seeming) grammatical solecisms[17] but failing to marshall sufficient evidence to hang the novelist for mass-crimes against the English

---

[16] Robert Nye's complaint in his review of *The Twyborn Affair* (1979) that the sentences are "ineptly constructed" exemplifies this failure to recognize stream-of-consciousness techniques.

[17] One example must suffice as illustration. Both Oliver (1958:49) and Brissenden (1959:411) are exercised by "a kind of wilful (but pointless) disregard of the rules of syntax" in White's use of relative pronouns in *Voss*. But they fail to see that this "un-English" way of positioning "of which" does not occur outside of this one novel, is doubtless meant to suggest a coloration from Voss's German, and has a local mimetic or iconic effect which conveys the disjunctive relationship between mental states and external situation. One example in the English editions runs like this: "It was an obscure and wretched situation, in which his knees were pressed together to avoid skirts, but of which, soft suggestions were overflowing" (Eyre & Spottiswoode, p. 61, Penguin, p. 56). No reviewer of the American edition could have taken exception to White's grammar or punctuation here, as the sentence there concludes: "to avoid skirts, but soft suggestions of them were overflowing" (Viking, p. 51). Once consideration is given to a possible mimetic correspondence between language, scene and psychology, the smoothing-over Stateside can only be viewed as the damaging act of a sorcerer's apprentice. In other, non-iconic contexts in the novel, it can be remarked that White's employment of postposed "of which" reveals a preference for direct and syntactically balanced linkage, and is fully in accord with normal relative structuring. There was no need for Koch-Emmery (1973:140) to mount an eccentric prosodic argument for White's "of which" construction as preserving "the equilibrium of sounds". White's practice consistently exploits the potential of the English language to precise purpose.

language; the relative uniformity of the descriptive terms employed (for example, White's style, it seems, is peculiar or idiosyncratic, or invites one to look for misprints);[18] and a disinclination to elaborate by way of illustration, proof or argument.

Non-specific "linguistic" observations lacking clarifying exemplification are legion.[19] Attempts to be more specific about the "grammar" suffer from diffuseness; some aspect or other will be identified, without any sense of the phenomena standing in any general relation to each other. Lawson (1979:292) is an exception in arguing that the "grammar" is "disjunctive" because it reflects flux and epiphany—the sole attempt to provide a general explanation for this aspect of White's style.[20] Scatter-shot compilations of style-characteristics—for example, "elision, asyndeton, parataxis, elimination of pronouns" (TLS 1966) or "unexpected punctuation, unusual inversions, emphatic auxiliary verbs, paranomasia [sic]" (Crowcroft 1974:50)—do not take us far towards either rejection or understanding of White's style. Heseltine (1963b) makes the first attempt by any critic to deal analytically with details of White's style; "Like it or lump it, his style is the very linchpin of what he has to say" (74), an assertion that consciously rejects what Heseltine takes to be the dominant approach to White's fiction.[21] For Heseltine, to mention single fictional events or "images" in one of White's novels, or to generalize (incorrectly) about the "pathetic fallacy",

---

[18] Idiosyncratic—for example: Muir 1941; Stern 1958:52; Brissenden 1959:410-11; Martin 1959:55; Burgess 1961:49; Walters 1963:38 and Herring 1965:20 (both claiming "eccentricities"); Heseltine 1963a:212; Brissenden 1969:25; Schermbrucker 1973:18; Brady 1974: 142-43; Crowcroft 1974:50; Hadgraft 1977:44; Dinnage 1980:25; Sharrad 1984:211. Misprints: Ricks 1962; Miller 1966

[19] "Jerkiness of ... style" (Times 1956); "strange jolting rhythmms and unpredictable syntax" (Lodge 1981); "staccato or broken or jerky pieces" (Thomson 1966:23); "strangulated prose" (Duchêne 1966); "contorted syntax" (McLeod 1974:440); the "tortured 'grotesque' manner of White's language" (Scheick 1979:144); "a dislocated and sometimes illiterate syntax" (Hope 1963:13); "oddities of construction and syntax" (George 1961); "the short, crystal, not always grammatical sentences" (Stern 1948:5); "the trick of the broken sentence" (Barnard 1956:159); "disconnected grammar" (TLS 1962); "dislocated" or "lopsided" syntax (Walsh 1973, 1974:200, 1976:9, 1977 passim). Attempts at specification can result in unhelpful vagueness: for example, "harshly syncopated commas" (Duchêne 1966).

[20] "Tricks of syntax—like the islanding of a verbless clause" (King 1966); "the short sentence whose verb is stuck in the groove of the present participle—'All the time gently stroking her thigh'" (Times 1964). Myers (1978:103) finds irritating the "mannerism" of "elision" and "beginning the sentence with a conjunction or a relative pronoun"—a widespread sentiment (eg, TLS 1964); Shrubb 1968:11—"the conjunctions that don't join, the nonsentences"; Stilwell 1964—"ugly fragments of sentences"; Naipaul 1964—White "declares war on punctuation ... chops up a single sentence into several little pieces".

[21] "In general, those who discover greatness in White's fiction, discover it in spite of, rather than because of, his style" (Heseltine 1963b:61). My introductory comments should have indicated that the case cannot be put quite so categorically as this, though it is true that "most of the reservations felt by critics generally have centered on the prose" (Crowcroft 1974:50). But there are very few critics indeed who (like Green 1973b:23 or Peter Porter in White 1982:[5]) have gone so far as to make the absurd claim that White's style is not a (central) determinant of his novels' power.

suffices to illustrate "style" until near the end of his essay (72–73), where he shifts tack in the direction of language. White's "responsive" syntax is "calculated to render, before all else, streams of individual consciousness"; typically present are conjunctions of abstract and concrete, "incomplete sentences" starting with "So", conditional constructions, and "eccentric punctuation" (this last not illustrated). Apart from having a good try at "imagery", critics since Heseltine have simply not accounted for White's style. As I have already declared, there is to date[22] only *one* study of *one* important ramification of his style, and that is Hilary Heltay's dissertation on White's use of the articles. Given the nature of her specific focus, she has space only for an (incomplete) listing of style-features peculiar to White:

A preliminary analysis of selected passages of White's prose ... yields a number of areas of grammatical structure where his usage deviates from the habitual and conventional. These are, to name the most immediately obvious, word order, inquits, restrictive and non-restrictive relative clauses, *of*-genitives, prepositions, continuous aspect, emphatic *do*-aspect, and the articles. [Heltay 1983:15]

Were I similarly to pass in review (and preview) such discrete features in White's fiction as have been held to be "stylistic", I would categorize and evaluate them as follows.

For a start, I would clear the decks of anything White's critics have attached to "style" that is not, as such, accessible to stylistic analysis—indeed, that would evanesce if analysis were attempted. This includes "mannered" style—on both functional and ontological grounds, a discountable claim, or one that is translatable into more precise, and defensible, terms. I seriously doubt that White's is a naturally "pretentious" or "inflated" prose. Such a claim is discountable on functional grounds; within the "visionary" or psychological system of relationships and correspondences set up within the novels, it is hermeneutically undemonstrable. That White's language is "obscure", "portentous" or "mystical" is similarly discountable on functional grounds, and by appeal to the principle of the *archilecteur;* the designation "mystical" can be embraced as a valid condition of the represented world, within its own normative system, and on ontological and epistemological grounds.

I would agree that poeticity is central to White's style, but would disagree with the contention that the poetic is an irksome and illegitimate quality in prose

---

[22] Book-length studies are now paying slightly more than lip-service to the matter of style and narrative technique; but Wolfe (1983) is unsystematic and misinterpretative in this regard, his position (that of an old-fashioned prescriptive grammarian) placing him among the ranks of those who cannot acknowledge the inseparability of content from form. Carolyn Bliss, who has written one of the most reliable studies of White (1986), nevertheless essentially draws on earlier critics (not including Heltay) in regard to stylistic features, pressing the latter selectively and without analytical rigour into the service of one central "visionary" and thematic thesis. Although she has sensible things to say about narrative technique, correcting some critics' misconceptions, her terms of reference do not capture the linguistic individuality of White's procedures. Edgecombe (1987) deals impressionistically with a scattering of obvious iconic effects; his book-length study (1989) of White's "vision and style" does not provide the balanced elucidation of style-features that his chosen author by now deserves.

narrative. (For a valuable summary of arguments from linguistic criticism against any essential polarization of "poetry" from "prose" in the novel, see Bronzwaer 1970:1–24.) That White's prose is uncompromising I would also grant. For a multitude of reasons deriving from the seamless continuity between White's world-view and his artistic expression, its delights reside in its difficulties. But uncompromisingness or difficulty, though qualities, are not discrete objects of stylistic investigation. At best, one can confirm or demystify the former (which have to do with reader-response) by clarifying the latter. Poeticity, on the other hand, can be analyzed stylistically (and customarily is—in poetry). Features that are commonly regarded as the stock-in-trade of the "poet" include synaesthesia, which both Kiernan (1980) and Bliss (1986) discuss in relation to White's style. The presence of synaesthesia can be readily acknowledged, and is an important consideration in that area of style which is traditionally termed "imagery". Imagery, metaphor, symbolism and the like make up a potentially limitless field of investigation. There are easy pickings here for anyone interested in White's artistic creativity—and this is precisely the trouble with the studies of White's "imagery" that have been attempted to date. There has been valuable clarification of patterns of figuration in individual works. But, with few exceptions, endeavours to "crack the code" and come up with a grand genetic scheme of figurational technique in White have turned out to be so many essays in thematic axe-grinding. What is still missing is an examination of White's figuration that reveals just how "uncompromising" and "poetic" it is. But the present book is not the occasion on which to present such a study (I have limited myself to illustrating analytically, in ch. 12, how White's approaches to verbal signification interact within *The Solid Mandala*). This, I trust, explains my disinclination to do more than nod to the presence in White's language of such phenomena as synaesthesia and the pathetic fallacy (the latter being dwelt on by Barnard 1956, Heseltine 1963b, Core 1974/1977, and Bliss 1986). On the other hand, there are good, general linguistic grounds for including in a study of style such features as punning or paronomasia (mentioned by Crowcroft 1974, and dealt with in ch. 8.VIII below), syllepsis (examined by Heseltine 1963b and Bliss 1986, and covered in ch. 8.VII), and the normally innocuous graphemic technique of capitalization (referred to only by Morley 1972, and treated in ch. 8.VI below).

There are more specifically grammatical and idiomatic aspects of White's language that require discussion in terms of style. Several are somewhat peripheral matters. Mentioned only by Heltay (1983) are restrictive and non-restrictive relative clauses and prepositions; these are treated below in ch. 8.IX. White's preference for "that" over "which" (Crowcroft 1974) is an almost negligible matter, which I treat in passing. Unattached participles (Oliver 1958, Naipaul 1964) constitute true solecisms rather than being style-features, but can often be defended.

Some style-features are interesting precisely because they are not constants. One such is the emphatic *do*-proform (Heltay 1983; perhaps also Crowcroft 1974: "emphatic auxiliary verbs"). This is not conspicuous in *The Solid Mandala* (see instances on pages 225, 274). It is most frequent in *Voss*, where it correlates both with the central male protagonist's peculiar cast of will and with typically nineteenth-century modes of "argufying", to use William Empson's term; it is less conspicuous in *The Tree of Man,* and is merely occasional in the other novels, whenever tight cohesion is required with something situationally implicit in a preceding stretch of narrative. That is, proform emphasis is an obliquity of figural or character-consciousness, involving mental concession, like conditionals. Grammatical features that have been regarded with some puzzlement may occur very seldom in White's narratives, yet throw light on other style-features with which they co-occur. One such is "transitive verbs used intransitively" (Shrubb 1968); I refer to this phenomenon in passing, and, with specific reference to tagging procedures with direct speech, in ch. 8.IV and ch. 11.

Tags or "inquits", though they are included in Heltay's shopping-list (and are possibly meant by Yaffe 1958 and Pringle 1961), have never been discussed by White's critics. As, however, White's narrational framing of dialogue is far and away the most revealing and "Whitean" style-characteristic, I have examined it at length (ch. 11). The next most pervasive aspect of White's style is his "elliptical" or "jerky" syntax, "disjunctive" grammar, etc, which I term "ataxis" and discuss in ch. 10.II. In contrast to the "inquits", this complex phenomenon has disturbed most of White's critics. The lack of adequate stylistic and linguistic categories in White-criticism to date means, however, that vague references must be interpreted generously whenever one attempts to meet criticisms. The frequent adversions to White's "punctuation" are a case in point. Related to the matter of "disjunctive" grammar are the "incomplete sentences" with *So* that are mentioned by Heseltine (1963b). I treat this phenomenon within a broader frame of cohesion in ch. 7.III and ch. 10.I.

Some of the terms used by critics to refer to features of White's style are "ghost"-categories only. "Asyndeton", for example (*TLS* 1966), is not characteristic of *The Solid Mandala.* Asyndetic constructions are not conspicuous in the other novels, either, though they do occur, particularly in that occasional sub-species of interior monologue which represents the nervous flow of direct thought. Asyndesis is not a typical style-feature in White as it is at the paratactic level of sentence-sequencing in, say, Vonnegut or Hemingway (see Levin 1951), or at the intra-sentential level, as in, say, Faulkner (see Weber 1969). "Parataxis" (*TLS* 1966) is not characteristic of White's prose. The reviewer may have been having a shot at what I term "ataxis". It would be interesting to know what the following critics mean by their characterizations of White's prose: "word-order" (Heltay 1983); "unusual inversions" (Crowcroft 1974); "mannered inversions" (Duchêne 1966). So far as I can tell, there is nothing amiss with White's "word-order", or nothing characteristic apart from the positioning of "of which"; and "inversions" without exemplification must remain a typical "ghost"-category. As for "elision" (*TLS* 1966 and Myers 1978): is "ellipsis" what is meant here? If so, what kind? Perhaps this is the same as "disjunctive" grammar, or the "elimination of pronouns" (*TLS* 1966). If ataxis is meant, then the pronoun is not "eliminated" from the construction, anyway.

Equally elusive are such categories as "elusive pronouns" (Balliett 1961). One can play the guessing-game, however, and give the critic the benefit of the doubt—perhaps what is meant here includes White's use of "you" (as mentioned in *TLS* 1961, Ratcliffe 1973, Holloway 1983 and Bliss 1986), which is examined below (ch. 6.III) in the context of narrative method. White's techniques of "understatement" and "evasion" (Corke 1957 and Taubman 1979 respectively), insofar as they are grammatically explicable, are treated within a much broader frame of indeterminacy, ambiguity and cohesion in ch. 7.II and ch. 8.II.

The continuous or progressive aspect (Burgess 1961 and Heltay 1983) is central to White's narrative style; in ch. 7.I, I extend discussion of aspect to include the perfective. This is a technique for establishing perspective, as is White's use of the articles (Heltay 1983). I consider the articles as such only briefly, but within a much broader frame of deixis and cohesion, in ch. 9.III. If these two conspicuous style-features are explicable in terms of narrational requirements, so are White's conditional constructions, which have been pointed out by Heseltine (1963b) and Bliss (1986). These constructions are treated where they rightly belong, within a complex, modal frame of reference (ch. 6.II and ch. 7.II) which is one of the main muscles working the heart-pump of White's narrative style, but which has never been dissected by the writer's anatomists.

This does not exhaust the range of style-topics that could be addressed, or are addressed in the following; I have merely sought to respond in terms of my own intentions to existing critical commentary on White. One of the underlying theses of the present study is organicist in nature—that wherever one looks when contemplating White's narratives, one finds (sometimes bizarrely) magnificent "motoric subsystems" whose immediate function might be to vitalize some apparently local "organ", but whose ultimate *raison d'être* is to keep in balance the whole body and soul of the work.

IV   Style, form and content

I lingered on "mannerism" (section I above) because I wanted to get the topic out of the way. The term is a vague encoding of a wide range of reader responses to a wide range of stylistic or discoursal features that can be treated more rewardingly under concrete headings. The position one takes up, however tentatively, towards matters of style and narrative discourse is decisive for the attitude one adopts towards White's fiction in general—in this respect, I am an almost unreconstructed monist as far as style is concerned. But I should perhaps make my position even clearer.

At a time that had not yet witnessed the resurgence of interest in formal systems of rhetoric, W.K. Wimsatt felt obliged to remind us that, as readers and critics, we should not throw out the baby with the bathwater: that because most theorists of note since the seventeenth century have affirmed the identity of style and meaning, and have rejected the Quintilianesque view of style (rhetoric) as ornament—as a "scum" on top of meaning—this need not mean that figuration, too, be cast out (Wimsatt 1941:362–64). Some implications of Wimsatt's view of things have less relevance here. One is "prose rhythm" as a critical term (and, possibly, as a style-index); a good prosodist like Wimsatt can take the application of "rhythm" to prose fiction only as a metaphor, suggesting significant irregularity and emphasis, rather than "measure" or "regularity". In the present study, I shall not be concerned with prose "rhythm" as a style-feature. I occasionally use the term "device" for an expressive feature of style; but I do so loosely (like those who use the term "mannerism"), as a slackly swaying rope-bridge leading far away from any suggestion that such "devices" are separate from meaning. To alter the placement of words in a sentence is not to apply a device in order to emphasize *a* meaning: "a change of emphasis is a change of meaning" (Wimsatt 1941:372). Only by taking the notion of "rhetorical devices" to suggest that the device is independently and "additionally" expressive can one be led to think that the recurrence of specific features constitutes expressive repetition to the point of mindless inexpressivity, mannerist saturation, or empty play. "Bad style is not a deviation of words from meaning, but a deviation of meaning from meaning" (Wimsatt 1941:370)—from which axiom it follows that we must seek to infer the author's intention from what he actually writes, with due consideration of "the adequacy of the detail to his whole purpose". It is necessary, perhaps, to have a grammarian's eye for the integuments of language—but not for these integuments as anatomized isolates. Relation is all: indeed, the principles of internal decorum established by the text are everything in judging White's style.

Wimsatt's view would seem to collide with that of Riffaterre, who maintains that "*Style* is understood as an emphasis (expressive, affective or aesthetic) added to the information conveyed by the linguistic structure, without alteration of meaning. Which is to say that language expresses and that style stresses" (1959:413). Although Riffaterre maintains that the objectifying criteria of his system try "to account for facts economically, without artificial separation of language and style" (430), it is apparent from various (lexical) examples he discusses (423/427) that he comes close to believing in absolute synonymity—an "effect" can be different, but the "meaning" undergoes no "alteration". Riffaterre has, however, belatedly acknowledged that his definition requires modification (1959/1971:164–65)—in *language,* a given word (as a lexeme with potential synonyms or substitutes) does not differ in "meaning" from certain others. But in a *text,* a word's specific contextual embedding leads necessarily to an "alteration of meaning", by a process of feedback or retroactive reading, a re-scanning of the words fore and aft. In his prolegomenon to a discussion of intertextuality (1980:625–26), Riffaterre makes the same point more technically. Useful in Riffaterre (1959/1971) has been his replacement of a linguistic norm (against which deviation can be measured and regarded as a style-feature accessible to independent normative evaluation) by the notion of the stylistic context as a "norm" or "a linguistic pattern suddenly broken by an element which was unpredictable" (1959:427/1971:184). This, of course, has affinities with foregrounding procedures, but can more easily accommodate and account for the "distinctiveness" of seemingly plain styles. The chief drawback (as Warning suggests, 1975:27–28) is the narrowness with which Riffaterre demarcates his linguistic microcontext. Valuable in Riffaterre is his reliance on subjective responses as indices to objectively verifiable stylistic stimuli in the text. The process of objectification begins with the discarding of evaluations that rely directly on these subjective responses, or which are steered by the reader's normative-prescriptive linguistic conditioning. The style-features that I have singled out for closer examination have in many cases been attacked on grounds of normative inadequacy. I endeavour to show, conversely, that these breakings or ruptures are objectively explicable in terms both of their immediate linguistic context and of their broader contextual function (particularly within patterns of convergent style-features—which Riffaterre takes into consideration; and within macrocontextual patterns of recurrence—to which Riffaterre grants little attention).

Everything of general validity relating to style can be found in a beautifully argued essay, "On Style", by Susan Sontag (1965/1982), which I would always fall back on as my last line of defence (should my own formulations above have failed to convince readers of White). Sontag writes of the untenability in theory of an antithesis between content and style, and of the extreme difficulty of practising criticism *without* maintaining this duality—if only by isolating "style" for examination. She notes how works of art may be called good, but their style careless or bad; complex styles may be praised, but it is the fantasy of an art without artifice (Barthes's "zero degree of writing") that is the contemporary religion. Apropos the "mannerist" debate: if the *artist* distinguishes between manner and subject, and is at most ironically distanced from his subject matter, the result may be "a rhetorical overlay that is stylization". It is a mistake to regard a work of art as a "statement" or to judge it for its moral or ethical "content"; "the knowledge we gain through art is an experience of the form or style of knowing something" (Sontag 1965/1982:142–43). Further, "Style is the principle of decision in a work of art, the signature of the artist's will" (152); form as style "is a plan of sensory imprinting"—some principle of repetition or redundancy, alongside our perception of variety, is necessary for us to be able to understand works of art (154); and "every style is a means of insisting on something", even if this involves a radical narrowing of focus or even silence (155). Each and every one of these statements has a direct and clarifying bearing on White's use of language, and on his critics' response to the latter—only a handful of whom have acknowledged the centrality of his style. And even their gestures of solidarity tend to promote scepticism.[23]

---

23 Ghose (1979:262–66 *passim*/1983:79–87 *passim*) balances structural stereotypicality in White against Flaubert's maxim about style being "une manière absolue de voir les choses"; more problematically: "He does not win the reader with his form but with his thought, and his principal attraction to writers is the quality of his prose"; Spinucci (1979:41), albeit advancing a doubtful aesthetic, writes that White "is one of the very few contemporary novelists in whom style cannot be regarded as a dress or as an alien covering, but becomes the incarnation of thought and vision". Spinucci's words are a steal from De Quincey, who is quoted by Dutton

Style is the artist's handwriting. Walter Pater saw literary art as the transcription of the writer's personal perception of the world. It is not, as in realism or naturalism, a submission to Nature through faithful imitation; Nature, rather, is subjectively transfigured. This transfiguration involves (indeed, is) the hallmark of personal style, which is not measured by broad conformity with schools or historical periods. Pater's aesthetic theory is, so far at least, innocuous enough to accommodate Patrick White's practice. From here on, however, I see the ramifications of Pater's theory (and his own literary practice) as going in one direction, while White's style strikes out in another. Pater regards the search for the right word as a dedication to the magic power of language, which permits the poet to triumph over an unreliable, non-subjective world that is partly "out of joint". White's struggle with the "rocks and sticks of words" is not like Pater's celebration of the artist's subjectivity, but is an encoding of *generally* subjective processes as they cope with the world. White precisely explores indeterminacy as it characterizes our perception of objects in the world. Although both Pater and White are archaeologists of meaning, Pater advocates a novelty-seeking investment in archaism and neologism as a way of resisting everyday language, whereas White's language is rooted in the everyday.

Wolfgang Iser has shown how Pater's stylistic theory and practice lead to a truly "mannerist" preoccupation with transcending the world of objects by creating "natural" artifice, and by elevating the part above the whole.[24] The old unity of the world is replaced by the unity afforded by the artist's all-embracing subjectivity. Iser, with support from Nietzsche, views this as literary decadence. I could not place White here. Iser persuasively analyzes passages from Pater to show how the parts do not add up to a whole, but float in a shimmering mist of impressions, incongruities, and indefinable associations. White, because his style ultimately and unceasingly makes us feel the hard surfaces of the objective world, does not allow his language to dissolve into a concatenation of subjective "subjects" with a life of their own. This last was not always Pater's intention: his ultimate but seldom realized aim was that stylistic nuances should forge a mysterious unity. White's style, for all its surface appearance of incongruity and indeterminacy, does achieve the mystery of unity,[25] wherein all elements of expression work together to shape a tangible world.

(1971:30) as being "completely relevant to White". Dutton, unfortunately, never shows clearly what he means by "style", ranging as he does in his discussion from narrative method, tone and metaphor through structure and actional detail to paragraph-length and theme.

[24] In these two closing paragraphs, I am indebted to Wolfgang Iser's consummate discussion of Pater's theory of style (Iser [1960]1987:46–60).

[25] For this phrase, cf Patricia Morley 1972.

3

NARRATIVE AND MEMORY

I Introduction

The blurb on the Penguin edition of *The Solid Mandala* may be said to encourage certain expectations and presuppositions on the part of a first-time reader:

> This is the story of two people living one life. Arthur and Waldo Brown were born twins and destined never to grow away from each other. They spent their childhood together. Their youth together. Middle-age together. Retirement together. They even shared the same girl. They shared everything—except their view of things. Waldo, with his intelligence, saw everything and understood little. Arthur was the fool who didn't bother to look. He understood. [blurb-layout simplified here]

Note the emphasis on shared yet contrasting lives (the stuff of conflict), and on linearity. The reader might vaguely expect to find a set of alternating chapters treating the twins contrastively and chronologically from childhood to retirement; with such a central constellation of characters, however, so many other possibilities for structuring a narrative could be entertained that the blurb can really be seen as, at best, a sort of guideline to the novel's thematic concerns.

The reader is more likely to have an unarticulated body of broad structural expectations tested by the macrostructural organization indicated on the contents page of the book. There the novel is divided not into chapters but into four sections or (as it turns out, chapter-less) parts. Judging from the page-beginning for each section, there is no symmetrical disposition of quantity among these four sections:

1 *In the Bus* (12 pages)
2 *Waldo* (193 pages)
3 *Arthur* (81 pages)
4 *Mrs Poulter and the Zeitgeist* (22 pages)

Section 1 seems to indicate the scene of the action for that section, 4 has something to do with a character subsidiary to the two central ones named in the blurb, 2 and 3 are in total much larger. If the central characters figure in 2 and 3, they might not figure large in 1 and 4, or might be treated together with other characters in what looks like a prologue/epilogue structure (this is in fact the case). The Waldo section is two and a half times as long as the Arthur section. This might suggest that Waldo is the more important (he is "treated"—a provisional formulation—before his twin brother). Or perhaps (given the blurb's emphasis on shared characteristics) more information common to the twins will be presented first, together, and under a heading which suggests better access to such information. In which case Arthur could be seen as being more important than, less important than, or as important as his brother. None of these speculations need prove justified. What the reader takes in from the very first sentence of the narrative proper could stand to correct, adjust or re-channel prior assumptions—even something so minimal an assumption as that the novel will be presenting us with the significant lives of Waldo and Arthur.

The actual disposition of such macrotextual features is as much a matter of style as is the microtexture of diction. These and other areas of style are intimately interwoven, or overlap, or exert "feedback" influence on each other. Whatever the level on which the analyst of narrative decides to operate, the determination of stylistic valency is fundamental. To a greater or lesser extent, it should be possible provisionally to allocate stylistic features of White's fiction to one of two broad categories.

(1) A given feature may be the expressive trace of White's own mind: for a given text (and, perhaps, for the *oeuvre*), such a feature would recur. It would be distributed with catholic impartiality throughout the narrative. It could be said to be an index to the author's idiolect—or, less naively, to the idiolect he has established for his implied author or his narrator where distinct from the characters. It need not only reflect an idiolect in the sense of representing speech or potentially articulable thought, but also idio-*lexis* in the sense of narrating or enunciating the preverbal or the non-verbal. Such an auctorial "mind-style", when it is mediating the perceptions, reactions and inchoate states of fictional characters, could be seen as essentially indicating pre-individual or universal aspects of human psychology. We therefore cannot speak of such a style as being employed to delineate specific characters.

(2) On the other hand, the presence of a given feature may be discontinuous with the whole of the text, and may occur and recur only under quite specific narrative conditions—conditions which cannot simply be explained in terms of the limited co-occurrence of certain universal or pre-individual psychological situations or states. At the very least, the implied author is then at a mimetic, parodistic, or ironic remove from his "own" store of mind-style features. Tension between the (epistemologically) universal and the specific can result. At the most (and this is no restriction), the position of "zero-degree" narration has been voluntarily—intentionally—vacated, the narration surrendered to a character. The mind that speaks is made to do so from within the narrative flow. This can be achieved by superficially conspicuous, but formally and linguistically "simple" operations of transformation (eg, the so-called "interior monologue"). Or less conspicuous, more complex operations may be carried out—the combining of character-specific style-features with "universal" or text-pervading style-features representing the characters' mental states and reactions in general, or the implied author's mental disposition, or both of these.

Although it is important to maintain the distinction between these two categories—without it, one cannot really establish a *particular* novel's nature as a verbal construct—it is hard to draw the line. We usually proceed by deduction, establishing isograms of stylistic particularity or generality according to our perception of relative absence or presence. It is easier to isolate pervasive style-features than it is to allocate such features within, say, passages of free indirect discourse with frequent slipping into other diegetic modes.[1] *The Solid Mandala* provides a better basis for testing assumptions about mind-style versus, say, character-specific styles than do many of White's novels. It is clear from even a first reading that the "same" events have been narrated at least twice, in discrete sections.[2] It is also clear that the narrative perspective is, in each section, established to maximize consonance between action and character-psychology. At one important level of the discourse, each character is telling his own story through his own subjectivity in his own section of the novel. This subjectivity is structured narratively by the implied author in such a way that its specificity stands in significant contrast to another. Otherwise there would be no point in telling the tale twice over. The over-arching significance of the novel cannot reside alone in the nature of the events recounted: it must reside in the construction that the characters themselves place upon these events. Accordingly, style-features may mediate or express either the implied author's view of events and character, or a character's own view of events, of himself, and of others. In order to get at significant (or significating) style-features and to allocate them to the relevant domain, one would ideally need to begin by examining indexical features of the narrative which do not necessarily have to do with style in the narrower sense.

One such index could be that of semically indicative or "characterizing" verbs: ie, those which serve to corroborate, through their particular, contrastive constellation, what has already been gathered from a consideration of narrative structure (see ch. 8.III below). Another index, which has customarily been examined in a very selective and partial way only, is potentially much larger, and constitutes all those semantic correlates of narrative events which show salience through repetition and variation (see esp. ch. 12 below). These may be called proairetic (actional) and hermeneutic (thematic) persistencies which correlate with the semic (character) code: and, indeed, also serve to constitute that code.[3] Anything can come within this category—persistencies of "thought" and lexis,

---

[1] I derive the terms "diegetic" and "diegesis" from Genette (1980:164–85), and implicitly or explicitly juxtapose them with "mimetic" and "mimesis", simply to distinguish the illusion of direct speech representation (pure mimesis, customarily within quotation-marks) from all other modes of regulating narrative information.

[2] A parallel situation does not exactly obtain in the case of Faulkner's *The Sound and the Fury;* but the explicit sectional structure makes it easier for the reader to latch onto, say, the style/character correlations in Benjy's section. It is much more difficult to establish such correlations in narratives with a through-composed structure like *Absalom, Absalom!* or *Light in August.*

[3] These codes are some of the signifying systems developed by Roland Barthes (in their fullest application, in Barthes 1974). In connection with *The Solid Mandala*, the hermeneutic code is the most interesting one, involving as it traditionally does the intimation of "enigmas" which the reader, in his desire for "truth", endeavours to solve. It is from Barthes (and, in his wake, Genette) that I derive the useful concept of the *leurre* or "false clue", to which I make occasional reference elsewhere.

especially of a descriptive valency; tropes, (trans)figurative procedures, "simile", metaphor, symbolism—so long as it is not itself an element in the mode of discourse proper (eg, deixis, cohesion), a salient linguistic marker (eg, a syntactic pattern or aspect-marker), or a rhetorical feature (eg, syllepsis).

The broadest index of all is the macrostructure of the narrative, in terms of the correspondences between *fabula* and *sujet*, or story and discourse, This is the index (within *The Solid Mandala)* that I shall be treating in this chapter, as it casts the clearest light on the subjective selectivity of Waldo and Arthur, as well as corroborating much of the stylistic patterning of the narrative at the level of lexis and syntax. I shall be referring to "narrative" instead of "plot", and to "discourse", "narrative discourse" or "narration" when talking of aspects of the mediation of narrative.[4] Causality, of course, is ubiquitous at both the macrotextual and the microtextual levels of the narrative. The generations and transformations of the main events in the history of each character in White's novel are themselves part of the narrative, and are so represented as to delineate Arthur's and Waldo's own position as victims of causality. Hence the obligation to consider in full the associative interrelation of textual detail as well as the more explicit interrelation of events.

II Narremic structure and the twice–told: preliminaries

I have attempted below ("Narremic reconstruction of *fabula*") to reconstruct the story or *fabula* of the Waldo and Arthur sections by dividing the narrative into "narremes" and redistributing these chronologically. The reconstruction was originally intended as an appendix. As, however, placing this schematic information at the back of the book would have involved much awkward shuttling back and forth, I have chosen instead to interrupt the main text here. Immediate rehearsal of the actional sense of the novel will, I hope, serve to provide concrete points of reference for the analytical discussions in the next three chapters.

With various degrees of reduction, these narrative units might equally well be termed "functions" (at the level of story, *fabula* or *récit*) and "motifs" (at the level of narrative, *sujet* or *discours*). As both are heuristic abstractions, I shall use my own unitary term, and not these or the structuralist, action-oriented term "armature" (see Rimmon 1976:36-37). Only those narremes have been included which have event-character, or which are processes or event-sequences of clearly demarcated duration. I have thus been concerned with what Chatman (1978:31–32) calls *process statements* ("kernel" events, which are logically essential; and "satellite" events, which are not), rather than with *stasis statements* (IS-statements

---

[4] Thus following Genette 1980. Sternberg (1978:8–14) includes a useful summary and refinement of the Russian Formalists' distinction between *sujet* and *fabula*, though he is concerned only with its application to the question of narrative expositions or beginnings. Although I have consulted with interest Rimmon[-Kenan] (1976:esp.36–41), her clarification of the forest of contradictory French-structuralist terms has succeeded only in leading me back to *sujet* and *fabula* here as a shorthand indication of a more sophisticated approach to the temporal dispositions of story/plot.

communicating "existents", such as characters and their traits, or setting and its impingement upon the mind of a character). Much of the microtexture of the process statements that I have reduced to narremes consists, of course, of stasis statements (descriptive passages, indications of mental and emotional states), which also occupy the gaps or interstices I have indicated in the synopses of the narremes in discourse-sequence. Consideration of these is mandatory in an investigation of psychological or subjective narrative; but I shall withhold such consideration until later, except for incidental remarks necessary to render intelligible the psychological motivation of the discourse-sequence.

The chronology is built up out of 116 narremes or story-units. A further 8 narremes have been included to cover the extension of the event-horizon through Section 4. The "fit" of Section 1 into the overall scheme will be discussed separately. All the narremes have been numbered for reference purposes, and are "stepped" to make it clear whether they occur within Waldo's or Arthur's section alone, or are in some degree "twice told".[5] Some of the narremes could have been divided further, others perhaps merged where they are adjacent. The *reader-response* principles upon which the selection of narremes was made are at once simple and complex. They derive from the relative salience of given events to the reader's eye (after at least a second reading), and from the less overt pressure exerted by the presence of manifold details, leitmotifs and echoes at the microstructural level. The reader may be shocked (or amused) to find in the narremic synopsis and in my general discussion of the novel considerable reference to the precise age of the characters, to specific years, and to historically "real" events and places. I am fully aware of how fallacious it can be to subvert and constrict a fiction by treating it as though it were historically "real". My motives for engaging in temporal archaeology lie elsewhere and will, I hope, explain themselves.

NARREMIC RECONSTRUCTION OF FABULA

1. A. at *Götterdämmerung* in England with relatives (A216–17)

2. A. on sea-voyage from England (after Capetown; A215–16, A218)

3. Brown family lodging with the Thompsons in Barranugli (A218)

    4. Mr Brown at the bank in Barranugli; twins visit bank, meet the invalid, Mrs Mackenzie, upstairs (W52–53 / A218–19, A220–21)

5. The twins begin attending primary school in Barranugli (A218)

    6. The Browns inspect land in Terminus Road, Sarsaparilla, guided by Mr Allwright (W37 / A221–23)

    7. The Browns have house built in Terminus Road; Mr Brown has Greek pediment built on (W36–37 / A223)

    8. Mr Brown reads to the twins from the Greek myths (W33 / A223–24)

---

5 Page-numbers within the reference-text of *The Solid Mandala* (Penguin edition 1969) are keyed by letter to the four sections of the novel: B = "In the Bus"; W = "Waldo"; A = "Arthur"; P = "Mrs Poulter and the Zeitgeist". This notation-system is used throughout the study, as differentiation of source-matter is crucial to my main arguments.

9. The twins are exempted from religious instruction at school (A224–25)

10. The twins' last visit to the bank; Mr Brown looks strange (W53/54; possibly W34, W136)

11. W., "at the leggy stage", overhears his parents talking about their tradition-warped relatives in England, and about the freedom of life in Australia (W48–49; W126: "his parents' unhappiness, viewed through the glare of yellow grass")

12. The Misses Dallimore pay a visit (W24, W49–52)

> **13.** A. helps Johnny Haynes with maths, receives marbles as reward (W42 / A228–29)
>
> **14.** W. reads out Gothic school-essay; Johnny Haynes teases him with knife; A. comes to the rescue; Mr Haynes visits Browns to complain about A.; Mr Brown's "collapse" after visit (W43–47 / *A229*)
>
> **15.** W. announces plan to write a tragedy (W38–40 / A229–30)
>
> **16.** A. acts out his cow-tragedy (W38–40 / A229–30)
>
> **17.** The twins are given piano lessons (W91 / A231–32)
>
> **18.** A. is shifted from piano-lessons to bread-making (W35–36 / A231–32)
>
> **19.** A. is apprenticed at Allwrights' store, and W. starts at Barranugli High (W59–60, W75 / A232–34)

20. Mr Brown tries to explain sex to W. on the train to Barranugli (W77–79)

> **21.** A.'s grocery-deliveries to, and contact with, Mrs Feinstein (A240–42)
>
> **22.** A.'s grocery-deliveries to Mrs Musto; A. discovers mandala-definition in book at her house (A234–39; and is told that W. is to be invited to a party there, along with the Feinstein girl)
>
> **23.** A. asks his father the meaning of the word "totality", on the Sunday after the weekday of **22** (A239–40)
>
> **24.** W. tells A. he has been invited to Mrs Musto's; A. gives W. a message for Mrs Musto; W. meets Dulcie Feinstein at Mrs Musto's tennis-party; D. tells him an anecdote about a pierrot; W. walks D. home (W86–98, W123 / A238–39; W87: *W. aged about 16;* W123: *late summer, early 1909*)

25. W. invited to Feinsteins'; Len Saporta, D.'s man-friend, is indisposed and cannot come; D., with a cold, plays the piano; Mr Feinstein talks about enlightened Jews (W99–106; *occasion:in the "holidays before the end" = August before the last term of school, 1909*)

> **26.** W. and A. visit the Feinsteins'; D. plays the piano; W. gets diarrhoea; W. finds D. and A. discussing the pierrot (W107–13 / A243–45; *late spring/early summer of 1909: phlox and white hydrangeas in bloom, and there are thunderstorms*)

27. W.'s end-of-year exams, interview, and acceptance at Sydney Municipal Library (W114; *end of 1909*)

28. On his seventeenth birthday, W. starts work at the Library (W121–22; *early 1910*)

29. W. gets to know Walter Pugh at the Library, boasts of (fictional) sexual exploits with D. (W122–23; *no earlier than mid-1912: Walter Pugh is Waldo's senior by 18 months, W122*)

30. D. tells A. that she and her mother are sneaking off to Europe (*W123–24,* A245–46; *early winter: A245; mid-1912*)

31. A. tells W. that D. and her mother have gone to Europe "on a visit to the relatives" "to learn the language" (W123–24; *an extended Grand Tour in reverse; at this stage the Feinsteins have only recently left, as A. speaks in the -ing-future of their intentions*)

32. W. enters the grounds of Feinsteins' "Mount Pleasant" and peers through slats in shutters; discovered and rebuffed by Mr Feinstein; talks antisemitically at the family dinnertable (W124–25)

33. W. tells Walter Pugh that D. has sent him a letter from Brussels (W126)

34. D. sends A. a postcard from the Italian lakes; A. claims later that he told W. this, and that the latter must have forgotten the fact (W132 / A247; **firm date:** *14 April 1914, A247*)

35. War breaks out in Europe (W126–27 / A247; *August 1914*)

36. A. meets D. after the Feinsteins' return from Europe (A247–48; *W130, W132: "Not long after the outbreak", "there was a submarine"; probably before the Lusitania incident in May 1915*)

37. Walter Pugh enlists; farewell party at home of Walter's married sister Cis, at which W. sings (W128–29; *Walter possibly sails with the A.I.F. as early as December 1914*)

38. Walter Pugh killed in battle; Cis appears at Library, offers W. her brother's few poems, "so unlike her brother" and written overseas; W. declines the offer (W129; *possibly Gallipoli 1915–16*)

39. Len Saporta sends D. a Star of David from France (A249; *any time between late 1916 and early 1918*)

40. Len Saporta returns with shrapnel wounds (A249; *1916–18*)

41. A. visits Len Saporta in his Sydney carpet-shop, and sees the mandala in a carpet (*W30*, A249–51; *"towards the end" of the First World War*)

42. A. visits Mr Feinstein's music-shop, sees a pierrot on some old sheet-music, and composes a pierrot-song in the tramcar on the way home (A248)

43. W. encounters D., who invites him to come and see her postcard collection from the trip to Europe (W130–31 / *A248*; W131: D. has by now started working at her father's shop)

44. A. and W. visit the Feinsteins by invitation; A. sings his pierrot-song; D. plays the piano; W. sings; D. weeps (W131–40 / A248–49; W139: *in "their wartime garden", 1916–18*)

45. End of War (*implied, W130*); A. celebrates the "Peace" in Sydney (A251–52; **firm date:** *11 November 1918*)

46. Mr Brown retires "a year or two early" (W158; *aged 58 or so; in 1920 he "had retired, but had not died", W140; 1919–20*)

47. The asthmatic Mr Brown tells W. of his reasons for leaving England, and about W.'s own chances in life (W145–46)

48. The Poulters arrive to settle in Terminus Road, at first in a hut, then in a house; early contacts; Mrs Brown's negative attitude to Mrs Poulter (W61, W140–42 / A256; *"perhaps about 1920", W140*)

49. A. soon begins visiting Mrs Poulter; once he asks her why she married Bill Poulter (*W140–41, W144* / A256–58)

50. W. courts, but fails to make a friend of, Bill Poulter (W142–44)

51. W. as voyeur, spying on Mrs Poulter at her toilette and lovemaking (W61–62)

52. Mrs Brown has an "operation" for removal of a breast (W120 / A256; *in the same year the Poulters came: ie, about 1920, A256*)

53. A. tells Mrs Poulter about his mother's mastectomy, and tries unsuccessfully to get Mrs Brown to talk about it (A256; **firm temporal datum:** *A. is almost 28 years old*)

54. A. hears that Mrs Feinstein has died; he visits D. in the Sydney house to offer his condolences (A252–53)

55. On a walk with Mrs Poulter, A. sees a Chinese woman under a wheel-tree, dances his mandala-dance, and gives Mrs Poulter his gold mandala-marble (A262–67; *a public holiday in summer; recalled in: "After he had given [two] marbles", A228*)

56. A. tells W. about Mrs Poulter, the Chinese woman and the wheel-tree (W145)

> **57.** The Brown parents reveal strong signs of hostility towards Mrs Poulter (W144, *Mr Brown only* / A267)

> **58.** A. dreams a tree-dream about D. and Mrs Poulter; next day, A. and Mrs Poulter go for a walk, and talk about Christ; walk terminated prematurely; A. has a crucifixion dream, and temporarily loses his "special" marble (A260-62)

> **59.** Mrs Poulter is frightened one evening by A.'s practical joke; she hedges about the possibility of further walks together; A. goes home in tears (A259-60)

60. W. overhears Council workmen talking scornfully about Bill Poulter, and making sexual innuendoes about Mrs Poulter and her walks with A. (W146-47)

> **61.** A. visits Mrs Poulter, who tells him that there will be no more walks, because "they" and her husband don't approve (*W148* / A268)

> **62.** W. forbids A. to go on walks with Mrs Poulter; A. replies that the matter has already been settled (W147-48 / A267, A268)

63. Mr Brown gives the Poulters an old raincoat (W161)

64. W. hears that Mrs Feinstein has died; he is unable to complete a satisfactory letter of condolence, and decides instead to visit D. with the vague intention of proposing marriage (W148-49)

> **65.** A. visits D., uninvited, at "Mount Pleasant"; she invites him to her wedding with Len Saporta, but he says he cannot attend because of W.; he gives D. his blue mandala-marble (A253-56; *A228: marble-gift recalled as for* **55**) / W. also visits D., and discovers A. already sitting with her; W. "proposes" to her, is disabused, and is introduced to Len Saporta (W149-58)

[**66.** "By this period" (prior to **67**) W., it is claimed, has started a fragment of a novel (titled later *Tiresias a Youngish Man*), and has "written several articles" (W70; but cf **80**)]

> **67.** Mr Brown dies; W.'s and A.'s differing immediate reactions to this event (W69-74, W120, W161 / A269-70, A274; **firm date:** *1922, W120 /A274*)

68. D. marries Len Saporta (A274)

69. Mr Feinstein suffers the first of three strokes after his wife's death; the Saportas go to live with him in the Sydney house; A. makes frequent visits there (A274)

70. W. contemplates himself in the mirror on his thirtieth birthday (W119-20; *1923*)

> **71.** Before the birth of the Saportas' first child, Len tells A. that it will be named after him (A275-76)

> **72.** A. pays a visit to the bedridden, speechless Mr Feinstein; they gaze at each other in silence, after A. has said that the Star of David is a mandala (A277-78)

> **73.** On A.'s next visit to the Saportas (after the birth of Arthur/Aaron: D. is lactating), D. tells him that her father has died (A278-79)

74. W. and A. are told by Mrs Brown to move into their parents' double bed; she will move into the boys' room (W174)

> **75.** Mrs Brown starts getting senile and dipsomanic (W164-68 / A270-71)

> **76.** Mrs Brown becomes chronically ill; W. will not call in a doctor for her when her state becomes acute (W1617-70 / A272)

> **77.** A. offers W. his third mandala-marble, which W. rejects (W169 / A273; *"during their mother's last illness"*)

> **78.** Mrs Brown dies, and is cremated (W167, W170-71 / A273; **firm date:** *1932, "ten years after ... her husband", W167*)

> **79.** W. has an accident in Pitt Street, Sydney, and breaks his pince-nez, while running away after an encounter with the Saportas and their two children, including

the boy called Arthur; A. visits W. in hospital (W63–68, W171, *W173* / A279; **firm date:** *1934, W63: "a couple of years later"—ie, after* **78**)

80. W. has one of his fallings-out with his younger superior, Crankshaw, at the Library (W70, W171–73 / A279; *after the "distressing incident",* **79:** *with three marriageable daughters, Crankshaw must be in his mid-40s, W. almost 50–cf* **87** *; early 1940s: "A second war had broken out", W173–74, "was going on", A280*) ["This was the year" of W.'s literary "activity", W173; is the "lady novelist" whose invitation W. declines, W173, the Miss Huxtable whose question he answers so sternly, W71? Cf **66**]

81. The "big new Public Library" (including the Mitchell Library, W182) is opened (W177; *1942, "a couple of years before" W. resigns from Sydney Municipal*)

    82. A. begins reading secretly at the Public Library (A279–80)

83. W. resigns from Sydney Municipal Library (W175–77; *1943*)

    84. W. applies for and moves to the Public Library (W177, W182 / A279–80; *1943; "The Peace" is "a couple of years after his momentous transfer", W182*)

    85. Both W. and A. are (separately) accosted and propositioned by women in Sydney on V–Day (W184 / A280; **firm date:** *11 August 1945*)

86. W. buys a large doll in Sydney and gives it to Mrs Poulter, after drinking in the pub with Library colleagues (W184–86; *September–October 1945: "some weeks" after "the Peace"*)

87. A. brings home a puppy (W178–79; *1949: "six years" after W.'s "momentous transfer"; A. now aged 56*)

88. Shortly after **87**, W. also brings home a puppy (W179–81)

89. One Sunday, W. is alone in the house when a man and a woman pay a visit; W. hides, and realizes that the man is Johnny Haynes (W187–91; *1951: "a couple of years after they got the dogs"*)

    90. Mr Allwright dies; Mrs Allwright continues running the store (W60, W203 / A282; **firm date:** *1951, W203*)

91. A. discovers the Tennyson poem; W. weeps (W195–96, *"Waldo had sat down"—Past Perfect places this before* **94–95**; *A. as intruder, W195, before the narrating of* **95**, *W191*)

    92. During a rainstorm, W. asks what A. is thinking, and bursts into tears (A282–83)

        93. At the Library, Miss Glasson causes W. to notice for the first time that A. is reading there; after a heated exchange, W. commands A. to leave (W196–202 / A283–85; *1951: "two years before Waldo's retirement", W202; A. is still working for Mrs Allwright*)

        94. A. takes flour to Mrs Poulter from the store, entering unawares to find her dressing a doll (W194 / A288–89; *1951 or 1952; P299: Mrs Poulter takes the doll away and buries it, probably after A. sees her with it*)

        95. Later the same night as **92:** W. finds a dress-box to hide his "papers" in, then sees his mother's blue dress, putting it on in front of the mirror; hearing A. returning with the dogs, W. changes frantically into his own clothes; A. enters, telling him about Mrs Poulter and the doll; W. stows the dress behind the copper (W191–94) / A. has actually seen W. in the dress before he enters to tell W. about Mrs Poulter (A291)

        96. Mrs Allwright sells the store just after W. retires from the Library; A. is also compelled to "retire" (W37, W202–204 / A286; *1953: the twins must be around 60 years of age for W. to retire from a public service job*)

    97. A. starts writing poems in secret (A290)

98. A. goes on walks with the dogs on weekdays now as well; on one occasion he looks at the wheel-tree and the Chinese woman (A286–87)

99. W. starts taking A. on strenuous walks, for health reasons and to fill in their mornings (W210 / A292; *early 1960s: Vietnam war penetrating Australian media consciousness—cf Mrs Poulter and television [introduced to Australia in 1956], P299, P302. The dogs are "nearly as old" as their owners: ie, in their old or late middle age, P20, which could make the dogs as old as ten [= 1959] or, exceptionally, in their late teens [= early 1960s]. The twins were born ca. 1893; Mrs Poulter is younger than A., A263, and is 67 at the time of W.'s death, P296. If she is, say, two years younger than the twins, this makes them about 69 at the time of W.'s death, and the year can be fixed at ca. 1962—which correlates with the circumstantial deduction at narreme* **96**)

100. On one walk, A. asks W. about cremation (A274)

101. W. shits the bed, and must be cleaned up by A. (W211 / A292; *this could be the result of a mild stroke occasioned by exertion on the walks*)

102. More walks; A. questions their efficacy; W. defends them (W211 / A292)

Actional Present (early 1960s, around Easter)

WEDNESDAY

103. A. gets a heart-tremor (W24–25, W31, W55: *adverted to in actional present* / A292: *recall of, at undefined moment*)

104. The twins set off for a walk (which W., as always, intends should induce A.'s death through a heart-attack), go along the main street to the edge of town, and enter the road leading to Barranugli (W23–31, W54–61)

105. W. (and, it turns out, A.) sees Mrs Poulter on the 8.13 bus to Barranugli (W60/62)

106. W. is almost knocked over by a passing truck; A. reminisces about deaths (W63, W68–69)

107. The twins turn back along the road, W. walking ever faster until he stops, in danger of a seizure, in front of a rosebush in the "glossier" section of Sarsaparilla (W114–19)

108. The twins open the gate and re-enter the house (W204)

109. After their midday meal of bread and milk, A. quizzes W. about "love"; W. is upset, and retires to his "papers" (W204–8)

110. In the evening, W. breaks down in tears, lies in bed comforted by A.'s embrace, and dreams of D. (W208–209)

THURSDAY

111. W. wakes early and washes the dishes; A. gets up and tells W. he has dreamt about him; they set off on their walk (W209–10)

112. The twins return as usual and have their bread and milk (*inferred from iterative diegesis, W210*); A. discovers the blue dress stuffed behind the copper, and shows it to W.; A. throws the dress away (W211–12 / A292–93)

113. W. discovers a poem by A. in the corner, and tears it up after reading it aloud at the apologetic A. (W212 / A293)

114. About 4pm, W. goes out to the incinerator and burns all his papers (W212–13 / A293–94)

115. W. lies down in bed, apparently with a seizure; A. finds him there; W. clutches at A., cursing his poem, and dies (W213–14 / A294)

116. Releasing his brother's grip, A. flees, inadvertently shutting the dogs inside the house (A294)

The Aftermath (Section 4)

THURSDAY

117. A. runs babbling through paddocks, takes the train to Sydney, wanders around, and spends the night in an alleyway (P305–306; *"'Is it Friday termorrer?'"—this and* **122** *form the basis for plotting the daily sequence of* **103–24**)

FRIDAY

118. A. loses his knotted mandala, wanders half-asleep until daybreak (P306–307)

FRIDAY TO FRIDAY

119. A. wanders round Sydney for days, not keeping track of time, once entering the Library (P307)

FRIDAY NIGHT

120. A. keeps a secret vigil over the Saportas as they celebrate the start of the Jewish Sabbath, then goes away (P308–309)

SATURDAY

121. In the morning, A. takes the train and the bus back to Sarsaparilla and Mrs Poulter (P309)

122. Mrs Poulter discovers W. lying dead on his bed, mutilated by the dogs (P301–305; *"a Saturday afternoon", P301; temporally preceded by Mrs Poulter's mediated interior monologue, P295–300, opening into her realization that she has not seen W. or A. "since when", P301; putrefaction has set in, P302, and is advanced enough for Mrs Poulter to smell it from a distance*)

123. A. appears at Mrs Poulter's house, and says he has killed his brother (P309–10).

124. Mrs Poulter comforts A., who is taken away to the mental home by the police; Mrs Poulter prepares her husband's evening meal (P311–16)

The first thing that becomes clear is that not all of the events in which Waldo and Arthur are involved are explicitly twice-told. The reason may simply be that certain events are experienced by one character only and are not directly accessible to the other.[6] I am not talking here of *ultimate* accessibility, as when we assume that Waldo may well have learned eventually the origin of Dulcie's Star of David (cf narreme **39**), eventually hears (**64**) of Mrs Feinstein's death (**54**), learns from Arthur (**31, 34, 56**) about Dulcie's trip to Europe, her postcard to Arthur, and the Chinese wheel-tree (**30, 55**); learns, through accidentally meeting Dulcie, of her early return from Europe (**43**, long after Arthur, **36**). Ultimate accessibility is also bound up with partial prior informedness, as when it is clear that Arthur knows in advance that Waldo and Dulcie will be brought together at Mrs Musto's tennis-party (**24**), or when Arthur tells Waldo that he has found Mrs Poulter with a doll (**94**).

More interesting are cases in which events are experienced to some degree by both Waldo and Arthur, or are accessible to the subordinate party by direct observation or awareness of the social situation, but in which these events have

---

[6] For example, in Waldo's section: narremes **11, 20, 25, 29, 32–33, 37–38, 43, 47, 51, 60, 64, 70, 86** and **89**; in Arthur's section: narremes **1-2, 36, 39–42, 45**, part of **49** and **53, 54–55, 58, 61, 69, 71–73, 82** and **97**.

been narrated in one section only.[7] Both twins make the last visit to the bank (**10**), but only Waldo finds this visit significant, in that it is associated with a painful sense of rejection by his father. In narreme **12**, there must be reasons why Arthur, whose interest in people is broader and more generous than Waldo's, should not have found the visit of the Misses Dallimore significant, inasmuch as his social role—at least as mediated through Waldo's recollections— was one of lively engagement. It may, conversely, be that Waldo centres on this incident purely because of his own psychological and social inclinations; absence and presence need to be weighed against each other. The various stages of his brother's career (eg, **27, 31, 66, 81**) seem not to interest Arthur until towards mid-life (**84**). Other domestic incidents *qua* incidents (changing bedrooms, **74**; buying the puppies, **87–88**) are not noted in Arthur's section although these actions have consequences (and the consequences are presented as matters of long-established fact). Waldo, as a sickly child at home in England, would have been aware that Arthur had been taken off to the opera by his relatives (**1**); he would surely have learned from his parents that Arthur had attempted to climb over the ship's railing during the voyage out to Australia (**2**). But these events do not occur in any form within Section 2. Nor do other events which have "genetic", social implications as beginnings: the twins' entry into Australian primary-school life (**5**, with its stress on the difference between the brothers and on the social function of language); the intermediate stage of lodging with the Thompsons (**3**, again with a stress on difference, this time cross-cultural); the preliminaries to housebuilding (**6**; here, of course, the focus is rather on Mr Allwright and the fascination he generates in Arthur).

Further, given Waldo's rationalist bent and propensity for *Schadenfreude*, one might have expected the incident of Mr Brown's notes pressing for exemption from religious instruction (**9**) to be at least touched on by Waldo. Instead, the exchange of letters is given verbatim in Section 3. More important still, in view of the characters' selective recollection, is the fact that the incident should have been mentioned at all in Arthur's section. The most interesting elision within the phase of childhood and adolescence is the complex of events (**14**) in which Arthur defends Waldo from Johnny Haynes. The narration-time devoted to this in Section 2 leads us to conclude that the incident remains of some emotional consequence for Waldo; but we cannot assume that its very veiled occurrence in Section 3 means that it has been of little consequence for Arthur.

Of the events that are "twice told", those that are temporally sequent in the telling have already been mentioned, but repay closer examination. Such tellings are productive of situational irony. In only a very few instances, however, is the reader privy to this irony at the first reading. The sequencing of narremes can involve not only a withholding of awareness from the character, but also a withholding of awareness from the reader *that* the character is unaware. In one case (**94**), Waldo must know through his own actions (**86**) why Mrs Poulter has

---

[7] In Waldo's section: narremes **10, 12, 14, 27–28, 63, 66, 74, 81, 87–88**. In Arthur's section: parts of **1** and **2**; **3, 5–6, 9**, part of **49** and **53, 68, 98**.

come to possess a large doll; and we know that Arthur is not cognizant of the antecedents of the scene he recounts verbally in Waldo's section. This is apparent on a first reading. But the pathetic, near-tragic dimension that is missing will be ultimately supplied only in the diegetic representation of the scene in Arthur's section. In other cases, the reader is trapped, until a second reading, within the non-privileged states of awareness of one or other character. In Section 2 (**64**), Waldo is represented as hearing that Mrs Feinstein is dead. On his acquisition of this knowledge depends a fateful train of events triggered off by his egoistic fantasy of proposing marriage to Dulcie on the pretext of offering her his condolences; Waldo finds Arthur already at the house with Dulcie, who wears mourning. At no stage in this latter scene (**65**) does Waldo construe Arthur's presence as having to do with Mrs Feinstein's death. He is so filled with his proposal-scheme that he takes the physical attitudes and words of Dulcie and Arthur as having something to do with *eros* and courtship rather than with *agape* and death. That Arthur has come neither to console nor to court—he has already offered his condolences on a previous occasion (**54**), and is seeing Dulcie on this later occasion because of a vague invitation which Dulcie had in the meantime forgotten—is effectively *suppressed* or *elided* narratively under pressure from Waldo's closed perspective.

In Section 2, Arthur tells Waldo (**56**) about seeing the wheel-tree with Mrs Poulter. The incident (given mimetically: ie, dialogically, not at the remove of diegesis) can have as little significant impact on the reader at this stage as it must originally have had on Waldo: he shudders, while we are still as mystified as in Section 1 (p. 13) when Mrs Poulter mentions the epiphany to Mrs Dun. It is only in Section 3 (**55**) that the wheel-tree epiphany takes on its full significance in the context of Arthur's mandala-dance. And it is only on our second reading that we realize the extent to which Waldo is closed off. It could be said that we are closer to the intense, self-sustaining solipsism of Waldo during our first reading than we are during any subsequent readings; we are gradually pushed off the analysis-couch and over towards the psychiatrist's big leather chair.

In the other major cases of delayed revelation, a double irony of situation is brought home to us on later readings only. One irony is purely situational—the fact of Waldo's non-awareness of Dulcie Feinstein's return from Europe (compare the narremic sequence **31, 34, 42**). The other, associated irony reveals through narrative sequencing something about the nature of Arthur that contrasts with our developed (or reflexive) image of him as "simple" in the sense of being open and direct, and conveys with awful implacability how far *he* is prepared to go by way of secrecy (if not deceit or self-deceit) to protect his interests—a trait we normally associate with Waldo. Compare the narremes **44, 34, 36** and **42**: it is only when we get to the last of these (A248, well into Arthur's narrative) that we can be certain Arthur has lied to his brother about having already informed him of Dulcie's postcard and her return. But there is no indication in Arthur's section of his moral and emotional reaction to what he has done. All of these various dissonances add greatly to the motivational complexity of the novel and to the reader's active involvement in the reconstitution of character.

It goes without saying that it is ultimately the author who selects the events that are narrated. But, with this novel, White makes his selection in such a way that it is fully consonant with the characters' making *their* selection. If the often extreme dissonances of perspective in the twice-told indicate Waldo's and Arthur's psychological makeup, questions arise concerning the precise nature of the narration. A *structurally* psychologized narrative can hardly rely throughout, or even intermittently, on what have been termed (Cohn 1978:esp.14) *psychonarration* ("the narrator's discourse about a character's consciousness") or *quoted monologue* ("a character's mental discourse"—interior monologue). Can the novel be predominantly in *narrated monologue* ("a character's mental discourse in the guise of the narrator's discourse", including free indirect thought and its close approximations) when the "narrator" narrates in the "guise" of the characters? Exploration of this problem should gradually reveal the radical nature of White's narrational modes, and should help in the determining of recurrent features of style. But, first, a closer examination of what I have termed *psychologized structure.*

III   Memory and recollective structure

Quite early on in Section 2, when the twins have only just set out on their walk, three statements occur which help focus the psychological genesis of the narrative's structure. I shall touch on these by way of anticipation, though the normal reader is unlikely to interpret them metatextually as I am doing:

(1) Arthur spoke quite briskly. Time, it appeared, removed him quickly from the sources of pain. Sometimes Waldo envied the brother who did not seem to have experienced—though he should have—the ugly and abrasive roughcast of which life was composed. [W25]

As they approach the dilapidated gate opening onto Terminus Road at the end of the garden path, Arthur remarks that it "will fall to bits any day now".

(2) He was right. Waldo dreaded it. Averted his mind from any signs of rusty iron, or rotted timber. Unsuccessfully, however. His life was mapped in green mould; the most deeply personal details were the most corroded. [W26]

And, just as they are passing through the gateway:

(3) Suddenly the smell of rotting wood, of cold fungus, shot up through Waldo's nose. He could hardly bear, while exquisitely needing, the rusty creaking of his memory. [W27]

All of these passages have to do with the impress of time on the psyche—specifically, with the ability to cope with the personal past (which is what defines the self), with the roughcast of life, its surface accretions. By the time passage (1) occurs, we are three pages into Section 2, which, so far as we can determine, has the twins as *old* men (as seen, perhaps, by the two old women from the bus window) about to set out on a walk; by hindsight, one can term this area of the narrative the *actional present.* In terms of action and time-lapse, they have put on their coats, moved out of the kitchen, and stumbled hand in hand, against the wind, down the broken brick path to the gate. These three pages are already saturated with the past, however, through Waldo's consciousness. Arthur is sitting in "*that old* leather chair with *the* burst seat where mice had nested *the other winter,* the woodwork *scratched* by dogs reaching up to claim right of affection. Arthur sat in *their father's* chair". This first paragraph of diegesis locates the chair in time, not space, its physical character being seen familiarly (note the undistanced deixis) through the traces or *striae* of the past. Arthur is helped into "*the old* herringbone coat", which is specifically identified as "amongst the things discarded by Uncle Charlie, some of which were lasting for ever". Their dogs are repeatedly designated as "old". The kitchen smells had "set almost solid" in the kitchen; "nothing would free" Waldo's oilskin "from the weathers which had got into it". There is at least one specific recollection (of Waldo's planting a gooseberry bush which fails), one attempt at recollection disguised as mental habit ("Sometimes Waldo would look at his brother and try to remember when he had first been saddled with him"), and pervasive references to habit, all construable as Waldo's thoughts.

As the radio-announcers put it, this walk will be "a trip down Memory Lane" for Waldo.[8] Section 2 is organized around the actional present of the walk (narremes **104–8**), which is broken persistently but irregularly by the irruption into it of Waldo's memories. The condition of the gate, and the opening of it, are explicitly and implicitly to be linked with the opening of a gate into the past. Waldo fears not so much the evocations of transience and personal mortality (the future); the rust and the rot hide, rather, traces of what was before, and it is this that he fears yet needs. The realm of Thanatos or quotidian life-time and clock-time is displaced by the realm of Hypnos or the dream-time of memory. The reader will experience how strong this need is, how Waldo's solipsism leads him to seek out "the most deeply personal details", how these details have been overlaid by the mould of rationalization, the roughcast carapace of self deception and prevarication; how they have been corroded by hurt and resentment—how reluctantly, yet obsessively, and with what inefficiency and rigidity, the gate of memory creaks open for him. Waldo sees time, for Arthur, as a stream bearing him away from "the most deeply personal details" of the past (which are the painful ones). In this reference to pain, there is a characteristic equivocation. It is clearly the traces of the *physical* pain of Arthur's early-morning heart-tremor (narreme **103**) that Waldo sees his brother as now being oblivious of. But the references to the Poulters and to being "beholden" are significant at a second reading, once we know (narremes **61–62**) that Waldo, deep in the past, had been

---

[8] By far the most stimulating concise statement on the nature and function of memory and time in *The Solid Mandala* can be found in Beatson (1976:71–73); Beatson employs Jungian categories ("ancestral memory" and, more questionably, "collective unconscious") to elucidate the general characteristics of the narrative structure. Apropos the organizational centrality of the walk: Argyle (1967:59) suggests that the whole action can be linked with the "prevailing image of the journey"—the bus-trip in Section 1; the walk in Section 2; Arthur's memory of the voyage to Australia in Section 3; Mrs Poulter's contrasting stasis in Section 4 (which, however, ends by suggesting that "her actual sphere of life" is "an inevitably circular journey through the past"). Arthur's section is insufficiently accounted for in this pattern-seeking. One would need to buttress the initial moment of memory with thematic (not actional) illustrations of Arthur's spiritual voyage through life in order to make the motif "structurally" convincing.

responsible for severing a relationship between Arthur and Mrs Poulter which had been based on their being spiritually "beholden" to each other; a severance which cannot but cause *emotional* pain. Has Arthur been removed quickly from this source of pain as well? Does his briskness of manner reveal or conceal?

By and large, we do indeed find that Arthur's section moves like a stream from narreme to narreme in fairly strict chronological sequence. He seems able to cope with time (or time handles him gently)—until we examine the narrative in detail. It then becomes evident that there are whirlpools and eddies of pain in Arthur's *historia,* too, all the more affecting for the general serenity of flow which otherwise obtains. I mentioned rigidity earlier: by contrast to Arthur, the roughcast-metaphor and those of accretion and corrosion point to a kind of stasis and immobility, a declension into entropy, at the centre of Waldo's being. The "past" in Section 2 is clotted, disjunctive; Waldo is continually turning in his tracks, retracing or dwelling on discrete or frozen moments, eliding whole tracts of time. The actional present, too, is clogged with the mental detritus of Waldo's past, so that the intrinsic forward dynamic of the walk is dissipated by Waldo's being constantly dragged back into recollection. Not only are his mental perceptions of current sense-data always burdened by the connections these data generate with the past; these data *are* for Waldo embodiments of the past, and constitute fragmentary, mute, historical tableaux. In Section 2, further, Arthur is instrumental in *actively* precipitating Waldo, against his will, into the past. Arthur is able actively to retrieve both those "deeply personal details" which have caused pain and those which have brought joy. But, for Waldo, Arthur is only the "getter of pain"; so that Arthur's breathless, re-experiencing engagements with the past, his loud encouragements to "'remember'", are persistently countered by Waldo's evasions and rigid resistance, by the dull inward throb of frustration, hurt and resentment.

These emotions are not expelled by enforced or willed recollection. The intercalation of past and actional present is the author's design; Waldo's secret intention that the walk should kill off his brother (the guarded solicitousness about the heart-tremor, and various occurrences along the way, betray as much) is explained—or justified—with implicit reference to the pain Arthur has caused him in the past. What was meant as a walk with death or to death, however, is provisionally transformed into a review of two interpenetrating lives. By the end of the walk, Arthur is stronger than ever (filled with life), and it is Waldo who is debilitated. The phase of immersion in memory is closed at narreme **108**, when "the two old men returned from the walk which wasn't Arthur's last, pushing at the gate which had not yet fallen down":

For the moment at least, Waldo saw, Arthur could not die. If they hadn't been knotted together by habit he might have continued resenting Arthur's failure to accept the plan he didn't know about. [W204]

After the gate of memory is closed again, there are three transitional narremes **(109–11)**, conveyed only in Section 2, which mark Waldo's failure in the face of love. Arthur's vitality breaches Waldo's passive resistance, and the latter succumbs in tears to the embrace of love; Waldo attempts to retreat once more from this embrace the next morning, but is vanquished by Arthur's recounting to him a "love"-dream involving Waldo. The remaining narremes (**112–16**) are the only ones that are twice-told in strict chronological sequence. Whereas in Section 2 Waldo is located in the realm of the actional present from the moment he passes back through the gate (**108**), the past's onslaught on him is continued from without, in the person of his brother, whose essential role up to the end is to uncover the past (love and failure; Arthur's strength and Waldo's weakness; Mrs Brown's blue dress hidden behind the copper) or to be uncovered (Arthur's secret poem as a confirmation of Waldo's failure of creativity); Arthur's dream of Waldo's fear of procreation fits this role, too. The trigger of the dénouement proper is constituted by the two *physical* acts of discovery: of the blue dress (we learn from Arthur's section that this act is disingenuous—Arthur knows that he is confronting Waldo with an emblem of his sterile solipsism and self-love); and of Arthur's poem. These discoveries lead directly to Waldo's synecdochic destruction of self in the burning of his papers (his "life"), and to his actual self-destruction in a paroxysm triggered by hatred. This last phase is all that is given of the actional present in Section 3 up to Waldo's death, save for the heart-tremor before the walk of the preceding day. The overall structural scheme is densely compact and fiercely implicative. But perhaps I've made it seem all too easily explicable; given the necessary interpretative baseline of at least two readings-through, couldn't any responsible reader have got things straight? Including, of course, the critics? Is a structural analysis like mine really *necessary*?

IV   An excursus on (mis)readings

Before discussing the narrative structure in more detail, I should like to review those observations of the critics that touch on matters of narrative discourse, structure, and (as a necessary precondition for the perception of structure) story. In a longish treatment of *The Solid Mandala,* Patricia Morley (1972:202–203) restricts her comments on structure to a comparison of the novel with *The Sound and the Fury.* "Both novels have four parts which are viewed from four different perspectives"—but in White's novel, there are more than four character-perspectives, and they are not evenly distributed (Mrs Poulter *and* Mrs Dun in Section 1; Mrs Poulter again in Section 4, alongside Arthur and the police sergeant).[9] "Both handle time impressionistically rather than chronologically, and manage to give the effect of telling us everything that passes during the course of many years while actually concentrating on a few central events"—apart from the fact that "chronological" sequence is a feature of *story* but not of *narrative,* the frame-narrative of Section 2 is strictly chronological (actional present), as is Arthur's section (at first glance). The novel does not give us the impression of

---

9 Argyle (1967:59) also sees Sections 1 and 4 as being exclusively Mrs Poulter's view of the brothers. Morley attributes Arthur's domain in Section 4 to an "omniscient narrator"; I shall examine this point later. Bliss (1986:101–2) sees the double perspective of Section 1, but misrepresents the actual narrative perspective of Section 4 by having the events "filtered through the responses" of too many miscellaneous characters.

"everything that passes": it is crucial to the meaning of the novel for us to realize that there are yawning gaps and suspicious compressions in Waldo's section, and an almost total absence of a public, social dimension in both Sections 2 and 3. There *is* an "impressionistic", subjective handling of time, and a concentration on "a few central events", but the three *conspicuously* twice-told events here are far from being the only important ones.[10] Additionally, the characters' perspective in White's novel is combined with "the author's viewpoint"—a statement which raises more problems than it solves. Comparison with Faulkner's novel in such terms is unproductive, encouraging a misleading impression of structural, perspectival and quantitative balance in White's novel; similarities at the level of temporal microstructure aside, the two books are not really comparable.

Whereas Morley stresses the quadripartite structure as one facet of the quaternary symbolism operating in the novel, others compare the structure to a mandala—there is a beginning, a middle, and an end, but not necessarily in that order (Argyle 1967:59). Without mentioning and explaining the four-part, partly twice-telling structure, Walsh sees the "actual structure" of the novel as being concentrically mandalic.[11] This has no relevance to the novel in any normal, narratological sense of "structure": it is a kind of meta-proposition, at best applicable to the varying degrees of dramatic or psychological emphasis within the *sujet*—but even here the gradation is wrenched out of perspective as soon as one starts considering the relation between character and theme. Symptomatically, it is often unclear whether Walsh is generalizing about the whole narrative or making a point about some discrete section of it; his account of what happens when is quite simply incoherent. To illustrate that "the story begins with a bus journey", he draws mainly on material from *Waldo's* section. Conversely, he manages to equate his concentric, non-linear, alogical, emotional structure with the *whole* of the narrative, rather than with Waldo's section. What about the linearity of Arthur's section? Of the bus trip? Of the walk in the actional present? Of the dénouement, and its aftermath in Section 4? Is it the narrative technique that has a different "logic", as Walsh suggests, or is it (via the author's craft) Waldo's memory that is non-linear? Michael Cotter (1978:22–23; followed by Bliss 1986:101) also claims that "the structure of *The Solid Mandala* approximates a mandalic symbol". What Cotter has to say about "concentric, bilateral and quadratic" "symmetries" is vitally important to the analysis of the novel. But, like Walsh, Cotter takes the "central image" of the story (for, one can agree, it *is* an immediate image on the event-horizon of the

---

10 Morley mentions the afternoon at the Feinsteins', Waldo's Encounter with the Saportas, and the confrontation in the library. But equally "central" double tellings are Waldo's transvestite scene, the visits to the bank, Mr Brown's (habitual) recounting of the Greek myths, the severance of Arthur's relationship with Mrs Poulter, the death of Mr Brown. And there are also conspicuous single tellings that require inclusion.

11 Walsh 1969, 1974:208 and 1977:87. The structure is "composed of a series of similar movements or concentric circles": ordinary people, like Mrs Poulter and the Sarsaparilla community, in the outermost circle; inside this, the Brown family; then the "most intense circle of the brothers"; within this, "the light-imprisoning, solid mandala itself".

narrative, taking protean forms, as well as functioning symbolically) and has used it to elucidate character-constellations and theme. This heuristic analogy perhaps applies to the novel's "moral structure", but not to its narrative structure. Nor need it be assumed that White intended to provide an analyzable equivalent or simulacrum of the visualizable (and, Cotter fails to mention, non-standardized and polytectonic) form of the "typical" mandala in the narrative structure.[12] Nevertheless, for non-narratological purposes Cotter's system of correspondences is ingeniously and cleanly argued.

Commentators tend to view Arthur's section as somewhat subsidiary. This is reflected in the identification of total resemblances when it is crucially important to note that such resemblances are only partial. "Arthur's recapitulation covers the same time-span as Waldo's, the same events and characters appear" (*TLS* 1966): no—the time-span begins significantly earlier in Section 3. Morley says about Section 3 only that it "retraces most of the events covered in Part Two, this time from Arthur's point of view"; this comment suggests that the task of Section 3 is merely to establish, within a secondary world, the real nature of Arthur. What Arthur's section in fact achieves is: to confirm what we must already have surmised, by our relativizing of Waldo's vision, about Arthur's nature; to resolve the psychological lacunae in Section 2; and, not unimportantly, to provide a framework of events *not* "covered in Part Two". More significantly, perhaps, there is a tendency to conflate the two central narratives in the discussion of everything from character through "imagery" to theme, without due regard for the differences with which these are structurally mediated. "Even within each narrative we move back and forward in time" (Scott 1966); no—we are, essentially, moved only forwards in Arthur's section (aside from the fact that the narrating is a single act of unbroken, unsignalled retrospection); The *Times* (1966) review, Walsh and Brissenden (1969:37) reveal a similar insensitivity to this contrast.

There is a fundamental disinclination on the part of many critics to stand back and see how aspects of the narrative work together. If Walsh (1977:85) can say that "this spare novel ... is one of the most beautifully organised of White's works", while Argyle (1967:65; like Wardle 1966) can criticize "the faulty arrangement of the novel's sections", its "lax" structure, both see White's world-view (and resulting tone) everywhere. Argyle suggests that readers may not even bother to *finish* the novel because White's own store of "acidic comment" blocks any sympathy or credibility for Waldo. Waldo may upset us in his treatment of Arthur and in his attitudes to all outside of himself. But a novel does not have to match one's own credo about human nature; there are, anyway, many real-life situations in which we are compelled to understand and accept the perversity of close human relationships precisely because the inner mechanism of such

---

[12] The structuring of time and events in respect of human consciousness is more easily approachable through some such pragmatic metaphor as Joseph Frank's "spatial form" than through any concept of mandalic structure. See also Tacey (1988:xviii–xix/123), who maintains that White's use of the mandala as a "circle image" is a misnomer (even in Arthur's apposite employment of the idea in the present novel).

relationships lies beyond our ultimate judgement. All we can do is try and construe the habitual motivations that bind together human beings whom we as outsiders may find shocking. Apart from which, Argyle has been misled by the defensive rationalizations of Waldo's own rhetoric (by the "narrating" of Section 2), and has failed to see that every token of impregnability hides a breach or wound. The discourse is made to reveal character, not to act as a goad to our contempt. When Waldo's second-hand transcribed wisdom is echoed in the phrase "Youth is the only permanent state of mind" (W119), Argyle is first baffled by the source, then makes the statement a generalization by White.[13]

---

[13] I am not disputing the *psychological* presence of White in his central characters; I am positing as highly problematical the notion that "attitudes" held at the time of writing by the "whole" person called Patrick White are identifiable with that broad spectrum of sublimations, inchoate emotions, prejudices and id/ego conflicts within developing and disunited personalities or the halves (or quarters) of the one "twin consciousness". "I see the Brown brothers as my two halves .... Waldo is myself at my coldest and worst" *(Flaws in the Glass*:146-47), and Bill, Mrs Poulter and Dulcie Feinstein are based on acquaintances *(Flaws:*139/146-47/260). The "fatality and foreboding" in the novel are biographically preconditioned, likewise its ambivalence and transitoriness; at Castle Hill as in Terminus Road, the trees encroach on the house—and White writes, against the prospect of the need to quit "what had become a suburb", "in the dark dining-room at the centre of the house" *(Flaws*:146), as Waldo, too, crouches scribbling in his dark sanctuary. Like Arthur, the boy White is inquisitive, prepared "to open any unopened door" *(Flaws:*18); like Waldo, he is conscious of his own "not exactly cold" eyes *(Flaws:*174), whose "discs of beige flannel" *(Flaws:*3) in boyhood are shared by Waldo and the Saporta children; like Waldo, he suffers from an "inability to forgive" and from sleepless nights; and White has given Waldo his own filthy, fat-splattered oilskin *(Flaws:*12/139-40/144). Dogs are ubiquitous in both households, real and fictive. Like Arthur, White milks cows and makes butter *(Flaws:*8/138). Mrs Allwright and Mrs Dun have much of the dull intolerance of certain of White's Castle Hill neighbours. The Feinsteins' Sydney house looks onto Centennial Park like the Martin Road house White shifts to from Castle Hill *(Flaws:*148-49; Marr 1991:497)). Mrs Allwright administers a punitive drink of vinegar to Arthur (A233); as a child, White is compelled by his aunt's cook, disastrously, to drink a glass of vinegar *(Flaws:*107). Other childhood details are embroidered into the novel's texture: Arthur's visit to a "red-plush theatre" and the shipboard figure of the Primrose Pompadour; Arthur as reveller with his paper whistle at the end of the Great War; the consciousness of language implanted in Waldo (cf Marr 1991:73/37/40/35). Arthur's struggle to act out the cow's birthing-agony, and feeling the calf's head "twisting in his guts" (A230), is an emblem of creativity confirmed by White's own connection between the potentially abortive grappling with the novels within him and his "actual experience of a calf twisted in a cow's womb" (cf *Flaws:*139). *Myths of Ancient Greece* makes an indelible impression on both White *(Flaws:*32-33; Marr 1991: 51) and Brown. Paralleling the suffocating oppression of asthma in Section 2 of the novel (the ailment is shared by Waldo and his father) is the asthma White suffered from all through his life (and which provides a persistent ground-tone throughout the autobiography: see *Flaws:*5/28/34/139-40/144; Marr 1991 *passim)*. Even poor Goethe, who receives such a sneering comeuppance from Waldo in the novel (W118-19/130/211), is already there in White's thoughts during his long German holidays away from Cambridge in the 1930s: "a genius who founders in his hypocrisy and pretensions as a human being .... a padded monster"; "the intolerable Goethe, inferior to his self-abnegating disciple Eckermann" *(Flaws:*40/154). White's search for wholeness within his own shattered personality, which was aided by talks with the painter Lawrence Daws in 1963, found a path in Jung's mandalas (Marr 1991:451-52); this is reflected in the novel, as is White's encounter with "'a Queensland wheel-tree in flower .... Very Jungian'" (White, cited

Further, we are apparently led to despise such thoughts because it is Waldo who entertains them (Argyle 1967:64–65). But there is no internal evidence that White is betraying his own deeply-held beliefs (and such attitudes as Waldo's here are positively conveyed in other books of White's) in having an unpleasant character endorse them. Far from laughing at Waldo, White has him convey his own ethos of unconsummated, vicarious prolongation of life, of youth. The sentence Argyle has difficulty in attributing is Waldo's own; it is not some auctorial fulcrum balancing Waldo's actions in the present against his slipping back into the memory of his thirtieth birthday. All of the transitions in the discourse are psychologically motivated, and are not subjected to an omniscient narrator's thematic irony.

Yet others miss the close relationship between the character-centred subjectivity of narrative mediation, the actions and events mediated, and the narrative structure. This can extend to the perception of character and society. Many take it for granted that Arthur is a clinical case of simple-mindedness, not considering how this impression is fostered by Waldo's subjective view *and* belied (at a clinical, not just a metaphysical or symbolic, level) by a myriad unequivocal details in the text.[14] Walsh (1977:89) *endorses* the view, mediated by

---

in Marr 1991:451). Like Mrs Poulter (B17), White and his "opposite neighbour" grew flowers and tried to sell them (*Flaws*:138–39); more specifically (in terms of the novel's symbolism; see ch. 12 below), these flowers included the shasta or oxeye daisy (*Chrysanthemum leucanthemum*), which, like Mrs Poulter's white "chrysanths", is a white "day's eye" or mandalic sun-symbol. White enjoyed an intense friendship with the Jewish refugee Klári Daniel, née Diamant, who helped him in his investigations of Jewish lore while writing *Riders in the Chariot* (Marr 1991:294–95, 362). Although the breach in their friendship in 1966 is depicted by Marr as being caused partly by White's impatience with her mothering and her out-dated intellectualism, and partly by Daniel's distaste for the violent climax of *The Solid Mandala* (Marr 1991:455), there are grounds for suspecting that she was not happy about her fictional transmogrification into Dulcie Feinstein (the surname being itself a sly version of "Diamant"—see ch. 12 below).

None of this essentially *affects* our understanding of the novel. But it is surely a fascinating confirmation of the psychohistorical wellsprings of White's art.

[14] As this aspect has to do with character constitution, I have not included it in the present study. Briefly, there is considerable evidence in the text pointing to the probability that Arthur is, at one level, represented "synthetically" as an epileptic ("holy vision"; psychomotor disorder: aura, psychomotoric seizure, catalepsy, narcolepsy, hyperaesthesia, tonic contraction, respiratory failure, phonational difficulty or aphasia, cyanesis). White's second cousin, Philip Garland, who was born brain-damaged, was the model for Arthur. White visited his cousin Peggy Garland in Wellington in 1961, three years before beginning *The Solid Mandala*. He was fascinated by the fourteen-year-old Philip, who was fat, clumsy, and had stopped growing physically at the age of ten. The boy liked talking to strangers, often came out with highly unconventional and mature opinions, could not bear the sight of loneliness and suffering, loved listening to classical music, was an avid reader of children's books and could read aloud from newspapers "with great fluency but almost no understanding", and "was fond of a bag of glass marbles". (For these facts, see Marr 1991:272, 375–77, 449; a neutral biographer, Marr does not make any connections—nor is Philip's disorder clinically specified.) Apart from the arrested growth, all of these traits found their way into Arthur in some form or other. White inverts one trait—Philip's aversion to being kissed and embraced—and, by introducing the generalized symptoms of epilepsy, reverses the direction taken by the

Waldo, that the garage mechanics hide their embarrassment at Arthur with "exaggerated bonhommie" (W59), when all the discoursal evidence of the local context, supported by what we learn in Section 3 about Arthur's acculturative flexibility, indicates that the only person who is embarrassed is Waldo himself. The discourse of the whole narrative has been read as being somehow reliable, non-ironic, auctorial, and not as dynamized via the characters. For Walsh, it is White who shows "witty disdain" towards the denizens of Sarsaparilla, "a measured and delicate compassion" towards the Brown parents. If these sentiments are felt in Waldo's section, why should White change his "attitude" in Arthur's section? Is it not the *reader* who shows compassion for the Brown parents, resolving Waldo's alternations between fierce negativism and calculated indifference (towards his father), modifying his excessive and self-serving adulation of his mother? Is it White being "compassionate" in Arthur's section, or is it Arthur being both pitying and understanding (which is a different matter)?

One would expect such broader (and apparently straightforward) considerations of narrative events and their mediation to be presented accurately. Some few accounts of the novel manage this; others, written by respected and confident critics, do not. I would suggest at the outset (ie, before summarizing various other critical attitudes) that a good number of professional novel-readers, whether they have responded negatively or positively to *The Solid Mandala*, have not been alert to the book's subtle clarity of representation. The result is either misprision or a welter of conflicting readings.

There are, first of all, matters of narrative event which are got plain wrong, or which are regarded as being unclear when they are not. Argyle (1967:57) has the ladies in the bus "passing the brothers on their last walk", while Tacey (1988:139–40) has Waldo dying at the end of the narrated walk; this actional-present walk is in fact the *penultimate* one (narremes **104–8**). For Wolfe (1983:145), it is Arthur's "first long walk with Waldo".[15] Bliss (1986:106) surmises that the same walk "takes place probably only a few days or weeks before" Waldo's death, and gauges it as occupying "nearly two thirds of the book", when it actually takes up no more (in pages) than 15%. Bliss also has Arthur reappearing in Sarsaparilla on the Saturday of Easter rather than on the Saturday a week later. Of the twenty or so critical accounts of the novel that potentially had room for a brief run-through of the significant plot-details, many do not mention the mortal dénouement. A few, availing themselves of the convention that you shouldn't give too much away and spoil the reader's fun, are coyly non-committal.[16] Some get it right, by going no further than is absolutely

---

behaviouristic manifestations of Philip's "fits of anger and destructiveness" (Marr 1991:375), which were to place him (like Arthur) in an institution. In different ways, Philip and Arthur are both *idiots savants*.

[15] Wolfe has particular trouble with narrative ordering. He seems to take propinquity of narrated events on the page to mean temporal propinquity (cf. Wolfe 1983:145/147/148/151/152ö there are misallocations of this kind on every page).

[16] It is a "devastating climax" (McCabe 1966), a "horrifying climax" (Herring 1966:74); Waldo dies "in rather mysterious circumstances" (Scott 1966) or "under circumstances of

necessary and taking Mrs Poulter's interpretation in Section 4 as being essentially
true: ie, that Waldo dies of his own hatred; or it is claimed that the reader cannot
know the truth.[17] Others see Waldo's death as (1) an act of fratricide by Arthur,
as (2) a "*coup-de-grâce*" by Arthur after Waldo tries to strangle him, (3) as an
unmalicious, self-defensive strangling by Arthur, as (4) a revengeful suicide, as
(5) Waldo's manipulation of his own murder by Arthur, or—correctly—as (6)
Waldo's simple demise while trying to attack Arthur physically as a result of
finding his poem (narreme **113**).[18]

In other instances of misreading at the level of event, it is usually just the one
critic who has seen fit to mention the plot-detail at all. Ratcliffe (1966) claims
(because of the library incident, narremes **82** and **93**) that Arthur discovers
Dostoevsky *late* in life, failing to pick up the various clues to Arthur's awareness
of his father burning Dostoevsky (before 1922) and to Arthur's covert adolescent
reading of Mr Brown's books (familiarity with which motivates his later selection
of such writers as Dostoevsky and Lewis Carroll for concentrated study from the
early 1940s on). The twins' lives, apart from earliest childhood, are coterminous
with their occupation of the house in Terminus Road—not, as Holloway thinks
(1983:157), only "the long later part of their lives". Intriguingly, readers have
had trouble determining how Arthur comes to identify his marbles with the
mandala: some think that Arthur has already given the name "mandalas" to his
marbles, or has at least got the idea of the mandala in his head, *before* he
deliberately consults the term in Mrs Musto's encyclopaedia. The discourse is
perhaps oblique in its mediation, but it in no way permits such a reading.[19]

---

peculiar horridness" (Brissenden 1969:39), or as a "horrible release" (Avant 1975). In four of
these cases, it can be suspected that the actual death scene has been conflated with its
aftermath (Mrs Poulter's horrible discovery).

[17] Those accepting Mrs Poulter's view include Herring 1966:77, *TLS* 1966, Wilkes
1969a:108 and 1969b:96. Miller (1966) maintains that "there are three versions of Waldo's
death but no amount of collation could establish what exactly happened. Why should we not
know? An affected, strained, stuttering imprecision is preferred". Miller is himself imprecise.
There are either *two* "versions of Waldo's death" (diegetically, in terms of actual narrative), or
five (in Section 4, two extra "mimetic" statements—Arthur's claim that "'After Waldo died—
after I killed him—I ran away .... I'd killed him. I killed Waldo in the end'", P310, and Mrs
Poulter's claim that "'Waldo was ready to die .... He only took such a time dying'", P310;
and her two later thoughts: "Waldo ... dead, or killed"—by the dogs; and "Waldo can of only
died of spite like a boil must burst at last with pus", P316).

[18] 1: Byatt 1967; 2: Watson 1971:165; 3: Tanner 1966:114–17; 4: Oliveriusová 1971:211;
5: McCulloch 1983:42; 6: Bliss 1986:105–6/110 and Tacey 1988:144.

[19] Before narreme **22** reference is made *only* to "those/his (glass) marbles" or "the smaller
sphere". At Mrs Musto's, Arthur wanders about the house touching various objects, including
"the marbles of Mrs Musto's solitaire board"—whereupon: "Something was nagging at him in
the library". In a tense paragraph detailing his physical and emotional excitation, Arthur looks
through the books, finding "what he must have been supposed to find". And it is after this that
he reads out the encyclopaedia definition of the mandala. What has he been prodded to look up
in the books (given also the fact that we have already been alerted to his association of Mrs
Musto with knowledge of "the Word", W85)? Clearly, the word "marble" (cf. the solitaire
marbles)—it is his marbles that he has already invested with significance. How does he come
across "mandala"? By riffling alphabetically through the *M*-volume (there is probably an

It might be objected that such misprisions have to do with "interpretation" in a wider sense, and that I am exceeding my brief. I would counter by suggesting that they are all "misreadings" in a narrower sense: they represent a failure to respond adequately to the narrative mediation of events, and thus to discourse-structure and stylistic detail. Even in the critics cited, however, there is usually a recognition that the narrative sections have been contrastively subjectivized or allocated to "differing consciousnesses".[20] Rather few commentators point to the specific structural *purpose* of the twice-telling narratives, which is the provision of checks and balances.[21] There is still a need for an investigation of narrative perspective and structure that can help invalidate claims that Arthur's section is conditioned by his incoherence, confusion and inarticulateness (Miller 1966, *TLS* 1966), or that Waldo is "presented" with such near-malicious "comic distancing" in respect of his brother that the reader can only view Arthur's liking for Dostoevsky, revealed in Section 3, as "preposterous".[22]

V   The major narrative divisions of Waldo's section

In Waldo's section, double paragraph-spacing marks transitions between the actional present (the walk) and the narrative past (the intensive operation of

---

illustration to draw his attention, which is naturally attuned to visual patterns of symmetry). The congruence between "the Word" on mandalas and his unarticulated conception of the marbles' significance leads him to assume reflexively that this is no fortuitous encounter, but itself part of some greater design ("what he must have been supposed to find"—*find*, not "look for").

[20] Sections 2 and 3 are "told" from the "view", "point of view" or "viewpoint"—or through the "eyes"—of Waldo and Arthur respectively: Heltay 1973:101; Herring 1966:73; McCabe 1966:36; Phillips 1966:32; Scott 1966; Tanner 1966:114; *TLS* 1966; Avant 1975; Brissenden 1969:37. Byatt (1967:74) makes this general point acutely: Waldo's "memory has an excellent shutter system, excellently evoked". Miller externalizes the mechanics of the structure ("one twin succeeds the other as *a focus for a narrative* of the same events") before admitting grudgingly that there is an "attempt to reproduce the subjective character" of the twins' experience. Mackenzie (1969:241–42) wittily discusses the novel's psychological, Jungian motivation at the level of character and theme, but not at the level of narrative structure, discourse or style. Indeed: he explicitly devalues discourse-features: *"The Solid Mandala* implicitly rejects stylization .... Because it follows out ["double"] thoughts systematically, it would seem almost as if White could not help this stylized doubling, which is a kind of necessary evil".

[21] Herring 1966:74, Brissenden 1969:38, McCabe 1966:36, Scott 1966, Burgess 1966, Byatt 1967:74.

[22] Kiernan 1971:130. Like Walsh (to the extent that the latter attributes "consciousness" to the narrative but not to the characters, *and* seeks the author's judgement in every narrative statement), Kiernan does not maintain a distinction between presenting and representing, between auctorial values and endorsement of character on the one hand and mediated character-values on the other. It is Waldo, not White, who makes Arthur "preposterous"; Arthur's section sheds a different light on his reading (and on his capacity to do so).

Waldo's memory).[23] These transitions or interfaces help indicate the extent to which the shifts are subjectively initiated (see Table 1).

Table 1: Waldo's section

ACTIONAL PRESENT (first narrative)			NARRATED PAST (second narrative)			
	Number of pages and page-span			Page-span		
			narremes	and number of pages		
A	8	23–31	**-10	31–54	23	A^1
B	6.5	54–61	48–70	61–62*	1.3	B^1
C	1.5	62–63*	-- 70	63–68	6	C^1
D	0.6	68–69	67–27	69–114	45	D^1
E	5.3	114–19	70–96	119–204	85	E^1
F	10	204–14	**-**			
A–F:	32				A^1–E^1: 160	

*No space in text between B^1 and C.
**Initial and/or closing narremes not clearly present.

It can be seen from the narremic reconstruction and Table 1 that only about 20% of Section 2 (and less than 10% of the whole book) is devoted to the time of the narrating (the actional present), which covers no more than about 36 hours of real time (the time taken for the walk in A–E; the remainder of the Wednesday and the events of the Thursday packed into F). The other 80% consists entirely of what Gérard Genette terms *external analepses*.[24] In narrative terms, the sole function of external analepses "is to fill out the first narrative by enlightening the reader on one or other 'antecedents'" (Genette 1980:50). In *The Solid Mandala*, this is also true, but the reader may not immediately realize that this is so, as the retrospections are subjective (character-mediated), not objective (narratorially elucidatory)—a distinction which is not a matter of temporality but of mood (Genette 1980:39). It takes some time to grasp that the inexorable first-narrative progression forwards is connected with Waldo's willed effort in the present to bring about Arthur's death, hence to grasp the fact that the second-narrative programme is in one respect a retracing of those sources of pain that have cumulatively induced Waldo to forge his fratricidal scheme.

A^1 seems occluded at its inception by the absence of any event-narreme that can be clearly located temporally. It would, however, fit somewhere between narremes **7** and **8**; the Browns are already settled in their Sarsaparilla house and Waldo has recovered from his illness but must still stay home from school occasionally. A^1 closes on Waldo's misery after the last visit to the bank in

---

[23] A copy-editing error introduces an additional space into the American edition (Viking, p. 76, between "seeded thistles" and "When his thoughts") where there is no shift of time-planes.

[24] Genette 1980:49–50. An *analepsis* (in "cinematic" terminology: a flashback) is "an evocation after the fact of an event that took place earlier than the point in the story *[histoire* or diegetic "plot"] where we are at any given moment" (40); an *external analepsis* is an episode "whose entire extent remains external to the extent of the first narrative": ie, the temporal level of narrative against which "anachrony is defined as such" (48–49).

childhood. B^1 opens with the Poulters' arrival in Terminus Road (around 1920), proceeding immediately to, and closing with, Waldo's act of voyeurism (probably a year or so later). C^1 is concerned solely with the Pitt Street Encounter in 1934. D^1 opens with Waldo's discovery that his father has died (1922), and closes with Waldo's acceptance as a library trainee at Sydney Municipal (end of 1909). E^1 begins in 1923 (the year after Mr Brown dies) with Waldo gazing in the mirror on his thirtieth birthday, and closes about 1953 with the twins' retirement. If we were so unobservant or naive as to conclude that each of these five bracketings of retrospection possessed its own forward temporal flow, the narremic disposition would look something like this :

Figure 1: Temporal scheme

1900	1910	1920	1930 *	1940	1950
[A^1]		[B^1]	[*C^1]		
	[D^1][	E^1			]

We know that the internal organization of each bracketing [ ] and the [*] for the point-time episode C^1) is actually achronous, with the exception of B^1 (whose two narremes are sequent) and C^1 (a single narreme). D^1 would be temporally sequent, however, if the initiating narreme of Mr Brown's death were granted special status and divided off. Although achronous in detail, A^1 and E^1 *generally* observe a forward temporal movement. Elsewhere, it will be the temporal dissonances that require attention; here, what is at first of interest are the following general features.

Waldo's retrospection does begin with the earliest phase of his *historia,* his childhood. The next segment focuses on Mrs Poulter and Waldo's covert, post-adolescent sexuality; in terms of narration-time, it is the briefest retrospective segment. The third segment, the second-briefest narrationally, focuses on Waldo and Dulcie Saporta after (in terms of the *fabula*) the frustration of Waldo's notional sexual attraction to her. The fourth segment, the second-longest narrationally, has its inception in Mr Brown's death but goes back to focus on sexuality, then on the first meetings with Dulcie, and finally on Waldo's preparations for his library job just before his seventeenth birthday. The last and longest segment begins just after Mr Brown's death, but then takes up from Waldo's seventeenth birthday to deal with his first experiences at the library. There are further meetings with Dulcie, Waldo's marriage-proposal, and his voluntary severance of contact with her; Waldo's severing of Arthur's contact with Mrs Poulter; the death of Mrs Brown; Waldo's temporary establishing of "contact" with Mrs Poulter through the plastic doll; and his last experiences (also a severing of contacts). These narrative rubrics indicate that all the segments together observe a general movement forward in time.[25] There is a fairly

---

[25] Inasmuch as Faulkner has already entered the discussion, it is interesting to observe that Richard P. Adams (1968:237–39) cites analytical studies of *The Sound and the Fury* to show

efficient coverage of Waldo's personal relationships with Dulcie and Mrs Poulter. There are cross-bracketings (eg, in terms of desire and loss or relinquishment; of the seventeenth-birthday nexus, to bind E^1 to D^1; of the beginning and the end of Waldo's library career, to provide internal bracketing support for E^1; of an early significant "withdrawal" of Waldo's father at the end of A^1 and the final loss at the beginning of D^1). Finally, three of the five segments are oriented around the period in which Mr Brown's death occurs: the opening bracket of D^1 touches the event, while that of E^1 stands immediately after it; and B^1 spans the period. On the basis of such raw data, so disposed, it would theoretically be possible for a writer to construct a fluent, logical, "objective" narrative of Waldo's life. It would, however, be highly questionable whether he could bring it off if he were asked, at the same time, to respect the fact that the analepses are embedded in, or intercalated into, the flow of the actional present. I would suggest that the narrative structure presents a *prima facie* case for subjectivized narrative (as evidence of subjectivized narration). Is any support for such a suggestion to be detected at the narrative interfaces themselves? The reader, I suggest, should have the text of the novel to hand as a necessary accompaniment to the following observations, which—because this degree of analytical attention is necessarily space-consuming—must be restricted to one narrative interface only.

The transition A to A^1 (analytical sweep from the middle of W30 to the top of W33) takes us out of Terminus Road via Waldo's bitterly envious thoughts about the prosperous middle-class area the twins are passing by. "Waldo yearned secretly for the brick boxes to an extent where his love had become hatred. He would have to control, as he had always known how to control, himself, his parents, his colleagues—and his brother" (W30). What starts off looking like non-Waldovian, psycho-narrational social criticism ("brick boxes") is relativized later when we learn how decrepit the Browns' house is: how much more reassuring for Waldo the idea of brick, how consonant with his reclusive, rigid, solipsistic personality the (objectively reductive) "box". The paradoxical phrasing is consonant with Waldo's instinctive reduction of "love", away from people and onto things, which are more controllable. The statement is also a sidling, covert translation of Waldo's present high-pitched mood—we are nudged back to "He hated his brother", his inward reaction to Arthur's whimpering about the mandala in Saporta's carpet. Arthur's remarks about this (W28) remind Waldo of the Encounter (W63ff., a scene finally clarified only at W150); this, and talk of Mrs Poulter, Waldo's writing and other topics have provoked Waldo to "hatred". Hence his gradual speeding-up as he walks hand-in-hand with his brother.[26] The

---

that rough chronological order is maintained throughout in terms of structural emphases, however strong the suggestion of "chaotic stasis".

[26] Waldo is "sidling brittly" at the start (W26); he walks "primly", while Arthur is "not exactly running, but lumbering" (W27); then "puffing" (W28); Waldo yanks at Arthur's hand, and is "striding now" (W30–31), while his brother has "to run to keep up"; Waldo's physical reaction to Arthur's mention of the carpet, and to Mr Dun's seeing him with his dill brother, is that "he could not walk too fast".

hatred for what he cannot have is linked with the hatred he feels for Arthur, the burden thwarting the realization of his middle-class fantasies, who is agitating him into physical efforts to get away from him. Waldo once kept himself (and his now-dead parents, his now-retired colleagues) under control; but the statement of resolve in free indirect thought (cf the modal "would")[27] is not under control—and nor is Waldo. But the strongly pointed sentence-ending indicates that, for him, it is Arthur who is out of control. The controlled reticence of the next paragraph (the twins' "united" breathing, a motif in the novel; the modal understatement that his breath "might startle a stranger") reveals Waldo attempting to cover up his physical turmoil. He *self*-protectively, correctively advises Arthur to keep calm because of the danger of a heart-attack—to conceal what we later find is a desire to *control* Arthur (by tugging him along ever faster) so as to induce his collapse. Waldo's thoughts about Arthur's "anxiety" are a projection of his own mental state; Arthur talks optimistically (the sentence "But would immediately cheer up" is superficially "habitual", but refers to the present moment) about all he might have done to support them financially. Waldo's secret yearning swells again, and he fantasizes scenically ("So they were sitting down to dinner in one of the brick boxes") about the luxury they could have had. But it is Arthur's presence that has thwarted Waldo's dream.

The fantasy-prolepsis immediately yields to a related analepsis, when Waldo recalls his father's habitual words. The "hot dinner in the middle of the day" is also a specific proleptic trigger explaining the otherwise overdetermined piece of diegesis that follows. Apart from which, we "catch up" on the reference contrastively much later, when we read that the habitual midday meal of the old men is just bread-and-milk. What makes Waldo "hold himself so rigid" is his own contrastive association with Arthur's bread-and-milk meal. His unarticulated mental scenario envisages *no* further midday meal (cf Arthur, A206: "'I forgot it's only middle of the day'"), as he expects Arthur to be dead by then. This is his last dark secret. "In some ways you were so close you did not always notice"—this colloquial pseudo-vocative free indirect thought relates contrastively to an earlier statement, "Because they were brothers, twins moreover, they shared secrets warmer than appeared" (W28), whose word "secrets" supplies the suppressed motivation for Waldo's later observation.

The remaining paragraph in the actional present seems at first glance to stand in only the loosest of relationships to what has preceded it:

(1) Waldo freed his hand. (2) The wind getting in behind his spectacles had stung his rather pale eyes. (3) It was so many years, he realized, since he had looked at himself without his glasses, he could barely see his youth's, not to say boy's, face. (4) Only sense it. (5) And that, though less concrete, was more painful. (6) In more normal circumstances there were only the scars where the acne had been on the back of his neck. [W31]

The state of Waldo's smarting eyes is actually a welcome pretext for him to disengage himself from Arthur to take off his spectacles—just in case Arthur *has*

---

[27] Fuller reference to the technical terms "free indirect thought/speech/discourse" (approximately equivalent to *style indirect libre* and *erlebte Rede)* can be found in the detailed examination of style-features, below.

"noticed" something untoward in the pressure of his hand. The perspective of "rather pale eyes" in (2) resembles narratorial analysis, but we learn in due course to take such objectifications as functions of Waldo's reflexive consciousness—he is forever mentally gazing in the mirror. An earlier, similarly "external" association of eyes and spectacles is actually Waldo's mental projection of an appropriate visual accompaniment to a carefully enunciated warning.[28] Sentence (3) supports the subjective centering of (2): it implies that Waldo has "looked at himself" (in the mirror) *with* his glasses on, and has retained a mental image of his spectacled self. But this image has not been reinforced enough for him to be able *now*, in his mind, to see clearly "his youth's, not to say boy's, face". Why does the subjective analepsis into childhood and adolescence, arising from the effect of the wind on his old man's eyes, occur at this stage of the narrative? It is evident from the immediate context alone that Waldo's freeing himself physically from Arthur has liberated him into egoistic introspection. But only repeated readings reveal just how obsessively the simplest of phrases is bound up with past events: there are, namely, two specific moments of *seeing* that have returned to Waldo at this point.

The earlier moment (his recollected "boy's face") occurs immediately after his father's death (W74). Waldo, after initially fleeing from the enormity of death, is encouraged by Arthur's rawly emotional reaction to demonstrate pridefully his *control* over the situation and over what he likes to think is his mother's helplessness. Waldo handles the formalities: but it is Arthur who, by comforting their mother, is ultimately the emotionally practical one.

So he continued watching Mother as she smoothed back Arthur's moist hair, looking into Arthur's face, into the avenue she hoped to open up. Finally Waldo saw them only indistinctly, because he had deliberately taken his glasses off.

This, too, is prepared for on the previous page: Waldo sees Arthur holding their mother, who is looking "into his blurry face, which perhaps was less confused than it should have been" (cf "anxiety .... But would ... cheer up", W31); "Standing above him his brother appeared huge":

If only he could have focused on Arthur's face to see what Mother was looking for. Because whatever it was she might find would soon be buried in words. The little boy on the step below stood craning up, wriggling his nervous, white worm of a neck to see. But could not. The sun was shining on his glasses. [W73]

The later moment (in *historia*-time) occurs on Waldo's thirtieth birthday, in the year following his father's death. As he gazes in the bedroom mirror, he wonders whether anybody "realized there was still the little boy inside him, beside his other self, looking out. His eyes, like his mother's, were blue, though his were watered down":

According to mood, he might take his pince-nez off, blurring the image, allowing his imagination to play amongst the hydrangeas, or alternately he would clip the lenses firmly on,

---

28 "The sun caught the gold of his spectacles with a brilliance which turned the skin beneath the eyes to washed-out violet" (W29; I analyze this later. In (2), the editorial gloss of the word "rather" is a giveaway—Waldo's subliminal twitch of regret, disguised as judicious modification, at not possessing the strong blue aristocratic eyes of his fantasized ancestors.

and refuse himself any avenues of escape from that intellectual ruthlessness he knew himself to possess. [W120]

Sentence (3), then, in the first quotation above, is not only an internal analepsis (we can perceive that Waldo is thinking back), but also a *germinal prolepsis* of two later analepses. Pouring back into the actional present at W31, but unarticulated there, is Waldo's concomitant resentment at Arthur, who—in his "anxiety" and intuitive capacity to comfort—usurps Waldo's "control" over their mother. In the actional present, Waldo shrinks from Arthur's flood of words; in the past, Waldo anticipates that the moment of silent communion between Arthur and Mrs Brown on the veranda must be analyzed quickly to his advantage before it is dispelled—as it is—by Arthur's return to the brisk, practical consolation of "words". In the past, "little" Waldo is shut out, unable to "see", to understand Arthur's magical, calming "control", and is dazzled by the sun. In the actional present, he is "blinded" by the wind, not the sun. In the later scene, there is ample proof of Waldo's cultivation of a visual self-image to explain the seemingly "objective" presentation of his eyes and spectacles (W29/31). And the implicit conjunction of "ruthlessness" and death is latent in the actional present as well. Waldo needs the self-control of "intellectual ruthlessness"; the "avenues of escape" (into emotion? love?) that he refuses echo the enigmatic "avenue" he sees his mother seeking in Arthur's face: is she reading his face like a mirror—for emotion? love? This self-control will enable him to exercise his fratricidal will (walking Arthur to death down a different "avenue", Barranugli Road), just as he assumed he was acting in accordance with this principle upon his father's death, and preened himself on the cultivation of that principle once he got his mother to himself later on.

The blurring of Waldo's inner vision is what is depicted; and the word "sense" also takes up from the suggestion in "notice" that there is something empathetically conveyed through the "sense" of touch. The pivotal thematic word is "painful"—the sensing of the blurred outlines of the deepest personal past leaves more room for subjection to uncertainty, hurt: to see clearly in memory is to relativize the painful, somehow to tame it. Waldo is himself thematizing memory, and the closing sentence (6) takes us away from the visual again back to the tactile, and implicitly back to the earlier metaphor of the encrustation of "his life" by time. What the aged Waldo can still feel without pain are *only* the physical traces of *physical* discomfort in adolescence.[29]

Thus the increasingly introspective run-up (end of A) to the first transition. The governing impulse in the initial narrative analepses of A^1 is Waldo's actional-present consciousness of his own shaky state of health in old age—hence the content of the first analepsis, which dwells on Waldo's sickliness as a child. The immediate linking index is that of Mrs Brown touching the boys' hair. This is primarily a tactile memory, which is linked with the scene of Mr Brown's death, when Waldo sees his mother smoothing Arthur's hair. A third element

---

[29] We later determine an intercalation of this reference with another expression—this time, of pained anger at those Waldo must work under at the library; the reference there is to squeezing pimples in the *mirror*.

feeding into this recollected detail is Waldo's persistent perception of Arthur's hair in the actional present (W23/26/27/31), and the mental reflection on the habitual cutting of his brother's hair (W26) with its own specific analepsis to boyhood ("It had seemed much coarser when Arthur was a boy"). The first external analepsis immediately develops its own momentum, of course, and its further internal development need not concern us here. There are, however, elements in the subsequent analepses which can be linked with the "content" of Waldo's consciousness in the actional present. There is the continued stress on Arthur's hair in Mr Brown's fondling of it (W32/33) "in the beginning". Waldo reflects on (or reflects on his reflecting on) the way Mr Brown at some stage "went off" Arthur, continuing to give him affection, "but more like some dog you'd got, and he couldn't help himself" (W33). Compare Waldo's first-narrative reflection on how he would "try to remember when he had first been saddled" with Arthur (W25), which builds on "duty" at the opening of the section (W23). More centrally still, and anticipatorily gathering up several later analeptic strands: "If Arthur had been, say, a dog, he might have touched the back of his head. That hair" (W27). The mirror-implication (W31), too, is played out in Waldo's recollection of habitually kissing the looking-glass in childhood (W32–33). Waldo's secret intention in the present of severing the bond with his twin shows in his contrastive recollection of the boyhood strength—even positiveness— of that bond. Waldo's unmediated suspicion that old Arthur is too robust to fold beneath the exertions of the walk surfaces analeptically in Mr Brown's reference to Arthur's strength (W33) "in the beginning", anticipated by Waldo's first-narrative reflections (W26). Waldo's sterterous breathing is "united with Arthur's" in the first narrative; "even their breathing was inextricably intertwined" in childhood (W33). The closing sentence of the first narrative (the acne-scars) not only connects old age logically with the internal free direct-speech analepsis to adolescence ("Not Waldo, George, it only brings the pimples out", W28); the topical framing ("Arthur had been Dad's favourite, in the beginning", W28) is a direct prolepsis of the second-narrative analepsis ("Arthur, whom Dad loved best in the beginning").

One cannot, therefore, speak of a direct line of association at the interface between present and past at A/A^1. The information in the last actional-present paragraph has stronger connections with discrete events that are narrated much later than it does with the immediately following analepses. The many scattered internal analepses within the first-narrative segment, as well as Waldo's mental reactions to present event-stimuli, function proleptically to interlock both with the initial analepsis of the second narrative and with the analepses that are narrated much later. There is, finally, an inexorable thrust of oblique cross-reference which serves to make all this pro- and analeptic detail interlock motivationally with Waldo's present intentions, mood and physical condition. Not to mention the fact that the first of Waldo's integrated recollections, where Mrs Brown is introducing her sons, also functions scenically as a narrative meta-introduction of the twins after the mimetic and diegetic ones of Section 1 and the one in the actional present of Section 2. The narrative symmetry is complete.

What should be emphasized, however, is the high—for the reader, unnervingly or even confusingly high—degree of autonomy granted to the play of mental reflection. Although the ghostly trace of narratorial mediation is (necessarily) sensed in the representational strategies of syntax, what the reader is essentially experiencing is a direct confrontation with consciousness, not character. Whereas the narratorial mediation of character is necessarily freighted with the burden of emotion and moral attitude, the mediation of mental perception and recollection is not (for all the talk of "duty", "hatred" or "pain"). It is *our* task to extrapolate from the cold and measured diastole of consciousness, in order to determine the emotional and ethical effects which Waldo's *controlling* upper consciousness is at such pains to conceal, rationalize or transform. In this regard, then, we can understand why it is that both the clearly presented and (for us) the highly oblique and opaque retrospections in the actional present have equally a sense of the self-evident about them. It is not narratorial arrogance, portentousness, or wilful obfuscation which generates this impression. *Everything* is self-evident and familiar to the retrospecting consciousness. *Narratively,* it constitutes the logical extension into structure of the deictic, referential intimacy that is evident *narrationally* at the grammatical level of discourse. The task of the implied author is so to distribute the particle-traces of memory that patterns are ultimately retrievable. And the possibilities of controlling this distribution reside primarily in linguistic and stylistic resources.

Not only is the same structural dynamic observable everywhere else; the effort of structural analysis alone, when applied resolutely to answering questions relating to "opacity" or "obliquity" of discourse, consistently produces fully satisfying interpretative results: the associative correspondences at every level of phrasing are rewardingly rich. They can be as complex and nuanced as in the present example; the remaining transitions are comparatively straightforward, both in their inception and in their closure, yet with the same interlocking of significant verbal detail. The transitions, interestingly enough, reveal ever-decreasing *amounts* of such detail. By the time we get to the closure D^1/E, both the analeptic and the actional-present segments are equally imbued with the presence of an intensely active consciousness. In memory, Waldo has been left, so to speak, at the gateway to adult working life; the optimistic closing note seems not to connect with the unnerving, obscure actional-present statement that succeeds it: "The preliminaries to dying, to what in the end is the simplest act of all, were so endlessly complicated" (W114)—"were", not "are": this is not just an existential statement. It turns out that most of this segment circles the topic of dying, and this opening sentence is an instance of Waldo's will and present awareness assuming the upper hand over the flow of memory. The converse proof of this is the fact that the last segment of analepsis takes up again, after an initial hiatus (the thirtieth birthday) *exactly* from where D^1 breaks off (seventeenth birthday and library job), as though a continuum of recollection has been disturbed by the irruption of the actional present and Waldo's impatient anticipation of Arthur's death. The linkage between E^1 and F is managed chiefly through the sheer congruence of externals at the temporal level. At the end of the closing analepsis (W204), the brothers are retired—there is nowhere for Waldo to go now psychologically except into the realm of habituality. And it is precisely this topic that is taken up in the first narrative. The underlying need for intensive, formalized analepsis has been abated by virtue of the fact that this walk "wasn't Arthur's last". The gate closes behind memory and behind Waldo's thwarted plan. What we now experience are the crushing effects of Arthur's vitality on Waldo's habitual assumptions. The whole infrastructure of Waldo's mental life is swept away in an orgy of unmasking.

VI   Time relationships in Waldo's section

An examination of the narremic reconstruction of the *fabula* (section 3.II above) might lead one to conclude that it must have been a relatively simple matter to set the events of the narrative in strict chronological order: but this is far from being the case. I would suspect that almost as much effort is required to disentangle the chronology as is needed to order the events of Faulkner's *The Sound and the Fury*.[30] The two nodal dates in Faulkner's novel (fixing the various "actional presents" of 1910 and 1928) are clearly, formally and immediately anchored in indicated public time. In White's novel, the actional present of Waldo's section (A–F in Table 1 above) is not. Although we are aware (from social specifica as early as Section 1 and from Waldo's anterior temporal fixings in the memory-segments A^1-E^1) that the walk must be taking place some time after the Second World War, it is only at narreme **96** in the closing pages of his section that we can place the walk (with some computation) after the mid-1950s; and only in Section 3 do we glean enough clues from social specifica to revise this forwards to the early 1960s. On the other hand, White's narrative is ultimately more directly helpful than Faulkner's in the provision of nodal dates within the retrospective segments, from which the reader can extrapolate "radials". In its temporal structure, Faulkner's novel seems more fragmentary, more psychologically paradigmatic. Both writers are fascinated by the metaphysics of time; but although their characters are obsessed by personal history, Faulkner's seem less committed than White's to the indexing of this (mental) history through the notations of public time. But this impression changes once one begins to reflect on just how and where specific temporal data are mediated in *The Solid Mandala*; on what data are conveyed; and on how we assimilate these data. Table 2 (next page), on the recursive ordering of temporal relations in the narrative, includes few of those events for which temporal placing is crucial for psychological interpretation. Furthermore, events are seldom formally localized temporally whilst they are receiving their fullest treatment in the narrative sequence, but usually much later in the context of some other event.

---

[30] See especially Edmond Volpe (1964:353–77). Volpe does not explain how he reaches his conclusions on chronology; the novel must be re-read in conjunction with the relevant appendix.

The first two segments of recollection (A^1 and B^1 in Table 1) are not internally assignable to any year or span of years. We know the first concerns the boys' childhood, but not *when;* and the voyeur-scene is said only to have occurred when Waldo "was quite a bit younger" (W61)—not necessarily in adolescence. The third formal analepsis, the Encounter in Pitt Street (C^1; **1.6** in Table 2), is furnished with a date (1934), and incidental detail would allow us to assume that Waldo is an adult. But as we have no clarification as yet about his past relationship to Dulcie (though there is no shortage of fragmentary glimpses), we cannot assume that the reference to her "middle-aged body" (W64) must also apply to Waldo. In analepsis D^1, we learn *that* Mr Brown has died, but not *when,* except that Waldo is now working at a library. We cannot tell from "Waldo by then was working at ..." (W69) whether this is his first or a subsequent job. Is he still in his late teens, in his twenties or thirties? That he has "a man's body" and is "a man strutting" at the library (W70–71) does not clarify matters. Relativization comes only afterwards, when Waldo is "tempted to re-enter his own boyhood" (W74), although it is the "landscape" of adolescence rather than "boyhood" that he now moves through. By the time we get to the end of Waldo's first meeting with Dulcie, it is plain that he is somewhere in his mid-teens and in the last terms of high school (W98–99), with job prospects ahead; after two more meetings with Dulcie, we know he has been accepted at the library (W114). But we don't know when all this takes place on the *non*-personal scale of public time, dates and years.

We have been enabled to make two inferences, though. First, the Dulcie of the Encounter furnishes a rough time-span, reaching from her "middle age" of 1934 back to a putative adolescence early in this century (or not so early, if Waldo is implying that she is "middle-aged" in body, not in years). Second, we can narrow down "by then" to permit us to locate Mr Brown's death within close temporal range of Waldo's taking up employment at the library—but we don't know *how* close. In swift succession, however, the next analeptic section (start of E^1) provides four important pieces of temporal data. Waldo has his thirtieth birthday (W119)—the *year* we do not discover here. "Today I am thirty, he had calculated"—free reported thought, in the present, of the past, recollected from a later vantage-point. The second clear date is given (W126) in association with Waldo's mother's financial dependence on him: Mr Brown (erstwhile breadwinner) died in 1922 (**1.5** in Table 2). That is to say, whereas 1934 is specified at the time of the narrating of the event, 1922 is dropped into the narrative after the narrating of the event, and is thematically subordinated. By means of a brisk associative side-step, we learn that it was on his seventeenth birthday that Waldo started at the library (W121)—again, the *year* we do not discover here. "At seventeen ... he had presented himself"—recollection from the actional present *or* internal recollection on his thirtieth birthday. In the course of recollecting an early scene at the library, Waldo then calculates that he was "only sixteen, was it?" when he "confided in Dulcie Feinstein that he was going to be a writer" (W123).

The earlier scenes with Dulcie and his exam-preparation are now localizable according to Waldo's age—but we still do not know the *years* in historical time. There is no explicit fixing of events occurring between the time Waldo joins the library and the outbreak of the Great War. We never find out when (in what year) Dulcie leaves for Europe. Her imminent departure, as conveyed to Arthur in Section 3, can at best be allocated to a season (either winter or the following spring). In Section 2, at one point in Waldo's early career at the Library he is transported by reading a poem; he tells Wally Pugh a fiction about possessing Dulcie sexually (using as details various bits of knowledge he has picked up from his three meetings with her); Pugh shows him three poems he has written, and Waldo, sticking mentally to his principles, renews his resolve never to show anybody anything *he* has written. He recalls one exception to this—when he confided in Dulcie at Mrs Musto's; but, it is implied, she is not around now to remind him of this. "And *not long after that,* Mrs Feinstein *had taken* her daughter away. So it was told" (W123). There follow Arthur's words giving details of the trip to Europe. The deictic coreferent would appear to be the occasion of Waldo's confiding in Dulcie when he was sixteen. As Waldo has distanced himself from the youthful stupidity of being sixteen, we might conclude that he is considerably older at the time Walter Pugh shows him his poems; but it could just as easily be adolescent vanity, and Waldo's exercise of superiority.

It is clear from the occasion when Mr Feinstein catches Waldo trespassing on the Sarsaparilla property (W124) that the sexual fiction antedates the trespassing, but there is no easy way of determining the diachronic proximity of the various events. "On a later occasion" (W126)—we take this to mean after the trespass, but it could instead be a thematic reference to the sex-fiction incident: Waldo tells Walter another fiction about getting a letter from Dulcie, who is said to have been in Brussels. The content of the two Dulcie-fictions is temporally stepped, indicating that Waldo is processing recalled details from successive incidents. The sex-fiction reworks only the negative data (Dulcie's pink dress, dark hair, swarthiness, hairiness) conveyed in the narrating of the first meeting (at Mrs Musto's). The Brussels fiction reworks data[31] from the later visit to the Feinsteins' with Arthur. The Brussels fiction, we might assume, follows closely on Arthur's telling Waldo about Dulcie's departure for Europe and on the second visit to the Feinsteins': Arthur's account would then corroborate this—his mention of being the only one to know of Dulcie's upcoming departure follows on smoothly from the dying fall of the twins' visit to the Feinsteins' (A245).

The implication, when we combine the two narratives, is that Arthur cannot resist blurting out his secret knowledge to his brother. The time-scale implications, however, run counter to these assumptions. In terms of the later datability to 1910 of Waldo's start at the library, this would mean (improbably) that Dulcie leaves for Europe in 1910—the Grand Tour would then last four years

---

[31] The Beethoven piano sonatas. This is Waldo's willed embroidery of what he hears Dulcie playing while he is trapped in the bathroom (W110)—music which, according to Arthur (A241), was études, polkas and gavottes. It is Waldo, late in the War, who first challenges the reluctant and unpractised Dulcie to play the Moonlight Sonata (W134).

or more. Arthur, too, needs time (in the narrative gap after first meeting Dulcie face to face, W109/A244) to establish a relationship with her that can explain the intimacy of their winter walk in the Sydney park (A245–46). Waldo fills in *his* gap of total withdrawal from the Feinsteins' circle even before his seventeenth birthday, by means of compensatory fantasies about Dulcie. Loath to admit to himself that Arthur had been privy to the Feinsteins' travel plans for some time before informing his brother, Waldo pushes the departure subjectively back into the proximity of his *own* meeting with Dulcie ("not long after"). In the text, the statement is momentarily ambiguous if one underrates the relativizing force of the past perfect "had taken". It is as though the Feinsteins' departure were being related to the occasion on which Walter Pugh shows Waldo his poems, instead of to the afternoon at Mrs Musto's. The temporal relations are rendered opaque by the discourse, which mediates a sea of consciousness whose surface may seem calm but is rippled ambiguously by subliminal currents.

At the same time as there is an attempt to stretch temporal extent on the level of personal events, there is an attempt to compact duration on the level of public events, thus reflecting Waldo's self-preoccupation. That Waldo's existence at the library is a kind of timeless or temporally flexible zone in which he can give full rein to his fantasies is indicated by the way in which the outbreak of the Great War is conveyed in the narrative. It is the world of the Brown family in Terminus Road—and not Waldo's world at the library—which has "contracted before the pressure of events. Because War was breaking, had already broken out" (W126; **1.2** in Table 2). Here there is grammatical iconicization of Waldo's perception of public events as blips, so to speak, belatedly registered on the radar of his temporal awareness. As far as Waldo's work is concerned, "they had put him on the catalogue. So the least desirable part of his life was war and all that it implied" (W127). The first cataclysm of this century is seen only as a threat to Waldo's personal desire for rigid order. Under the weight of Waldo's unacknowledged sense of self-preservation, the war's significance—its unignorable, specific *there*-ness in time—continues to be subordinated to his hatred for the vitality of those who have enlisted; to the public acclaim awarded to them; to his sub-sexual fantasies about Dulcie (and her mother) "stranded somewhere in Europe".

So far, the only dates we have are (a) 1934 and 1922 (which locate single events and serve only loosely to relativize anterior time-*spans*), and (b) the outbreak of the war, which, along with the vague proleptic analepsis "towards the *end* of the War"—the specification of the Armistice comes only in Arthur's section, **1.3** in Table 2—serves as a frame for the non-specific localization of other events. The arrival of the Poulters in about 1920 is the next fairly firm date (if we can trust Waldo's memory), and this is located in relation to Mr Brown's retirement (W140). For the next 25–30 pages, the temporal relations of the events and processes are internally regulated with the barest explicit connection with the rough time-scale already established. We are at first aware that the events recounted are firmly pressed into the two-year period before Mr Brown's death. The central incidents concern Waldo's secret hostility towards Mrs

Poulter, his learning that Mrs Feinstein has died, and his use of this knowledge to visit Dulcie and propose marriage.

Table 2: Recursive ordering of temporal relations

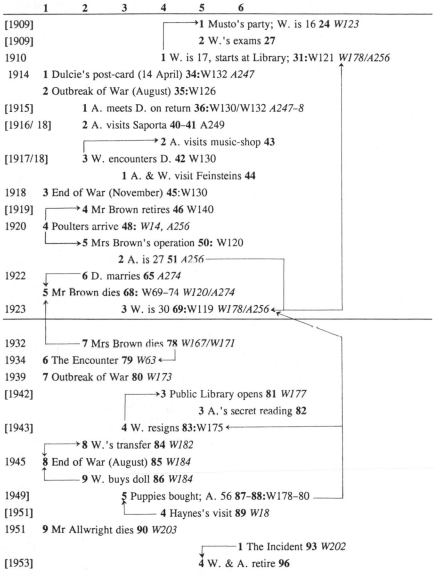

	1	2	3	4	5	6
[1909]					→1 Musto's party; W. is 16 **24** *W123*	
[1909]					2 W.'s exams **27**	
1910					1 W. is 17, starts at Library; **31**:W121 *W178/A256*	
1914	1 Dulcie's post-card (14 April) **34**:W132 *A247*					
	2 Outbreak of War (August) **35**:W126					
[1915]		1 A. meets D. on return **36** W130/W132 *A247–8*				
[1916/ 18]		2 A. visits Saporta **40–41** A249				
		→2 A. visits music-shop **43**				
[1917/18]		3 W. encounters D. **42** W130				
			1 A. & W. visit Feinsteins **44**			
1918	3 End of War (November) **45**:W130					
[1919]	→4 Mr Brown retires **46** W140					
1920	4 Poulters arrive **48**: *W14, A256*					
	→5 Mrs Brown's operation **50**: W120					
			2 A. is 27 **51** *A256*			
1922	6 D. marries **65** *A274*					
	5 Mr Brown dies **68**: W69–74 *W120/A274*					
1923			3 W. is 30 **69**:W119 *W178/A256*			
1932	7 Mrs Brown dies **78** *W167/W171*					
1934	6 The Encounter **79** *W63*					
1939	7 Outbreak of War **80** *W173*					
[1942]			→3 Public Library opens **81** *W177*			
			3 A.'s secret reading **82**			
[1943]			4 W. resigns **83**:W175			
	→8 W.'s transfer **84** *W182*					
1945	8 End of War (August) **85** *W184*					
	9 W. buys doll **86** *W184*					
1949]			5 Puppies bought; A. 56 **87–88**:W178–80			
[1951]			4 Haynes's visit **89** *W18*			
1951	9 Mr Allwright dies **90** *W203*					
				1 The Incident **93** *W202*		
[1953]			4 W. & A. retire **96**			

The most interesting skein of incidentals relates to Waldo's attitude towards Mrs Poulter. His is the kind of negativity which, given the right combination of stimuli, festers into the surrogate possession and revenge-violation of voyeurism.

It is "logical" for Waldo, after reflecting on his (perfectly reasonable) denial of love to his parents and on his (patently artificial) "exercise in loving Dulcie" (W56), to slip sideways into a recollection of love's desperate reduction to solipsism and obliquity in the secret observation of the physical love of others. The main transition **B/B¹** has Waldo glimpsing Mrs Poulter's face at the window of the passing bus (W60), and the conjoined analepses which follow are his recollections of her. In thematic terms, one could say that the link rests on *secret seeing:* Waldo doesn't let on to Arthur that he has seen her; and he certainly doesn't reveal his presence when he spies on her as she stands naked before the washstand basin. The secret of Waldo's murder-plan is also being guarded here as well when he yawns, "till remembering why he had chosen to commit a deliberate assault on distance on that morning" (W60). The phrasing itself betrays both violence and violation; and the walk is much longer than usual. Along comes the 8.13 bus. The informally gnomic observation "Look into a passing bus, and more often than not you will see something you would rather not" sounds almost comically portentous, not to mention untrue. It is in fact Waldo's *retrospective* attempt to suppress the impact of seeing "something" (someone) he "would rather not". "Smeared mauve against the window Mrs Poulter's face was too stupid exactly to accuse Waldo"—another of Waldo's mental ploys which doesn't come off: the slanderous reductiveness of the description, like a painting by James Ensor, cannot remove Waldo's feeling that Mrs Poulter has in fact somehow accused him. The word "accuse" is out; its concomitant, "guilt", will not be far ahead (Waldo, after seeing Mrs Poulter's breasts and private parts: "He had never felt guiltier", W61). That vague word "something", which fits the aphoristic generality so well, is multifunctional as so often in White: it suppresses as long as possible, thus betokening Waldo's mental evasion; it reduces a person to a thing; it includes the person within that *Verdinglichung,* so that the evasion is of a personal *situation.* More than one situation, potentially, as Waldo's snorting laughter seeks to shrug off. We should remember that the passage of the bus is also covered in Section 1, the actual description of how the twins look being conveyed through Mrs Dun's eyes. At two points after the bus has left the old men behind, Mrs Poulter is curious as to why the Browns are "so far from Terminus Road"; she has glanced back over her shoulder "as if hoping to confirm something" (B20/21). If we ignore Mrs Poulter's own view that "'what goes on in other people's minds is private'", is there something in her surprised face that leads Waldo to imagine for a moment that she has seen through his plan to walk Arthur to his death—something in her facial expression that triggers off his feelings of guilt? We must at least posit that Waldo has *already* been recollecting the voyeur-scene, and that the formally posterior analepsis is therefore not *psychologically* posterior to Waldo's seeing Mrs Poulter on the bus. His artificial manner can be put down to the forced sniggering of somebody who is hiding a sexual secret. What Waldo imagines Mrs Poulter cannot "accuse" him of *is* his voyeurism of long ago. For Waldo, whose whole existence is based in secrecy, is revelling in what he regards as a double situational irony: how *doubly* unusual ("It was unusual", thinks Waldo), in the conjunction of his thoughts of her and her actual passing-by, that Mrs Poulter has gone through life never realizing how intimately he has intruded on that life; and how amusing that Arthur, the one who has been talking about Mrs Poulter ("one of the fifty-seven things and persons Waldo hated", W58), has apparently failed to notice her in the bus. A visual conjoining of the two moments of Waldo's secret seeing is found in the bus-window/house-window symmetry.

How does the analepsis open (W61)? It does so by taking up from Waldo's recollection, in the middle of segment **A**, of Mrs Brown's carefully fair-minded appraisal of Mrs Poulter as a "young woman" (W27). Why should Waldo at this point in A^1 remember spying voyeuristically on Mrs Poulter? At W28 there is a prolepsis of secrecy and concealment, with Waldo and his mother "hidden in collusion" while Mrs Poulter calls to Mrs Brown from outside the house; so that we already have the germ of a subliminal association in the narrative. The voyeurism-analepsis is cleverly framed by the variation or re-employment of verbal details. Waldo spies on Mrs Poulter "in one of his less *oblique* moments"; after the return to the actional present (W62), Waldo is "tempted to glance, if only *obliquely,* at Arthur". Waldo leaves the Poulters' house `crunching` on flowerpots; in the next sentence he is *trudging* along Barranugli Road. Then, in a parallel to the upset Mrs Poulter *crushing* her chrysanthemums in the bus (B20) just after glimpsing the twins, Arthur breaks his silence (or compelled secrecy) by observing how the "'chrysanths'" will get *crushed* on the bus (W62)—and Waldo must face the fact that Arthur, too, has seen Mrs Poulter riding by and hasn't mentioned it immediately. This is formally a continuation and resolution of Arthur's talk about Mrs Poulter and her flowers (W27), evidently at a time before the bus has set off. It will be seen that the impulse to symmetry in the details of narrative structure is marked; that the specific stimuli for the inception of analepses are suppressed or unarticulated; that these stimuli, though they take a myriad forms, are predominantly analeptic germs within the first narrative, triggered off by its events rather than being the events of the first narrative themselves; that the analogy of widely separated neural synapses "sparking" to produce an "explosion" in some central ganglion is perhaps not too farfetched an analogy; and that egress from the state of concentrated recollection coincides with the conveying of some *physical* detail.[32]

---

[32] Here, in B^1, it is the tactile "jolt" of Waldo crunching over the flowerpots. In A^1, to take another example, it is the willed shrivelling-away of Waldo's despair at his father's despair as revealed at the bank: release of feeling comes only when he crushes a brown slug in the garden after the return home. The bank scene and the discontinuance of the boys' visits there are, incidentally, not simply to be explained by the fact (nowhere adumbrated in the narrative) that Arthur is felt as a too conspicuously shambling public embarrassment to Mr Brown. That Mr Brown, who "very seldom looked up" (W53), should now be "looking out from the cage in which he stood" (W54) has broader emblematic importance for Waldo. This is underscored by a proleptic use of the modal "would remember", explicitly linking the bank scene and Mr Brown's dead eyes with the later analepsis of his death: "More distinctly even than the morning he found their father dead Waldo would remember the morning of their last visit to the bank". Although this reads in isolation like a classic proleptic "advance notice" as in a nineteenth-century novel, it has not been classically positioned *prior to* the scene to be

But the voyeurism-incident cannot be placed according to temporal indices. It can, however, be located circumstantially through the collation of recurrent verbal detail, even though there is no further mention of the incident. Mrs Brown's generous opinion of Mrs Poulter is stressed at three points: when the initial settling-in is narrated (W141); after the act of voyeurism (W144; hereafter termed the "after-phase"); and before the specific recall of the voyeur-scene (W61). Mrs Brown seems hostile towards Mrs Poulter after she hears Arthur talking about her (W144)—but Waldo's narration has obscured the implication that his mother has been alarmed enough already by Mrs Poulter's talk of cancer to distance herself from her publicly *and* to react negatively whenever her name crops up (W141–42). She is facing an operation for breast-cancer, after which Arthur's talk about the pigeon-breasted Mrs Poulter reminds her of her loss (A256). Waldo's negative attitude towards Mrs Poulter is there from the beginning (W61/140/144), and surges up self-protectively when he sees her in the bus (W60). His negativity is compounded with sexual attraction, fed by adolescent thoughts about a prostitute (cf W78 and W140, with the recurrent stair-motif). Waldo is attracted to Mrs Poulter, sharing his mother's standoffishness but aware of a sexual pull (W144, "But knew she was there"). Arthur's romantic description of her hair (W144), at an earlier stage (cf W141, A264) before the Poulters have built their house, fuels his desire or curiosity, as does a subliminal wish to get even with Bill Poulter for rejecting his intimate intellectual overtures. Several key physical details from elsewhere are mentioned in inversion or in transmuted form within the voyeur-scene: the hair-washing that Arthur has openly claimed to have seen contrasts with Waldo's secretly witnessing Mrs Poulter washing her whole body, including her secret hair. The after-phase paragraph (before which the unlocated voyeur-scene would chronologically belong, W144) puts what Arthur has called Mrs Poulter's "lovely hair" in a positive light, as it were (exceptionally for Waldo, who elsewhere has a horror of hair)—the "certain lights" being a recall of the "yellow light" in the house. The mention of "firm flesh" in the after-phase (W144) is an

---

specified, but has been added on. The implied emphasis is not on the impact of the scene on Waldo, but on the inexorability of memory itself. Waldo has a distaste for things brown or liquid, a preference for the blue and the dry. At the bank, his father's brown, "normally liquid eyes" are "set like glass inside the cage". It is not Arthur's presence alone that explains this stare—for Waldo, the death of the rational soul, imprisoned in circumstance; it is the fact that Arthur's habitual behaviour has "tainted" his father's social credibility and has caused him to be passed up for promotion. Before the two bank episodes (the relaxed early visits, W53; the epiphanic last visit, W54) comes the narrative of the Dallimores' visit, with its reinforcement of Waldo's secret desire for genteel, "blue-eyed" ancestral antecedents. More centrally, the ladies' suggestion that Mr Brown will be promoted to Head Office meets with a conspicuous silence, and Arthur's later repetition of the suggestion with Mr Brown's blank pessimism. It is before the ladies' visit that the bank-visits have been discontinued "because Dad no longer wanted it" (W53). Waldo's arid, rigid, "blue" equilibrium can be re-established only by the symbolic extinction of his father's brown liquidity in the crushing of the slug. The process of recollection re-enacts pain; the actional extermination or transference of pain marks the closure of this narrative phase of recollection.

uncharacteristically sensuous detail, subverting Mrs Brown's descriptions, and secretly recalling the light's transformation of Mrs Poulter's flesh (W61). Whereas she elsewhere has a high complexion (W61/141), the light has bled it here (W61); her complexion is recalled after the incident (W144). During Waldo's wooing of Bill Poulter, the latter is described as scraggy (W141)—the specific epithet that is minimized during the voyeur-scene (W62). Although the first sentence of the after-phase is sensuous, even sensual, it is also innocent—as Mrs Poulter was innocent of any complicity in Waldo's scopophilia. The next sentence (W144) implicitly contains the emphasis "There was nothing you could have accused *her* of", evoking the concept of "guilt" in the voyeur-scene and linking with "accuse" in the actional present (W60).

The voyeur-incident can be placed before Mrs Brown's operation and after Waldo's overtures to Bill Poulter. The temporal localization of the B^1 analepsis depends almost entirely on the degree of attention we bring to bear on the figural discourse. Other, equally ubiquitous techniques of indirect temporal binding can be found in the novel. One good example is related to what has just been discussed. Waldo's tangle of repulsion, attraction and sexual guilt towards Mrs Poulter, and the transfer outwards of his own drive for status and secrecy, result in his successful effort (abetted for other reasons by his parents) to sever the contact between Arthur and her. Severance is built into the narrative structure: what now follows is the puncturing of Waldo's hopes of marrying Dulcie (narreme 65, W149–58). This resolves the enigma, set up by narrative sequence, of Waldo's extreme reaction to meeting Dulcie and Saporta in 1934. It is no accident that the mental and actional images accumulated as Waldo leaves in humiliation, self-pity and self-protective scorn are those of Dulcie as a Great Earth Mother, of his checked compulsion to run, of his unchecked weeping "for the tragedy of this ugly girl" and removal of his pince-nez to wipe his eyes. In 1934, there were (narratively) or will be (chronologically) the Saportas' children and their mother, Waldo's unchecked, headlong flight, his broken pince-nez, and his weeping in the hospital "for Dulcie he would have liked to think".

There is now a brief narrative recursion delineating once more the asthmatic retirement of George Brown ("Dad *had* retired a year or two early", W158–61), especially *his* relation to Mrs Poulter and her "sacramental" charity towards him in his illness. Also repeated in variation are Mr Brown's unsuccessful attempts to communicate to his sons his heritage of insight about life in Australia (W160, recapitulating a scene at W145–46). The later scene is narrated with terse, dismissive irony, as the full force of Waldo's rejection of this wisdom—and of his father—has already been expended in the earlier scene. Mr Brown's death is noted once more, this time in a single dismissive clause, and the narrative proceeds onwards by shifting to Waldo's encouragement of his mother to reveal the "secrets she had been waiting to tell" about the past in England. Waldo can only look back: his procreative extension of self through Dulcie (or at least through her son's name) now thwarted, he seeks the mythic "Waldo" in the Thourault family history. But his father's presence persists, mocking his son's sterility through the paper bags of dry seed rattling in the wind.

Mrs Brown's decline into dipsomania, early memories, amnesia, senility and final illness is charted down to Mrs Poulter's reappearance in the role of Caritas, entreating the stubbornly blind Waldo to fetch the doctor (W167)—at which stage there is a proleptic reference to his mother's coming death "ten years after ... her husband" (**2.7** in Table 2), followed by a further phase of decline, then the final noting of her death (W171, **2.7**) "a couple of years" before the Encounter. Actually, the link is between Arthur's "delicacy" in not bringing up the Dulcie/Saporta business at the cremation (which Saporta has arranged) and his "recapitulation" of "the whole Feinstein–Saporta history" after the Pitt Street accident, "a couple of years later". Mrs Brown's year of death is thus established by a prolepsis within an internal analepsis (back to 1922), and by a repeating analepsis (recalling the already narrated but chronologically posterior event in 1934). The explanation for this double locating of Mrs Brown's death within such a brief span of reading-time lies in the narrational manifestation of obsessive groundswells within Waldo's unconscious, not in an implied-auctorial trick to help the reader.

There are now two phases of analepsis (W171–86) centering on Waldo's existence at the library. The second of these phases broadens to include Waldo's relationships with Arthur (reacting to Arthur's dog by getting a puppy of his own, W180) and Mrs Poulter (the doll). In both cases, the central event is the indirect establishing of a relationship. Waldo's giving Mrs Poulter the large and ugly plastic doll is psychologically implausible (cf W185), but involves various contributory antecedents: the theme of sexual attraction (the voyeurism); the theme of frustrated procreativity (Dulcie/Saporta); the compensatory but grotesquely negative re-establishing of a bond with Mrs Poulter which had once been her bond with Arthur (it is only in Section 3, where Arthur explicitly becomes her child-surrogate, that this symmetry is clinched). This second phase involves relatively clear narrative presentation. The fixing of the events in time, however, involves their intercalation with details of Waldo's *earlier* experiences at the library. Our efforts to follow the temporal localizations involve us in some breathless shuttling back and forth, ever at the mercy of the labyrinthine interconnections wrought by Waldo's increasing paranoia.

These interconnections are ultimately established, with clarity, in relation to events occurring during the Second World War. The first phase of analepsis (W171–77) seems to take us from the years immediately following Mrs Brown's death and the Encounter (1932–34) up to Waldo's resignation from Sydney Municipal at some as yet unlocalized time during the war, with one minor internal analepsis (W174–75) to a time "not long after Dad died", when the twins shift into their parents' bedroom. So much of what is recounted occurs on the level of *habitual* action, however, that there are details relating to Waldo's literary activity and his galling relationship with his library superior, Crankshaw, that are temporally *mislocated* under pressure from the unconscious. As with the previous war, then, the narrative elides true temporal relationships, this time not pushing incidents further into the past but pulling them forward into a later period.

Crankshaw is already "playing up" by gently questioning the accuracy of Waldo's work "a long time" before Mrs Brown's death (W166–67). After the narrative of her death and cremation, and a reference to the Encounter and Waldo's loss of his pince-nez, Crankshaw re-enters. By this unspecified time he has been promoted to Librarian, though "several years" Waldo's junior (W171) and has obviously been Waldo's superior from the 1920s onwards; like his father, Waldo has been passed up for promotion. On the "first of several progressively intensifying occasions" (W172) when Crankshaw begins asking his mild questions about Waldo's working conditions, the latter magnifies these questions paranoically into a conspiracy against him. In this scene, Crankshaw is presented contemptuously as having three marriagable daughters, so this tense exchange must have taken place in the late 1930s (Waldo thinks back on that occasion to the "distressing incident" of the Encounter, the feel of his spectacles linking the two scenes, W173). This scene is explicitly associated with Waldo's literary activity:

This was the year Waldo Brown began what became a considerable fragment of his novel *Tiresias a Youngish Man*. He was invited, too, in a roundabout way, to address the Beecroft Literary Society, and did, or rather, he read a paper on Barron Field .... Finally, a lady novelist of the Fellowship, [*sic*] had asked him to an evening at her home, to which he hadn't gone, for scenting sexual motives behind her insistence.

With all this, it was incredible to think a second *war* had broken out, though of a different kind. [W173]

The activity, though relished as if following in swift succession, is actually so slow that the start of the war (and, from the next few remarks, specifically Japanese entry into it in 1941 and the gassing of the Jews, not publicly known until late 1942 at the earliest) cuts across this succession and is not even noticed by Waldo. When he does start noticing, he is psychologically, not socially, preoccupied, his attitude differing from his reaction before the Great War: earlier, "he could never in any way take part" and would anyway have been physically unfit (W127); now he "could have outmarched the most virile of them"—but "to the big new Public Library they had opened a couple of years before" (W177). The time-data are subordinated offhandedly, vaguely, to Waldo's mood of high expectation that he is going to win *his* "war" against Crankshaw by resigning.

But the alert reader will have retained a memory of a parenthetical comment in the main segment dealing with Mr Brown's death (W69–70), where the closest textual analysis fails to dislodge the conviction that the temporal centre of narration is the morning of Waldo's discovering his father's body in 1922. There is no suggestion that Waldo's thoughts relate specifically to events or states occurring or obtaining later than 1922. Consider, then, the information that is given in parentheses:

(Waldo *by this period* had written several articles, there was the fragment of a novel, and he had joined the Fellowship of Australian Writers.) [My emphases.]

This seems to parallel the information given at W173, at least generally. Two of the three correlative references so far—to the novel-fragment and to the written articles—are compromised in terms of both their extent or completeness and the "period" in which they were written.[33] The third is quite inconsistent with a temporal locus of 1922: Waldo could only have joined the Fellowship at the earliest in 1928, the year of its foundation in Sydney. This fact validates the location of the lady novelist's invitation as some time in the late 1930s or mid-1940s. The parenthetical comment at W70 does not and cannot figure, no matter how one tries to twist and turn the possible temporal reference of "by this period". Is this parenthesis, then, a mistake on the part of the author? I think not. There are other instances of parenthetical comments which possess more than doubtful truth-status (W129–30, for example). Instead of being narrator-focalized "intrusions", they represent an especially alert state of mind, in which a character is engaged in a blithe, or resolute, rewriting of "reality". The present rewriting contains three separate topics at least. Only in the rewriting do they co-occur: ie, we are being *led* to assume that the time-markers "by this period" and "this was the year" gather together events, states and processes which belong together by temporal logic. In "reality", they need not; the rewritings are subliminally willed or wishful concatenations or collations of temporally discrete data. Indeed: a strong case could be made, on the basis of "intertextual" resonance alone (the *historical-literary* time during which Waldo was most likely to have made a quasi-creative reader-response to Crankshaw's Catholic friend, Patrick Joseph Hartigan, alias "John O'Brien"; to the nineteenth-century "Austral Harmonist" Barron Field, producer of all of six poems; to J.G. Frazer's *The Golden Bough;* and to T.S. Eliot's reworking of myth), for dating the sole existing "fragment of a novel" to the early 1920s. The fabrication of a *cohesive* complex of literary "life" is needed by Waldo's mechanism of recall when he is reliving the discovery of his dead father: the presentation of the scene—Waldo strolling in the garden, waiting to capture wingèd thoughts in his notebook—is deliberately poetic, a way, once again, of stemming himself against association with his father's failure. After the scene with Crankshaw, a similar fictive complex is needed to make Waldo look successful in his own eyes, as a means of raising himself (as a "superior subordinate", W173) above a man who has effectively put him in his father's existential position.

It may be objected that, if these temporal localizations are mediated so unreliably, Waldo is hardly the one to depend on for any of the other temporal

---

[33] Compare, in connection with those "several articles", the following indications of barely inceptive or merely "conceived" literary activity. During the Great War, after Walter Pugh's death, "he went so far as to begin a poem" (W129)—he doesn't, then, complete the poem, and even to have gone "so far" is further than usual. If Waldo gets a "thrill" at coming across the lines years later, it is not so much because of the clichéd sentiments expressed as because this is the *sole* evidence of poetic creativity, which remains frozen at the stage of the would-be, as expressed during a pre-war visit to Dulcie's: "Waldo wished he could have conceived a poem. He had not yet, but would—it was something he had kept even from himself" (W110). After the Second World War, he "almost wrote, not an article, more of an *essay* …. almost composed a poem" (W183). One begins to suspect that the "paper" he has "left no stone unturned" in writing has been his life's work; he does not "address" the literary society, because he has not been invited on the basis of previously published work.

fixings. I can only answer that the degree and kind of deviation depend very much on what we gather is closest to the deepest sources of Waldo's pain—and his investment in his role as Secret Writer and his quest for status are among these deepest sources of pain; for he continually runs up against the obstacles placed before him by his own closed vision. A very few events that have scarred him deeply have such a public or social dimension to them (the coming of the Poulters; the death of his parents; the Encounter) and have—Waldo believes— been so successfully exorcized through his scorn or psychological compensation that he is able to place them in time without any displacement tactics. There is a "middle"-status aggregation of events which seem not to have caused lasting psychical lesions. In most of these Waldo sees himself as having the situation under control (although the exercise of control is the outgrowth of pathological states of paranoia or deprivation). Here he employs a comparatively clear temporal notation, but one where the chronological sequence is presented in "secret" or shuffled narrative relativities. One example of this is the sequence (a) shift to the new library > (b) buying the dogs > (c) buying the doll > (d) the visit of Johnny Haynes (W177-187), where there is a thick skein of time-references that takes quite some effort to unravel into linear logic. I suspect that few readers would actually think to make the necessary computations. My experience after repeated readings is that one is so immersed in the flux of Waldo's recollections that it never occurs to one to impose the external logic of strict calendar time. If one actually does so, however, concealed and significant relationships are revealed. But, until this is done, one is truly under the sway of Waldo's rationalizations and his retreats from temporal particularity. Not only does one experience the *Eigendynamik* of memory; one is also, with part of the reading mind, forced into collusion with Waldo and one's reflexes become perhaps as subterranean and unconscious as Waldo's own.

4

DOUBLINGS

I   Narrative frequency and ordering:
Examples of double telling

The various temporal dissonances in Waldo's section discussed so far can be accounted for by the fact that certain events in *The Solid Mandala* are "twice-told". What I want to look at in the present chapter is the question of *frequency*, or the *fabula/sujet* relationship in respect of the number of times events occur and the number of times they are narrated. The main focus of attention will be the two central narratives (Waldo's and Arthur's); but the far-from-peripheral presence of the initial section ("In the Bus") also invites analysis.

The instrumentarium of analysis most suited to my purpose is supplied by Gérard Genette (1980:114–16), who sets out the main categories of narrative in regard to frequency:

1) The most common form of narrative is *singulative*, where a single event in the story or *fabula* is recounted once in the narrative or *sujet*.

2) In *iterative* narrative, repeated habitual or analogous events in the story are summarized or synthesized "sylleptically" in the form of a single narrative utterance. Classically, iterative narrative (like description) is a subordinate technique which frames passages of singulative narrative. The *paradigmatic* use of *singulative* narrative (where a particular event is narrated as an example of others) can, in respect to the tricky structure of *The Solid Mandala*, be taken as a sub-class of the iterative.[1]

3) *Repeating* narrative occurs when the same unique story-event is told more than once in a narrative, with stylistic variations and/or variations of narrative perspective (*multiple focalization*: Genette 1980:190).[2]

Broadly speaking, the whole of Sections 2 and 3 of *The Solid Mandala* (except for the "present" *events* of the actional present) is a repeating narrative, together with much of the mimetic representation (dialogue) of Section 1. One cannot, of course, rely on a formal classification of narrative events by, say, the time-

---

[1] Genette 1980:116.*n*6; cf Lämmert 1955:84 on eclectic or metonymic condensation; Genette 1980:121 also uses the term *pseudo-iterative*.

[2] In terms of the ordering of narrative time, the epistolary novel often exhibits such repetition. Narratives may contain *repeating anachronies* and advance notices (Lämmert 1955:122–28; Genette 1980:54–61/73). These are brief internal analepses or recalls involving postponed significance or reevaluation, and brief internal prolepses or allusions to events that will later be told in full. Such anachronies are not only *generated* by narratives with a broadly repeating structure, but can also *give* to narratives differently organized the fleeting look of repeating narratives.

adverbials attached to them. A statement like "He read to them sometimes about the Greeks", and all the habitual detail adhering to the statement (W33), constitutes a stretch of *iterative* narrative—but it must be classified at another level as an iteratively mediated part of a *repeating* narrative, once we have come across the same events described in Arthur's section ("Dad would read them the Greek myths", A223). Similarly, a stretch of *singulative* narrative ("Then, on that morning of dew and light", W70) is part of a *repeating* narrative with respect to the number of occasions Mr Brown's death is noted within Waldo's section and within Arthur's, no matter how fully or summarily the event is treated.

My concern here is the analysis, not of frequency and narrative ordering as such, but only of such aspects as might cast light on the ways in which the narrative is organized by, or around, the subjectivity of the central characters. One representative group of repeating-narrative segments, with subdivisions, might be the following:

A: The bank (W52–54, A218–21).
B: Building the house (W36–38, A221–23).
C: The twins' Greek tragedies (W38–41, A229–30).
D: Dulcie and her family.
E: From the end of the actional-present walk to Waldo's death.

A combines iterative narrative with point-time (punctual) incidents, and is essentially told twice only. B and C are also told twice only, but their reach is greater and more complex in terms of the interlocking between certain details and other events and temporal phases in the narrative. They are, for one, dovetailed into one another, are alluded to motivically in connection with the passage of time, and are syncretized with Mr Brown's death.

The central complex of data embedded in the narration of C (the house-building) is tangential to the event-surface. Waldo's narrative does not mention that the building-site is in Terminus road; only later, at the end of the playground-torture scene, does he focus on the road "where nobody else had begun to live, or some perhaps, in the past, and given up" (W45). Arthur, by contrast, provides a practical gloss on the name "Terminus", which is seen as "already theirs" (just as, in Section 2, the very house of the Browns is to be painted brown): the road is "close to the station, practically planned, in fact, for Dad". If this refers to George Brown's requirements in commuting to the Bank, the statement is also germinally proleptic for his fate in life, which is to end where he began. In Arthur's narrative only, the following scene occurs: On the way to the building-site, Waldo is annoyed, Arthur amused, that Mr Allwright will not tell the boys the secret of "a ruined house standing amongst fruit trees which had been allowed to grow wild"; Allwright intimates that "too much imagination" could get the lads into trouble. For Waldo, the word "Terminus" has an ominous association with an area of experience (death) he deeply fears; his relative clauses (W45, quoted above) are diffident, and implicitly augment what has been the triggering moment of the playground bullying-scene, which is the content of the essay he reads to the class. By describing in the essay a decrepit, deserted old house "among the pear trees", and embroidering this with speculation about murders, he compensates for Mr Allwright's withholding of the house's secret, and gets into trouble for giving his "imagination" free play (W43–44). There are thus three "versions" of the ruined house: in the building-scene, the immediate and scenic (Arthur's recollection from the present); outside the building-scene, a recollection in the past (Waldo's characterization of Terminus Road); and, similarly outside the occasion on which its "original" is registered, the "artistic" transformation (Waldo's essay). Whereas Waldo's account of the Browns' house darts forward to momentary contemplation of its decline, Arthur's accepts the "brown weatherboard" on its own terms, as it does the ruined house—in macrostructural terms, however, the occurrence of the latter is also an emblematic germinal prolepsis of the similar final state of the Browns' own house, whose physical decline and enclosure by trees and undergrowth are stressed descriptively in both Section 2 and Section 3. Whereas the building of the house and the Greek pediment is presented by Waldo in strict chronological sequence interrupted by negative futurity, Arthur, who has an acute awareness of the positive enthusiasms of other people, disrupts the chronology in a mood of empathetic anticipation. Narrative quantities reflect psychological pre-occupation—not the house (as with Waldo), but Mr Allwright, is pursued by Arthur into the future beyond the immediate confines of the house-building.

The correct understanding of **D** depends on our perception of the relationship between incidents which the twins experience together (their visits *à deux*) and those which they experience separately. Strictly speaking, the latter are by nature singulative except when they crop up in truncated form elsewhere, in the form of mental recall or association; this is frequently the case with apparently singulative events in Waldo's section. But the effort of both twins mentally to bridge the gap between what they have individually experienced and what the other has experienced leads to a situation in which singulative events may become encoded in the discourse of the other. This is a clear case of the implied author allowing his narrative to exercise its own revelatory strengths—on the backs of the characters' psychology, so to speak. But it is also frequently clear in **D** that, although temporal markers are few in comparison with the much more densely narrated **A–C**, the configuration of the narrative depends not so much on action as on Waldo's and Arthur's mental construction of event-relationships. My schematic analysis of **E** is prompted not so much by technical considerations as by the fact that two apparently discerning critics get this "ending" wrong. The narremic reconstruction (ch. 3) shows very coarsely the results of my sequencing activity as a reader, but not the steps by which my conclusions were reached. I have selected three of the five examples **A–D** for closer analysis.

THE TWINS' GREEK TRAGEDIES

In Section 2, the consecutive scenes (Waldo's proposition, then Arthur's playlet) are so treated. The point of inception is not temporal, but marks Waldo as the focus of information ("It was Waldo who disturbed the peace" of the previously-mentioned "hot brown box" of the family house). Waldo declares he will write a play, Arthur appears, asks if he can act in it, and is rebuffed. There is a shift to *habituality*: Arthur's breathing when Waldo wakes in the night, his searching eyes in the morning: this is enough "sharing" for Waldo. Arthur is not "put off", and acts out a distressed cow; Mr Brown diffidently calls a halt, as does Mrs Brown, who remains seated on the veranda when her husband limps inside. Waldo resolves to write a quite different play, and lingers "on the stage which no longer contained their wooden play". In Section 3, Arthur's telling is half as long as Waldo's, but is curiously and obliquely prefaced by material that has already been "holographically" encoded in his telling of **B** above. Two iterative-narrative paragraphs precede the actual incident, and are generated by the "descending darkness" of one early morning, after the twins have lain together as always, when Waldo is bad-tempered:

It was the kind of moment when Arthur sensed he would have to protect his brother, who was too clever by half, who read essays aloud in class, who liked books, and who was said to be their mother's darling. Because of it all, Waldo needed defending from himself and others. [A229]

The iterative follows: though Arthur cannot "take time off" like his brother, he does "look up a book on the sly". "In the meantime there was his family", whose frailties are listed. This *seeming* iteration is then anchored to Arthur's habitual *and* point-time perception of the family "sitting on the classical veranda" "as he went down to milk". The next paragraph has a *logical* inception: "So Arthur had to go carefully". He tries to keep quiet with the milk-bucket, then returns from milking, knowing the others are still on the veranda. "Still. With Waldo going to write some old tragedy of a play. Arthur had by some means to distract".

Arthur's account relates to the housebuilding and housepainting scenes by a skein of largely iterative, not singulative, details. (1) The family on the veranda links up with "in the beginning" as narrated in Waldo's version of **B**. (2) Arthur's views on the family echo and augment Waldo's in **B** when the paint is discussed. (3) Mention of the school-essay and defending Waldo encode the outcome of the deserted-house fragment in Arthur's version of **B**; Arthur's time-sequence here is chronological, unlike Waldo's. (4) The boys' sleeping together appears in the middle of Waldo's **C**. Waldo's bad temper as detailed by Arthur is the reaction to the sight of Arthur's early-morning eyes as detailed by Waldo. (5) Arthur, in observing that Waldo likes books, matches the fact that a literary source (Aeschylus) motivates Waldo's selection of the genre of tragedy.

In Waldo's section, Arthur's actions appear spontaneous, and limited to after his return from milking. What Arthur's iterative-narrative preliminaries do is provide the secret motivation for his actions. Both versions relate scenically to the veranda; both encode scenic and actional analogies between the Greek pediment and the Greek tragedies—Waldo's explicitly at the close, Arthur's implicitly at the start.

In the presentation of Arthur's cow-tragedy, there are further details which corroborate or contrast with Waldo's version. (6) Arthur abbreviates his actual proposal ("and said more or less"), whereas Waldo's account has him being *coaxed* to "blurt out" the details after a much fuller "good-tempered" announcement. Arthur's section reveals that he is hiding tears for Waldo by a display of distracting good temper. Arthur pretends to take up, impromptu, from Waldo's words as he approaches with the full milk-pail; in fact, his efforts to keep quiet while milking have been because he is *listening* to the distant conversation. This casts a new light on Waldo's narrative incipit: in preventing the bucket from clanking, Arthur has generated an atmosphere of "peace"—which Waldo's proposal disturbs. (7) Aware that the family think him mentally limited (A230), Arthur appeals to the universal law of psychological verisimilitude in proposing a cow as subject—not to Mr Brown's scepticism about its generic suitability (W39). This contrasts with, yet confirms, Mr Brown's reaction to Waldo's own proposal: "'You'd better learn to live first'". (8) Waldo's discourse depicts Mrs Brown's reactions so positively that Arthur's phrase about "their mother's darling" is thereby confirmed. Arthur perceives her more clearly: "Mother suddenly tried to throw the expression off her face", her call to halt being repeated almost verbatim from Waldo's segment. (9) Arthur's disingenuousness is apparent from his narration; in Waldo's, there is only the noncommittal notice Waldo takes of how Arthur seems to stop acting "as though he had been going to". (10) The equivalent to Mr Brown's getting up and limping inside is, in Arthur's narrative, a longish passage which both reveals Arthur's emotional acuity and also fills in a narrative gap in Section 2 caused by Waldo's self-preoccupation. In Section 3, only Mrs Brown suggests that Arthur desist—at which moment Arthur "felt Dad turn against him". Waldo's narrative provides Mr Brown's specific words before his wife speaks. Section 3 makes it obliquely apparent that Arthur attempts to accompany his father "off stage" as he limps away. His apparently false apprehension of the others' empathy for his dramatic rendering leads him to try and empathize with his father and his bad leg.

(11) Waldo's narration struggles to avoid conceding that Arthur's playlet has touched the audience: the very syntax, however, reveals how shame has turned to terror: or, later, that it was "ridiculous, when not frightening", to think that Arthur could have thought of such a play. If Arthur "of all people" could do this, then Waldo is endorsing the validity and force of the theme, just as Mr Brown has conceded its cultural—if not generic—validity. The father is clearly thinking of the Greek myths he has told the boys (W33/A223—in each case preceding both the Greek pediment and the Greek tragedies). And it is reasonable to assume that Arthur, burying his head "in their cow's side" while milking, has also had the myths of Io and Hera at the back of his mind. Arthur's theme of the yellow cow and her stillborn calf is, incidentally, a germinal prolepsis of his later empathy for Mrs Poulter, who has lost her child and eventually "adopts" Arthur in its stead. (12) In Arthur's section, everything points to his having been elevated by

the *furor poeticus* to create a rounded (if abbreviated) work of art, which is also a work of artifice to the extent that the whole exercise is his attempt to protect his brother from displaying his inadequacy. This contrasts—germinally for the whole tenor of the novel's action—with Waldo's declarations of *intention*, feeding off literature and ego rather than life and experience, to "write a play". Arthur's dramatic *ekstasis* is a surrender of self to empathy; when checked by his parents' doubts, Waldo, by contrast, "began to sidle. He was never easily carried away" (W39).

It should be evident how inescapably reliant we are on both narratives for the resolution of meaning, not least in regard to the different ways in which events are placed in relation to habit, to the merciless salience which Arthur's narrative grants to actions that are submerged in Waldo's obliquities, to the serenely clear emotional centre of Arthur's narration, and to the tense stand-offs between extremes of feeling and vision in Waldo's.

DULCIE AND HER FAMILY

Waldo's earliest meeting with Dulcie Feinstein occurs at Mrs Musto's tennis party (W89ff.). The reader has already "eavesdropped" on dialogue (W28–29) and free indirect discourse (W56–57) during the actional-present walk, on dialogue and free indirect discourse during the Encounter-incident (W63ff), and on dialogue during Waldo's adolescence (W80)—all of which serves to connect a "Dulcie" with someone called Len Saporta, and closely (even romantically) with both Waldo and Arthur. In every instance, these relationships have been questioned by Waldo; at the first mention of the name Dulcie, it is clear that there is something Arthur has touched on that Waldo does not want to be reminded of, and that Arthur is hesitant about admitting that he has seen "them" (people named Saporta) within recent memory. In the first actional-present passages, the topic of Dulcie has been prefaced by reference to the glittering of Waldo's spectacles. The thought-sequence in the second passage is full of details that are clarified only much later:

How dreadful if Dulcie. But she hadn't. It was the kind of near-slip which made him hate Dulcie's judgment rather than deplore his own temporary lack of it. Suppose his exercise in loving Dulcie had been forced to harden into a permanent imitation of love! The intermittent drizzle of resentment is far easier to bear, may even dry right up. It had, in fact, until Arthur. [W56]

The Encounter in Pitt Street (W63ff.) explains few of the earlier obliquities and introduces some of its own. A motivic continuation of the detail about the spectacles can be sensed at the start, in the reference to Waldo's "broken pince-nez". Waldo's detestation of Saporta is mentioned, but not explained—except that the separate "Dulcie" and "Saporta" of before are here married. The reference to "loving" in the above quotation connects somewhat with Waldo's noticing in the Saportas' children "the absence of those qualities with which Waldo might have endowed *the children he had not got with Dulcie*". Waldo's relief (or triumph) is suggested at the fact that the Saportas do not mention Arthur. Then comes the blinding, literally staggering revelation that their boy has been named "Arthur": Waldo, brimming with nostalgia and certainty, has been expecting his own name. In a turmoil of semi-coherent thought and feeling, Waldo flees; the scene is rounded off by his losing his spectacles. Dulcie drops out of sight again until Arthur tries to console Waldo in his attempt at "growing his first moustache" during his last year of school. When Arthur mentions liking "Dulcie", who, he says, "'will probably grow a moustache'", Waldo erupts: "'You know nothing about *any* girl!'" (W80). "Nor did Waldo. Nor did he want to". This all would indicate that Arthur thinks Waldo knows who he is referring to: ie, that he has already spoken of her; Waldo's denial, following on an embarrassing sex-lecture by his father, could be either of a personal and social acquaintance or of a "biological" acquaintance with girls in general.

At the tennis-party, there is considerable narrational equivocation regarding the girl who is called Dulcie from the very first of her actions. Deictic indications (eg, "the girl Dulcie", "this ugly dark girl") are that Waldo does not know her— or even *of* her. As cultural connections in their conversation slowly whet Waldo's interest, he notices "a dark shadow on her upper lip" (W92), a detail which is repeated, along with: "Arthur had been right, Waldo realized. Dulcie would probably grow a moustache" (W94).[3] This establishes the temporal sequence (Waldo grows his moustache, then goes to the party), and the fact that Waldo recognizes this as the girl Arthur mentioned on *one* prior occasion; Waldo's referring to her as "Dulcie" is not an index of familiarity, but an echo of Arthur's own words. From Waldo's subsequent query about whether Dulcie knows his (unnamed) brother, we can deduce that Arthur *has* told Waldo about *a* Dulcie whom he has encountered as a customer at Allwrights' store (W95). Although Dulcie apparently does not know his brother, Waldo hopes that "perhaps Dulcie Feinstein would continue in ignorance of his uncontrollable twin" (W95). Waldo wishes to make Dulcie his secret, denying that the two spheres of public and private life (the shop; personal contact) can come together, taking thankful refuge in the ambiguity of a later question from Dulcie to deny his brother ("'Your brother, ... is he anything like you? Is he older?'" "'No,' he said"). But it becomes increasingly hard to uphold the separation of spheres when it is *clear* from an invitation to Waldo from Mrs Feinstein that Arthur has been left out *because* Dulcie knows him. Arthur then enters to talk with familiarity about the Feinsteins' house and Dulcie's piano-playing—but he does not still Waldo's secret hunger for more information, preferring to frame his knowledge of the Feinsteins in a purely commercial context.

---

3 All these references to Dulcie's hirsuteness have been prepared for by an oblique parenthesis during the Encounter-scene: "... looking at her, at her heavy moustache—he had been right—..." (W65). Although Arthur is mentioned at the very end of the sentence, "he" here can only mean Waldo: so that by 1934 an opinion originally expressed by Arthur has been expropriated by Waldo. This is a good example of the way in which the pressures of rationalization warp Waldo's memory and relation to truth.

Because of the limited and prevaricatingly *withholding* nature of Waldo's articulation, we are confronted on a first reading with the enigmas and shadows he confronts and generates, and are forced into a parallel condition of guesswork, suspicion and irresolution. Despite our efforts to lessen our incertitude by seeking Waldo's motivation in incidental turns of phrase, uncertainty remains as an aura conditioning the narrative. Behind specific uncertainties (those centering on Waldo's drive to keep things to himself) lies the structure of the narrative itself. Enigmas may vanish as patterns of causative ordering are completed or reshuffled; but the macrostructural twice-telling withholds knowledge from us that is also withheld from Waldo. This is circumstantial evidence for the absence from the narrative of an omnisciently analytical auctorial voice. The deductions made are, so far, Waldo's.

The obliquity of Waldo's narrative (ultimately the consequence both of the self-evidence to him of his mental referents and of his urge to rationalize away the painful), coupled with the referential self-evidence to Arthur of what he recollects, means that matters of texture and detail will still have slipped our attention even by a third reading. However, what Waldo *doesn't know* in *fabula*-sequence up till W99 is comparatively clear: he cannot know that Mrs Musto has issued invitations to Waldo and Dulcie after discussing the matter with Arthur (A238–39); and he cannot know the precise extent to which Arthur's prior acquaintance with the Feinsteins is personal, not commercial (A240ff.).

In Waldo's narrative, we have got used to him wishing his brother to be on the *outside* of the relationships he covets. His suspicions that Arthur may be *already inside* are allayed for us through the peculiarities of his mental discourse. When we get to Arthur's section, a leitmotivic pattern of mental attitudes about relationships begins to consolidate itself. When Mrs Musto swears him to *secrecy* about her plans for Waldo, Arthur suspects he will lose her to his brother (A238); similarly in the case of the Feinsteins, "who might have become his private property" (A239)—the first mention of the latter in Arthur's section. This strand of possessive *concealment* is embedded in a framework of *discovery*: the mandala-definition in Ralph Musto's encyclopaedia; Mr Brown's failure to uncover for him the meaning of "totality"; Arthur's manipulation of a pocketed marble in a "frenzy of discovery" (A240)—this last followed by the plain statement: "Arthur discovered the Feinsteins too".

Iterative narrative characterizes the phase of Arthur's grocery-deliveries to the Feinsteins. The first meeting is marked by Arthur's curious use of the (customarily phase-time-marking) adverbial "in the beginning", and further point-time references distinguish clearly between Arthur as the guest of Mrs Feinstein and the distance maintained between Arthur and the "young girl inside" practising the piano. In Waldo's section, Arthur mentions the Feinsteins' brass bell and Dulcie's piano-practice separately (W99); in his own section, the bell, the music, and Mrs Feinstein's admonition link the need for silence with the need to avoid distracting the girl. Arthur's remark about Dulcie's moustache (W80) is based only on speculation: "he had, he thought, once, at the store", seen "a skinny girl with a dark shadow on her upper lip, standing probably having the sulks" (A242). At Dulcie's home, Arthur can only press his face against the glass, looking "at Dulcie Feinstein's back" as he is agonized by the beauty of the music she plays (A241). This fairy-tale or romance element of the "faceless mystery" or name without a face and the longing prince as outsider is kept distinct by Arthur from the other manifestation of the girl as the face without a name at the store. The "real Dulcie", it is nevertheless implied, would be an amalgam of the two. Arthur quizzes Dulcie about Waldo and receives an "uncommunicative reply" (A242): almost a mirror-image of Dulcie's negative reply at Mrs Musto's (W95), and with a similar echoing of relief—he can keep the Feinsteins "as part of his own secret life, which was naturally so unsuspected nobody tried to enter it" (A242). Arthur's idea of "secret life" stresses "life" rather than complete secrecy. He will always try to conceal: but, unlike Waldo's, his innermost compulsion is to *reveal* and *share* his experience of other people's lives, even against his protective desire. This is retrospectively confirmed in Waldo's section *immediately after* Arthur mentions Dulcie's moustache. Waldo's secret acts, it is implied, are an egoistic aggrandisement of self, unlike Arthur's, which are conceived as a selfless protection of others from Waldo's rapacious ego. Waldo is in an ironic double bind, however: his drive to reinforce his ego from within means he cannot reinforce it from without, in the mirror of social relations. Hence, partly, his obsessive contemplation of the social and cultural status of others (Mrs Musto; the Feinsteins; his mother in her past) and his own paralyzed inability to immerse himself freely in the social milieu he imaginatively feeds off.

Waldo's first visit to the Feinsteins', which precedes that of the twins together, is not mentioned as such by Arthur; Arthur's chief fear on the joint visit is his brother's lack of social flexibility, and he cannot determine how often Waldo has visited the Feinsteins already on his own (cf A243). We know already that Arthur's fears are justified. His first visit alone is overshadowed by the fact that Dulcie has a cold and has an "angry sullen look" (W102)—which correlates with Arthur's memory of a sulky girl in the store. Arthur's "real Dulcie" is not present for Waldo, who cannot respond to her piano-playing (W101). When Mrs Feinstein asks him to bring Arthur the next time, and intimates that he has already been there, there is the first open admission in Waldo's section of the latter's fundamental uncertainty: "Waldo looked at Dulcie, who at least on that occasion had been inside practising the piano .... He could not be sure whether she had already made his brother's acquaintance" (W106). Waldo's deduction here from what Arthur has told him about Dulcie's piano-playing (W99) is an ironical asymmetry: Waldo can look at the girl (in the face), Arthur could not. Waldo's subsequent fearful thoughts on the smashing by Arthur of a relationship he is beginning to cherish are comparable to, and subtly different from, the references in Arthur's section later (A238–39/242), and reflect differences in character.

Arthur emphasizes that the joint visit is "the first official, socially ratified meeting with Dulcie Feinstein" (A243)—meaning he will get to see her face to face. In Waldo's section, he refers only to looking forward to meeting *Mrs*

Feinstein socially (W107)—in keeping with the fact that the invitation he manages to "discover", despite Waldo's attempt to maintain his secret relationship by concealing it from him, stems from the mother. This attempt is not mentioned in Arthur's own narrative. The various phases of the visit itself are, as expected, narrated with differing evaluations and emphases. Omitted from the respective sections, of course, are details occurring when the twins are spatially separated. Arthur, however, can at least intuit that the afternoon, instead of being Waldo's "under the dripping hydrangeas with Dulcie ... would become Waldo's tragedy, because he wouldn't know how to act" (A245). Although Waldo is not interested in the hydrangeas (W112), the motif of the hydrangea-garden plays a conspicuous role throughout the novel. Waldo, too, has a curious proleptic thought: "From this occasion he *would remember* her breaking up into the crumbly fragments of greeny-white hydrangeas. Her dress, at any rate" (W112)—if not, we might add, herself before Waldo's romantic blandishments.... Checking back, we find that Waldo "had received" Dulcie "jealously, expectantly, into his mind, and allowed her to drift there passively" (W106). He continues to hold the advantages of Dulcie and her family in thrall; this mental storing-up, or passive cataloguing, is achieved by a process of recollection throughout the relationship: "So Waldo continued remembering" (W106). He is aware *at that time* of his relationship with Dulcie consisting of an accretion of romanticizable details which he abstracts from their original context and idealizes. The aspectuality of "would remember", then, indicates Waldo's recollection in the past at some future date, and also the selective operation of his memory.

The moment at which Dulcie and Arthur meet face to face overwhelms him; he senses that she finds his babble about her father's prayer-cap "distasteful"; once he gets close enough to her, however, he sees her own initial awkwardness dissolving in their mutual gaze and touch, like the opening of a flower or the breaking of virginity (A244). There is no cause to doubt the validity of this epiphany. Waldo, however, sees the confrontation as distressing to Dulcie because of Arthur's "imbecility", which she conceals as a reaction of distaste for religious superstition (the prayer-cap). This misconstruction proves fatal to Waldo's relationship with Dulcie. Although, on both this and the previous visit, he has correctly gathered that Mr Feinstein is an "enlightened" rationalist (which suits Waldo's own upbringing), he projects these beliefs onto Dulcie, later failing to see how important religion has become to her—and how much Arthur understands of, and has contributed towards, this rebirth of spirituality (or myth). One detail Waldo omits is that "fear that something precious might escape [Dulcie] was making her take [Arthur] by the hand" (A244)—this occurs *after* Waldo in his frantic embarrassment has tried to "drag him off" Dulcie (W109). Arthur's narrative suggests that Dulcie agrees to teach him the piano after he has asked her to, and that she is overjoyed to register this bond of music. Waldo's narrative suggests that Dulcie is only trying to humour Arthur in his wish to learn the piano, as she is embarrassed by his intimate comments about human communication. Dulcie's and Arthur's joint piano-playing is for Arthur "the most exquisite *fulfilment*" (A244). As in the incident of the Greek tragedy, we have on the one hand Arthur's access of improvisation, which, for all its lack of control, Dulcie understands. On the other (literally on the other side of the house), Waldo is *emptying* his bowels, and wishing poetic creativity could come shooting out of him "with the urgency of shit and music" (W110). Waldo returns to witness the laying bare of one of his own secret experiences: Dulcie and Arthur discussing the pierrot sitting on the moon, the significance of which had eluded Waldo at Mrs Musto's. Waldo senses "for the first time" that this is "Dulcie being herself" (W111). This is, of course, the "real Dulcie", whom he has already had the opportunity to experience, and whom Arthur is only now experiencing in the flesh. It is not clear to Arthur, as it was not clear to Waldo, what Dulcie finds so amusing about the pierrot on the moon.[4] But Waldo is only horrified at Dulcie's discussing the difference between *amour* and *love*. Waldo tries to see Arthur's role here as subservient, but it is clear from Arthur's section that it is more active, socially tactful and intelligent than Waldo can make out. What Waldo chooses to take as Dulcie's formulation is actually a conflation of Arthur's own observation with Dulcie's reply. It would be possible to doubt Arthur's version—there is *no way* of telling for sure, for example, whether Dulcie's behaviour is genuine, immediate communion or initial embarrassment *overcome by* real fascination—were it not for the revealing, rationalizing emphasis in Waldo's narration.

There are subsequent developments in the Dulcie/Feinstein relationships to the twins, of course, but these need not concern us here—except to indicate that the obliquities deriving from the passages mentioned earlier on (W56 and the Encounter) are clarified later in both narratives. We discover that Waldo's "near slip" and his reference to "loving Dulcie" correlate with his fantasy of a marriage of convenience with her, his fortunate inability to express this wish unambiguously, and the appearance on the scene of the already-confirmed suitor, Len Saporta (W149–50/153–54). Arthur's hesitation about specifying when he last saw the Saportas (his secret family) is explained when Arthur reveals that he has been visiting the Saportas "all through the two children and several miscarriages" (A275–79). Waldo's anticipating that the Saportas' boy-child will be named after him is based on his fantasizing extrapolation from knowledge imparted by Arthur (W167–68, during Mrs Brown's wine-soaked years before 1932) that Dulcie (known to Waldo then only as "'Miss Feinstein'") is the mother of two children.

---

[4] Which is that it is the *pierrot lunaire*. She has made the connection between a pictorial image and the words it stands for, rather than simply laughing at some incongruity in the elements of the image. No symbol-hunting critic, in pointing out the moon-element of the incident, has so far asked why Dulcie should react as she does; it isn't exactly self-evident. The phrase at least, or even the baroque decor of the *commedia dell'arte,* would be familiar to Dulcie. There is circumstantial evidence pointing to Dulcie's association of Arthur's appearance with that of a pierrot-like buffoon or clown. While working in her father's music-shop, Dulcie may have come across an illustration of the pierrot on the same sheet music Arthur has used for the basis of his own pierrot-song. There is also, subliminally, an association between the pierrot and Arthur as the steadfast Clown (*pierre* = rock) and as "lunatic".

FROM THE END OF THE ACTIONAL–PRESENT WALK
TO WALDO'S DEATH

Arthur's narrative does not recount the actional-present walk or the walk the following day; only the very last, "mortal" phase is twice-told. Certain "doubling" details crop up, but these are states, acts and gestures which, in Waldo's section, are not unique but typical.[5] Reference to them in Section 3 is not punctual (point-time) but statal or iterative; and there is insufficient contextual detail to show that they refer obliquely to the actional present of Section 2. Causality and order must be established carefully and indirectly by the reader, with close attention to discourse details rather than to the superficial sequencing on the page (if the latter, linear approach is attempted, ambiguous time-markers and deictics combine with the obliquity of reference to throw one off course or off the scent).

Waldo gets "diarrhoea"[6] in bed one night: in Section 2 the complaint is only indirectly specified at first ("the night he woke to discover the worst had happened", W211), is related not temporally but associatively to what precedes, and is drawn from the indefinite continuum of the recent past. Arthur's section names the complaint, in phrasing that is echoic of Waldo's but deictically firmer ("That night, for instance, the worst happened in bed", A292), and connects the cleaning-up with Arthur's habitual self-sacrificial attitude (anticipatorily, Arthur performs "for Waldo the humblest tasks", A291, then specifically "the humblest task of all", A292). In Waldo's section, the diarrhoea-incident is *embedded* discoursally in the sequence of walks.[7] Waldo starts the walks *ostensibly* for the good of their health, without any specific ailment being involved; in trying to drive Arthur so hard that he collapses, Waldo starts breaking down himself—first at home in bed, but probably through general difficulty while walking; then radically, near the white roses, through panic and over-exertion on the morning Arthur has his heart-tremor; and finally, after a chain of rapid emotional shocks,

---

[5] For example: mention of the front gate (A291; cf W26); "It was his brother who kicked" (A292; cf Waldo kicking Scruffy, W119); "Or turned his face away" (A292; cf Waldo, who "averted his face from something", W28).

[6] I'll call it this, though it is less likely to have a bacterial origin than to be the loss of sphincter-control typical of senescent incontinence or a mild stroke. Thematically, of course, there is a mocking echo of Waldo's youthful diarrhoea at the Feinsteins', when he wished his creativity could flow so easily. At the end of his days, Waldo's *physis* is undermining, during sleep, his conscious will to maintain control. It is no accident that events centering on the bankruptcy of Waldo's willed "creativity" follow pell-mell upon his nocturnal bed-soiling.

[7] "Waldo thought he couldn't allow himself to fall asleep ever again" (free indirect thought or psychonarration with a neutral tag). "And find *that*" (free indirect thought with syntax- and tone-marking). So far Waldo is ostensibly thinking with horror of having to find the dogs in bed with him; but also evoked is the embarrassed discovery of his diarrhoea. "Only walk, which is another kind of sleep" (elliptical continuation of psychonarration, or fragmentary free indirect thought). This last has a gnomic, "reflective" component. Then, foregrounded by separate paragraphing, but grammatically and logically attached to the gnomic sentence: "Which they did every day". This is not a thought about something *now* inceptive, but a reflecting back on an already obtaining, iterative situation.

in bed a day later. This is clearest from Arthur's section (A292), which has two paragraphs detailing "the morning" of Arthur's heart-tremor; Arthur's narration takes it for granted that this is the morning of the actional-present walk. In Waldo's actional-present narrative, it is clear that this heart-tremor has occurred "earlier that morning" (W55) as chest-pains (W24) and is *the first sign* that Arthur's heart may be starting "to give trouble" (W30). "After the warning" to him, Arthur feels fine, but Waldo feels terrible (A292; confirmed W31/119)—Arthur's vantage of narration is the phase after the actional-present walk.

Waldo's "*had* prescribed" the walks (A292), which have thus already been long in effect, and the *usualness* of walking together along Barranugli Road is clear from the first narrative (eg, W60). When Arthur tells the manager of Woolworths that he won't be working that morning because "'We're going for a walk'" (W55), this is only because the twins wouldn't have met him on their way past during their previous walks, as only *this* morning was he "parking early" (W55). A false expectation that this is the *first* long walk is raised by this thought: "They were walking on in the direction Waldo knew now he had not chosen: it had chosen him" (W57): but the "direction" of Barranugli involves long walks whatever road is chosen, Waldo has long since been taking this direction, and it is the implications of "being chosen" that interest him here. The most obvious signal that the walks are already habitual is given by a passage which is located in the late 1950s at the earliest, but which is sandwiched between events centering on 1932 and events after 1922: "They were walking up Terminus Road, *up the last hill before* Sarsaparilla" (A274). The spatial indices show that they are outside town and returning home—and, except in boyhood, they have never done this together *until* Waldo's walking-programme. The first big problem in Waldo's section is: the general fact of a walking-programme is first narrated (in the preterite, not the past perfect) *after* the return from the actional-present walk: "Every morning, sooner or later, they went for the walk, longer, and then longer, Waldo always hoped" (W210). But so is the incident of Waldo's diarrhoea. The latter has arisen associatively out of the mention of food (meat); the mention of food (meat) has arisen associatively out of the mention of the bread-and-milk habitually consumed after the walks. And it is after the diarrhoea-incident that there is a summary confirmation of the walks ("Which they did every day", W211) and Waldo's remark to Arthur ("Once ... he said") that these walks must be doing them good. The walk along the main road would have been the longest yet taken, were it not for the fact that they (Waldo out of exhaustion; Arthur out of boredom) agree to terminate it prematurely. This is why Arthur gives the dogs the mutton flaps although it is only midday, as he is used by now to getting home later (W206).

After the actional-present walk and the afternoon and night that follow, there is an indication, as the twins stand in the early-morning kitchen, that they are to embark on another walk. Although they both know the pattern by now, they still ask each other what they are going to do each day. This particular exchange (W210) is more pointed than usual, however. Arthur asks "'What walk?'" because he thinks Waldo is not up to it (after what Arthur saw of him the day

before). That Waldo should choose the same boring main-road walk again is
cause enough for both of them to try and read the other's intentions or reaction.
"So there was nothing for it but to go"—Waldo has met his match, is giving
himself over to his fate: the futile attempt to wear down the indomitable Arthur,
in the full knowledge that he is only wearing himself down. What follows is a
suspension of the actional-present action. Instead, there is the last fluttering of
Waldo's memories, dwelling on already established habits (the walks; his
feverish note-taking; the exchange concerning the efficacy of the walks; his recall
of a recent sign of his own increasing physical debility—an *omen* of his near-
collapse on the actional-present walk, not a consequence of later walks). "If
Arthur made no other attempt to convert Waldo to the love he preached"
(W211)—reference here is to the day before; "no further attempt" does not open
out on a vista of potential later days, but is restricted to attempts not made on *that
day*.

The point is that there is nothing special about the last actual walk that would
warrant its being narrated. We know it will follow its established pattern. Waldo
will keep himself under better control—but the nervous strain will contribute,
along with the ensuing "revelations", to his total collapse and death. The
"absence" of the last walk and the last midday (or post-midday) meal make even
more irruptive into figural reflection the peculiar way in which Mrs Brown's blue
dress is introduced into the narrative: "When Arthur produced something he had
found" (W211); "If Arthur picked up from behind the copper that old dress ..."
(A292). The scene of this discovery can be deduced as a specific instance of
habitual locality already established iteratively: Waldo sitting outside with his
papers, after the last walk, engrossed in sorting through what he has written.[8]

Argyle (1967) and Tacey (1988) think that the actional-present walk is the
brothers' "last walk" together; but there must be one more walk after the
actional-present one. Mackenzie (1969:248) summarizes the final sequence thus:
Waldo discovers Arthur's poem; crazed by this revelation, he "turns arsonist and
destroys his own Writing"; *then* he takes Arthur on long walks in order to kill
him of a heart attack; Waldo kills himself instead of killing Arthur. But there is
no "then". Waldo's physical demise follows on immediately from the burning,
and thought of burning his papers is already father to the act itself on the
actional-present walk (before the rest of what Mackenzie details), even before the
act is precipitated by Arthur's poem. Bliss's supposition that the whole of the
actional present in Sections 1 and 2 occurs *several walks before* the mortal

---

[8] Getting the discourse straight at this point is crucial. It begins iteratively: "*Mostly* he
corrected ... he *would* also write". There follows an analepsis: "On one occasion he *wrote:*"—
this obliterates consideration of temporal framing (ie, "he *had* written") because it is quoted
while Waldo is reading it through. Into attendant reflection ("He kept everything now")
intrudes the quasi-conjunctive "When"–sentence about the blue dress. Arthur's approaching
Waldo is governed entirely by consideration of his own intentions *while* he acts. Before
Arthur's identical question in both narratives ("'What is it, Waldo?'"), the close of one
diegetic sentence forms a distorted mirror-image of the other: Waldo is governed completely
by the past ("or respect for posterity") and only pretends to sift his material; Arthur's thoughts
turn on the past forcing itself on "those who have participated".

dénouement explodes the otherwise sensitively established temporal rapport with Section 4. Such an assumption as hers probably derives from a misconstruction of the *seemingly consecutive* narrative detail at W210–11 and A292.

The interesting thing is, rather, that the peculiar ordering of the narrative reveals a sudden collapse of the two old men's capacity to keep recent temporal events under strict diachronic control, and their unawareness that anything is amiss. The triumph of the narrative technique here resides in the fact that a non-intensive reading can trick the reader, too, into assuming that nothing is amiss. Limits are imposed on a narrative of recollection that is so interiorized as to dispense with logical temporal linkages (the complexities of Proust, by contrast, are invariably kept under clear, formalized, albeit obsessive verbal control—which is one reason that Gérard Genette and others have found in him no shortage of categorical examples). One of these limitations is signalled by the frequent exposure of the psychological sham of figural consciousness as soon as it comes up against the fact that fictions have endings or closure. The blurred line between mediated recollection and mediated "immediate" experience becomes almost erased, along with diachrony and rigorous tense-markings. The reader who steps back is faced with thinking the unthinkable: is there a fixed temporal vantage-point for retrospective narration? In Section 2, we assume that Waldo recalls as he walks, and that this structures the oscillation between actional present and past. In Section 3, we don't get the feeling that Arthur is *situated* on the walk. In Section 4, we can imagine Mrs Poulter sitting in her house, reflecting and remembering, and her temporal situation is gradually sharpened from vague early 1960s to a specific time in the course of a week that is posterior to the climax of Sections 2 and 3.

We see the tricks of narration in Section 2 that allow verisimilitude of direct experience to "kill" the narrative at the moment of Waldo's loss of consciousness (ironically, perhaps *self*-consciousness—is death the only cure?). There are no difficulties for Arthur at the end of Section 3: he is to live on. But we are nagged with doubt about the differing structures. When Waldo, in Section 2, goes back in through the gate, the narrative moment is as satisfying, as completive, as the kind of good Sunday lunch the twins never have. On a second reading, we may start feeling uncomfortable with strong temporal deictics ("*That* morning", W209) which thrust so far *back* that we sense analepsis or recall at work, with plenty of time still to go. We may become disorientated by iteratives that suggest action past and action to come, and point-time markers that promise the same. But, as I have suggested, all these matters have reference to a strip of time which is anterior to the completed actional-present walk: a strip which is unsituated except, inferentially, as prior to that walk—or as reviewed in the *wholly ellipted* last walk. In Section 3, Arthur *recalls* the second-last walk (essentially: its prelude) and—fore and aft of that recall—events prior to it. We are not disturbed by the deictic "*That* night" (A292), as it is locked into an exemplification. "*The morning* he got the shock" (A292) is no shock—no feeling here that we are thrust back into a past far from the moment of recall; it could, indeed, be a piece of narration in the process of moving *forwards*. Questions of temporal relation are then thrown up by the slalom-race of past-time references that follows. Ultimately, we are compelled to accept the fact that the lack of a vantage-point for memory in Section 3 is consonant with Arthur's lack of an intensely self-reflexive consciousness compared with Waldo, and with his greater experiential involvement. The narrative and the narration are more innocent. Arthur's narrative reads more conventionally than Waldo's; we notice much less often, if at all, the wrenchings of sequence and the many rationalizing or mistaken apperceptions.

II   Other 'ingeminate' parallels and repetitions

As well as the double-telling that is intrinsic to the novel, and the patterns set up by indexical detail (description, metaphor, etc.), there are various other kinds of repetition or variation in the narrative that prompt the reader to make interpretative connections. (It is not so much the act of interpretation that is at issue here, as the specific stimulus to interpretation set up by the narrative structuring.) Like Waldo and Arthur, who are dizygotic twins exhibiting some degree of interpenetrative consciousness, these are "ingeminate" echoes in the discourse. They may be a simple matter of phrasing, or of the angle from which an object is described—these phrasings occur in both of the central sections. Waldo, for example, asks his mother: "'Why did you marry Dad?'" (W145) and Arthur asks his "friend" and surrogate-mother: "'Why did you marry Mr Poulter?'" (A257). In the train, Waldo cannot help "looking at his father, at the sweat shining on the yellow edge of his celluloid collar" (W78); before the cow-tragedy scene, Arthur thinks: "poor Dad, very little made him sweat under his celluloid collar" (A229). Not only the direct speech but also a statement registering Arthur's emotional state (and "fronting" Waldo's last lunge at his brother) occurs in both narratives at the end: "'Waldo!' Arthur was afraid at last. 'What are you trying to do to me?'" (W213, A294). There is the occurrence of the same oblique reference to Arthur in both sections: "His body might topple, but only his body" (W55, A240: discussed below). The bed "jingling brassily" in Arthur's mental analogy at the end (P305) is already there in the "brass balls" and "dislocated iron" of the voyeur-scene (W62), and when Arthur rises in the morning, "in a flurry of iron joints, a ringing of brass balls" (W175).

A scene adverted to in some detail in the earlier narrative (eg, Arthur's talk about being misrepresented as withholding Mrs Musto's change, W60) may appear only in the barest summary in the later narrative ("the incident of Mrs Musto's change", A233); or, within the same narrative, actions or explicit reports (eg, Mrs Feinstein's excusing Saporta's absence because he has cut his hand on the glass knob of a door, and had "'the *grippe* or something'" on an earlier occasion, W138; or Waldo's weak joke about not mowing the lawn on a Sunday, W156) can subsequently become so compressed in figural thought that only the alert reader will remember the motivating memory ("Waldo could not think of a better answer than Saporta's own—unless a glass door-knob and the

'flu", W156; "He still heard the slash of the lawn-mower running itself
deliberately against the stones", W160). Hundreds of pages may elapse before
the reader realizes that an apparently general observation has a highly specific
correlative in a character's personal history (eg, the business about the ruined
house). Connections between events may be established explicitly (as with Mr
Brown's double "withdrawal" from Arthur, A230/269); or the surreptitiousness
of childhood may find exposure in old age. In boyhood, for example, Waldo
makes sure that Arthur, not himself, is caught picking his nose (W37); in his
immediate pre-retirement years, Waldo's colleagues catch him out picking his
nose (W203). Whereas the reader is left to catch the irony here, the symbolic,
framing import of Arthur's upward climb towards the sun (A215, P314–15) is
established in the narrative by clear prolepsis (A265). Waldo's adolescent sex-
fantasies on the train (W77–79) underlie his realization in old age that he is like a
"dirty old man dribbling in a train" (W190), and the figures of Haynes and his
woman serve as phantom revenants from his adolescent memories of prostitutes
and their customers. Much more submerged is the connection between Arthur's
talk of the "salon" (W112) and Waldo's thoughts about his brother's "innocence"
(W26).

A few broader continuities are worth mentioning, raising as they do questions
about the thematic significance of scene and situation. Waldo, shocked by the
intimacy of kissing his father, suddenly feels he is a "stranger" (W34); when he
sees Dulcie embracing her father, he grows "guilty with his own foreignness"
(W105); and, when confronted by Mr Feinstein while snooping outside his
house, he is "transformed forcibly into the complete stranger" and is prompted
by feelings of guilt for thinking dirty thoughts about Feinstein's daughter (W124).
At the Feinsteins', there are "fleshy leaves plastering the windows" (W112); at
the end of a later visit, Waldo sees Dulcie's figure against the glass door, and
remembers "seeing a fern pressed under glass, the ribs more clearly visible"
(W140); listening to Dulcie playing the piano, Arthur strains forward: "his flesh
pressed against the pane must have been turning that sickly-plant tone of green,
of faces forcing themselves behind glass" (A241). If the affinities here are
transformational, recurrences elsewhere can be seen as silently ironic, widely-
spaced reinforcements of central ideas. There is, for example, Waldo's Writing
as a sickness (W29) and his mother first treating him "as though he were sick or
something" and then asking about his Writing (W82); or his Writing as being
"like a natural function" (W93) and the episode of the diarrhoea at the Feinsteins'
(W110). Inter-narrative symmetries may harbour crucial indices to character:
Waldo's "secret vice" is naming the cars, his "other" vice what he would do "if
Arthur died" (W115); the first of Arthur's "two preoccupations" is Waldo, and
protecting him, while his "second obsession" is "the Books" (A280), whereas, in
Waldo's view, "Arthur had not cared for books" (W33). There is the contrast
between Waldo fleeing from his dead father, then gathering himself to sprint
resourcefully across the road (W70–72), and seeing his dying mother, already
looking dead, then his alienated blundering across the road (W170). With his

father, Waldo takes over from Mrs Poulter; with his mother, he gives himself into Mrs Poulter's care.

The most persistent pattern, finally, has to do with secret vision, and a number of major episodes serve as points of focus for a myriad other indications of the microstructural working-out of this theme. Mr Haynes predicts that Arthur will be "'peering in at the windows'" (W47); Waldo peers in through Mrs Poulter's window (W61–62), through the "slanted slats" at the Feinsteins' house (W124) and through the "slats of the ... fan" in the transvestite scene (W193). Arthur peers through the window at Dulcie practising (A241) and at Waldo peering in the mirror (A291). Waldo peers through the window at his dead father (W70) and Mrs Poulter peers through the window at the dead Waldo (P301). The idea of secret knowledge is conveyed at the moments in Sections 1 and 2 when Mrs Poulter (and Mrs Dun) peer out the bus window at the two old men, and Waldo (and Arthur) look in the same bus window. Secret observation is conveyed in Section 2 when Waldo conceals himself from Haynes (and looks through the window) and (together with his mother) from Mrs Poulter; likewise in Section 4, when Arthur peers in the Saportas' window.

None of the various parallels and repetitions mentioned here gives the slightest impression of being contrived or artificial. As at so many other levels, the discourse functions by analogy, connotation and echo, in the elegantly efficient and condensed manner (*sic*) of poetry. Sometimes these echoes are irreducible existents, where it is not possible for the reader to determine *which* is source and which the phantom double. A tantalizing instance is the schematic correspondence between Waldo's fantasy-memory from early childhood of a neurasthenic woman standing "on the half-landing at the elbow in the great staircase" (W192) and Arthur's boyhood experience of suddenly encountering Mrs Mackenzie (who has some sort of nervous ailment) on "a little half-landing" "almost at the top of the stairs" at the bank (A220). Peter Beatson, in his book, writes of the presence in the novel (or in the psychical makeup of its main characters) of the Jungian "collective unconscious", Manfred Mackenzie of "twin consciousness". It really does appear to be the case that the kinds of mutual and reciprocal informing within *The Solid Mandala* can ultimately be explained in terms of these concepts (or in terms of "ingeminate" empathy), at all levels of narrative discourse and narrative structure.

III   Expositional signification in Section 1

The reader is likely to take Section 1 of the novel for granted, overlooking the high degree to which it also contributes to the process of mutual and reciprocal informing that I have been examining. There have been a few quite strongly dissenting opinions about the section—for example, Ratcliffe (1966): "a rather gauche presentation of the facts (and some uncomfortably patronising dialogue)"; or Brissenden (1969:39), who senses "an art of deliberate artifice and contrivance about the narrative, which [he finds] irritating and distracting". Now, White does have the Jamesian propensity to avoid diegetic block-exposition in favour of the scenic or mimetic mediation of information through the direct speech of what are traditionally called "reflector"-characters. Exposition can be a tiresome burden for both author and reader (as is shown in many comments and analyses by Sternberg 1978, for example). Significantly, no amount of microanalysis of Section 1, if conducted artificially under the constraints of "first-reading" conditions, can determine the particular significance (or, of course, later relevance) attached to the information imparted about the past by Mrs Poulter. Dialogic mediation, coupled with the utmost restraint of diegesis in sticking to the local context (the conversational process), prevents any possibility of *formal* prolepsis. What we do find by hindsight, however, is the overwhelming presence of germinal prolepsis or advance mentions.[9] For the purposes of the present novel, advance mentions in Section 1 fall into two main categories: those that are recalls or memories, and those that anticipate events later than the immediate actional present.

Mrs Poulter's recollections are conveyed mimetically, while anticipations of the novel's dénouement are largely diegetic. Insofar as the substance of what she says touches on the *historia* of the Brown family, the information serves two purposes: it provides a rough semic or characterological framework for the reader's initial placement of the twins in the first or actional-present narrative of Section 2; and it provides a third "telling" of events which are recalled in the second narrative of Waldo's section and confirmed or modified in Arthur's. If we take only those statements that correspond to temporally localizable events (as in the narremic reconstruction, ch. 3 above), what Mrs Poulter says has no intrinsic significance apart from the fact that a kind of summary is given of various stations in the Browns' lives. It is less the events themselves than the various perspectival constructions placed upon them that are important in the reader's search for meaning in the novel. Mrs Poulter's "proto-narremic" information can be shuffled into chronological sequence; the many correspondences with the later narratives include the following (keyed to the relevant page).

The topic of the veranda "'in the classical style'" (narreme 7) arises naturally out of the women's conversation (B15). In the main narratives, it has "satellite" status, being tangential to character-relationships. In terms of theme, however, the Greek pediment is richly emblematic for Mr Brown's world-view, and is made to contrast with the "personality" of the Australian setting and (in a different way) with the essential mind-set of Waldo. In Section 1, where the veranda-topic gets its fullest treatment, Mrs Dun's responses are typically impoverished and inarticulate—a shrinking from language and conceptualization, a mentally closed, rigidly bounded empiricism. This anticipates the scepticism of the builders in the later narrative. In order not to "lose" her potential new friend, Mrs Poulter, for whom knowledge of the "Greek" veranda lends her self-

---

[9] These are "simple markers without anticipation, even an allusive anticipation, which will acquire their significance only later on and which belong to the completely classic art of 'preparation'" [Genette 1980:75–77].

importance, tries to dissociate herself from the architectural values implied, but cannot help revealing to the reader her awe at and respect for Mr Brown's educational and socio-economic status. The topic thus provides an initial social focus on two character-constellations.

Arthur is said to be "'clever with figures—in spite of all'" (B16–17). An existent rather than an event, this is part of a temporally localizable narreme (13) of iterative behaviour during Arthur's primary-school years, though Mrs Poulter naturally sees the applications of this gift in Arthur's later practical life. The contrast she so succinctly suggests between Arthur's mathematical capacities and his being "'not all that bright'" is subsequently elaborated in even more subtle shadings in Sections 2 and 3. The assignment of the boys to Mr Allwright and "'the books'" (B16–17) corresponds to narreme 19 (where Waldo is "put to the books" at high school) and narremes 27–28 (the library-job). It is out of these "kernel" events that the whole chain of incidents is generated which brings the brothers into contact with other seminal characters, and which provides both the behavioural context for most of our judgements on the twins' personalities and the circumstantial matrix for the inexorable progress towards catastrophe.

If only because the details are so exotic at a first reading, it is possible to sense the epiphanic significance of Mrs Poulter's reminiscences about the Chinese woman and the wheel-tree (B13). The reach of this advance mention is enormous, its enigmatic status being heightened by the way in which it is "repeated" later. What we get in Waldo's section (narreme 56) is Arthur's direct-speech mention to Waldo after the event. At both B13 and W144, Mrs Poulter and Arthur respectively are exposing themselves to people incapable of empathy; on both occasions, the delivery is hushed, the contextualization unclear. Withheld by Mrs Poulter but provided by Arthur is the fact that it is on *her* initiative, and in Arthur's company, that she sees the wheel-tree. In Arthur's section (narreme 55), the incident itself is narrated, some 250 pages after its first mention. It is made explicit at this point that the incident will be an indelible memory for Arthur, but his report of her reactions at various stages suggests that none of her experiences (the wheel-tree, the blackberrying, Arthur's mandala-dance, the gift of the gold marble) will have any lasting impact on her. The exposition thus enables us to "read" beneath the superficies of Mrs Poulter's reactions in Section 3, and to assent fully to the closing of the circle in her narrated monologue in Section 4 (P300), where she gives unequivocal testimony to the centrality for her of the wheel-tree episode.

The statement that "'Mr Brown was the first to die'" (B16) corresponds to narreme 67, and is even matched by verbal detail in Waldo's section (W69), which also states that Mrs Poulter was present on the day Mr Brown is discovered. In Section 1, the topic of the parents' death seems awkward for Mrs Poulter; but it is only later that we can resolve her attitude here as signifying more than ritual reticence. More important is Mrs Poulter's answer to Mrs Dun's query about the cause of death: "'Mr Brown, so they say, was disappointed in his sons. Anyways, Arthur. Arthur had been his favourite'". A similar connection is made by Arthur after he finds his father dead (A269, on Mr Brown's second "withdrawal"). This oblique allusion is rendered less so by prior reference to the distraught Arthur "bursting out on the classical-tragic veranda"—which takes us back to narreme **16**, Arthur's cow-tragedy on the veranda, and his father's rejection (A230). Waldo's section has already confirmed Mr Brown's affection for Arthur: once in a brief analepsis in the actional present (W28), twice in the recollections of the second narrative (W33/35). Section 2 avoids specifying when Mr Brown's attitude towards Arthur changes, whereas Arthur's narrative registers a particular moment of estrangement (or, rather, Arthur's awareness of something in his father's attitude that may already have been there as early as the bank-visits). Whereas Mrs Poulter tries to make the source of her knowledge hearsay, it is later clear that Arthur must have confided in her that his father has distanced himself, though only she would know the reason why. That she modifies her remarks to exclude Waldo is richly ambiguous. We infer retrospectively that she has observed that Waldo, too, has proved a disappointment; but she can in all fairness only make an informed judgement in Arthur's case. Waldo's narrative similarly reveals through concealment and tangential reference. It is nowhere stated that Mr Brown is disappointed in Waldo (or that Waldo knows or feels this), but there is much presentation of the Oedipal awkwardness of the father-son relationship, and a concentration on formulations indicating how close Waldo wants to be to his mother (W28/59). Such explicit formulations, however, do not occur in the fully analeptic second narrative, but in the fragments floating in the stream of the actional present, and tend therefore not to be articulations of Waldo's attitudes *in* the past. These attitudes are conveyed much more obliquely in the second narrative. What is foregrounded is a series of inarticulate confrontations between Waldo and his father (the bank scene, W54; the home-coming scene, W34; the train-scene, W76–79) which suggest Waldo's disappointment in his father rather than vice versa. Existing criticism of the novel has never really managed to explain the significance of these scenes; but it seems clear that Mrs Poulter is telling the truth when she says that Waldo, too, disappointed his father—or, rather, that Waldo is made to feel guilty or ashamed by complicity, through sensing how his father's hopes for Arthur have been dashed, and how Waldo cannot take his brother's place in Mr Brown's affections because his very personality prevents any rapprochement (cf W34).

The focus on the dogs (initiated by Mrs Dun, B20) is justified partly as a foreshadowing of the dénouement, and partly because the animals are a constant presence in the narrative of the twins' declining years. The information also helps narrow the dating of the actional present (cf narremes **87–99**). Only here do we learn that it is Waldo's dog that bites: a nice point of correspondence between animal and master. The narrative is also allowed to play a joke of anticipation on the reader, by having Mrs Dunn employ the adjective "scruffy", which turns up later as the name of Arthur's puppy.

In terms of mimetically conveyed information, Mrs Poulter effectively covers the life-span of the twins from early childhood emigration to retirement, and touches on several incidents and relationships central to the later narratives. The only important stations in the Browns' lives that she doesn't mention are those which are presumably not made accessible to her (the Feinsteins; the library incident). The ways in which she presents her view of the past are useful benchmarks for the evaluation of later accounts of the same data; and some information is given only via her view of things. Mrs Poulter, it is made clear, has long been interested in the Brown family, knows a lot about them, and is particularly protective of Arthur Brown; but the reader is never given the impression that any particular piece of information conveyed offers a proleptic opening into the later narratives. Although the social distance of the Browns from the likes of Mrs Dun and Mrs Poulter is highlighted, the context of old ladies' gossip and Mrs Poulter's own charitable disposition contribute to making what is reported sound terribly ordinary in comparison with the women's fascinated involvement in other people's lifelines.

Scenic or mimetic information that can be connected up with later narremes is, however, only the most rudimentary of expository levels in Section 1. There are such details as those noticed by Mrs Dun (B19): for example, the old men's coats, one a stiff oilskin, the other "yellowed herringbone". In the actional present of Section 2, much is made of these garments, which we gradually associate with the personalities of those wearing them. Waldo's stiff, creaking oilskin, like his nature, is permeated by the weathers of life however much it protects his brittle self from life's thorns (W25/30/56), however hard he tries to sidle past obstacles (W25/116). Arthur's tweed coat is as "inexhaustible" as Arthur (W23) will prove to be. Waldo places the safe inflexibility of "duty" before "the snares of sentiment set by inexhaustible tweed". The statement itself is a snare. The parenthetical gloss that follows, with its reference to Uncle Charlie's discards, suggests that it is the reminders of what we later discover is the family's distant English past that Waldo mistrusts: the reminder of *quality*, whose absence in Australia Waldo resents and tries in fantasy to compensate for. It becomes clear later, however, that the "snares of sentiment" are set up by Arthur when he broaches the subject of love after their walk (W207–208). Whereas Waldo's narrative refers to the herringbone coat at the start, Arthur's does so towards the end (A289); on both occasions it is made evident that the coat had belonged to Uncle Charlie. White has *in-vested* the twins with Charlie's presence. From the visit of the Misses Dallimore, we learn that Uncle Charlie Thourault (or Lord Tolfree) is the liverish father of Mrs Brown's cousin Mollie, with whom contact of sorts was maintained. It is significant that, though Mollie is a poor correspondent (W50), Mrs Brown hangs on the connection even in her dotage when it is clear that no letters will come (W165), and that the connection is essentially one of charity (cf the bank-drafts, W50). It is not charity that Waldo is reminded of whenever Uncle Charlie is mentioned, but status and his mother's family's illustrious past (W51/165). Only at the beginning of Arthur's section is Charlie's character put into sharp focus. His intentions in taking Arthur to the opera seem not to be the purest (A217); by the evidence of what he says, he is a cynical, overbearing and brutal man, talking obliquely about Arthur's disability and Mr Brown's religion and dismissing the opera-visit as an "'unrewarding experiment'". He offers cold, false charity, blind in his arrogance to the fact that Wagner has touched Arthur's spirit. Waldo in his desperate strivings for class and intellect is a truer scion of the "family" than he can imagine. And the coat that Arthur wears is the discard of false charity, which Arthur wears because he is humble. Mr Brown, says Mrs Poulter, gave her an old raincoat for Bill to wear (B15-16; the equivalent of narreme 63). In the context of Waldo's section, this act is a parody of Mrs Poulter's numerous acts of charity towards Mr Brown in his illness. Although Mrs Poulter has hinted to Mr Brown at her lack of worldly goods (W161), her acceptance of the raincoat is represented to Mrs Dun as tactfulness. Though neither section is clear on the motives for this gift, the exposition does at least supply its aftermath: Bill throws the coat down the gully. We have, then, an index to Bill Poulter's resentful pride, which is not touched on elsewhere and which places in perspective the ailing Mr Brown's joking *acceptance* of his neighbour's charity (W159-60).

The whole problematical business of charity opens out into the texture of the novel from the small detail (B18) of Mrs Poulter's trying (self-therapeutically) to protect the brothers by taking them a baked custard. Waldo's "candid though unostentatious charity" towards his clumsy brother is merely a tactic for gaining the observer's sympathies for himself (W75). Arthur, recollecting the time when Mrs Poulter "sat with him on the grass", is uncertain whether she "burned with him in a fit of understanding or charity" (P309)—he perceives the difference of commitment involved. Waldo, ever suspicious, makes her charity into a strategy rather than an impulse (W141). Mr Brown jokes feebly about her "'making a sacrament of food'" when she brings her puddings (W160). The essential point about the early mention of the sacramental, neighbourly custard in Section 1 is the way in which it dovetails into the revelations of Section 4. There, when Mrs Poulter goes to the Browns' house after not seeing them for days, she carries her custard "as a protection"—but this time for herself, against her intuition of the worst. White skilfully provides an objective correlative in the custard for the physical revulsion Mrs Poulter feels, a physical reaction already prepared for by a skein of connotations in Section 1 relating to communication rather than to communion (B20-21: the bus spewing out its gobbets; Mrs Poulter's fearful expectation of swallowing and choking). Gagging on lumpy custard can be one of the less happy memories of childhood. On seeing Waldo dead, Mrs Poulter "could feel her own cries stuck in lumps in her stiffened throat" (B15). This is transferred, along with Mrs Poulter's anecdote about the "community spirit" of taking food to the laying-out ritual for the fellow who "'cut 'is own throat'" (W160), to the revolting image of Waldo's "throat open on the gristly apple", with its grisly revitalizing as a food-image of the dead metaphor of the Adam's apple. In a grotesque parody of communion ingestion, Waldo's dog Runt crouches on the floor, "swallowing down" what he has obviously torn from his master's throat. Hanging on Mrs Dun's words in the bus, Mrs Poulter feels as though she "were waiting to swallow down some longed for communication while half expecting it to choke her if she did" (B21). In the discovery-scene, "She could not scream. The sounds were knotted up inside her" (P302). This time, she does not "return the better" for having gone on her errand of charity—not physically better at least: but the revelation does prove salutary to her understanding in other respects (P302–303). There is further serious play with the custard's vomitous appearance, when a young policeman is overcome by nausea after seeing the dogs eating Waldo.

Connections are also made elsewhere between the ritual of ingestion and the rejection of food. Waldo twice rejects Dulcie mentally on covertly antisemitic grounds, food sticking in his throat (W65/125). If rejection is associated with food in a ritual context, so are other narrative moments. The crisis of Waldo's rejection of Arthur is resolved temporarily after Waldo collapses in tears during the post-walk lunchtime: a subtext of communion (W208) is revealed when the twins merge into one another through the agency of Arthur's lovingkindness. Arthur's ultimate estrangement from the family life of the Saportas, which he had helped create, is dramatized by him observing their Jewish mealtime ritual from afar, helpless after Waldo's death to "test their lovingkindness" as proclaimed in their readings from Proverbs (P309).

The reason why the brothers are so far from Terminus Road (B21) is sought not only by Mrs Poulter but also by Arthur (W25/63), and the oblique unravelling of Waldo's sinister motives forms a central strand in the later narrative. Indeed, it could be said that Mrs Poulter gets her answer in her discovery of Waldo's corpse, the mocking emblem of the reversal of his plan for Arthur's demise. There are other ironic contrasts, including the fact that two fundamentally opposite characters (Mrs Poulter and Waldo) should have (for different reasons) the same worshipful attitude towards "the glossier side" of Sarsaparilla (B13; W30/58/118). In their own ways, of course, both have dreamt of escape from the terminal state of Terminus Road: Mrs Poulter from her "blank box" (W141); Waldo from the coffin-like, "disintegrating wooden box" of the family house. Changes are also rung on the implication that Mrs Poulter habitually keeps an eye on her neighbours behind their now overgrown hedge across the road (B14–15/20). The grand-guignol doubts about spying beyond the hedge which Mrs Dun expresses are all too savagely confirmed, even down to the proleptic association of the old men with biting dogs (B20). "Mrs Poulter, trying to mind her own business, failing to outstare the hedge opposite", embarks on the last, fateful walk across the road. The curiosity which Waldo mocks (W185) is verbally paralleled here, and in the "dialect-contaminated", garbled syntax later when she risks a look through the twins' bedroom window: "She wasn't going to not exactly look, but glance, to see ... " (P301).

The matter of the ladies' "friendship", so hesitantly and humorously mooted in Section 1, is ultimately resolved in Section 4, in the disillusionment of Mrs Poulter's quoted monologue (P295), which includes further references to curiosity, and is coupled with Mrs Dun's frightened reaction in the bus to seeing the Brown brothers. If at the beginning of the novel the "situation" of friendship "had not been proved unbreakable" (B11) and a common interest in the Brown twins "could be about to set the friendship of the friends" (B15), Mrs Poulter's horrified communication of finding Waldo's corpse does not bring the terrified

Mrs Dun any closer: the latter refuses to admit Mrs Poulter to her house, and has thus "broken their always fragile relationship" (P303). The unspoken terror that Mrs Dun feels about the Browns is expressed in terms of the features of the town "fluctuating strangely through the glass" of the bus-window (B21); in the rejection-scene, Mrs Poulter begins "to recede, like Mrs Dun, as through water, only it was glass". That Mrs Dun behaves in the bus as though she has never heard of the twins (B14) is Mrs Poulter's impression; in Waldo's section, however, we find Mr Dun's "small mean face recognizing" Arthur (W30), as Arthur recognizes him, so the Browns will already have been the subject of prejudiced talk in the Dun household.

The narrative moment of seeing the twins is presented in reverse perspective in Section 2 (W60/62), and the corresponding moments are bound together by continuity of detail, specifically that connecting Mrs Poulter's market-bound chrysanthemums with her protective gestures towards Arthur in her conversation with Mrs Dun (B18/20). Early on the walk, Arthur mentions having seen Mrs Poulter picking "'White Chrysanths for Mother's Day'" (W27), and specifically associates this with the bus to Barranugli. Waldo's crunching of the flowerpots in his memory of spying on Mrs Poulter segues into Arthur's remark that "'Those chrysanthemums will get crushed in a full bus'" (W62). An intense rapport between Mrs Poulter and Arthur is intimated via these flowers; this rapport can only be guessed at in Section 1 through the judicious interpretation of the symbolic placement of detail, and it continues to be expressed without heavy-handedness. References to chrysanthemums bracket Sections 1 and 4, with the help of other image-clusters (eg, the real "little black curly pig" that is also her dead baby daughter, P298; the "curly pig" that is her surrogate son, Arthur, P300). It is only after these intercalations, across the whole span of the narrative, have been established that speculation is possible concerning the rich symbolic ramifications of individual details, of which the chrysanthemum-complex is central. Throughout, the organic totality of the narrative is permitted expression without the intercession of linking narratorial analysis; this extends to Arthur's acceptance of Mrs Poulter's love of flowers (A258 and elsewhere) and to the echoing of the graphically emphatic phrase "She professed to Love All Flowers" (B17) in Waldo's section (W141).

Numerous other details in Section 1 are submitted to significant variation later on. Mrs Dun sees *both* men, with a meiotic inflection, as "stumping, trudging, you couldn't have said tottering" (B18). Waldo sees himself as walking carefully, but Arthur (also with a meiotic inflection) as "not exactly running, but lumbering and squelching" (W27). Themes which figure large in the main narratives are touched on in less central relation to the ladies: cruelty to others and the protection of the defenceless (B17–18); the notion of a sense of duty, here applied to Mrs Dun (B16);[10] Details of the Sarsaparillan setting, such as the

---

[10] Present later in Waldo's mental litany of the burden and responsibility of caring for Arthur (W23/28/33/41/76/146/187); in Arthur's sense of duty towards Waldo (A282/291–92); in Waldo's fantasy-projection of Dulcie as his "dutiful wife" (W152); in Mrs Poulter's thought of Arthur as her "joy and duty" (P311).

"sudden stench of crushed weeds" (B14), recur as the oppressive percepts of other characters inhabiting the same environment (W34/43). The peculiar metaphor of the eyes of the old women following "the tunnel which led inward, through the ragged greenery" (B14) recurs with various shifts and connotations of constriction and intensity.[11]

Careful yet inconspicuous reinforcement is given at later stages to many other details in the exposition. Much of this relates to the fleshing-out of Bill Poulter, who would otherwise remain more of a sideline figure than he actually turns out to be. Mrs Poulter recalls why she and Bill came to live down Terminus Road "'in those days'" (B12–13; narreme 48). Mrs Brown later echoes closely (W140) Mrs Dun's question about the Poulters' motives, but these reasons are not at first recorded in Waldo's section (W61). It is Arthur who augments (W140) Mrs Poulter's remark that they were "'country people'", but he doesn't advert to Bill's "'nerves'" as a reason for moving south: this is left to Waldo's distanced, non-committal account (W141) of what Mrs Poulter has told his mother. It is significant that the topic is hardly touched on in Section 3: only the fact of the Poulters' arrival, and a repeat of Mrs Brown's class-conscious question "'Why here?'" (A256). An *enigma* is fostered from the outset (Mrs Poulter's subsiding into sadness) by the withholding of ultimate motivation. It becomes circumstantially clear that the Poulters' intentions as glossed by Arthur ("'To be more independent'", W140) will not be fulfilled: Bill's "temporary" Council job is a dependency he is never able to escape from, and must contrast for him with the eccentric, relative "independence" of the brothers' life-style. In both Sections 2 and 3, however, Arthur defends the Poulters' existential decision (W410, A256), and we can infer the tragic banality and pain of their life from non-localizable conversations between Arthur and Mrs Poulter and from details about Bill's mannerisms. The most telling piece of indirect information comes on the day of Arthur's mandala-dance, when Mrs Poulter tells him her romantic, big-city daydream of being swept away by a middle-class "professional man" (A264). Bill's failure in life down Terminus Road is an extension of some unarticulated earlier failure, and Section 1 plants the germ of this surmise. The laconic reference to "'Bill's nerves'" (B12) is expanded in Section 2 (W141) and his neuroticism confirmed by his wife in Section 4; his favouring of a tooth (B18) is likewise noted in passing (W143, P315), as is his rolling of cigarettes (B13–14, W143). Bill ignores his wife at work and at home (B13/18); his in part banal and

---

[11] The world of the Browns is isolated from the world at large, "at the end of the yellow-green tunnel called Terminus Road" (W126). Waldo is "possessed" by the blue dress he is about to put on: "His breath went with him, through the tunnel along which he might have been running" (W193). Arthur and the paralyzed Mr Feinstein sit "looking at each other from opposite ends of the tunnel, in a light of ... momentary intensity" (A278). And, after Arthur's week-long ordeal of distracted wandering around Sydney, Mrs Poulter remarks, with more relevance to Arthur's benighted agony than she can realize: "'You look as if you was dragged through a tunnel!'" (P305). St Pierre (1978:102–104) has an interesting discussion of tunnel-symbolism in White's novels, in terms of the quest of consciousness and "a nightmarish system of being". St Pierre's effort to locate an all-embracing paradigmatic basis for the tunnel in White leads, however, to a stark neglect of the image's expressive flexibility.

in part near-tragic alienation is differentially exemplified later (W61/142, P297/316).

Yet another correlation of details about the Poulters functions like the complementary images in a stereopticon, an image in depth being achievable only by synoptic viewing. Mrs Poulter states that Bill wrote all their letters, but would hide from visiting relatives (B20); the letter-writing proficiency is confirmed near the end (P297), and there is a hint that Mrs Poulter is estranged from the up-country people they left behind (A258). The interesting thing that comes through from the combination of these references is the couple's chiastic relationship regarding communication: Mrs Poulter (like Dulcie except in her one polyglot postcard, W97/A246–47; and like Arthur apart from when he is writing secretly for himself) cannot cope with the written word but is (like Arthur) untroubled by direct verbal communication. Bill cannot perform the latter, only the former. The function in this constellation performed by Bill Poulter leads to the possibility— otherwise obscured by the antagonism of Waldo's discourse—that Bill is Waldo's counterpart. Both can "communicate" on paper, exercising control over artifice (even if this communication, in Waldo's case, only reaches the destination of the self); both are savagely resentful and denigratory, or self-protectively standoffish, in direct verbal communication, which for everyday purposes is kept to a minimum. Both have a terror of social contact so strong that they have to hide away from visitors. Both are puritans, shunning contact and flinching from any suggestion in others (or themselves) of sexual ambivalence. Both feed off "principles". Both have ambitions, but turn out to be failures. Both are obsessed by the minutiae of their own decaying *physis*. Both are somatically scraggy types. Although they are polar opposites in respect of literary interests, and "Antipodal" in cultural allegiance, they are like fish out of water in the gothic entrapment of suburbia, living by their own perversion of the code of rationality. No wonder Waldo should feel attracted enough to Bill to embark on an intellectual love-affair (the Old World bringing enlightenment to the Austral Savage—another version of Dulcie as the "dutiful wife")—and no wonder like repels like, shunning his distorted image in the mirror of the other.

It is the silent tentacular reach of the initially non-committal data presented in Section 1 which stimulates the reader to such constructions of character. This applies equally to almost surreptitiously pursued juxtapositions of social and ethical character traits (Mrs Brown's status as a "lady", for instance: B16, W59/142; or the weightings of the epithet "good" as applied to Mr Brown: B16, W145/A258). Finally, Mrs Dun's outsider's subjective view of which brother is leading on the walk and which is the bigger (B19) serves as a subtle *entrée* into one of the most persistent strands of exploration and relativization in the later narrative: the complex undeclared struggle as to which twin is the stronger, which his brother's keeper, what the metaphysical correlates are of stature, physique, control of self....

I have examined only one small corner of the text. A similar dynamic of germinal prolepsis, "holographic" encoding, variation and resolution operates throughout the narrative—all without any discoursal manipulation beyond the radius of unglossed mimesis and subjectively focused diegesis. The seemingly innocuous, often entertaining exposition of Section I itself is far more than a satiric anatomy of "working-class" attitudes. It subtly provides the initial traces of the essential surfaces of the ensuing narratives: memory; subjective perception and its tyranny over the ethical dimension of human relationships; and the journey towards wholeness, a destination Mrs Poulter herself can reach only imperfectly by immersion in the inwardness of "her actual sphere of life" (P316).

5

TIME AND THE NARRATIVE MOMENT

I   Temporal indices to recollective
figural discourse

QUANTITATIVE AND CONTEXTUAL CONSIDERATIONS

In this chapter, I want to take a closer look at the ways in which events are explicitly structured in terms of when they occur, and at the perspective from which action is viewed. The reader expects, as a rule, that time-markers are a "neutral" category. This is particularly the case when it can be assumed that a narrator is present who is dissociated from the consciousness of the characters proper, and who is organising the "telling" and "showing" of events in accordance with a non-figural perspective. If, however, time-markers occur in differentiated patterns which upset our assumptions about narratorial impartiality, we have to seek the source of authority elsewhere. If, subsequently, it can be shown that the organising authority resides in, or reflects, the subjectivity of the characters themselves, then other aspects of ordering and perspective must come under review—including phrasings which seem to betray the presence of an omniscient or auctorial narrator.

We are continually made aware of the irruption of memory into the first, linear narrative of Waldo's section. The causal burden of the past weighing on Waldo's present consciousness is iconically indicated by the fact that the past is given progressively more space—it displaces the present. The first analeptic segment, with six localizable incidents, covers about seven years of childhood. The next section is partly embedded formally in the actional-present narrative after brief retrospective phases; the voyeur-incident covers an hour or so one night when Waldo is probably in his late twenties, and is an anticipatory irruption resolved thematically much later in the analeptic narrative. The Encounter covers an afternoon in Waldo's middle age. Longer than the previous irruption, it centres on the fourth of the quaternity of focal characters, is similarly anticipatory and singular, covers more real time, and is set off from the actional present at both ends: the pressure of the past is being exerted more strongly. Twice as long as the initial analeptic phase of Section 2, and covering twice the time-span, the fourth segment carries on from it by dealing with adolescence and early adulthood, and is structured upon about the same number of "datable" incidents. There are, however, more unlocalizable significant incidents than in the first phase.[1] The last recollective phase covers half a century, from when the twins are seventeen to when they are in their late sixties. There are both more "datable" incidents and more punctual but unlocalizable ones, and a geometrical increase in the space granted to descriptive and iterative narrative. Incidents conveyed scenically (through dialogue) increasingly form a pseudo-iterative part of the latter (eg, W158–69).

Thematic preoccupations are reflected quantitatively. Waldo's relationship with Dulcie occupies some 30% of the analeptic narrative. Next come those incidents revealing Waldo's failure as an artist and thinker, and his general failure in life (11.5%; excluding moments of artistic failure in connexion with Dulcie and Walter Pugh); then come his various other failures to establish relationships (Bill Poulter; the dog), his shrinking from or distortion of relationships (Pugh; Mrs Poulter; Crankshaw), and his interference in the relationship of Arthur and Mrs Poulter (9% in all). Fourth in magnitude are Waldo's fantasies of ancestral status (7%), fifth his broken relationship with his father (6%). Such a correlation as this cannot be made for Arthur's narrative, as the various people he comes into contact with are, so far as particular incidents are concerned, allowed to exist in their own right: ie, there is no strong reflexive component "contaminating" what is perceived. Arthur interacts most with Mrs Poulter (19%), then with Dulcie (14%). Some 8% of the punctual narrative is devoted to confrontations with Waldo, and the same percentage can be divided up fairly equally among the various familial radials of Dulcie and, contrastively, between Mr and Mrs Allwright. Mrs Brown figures far more prominently in point-time scenes (6%) than Mr Brown (1.3%), while persons who are ignored by Waldo or treated only in iterative narrative or as subordinate to Dulcie receive considerable space (Mrs Mackenzie 3%; Mrs Musto 6.5%). There are no incidents, except for two brief paradigmatic pieces of dialogue with Mrs Allwright and with Waldo, that cannot be localized temporally in Section 3. Nor is there any bunching of incidents that has significance beyond the fact that these incidents occur successively when they do.[2]

These kinds of narrative selectivity represent two distinct mentalities. It might be countered that a writer would hardly try the same structural "tricks" in two consecutive narrative sections when it is evidently enough to represent the primary framing narrative once in Section 2 (and, of course, with its mid-point proleptically in Section 1, its aftermath in Section 4). It is, however, also unreasonable to assume that a principle of variety for variety's sake has been

---

[1] In the first: Waldo's rejection of his father's clumsy gesture; Arthur using the word "vocation"; Waldo refusing to learn to milk the cow (all W34–36). In the fourth: Waldo running ahead of his father; the argument about Waldo's moustache, and Arthur mentioning Dulcie's; Arthur, and later Mrs Brown, asking about Waldo's writing (W76–82).

[2] Cf the phasing of the constellations Mrs Feinstein > Dulcie > Mr Feinstein > the Feinsteins > Leonard Saporta > Dulcie (A240–56); Mrs Poulter (A256–68); Mr Feinstein and the Saportas (A274–79). The shift to Mrs Poulter is a natural one; when Waldo then severs the contact, the narrative reverts to a relationship that has continued "behind" the one actually narrated.

pursued. After all, both Section 2 and Section 3 continue past the hypothetical, internally teleological end-point as envisaged by Waldo; and it is only the pressure of events in the "extra time" after the next walk that causes Arthur to undergo a process of final discovery. It is the apparent serenity of Arthur's ordered narrative—where everything seems to be under the control of some intuitive higher understanding—that makes this discovery so deeply affecting for us: indeed, so tragic. Arthur may have been able to foresee his brother's blindness, but he has been unable to anticipate that Waldo's end will take the form of self-destruction born of hatred and fed by Arthur's own indomitable love: *mythos* determined by *ethos*.

Theoretically, it would have been possible to tell (and show) the intertwined fates of these twins with the minimum of contrastive temporal and structural reordering. But the further away we get from the narrative as it stands, the more the implied author would have to step forward in the guise of an overt narratorial presence. The implied author is only minimally present in Section 1 as a covert, ironic mediator, and does not take from Mrs Poulter and Mrs Dun their central function as observers and reporters (of limited vision) on the social periphery of what they must interpret. This narratorial function can no longer be exercised in Section 4, once the relationships between Mrs Poulter and the Browns have been represented in full from the twins' viewpoints: we are plunged immediately into eight pages of free indirect thought.

To what extent does "auctorial" narration—overt, or noticeably covert—play a role in Sections 2 and 3? We can provisionally assume that the discourse is prevailingly narrated monologue (with a covert narrator doubling for the focal character). But is consciousness also represented via psychonarration or dissonant narration? 95% of White's critics believe that overt, analytical, auctorial narration is his most conspicuously employed mode. How much quoted monologue or covert, consonant narration is there, where the narrator merges with the character?

We assume that Waldo is represented as recollecting in the analeptic sections: what is being shown is the mental activity of a figural consciousness. One of the earliest external analepses occurs in the actional present of A (W27–28). Triggered by Arthur's asseveration that Mrs Poulter is "'such a good neighbour'", there is free direct speech with an iterative tag: "Mother used to say". The next sentence, "Doors closing", seems to extend the tag, but its disjunctiveness indicates its function as a contiguous fragment of preverbal perception (quoted monologue) prefacing the narration of an event: "Waldo remembered sitting alone with his mother, in the dining room, at the centre of the house, while Mrs Poulter roamed calling round:" (followed by free direct speech). This sentence is psychonarration if we go by the verb of mental process and the personal name rather than pronoun. But the syntax represents the scene psychospatially, it is possible to imagine Waldo being conscious of remembering, and there is nothing in the language to prevent us personalizing it ([I (can) remember sitting alone ...]); narrator and character merge. None of the major analeptic inceptions A^1–E^1 is signalled by a psychonarrative verb of recollection or thinking. A^1 is scenic-mimetic, and the diegetic sentences can be personalized via "I"—pronominalizing; indeed, there is already a personalization in the use of "Mother". At B^1, "Mrs Brown admitted from the beginning that Mrs Poulter had her good points" is consistent with figural narration. The temporal reference is internally regulated against Waldo's personal history (the "beginning" is not narratorially specified), and the formal "Mrs Brown" is not necessarily a distancing from Waldo's consciousness. C^1 begins: "Yes, Waldo Brown had been hit somewhere in the middle stretch of Pitt Street, it must have been 1934". The affirmative is a response to Arthur's question, "'Remember?'", and marks Waldo's mental response; the full personal name correlates with his retrieved sense of his exposed public self. The suppositions "somewhere" and "it must have been" are consonant with the effort of recall, not with external-narratorial hesitancy. The very presence of asyndetic juncture ("Pitt Street,|it must ...")— which occurs extremely seldom in White—is a colouring of informality that bears witness to the immediacy of figural thought rather than to the presence of a dissonant, laid-back narrator. "He did not like to think about it now" relates punctual past time with iterative recent past to imply a gloss of reluctance on the present enforced act of recall. The remainder of the paragraph explains this reluctance in terms of the painful recollections evoked, leading progressively back via evocations of the children to the idealized qualities Waldo wished them to have long before the shattering of his procreative dream. The prose is consonant with the recursive logic of Waldo's memory, and the details of the discourse-style correspond to Waldo's typical mode of thought. D^1 parallels the presentative mode of C^1, in that it starts thematically with a statement about the incident to be treated before again mentioning Waldo's habitual reluctance to remember. In neither case is the actional present linked to the remembered past by narratorial analysis of Waldo's emotional reaction to these surges of recollection. What (for all the differences in phrasing) would count as a redundant repetition of habitual attitude makes sense if seen as Waldo's attempt to maintain emotional equilibrium.

I maintained earlier that the inception of E^1 is not characterized by psychonarration. The gnomic initial statement, "Youth is the only permanent state of mind", would normally be judged as a general, "non-fictional" truth issuing from a maximally dissonant narrator who wishes to direct the reader's attitude towards narrative particulars which may contrast ironically with this truth (Chatman 1978:243–47). Neither Chatman nor Cohn (1978:28/31) seems to entertain the possibility that such "ex cathedra" statements could be wholly figural (either quoted monologue or direct thought-representations). The theme of the sentence is the same as in the immediate vicinity, but it does not interface with quoted monologue (Cohn's criterion for narrator-character consonance).[3]

---

[3] "A present-tense statement that leaves the reader uncertain as to its origin is ... a certain sign of a successful merger" between narrator and character. An "equivoque is created when a text shifts to a gnomic or a descriptive present in the immediate vicinity of a quoted monologue .... A sort of disincarnated narrator-consciousness can enter the scene with a statement cast in a gnomic present". But where figural thoughts finish where this voice begins,

Before the typographical space, there has been a long section of narrated monologue or free indirect thought interspersed with the aphoristic forms of Waldo's own thoughts that he intends copying in his "current notebook". The exclamatory-interrogative or *wh*-form of this sentence interiorizes it: "How much less exposed to destruction was the form of youth, even with time and memory working against it" (W119). A few sentences later, there is one of Waldo's thoughts, in the gnomic present, and italicized as though Waldo were already visualizing it in written form. Then: "He liked that, he would write it down. For his private pleasure. And the bit about form of youth, time and memory. In that way he would continue living .... In spite of Arthur. And Goethe". This free indirect thought precedes the space and the thematic, gnomic sentence in question, after which there is a return to the past tense: "There was no stage in his life when he hadn't felt young—he insisted—except sometimes as a little boy". If we take the gnomic sentence as dissonant and non-figural, we will react similarly to this last sentence, taking the conspicuous parenthesis ("—he insisted—") as an embedded tag for a nominal sentence of reporting. But the past perfect "hadn't felt" is also the standard tense for memory in narrated monologue (although, once registered, it need not be continued; Cohn 1978:127-28). "He insisted" would then function iconically as a transcription of figural consciousness—of Waldo's perception of the imminent invasion of his claim by countless miserable exceptions, and of his hasty inward steeling of himself against this. A verb which would normally tag speech or an objectively reported mental act in psychonarration is here part of narrated monologue.

If we pursue analysis of this passage a little further, it becomes clear how crucial to the interpretation of character it is to identify the discoursal frame correctly. Waldo's insisting is in the actional present still, but he is already on the threshold of memory—indeed, his feeling is already being narrated as memory. The paradoxical close of the sentence is no paradox when we consider how children lack any basis for comparison, so cannot feel young in contrast to feeling old. Waldo follows out the logic, but then turns the notion of awareness on its head to imply that he did not feel young when he was a boy only because he felt old: "If growing old is to become increasingly aware, as a little boy his premature awareness irritated his elders to the point of slapping". Note the (necessary) continuation of the gnomic present in the hypothesising clause, and the distancing use of "elders" (the parents) to make a Waldovian witticism. The next sentence, with a logical connector to indicate that these musings have, as it were, been theoremic, returns to the gnomic present: "So there are, in fact, no compartments, unless in the world of vegetables". Youth and age cannot serve to compartmentalize human life-phases, only non-human ones. But the very opacity of the statement indicates that this is a dangerous generalization: Waldo is abstracting illegitimately from his specific case. On the back of this present tense, the next paragraph slips effortlessly into free direct thought, with a recollective

---

or begin where the voice finishes, and the theme is the same, vocal unity is suggested. (Cohn 1978:75)

past-perfect tag suitable for narrated monologue: "Today I am thirty, he had calculated". This cuts the ground away from under the previous rationalization (ie, that you're as young as you feel). Waldo tries "to accept the incredible" (that he is getting older): "Sometimes he wondered whether anybody realized there was still the little boy inside him, beside his other self, looking out". This iterative statement tries to draw attention away from the fact that it is very much at this moment in front of the mirror that Waldo realizes the gap between objective truth (he is getting older) and desperate subjective conviction (he is still the boy he always was). Further reflection by the reader on the implications here could set the brain spinning. There is, for one thing, the obvious corollary that the little boy of memory is, by the figural narrative's own deposition, prematurely aware and therefore already infected with age. Waldo's mother soon confirms this: "'I think, dear, you were born thirty'". But the fact that Waldo can so readily rationalize even this away, and with the repeated use of the word "compartments", confirms that the whole of the initial paragraph with its gnomic statements is Waldo's thoughts. It is Waldo who is imputing to his mother (her timelessness) the realization that he has nurtured. This is represented mental assumption, not privileged narratorial analysis of a factual situation.

CHIEFLY ADVERBIAL CHARACTER–SPECIFIC INDICES

In the above example, formal temporal linkage is much less noticeable than the logical and discoursal ordering of a temporal theme. In the normal analysis of narrative ordering, we usually depend on the classification of time-adverbials to sort out types of temporal ordering. (Genette's discussion of frequency in Proust, for instance, devotes some twenty pages to adverbials revealing the novelist's "intoxication with the iterative"; Genette 1980:123–43.) If we take first those cases in *The Solid Mandala* in which events are introduced by non-specific point-time adverbials ("Once", "on one occasion", "One Saturday morning", etc.), we find that there are no more than about 40 in the whole of Sections 2 and 3, with no conspicuous difference in the degree of occurrence. These unique yet representative incidents typically follow on immediately from passages of iterative narration, but their temporal embedding in the iterative flow is seldom accompanied by the past-perfect tense (there are exceptions at W48/76/121/175/178/195; A243/259/288). The relationship is usually left to the reader to construe, on the basis of implicit subjective logic. The prevalent frame in Waldo's narrative is introspective (inward reactions to states and behaviour), in Arthur's actional (social relationships). Attention-focusing initial placement of point-time adverbials is avoided with what are obviously major events. Exceptions are the voyeur scene and the library incident, and it is precisely here that the relevance of the iterative frame is most obscured: the reader is forced to probe for logical relationships. In the two tellings of the library incident, free indirect discourse precedes, not iterative narrative, and an ostensible uncoupling of the events' inception from the temporal frame is achieved by the subjective occurrence of the past progressive ("One day ... Miss Glasson was standing at his elbow", W196; "one morning ... Waldo was sitting at the same table", A283).

Some 83 out of the total of 102 narremes before the actional present are anchored in unique events. Of the 83, almost half are narrated without a specified time-frame. Only seven are introduced solely by an unspecific point-time adverbial in initial (focal) position. A further five such adverbials are innocuously embedded or tacked on, and there are three or four borderline cases. Only about 20% of the unique-event narremes are signalled non-specifically. By comparison, 33% of the unique-event narremes are signalled by specific relational adverbials of point-time, and this group happens to be more significant in determining the presence in the narrative of figural consciousness. Specific punctual adverbials fall into two general classes: those that (a) relate an event to a previous (explicit or implied) reference to that event and/or are attached to an internal definition of an event which, in turn, is related to a particular detail of that event; or those that (b) relate an event to the time of another event. The two categories are not always mutually exclusive. "On that night" and "The night the prowler came" exemplify the two subclasses of (a). The first adverbial is externally deictic (anaphoric, or pointing back to a previous mention of an event); the second is internally deictic (cataphoric, or resolved here by the relative clause after it), but may or may not be referring back to a previous mention. "The third time", "And then", "Two years after" exemplify (b)—whereby the function is either sequential or relational. These, too, are externally deictic, and may be internally deictic if earlier information is repeated ("Two years after Dad died"). All such deictic time-references presuppose the self-evident status of both the events and their temporal placement: but, in any conventional terms of a compact between narrator and reader to ensure that the coreferent of deixis is clearly prepared for, most of these time-adverbials fail conspicuously to adhere to such a compact in White's novel.

"That Sunday morning he went across to Bill Poulter" (narreme **50**, W143). Here the temporal coreferent occurs half a page earlier: Waldo's decision, while returning from work "on a Friday night", to seek out Bill. "That Sunday he decided to ask help from somebody" (**23**, A239). Here there is no temporal coreferent, only a mental one: "the thought of the mandalas" as Arthur makes his grocery-deliveries. We have to follow back from this to his discovery of the mandala-definition before "that Sunday" can be construed as the Sunday following Arthur's exploration of Mrs Musto's house. "As they walked up the hill to Feinsteins' on the day" (**27**, W107): the temporal coreferent ("the Saturday") comes half a page earlier. "On that night, when he unavoidably missed his usual train" (**83**, W184): there is no temporal coreferent, only Waldo's visit to a Sydney pub. "The afternoon Waldo had to go to Feinsteins' he arrived late" (**26**, W99): as with the next visit, the temporal coreferent occurs half a page earlier ("on the Friday"). A contrasting instance of the narration taking punctual time for granted is: "That morning the old Municipal ... was spreading snares" (**83**, W175). The closest prior coreferent, over half a page earlier, is: "Waldo could not feel concerned on such a clear morning", which is itself deictic, linking with Arthur's spoken comment: "'You had the blues last night'". All of these specific adverbials stem from a non-specific adverbial, "On one occasion", which is then evasively specified: "during the night, during the despair". "The despair" paraphrases the vaguer "Only at night his doubts would return" a page earlier. "The despair", however, breaks the rule of close cohesion: the emotional state is familiar to Waldo but not explained to the reader. We must connect it with the difficulties Waldo is having with (or making for) Crankshaw. Waldo's direct speech on the "clear morning" hints at a showdown with Crankshaw, but explanation is withheld—from Arthur and from the reader, who cannot even be sure that Waldo intends to do something on that day. The paragraph before "That morning" is conspicuously iterative, moving away from point-time: "Actually Waldo was surprised he had succeeded in forming any kind of plan during the years of anxiety and stress". The "plan" is not positively admitted, nor its intended execution on a particular day. It is only made clear one page later that Waldo is resigning from the library. "That morning" carries not just temporal reference, but also refers specifically to Waldo's secret intention, which is kept unspecific to the point of not being present except in Waldo's consciousness. The reader is on the outside looking in: he can register figural intention, but not figural motivation, which is deliberately occluded.

The technique of providing a first temporal specification in the guise of smooth paraphrase is exemplified by: "It came as a shock on such an evening when ..." (**60**, W146). The coreferent is iterative and temporally less specific: Waldo's daily "return to Sarsaparilla, by ... summer light, or ... winter dark". The chief function of this kind of deictic economy is to bind occasion to (in this case contrastive) subjective mood: the temporal marker is not simply a temporal marker. Temporal location, especially in Waldo's section, is often almost wholly subordinated to the act of mental recall itself. "Waldo remembered with difficulty the occasion" when he first saw the Poulters (W140); this "occasion" is not immediately specified. First there is an allusion to the building of the Poulters' house, and only then: "but before that, yes, he could remember the day the man and woman" measured out the site. The "difficulty"· of recall is iconically represented, the first occasion being narrated in free indirect thought. The handling of time within a subjective frame of reference is also apparent in the library scene where Walter Pugh's sister makes a visit with her brother's poems. "Waldo had to remember the morning Cis came into the Library. He knew it must have happened, because she was in black" (**38**, W129). There is none of the summary anticipation of an event's focus that we find in conventional narrative ("came into the Library [to tell him of Walter's death]"). Emphasis is equally on recall and on Waldo's inference at the time that "it" has happened. Phrase-juncture creates a fruitful ambiguity: Waldo has seen Walter off to war, and "the incident was one to forget" (he tries to make it insignificant because it was retrospectively too embarrassing to keep in mind). Waldo is forced to remember both the leavetaking (on the morning Cis turns up) and the morning of her visit. The latter prolepsis is actually fulfilled several times in the later narrative. The main point is that the syntactic placement of "the morning" conveys the character's awareness of the visit's significance. The impulse of recollection has already produced a prolepsis a page earlier which looks like a narratorial aside but is actually figural recall: "(Wally, in fact, was so good at war he got killed for it, and they sent a medal to Cis)" (W128). This is full of Waldo's bitter (and self-protective) irony, not White's. The particular manner in which Cis's visit is narrationally set up has less to do with the impact on Waldo of Walter's death than with the fact that Walter's poems have come back from the grave to mock Waldo's non-creativeness.

Arthur's section is full of cataphoric point-time reference: for example, "The night of his outburst Waldo congratulated Arthur" (62, A268), or "The night Arthur ... brought the flour ..., Waldo was acting or celebrating something" (95, A291). In such cases, the actional coreferent has already been narrated, but has been interrupted by internal analepses of a page or more in length; "The night" is thus taken as given. It is significant that the incident of Waldo clothed in his mother's blue dress (the second quotation) should be relived in Waldo's section with no punctual time-frame, and should be introduced in Arthur's by the past progressive. The verb-aspect effectively cuts across point-time, suggesting both that Arthur assumes Waldo's dressing-up had been going on while he was at Mrs Poulter's, and that Arthur's moment of covert perception is subjectively mediated by the narration. In narreme 41 (A249), the focus of Arthur's visit to Len Saporta's carpet-shop is on the time-frame, and the fact of the visit is taken as "old" information—but it is only so for Arthur, not for the reader, for whom there has been no previous mention of the visit. It has, as it were, already been silently recalled to mind. Not until after a long parenthetical excursus filling in miscellaneous bits of prior information about Saporta and Dulcie do we come to the actual recounting of the visit: "Anyway, Mr Saporta had returned, and the day Arthur went to his shop, approached ..." (A250). Here we find an informal discourse-adjunct of narrative resumption ("Anyway"), acknowledging the excursus; a past perfect résumé of earlier information; and a punctual adverbial that refers back to "visit" but is explained only by the following relative clause. The narrative tone throughout indicates that this information is self-evident, and actively recalled. Narreme 22 (A235) is more radically cataphoric than 41. An iterative paragraph has been devoted to Arthur's exploration of Mrs Musto's house. The singulative incident begins: "The morning he went so far as to explore an upstairs room Arthur was surprised to find Mrs Musto standing in her bloomers and camisole". In terms of sentence structure, the temporal subordination is iconic, the moment of surprise drawing behind it, as it were, the linear trace of Arthur's actional intention; temporality is spatially organized, to lay bare the linear constitution of Arthur's specific recollection. The interesting thing macrostructurally is the situational parallel with Arthur's encountering Mrs Mackenzie in her nightgown upstairs at the bank.

Many relational and sequential adverbials are employed unexceptionally in providing a clear frame for narrative events. Others are diegetically linked to a process of figural recall, and may be inceptive (the narration of the incident following immediately: "It was, he thought, the occasion of their last visit ... that

Waldo noticed ..."; **10**, W54). Prolepsis may occur ("It was Sunday, Waldo would remember"; **89**, W187), sometimes non-inceptively ("From this occasion he would remember ..."; **26**, W112). These last two cases are problematical. The claims that Waldo "would remember" are not honoured in the narrative; the claims must be iterative summaries of what has stuck in Waldo's memory. Is Waldo, while recalling a specific event, also recalling moments of recollection prior to the specific analepsis? This would mean that the ghostly presence of the first narrative (actional-present recall) can be felt even deep within long sections of analepsis which have no formal evocation of that first narrative. Waldo's radical subjective immersion in the moment recalled is exemplified after an iterative paragraph dwelling on Waldo's train-trips to school in the company of his father: "Seeing them off in the early light that first morning, Mother said:". The deixis is not to an incident already "in" the narrative, but to an un-narrated incident already in Waldo's mind.

The range of indications that an active recollective consciousness is at work in Waldo's section is great and varied. There are purely narrative prolepses with no specific indication of mental function: the veranda already weathered in Mr Brown's lifetime, the day-bed infested with borer only when the twins retire (W37). An incident during adolescence is interrupted by a prolepsis to Mrs Brown's memories in the late 1920s (W80). There are occasional puzzling prolepses that seem to be resolved too soon (cf the contradictory time-scales of Waldo's references to Dulcie's watery eyes, W92–93). There are, as we have seen, explicit references to Waldo's remembering, to his reluctance to do so (W69), to the apparent difficulty of doing so (W140), to the certainty that an event would be remembered (W112/187), to the inevitability of remembering something already consigned to oblivion (W129). The process of past recollection combines psychological necessity and volition ("So Waldo continued remembering", W106), is a release from the burden of paternal presence ("Waldo was often tempted to re-enter his own boyhood", W74), is the rationalizing, vengeful retrieval of a painful but carefully filed memory ("he allowed himself to remember a dialogue", W179; this has been obsessively prepared for: cf W177/178). Waldo, hiding in the house, observes the prosperous stranger outside with his sexually exciting woman companion: "Again memory was taking a hand. He remembered" Johnny Haynes, who, when they were schoolboys, had warned him of hoarse-voiced women (W189). Free indirect discourse occurs constantly to mediate inward retrospection and prediction ("Certainly he had confided in Dulcie", W123; "How raw he had been formerly", W131; "Arthur ... probably wouldn't alter much", W131). Later events may be recalled germinally, only to be thrust away until later (W183).

There are few such wide-ranging analepses and prolepses in Arthur's section. Most are close to previously narrated events and establish a subjective perspective on causally linked incidents (A249/268/277). The most radical analepsis (and the only one in which an actual year is furnished with a date) is the leap back to 1922 from the mid-thirties (A274). The only significant use of a verb of recollection occurs in a passage near the inception of the most crucial incident in Arthur's section (the wheel-tree and the mandala-dance): "And under the tree was standing the Chinese woman, whom he often remembered afterwards" (A263); the act of remembering is then elaborated reflectively: "There was no great reason why he should remember her, except as part of the dazzle of the afternoon. For that reason he did" (A263). There is no stress elsewhere on the process of memory, because it is as effortless to Arthur as this quotation suggests. Retrospection goes constantly hand in hand with prolepsis or foreknowledge. After the central walk with Mrs Poulter, before Waldo and his parents cut off his contact with her: "The perfection of the day saddened him in retrospect. He knew it could never recur" (A267). Arthur's initiation into the mysteries of bread- and butter-making give him "a satisfaction more intense than any he experienced before the coming of Mrs Poulter" (A232)—which is narrated some twenty pages later. The night-time embrace of the twins in their boyhood is connected with a passage (quoted at A229) "in the old book Arthur came across years later"—possibly the same book by Jung that Arthur consults in the 1940s (A281). By far the most resonant of the few prolepses in Arthur's section is the earliest one: "Arthur could not tell, but found out later Granny was right, that even dogs are less brutal than men, because they are less complicated" (A217). The dogs do not recur in Section 3 until the dialogue of the library incident (A284), but are thereafter a continual presence until the very end; the prolepsis thus spans the whole section. If we did not have the conditioning prior existence of Waldo's narrative and the inchoate, internalized, unpunctuated, *Portrait*-like beginning to Section 3 (A215), we would have to construe "Arthur could not tell" as auctorial intrusion (as what Genette 1980:197 has called "the excess of information or paralepsis, ... an inroad into the consciousness of a character in the course of a narrative generally conducted in external focalization"). It seems evident, however, that the statement is Arthur's own retrospective reading of his state of awareness in early childhood. There is plenty of evidence, before the mortal dénouement, of Waldo's brutality and complexity, and of the closeness of the "brute" dogs to the mandalic wholeness and clarity that Arthur himself strives for. This business of "finding out", of discovery or learning, is absent from Waldo's section.[4]

Even when the narrator is the "hero" (as in many first-person narratives), he almost always commands more information about himself than is conveyed in the narrating (Genette 1980:194). Similarly, a narrative focalized internally on the figural consciousness, as Waldo's is, will—even in a context of explicitly framed mental recollection—tend to maintain distinctions of identity and perception between the character recalling in the actional present and the character experiencing in the past. It would impossibly complicate the narrative if the narrated recollections were constantly relativized against later knowledge.

---

[4] Compare, in Section 3: "for he never found out whether ..." (A221); "as Arthur got to know" (A222); "Arthur learned in time" (A225); "which, he now realized, she would never notice" (A244); "it would become Waldo's tragedy" (A245); "Arthur sensed on his way through life that ..." (A250); "He had always known that" (A255); "In the beginning he had wondered ..." (A290).

Indeed, this would take the wind out of the narrative's sails, and it would cease to have any forward momentum. The past narrative in Waldo's section, then, cannot be meant to represent the fully psychologized recall of memories, save within the narrower context of internal analepses. Waldo's memories, especially the inceptive ones (A^1–E^1), are not conditioned by his later knowledge of their significance.

TEMPORAL AND PSYCHOLOGICAL DISJUNCTIONS

There is one case that indicates well the problematic nature of Waldo's memory processes. In his youth, Waldo is transported with almost sexual delectation by some lines of poetry he comes across at the library, then shuts the book guiltily (W121–22). After refusing to take custody of Wally Pugh's poems, Waldo tries unsuccessfully to write a war-poem. A parenthetical paragraph then tells how he discovered, as an old man, the fragment of this war-poem, together with "that other fragment of his youth" (W129–30)—the lines quoted indicating to us that it is from Tennyson's "Fatima". At the end of the paragraph, however, we find Waldo claiming these lines as his own creation, whereas we would assume that he knows they were hurriedly scribbled down from the book he perused in his youth. Before the library incident in the early 1950s (W195), Arthur finds a sheet of paper with a poem on it. He makes it clear that he knows it is by Tennyson and that his brother has copied it out; it is the same text as in the earlier quotations. Waldo's nervous probings reveal ("too brutal for Waldo") that Arthur has read poetry in their father's old anthology. If "Fatima" were in that anthology, and Waldo did not first encounter it there, then this is an irony (Waldo has always prided himself on his reading while playing up Arthur's lack of interest in books at home) anticipating the later discovery that Arthur does his secret reading in the public library and could have been encouraged by his father's anthology to acquaint himself more thoroughly with Tennyson. What is important is that the incident narrated at W129–30 pre-dates the one narrated at W195—in which case Waldo unwillingly realizes only in the third narrated incident that he has wrongly transferred authorship of the poem from Tennyson to himself.

The unmasking by Arthur has no influence on the representation of Waldo's self-satisfied discovery "as an old man". In both, the word "copied" is employed with all its rich ambiguity of motivation. By pathological suppression, Waldo has imposed his own authorship, and is shocked out of suppression by Arthur, who can see the truth. What was safe as a fantasy come true is put at risk once this "fragment" of his secret substitute-life has been exposed to another consciousness. Waldo's cover-up comment that Tennyson must have had difficulty "'in remembering what he had written'" (W195) applies to himself as well. The discrete recall of events is mediated as directly experienced at the time, cut adrift from the qualifying mode of hindsight. Waldo's recollection of finding the poem is given when it is given because it accords associatively with his self-deceiving mood after Wally Pugh's death. This would also explain the relative paucity of formal prolepsis in Section 2. Events that are merely contiguous to Waldo—in which he is not himself the central, actual or potential, actant—are denied the status of narrative moments in a linked *historia*. Waldo thus struggles against time, though he is tyrannized by the past.

Arthur, I repeat, suffers no such tyranny—or so it seems. I did mention that the surface of his narrative is not entirely untroubled at the level of structural disposition. The first significant anachrony or shift of temporal order is the introduction of the Feinsteins (narreme **21**) after the narrating of Arthur's visit to Mrs Musto (**22**). Although both the twins have met Mrs Musto frequently on their boyhood walks (W83–84) and the Brown family have been invited to her place (W84–85), Arthur's one-to-one acquaintanceships with Mrs Musto and the Feinsteins date from the same time (his release from the store to do outside grocery-deliveries, A233), but his interest in the Feinsteins precedes Dulcie's appearance at the shop while Arthur is still working indoors, and thus antedates his personal contact with Mrs Musto. The belated introduction of Arthur's first encounter ("in the beginning") with Mrs Feinstein is a narratively normal filling-in (not all relationships can be narrated at once). Psychologically, however, it reveals a secret relationship that Arthur had wanted to protect; this is narrationally retraced under emotional pressure only now that it is at risk (cf A238–39).

The next pressure-point is constituted by two major implicit ellipses (Genette 1980:108): one between Arthur's first visit to the Feinsteins' and his walk in the park with Dulcie (A245), the other between the walk in the park and receipt of Dulcie's postcard (A246). Whereas Waldo's narrative for this stretch of indefinite time is filled with the presence of Dulcie, Arthur's does not even have iterative bridges between the various events. The narrative does, however, refer to Dulcie as being "focussed ... in the crystal of his mind", and there is one statement that suggests Arthur has been thinking of her during her absence, by virtue of the fact that the discourse is at pains to excuse the paucity of her contact (A246–47). Arthur's thoughts after the outbreak of war also imply that he has imagined the Feinsteins as being both not really absent and also safe in their absence (A247). This second ellipsis indicates that Arthur protects his friends without being anxious about them. The first ellipsis takes the establishing of a personal relationship for granted (even Waldo notes how Arthur talks to Dulcie, for the very first time, "as though he had met her before, and she was only, as it were, re-appearing", W109—though there is an irony of prior "meeting" here)—so it can be passed over. Besides: the relationship is secret. The ellipsis in Arthur's section reflects Waldo's (and our) state of knowledge.

The next instance of narrative achronicity is the "nocturnal rapist" joke which Arthur plays on Mrs Poulter (narreme **59**, A259–60), in response to Mrs Poulter's practical joke with the "severed finger"—these incidents are uncoupled from a chronological frame ("Once ..."; "And once ..."). It is here, for the first time outside Waldo's narrative, that Arthur's habitual walks with Mrs Poulter are mentioned. The prior placement of Waldo's narrative allows us to construe the sense of the mention of walks here, and to feed into the narrative an aura of fatefulness and portent. The aura of anticipation is absent from Waldo's narrative. No sooner are the walks mentioned in Arthur's than they are threatened; a close relationship established dialogically over the previous four pages is already under threat of dissolution. Mrs Poulter withdraws from Arthur (as, it is suggested, she not infrequently does: A260), who goes home in tears. The "pictures of contentment" associated with Mrs Poulter's plenitude that flicker before his eyes recur in the symbolism of his mandala-dance (55, A266). These pictures are presented as fresh, new information in 59, as ritually familiar in 55, so one might expect the practical-joke incident to precede the dance-episode. This is not the case. On both narrative occasions, an independent process of mental association is narrated; the earlier mention is, at the most, a concealed proleptic recall of the most intense epiphanic ritualizing of these "pictures" in the mandala-dance scene, which itself ends with Arthur's intuitive fear of losing intense contact with Mrs Poulter (A267). What follows is an account of the Brown family's resistance to Mrs Poulter, a condensed version of Waldo's ultimatum of severance, and recall of the evening Mrs Poulter calls off the walks because of resistance from Arthur's family and her husband (narreme 61).

We have been conditioned to expect Arthur's narrative to move forwards in time (despite the ellipsis just mentioned, we feel that the narrative progression is smooth, not jagged like Waldo's). The anachronous ordering of narremes 59 and 55 is not furnished with temporal markers. What we have instead is a negative/positive alternation of scenes. (A256–67) between the involvement with Mrs Poulter and threats to that involvement, all funnelling out of the statement (W25) about the twins' relationship and the hint of severance by the knife. After the practical joke is narrated, and before the narrating of the mandala-dance, there is an account of a Sunday walk with Mrs Poulter, which is framed temporally by Arthur's symbolic dreams (one the night before, the second in the night after the walk; narreme 58, A260–62). The tree-dream (related to the Jungian account of the Tree of Life) is uncoupled from the event narrated before it ("Once Arthur dreamed the dream"). Its symbolic content and deixis ("the dream") make it derivative from the wheel-tree and the mandala-dance occurring earlier. In this latter incident, Arthur touches Mrs Poulter's smooth hair; in his dream, her skin is not smooth as expected, but "rough, almost prickly bark"—a negative omen of her own increasing resistance to Arthur under social pressure since the wheel-tree walk. But the placing of the wheel-tree walk ("This time it was a holiday") and the crucifixion-imagery of the mandala-dance suggest that the dream and the Sunday walk with Mrs Poulter's talk about the Crucifixion and Arthur as her surrogate-child have been subsequently built into the ritual of the dance: "all that was spoken and acted was as inescapable as conviction and dreams" (A264). However, "This time" can be contrastive without having a sequencing function. Moreover, the Sunday-walk conversation can just as easily flow topically from the mandala-dance scene. The strongest sequencing index is the behaviour of the two characters. During the wheel-tree walk, Arthur expressed happy energy, whereas the Sunday walk is overshadowed by his melancholic lethargy; the benevolently warming sun of the wheel-tree walk has become "the raw sun ... sawing at them". On the wheel-tree walk, Mrs Poulter was at her most accessible; her chirpy friendliness on the Sunday walk cannot hide the fact that she now ranks the otherworldly covenant with Christ and the church higher than the this-worldly mandala-covenant with her as already expressed in Arthur's dance. More significantly, the Sunday walk finishes abruptly: Mrs Poulter has taken a convenient short cut—but it is the roundabout-ness of the walks that Arthur loves. She is avoiding walking along the neighbourhood streets in Arthur's company, thereby denying her own prevailing attitude as expressed earlier: "That Arthur Brown. Harmless enough. Nobody could ever accuse you" (A259). This is the sole instance of an irruption into Arthur's narrative of another character's mental discourse (Mrs Poulter's free direct thought). Finally, the ritual covenant of giving Mrs Poulter the gold marble has its subsequent, bathetic antithesis in Arthur's temporary loss, under the po-cupboard, of his own "special" marble (A262). This is a symbolic separation from self, just as the gift to Mrs Poulter was a symbolic inclusion of her within his protective self. The drive for wholeness, culminating in the mandala-dance, is subsequently set at risk.

The very structuring and disposition of narremes **55–62** in the two central narratives (and more specifically in Arthur's), with all the withholding of external ordering-markers, conveys Arthur's hesitant re-entry in memory into the most traumatic experience of separation he must suffer before the final separation from his twin. He cannot recollect serenely the epiphanic highpoint of his relationship; what he recollects first is his own fatal false step (scaring Mrs Poulter). It is psychologically plausible that he should then explore that prior phase of halfhearted allegiance by Mrs Poulter, and despondency on his own part, that is the result of general contamination by the Brown family's disapproval. Only after the pain has been got out of the way is Arthur able to recall in its untouched totality the perfection of the holiday walk. It is no accident that the actual phase of gradual estrangement, like the culminating and temporally inverted calls to terminate the walks, should be narrated with such fatalistic dispassion.

II   Omniscient narration?

I wish to examine here the question of how far the narration is dependent on what is traditionally called the "omniscient narrator". Discussion of this topic has been bracketed off for two reasons. First, such narration would be the exception rather than the rule in *The Solid Mandala;* indeed, one cannot even speak of the presence of a regular or even intermittent alternation of "omniscient" and "personal" or "figural" narration. Second, the presence of "omniscient" narration in a given text can be proven largely by contextual inference and does not require the deployment of formal test-categories. To put it more bluntly: this novel, and at least White's other fiction from *The Tree of Man* (1955) to *Memoirs of Many in One* (1986), constitutes a body of work that explores consciousness through narratorial representation of it. White's narrational techniques ingest modes of representation whose surface structures resemble traditional (and modernist) "omniscient" techniques but which are subverted.[5] To disprove assumptions that such techniques are actually traditionally employed, it is necessary (and possible) to enlist support from both contextual and discourse-technical analysis. Isolated instances of what looks like "omniscient" narration in the present novel have already been "defused" in passing by the application of this approach. The analysis of White's "individual" style in the chapters that follow necessarily adheres closely to discoursal categories that not only underpin the fully subjectivized narration in *The Solid Mandala* but are also ubiquitous in the other novels, and must therefore have the same or similar functions.

To rehearse Genette's categories: omniscient or non-focalized narration reveals more than the characters themselves can know. ("Omniscience" is a relative concept: in a truth-conditional sense, there can be no such thing narratorially or characterologically as "omniscience"—see Kuiper/Small 1986.) Although non-focalized utterances may sound Olympian and at an "objective" distance from the events narrated, the narratized discourse is the least distanced from non-verbal events in the telling of them. (This observation alone should give those critics pause who have complained about the obliquity, portentousness and "gnomic" quality of White's narratives: such qualities fit ill with the role of an "omniscient" narrator.) In Cohn's terms, we can also speak of the presence of dissonant narration (and, insofar as inward states and processes are mediated, of dissonant psychonarration).

In *The Solid Mandala,* the only fair test of the presence of non-focalized narration that can be undertaken is the analysis of Section 1, where one would most expect to find it. I submitted the whole section to analysis in order to determine the degree of inconspicuous slipping or *glissage* from one presentational mode to another (from, say, indirect speech or thought to free indirect speech or thought). Slipping is a matter of style, to the extent that a given configuration of perspective and distance ("telling" versus "showing") presupposes that the implied author has made presentational choices. Slipping is always markedly present in White's fiction, but is a feature shared to such an extent by countless other writers from Jane Austen to the present that it is comparatively ineffective as a discrete style-marker.

On page 123 below is the tabular scheme of findings for 22 lines of discourse (two passages, 1–8 and 1–11) towards the end of Section 1 (B18–19); the opening and closing words of each phase of slipping are provided. Non-focalized

---

[5] Reluctance to jettison the notion of omniscience in the face of subversive indices denying its validity persists in such efforts as those of Anthony Hassall to pin down the elusive representational mode of *A Fringe of Leaves*: the narrator is "omniscient in the sense of knowing all Ellen's life, but he does not claim to understand all that he tells"; "White has never extended the author's notional omniscience to an understanding of his characters that would explain them in a fictionally privileged way to themselves, to one another, or to the reader. For White, character remains an enigma fitfully lit by shafts of insight and sometimes illuminated by approaching death" (Hassall 1987:18–19).

perspective equals "omniscience"; external focalization is objective or behaviourist: the narrator says less than the character knows. In internal focalization, the narrator says what the character knows. Internal focalization can be fixed to the one character concerned at any point in the discourse, can be variable (shifting between characters), or multiple (different characters on the same events).

Table 3: Slipping in Section 1

| | PERSPECTIVE (FOCALIZATION) | | DISTANCE | |
	External/ Non-focalized	Internal	Narrative of Events	Words
1 *"I bet there is!"*	external			mimetic
2 *her/said*	narrator		diegetic	
3 *doing/with him*	narrator	fixed (P)	diegetic	
4 *He would/evenings*	narrator	fixed (P)	diegetic-mimetic	
5 *or that/it*		fixed (P)		transposed-mimetic
6 *and when/beer*	narrator	fixed (P)	diegetic	
7 *he was/in that*		fixed (P)		transposed-mimetic
8 *she/side.*	narrator	fixed (P)	diegetic	
1 *Then/trudging,*	narrator	fixed(D)	diegetic	
2 *you/infirmities -*		fixed(D)		transposed mimetic
3 *along/Sarsaparilla.*	narrator	fixed(D)	diegetic	
4 *The strange/up,*		fixed (D)	diegetic	transposed mimetic
5 *if only/mind.*	narrator		diegetic	
6 *She was/that.*		fixed(D)		transposed mimetic
7 *But she/men.*		fixed(D)	diegetic-mimetic	
8 *The one/hand.*	narrator		diegetic	
9 *It was/led.*	narrator			transposed thought
10 *But one/sense.*		fixed(D)		transposed thought
11 *She sensed/skin.*		fixed(D)	diegetic	

As a whole, *The Solid Mandala* obviously has multiple focalization. It is clearer to speak of a series of fixed focalizations than of variable focalization: Mrs Dun (D) is focally prominent at the beginning and at the end of Section 1, Mrs Poulter (P) in the middle stretch. *Diegetic* narrative "tells", includes interpretative speech-act verbs, and analyses speech and thought as action and event (the term "diegesis" is also applied more broadly to all narrative that is not "mimetic" or based in direct speech). *Diegetic-mimetic* indicates the presence of the implied author's words with speech-allusive components. *Transposed mimetic* "shows", and is free indirect thought. *Transposed thought* "tells" in the form of narratized quotation.

In Section 1, it is seldom that non-focalized narration appears in its "pure" form: ie, uncontaminated by character-idiolect. Of the 76 segments of slipping analyzed, only 20 (in the above extract, 5 and 8 in the second sequence) seem at first glance to be "telling" the reader something from "outside" the characters. If we pay due consideration to the pragmatic context (which is that of degrees of communication between two characters), we find that most of these statements mediate physical gestures or attitudes that are perceivable by, and arguably significant to, the counterpart-character, or mediate an inward state: ie, the narration is not dissonant. On only two occasions (B12: "to notice … life took its cleaver to them"; B13: "She had a certain relentlessness of conviction") is the mediated information not accessible to the characters themselves. "The eyes of the two women followed ..." (B14) is a determination which is solely within the purview of an observing narrator; but the resolution of the sentence mediates the preverbal mental state of both characters. "Her lips were slightly open" (B14) is outside Mrs Poulter's own somatic awareness; but the sentence similarly concludes with the mediation of inward state. The sentence "Nor did it help either lady to know the other could be involved" (B21), by equivocations on the word "involved" and on the factive/non-factive status of grammatical negation, mediates character-awareness and "privileged", contrary, narrator-awareness at the same time, to generate a solemn perspectival irony.

There is no need for the narrator to "stand back" from the two women in Section 1. If Mrs Poulter, as has been indicated, is exercising her memory, covering proleptically the ground that is to be ploughed more thoroughly and painfully later, it is also her consciousness that is represented as hopefully scanning her fellow-passenger, Mrs Dun, and her reactions. Opposed to the presence of memory in Section 1 is the immediate but imprisoned awareness of Mrs Dun, who is as outside the charmed circle of rememberers as we the readers are. Indeed: her revulsion on first glimpsing the old men is as much a rebounding from the surface of what is perceived (as much of an accommodating falsification) as the serene view of the anonymous reviewer who (although later, and in a way rightly, granting Arthur the status of "idiot genius") could see the initial presentation—or mediated perception—of the walking men only as a picture of "obscene senility" (*Times* 1966).

The question of the function of memory in the structuring of the narrative discourse, and of the extent to which this structuring implies the consonance of narrator and figural consciousness, seems to be rendered problematical by a sentence in Waldo's section: "To the end of his life Waldo cultivated his gift for distinguishing failures" (W82). It is inconceivable that Waldo can be recalling from beyond the grave or on his deathbed. To what extent is this "a momentary infraction of the code" where "the coherence of the whole still remains strong enough for the notion of dominant mode/mood to continue relevant" (Genette 1980:194–95)? The particular seeming infraction under inspection here is one which White must have found irresistible in its ironic fidelity to the truth of the narrative. It is, after all, himself (Waldo) whom Waldo distinguishes as a failure at the "end of his life", and it is this awareness of his total lack of distinction that kills him. I say seeming infraction, because (as in the last example mentioned above for non-focalization in Section 1) the sentence is really an instance of what Mikhail Bakhtin has called double-voiced discourse or heteroglossia.[6] It is only by taking the sentence in question in isolation, and not as embedded in the flow and flux of discourse, that the reader can classify it, on the apparent proof of actional circumstance, as "auctorial" or dissonant narration.

---

6 "It serves two speakers at the same time and expresses simultaneously two different intentions: the direct intention of the character who is speaking, and the refracted intention of the author. In such discourse there are two voices, two meanings and two expressions" (Bakhtin 1981:324).

The immediate context helps a little. The previous theme has been Mrs Brown's upsetting question about Waldo's "Writing", which he professes to want to keep secret (but the circumstance of others knowing about it suggests that Waldo has drawn their attention to his secretiveness in order to plump up his positive self-image as a writer). Mr Brown, for all his reading, "had failed to be a writer", "Waldo was suddenly convinced". Now, Mr Brown's death has already been narrated. That Waldo should notice that "Dad seemed unaware" of his son's writing is a hint at Waldo's pain at not being acknowledged as a writer, not—as Waldo insinuates—because his father was jealous of his son's achievement and ashamed of his own failure. This is an instance of consonant psychonarration that allows the reader to separate out the underlying truth of mental acts from their patina of fiction, and thus to determine an irony in the narration which is not dependent on any voicing through a narratorial commentator. In the sentence in question, the phrase "to the end of his life" reflects an unarticulated contrast with the death of Waldo's father, while the clause "cultivated his gift for distinguishing failures" is an extension of Waldo's sudden conviction about his father. In the listing of "failures" that follows, Waldo narrows the spatial radius of his concern to Sarsaparilla, scornfully detailing its inertia, its entrapment in steaming yellow grass. He must, of course, leave himself out, though we become aware (if we are not already so) that he himself is the prime failure of the suburb. That he should bring up Johnny Haynes at the start, only to discount him for lack of hard evidence of failure (he was "suddenly convinced" about his father's failure, but "couldn't make up his mind" about Johnny: the discourse exploits symmetry), has to do intimately with Waldo's writing, which he hoped made him better than Haynes in school. At the same time, he feared Haynes's opinion of his writing, and with good cause. As we discover later, Waldo knows that Haynes, never so good a pupil as he, has become an M.P.—not exactly a mark of failure, except that it is the kind of success that Waldo can envy but not deeply so, as it does not impinge on his realm of intellectual desire.

The bond of secret or invisible discourse is one that is not exhausted in the threads of mental association which I have adumbrated so far. The concealed datum of Haynes's public success is anticipated in the diction of the problematical sentence preceding, which is couched in the rhetoric of public laudation with its talk of "distinguished success", the cultivation of "gifts", in the lifetime of public personages. Later, in the actional present, Waldo indulges in his "secret vice" (symmetrical with his Secret Writing) of imagining what he would do "If Arthur died". The quoted monologue shifts subtly from the acquisition of material symbols of status (the complete Everyman Library) to the acquisition, through influence, of social status:

the land the developers were after if Anglesey Estate then why not Browns' place Terminus Road see an alderman no alderman was so dishonest you couldn't teach him a point or two approach a minister if necessary the Minister for Local Govt if only Mrs Musto were alive and say it is imperative imperative was the word that W. Brown of honourable service should end in a blaze of last years. [W115]

On the occasion of the stranger's visit to the brothers' house:

Waldo remembered reading some years earlier, before the demands of his own work had begun to prevent him following public affairs, that Johnny Haynes was going to the top, that he had become a member of parliament—if you could accept that sort of thing as the top—and been involved in some kind of shady business deal. Exonerated of course. [W189]

The presence of the successful man (Haynes) which pervades all three contexts allows us to see what is Waldo's mental projection of personal success-fantasies at W115 (the "public" diction of "W. Brown of honourable service"; the slip of involuntarily going from Arthur's death to an incorporation of his own "end" into his blazing late career; in short, the imagined obituary) as prefigured in our problematical sentence. What at first looks like auctorial, dissonant perspective is only so as the by-product of the heteroglossic or double-voicing capacity of discourse. It is Waldo who includes the "end of his life" in his recollective discourse; the language of public laudation is the mental writing of his own obituary.

It has not been my intention to argue that the novel makes no use of "omniscient" narration; there do seem to be occasional real infractions of the dominant mode. But one must inspect the territory very carefully before claiming that this or that passage or sentence is an infraction. The modality of the sentence just discussed could only be finally established, in stages, over a hundred pages further on in the narrative. At each stage, the information provided is trimmed to the requirements of the immediate psychological context. The last piece of information that we pick up about Haynes is the closest, in narrative presentation, to "basic" or expository material, but it "behaves" as though nothing at all has been stated or implied before. The diegesis avoids referential cohesion, because the three occasions on which Haynes/the M.P. occurs are discrete mental occasions, subliminally interconnected, but not consciously.

Sometimes there seems to be no convincing detail elsewhere that can help invalidate initial assumptions about the presence of non-focalized narration. There is one example in Arthur's section: "It was the embroidery of life on which they were engaged. They followed no particular pattern and could seldom resist adding another stitch" (A258-59). As with most plural referents, it is difficult to take this as representing Arthur thinking for himself and Mrs Poulter. Although the elaborate metaphor is domestic, it is not necessarily commensurate with Mrs Poulter's way of thinking (and is not a metaphor specially handcrafted for this context, as it occurs in other novels by White). Apart from which, it is an analytical representation of habitual verbal action rather than of preverbal thought. Prior references to Dulcie Feinstein's embroidered dress (W103, A244) fail to confirm that the metaphor of Arthur's and Mrs Poulter's talk is generated via Arthur's consciousness. The next paragraph, already quoted above ("That Arthur Brown. Harmless enough. Nobody could ever accuse you") might confirm this; it is quoted monologue representing Mrs Poulter's thoughts about Arthur—but not Arthur's mental projection (or inner dramatization) of these thoughts. The idyllic tenor of the preceding diegesis is undercut by what the thought reveals, but not too much.

What could be taken as narrator-comment and as the dissonant psychonarration of a mood felt by both characters has given was to a piece of narration which in one sense jars (because the narration has previously stuck close to Arthur's perceptions); but, in another sense, it is the only solution. A formal psychonarrational move away from twin focalization—something like: "Mrs Poulter thought that Arthur Brown was harmless enough; nobody could ever accuse her of anything improper if she talked to him"—would mean a bumbling incursion into what is one of the central harmonious relationships of the book, and would distance Mrs Poulter too much from the object of her charitable affection. Quoted monologue sounds spontaneous; narratorial analysis would have made Mrs Poulter sound calculating and hypocritical and would render the "embroidery"-passage puzzlingly universal rather than bivocal. Another problem of perspective is raised by the next sentence: "From her house, like a houseboat moored in the backwaters of grass, Mrs Poulter would often beckon". Are we to assume that the metaphor—which has already occurred twice in Waldo's section (W141/185–86)—is narratorial, or entailed by Arthur's mode of perception? The logical conclusion is to treat the reappearance of the metaphor here (like so much shared indexical detail elsewhere) as confirmation of one stratum of perceptual affinity between the otherwise dissimilar twins—whence the circumstantial confirmation that the narration at this point is consonant psychonarration, not auctorial perspective.

It is customary to regard external somatic indices as non-focalized (perspective from without), so long as the context does not reveal that a character is viewing himself (in one of "the many cumbersome 'mirror views' in modern fiction", Booth 1961:172). The degree of figural awareness mediated in the following passage is a case in point:

(1) Nobody could remember, not even Arthur Brown himself, when he developed his head for figures. (2) The gift was found growing in him, as naturally as hair, for instance. (3) He was safest with numbers. (4) The steel springs of clocks could not be unwound so logically. (5) Arthur's awkward fingers would become steel tentacles reaching out for the solution of his problem. (6) What Waldo called those messy-awful melting-chocolate eyes would set hard in the abstraction which should have been foreign to him. (7) How did he do it? (8) He just knew. (9) And immediately after, was laughing it off. (10) The brown sloppy awful eyes had a squint in them too, or in one of them. [A231]

The statement in (1) derives from what has been said by others about Arthur's gift. The presence of the full name usually signals non-figural focus but, as I will be arguing later, functions here to signal the character's own awareness of himself as the object of public attention. The passive in (2) evades the question of who finds the gift, but the insouciant addition of "for instance" points to this being a recollective mental report, with subjective focus. (3) could be either psychonarration (dissonant: auctorial analysis of a relative sense of security not apparent to Arthur; or consonant: Arthur's conscious valuing of this refuge in numbers) or narrated monologue (directly convertible to first person). The word

"safest" is equivocal—the world of numbers is more stable for Arthur than the
concrete world, thus offering him greatest security of perception; his gift,
whenever he exercises it, protects him from baitings by his classmates because
Johnny Haynes depends on his mathematical wizardry. The unequal analogy in
(4) could be auctorial, or within Arthur's experiential purview. It could be Arthur
who is aware in (5) that his fingers are usually "awkward", who is conscious of
the transformation into somatic certainty—counting mentally on his fingers—
caused by his engagement with mathematical problems; "his problem", rather
than "a problem", maintains close focalization. Arthur's awareness of what his
own eyes look like is based non-committally in (6) on his brother's verbal
opinion.

But how can Arthur know that his eyes "set hard ... in abstraction"? Is this
the view of those watching him, and is it they who find this "abstraction"
"unusual"? I would suggest that the awareness of state is Arthur's own—that it is
somatic, preverbal inference. There are also external links with Arthur's
psychological investment in the transparent permanency and hardness of his
marbles. He is aware that others think his behaviour here is "foreign" to what
people assume is his nature. The narrated monologue or free indirect thought of
(7) transcribes the others' reaction, as (8) does his spoken reply and/or inward
awareness of intuitive certainty. (9) is in figural focus, as the progressive aspect
indicates, along with the inexplicit deixis of "it". Sentence (10) is the crux: what
informative purpose does it serve? The reference to the squint seems to lie
outside the theme of the paragraph, the information gratuitously superadded
("too"). Its "after-thought" status seems underscored by the improvisatory
correction "or in one of them". Is this auctorial casualness, or is the perspective
that of Arthur's classmates, sharing Waldo's perception of Arthur's eyes? It
would appear that the discourse is once again double-voiced. On the one side
there is a mediation of the outside observers' perception of Arthur's eyes
(reference to the squint tying in with the subjective negativity of "sloppy awful",
to hint at the "evil eye" of supernatural giftedness). On the other side there is
Arthur's own perception of his eyes as being upsetting to the observer—he keeps
his modified citation of Waldo's description at arm's length from his own
unspecified evaluation by using the definite article; the squint is subliminally to
be linked with the flaw at the heart of his marble-mandalas.

How can we know that a somatic outside view is accessible to Arthur? This is
easily enough done on a second reading of the novel, after we have registered
that it is not only Waldo who looks in mirrors (cf Arthur's catching sight of his
reflection in old age, A290). Arthur also has reflexive awareness of his own face,
his own soma and his awkward relationship to it. On his winter walk with
Dulcie, "he reckoned his face wouldn't have collapsed yet into its normal
shapelessness" (A246). He knows from Mrs Allwright's reaction that his face is
revealing his "withdrawal into himself", drawing attention "to the luminous edges
of his face, where at any time the skin was of a whiteness to suggest blue"
(A242)—his physical appearance would at some time have been accessible to him
via the mirror. By contrast, "he knew the flames of argument must be colouring

his face in the way which distressed strangers, even Waldo, most. But for the moment he was almost glad he couldn't control himself" (A284). Either by self-observation or by somatic inference, Arthur has a physiognomic self-image, and attempts—or not—to control public manifestations of that physiognomy (quite counter to the impression evoked in Waldo's section that Arthur's *physis* is neither consciously under, nor consciously out of, control). This somatic self-awareness extends to his inferences that his physical features are differently proportioned, as when he is kissed "on his large face, slobbery with the joy of fulfilment" (A252)—this is not unlike an adult's sudden awareness of gross stature when embraced or kissed by a child. Discoursally, Arthur is conscious of his "unmanageable hands" (A244), "his stumbling", munching and hobbling (A246), his walking "steady enough" (A285). A lyrical passage on the winter walk with Dulcie looks like external non-focalization: "They were the long-legged lovers, confidently offering their faces to receive each other's gentleness as they moved in perfect time, in absolute agreement" (A246). But the lyricism is Arthur's projection of desire, undercut at the close of the scene, with Dulcie "looking so far into the distance, she had already left him" for Europe. The detail "long-legged" derives from Arthur's earlier sighting of "the swamp-hen strutting blue-enamelled through the weeds". Later, during his relationship with Mrs Poulter, "They crossed paddocks, they stalked like turkeys through belts of thinned out scrub". The bird-analogy is not auctorial so much as Arthur's somatically conscious gloss on their manner of walking. It is, too, a qualitative reduction of the earlier lyrical oneness with Dulcie—ungainliness rather than ease, but still Arthur's self-consciousness at work.

The remaining external somatic indices in Arthur's section clearly mediate his own physical perception, even when couched in metaphor.[7] In comparison with Section 3, Waldo's narrative is full of details about the central character's physical appearance which might lead one to conclude that the perspective is that of an outside observer—but which serve chiefly to signify an extreme of figural self-consciousness. The many references to mirror-gazing provide circumstantial motivation for many self-dramatizing "external views". "The sun caught the gold of his spectacles with a brilliance which turned the skin beneath the eyes to washed-out violet" (W29)—this is actually bivocal, as the reference to violet skin establishes ironically Waldo's momentary identity with Saporta, the person he is thinking about (cf the "beige flannel circles" round the eyes of the Saportas' son, eyes which Waldo attributes to Dulcie rather than to "ox-eyed" Leonard, W65/117). Waldo's inward picturing of the appearance of his eyes and spectacles here and later (W56) is substantiated by details of the mirror-scene on his thirtieth birthday (W120), as are such projections as his consciousness, when fleeing down Pitt Street, of "sticking out his jaw, a pronounced one in its delicate way" (W67; cf "his chin less pronounced" through his spectacles, W120), of "his usually nondescript hair", on the morning of his father's death, glittering "with

---

[7] "He blathered, jerking his head against the gag" (A219); cf his consciousness of himself, while dancing, as a shabby scarecrow, his fingers "bundles of thawed flesh" (A289).

sunlight and the brilliantine" (W70). Even such a romanticized, clichéd statement as "during his boyhood strangers were moved by the streaks of water in his innocently plastered, boy's hair" (W74) connects with the brilliantine he resorts to in later years. The projection of an unreal image of his recollected boyhood self onto a recollected scene from adulthood both presupposes Waldo's intimate visual acquaintance with himself in the mirrors of childhood (his "innocence" belied by his openly admitted precocity) and anticipates the image of the child within the mirror of his thirtieth birthday (W73). Waldo's intense somatic awareness can find expression, too, in the enclosing, symbolic paraphernalia of clothing (W25/30/63).

These are self-elevating, self-protective, pathetic, heroic or aggressive images. Nobody is externally observing (except, circumstantially, his brother) when, before Waldo carefully enunciates his unwillingness to talk about the Saportas, it is stated that he "averted his face from something" (W28). It is Waldo who knows what that "something" is: he won't tell, but will show, through a deliberately imagined histrionic gesture of distaste, what he is reacting against—all for the benefit of Arthur. Standing in the playground while Arthur is demonstrating his mathematical prowess, "Waldo kicked the ground as though he were a little brother waiting" (W42). If the gesture is involuntary, it is recognized by the self-conscious Waldo for what it is. That "he failed for the moment to notice the smell of mucus in his nostrils" (W56) is only an indication that Waldo himself realizes retrospectively the absence of an habitual self-conscious "reflex". When Johnny Haynes is pricking at Waldo's neck with his penknife, what might appear to be an externally balanced, observed fact is actually a projected *irrealis*: "his gooseflesh must have been visible as the blood shot out in little jets of scarlet fountains" (W44). Even highly negative external descriptions of Waldo are to be read as his own self-flagellating mental voicings of the perceptions he imagines outside observers would entertain: "But Waldo was born with that small head, with what you might have called that withered-looking face, if you had been inclined to unkindness. The heads of father and son were both, in fact, carved in rather minute detail" (W33). Contextually, there is a struggle of rationalization going on in Waldo's mind: he hastens to claim that his father is affectionate towards him, then implies that Mr Brown might have been put off by his son's inherited appearance—when in fact Waldo is silently cursing his father for that inheritance. What Waldo sees of himself in the mirror of his mind he immediately withdraws from: as much as anyone, it is himself he accuses of unkindness. The "that"-deixis is a double voicing: of the imagined perspective of those outside observers who know of (and, worse, would talk about) his withered face, and of Waldo's self-hatred, which is deflected into an attempt at objectivizing here, and is overlaid by self-aggrandisement elsewhere.

In cases of plural reference to the twins in Section 2, it can be assumed that the "outside perspective" is Waldo's—his awareness of his brother and himself as an entity. This means, of course, that any comments on inward state arise out of Waldo's assumed authority—sometimes with interesting results. There is, however, always a kind of double-voicing whenever the appellation "the Brothers

Brown" occurs: although even Bill Poulter can employ this referential formula quite unknowingly, it is an ironic thematic voicing of the identity-relationship established towards the end of Sections 2 and 3 in the library incident: the Brothers Brown/Brothers Karamazov analogy. "The Brothers Brown had almost emerged from the subfusc vegetation ... into the world in which people lived" (W30). As already indicated, this middle-class "world" is Waldo's model, not the implied author's, and it is characteristic of Waldo to hoard, treasure and lovingly apply such dusty latinisms as "subfusc" (the word occurs later with reference to himself, W183).[8] "The wind might have cut the skins of the Brothers Brown if they had not been protected by their thoughts" (W23); Waldo is assuming that Arthur, too, is "protected", but only because he hopes this is so—his words immediately following are concerned with Arthur's physical welfare, while his thoughts and desires are not at all protective of his brother. "Nobody seeing the Browns now connected them except in theory with the past" (W60); this is Waldo's inference or assumption, not an external observer's. Similar arrogations of perspective are involved elsewhere.[9]

One long passage with interspersed direct speech (W54–55), set in the actional present, looks like "privileged" narration about the two brothers, except that some of the claims made look a little askew if applied retrospectively to Arthur. The particular kind of detailed analytical familiarity with the tangibles of the neighbourhood fits Waldo's collative mind-set, but not Arthur's. Further along, the "two old men" are described as "each examining himself, separately, secretly" in the plate-glass windows of Woolworths. It could be argued that this examination is an open secret to the men themselves, who are each conscious of what the other is doing. "On the whole each was pleased, for reflexions are translatable symbols of the past, Chinese to the mind which happens to be unfamiliar with them". The aphoristic obliqueness here is characteristic of Waldo. The summary evaluation does not fit in with what we learn later about Arthur, whose involuntary reaction to seeing his reflection in Woolworths' window on an earlier occasion (A290) is one of shame at being old, rather than one of pleasure. It is Waldo who uses mirrors to retreat into the past. Waldo continues to impute to Arthur his own willed consciousness, after mentally "objectifying" how they must appear to the public gaze in their senescence: "Some of those who noticed the old blokes might have seen them as frail or putrid, but the Brothers Brown were not entirely unconscious of their own stubbornness of spirit". There follows a verbal evasion of the hard facts of

---

[8] Argyle (1967:65) typically takes the word as being one of White's own "favoured oddities" and a sign of linguistic "laxness" attributable to the author.

[9] "The Brown boys never stopped, it seemed, marching up the hill to school" (W41), or "the Brown brothers were alone as usual, at last" (W45). "Yet as soon as Mrs Musto had dismissed them, he and Dulcie began to behave mechanically .... the acquaintanceship was so obviously closed" (W95–96)—Waldo assumes that Dulcie will be feeling as self-conscious as he is. "If Waldo did not criticize further, it was because they did forget" (W206). This is not an omniscient commentary on the brothers' separate minds (with a "Whitean" use of the concessive do–proform): the emphatic "They both forgot" that follows indicates Waldo's need to speak for the two of them.

Arthur's early-morning heart-tremor, which is Waldo's evasion: "Arthur ... whose mechanism had in some way threatened his continuity earlier that morning". This distanced diction contrasts with the simple syntax used to delineate Arthur's behaviour at Woolworths (earlier on this page). There is no way of telling whether the latter is non-focalized narration of events which Waldo himself has not witnessed (we learn later that Arthur used to spend mornings on his own while Waldo did his Secret Writing), or whether it is figural transcription of what Arthur has told Waldo about his adventures at Woolworths.

After the oblique reference to the heart-tremor, the passage closes with a focus on Waldo: "The drier, more cautious Waldo walked taking greater care in spite of the strength of his moral convictions". The first sentence of the next paragraph—"Everybody to their own"—seems to indicate a shift back to Waldo's thoughts, via "moral convictions", from some more general perspective. That Waldo's perceiving mind is actively involved now can be seen by the introduction of the personal pronoun ("Over his shoulder") in the fourth sentence of a paragraph which has no formal name-antecedent apart from "Waldo" in the previous paragraph. But it is possible by hindsight to see this, too, from the extent to which Waldo is obsessively conscious of his own somatic "dryness" (for him a positive quality) and of his need for caution and control. The sentence also has a subtext of secret desire: he takes "greater care" than Arthur (who is by nature seemingly carefree) and depends on the "less care" taken by his brother to kill him off. "Moral convictions" get hastily smuggled in at the end in order that Waldo can paste over his immoral conviction in willing Arthur's death. It is, of course, possible to take this last sentence as bivocally dissonant—indeed, as heavily ironical—psychonarration, pricking Waldo's pretensions.

There is no more radical a double-voicing in the whole narrative than two sentences which I have held over for discussion until now:

Arthur ... was still able to enjoy the gusty light of boyhood in the main street of Sarsaparilla, his lips half open to release an expression he had not yet succeeded in perfecting. His body might topple, but only his body. (W55)

This takes up from "stubbornness of spirit" and from an earlier reference: "Arthur, puffing, threatened to topple, but saved himself on Waldo's oilskin" (W28). With hindsight awareness of Waldo's secret desire that his brother should drop dead, it is easy to see the double judgement involved here: unctuous praise of Arthur's indomitability concealing disappointment that he has not "toppled". The modality of the statement might be Waldo's—but the voicing of it is part of the secret writing of the whole narrative. In Section 3, after Arthur has been disappointed by his father's inadequate tautological gloss on the word "totality", he leaves the room:

His lips were half-open to release an interpretation he had not yet succeeded in perfecting. His body might topple, but only his body. [A240]

In this later passage, located, as it were, in the "gusty light of boyhood", Arthur's mental equilibrium comes from feeling the mandala-marble in his pocket in "his frenzy of discovery". It seems no accident that the first reference to

Arthur's "solid mandala" should come before the uncanny verbal duplication at W55. Although it is possible to imagine Arthur being somatically conscious of his half-open lips (he is always conscious of the physical difficulty of articulating thought in words), it can only be an auctorial consciousness that is responsible for this parallel voicing in two discrete contexts.

On the few other occasions in Section 2 when "outside views" are conveyed, it is either made clear that Waldo's self-consciousness creates a narrative transcript of what he assumes others must think of the twins ("Waldo knew it all by heart from listening", W75) or it can be inferred that a passage of free indirect thought is his mental construct (for example, the thoughts of the "mother with kiddy", W114, where there is a metatextual joke: Waldo is "imitating" the thought of a woman who has overheard Arthur talking about the Allwrights: "Arthur would assume the voices of those who were addressing him"). Sometimes the narration is so fiercely deictic that one gets a distinct sense of the preternaturally sensitive Waldo observing himself through the eyes of other characters—as in the second of these two sequent sentences: "That the chauffeur did run Mrs Musto Waldo discovered by witnessing. Mrs Musto had just dismissed that boy—the brighter of the two Browns—who had come with a note of thanks from his mother" (W86).

There is perhaps a hermeneutic hitch in the determining of mood and voice, by virtue of the fact that borderline instances can only be resolved through an appeal to data present elsewhere in the text, hence similarly mediated. An iterative excursus in Waldo's section dealing with the behaviour and character of Mrs Musto (W84–86) offers a good example. None of the information present would be inaccessible to Waldo; indeed, the limitations of knowledge are specified:

Nobody remembered her husband, or knew whether she had ordered him out of existence so that she might enjoy a breezy widowhood. On the other hand Mrs Musto was bullied by her maids and the chauffeur Stubbens who wouldn't honk. [W85]

It is Mrs Musto who secures Waldo the library job, upon which she "retires".

She did not venture very far into other people's lives, because she had been bitten once, no, twice, in the course of human relations, and did not want to risk her hand again. [W114]

This latter passage is opaque compared with the former—conspicuously so, because although it cannot be clear from Waldo's narration what the revitalized dead metaphor of the bitten hand refers to, the datum is voiced clearly ("once, no, twice"). The earlier information about Mrs Musto's husband is syntactically ambiguous, and we are discouraged from connecting it with being "bitten". We might ask ourselves what advantage could accrue to an "auctorial" narrator who conveys an opacity so clearly; if we take the information to be Waldo's, we must assume that it is advantageous to him to have his thoughts mediated so allusively. In Arthur's section, finally, we discover that Mrs Musto's husband Ralph ran out on her while they were in Europe (ie, no initiative came from his wife), and that it was certainly no intention of hers to "enjoy a breezy widowhood" (Ralph is, indeed, probably alive and well in the States).

The "Gothick" touch in the public speculation is, of course, hyperbolic; and it is not indicated that Waldo thinks she has killed her husband off. It is simply that Waldo's narrative affords us no insight into the ways in which Mrs Musto has been "bitten", while Arthur's narrative makes it clear how she has been twice-bitten: first by her husband, then by the chauffeur Stubbens. The ostensible focus is on how Stubbens pushes Mrs Musto around (W86). The most Waldo notices is that she seems not surprised to see Stubbens without his cap, and that she does not let him touch her when he helps her on with her cardigan. Any implication that Waldo senses a "relation" between the two is overlaid by the Waldovian wit of the prose itself, and by Waldo's desire to see class-demarcations confirmed in gesture: "she shrugged herself into the sleeves, without letting him touch her though. Mrs Musto would come out shrugging off the advice ... of her servants". Details of what Waldo perceives are foregrounded through separate paragraphing here, but no conclusions are drawn. It is left to Arthur to catch Mrs Musto upstairs in her underwear, weeping over a row she has had with Stubbens, who seems not only to be her lover but, to her own despairing chagrin, even looks like her ex-husband. We can only conclude that Arthur has told Waldo, after the scene recounted at W86, about Mrs Musto's failed relationships—close enough in time to Waldo's final terms at school to enable him to make an ad-hoc correction to his previous state of knowledge about his patroness ("once, no, twice").

Other passages, which seem to reveal through analytical commentary the dominant presence of a non-figural narrative focus, can similarly be resolved as figural if evidence is drawn from statements made elsewhere. During the period following the Second World War, Waldo is much concerned to keep his colleagues at the library away from his private life back home in Sarsaparilla:

(1) ... Parslow had to be choked off. (2) Because Mr Brown of the intellectual breathers in the Botanic Gardens must never be confused with the subfusc, almost abstract figure, living on top of a clogged grease-trap and the moment of creative explosion, under the arches of yellow grass, down Terminus Road. (3) Waldo Brown, in whom these two phenomena met on slightly uneasy terms, would have suffered too great a shock on looking out *from behind his barricade of words and perceptions,* to discover some familiar stranger approaching his less approachable self—as happened once, but later.

(4) So Waldo, who was in frequent demand, continued to refuse, on principle, by formula. [W183] [My emphases.]

While the quasi-modal of necessity in sentence (1) implies no particular source of subjective authority, the necessity cannot be contextually external to Waldo himself; in (2) the modality is radicalized—"must" cannot be externally performative, and is actually a chief marker of the presence of "internal monologue" (see Coates 1983:40/54–57). Characteristically skilful use is made of the naming-gradient to indicate Waldo's mental image of his various selves: "Mr Brown" for the public literary persona; a descriptive (indeed, "abstract") label for the private persona Waldo is ashamed of and wishes to withhold from public scrutiny; "Waldo Brown" for the hypothetical norm or shell of reality housing these two fictions; and "Waldo" for the acting self. The clogged, statically additive syntax of (2) registers the degree of distaste and resistance with which

Waldo, wearing his public mask, encounters his entrapped private self. The sylleptic formula linking grease-trap and "creative explosion" is a double-voicing: Waldo's own dull despair comes through in the juxtaposition of decay and ever-inceptive creativity, but White is also there to allow the grim pathos to tip over into bathos in the connotation of drainage, lavatory and diarrhoea (already present in the scene at Dulcie's house, W110). Sentence (3) is itself "slightly uneasy" in its ponderous abstraction ("phenomena" neatly signals the inner man's awareness of the essential factitiousness of these personae), its diffident measuring of degree ("too great"), its evasive oxymoron and wordplay.

Only a reader who has failed to register the pervasive mental rhetoric that characterizes Waldo's sinuous consciousness will take this passage as a mocking, ironical drubbing of Waldo by an expressively autonomous, auctorial narrator. Readers do tend, however, to form general impressions of mood and voice on the basis of single revealing details of the verbal surface. If the modal verb of (2) signals free indirect thought, does not the italicized phrase in (3) point to auctorial analysis? Can it really be that Waldo is aware of the protective use to which he puts "words and perceptions"? First, it must be remembered that the "central" self who hides behind this barricade cannot but be aware of his own bifurcation: otherwise there would be no need for him to keep his two worlds apart. With his library colleagues, he trades in "words and perceptions" about literature, thereby creating the desire in Parslow to see the personal (and presumably contiguous) side of Waldo's "intellectual" self. At home, Waldo puts up, not the same barricade, but another, collecting "words and perceptions" to make literature, in an attempt to redeem what he knows is the failure of his real public self. His role as Secret Writer is underlined, in passages of consonant psychonarration, by metaphors of walls and barricades (W81/195), while his self-protectiveness in general is similarly conveyed (whether physical, W68; social, in emulation of his mother's voice, W72; or by metonymic extension through the house or the idealized suburban villas, W118/190).

Both the localization of action in time (temporal indices) and the perspective from which action is represented indicate that the narrative of *The Solid Mandala* is fully subjectivized. Contrary to prevailing expectations, White does not ripple the pool of figural modes of narration by appearing in the guise of an omniscient narrator to set the record straight. What look like exceptions prove on closer examination to fit the rule, are instances of "ingeminate" consciousness, or are residual traces of the "secret writing" of an echoic narrator who is "ghosting" for the principal characters.

I have already suggested that it is of considerable value for the study of White's narrative discourse and style to be able to draw on at least two narratives (a bit like having a test group and a control or placebo group in a pharmaceutical experiment). The present discussion, however, should have shown that the analysis of style and discourse does not have to depend on the twice-told, and that these two aspects are themselves crucially interanimative. If the discussion so far has had its incidental share of technicality, the chapters that follow are necessarily dependent on technical categories. They examine style-features which are dominant in *The Solid Mandala* and which can generally be explained in terms of this novel's narrational requirements. But these style-features have relevance for White's other prose fiction as well, irrespective of the specific nature of *The Solid Mandala*.

6

NARRATION AND CHARACTER

I   Introduction

The topic last dealt with—that of who does the narrating—shall continue to occupy centre-stage. So far, the discussion has involved probing the narrative for largely circumstantial evidence of subjectivized narration—for example, spatial aspects of point of view (somatic indices, etc.); the character-specific disposition of what might otherwise appear to be "neutral" temporal markers; patterns of causal manipulation in the overall structure of the plot which can best be accounted for in terms of the operation of figural consciousness.

From now on, the identification of narrational authority will involve combing quite specific (lexical and grammatical) areas of verbal texture. These discoursal features can be accounted for in terms of current narrative theory, or require adjustment of current theory. The particular sub-topics considered in the present chapter are, in terms of White's narrative practice, relatively inconspicuous (ie, they have either been felt to be "normal", acceptable aspects of White's style or have not even been registered as style-features at all). Subsequent chapters deal with the more conspicuous features of the verbal texture of *The Solid Mandala*; they have either been felt to be "abnormal" and unacceptable aspects of White's style, or they have been pronounced acceptably "deviant". Or (like the "inconspicuous" style-features) they have not been registered as features at all, even though stylistic analysis reveals that they are indispensably and specifically Whitean ingredients.

For the moment, however, I should like to stay with my guiding topic: that of narrative authority. Dorrit Cohn (1978:25) takes Wayne Booth to task for opining that "any sustained inside view ... temporarily turns the character whose mind is shown into a narrator". According to Cohn, an increase in psychological interest means that the *audible* narrator disappears from the fictional world; full figural consciousness takes the "energy" formerly residing in an "expansive" narrator— the narrator *still* narrates. And here, of course, we are back to the twin poles of prominent or distanced narrator and effaced or fused narrator: Stanzel's *auktorial* and *personal* (1979/82); Cohn's dissonant and consonant psychonarration; telling versus showing; non-focalized versus focalized narration. In free indirect discourse or narrated monologue,

as in figural narration generally, the continued employment of third-person references indicates, no matter how unobtrusively, the continued presence of a narrator. And it is his *identification*—but not his *identity*—with the character's mentality that is supremely enhanced by this technique. [Cohn 1978:112]

Ann Banfield (1982:65–67 and elsewhere) has, by contrast, argued for a "narrator-less" text: the nature of free indirect discourse being essentially the representation of figural consciousness, verbal or preverbal, and such signals as shifted tense and third person functioning merely as indications of the "source of the expressive point of view". Cohn, in response to earlier versions of Banfield's thesis, objects that the "narrator-less" text idea *cannot* account for "the continuity of the voice that refers to the protagonist in the same third-person form in passages of authorial commentary and of narrated monologue" (Cohn 1978:294–95.n30; see also Genette 1988:99–101)—which is the situation one believes one has encountered in *The Solid Mandala,* of course. Banfield's more recent work tackles the counter-claims of Cohn and others in great depth if from a narrow platform; the battle is still being fought, and will doubtless prove to be a war of attrition if not a *jihad,* both sets of mercenaries being well-armoured and provided with a limitless supply of *matériel.* My chief concern is with isolating those features of narrative discourse which have been employed by White and pushed here, pulled there, until they have taken on shapes of his own fashioning. In order not to over-dramatize the narrational originality of White, I also offer textual evidence to confirm the fact that he is quite capable of handling expertly those features of narrative discourse (especially narrated monologue) which are recognizably orthodox. As narrative analysis is inescapably quantitative in certain crucial respects, the burden of proof rests on my ordering of textural (*sic*) detail—here, however, I have had to select brief, quotable examples for discussion, referring the reader to page-numbers in the novel for the remaining unquoted instances. This has the possible disadvantage of rubbing the reader's nose in the text, but the decided advantage to me of not having to reproduce wellnigh the whole novel in decontextualized fragments.

Among the pitfalls of narrative taxonomies that assign *general* features to types of discourse is the nature of figural consciousness itself. Cohn, in setting up a dissonance-to-consonance scale for psychonarration, assigns characteristics which the sophistically inclined could equally well claim for the opposite polarity, given the right conditions and the right kind of author. For example, in Cohn's correct analysis of a passage from Thomas Mann's *Death in Venice* (1982:26–31), which is contrasted with Stanzel's typological favourite, Joyce's *Portrait,* the following elements (**1–4**) are claimed exclusively for psychonarration with maximal dissonance between narrator and figural consciousness (ie, Genette's external non-focalization). One might refine (**4**) by including Stanzel's rule-of-thumb for *auktoriales Erzählen:*

(**1**) "gnomic present statements", "ex cathedra statements, unmistakably set apart from the narration proper by their gnomic present tense";
(**2**) "speculative or explanatory commentary";
(**3**) the presence of "reportorial indirection"; "maintenance of subordination of the 'he thought (felt, knew) that' variety";
(**4**) "distancing appellations" (here: "'the aging man'").

(4.1) naming-gradient, with auctorial narration at one end, shading off towards the figural on a descending scale: auctorially sympathetic naming > auctorial periphrasis > characters' names > the personal pronoun. [Stanzel 1982:245]

I have already touched on the question of dissonant psychonarration. The matter of Waldo's psychological disposition has proved a stumbling-block to any easy assumptions that an implied-auctorial narrator is "intruding". The narration in *The Solid Mandala* can be checked off against the elements listed above. (1) Gnomic statements are exclusively the domain of figural consciousness (I discuss this aspect in detail below). (2) Speculative commentary in the novel is restricted to diegesis which (whether it looks like psychonarration after a gnomic sentence, W177; or like psychonarration with a "supposing"-sentence in its midst, A253) conveys the characters' self-analysis. (3) If it is "reported" that Arthur "saw that grief had destroyed her face" (A252) or that Waldo "knew that he was poor, pimply, stupid, and if not ragged, definitely frayed" (W87), we have got to evaluate the truth-content of the statements in accordance with our familiarity with the characters' capacity for percipience, and not take them as they are merely because they are "reports" of cognitive acts whose reliability is vouched for by a dissonant psychonarrator. (4) I take it that Cohn would not mean, by "distancing appellations", such terms as "a real dill" (A225) in an ostensibly "reportorial" context (it is clearly Arthur who "reports" the appellation to himself); but presumably the following would count, when Waldo goes outside to burn his papers: "About four o'clock he went down, Tiresias a thinnish man" (W212). It is, however, Waldo who must be using the appellation of himself, if we compare the citation (as he reads his notes) made a page earlier (W211). (4.1) Finally, I shall be showing later that all the naming in the novel is carefully graded according to the kind and degree of the characters' reflexive awareness at any given narrational moment, and is, on many occasions, a stronger index of figural consciousness than even the personal pronoun.

It is pointed out by Cohn (1978:28) that conceptual, analytical and abstract vocabulary can be used to describe the inner world of a character, thus removing the presentation of the inner life from the domain of the psychical experience itself: this does not occur in *The Solid Mandala* except in the form of Waldo's own protective self-distancings. Dissonant narrators, "without necessarily implying omniscience", can present the inner life from a pseudo-distance: there may be a "pose of speculative puzzlement". Seymour Chatman draws attention to the high proportion of expletive-*it* sentences involving clauses with "as if/though" in late Henry James:

It is the means by which the character's imagination is opened to speculation, but without suggestions of idle fantasizing .... It is a safe instrument, since no one—neither Strether [in *The Ambassadors*] nor his interpreter—is necessarily committed to it as the exact state of things .... In fact, the narrator is not even asserting that these were Strether's very words, that it was Strether who was metaphorizing; there is a delicate but clear distance suggested, and the authority for the simile is kept vague. That was how the situation "felt" to the *narrator*, whether or not the character would have expressed it in those terms. [Chatman 1972:73–75]

Booth (1961:184, confirmed by Chatman 1972:73–74.*n* 1) has indicated how elliptical formulae for receptive cognition with such verbs and structures as *seem*, *appear*, *be as if*, and many adverbial adjuncts of indeterminacy have conventionally been regarded as subterfuges by "objective" novelists such as Faulkner to conceal auctorial commentary behind pseudo-conjecture. Booth stresses the moral dimension, when in fact it is surely a matter of the psychological perception of surface appearances. In any case, the novel by Faulkner that is cited (*Light in August*) is unequivocally non-figural in its narration, so that the status of such comparative clauses really is part of the large and oft-discussed question of Faulkner's own epistemological philosophy as an artist. With James, this may also be the case—but *The Ambassadors* is a different matter as regards narration. However we ultimately place the "narrator" along the dissonance-consonance scale, the clausal structures that occur in James are there to convey the characters' mode of perception and apperception. What do we find when we turn to White?

II   Indices to figural (ap)perception

'SEEMING' INDICES

When we turn to *The Solid Mandala,* we find a lower incidence of *as if/though* sentences than in James or Faulkner; they also differ markedly in syntactic emplacement, as the distancing cleft-sentence construction "It was" (the hallmark of James's style in respect of comparisons) occurs very seldom: only some 12% of the total, in fact.[1] (Compare Table 4 on the next page.) Statements setting up the psychological atmosphere usually immediately precede the *it*–sentence, whose form is to a certain extent pragmatically determined: ie, no coupling of "as though" to the preceding is possible. The *irrealis* of the propositions after "it was" is marked in the instances listed in fn. 1: flaming angels, indecent proposals, being "cast off", games of billiards—none is left unexploited in terms of the broader context, all arise out of a figural consciousness (Waldo's) which is inclined to weld together mental extremism and emotional "control". "As though" constructions largely represent Waldo evaluating the gestures or facial expression of those he comes into contact with (eg, W38/134/136/162/135). There is often the implication—or the reader makes the inference—that Waldo's sensibility is overreacting to what he perceives (eg, "sucked her teeth, as though to defend", W102; also W151). Many occurrences indicate that Waldo has registered—without admitting it—some particular, inaccessible quantum in behaviour which happens to be a significant missed apperception in terms of what we discover from the rest of the narrative (eg, "asked as though he had met her before", W109; also W40/108/152/85). Willed assumption and presumption play a considerable role, concealed as these are by the disinvolvement conveyed by "as though". Waldo's assumption about his father's topic of thought is willed: "While Dad continued sitting, as though considering the problem Arthur was

---

[1] "It was as though he ... had been cast off", W48; also W103/45/144/cf B19/21, and—if we include verbs of inert perception and cognition—"It appeared as though she had ...", A235; also A273/W134/138.

becoming" (W47)—and "as though" is immediately re-used to focus exclamatorily on Waldo's self-pity: "As though Arthur was only Dad's problem". The same applies to his consideration of his mother's changed behaviour (W161), and to his arrogant (or blind) assumption that Arthur is "unable to think" or to give something thought (W57 and W113, both belied by ensuing narrative action). He *desires* Mrs Musto's attitude to be conspiratorial ("as though to conspire with him", W95), is ego-ridden enough to *see* Dulcie's piano-playing as confirmation of his daydreams (W101). "As though" can *blur* the fact that Waldo is indeed blaming his father (W94), or a pseudo-distancing can conceal his willed negativity (W66).

Table 4: Indices to figural perception and inference[2]

	WALDO		ARTHUR
	1	2	
INDICATIVE VERBS			
S *seemed*	6	22	11
S *appeared/looked/sounded*	3	13	3
it *seemed*	2	17	9
it *appeared/looked/sounded* (*as if/though*) 1	5		2
	69 (.363)		25 (.294)
MODAL STATEMENTS			
S *must have*	2	2	5
S *might* (*have*)	5	8	6
S *could* (*have*)	1	10	2
	28 (.147)		13 (.152)
ADVERBIAL CLAUSES			
as though	2	27	7
as if	–	5	1
	34 (.147)		8 (.094)
DISCOURSE MARKERS			
perhaps	1	5	3
apparently	–	7	1
evidently	–	1	1
probably	1	2	1
no doubt	–	4	–
obviously	1	8	1
doubt-markers:	20 (.105)		5 (.058)
certainty-markers:	10 (.052)		2 (.023)

When Waldo and his father are "struggling, as if in the one body" (W34), the somatic comparison reflects the dual awareness of temporary unity and the self-conscious desire for separateness. A very few comparisons are thought-associative and symbolic, as when Arthur is linked quite gratuitously with the dogs (W62), or when the burning of the book is subliminally connected with the burning of a dismembered penis (W199; this example is not just psychologically significant, of course, but also feeds proleptically into the narrative action). Some mental assumptions can only be shown to be false by careful attention to

---

[2] 1 = actional-present narrative; 2 = second narrative; decimal figures for each category = ratio of occurrence.

situational placement and expectable character-behaviour, as when it is evident
("She paused as though the language she was using might sound too daring",
W101) that Waldo's rigid attitude towards what he takes as Dulcie's
awkwardness is an effective screen against perception of the fact that it is his own
cramped and watchful silence that has made her awkwardly self-conscious.

One of the earliest "as though" clauses looks just like a sovereign auctorial
irony: "Lady callers had inquired about Waldo's Writing as though it had been an
illness" (W29); but we encounter a recontextualizing of it later in the second
narrative, with a clear, idiomatic tonal signal ("or something") expressing
Waldo's exasperation and irritation: "She ... would put on a kind of milky smile,
and walk softly, as though he were sick or something" (W82). This notion occurs
at least twice later on, both times analogically with bodily processes that are
"sick" and linked with "writing" (W93/110). There is nothing casual about
White's exploitation of this level of "seeming" discourse. By comparison with
Waldo's discourse, for instance, only once in Arthur's section does an "as
though" construction (supported by "it seemed") convey a mental assumption
based on generalities—and the result is a débâcle (A273). All of Arthur's other
"as though" sentences convey the reluctance with which he registers insufficiency
and negativity in the words and gestures of others (A235/239/226/227
(twice)/235/252/258/292/243).

It is normal to expect predications on "seemed" to convey judgements derived
from subjective impressions rather than from objective indications. Inert
perception and cognition are involved, without the mental percept ever attaining
the status of fact. Almost all "seem" statements in *The Solid Mandala* convey
figural consciousness.[3] They are not traceable back to an ironically speculative
auctorial voice speaking for the characters.[4] It is extremely seldom the case that

---

[3] Including Section 1 (B20 twice, B13: "'Oh, the crow,' her friend murmured, seeming
uneasy at the idea"; B18: "or that was how life seemed to have arranged it"). There is only
one passage where dissonant narration does make an incursion with an ironic conjecture: "Mrs
Poulter was a pigeon-coloured woman, whose swelling forms, of a softish stuff, seemed to
invite the experimental pin. Often got it, too. Mrs Poulter was sometimes moved to smile at
strangers, until they started frowning back" (B17). This passage comes just after Mrs Dun has
turned her attention away from her, and just before a recollective sequence focussing on Mrs
Poulter as a defensive victim of a victim (her husband, accusing her of being too soft). An
implicit connection is made between the name "Poulter" and birds/pigeons, and the idea of
"swelling" has been anticipated in "her plump glove" (B12). De-animation is effected by a
syncretizing of bird's down and clothing material, and the "experimental pin" is a vehicular
bivalency (the dressmaker's; or the taxidermist's). The sentence "Often got it, too" is not
narrator-idiolect but a representation (echoing Mrs Dun's terse remark about daylight
murderers: "'Often do, too'", B14) of the demotic of those "strangers" who make Mrs Poulter
their victim. This semic or characterological sketch is important for the thematic development
of the novel; although not consonant in expression with the character's self-awareness, it is not
totally external to the potential actants within the scene.

[4] Wolfe (1983:26) not only finds the dead hand of the author in "it seemed" constructions;
he also thinks the prose could do without them: "Linking verbs also subdivide ideas and
images, impairing coherence: 'It streamed out of the holes of the anonymous woman's eyes. It
was, it seemed, the pure abstraction of gentle grief.' *[Riders in the Chariot,* Viking, p.

Arthur gets things right when the predication involves the correctness of a subjective inference. He is right about his marble and, essentially, about his mother (A228/221). "Seemed" can imply Arthur's reluctant awareness of a personality-type different from his own, where he would have liked to find congeniality (A235); it may, in conjunction with the past progressive, suggest his gradual emergence from engrossed contemplation into perception ("she seemed to be, and was in fact, saying", A244). An active subjective component may be present (A272), and the resulting apperception factitious. Most of Arthur's "seemed" sentences involve misjudging people's gestures, reactions and moods (A218/231/247) or are inferential formulations, relating to his own social status, which are wide of the mark (A225/252). We never get this feeling about Waldo's predications. At the most, an available explanation for a fuzzy situation will be repressed (his failure to perceive that their slowness is the result of senile debility, W60). Sexual excitation may cloud his reception of sense-impressions (W61/62). The "seeming" may be a matter of a split-second before subjectivity is stabilized again (W93/105); inchoate emotion may be compounded with reluctance to take in what is registered (W124/125). His father's inward states are beyond Waldo, even where he could furnish knowledge that might help decode them. Instead, he skirts round truths about his father which might fall back on him, or constructs reductive inferences on what he only half-perceives or *will* only half-perceive ("if Dad seemed unaware ...", W82; W158/159). In taking his colleagues as "seeming" to be interested in him (W182), Waldo is conveying self-doubt, and the will nevertheless to be "wanted". Most "seem"-sentences have a connection with Arthur. Incomprehension of Arthur's physical attitude or presuppositions about his mind are hastily erased by reductive inferences (W58/200). Observations which "seem" to turn on Arthur's gestures and/or existential situation (W25/57) are actually muffled reflections on Waldo's own contrastive condition. Resentment of Arthur accounts for various tonalities in the "seem" statements: at the strongest, paranoiac overstatement ("the whole purpose of the dogs ... seemed to be to remind ...", W187).[5]

307/Penguin, p. 288] would stand more firmly as a single sentence, with a comma replacing the period after 'eyes' and the next four words omitted". But the paragraph context of this quotation provides a reason for the "it seemed" marker of figural awareness. The sight of Ruth Godbold weeping in public for the death of her husband is not only a contravention of Australian stoicism for the onlookers, but also a source of *Schadenfreude*—which, however, does not have as its object anything comfortably normal: and because the onlookers are in the presence of something extraordinary which has managed to disturb and move them, their desire to retain their "normal" perspective generates a reluctance to accept what they perceive. Hence the qualifying withdrawal from any form of statement which might confirm that what they witness is what they witness.

[5] Others include: the willing of a mental intention, to Waldo's disadvantage, in the expression in Saporta's eyes (W65); reluctant acknowledgement of the precise significance of Dulcie's dress (W65); reluctant surprise ("Mrs Poulter ... usually seemed to find an answer", W61; W141); condescension ("Arthur seemed to enjoy that", W60); a willed imputation of difficulty to Mrs Brown's active involvement with Arthur (W35); or secret pleasure, concealed by the casually distancing "seemed", in his assumption that Arthur may have fallen out of favour with their father (W33).

The distinction between "seem" and "appear" is scrupulously maintained, the latter carrying with it a strong sense of negative judgement—the object or situation perceived being somehow discordant with notional presuppositions about surface phenomena. Waldo does not endorse what "appears" to him ("the ... dogs appeared convinced", W24; W87) and views it negatively ("She appeared overheated", W89; W24), to the extent that a disruption of his ego threatens. The verb may occur when he is emerging from panic (W105), so that the stabilizing function of his intellectual awareness is to some degree again in force. What Waldo does not *want* to be so, only "appears" so ("Mother appeared to ignore them", W72; W111/190/200); what he *does* want to be so, "appears" so, whenever he is conscious of his own actions ("It appeared to convince", W72), approves the actions of others even though they are somehow factitious ("Then Dulcie appeared to be making a great effort", W109; W182), or is struggling against potentially humiliating appearances and needs to rationalize into existence something apparently more favourable (W154). Arthur is not given to registering surface phenomena in these ways. At the most, his two sentences ("But Mrs Mackenzie appeared too delicate to see any point", A220; A238) convey with the greatest delicacy a disparity between the perceived and his own unarticulated preconceptions.

Parenthetical "seeming" clauses are not there simply for stylistic variation, but provide a further nuance to the level of figural awareness. Where "it seemed" is truly medial in Waldo's discourse, it is designed not just to indicate the registering of a percept, but the way in which emotional reaction plays its part. Because *it*–constructions are impersonal, the way in which they interrupt the flow of a diegetic perception serves to dampen Waldo's full acknowledgement of the impact a perception has actually made on him. Closest to the intellectual end of the scale is the caution with which Waldo accepts Mr Mackenzie ("He was, it seemed, all right", W53). Then comes his potentially superior registering of his parents' impercipience about Arthur—but he cannot be certain that his assumption is correct: "At first, it seemed, they could not ..." (W35). Muted by medial "it seemed" are the unpleasant impact of his father's withdrawal of affection, his hunched posture in the bank, and the awfulness of his physical attitude in death (W49/54/70)—cold consciousness, however, is also stunned consciousness, so that "it seemed" is in every case double-edged. A clear perception of his brother's anxiousness is thrust away at arm's length by a medial clause (W68), as are complicitous guilt-feelings and the persistence of emotion (W61/54). Near-rejection, or grudging acceptance, of the realization that Arthur is unafraid is marked by the undercutting medial "it seemed" (W209). Introducing the train-journey episode with Mr Brown's embarrassing sex-lecture is a psychologically anticipatory sentence which does its best not to get Waldo emotionally involved, though he is: "Dad, though, was not unaware, so it seemed, painfully, of some of the responsibilities he shirked" (W77). Halting syntax, trickling out the sense awkwardly in gobbets, reflects Waldo's discomfiture in recall. The sentence declines iconically towards the end into vagueness.[6]

In one case, obligatory medial distancing suggests a furiously ironical mode of viewing a scene which for Waldo illustrates Dulcie's utter pretence ("trying, it seemed, to disguise", W133). Where Waldo's "it seemed" clauses occur terminally ("almost habitually, it seemed", W105; W109), a general inference is attendant upon the immediate perception of action; the "seem" clause may be syntactically "blocked" into end-position in a futile effort to avoid unpleasant truths (W189). White is not averse to playing with the notion of "seeming"—as in the mirror-gazing scene, when a falling lamp frightens Waldo out of his reverie: "When his heart crashed. So it literally seemed. He was left holding the fragments in front of the mirror" (W192). Clutching the dress, Waldo is clutching his shocked heart. The "seem" clause registers a perception involving confusion about what is happening; hence the grammatical revenge of using "literally" as a logical contradiction. Arthur's medial "it seemed" clauses are, on the whole, more tactful and less coldly distancing than Waldo's, and can even be shaded by concession (A242); the phrase may signal gradual awareness (A215, P307). There is otherwise always a hint of doubt about the objective foundation of his judgement (A250/260), to the point of inverting normal word-order to avoid head-on confrontation ("turned, it seemed resentfully, and went", A263).

DISCOURSE MARKERS

Discourse markers can be grouped formalistically (as indices to free indirect discourse) or pragmatically (as evidence of correspondences between discourse features and character traits in respect of figural consciousness). The first group relates to indices of modality and aspectuality in verbs, and consists of adverbials expressing doubt or certainty and "lexical fillers" expressing "an ongoing internal or external interchange".[7] Although there are no significant quantitative differences in the employment of indicative "seeming" verbs and modal-perceptual statements in Waldo's and Arthur's sections (though the internal distribution, and thus mind-set, may differ), there are differences in the distribution of discourse markers of doubt and certainty, and in a discoursal commitment to adverbial clauses of analogy—in each case by a ratio of roughly 2:1, Waldo as against Arthur. The difference with adverbials has to do with the characters' relative propensity to ratiocinate about psychological circumstance. Waldo tends to get caught up in processes of reflection and ego-reflexivity,

---

[6] Near the start, after a vague concessive "though", "not unaware" is meiotically suppressive and absorbs Mr Brown's reluctance; "*so* it seemed" is more cluttering than it need be, marking time—and distancing Waldo himself from any embarrassing empathetic involvement—but unable to halt the admission that awareness is painful. By contrast, a serene sentence like "Dad, though, was painfully aware of ..." would suggest Waldo's empathetic involvement in his father's emotional plight; hence the hedging, even on the matter of Mr Brown's consciousness being not only pained, but also painfully obvious.

[7] Such adverbials are *certainly, perhaps, maybe, probably*, and *yes, no, well, of course, after all, anyway, so, surely* (McHale 1978:265/269; see also Halliday/Hasan 1976:267–71).

whereas Arthur is much more up and doing. The small assortment of discourse markers in Table 4 above is attached almost exclusively to statements relating to visual perception, not to abstract or abstract-inferential modes of thinking.

The essential point about the disjuncts in Table 4 is the extent to which they entail rationalizations of visual percepts. Even "no doubt" can involve some whistling in the dark—to use it is to cover up the fact that one's judgements are based on inadequate or *doubtful* indications; something of the same attaches to "evidently". Three assumptions that Waldo makes about his father (with "obviously", "no doubt" and "perhaps", W34/33/34) are correct: but they derive implicitly from Waldo's feelings about *himself*. One use of "no doubt" is bitterly ironical, with Waldo pretending to impute intentionality (W113)—similarly at W131 and W65, where Waldo is probably correct about Dulcie's bourgeoisification; the edge given by "evidently" reflects Waldo's superiority about being able to judge Dulcie's general social condition from limited outward manifestations. The sole use of "evidently" in Arthur's discourse occurs in his dark night of the soul (P306), and could easily be mistaken for the commentary of a dissonant narrator; but it is essentially a sign that Arthur's discourse, like his perception, has been tainted by "experience" and is no longer innocent. The attitudinal disjunct carries an ironical touch in contexts where the "evidence" is so overwhelming as to make the very registering of an act of inference heavily superfluous.

The slippery disjunct among these is "apparently", whose assent to states of affairs that are scientifically unverifiable is the sole semantic base. Consequently, a wide range of Waldo's mental attitudes is mediated.[8] The only occurrence of "apparently" in Arthur's section is non-perceptual: a mild protest attached to his acceptance of a social restriction for which he can see no objective justification (A219). The use of "perhaps" in Waldo's discourse, as with "it seemed", involves much rationalistic wriggling.[9] By contrast, Arthur's discourse employs "perhaps" in purely intuitive reactions to aura or ambience (A238/275), and in one case self-protectively imputes emotion to Waldo before being exposed as a rationalization and deflated by the remainder of the sentence (A268): it is difficult for Arthur to practise self-deceit, but child's-play for Waldo.

In Waldo's discourse especially, "probably", "no doubt" and "obviously" have in common with non-perceptual or generalizing disjuncts like "of course" and "certainly" the fact that they frequently signal a kind of self-protective false consciousness asserting itself in the face of contradictory reality. On several occasions, assumptions are willed but patently false, or doubt immediately

---

[8] These cover: disapproving, sceptical surprise (W178/189); non-perceptual, neutral inference after the fact, about something unprovable (W167); concealment of incertitude and incomprehension (W152); the implicit supplementation, by Waldo's awareness of his own state, of insufficient indices to another's inward condition (W112/155).

[9] It can involve projections of his own mood ("Perhaps feeling that ...", W131); rationalization of his own embarrassing actions (W93); tortuous imputations of intention, based entirely on his own antipathy and untrue to the objective evidence ("perhaps so that ...", W131); and mutings of unpleasant truths ("Waldo had perhaps shrieked", W68; W73).

countermands an assumption.[10] One is a desperate assumption of certitude, a heavily concealed hope against hope: "No one probably would have guessed" (W58). An apperception may be willed by Waldo, but may rest entirely on his exercising of imagination on second-hand knowledge ("smelling no doubt of something exotic", W189); or it may be willed, but untrue in the sense in which *he* means the words ("Crankshaw was obviously stunned", W176; W153). A surreptitious gesture between Dulcie and her mother can become totally "obvious" to Waldo solely because of his sense of being excluded (W102). A boy's inference from adult conversation may pretend that it is the tone of what is heard that makes something obvious, whereas Waldo's precocious exercise of will also plays a not inconsiderable role ("It was obviously the only place to live", W51). "And obviously he did not want to tell" (W61)—this is a curiosity, in representing Waldo's thought that his own ostentatiously secretive behaviour must be enough to deter Arthur's questions: a purely volitional, only hypothetically perceptual, use of "obviously".

Of the remaining positivizing adverbials, none can be said to be enlisted honestly in Waldo's discourse. "Physical suffering, certainly, was something Waldo hardly experienced after early childhood. But Dad probably suffered without telling" (W33): here, "certainly" is doubly—duplicitously—concessive: it professes to find its contrastive resolution in the next sentence, which clinches a comparison between two kinds of physical suffering. In fact, the covert tenor is Waldo's noble stoicism in the face of his *spiritual* suffering. Most other uses of "certainly" are vaguely patronizing (W84/85/185) or try to conceal through airy concessiveness some ripple of uncertainty (W175). "Of course" is a jack of all trades in Waldo's lexicon. He can pretend after the fact to have known all along what the path of right action is; he may do so in order to obscure what he fails to do (W113—in the gnomic present), or to hide the hurtful consequences of what he does in fact do (W25, "What he should have answered, of course, was:"—in fact, the *wrong* thing said happens to be closer to the ultimate truth). He may simply be reassuring himself about the validity of his own shaky intellectual assumptions (W183; also "naturally", W127, and "admittedly", W91); he may be mistaken in his assumption—but this is the way he wants things to be ("Of course the men were laughing at Arthur, Waldo knew", W59; W194); or he may kid himself about future certainties in order to repress the hurt of present failures ("Its substance was bound to return, of course", W174). "Of course" can reinforce the strength of his paranoiac convictions ("Of course you could never tell", W95; W118), or of what he regards as his self-evident disadvantagement (W113). He can be bitterly ironical, enviously so (W95/127), or mockingly ("naturally" twice, W74; "really", W54–55). In his daydreams of delirious hedonism, Waldo provides himself with eager confirmation of the well-rehearsed familiarity of his fantasies, each "of course" leading him on from strength to strength (W116).

---

10 "She was embarrassed no doubt" (W64), "Modesty no doubt had imposed restraint" (W153), "Which was probably why he had been disinclined to remember" (W69), "It was obvious that they had both been waiting" (W149—non-perceptual); "He was obviously giving thought to ..." (W31).

Some uses of "of course" are purely psychological or precognitive markers (eg, to his sense of physical security, which enables him to make a pig of himself without Arthur seeing, W206). Waldo must assert in advance the truth of what is "in fact" a subjective distortion (W23/153), or must steel himself to approach unpleasant realities or distortions of reality (W102/33/161/201/212). As with "seemed literally", the text allows itself a little jokiness with the notion of factuality: "Now at least he was free, in fact, if not in fact" (W194), as also with "(un)fortunately" (W209), the last time this frequent emotive marker occurs in Section 2—Waldo is forever experiencing lurches of relief that his self-consciousness has been spared yet another humiliating exposure ("fortunately": W85/106/108/111/139/159; "unfortunately", W118).[11]

It is significant that certain of the attitudinal disjuncts occurring frequently in Waldo's discourse with a weight of duplicity only turn up in Arthur's during the carnivalesque, topsy-turvy limbo after Waldo's death, as though some of Waldo's ironic gall had suddenly begun eating into Arthur's soul ("certainly", P305; "evidently", P306; "fortunately", P305). Arthur's discourse employs the blandest of disjuncts to permit a concessive glimpse of his embarrassment ("in fact", A240/244). There is also no concealment or irony in the occurrences of "naturally": circumstances are regarded serenely as foreordained (A220/239/242/253), whereas the discourse creaks with Waldo's alacritous self-protectiveness (W74 twice, W127). The only duplicity arises in connection with "of course", which is sometimes enlisted to emphasize the necessity of negative experience ("In the morning of course he could barely remember", A260; A240/271), to rationalize away some fearful uncertainty ("Of course it was inconceivable that ...", A260; A244), or to offer reassurance that an act of deception or hurtfulness is pragmatically and logically inevitable ("Of course Waldo could not be told about that", A274; A273/293).

The remaining discourse markers—adjuncts and conjuncts in the main—generally follow the pattern outlined for the attitudinal disjuncts. Some few conjuncts actually do mark the discourse (eg, "as for", W106, P313; and, preeminently, the concessive-resumptive "in any case", W23/58, and "anyway": W38/87/191; A250). Other markers indicate Waldo's need to shrink from full acknowledgement of unpleasant facts, as in the use of "rather" and "not ... quite"

---

11 Wolfe (1983:24) complains about "(un)fortunately" and the doubling of "in fact": "White's indecisiveness rankles the reader. Either Waldo is free or he is trapped; the Jew's wrapping job promotes either good or bad fortune. Had White wanted to define a middle ground, he should have rephrased the sentences, rather than resorting to parentheses or assigning the same word opposite meanings". It should be evident by now that it is, narrationally, not *White's* indecisiveness, nor, as Wolfe suggests, the sign of a "pitted" psyche (neither White's nor Waldo's nor Arthur's). There is no "middle ground"—this is a logical category, not a psychological one. I have intimated that a certain degree of bivocality may be present—a playing with the notion of option-excluding "logical" categories, at the metatextual level. But the central point is the emotive bifurcation, or oscillation between dominant and repressed perceptions and cognitions. This is surely a universal mental phenomenon; so that it is a dereliction of duty to absorb the words of a text as dead or neutralized data without constituting them in terms of one's own deepest experience.

("his rather tinny laughter", W97; W23/31/33/95/134/ 178/183/185; "Arthur's not quite controlled hands", W110; W85/161/176), his need to euphemize the sexual ("slightly more than intellectually excited", W182), or his coy self-congratulation ("the rather fine tenor voice", W26; W119; "quite boyishly", W175; W102). The use of "practically" points up the shrilly hysterical, old-maidish side of Waldo's nature ("her look had been practically indecent", W162; W184 twice, W186), while the compromising downtoner "enough" marks a pretence of casual concession to conceal prickly self-consciousness ("crossed the road naturally enough", W73; W56/97). "Perhaps, also, he was slightly, if only very slightly, stupid" (A250): this demonstrates as well as anything how hesitatingly Arthur approaches the adverse judgement of others. The occasional paraphrastic adjuncts show neatly the difference in the brothers' mental set, via jokey formulae: Waldo's are ponderously schoolmasterish, self-conscious last-ditch attempts to hide the cliché just uttered mentally: "must take the bull by the horns, as it were" (W142); one of Arthur's—unequivocally lent him by White—is a good joke on the double sense of "arrested", the conjunct signalling this: "He was, so to speak, arrested" (A220). Concessive conjuncts like "after all", "still" or "in any case" are almost always used to rationalize doubtful or unpleasant quanta ("for after all it was a good-will offering, not a bludgeon", W186; W153/186/195/208; "Still, there were certain details", W161; W131; "It was, in any case, the angle at which Arthur wore his cap", W23; W58), even in Arthur's case ("It was, after all, her right", P308; A281). Waldo's subsidence into frozen doubt, the *ad hominem* phrase still on his lips, is nowhere more tellingly captured than by the isolated conjunct in the following: "Wasn't most of anybody's? After all" (W195).

There are several emotive maximizing adjuncts which parallel the phenomenon of expressive adjectives with personal reference that are typical of free indirect discourse (eg, "the *wretched* Arthur", W174, or "*old* Feinstein", W106).[12] It is noteworthy that Arthur's discourse is not marked by such hyperbolic adjuncts—sometimes "juvenile" ones, like "horribly"—until the very end, just before the mortal climax, where the same juvenile marker occurs in conjunction with an imputation of "evil" intent normally characteristic of Waldo's paranoid discourse: "Which Waldo exaggerated *quite horribly* and deliberately" (A293). The term "hateful" is applied to Arthur's hair by Waldo (W45), and turns up in Arthur's dark night of the soul with negative reference to his own body (P305).

The largest single classes of locutions indicating mental processes are meiotic or "alternative", and have much in common with concessive discourse markers (including downtoners). A microanalysis of Section 1 reveals, in the diegetic texture, manifold indices to indeterminacy, uncertainty, insufficiency,

---

12 See Banfield 1973:22–23, McHale 1978:269. The adjuncts in question include: *"immensely* conscious" (W154); *"downright* painful/obscene/difficult" (W154/56/76); *"horribly* dry/detached" (W113/124); *"embarrassingly* educated voice" (W32); *"painfully* noticeable" (W38); "so *grotesquely* awful" (W40); *"sickeningly* physical" (W144); *"abominably* unprepared" (W148); *"obscenely* physical" (W151); *"exceedingly* dry" (W154).

inadequacy, negativity (including silence) and unpleasantness. The least number of these can be traceable to a coolly sure-footed but ironically self-distancing narrator; most can be resolved as mental hypotheses tendered by the characters, as their cognitive-emotional uncertainty, and as communicative negativity or inadequacy (as determined by the relationship between the two ladies). There is a good sprinkling of modal, "seem" and "as if/though" structures, and of such meiotic adverbials as have just been examined ("perhaps benefited more", "perhaps doubtful"). The *local* function is to imply unstated true degree and to reflect the characters' hesitancy or self-conscious discretion, whereby occurrences can also be speech-allusive (eg, "sat rather careful"). There is a foretaste, in such locutions as "you couldn't have said", "almost shouted", "if only momentarily", "it could not be denied", "not unpleasantly", of the more elaborate structures of understatement in Sections 2–4 of the novel. It is important to realize that, although the particular constructions in question ("*x*, not to say *y*"; "if not *y*, *x*"; "not exactly [, but]") are predominant in Waldo's section, at least two of the three also occur in Arthur's discourse, and one in Mrs Poulter's. A further meiotic device ("not" + negative adjective) occurs in Waldo's and Mrs Poulter's discourse but not in Arthur's. What conclusions might be drawn from these observations?

If a collocative structure is striking enough to be isolated as overproportionately represented in diegesis, but cannot be regarded as the idiolectal "tic" of one character, we can posit that (a) it is not so unusual after all, and reflects a common stratum of figural consciousness; or (b) it is not figurally oriented at all: ie, must be part of the idiolect of a superior function such as an implied-auctorial narrator; or (c) it reflects White's own mental set. The easiest way of resolving these alternatives is to state that a stylistic choice has been made (automatically involving semantic difference) which is exogenous to the specific mentality of the characters (ie, it does represent one of the ways in which White himself senses his own mental processes as operating), but which is employed narrationally to convey figural consciousness. The features are part of the "mind-style" of the author, but in no way imply the presence in the text of a dissonant narrator. There is complete empathy between the creating consciousness and the created consciousness at the level of the *general* movement of thought. At the level of particular contextualizations, however, the characters are left to their own mental vices and devices.

In the highly revealing "not exactly", for instance, it is clear that the various characters are responsible for different colorations of the same fundamental process of mental hedging and withdrawal. There is nothing in Waldo's discourse to match Arthur's delicacy about *not* expressing strong emotion towards a deceased friend ("he didn't exactly grieve for her", A252). Equally, there is nothing in the discourse of either twin that approaches Mrs Poulter's grammatically cocked-up expression of inquisitive propriety ("She wasn't going to not exactly look, but glance", P301). In Waldo's thoughts, projective malevolence can undercut the meiotic protestation ("did not hate Bill, not exactly, or not yet", W144). There is also a persistent withholding of the other member of the gradation when the rationalization relates specifically to Waldo himself. Both of Mrs Poulter's include both gradations ("not exactly tense, but waiting", P298), and one of Arthur's two ("and not exactly sleep, retire behind ...", A249; the other is extrasententially resolved). But only one of the several in Waldo's section admits both states, the dread that is denied and the "doubts" that are his corrected façade—intellection taking self-protective priority over emotion ("he did not exactly dread, he had doubts about ...", W162). The truth is, that the "positive" substitute is simply not available, no matter how earnestly Waldo tries to scale down his self-exposures or his unpleasant thoughts into something respectable. "'The children,' Waldo did not exactly gasp" (W65)—but he does "gasp". "You couldn't say she was exactly ugly" (W111)—but Dulcie is still "ugly" to Waldo, no matter how strongly she seems transformed in Arthur's presence: Waldo will never allow inner beauty (the kind Arthur apperceives) to take precedence over his subliminal doctrine of outward forms. "It was not that he was cold, exactly" (W152)—Waldo *is* as cold as Wally Pugh says he is (W123), just as his eyes are the coldest, the palest of pale, no matter how hard he tries to euphemize the fact (W31). Arthur, by contrast, is trying to reach for a truth about his own *physis* that yet eludes him; he is not trying to wriggle out of the hot seat. Similarly with the "not to say" and "if not" constructions.

None of these statements needs to be taken as a transcription of fully-articulated thought at some notionally mental-verbal level. It may be that the "pretty-pretty" formula is pushed to the foreground of consciousness, as a twitch of emotion or a mental or perceptual image, while the negative judgements ("vulgar", "uglily", "painful", "idiotic") are the little horned devils in Waldo's mental underworld, popping up to announce the truth—or his truth—from behind his pretence of intellectual expansiveness. At any rate, these devils do appear—or these toads do crawl out from beneath the rock of euphemizing consciousness—to the uniform disadvantage of everyone except Waldo.[13] By comparison, poor old Arthur is a model of transparent guile ("Arthur was fascinated, if not actually frightened", A226), or his self-consoling posture enlists our sympathy ("if not several postcards ... at least the card ...", A246), or his quaint infraction of the rules of gradation leads us to a higher psychological truth ("if not his study, his obsession", A283).[14]

The last feature to be mentioned here—the employment of *or*–clauses to undercut, modify, correct or otherwise obfuscate an initial assumption[15]—has in

[13] Waldo's include: "of physical, not to say vulgar appearance" (W155); "most irregularly, not to say uglily, placed" (W70); "extravagant, not to say idiotic, ideas" (W87); "plain. If not downright ugly" (W89–90); "capricious, if not downright idiotic" (W82); "which made her look, you couldn't say pretty, but healthy" (W150); "especially as a woman, more of a female ..." (W188); others at W70/73/83/87/150.

[14] At one level here, there is the admission that, though he "thinks", he does so unsystematically: he is not studious like his brother. But at the other—in the inversion of the order of intensity—there is a clear implication that one can get by quite well with one's obsessions, passions, emotions or intuitions.

[15] Examples: "to argue, or at least to wonder aloud" (W85); "was saying, or gobbling" (W109); "So Waldo slowed or was slowed down" (W119); "in the light of conquest, or love"

common with the others above (and, for that matter, with the pervasive conditional modality of the novel) the fact that it reveals the fundamentally dual, binary or "switching-mechanism" nature of psychological processes. These processes are mediated stereoscopically—those critics who complain of portentousness in White's fictions would do well to keep this in mind, and check their own cognitive apparatus to make sure that it is not monoptical, imposing on White's narratives the expectation that they deliver some bland, prefabricated, shrink-wrapped, take-it-or-leave-it product of an imagination working at quarter strength or from a universal lexicon of unitary narrative and psychological categories.

'SEEMING' MODALS

There is no clearer indication of the universal sameness of the mental processes mediated in the novel than the fact that modal verbs expressing primarily a character's subjective response to sense-perceptions occur almost equally often in Waldo's and Arthur's sections (cf Table 4 above). These modals constitute a step-down into a deeper realm of figural consciousness than is revealed in the *seem*–formulae or discourse markers of doubt and conviction (all of which are applied with scrupulous attention to their psychological gradability, as I have endeavoured to show). It is easy enough to classify modals in terms of the logical element in their meaning (necessity, permission, possibility). But an individual occurrence of a modal must also be judged in terms of the pragmatic element that adheres (or inheres), and which constitutes the specific shading generated by the "psychological pressures which influence everyday communication between human beings" (Leech 1971:67)—in the case of *The Solid Mandala,* pressures arising *within* figural consciousness and worked out, or off, within that consciousness.

This brings us to the first problem regarding modals of precognition. Nowhere in Leech (1971), Coates (1983), or even such comprehensive dictionaries as the *OED* or *Webster's Third* are there illustrative modal sentences remotely approaching (ie, validating) many of those to be found in this novel (and White's other fiction) that are based on *might (have),* let alone discussions of perfective usage in reported speech and free indirect discourse which could account for their "feel". One explanation could be that Leech really does mean "everyday communication", his discussions and those of Coates being drawn from standard linguistic surveys oriented towards everyday pragmatic—and, frequently, spoken—English. Preverbal thought and mental processes as diegetically mediated in fictional narratives are a different matter. Local contexts tend not to be explicitly helpful, as there is no communicative situation which could truly be called interpersonal. Thus, when it is a matter of conveying

---

(W158); "Then suddenly he noticed, or ... Mrs Poulter had" (W170); "She remained indifferent. Or ignorant" (W189); further: W116/141/153/171/187/188/190/211; "ignored him, or at least half" (A216); "Arthur did not care. Or he did" (A218); "more sympathetic, or inquisitive" (A238); further: A220/223/231/242 /269/270.

modality, only such sentential indicators may occur as would—notionally—suffice for the "narrating" monologist himself. Although it is "normal" for modal sentences (apart from those with *should)* to appear with suppressed conditions (ie, without *if*-clauses to clarify the modal nexus), sometimes this absence is felt as a gap in sense rather than as something we no longer even miss.[16] "Our team might have won the race" or "She might have left her umbrella at the station" require no recuperation of suppressed condition, or further contextualizing, for the sense to be immediately clear, whereas "He called it Scruffy, and might have created what he named" (W179) is of a different order of epistemic hypothetical possibility (Coates 1983:158–60), and the sense is surely not "clear", though it can be "felt" immediately.

The trickiness of the "seeming" modals in the present connection is not primarily that of their resolution into free indirect discourse or consonant psychonarration: I deal with this matter more fully below in the context of back-shifted modals. It is, rather, that they are open to multiple interpretations. Of the three in question, *must (have)* is the least problematical because furthest removed from the zone of non-inferential apperception and uncertainty. In the present tense, it is used of knowledge

arrived at by inference or reasoning rather than by direct experience .... a chain of logical deduction can be postulated .... There is an understandable feeling that knowledge acquired indirectly, by inference, is less certain than knowledge acquired by direct experience. Hence "logical necessity" can easily become weakened to "logical assumption" [Leech 1971:72]

—or even to a mere guess. In discussing epistemic, present-tense *must*, Coates (1983:41–42) speaks only of "an objective periphery meaning 'In the light of what is known, it is necessarily the case that *x*'"—not of guesses. When she comes to perfective *must have,* her only examples express confident inference, although the subjectivity of the proposition may be underlined by "hedges" such as "I suppose/fancy/would guess" (similarly with *might* [*have*]: 151–52). In *The Solid Mandala,* there is no way in which figural consciousness can be properly mediated by the insertion of such hedges, given the hierarchy of separate cognitive levels in the discourse. And given the divergent emphases of Leech and Coates, it is probably just as well that *must have* is as straightforwardly applied as it is in the novel.

For a start, the inferential nature of the modal allows us to assume that it is the characters thinking, without our having to commit ourselves to the absurdity of ever positing a non-figural narrator doing the thinking for them, or instead of them. The non-perceptual instance is represented in unproblematical statements, as is retrospective realization; even reflexive and non-reflexive inferences pertaining to figural *somata* are straightforward.[17] The only sentence that could

---

[16] Cf Leech's examples: "I'd hate to live in a house like that" (= "if I had to"); "I'd be inclined to trade that car in for a new one" (= "if I were you"). [Leech 1971:113]

[17] "Arthur must have felt it" (W31), "He must have been working on his glasses with the shammy" (A255); "The life ... must have been jingling ... all those years" (P305); "and his goose-flesh must have been visible" *(irrealis,* W44), "His flesh ... must have been turning that ... tone of green" (A241), "her throat must have been swelling" (W136).

make the reader at all unsure is: "Waldo went so silent he must have been offended" (A231). Arthur's discourse here persists in having a strong "present" feel about it, a confident immediacy, even after the context confirms whether the perfect infinitive is statal or passive. This is as it should be—the utterance from "he" onwards could equally well be made by a speaker judging from a "present-tense" vantage-point ("Waldo's gone so silent—he must have been/[something must have] offended [him]"). It is thus an advantage in past-tense narration to have this convergence of forms when the centre of focalization is figural.

According to Leech, the past-tense, hypothetical modal auxiliary *might* (*have*) implies "contrary to expectation", thus making "the expression of possibility more tentative and guarded" (Leech 1971:69/92/120–21). These paradigmatic, purely logical nuancings begin to look unhelpful when one inspects some of the *might* (*have*) sentences in *The Solid Mandala*. In the sentence already cited, "He called it Scruffy, and might have created what he named" (W179), it doesn't help to haul the sentence up out of its direct modality via paraphrase ("and it was as though he had/and he seemed to have/and he had, perhaps, ..."). We must grasp the underlying idea—present in the narrative ever since a boyhood afternoon with Mrs Musto (W85; cf W87)—of the Logos made flesh, and on the central thematic notion that the dog regards Arthur as its god, worshipping him when he is present, contemplating "some abstraction of the man" when he is absent (W179). Extreme cognitive tension is implied in the use of this modal to represent Waldo's apperception: (a) the entertainment of a mere intellectual conceit; (b) the judging of this epistemic hypothesis as true to appearances but quite out of court in regard to reality; (c) a reluctant realization that the appearance is far closer to being a reality—far more *possible*—than the other shadings of the modal allow. Figural consciousness is, again, "split-level", dual. At the very start of Waldo's narrative there is the sentence, "But he sat, and might have continued sitting" (W23). Once again, the condition is suppressed. When we try to work out the sense, we reject the hypothetical root sense of the modal ("it would have been possible for him to ...") in view of the fact that the paragraph continues for three lines, describing where Arthur is clearly still sitting: "Arthur sat in their father's chair". Well, it seems Arthur *does* continue sitting, long past the modal statement. The next paragraph begins: "Waldo brought the two coats. He helped Arthur into his". So Arthur must be standing now: we can safely construe the modal as epistemic hypothesis ("If Waldo had not brought his coat and made him stand up, it was possible that Arthur would have remained seated"). But the simple logical inference is beside the point, in a way—psychologically, there are once again two factors operative: (a) Waldo, in retrospective narration, states a fact about an objective possibility; (b) *independent* of Waldo's pragmatically oriented awareness, there is his awareness of how "permanent" his brother's seated posture appears. The moment of figural apperception, with a projection or extrapolation in time, is the central datum here, as mediated by *might have*. The *less* customary sense of the modal is the paramount one as far as consciousness is concerned.

In the sentence, "He had not yet developed his asthma, though might have that morning in the tearing silence of the brown bank" (W54), "might have" sounds close to "could have"—but the modality dos not depend on anything physical in the atmosphere of the bank. It is, rather, something psychological—therefore less "in the tearing silence" than in Waldo's empathetic awareness. The "tearing" is the riffling sound of banknotes being peeled from a roll during counting, in the midst of an oppressive silence that "tears" at Waldo. It is associated in Waldo's mind with the wheezing of his father's asthmatic breathing: but, of course, not at the time of his actual visit to the bank. The analogy is superimposed on the scene in retrospect, the *tertium comparationis* being itself polysemous: the claustrophobic constriction experienced (a) in the bank by Waldo, (b) in the bank by his father (as recoverable via Waldo as inferring witness), (c) by Waldo, in his later life "under grass" in Terminus Road, and (d) by the asthmatic Mr Brown, shortly before and during his retirement. This "might have", then, is peculiarly hypothetical and "fictive". The fact that Mr Brown's shoulders hunch (in the next sentence) correlates with later descriptions of his asthmatically arching "gothic shoulders" (W159; cf W145); so that it is possible to construe the model as an epistemic hypothesis overlaid on an actual sense-impression. In which case, "almost seemed to have developed his asthma even then" is as valid a paraphrase of mental modality as "it would have been possible, given the psychological and physical circumstances of the bank, for Dad to have already shown a proneness to asthmatic attacks". Neither of these need entail an actual attack, merely the aura of one. The fact is, of course, that these possibilities are subsumed under the bizarrely imaginative and purely associative one.

Replacing "might have" with "could have" works quite well with most of the sentences in question.[18] But again, substitution does scant justice to the psychological particularity of the less usual modal, and may create more problems than it solves (eg, introducing a disruptive implication of "would have had the opportunity to do"). "Could have", besides, operates too close to the more resolute, pragmatic end of the scale of judgemental consciousness, and would sound correspondingly mundane and "out there". "Might have" is exquisitely inward: it expands in the direction of the consciousness receiving the percept, whereas "could have" expands in the direction of the percept itself. Anyway: the negation-test precludes full experimental replacement by "could have", which cannot always be used without a change of meaning—in "They might never have known each other" (A288), for instance, or "But she might not have heard" (A261); the latter compels one to imagine someone thinking: "But maybe she didn't hear me". This would represent the second, and secondary, mental operation—the primary one is essentially precognitive, a mere registering of uncertainty about an as yet unformulated disparity or dissonance between what

---

[18] About 33% of all the *might have* sentences are relevant here: "Poor Arthur, Waldo thought, and might have been loving himself" (W42); "Her face might have been mysteriously tattooed" (A263); further: W32/55/58/63/91/97; A240/254, P309-10.

is immediately perceived (that which the sentences do not detail in the way of physical gesture, etc.) and the perceiver's psychological disposition, expectations, and so forth. "Could have", too, brings with it its little disturbances.[19] The following are classically clear instances of inferential modality: "her eyes brimming once more, so it couldn't be with tears" (W93), "And very soon they were approaching what could be the lit house" (W97); but they are not perfective, resembling instead immediate thought. The sentence "He could have been hit over the head" (W47) momentarily suggests "It would have been possible for someone to hit him over the head", which is quite irrelevant; likewise in: "With the fag-end of her intelligence Dulcie could have sensed this" (W156). Even more confusing, on the face of it, is this sentence, with its disorienting time-phrase tacked on at the end: "She could have been sucking a lemon the moment before" (A254).

I think the kind of precision in psychological delineation that White is aiming at has a good deal to do with this shimmer of polyvalency in *might have* and *could have*. The only way for the reader to avoid the potential disaster of taking such modal statements in the wrong ("everyday") way is to accept them as operating at a deeper level of cognitive "sensing" (recipient-oriented) or "seeming" (object-oriented). This is a level that approximates neither to conviction nor to doubt, and nevertheless generates the feeling that one is caught in the midst of an act of perception rather than of some prefabricated, tidied-up simulacrum of it. With White, one is pretty close (this side of Joycean fragmentation of sense-perception) to being inside the mind of a character who is judging before he reflects upon the awareness that he is judging. This would help account for such sentences as "Poor Arthur, Waldo thought, and might have been loving himself" (W42). "Loving himself" would normally be felt negatively as narcissism, if we were to presuppose the presence of a recollecting figural consciousness. But it is actually the experiencing Waldo here, caught in that moment of "genuine" self-love that we can all experience whenever we are overcome by a surge of outward-directed, sentimental pity or sympathy. We can end up *almost* wondering whether our pity or sympathy is not a refraction from our feelings towards ourselves—but as soon as such an inchoate precognition

---

[19] 63% of the total number of *could have* modals are involved here: "She could perhaps be waiting to break out" (W153); "He could have been hit over the head" (W47). The modal is used not for potential ability in the object, so much as to suggest that a phenomenon is almost tangibly imminent: "Arthur could have been about to start the hiccups" (51–52; he doesn't *here*—but shortly); "Mrs Poulter could have been expecting Mrs Brown" (W72; Waldo's vague projected impression is then "confirmed"); "Waldo's throat could have wobbled for some repeated hurt he had to suffer" (W81; it undoubtedly does—but he thrusts the fleeting sensation away into the putative); further: W72 ("She could still have been soothing his withered leg")/95/97/117. There is an earlier instance, attached to direct speech from Mrs Poulter: "she could have been protecting Arthur" (B16). This is not an expression of conditional potential but of "impression to the observer"; it places us halfway between the narrator (whose narratorial externality would make "seem" more appropriate) and Mrs Poulter (the modal is appropriate to a tension of self-consciousness between personal involvement and her doubts about revealing this to Mrs Dun).

takes an articulate form, our sense of sentimental pity or sympathy evaporates or is compromised. *Might have* in this sentence catches Waldo at this uncritical, precognitive moment. In many instances of "might have", one could imagine "clearer", paraphrastic ways of getting at the sense-impression that is being mediated: "He might have done it, if Waldo hadn't shouldered him off" (W80) or "He made to do so/was on the point of doing so, but Waldo ...", for example. But it is precisely the non-analytical, almost iconic fuzziness of the modality that is appropriate here for a fleeting possibility which is essentially conceived in inward, mental terms (also: W85, A237/283, P312 twice).

The aspectual overlay on the modals is precisely applied in accordance with psychological principles. Take this example: "he put out his tongue and licked the air. It might have been barley-sugar" (W57). Arthur's gesture with his tongue must be involuntary—he is not some kind of basilisk actually licking the air. Waldo's associative mentality (picking up on memories of the humbugs Arthur got from the store when younger—if not on the jujubes he still consumes, jujubes not being barley-sugar) takes the gesture after the event, as it were, after the raw perception, and transmutes it into an *irrealis*. The end of the first sentence shows how the gesture seems: ie, willed; the modal sentence is logically consequent upon this immediate perception and refers to an already completed action. In two of the sentences cited and in the following, the tense is the "present"-looking past of free indirect discourse: "Waldo would not listen any more, though Arthur might be tired of telling" (W58); "But in this girl he might be addressing ..." (W93). The progressive aspect is more easily naturalized, since the act of surmising is taking place during a longer dynamic process; but the non-progressive modal makes one hear, again, the unmediated voicing of a "present" tense, even though it is just as logical for states to persist as it is for processes. Another source of interference at W58 is the *though*–clause, which one could be tempted to read in the present as "no matter that Arthur has become tired of talking about it". The clause is actually non-factive, its potentiality unexpended. Waldo, of course, wants to stay in command—after going to the trouble of mentally registering resistance to what his brother is saying (and probably signalling it gesturally as well), he doesn't want him to exercise free will and desist calmly, leaving Waldo with the empty mental rhetoric of his resistance. Waldo is registering only the vaguest inkling that Arthur is getting tired. The precognition is bivalent: Waldo doesn't welcome Arthur's possible change of mood if it is going to deflate his will; but he also desires it, because of the unpleasant subject-matter of Arthur's talk. The sentence about the "lit house" has the most interesting of the "present"-sounding past-tense or free-indirect-discourse clauses, as "the lit house" has no prior coreferent. What the sentence actually means is that Waldo and Dulcie are approaching *a* lit house which, Waldo surmises, is possibly/probably Dulcie's home. The deictic compression here is itself an index to Waldo's head-over-heels assumption, and the "could be" in free indirect discourse is another—whereas "could have been", though narrationally sound enough, would have conveyed too much doubt. The supposition with the *wh*–interrogative nominal clause ("what ...") is still conveying doubt, of course, but much less so than a sentence with all its elements spelt out.

It is, of course, possible for apperceptions to be stated, only to be denied. This occurs in the one modal sentence of surmise which does *not* have a suppressed condition: "Mother might have been grunting it if she hadn't been taught how to behave" (W32). Waldo's hearing a note of irritation in his mother's voice is already being rejected in the modal itself, even before the *if*-clause introduces its suggestion that the gentility Waldo so admires in her cannot allow his surmise to have any validity. Another Waldovian sentence, finally, is a perfect instance of a modal construction that bears an ironic weight unknown to the character expressing the thought: "In time, in the dusk, she might have forgotten about her family" (W40). Two informants whose native tongue is English took this sentence, in conjunction with the adverbial "in time", to be hypothetically predictive: ie, "in the course of the time yet to elapse, it would have been possible for her to forget her family". This interpretation is supported by the paragraph-beginning that immediately follows: "At least Waldo was the only one who had remained standing by". If Waldo had not been present, his mother would no longer be conscious of any of her family, and would be totally immersed in her own thoughts after the overwhelming experience of Arthur's cow-tragedy. But we must remember that: (a) "In time, in the dusk" is not entirely projective, as Arthur's performance has already taken place "in the dwindling light and evening silence"; that (b) Mrs Brown, who continues "sitting on the day-bed" while Waldo remains "standing by", goes into the house when her husband calls her, "as if nothing had happened", leaving Waldo behind; and that (c) Waldo is "officially her favourite" (W28), at least according to him, and has a vested interest in believing that he is in silent communion with his mother. The "at least" is a giveaway for a Janus-faced use of "might have". The volitional part of Waldo's consciousness is encoded in the hypothetical "root" sense of the modal (Coates 1983:161): Mrs Brown doesn't "forget" her family, because Waldo is there. The apperceptive, precognitive part of his consciousness is encoded in the hypothetical "epistemic" sense of the modal (Coates 1983:158–60): Mrs Brown *has* forgotten her family, despite Waldo's "standing by". "In time, in the dusk" (which passage of time, which ever-dwindling light Waldo, too, is experiencing) it *seems* to him, from his mother's abstracted air, that she is not taking cognizance of his silent, stalwart presence, not catching his "vibrations". He cannot face up to this: but his discourse would have to do so with such formulations as "seemed/appeared to have forgotten". The doubt in Waldo's mind about the truth of his willed assumption is retained in the use of that modal, *might,* which is at the greatest possible remove from active inference and conviction, and the closest to doubt and involuntary precognition.

III   Speech and thought: general aspects

LANGUAGE AS THEME

Language forms a complex and highly ironic thematic subtext in the novel. Words are constantly being reified in figural consciousness, but there are significant alterations of valency, which need to be viewed against the characterological preoccupation with language.[20] Waldo, Arthur observes,

preferred to speak English because, he said, it had a bigger vocabulary. Arthur did not care. Or he did. He developed the habit of speaking mostly in Australian. He wanted to be understood. He wanted them to trust him, too. Waldo, he knew, was suspicious of men, though Waldo himself was inclined to call them Australians. [A218][21]

Waldo is sharp to the unassimilated Europeanness of Mrs Feinstein's English. For all his espousal of the "rationalist stand", Mr Feinstein has not shut himself off from people or his adopted land like Waldo, and this brings Arthur closer to him: "He spoke with a fairly strong Australian accent, to make up perhaps for anything foreign about him" (W103). Waldo takes this assimilation to the demotic as camouflage, and is prepared to write Mr Feinstein off, were it not for the fact that he is impressed and flattered by his large "vocabulary" of rationalist abstractions (W103–104). Waldo collects, lists and selects words (W36), and "'exotic' ... was a word he had decided to adopt" (W94). Fascinated by Dulcie's knowledge of foreign languages (W97), he is forever cultivating his exotic vocabulary (W129/134/181/184), while his discourse has occasional nonce-formations ("prestiferous" = producing speed, in relation to the demands placed on the performer by the *Allegretto* of the Moonlight Sonata, W135) or words which smell of the lamp ("subfusc" = sombre-hued, W183). In "His hair was so *candid*" (W74), the italics play on his gloating knowingness about the word's etymology.

Waldo prides himself on his powers of lexical discrimination (which more often than not result in prevarications or the use of the Higher Cliché).[22] He is "fond of 'eschew'" (W162) and intensely jealous of Arthur's word, "vocation" (W35)—this is a nice lexical epitome of the twins' life-philosophies: intellectual avoidance on the one hand, mystical dedication on the other. Waldo is a nominalist, resenting what he suspects is Dulcie's withholding of the name of the Italian lake, appreciation of whose sensuous essence is secondary to him (W133);

---

[20] Compare, with this figural involvement with language, the narratorial and thematic-polysemic saturation of *Voss* with references to language, writing, and reading (see Lyon 1990).

[21] Cf White, who was caught on both sides of "the eternal barrier of speech" *(Flaws:*47). While at school in England, he "was reminded of the deformity I carried round—my Australian-ness. I hardly dared open my mouth for fear of the toads which might tumble out" *(Flaws:*13). After his return to Australia, he would notice how "a film gathered on the eyes of those faced with my accent" *(Flaws:*47).

[22] *"Distinction,* in fact, was how he saw it in writing" (W122); "not an article, more of an *essay"* (W183); "imperative imperative was the word" (W115); "inadvertently inadvertently was the word" (W117).

he is remote from the divinity of lexis ("thank God—Waldo would allow himself a *lapsus linguae* if the error had grown into the language", W59). He uses words and expressions as weapons of defence ("*de trop*", W98) and attack (particularly the gross Australianisms he deplores: W80/91/98/131). Nature is reduced to a heady, narcissistically cultivated catalogue of weed-names (W43/46) or to Linnaean latinisms (W63).

Waldo's words are "carefully phrased" (W72), and he sees Arthur as "insulting" him by his coarse pronunciation of foreign words (W132), which Arthur phonetically acculturates. He shudders at Arthur's bad grammar (W46/145), and notes disapprovingly that their mother fails to correct it (W107).

> "I'm that tired," Arthur used to say ....
> "It isn't 'that'. It's just 'tired'," Waldo used to say, ever so prim. It made Arthur giggle.
> [W42]

Ironies abound, however: Waldo's tyrannical, intellectual principles are betrayed by his practice. He is made in direct speech to use the Australianized "*petty point*" (W126; cf also White, *Flaws*:242), to match Arthur's diegetic "*pre-dew*" (A220) and "*etoods*" (A241; normal "*étude*" in Section 2, W100). But although the direct speech in Waldo's section mockingly transcribes Arthur's "*salong*" (W132) and "*peerrot*" (W111/133), Arthur is quite capable of *thinking* "*pierrot*" (A245), which is all that is important. Waldo is a poor teacher: instead of "correcting" Arthur's "that" to "so (very)" (or to the equally informal "ever so", which Waldo himself uses and which is ironically present in his discourse above), he effectively demands that an emotively loaded statement be reduced to mere factuality. Consider, finally, the diegetic subversion of *Waldo's* narrative by the very "solecisms" he criticizes, and their absence in Arthur's section.[23]

Waldo thinks that "'it's the language that matters'" (even though it is Arthur who "knew what to say", W113). Both twins react to words as single entities: as talismanic passwords to insight for Arthur (W196), and as instruments of power for Waldo. Arthur, too, collects them: "big chunks" or "necklaces" of words (W87). He bypasses Mrs Musto's plural emphasis on "*words*" in social communication, and is fascinated by the grammatical, mystical, unifying singularity of "'the Word'", the divine Logos (W85/87). There is an element of the humorously mundane in Arthur's fixation on meaningful "objects"—the "'shiny, polished'" word "'*God* ... is a kind of sort of *rock* crystal'", he says, much to Waldo's disgust (W87). Arthur makes the abstract (or foreign) concrete; Waldo flees the concrete into intellectual abstraction. What fascinates Arthur is the singularity-in-multiplicity of words. But, ultimately, knowledge does not "come to him ... through words, but by lightning" (P307): "'Words are not what make you see'" (W57). In those moments when he is most alert to the danger Waldo presents to his relationships, and when he is fully at home within his physical self, Arthur has no trouble with words, speaking briskly, or softly, or

---

[23] "But he did not mind *all that* [= so very] much" (W48); "not *all that* absently, Waldo could see" (W94); "he wasn't *all that* keen on coming" (W99); "his remark hadn't sounded *too* effective" (W96); "*Except* [(for the fact) that] Arthur was not *all that* innocent" (W208).

gently (eg, W25/26/145), or, like the "twinned" lovers in Sydney parks (A280), withholding speech altogether (A217) or at least the full implications of his thought (A223–24). When he does have difficulty with words, he hopes that those he loves "would see behind" them (A248). Words, ever physical approximations to the inexpressible, can be stumbling-blocks.[24] Waldo's perception of his brother's speech is expressed through ugly verbs of buccal hindrance (gulping, golloping, gobbling, blurting, slobbering, W39/47/109). A specific focus is provided by metaphoric analogies between words or concepts and food or drink, consumed or chewed (W25/28/39/125/193/199–200, A246).

By contrast, Waldo and the Feinsteins are much more delicate, "nibbling at a few last crumbs of conversation" (W137–38). In a narrational anticipation of Arthur's "shiny, polished words" (W87), Waldo rolls words in his mouth Demosthenically "like polished stones" (W36)—he doesn't munch his words, struggling to make them match his thought, or simply marvelling at their epiphanic perfection; he tastes them like a connoisseur, hedonistically. But they remain stones, ultimately "encrusting" his mind and his notebooks (W162), possessing no mandalic aura. In boyhood, the division between content and form is as complete as Waldo's collecting instinct ("his gift for composition persisted as vocabulary increased to *decorate* it", W74–75; my emphasis). By the end of his life, although he takes out his papers "to look out shining words" (W212), when "Tiresias suffered difficulties with his syntax and vocabulary, he found that words, turning to stones, would sink below the surface, out of sight" (W211). "By now he suspected even his own syntax" (W207): he is losing the struggle to impose abstract order, patterned logic, on what for Arthur are individually assertive substantials; hence the irony of Waldo's loss of control, in view of his attitude towards Arthur's imperfect syntax. In his last paroxysm, Waldo rejects Arthur's plea for forgiveness (for the "sin" or "blasphemy" of using words creatively)—a plea which for him is but "the warmed stones of words" (W213). In the only metaphorically comparable instance of verbal inadequacy on Arthur's part, it is neither the loss of memory nor the bankruptcy of intellect which leads to Arthur's being blocked in explaining "what was too big, an enormous marble, filling, rolling round intolerably inside his speechless mouth" (A278). He is facing Mr Feinstein, who has undergone a steep decline from rational, enlightened loquacity, through disillusionment and paralysis ("his tongue was noticeably clumsier"), to a speechless return to the Torah, or wisdom, of the Jewish faith he had originally jettisoned (A277). The marble in Arthur's mouth is a mandala of insight, so great that it is incommunicable except through the silent meeting of eyes down a tunnel of light. There is, then, in this scene, an imagistic recuperation of the Logos, expressed in the language of solidity.

All of the language in *The Solid Mandala* is solid. No part of it can be brushed aside as shimmering surface; if its surfaces are resistant to the reader,

---

[24] "Arthur was silent, stumbling" (W28); "[he] began his stumbling" (A245). Words, difficult to *ex-press*, "grated on the way out of him" (W29). He has to jerk "against the gag" holding back "the rush of words" (A219).

then by design. A novel that so relates the substantiality of language to the thematic significance of character is unlikely to fall short in its application of language to the narrational mediation of consciousness.[25]

DIRECT SPEECH REPRESENTATION

At the level of unmodified mimesis or direct speech (ie, outside the narrative discourse proper), establishing White's practice should serve as one useful contextual "norm" against which to determine and judge his discoursal procedures at other positions along the representational spectrum. The closer a narrative is to the mimetic end of this spectrum, the less auctorial or narratorial presence or interference there is in speech (see, generally, Leech 1981:318–36). In Section 1 of *The Solid Mandala*, White's practice cleaves close to the "norm" of direct speech, where the words spoken have quotation marks and a speech-tag ("'There's more life up this end,' Mrs Poulter said", B11). A narrator seems to be at least partly in control of the report, though the fact that over half of the speech-tags are limited to the non-interpretative "*x* said" would suggest that this control can be minimal or notional (see Chatman 1975:237–38). I shall be returning to this point later on. In the dialogue of the old women, dialect or sociolect features characterize their speech. At the primary level, we find such phonetic truncations as "mornin'" and "muckin'"; a generally impoverished articulation of thought; substandard accidence (eg, past-participial "spoke" for "spoken") and syntax (eg, ellipsis of adverbial conjunctions: "not like [*when*] you ..."). It is perhaps at the graphological level that the characters' location in the speech community is most obvious, although the presence of *eye-dialect* (misspellings or "illiterate" renderings of what would otherwise be standard Australian phonetic practice) points to the likelihood that White is not striving for

---

[25] A covertly Borgesian edifice of imploded, transcribed language haunts the macronarrative, too, at the level of action: namely, the Library in its various manifestations. The library at which Waldo works from adolescence onwards is institutionally the same as the one he transfers to: ie, both physical establishments are what is now called (since 1975) the State Library of New South Wales. The Sydney Municipal Library, was so named in 1909–10 after various intermediate re-christenings in 1845, 1869 and 1895, and dates back to 1826; the Mitchell Library attached to it was opened in 1910. Waldo's desperate attachment to the new obscures the actual state of affairs—the "big new Public Library they had opened a couple of years before" is a "new building" with the Mitchell "attached" to it, as though the latter were also "new". In fact, this main part of the Public Library complex (including the reading-room of the reference library which Arthur frequents and which is the location of the Incident) was added to the Mitchell and opened in 1942. Waldo's "functional" involvement with books is also his first flight into the world outside Sarsaparilla (yet a world of his own making) in 1910. His second flight, from that world into another, from the "old" into the "new" (yet essentially, institutionally, the same) dates from 1942, as does Arthur's first formal commitment to "the Books". These *termini post quem* coincide neatly with three major institutionalizations within the same pre-existing library complex. Indeed, the Public Library in its broadest specification (as the Public Library of New South Wales, 1895) is *ab initio* almost coextensive with Waldo and Arthur (born c.1893–94). These correspondences—between the body public of recorded knowledge and the printed word, and the body private of psychical and intellectual engagement with the Word as knowledge—are not fortuitous.

absolute realism but is, rather, exploiting a representational convention for non-objective reasons. I am thinking here of such things as "shillun'" (and not "shillin'") for "shilling"; "Yairs" for "Yes"; the reintroduction into speech of mistakes which would only occur in writing—thus turning graphemic inference into phonological intentionality (eg, "of" for auxiliary "have" in compound tenses). Such "Dickensian" representation has led many readers of White to see him as operating almost exclusively at a comic or satiric remove—probably because the showing of features that deviate from an assumed auctorial standard serves to stigmatize. It is only certain cultural and socioeconomic strata in White's Australian fictions that are treated in this way.

Boris Uspensky (1975:62–65) has indicated that this naturalistic rendering of the "how" of direct speech indicates that the narrator finds it externally conspicuous; neutralized phrasing would concentrate on the "what", thus reducing maximal distance (cf also Genette 1980:182–85 on Proust and "objectivization" through "stylized" speech). In White, however, "low-style" speech-characterization is not used (as Leonard Lutwack has argued for nineteenth-century fictional usage: 1960:214–15) to add a "quaint" flavouring to a uniform mode and to confirm the marginal status of the characters who speak like this. White's characters are not simply exoticized through their speech. At the same time as their language *locally* defamiliarizes them and robs them of their dignity, the accompanying diegesis works against speech to familiarize the reader with the characters' inner selves, and (in Section 1 at least) with their efforts to maintain dignity. Dialectal and conceptual distancing of the characters from author or reader is less significant in White than the distance of the characters from the central figures of the novel. Paradoxically, we infer this distance largely from what Mrs Dun and Mrs Poulter themselves have to *say* about the focal figures.

Elsewhere in the novel, White observes precise dialectal distinctions between characters. There is the broad substantial Australian of the Council-workers (W146–47) and Stubbens (W86); these are the only true parallels to the speech of the Poulters and Mrs Dun in Section 1 and, less so, of the drunks in Section 4 (P306). An exception to this is Mrs Poulter's own speech, whose characteristic informalities are carried over into extensions of reported speech (W142–43) and into her own narrated monologue or free indirect discourse (P295–305; though there are subtle, fragmentary retreats from her idiolect towards the end of the latter subsection, in the conveying of action and apocalyptic apperception after her climactic discovery). There is the juvenile *ductus* of Wally Pugh (W122–23), the sturdy, mild informality of Len Saporta and Mr Allwright (whose way of pronouncing "fellows" fascinates Arthur, A223), and the approximation to this of Mr Feinstein. Mrs Brown expresses herself in a precise, genteel fashion, eschewing informality; and she has her counterpart in Mrs Feinstein: the latter's speech is rendered normally in Arthur's section but with faithful attention to interference from German in Section 2 (eg, W100/111–12), Waldo having an obsession with syntactic aberrations. Waldo himself is coldly careful and sparing in his speech, except when his emotions get the better of him; Arthur's speech is informal, spontaneous, without phonetic distortions but replete with substandard syntax and affective markers.

DIEGETIC SPEECH ALLUSION

If we move across to the diegesis, we find an intermittent coloration by informal and idiomatic locutions. This is characteristically manifested at the level of individual speech-allusive lexemes or phrases embedded in strands of diegesis which are otherwise neutrally narratorial in lexicon; this phenomenon falls short of the phrasal integrity characteristic of straight free indirect speech or thought. One explanation of the phenomenon is that the narrator (or even the author) empathetically or ironically "ventriloquizes" either specific characters or a communal point of view (Leech 1981:349–50). It has, however, been doubted that the colloquializing of single scattered expressions can be construed as irony, only *extended* "personalization" (in the sense of free indirect discourse) being readable in this way.[26] At any rate, in Section 1 of White's novel, speech allusion serves to cancel any potential for "personalization". At best, it is a kind of ironical, negative empathy, using the characters' lexicon in a selective, dissonant way in order to foreground character-information without narratorial evaluation— the latter is left to the (implied) reader.[27]

Informality is more pronounced in Arthur's section than in Waldo's: but that it should colour Waldo's discourse at all could indicate a discontinuity between his public (direct-speech) image and his inward verbalizing.[28] Sergeant Foyle's

---

[26] Stanzel 1982: 248–56 *passim*. Stanzel's view of irony here derives from his assumption that the opinions of a character are mediated but are not shared by the "auctorial narrator". But this assumption must be based on context, whether the passages concerned are limited or extended in scope.

[27] Some typical phrasal examples showing ellipsis, structural or collocative coloration (I include in brackets the character who is being mimetically focussed on): "never let it be hinted that" (Mrs Dun, B11); "the sallow sort" (Mrs Poulter, B12); "it could not be denied" (Poulter, B12); "—no hope this side of the tea break—" and "Often got it, too" (collective, public persona, B12/17). There are, further, formal lexemic indices to age/class register, such as "the ladies", "the young girls", "young lady typists/young typists/young ladies" (Dunn and Poulter collectively), and various traces of informal, misplaced formal, or informally elliptical speech at the lexemic level, eg: "on account of", "the pay-as-you-enter", "kiddies", "chrysanths" or "long-winded" (all Poulter); "which ever library" or "creating" (Mrs Dun).

[28] Examples include: "having a whale of a time" (W28); "the old blokes" (W55); "not a bad stick" (W85); "got the wind up" (W99–100); "not all that keen" (W99); "the old nut" (W114); "the beastly treacle" (W176); further: W36/91/128/135/211; "a spot of trouble" (A224); "having a cry/the sulks" (A235/242); "a bob or two" (A243); "all that silly rot" (A244); "off his rocker" (A279); "crumbly as one thing" (A294); further: A233/237/253/271/282 /283.

In view of my earlier remarks about "solecism" and cliché in Waldo's discourse, it is well to remember that it can be the author's responsibility to *maintain* an aura of linguistic imperfection. The critic, in seeking to gun down such manifestations, may succeed only in shooting himself in the foot: "Sometimes a wrong word will leak in, as in 'He had even less clues to the whereabouts of Mrs Julian Boileau' *[The Vivisector, P180]*. Clichés like 'worn herself to a frazzle' *[Riders in the Chariot, P244]*, 'naked down to the soles of her feet'

perspective is also speech-coloured ("a blooming baked custard", P313; "the old boy", P314). Arthur, on a very few occasions, is inclined to wander off the rails of *le bon usage* ("you couldn't hardly count himself", A263–64; "if they wouldn't have seen it", A230). There are a few syntactic ellipses that could be put down to Waldo's "mental informality" (omission of nominal- or cleft-clause *that*, W69); discourse adjuncts ("anyway", W140) point to Waldo's own narrational regulation. A consistent recurrence of affective markers is noticeable: eg, "ever so prim/slightly scented/naturally" (W42/49, A241); "didn't say an awful lot" (A222); "puzzled Arthur a lot" (A226); "Mrs Musto was so upset" (A236; other *so*-intensifiers: A234/236/241, W50, whereby the last two mimic the locutions of the women present).

INTEGRATED SPEECH- AND THOUGHT-PRESENTATION

At no stage in Section 1 does the narrator assert any greater degree of control over *speech* than normal direct speech. The diegetic possibilities are not exploited.[29] Nor is there any particular need for such a dramatically busy conversation to be presented in any less direct manner. The most radical relinquishing of control (free direct speech as the words spoken and nothing else; the same, but with neutral speech-tags and a run-on into narration) is absent from Section 1 as well. Where ambiguity of reference can be avoided, White moves one step away from normal direct speech into un-tagged scenic presentation ("'It's the shops all right'", B11). Our feeling that speech has been "quoted" by a consciously "invisible" narrator may still be strong, but the characters are granted a great degree of autonomy.

Thought-presentation (see esp. Leech 1981:337–48) differs from speech-presentation in respect of narratorial access: the substance of speech can be mediated, but only the non-verbatim content of (generally preverbal) thought. Thus the norm for thought is shifted down the presentational axis to *in*direct thought, and in the opposite direction to free indirect speech (the latter is auctorially interpretative, the former is a move towards the active consciousness

---

[Riders in the Chariot, P131] ... cast further shadows on White's stylistic integrity" (Wolfe 1983:24). What makes "less clues" wrong, when Hurtle Duffield's discourse is persistently tinged with colloquialisms? "Fewer clues", anyway, is semantically incongruous with a plural of indefinite amount. "Worn to a frazzle" is the kind of informal hyperbole that fits Mrs Chalmers–Robinson's sociolect (it snuggles here against another cliché, "at the eleventh hour", which Wolfe doesn't pillory). The cliché also serves to connote the state of her hair, which is presently disguised cosmetically by her maid. The "soles" cliché (which is really an intensifying redundancy) is restored contextually to its full vigour when one considers its implication that the soles of the feet are not visible on a person who is standing. Duffield has burst in on his sister, Rhoda, obsessed with the idea of painting her—of capturing her flesh-tones and her form. His artist's perception is already, at this instant of discovery, analyzing the seen and the implicative: even the unseen soles of her feet do not escape his inward, projective vision. The "clichés" are *essential* to White's "stylistic integrity".

[29] These being: free indirect speech (tense/pronoun transformation, no quotation marks or speech-tag); indirect speech (tense/pronoun transformation, with a reporting or nominal clause); narrative report of speech acts (summarized conversation).

of the character). Common to *free* indirect thought and free indirect speech, however, is the impossibility of applying linguistic criteria alone to determine whether the discourse is character-thought or narrator-opinion. In Section 1, there are narrative reports of thought-acts ("Mrs Poulter decided not to bother", "Mrs Dun could not believe", "Mrs Poulter had hoped to avoid it") and "normative" thought-presentation ("Mrs Dun wondered whether she had ...", "But one was the leader, she could sense"). By far the most prominent form of thought-mediation is free indirect thought ("A young lady couldn't ..." and "If what Mrs Poulter said was true ...", B11; "It was so important to be decent", B12; "It was those stiletto heels", B13).

In the initial actional-present segment of Section 2 (W23–31), specific turns of phrase recollected from the past are "kept down" by narrational strategies designed to keep them part of the habitual past, to prevent them obtruding too brilliantly into the realm of present, active consciousness. A verbless statement can be made to look initially like Waldo's own thought: "Waldo's voice and Arthur's hair. So Mother used to say" (W26). The statement must be reattributed, then opposed in Waldo's thoughts. An example already cited ("So they were sitting down to dinner in one of the brick boxes", W31) starts with a past progressive (Waldo's projective imaginings). The sentence that follows ("A hot dinner in the middle of the day ... has its advantages, Dad used to say, you can put your feet up at night and read") starts by looking like a figural, gnomic justification of Waldo's projection, but we discover that it is tagged as unmarked direct speech from the past. In this way, we are made to "feel" Waldo's present-thought expropriation of his father's past utterances. Speech-tag placement and the absence of quotation marks make the thought "bi-temporal" in relevance.

Some unmarked, recollected direct speech is embedded in diegetic recollection ("hoping that too much water wouldn't squirt up into her face. Shall I fetch Dad? Arthur would ask", W27), but this is uncommon. There may, instead, be a devolution from Waldo's fixed attitudes (related in what looks like psychonarration: "But Waldo Brown, although he kept them, did not believe in touching dogs"), through reported speech with embedded tags to make sentences look like "self-reported" thought ("It gave them, he said, a wrong sense of their own importance"), to tagged direct speech without markings ("But why, Arthur would persist, I like to touch dogs", W27). Everything is kept in balance, as levels of recollective consciousness. Post-tagged free direct speech may illustrate, as immediate associations, an actional-present statement ("'She's such a good neighbour.' I am very fond of Mrs Poulter ... Mother used to say", W27), or tagless free-direct-speech dialogue may provide scenic illustration after an analytical, figural thought ("Arthur had been Dad's favourite, in the beginning. Who's coming for the ice-cream horn? Not Waldo, George, it only brings the pimples out", W28). The only *pre*-tagged free direct speech from the past is that of somebody *outside* the family circle, kept at a distance even in recollection of the scene ("Waldo remembered sitting ..., while Mrs Poulter roamed calling round: I don't want to intrude Mrs Brown on you", W28).

In the second or fully recollective narrative, direct speech is reinstated to its full, formal, scenic status. Direct thought is kept "hidden", without quotation marks ("How very yellow and horrid you are looking, Waldo thought", W34; "Poor Arthur, Waldo thought", W42). When direct speech is presented tagged but without quotation marks, this is customarily a sign in Waldo's narrative that the import of the statement has more than merely illustrative, discursive weight. "Because Dad never went to sports. If you take the trouble to invent gods, he said, you don't ..." (W33): this is recollected at a different psychological level than the opinion on Arthur in free direct speech which precedes it in marked form: "Once Arthur got a ferret .... I'm going to love it dearly, Waldo, Arthur confessed privately" (W41). This, like the preceding, forms the basis of a collection of obsessive moments (the "myth"-nexus, the "ferreting"-nexus), which find their way into other levels of the discourse later. There are downgradings into hybrid diegesis of what would have no significance to the acting figural consciousness if the reply were in direct speech ("Waldo said all right he would", W102). Mentally projective "scenarios" are not infrequent in Waldo's section, with unmarked direct speech: "Tell me, Dad, he was tempted to make a challenge of it—tell me something I don't *know*" (W78); "Then he would walk up the hill ... and say: Here I am, an intellectual" (W110). Recollective observation at a distance is usually signalled by a mixture of unmarked direct speech and reported speech, as in Waldo's immediate sexual memory on the train: "No man is all that attractive, she said, that there isn't a copy or two of him about. The man called her his copy-cat, and both laughed" (W78). Centrality of immediate thought, whether the expropriated opinions of others or personal reactions, may lead to an intrasentential rupture of past-tense diegesis. In the following example, an exclamation as free indirect thought is followed by past-tense diegesis; the reason-clause is invaded by direct citation, not by the reported speech that could follow "said Mother":

"The main thing," said Dad, [...], "is to lead a decent [...] life [....]"
O Lord. Waldo had not been taught to pray, because, said Mother, everything depends on your own will, [....] we can achieve what we want [...] if we are confident that we are strong.
And here was George Brown [....] Who had nothing to feel ashamed of. Except perhaps his own will. [W77; my elisions]

That this is an example of immediate figural involvement in the scenically re-created is indicated by the deictic fall back into "present" awareness ("And here").

The remaining instances of integrated speech- and thought-representation, right down to the interface with free indirect discourse.proper, can be laid out on one page: there is actually very little text, and a large variety of categories. The diegetic and paramimetic forms of representation in the novel have little about them that is predictable. It is Arthur's section (and his segment of Section 4) that has the simplest applications of any of the types, which are essentially the few conspicuous remnants in this novel of the stock repertory of mediative techniques common to the high-modernist mode of Dorothy Richardson, Virginia Woolf, Faulkner and Joyce.

1a. "Tagged" free direct speech: Not long after Dad died Mother had said: There is no reason why you boys shouldn't have this larger bed (W174); Again it was: how do you like it? what do you make of it? (A217); While pausing every few weeks to remind them: none of this is real, none of this is true (A223).

1b. Projective direct speech as thought: Suddenly he knew he would like to say: Dearest, dearest Dulcie (W139); She was not so soft as to say: I will keep you for ever (P311); Arthur did not know how to say it often has to (A239); also W162, A284.

1c. Direct thought: he derived some comfort from remembering: I am Waldo's dill brother of whom nothing is expected (P308).

1d. Parenthesized, un-tagged direct speech in recall: Once before Waldo had accepted, and eaten a sociable braise with Cis and Ern—we're going to treat you just as if you were one of the family—and Wally had spoken about his plans for the future (W126).

1e. Tagged direct "speech" (= thought): Oh God oh God, he repeated (W127); It is ridiculous, he panted, to think I may pop off (W119); So much—this time—for Crankshaw, said Waldo (W173).

1f. Un-tagged, italicized, iterative direct speech (generalized public opinion): *Arthur is the backward one ....Waldo is the one who takes the lead* (A256); also W121, A271.

2a. Reported speech followed by free indirect speech (if spoken explanation) or free indirect thought (if mental self-address): Waldo said he wouldn't go in. He did not care to look at her, because what was the point. Dead, he said, is dead. One had to be realistic about it (W170).

2b. Coloured reported speech with direct-speech elements, immediately taking on the status of free indirect speech (mostly tagged, sometimes un-tagged, sometimes [*] with syntactic rupture): Mrs Poulter told Mother the War had got on Bill's nerves sort of ... if only she could make certain, she would perhaps grow the violets, and post the leaves in a moist parcel (W142–43; 16-line paragraph); and she said yes she knew of Waldo (A242); Arthur said yes he would (A240); also W148–49, A216; *Cornelius, that rather ascetic Jew, heard that Mrs Brown lived at Sarsaparilla, and wasn't he perhaps acquainted with a certain family (W183).

2c. Tagged reported, projective "speech" (= thought): That a daughter became engaged while a mother was still high in her coffin, he prevented himself adding (W155).

2d. Parenthesized, un-tagged reported speech in recall: They made arrangements to meet, to discuss ... Picasso—it was so important to keep abreast—and Waldo smiled, agreeing (W204).

3a. Free indirect thought with psychonarrative tag: Now, he thought, he'd show her up (W134); How long now, he tried to calculate, had their mother kept to her room? (W170).

3b. Free indirect thought interrupted by a psychonarrative tag to represent a temporary deflection into Waldo thinking about his thought: Youth is the only permanent state of mind. There was no stage in his life when he hadn't felt young—he insisted—except sometimes as a little boy (W119).

3c. Free indirect speech in iterative past time: How did he do it? He just knew (A231).

3d. Free indirect speech in punctual past time: He was distracting the readers (A307); When he had written enough of them, as he intended, Walter was going to offer them as a volume, [shift to Waldo's mental commentary] and join the ranks of the Australian poets (W123); She would, of course. Written in coloured inks (A246).

3e. Mentally projective, coloured free indirect speech/thought arising out of "objective" diegesis: Arthur tended to fade out. Began to work for Allwright .... It was sad for Browns, ... You wondered what they talked about (W75).

AN INFORMAL INDEX TO FREE INDIRECT DISCOURSE

If one were to posit the presence in *The Solid Mandala* of an "omniscient" narrator, then it would be a conspicuously informal one in certain respects, and a formal one in others. The particular, indexical informality I am thinking of here is the use of the vocative ("you") to cover what has hitherto been the usual literary pronoun of impersonal reference ("one"). "You" correlates well with other indices to free indirect discourse, so we are not obliged to account for its presence in consonant psychonarration: "bowling along like your own thoughts" (B16); "Arthur was never what you could have called bad-tempered" (W29); "It was all very well to hang on to your brother's hand" (A229); "You couldn't say .... You had to keep up .... you couldn't very well expect ..." (P295–97).[30] It is clear from the free indirect discourse in Mrs Poulter's diegesis in Section 4 that this use of "you" is automonologic (though not part of quoted monologue), and that it is almost entirely self-protective, consolatory or rationalizing in its function. Deprived of a "friend" in the social domain, Mrs Poulter is governed by an interlocutory, "social" reflex in the psychological domain. When the narrative shifts further inwards, towards Mrs Poulter's reflections on her relationship with her husband, and towards the apocalyptic confrontations of her consciousness with manifestations of cruelty, horror and heartbreak, "you" peters out and disappears: the truly personal pronoun of experiential immediacy and deepest recollection is the third-person singular. Interestingly (or perhaps expectedly), much the same applies to the twins' narratives, where "you" is generally found whenever Waldo or Arthur are engaged in explaining to themselves moral or psychological categorizations—rather, explaining away, or rationalizing. "You", then, often signals unreliability in the discourse (though it is certainly not the only signal; and who really expects "reliable narrators", anyway?).[31]

---

[30] Other instances of Mrs Poulter's vocative discourse: "Like that blood-pressure thing was on your arm" (B20; also B14 twice, and Mrs Dun, B18), "Nobody could ever accuse you" (A259), "Only you forget" (P305, in the gnomic present), also: P298/299/302/303/315; Waldo's discourse: "In some ways you were so close you did not always notice" (W31); "But of course you never could tell" (W95); "You never could tell" (W173); "(though you never could tell; ...)" (W183); "But you could see that nobody would ever really understand" (W37); "You could see that behind the words their father was really hoping ..." (W146); also: W33/53/79/85/117/121/144/175; Arthur's discourse: "You couldn't exactly say *they* were *speaking,* because ..." (A283); "It was Waldo who took fright. You could see that" (A292); also: A220/222/224/246–47/293, in the gnomic present.

[31] It should be stressed that "you" in White's novels does not have the function of vocative narration that is the controlling reflexive perspective for, say, the character Damian Glover in Thomas Keneally's *A Dutiful Daughter.* Nor is it a sign of White's own awareness or complicitous intrusiveness, as the two or three critics who have noticed the "Second Person Familiar" seem to think. By and large, narratologists have not picked up on vocative function in represented speech and thought; Banfield (1982:297.*n*4) cautiously relegates *you* to a footnote and never considers the advantages accruing to free indirect discourse through the use of this pronoun.

EXPRESSIVE INDICES TO FREE INDIRECT DISCOURSE

Un-tagged, past-tense, direct questions are, like exclamations, expletives and other expressive features, customarily regarded as reliable signs of the fact that a shift has taken place in the diegesis from consonant psychonarration, or other mediative levels of discourse, to narrated monologue or free indirect discourse (see esp. Chatman 1978:201–203, Banfield 1982:30–32/203–204/210). Such indicators may stand alone, or may have on their periphery further discourse features signalling the operation of figural consciousness. Internal questions can be classified in accordance with the general psychological import of the immediate context; exclamations, epanorthosis (etc.) can be grouped according to phrase-structure. In no case is bivocality present (where the tonality could be determined as stemming ironically from an "auctorial" narrator).

Both Waldo and Arthur ask questions of a resignative nature: "But how could he tell her?" (W54), "What could he say to this woman?" (W180), "Mother had died, hadn't she?" (W192); "But what could you expect of her, or anybody else?" (W201); "How could he tell them of his dreams, for instance, except as something to laugh about" (A224), "... she would never notice. Why should she?" (A244). Waldo's discourse can have a heroic self-challenging aspect: "Was Dulcie playing an *étude?* He hoped it was an *étude*" (W110), "Would it escape without his assistance? Or someone else's?" (W136), "Was he strong enough?" (W136), "Could it be that this was one of the crucial points in his life?" (W119). This can shade off into exultation or self-congratulation: "(What price the Feinsteins now?)" (W114), "Was he vain to have lost faith in public sculpture?" (W117); Arthur can be excitedly reflective: "And if one wife, why not two?" (etc., A281), "Who was the Grand Inquisitor?" (A283). Waldo indulges in rationalization (sometimes fearfully: eg, W118): "but hadn't the whole botched mess ... helped give birth to that proven sensibility?" (W120), "But hadn't he given himself to books?" (W121), "Wasn't most of anyone's?" (W195), "Then, who else, finally, but Mrs Poulter?" (W185). Neutral reflection in Section 2 ("Or was it a dutiful one?", W152; "Had he actually experienced ... the icy vision?" W163; "Crankshaw, was it? and a priest", W201) can contrast with despair: "Who had inflicted Arthur on him?" (W68); "And why did Arthur keep on lumping him together with almost all the people they knew?" (W199); "Why were they always dragged back to this?" (W206). Both brothers suffer fear and doubt: "He knew this as he went away. Or did he, though?" (A260), "... would Waldo have hated him?" (A273); "What if it, if they all, stuck?" (A273); "and was it mirth? was it Mrs Poulter's?" (W62), "Was she laughing *at* him?" (W96); but only Waldo's discourse raises these emotions to the level of panic, especially in regard to other persons' behaviour towards himself (W56/65/90/131/153/166/172/186/194).

The only expletives are in Waldo's section: "Ugh!" (W120); "Pffeugh, the books!" (W121); "Indeed!" (W196). Waldo's vocative and apostrophic exclamations ("Tender Dulcie!" W154, "What hell!" W155, "Oh, Lord", W98) concentrate on "poor Crankshaw" (five instances, W171–72/177), Arthur's on "poor Waldo" (A245/A290 twice). In Waldo's discourse but not in Arthur's, these are generally made affectively explicit through an exclamation mark, as are deictic expressions, which do not occur in Arthur's section: "He liked that!" (W162); "Those peppercorns!" (W165); "From Mrs *Poulter!*" (W169); "His brother! This obscene old man!" (W196); "That was it!" (W130). Volitional and suppositional formulae occur in the discourse of both brothers: "If she only knew" (W67, A281); "If only he could have focused on Arthur's face" (W73); "If only he could have retired" (A282); "If it would only come shooting out" (W110); "If he could only have moulded music" (A232); "Supposing Feinsteins thought he was trying to cadge another meal?" (W105); "Supposing he had been wrong" (A253).[32] Miscellaneous tonal expressions[33] which have an expressive base can be found in both central sections, but only Waldo's discourse has the particular affectivity mediated by *wh*-formulations: "How raw he had been formerly" (W131); "How his heart contracted inside the blue ... ice" (W192); also W75/125/119/164/198 (all "How" except W189: "—what vanity").

Once again, the variety of psychological contexts is much greater for Waldo than for Arthur; in absolute terms, the frequency with which such emotive pressure-point indicators occur is greater, too, in Section 2 (more than twice as often for questions, when the gross figure is adjusted for text-length). The reader tends, however, to register absolute occurrences rather than relative density, and Waldo's section has more than four times as many questions, and twice as many exclamations and interjections, as Arthur's. Perhaps expectedly, emotional states are consistently extreme throughout Waldo's section, but tend to cluster towards the end of Arthur's with the gradual weakening of his carapace of innocence. In neither narrative, however, is recourse had to such expressive "flash-point" markers of emotional stress during the climactic closing scene—the prose deadens into statement, turns almost fatalistic; events strike consciousness with such an impact that there is no "time" left for the kind of inward resistance best characterized by *this* texture of free indirect discourse.

What Banfield (1973:21–22; 1982:202/311.*n*17) calls "contrastive stress" or, tautologically, "emphatic stress", and what I would term typographical or graphic emphasis, is regarded as an index to figural, reflective/non-reflective consciousness: eg, "As if *he* were the one a shingle short!" (W146, where there is also the unequivocal presence of an exclamation and, less unequivocally, colloquial coloration); "Arthur *seemed* content" (W194); "You couldn't exactly

---

[32] Also: "How dreadful if Dulcie" (W56); "Suppose his exercise in loving Dulcie had been forced to harden ...!" (W56); "Supposing, for instance, other boys found out" (W36); "If only the curtain on his mystery hadn't stuck halfway up" (A239); "If only Dulcie would declare herself" (A244); "If he could only have revealed himself" (P307).

[33] "Oh yes, he would have liked to" (W128; cf A291); "Oh well" (W115); "Well, he wouldn't have fallen for it" (W156); "not in its flesh, oh no, but ..." (W189); "He had thought it out, oh, seriously" (W180); "but before that, yes, ..." (W140); "because of, well, everything" (W167; cf A230); "oh no, it was rather ..." (W111); "As if Johnny Haynes cared" (W43; cf A285); "Though he hadn't met—well, perhaps one other" (W125; epanorthosis also at W114); "Was he a relative!" (A249); "So frustrating" (A282).

say *they* were *speaking*" (A283); "not exactly that Bill didn't *believe*" (P300).[34] Waldo, rather than Arthur, thinks in this emphatically differentiative mode. This graphic device is distinct from "deep" mental quotation (as in the italicized portions of Faulkner's *Light in August,* Waldo's "He would do how was it he would *blow everything*", W151, or Arthur's "—what was it? *collating* his notes—", A292). There are, however, borderline or dual-function instances: eg, "his hair was so *candid*" (W74), "you could not say *wilfully*" (W82) or "*because of*" (W64), which involve both affective emphasis and the "quoting" of a locution.

In general, the narrative discourse of *The Solid Mandala* scrupulously maintains characterological differences, except where psychological universals override such differentiae. Verbal, modal and adverbial indices to perception and judgement are fully consonant with modes of narration that represent the mental world of the characters. White's ability to differentiate character acutely is in full evidence both at the mimetic or "direct" level and at the diegetic or "indirect" level of narration.

---

[34] See also W26/65 (twice)/69/112/118/128/162/167/169; in Arthur's discourse: P307 (twice).

ASPECT, MODE AND TENSE

I   Aspectuality and free indirect discourse

The difficulties experienced by White's readers in coming to terms with features of his narrative style are exemplified by O.N. Burgess in a discussion of *Voss:*

We may find ourselves in occasional doubt over White's distinctive use of the past continuous tense in narrative sequences:

> Then Voss caught sight of the drawings.
> "What do these signify, Jackie?" he asked.
> The boy *was explaining*, in his own language, assisted by a forefinger.
> "Verfluchte Sprachen!" cried the German.
> For he was doubly locked in language.
> As the boy continued unperturbed, the man had to recover from his lapse. He *was looking.*

Sometimes, looking at this or that passage, I can persuade myself that this past tense form gives a designed impression of continuity and of things happening at a distance; sometimes I can convince myself that the concatenation of words ending in "-ing" provides a hypnotic and ritualistic effect. But, at other times, I can perceive no genuine distancing or ritualistic purpose behind the writing, and I am merely irritated. [Burgess 1961:50. His emphases; I have replaced the Eyre & Spottiswoode text with the Penguin, p. 274.]

It might have helped Burgess if he had maintained the distinction between *tense* and *aspect*, and had given some thought to the implications of aspectuality in the progressive form. There is no need to search for "distancing or ritualistic purpose" once one has understood that verbs in this form relate what is mediated duratively to a coexisting time-plane, and indicate (in White's usage at the very least) perspectival focalization on the perceiving consciousness of the character for whom awareness of the aspectualized action is most crucial.[1] Voss is *aware* of his own concentrated involvement in the process of listening to Jackie explaining, and *is* thereby "distanced"—hence his reaction. And Voss "was looking" because he has had to propel himself back out of his angry disengagement and into a state of concentration again. His awareness of his obligatory visual concentration (he is relying now solely on the sign-language,

---

[1] This is the central tenet of narratological investigations of perfective/imperfective alternation (eg, Ehrlich 1987), which check the significance of aspect against other features in the local discourse context (eg, free-indirect markers), rather than employing only linguistic, discourse-analytical explanations based on global discourse (eg, foreground/background features of temporality)

not the spoken language) is in tension *and* accord with the flow of communication which he rejoins.

The specific problems in the *Voss* passage did not have to be resolved by an appeal to general linguistic principles; it would have been sufficient to make an intelligent probe of the continuous forms within the meaning supplied by the local context. But (I repeat) a shift from the preterite or simple past to the past progressive does happen to represent a centering on the perceiving consciousness.[2] Not only is simultaneity implied—so that a three-dimensional sculpting of actional space is enabled, thus releasing narration from the constrictions of strict linearity or sequentiality; it is possible to use the progressive aspect as a delicate instrument for conveying the activity of figural consciousness. Most uses of the progressive are relational and not intimately involved with figural perception. For example, Waldo *knows* that the following (processual) state of affairs obtains: "Arthur was in the kitchen with Mother, who *was allowing* him to knead the dough" (W34); the progressive circumvents the "habitual" function of the preterite "allowed". Equally natural is the use of the progressive for the actional (or perceptual) continuum out of which a punctual act arises: "Once Arthur, who *was watching* the buttermilk gush out ..., laughed and said:" (W35). These are not the kinds of occurrence of the progressive that are likely to give the reader pause. Consider, however, the following, from the beginning of Section 2:

Then the older of the two dogs [...] threw up his head, and gave two ageless sexless barks. The second [...] began to scutter across the boards [....]

Waldo *was leading* his brother Arthur, as how many times, out of the brown gloom of the kitchen. [W24]

We should not rest content with the recognition that the movement of Waldo through and out of the kitchen is made simultaneous with the barking, then the scuttering, of the dogs. A kernel sentence such as "Waldo *led* Arthur out of the kitchen" could also be construed filmically as continuous (the verb implies movement), but a lot would be missing—and not only the temporal nuancing of the progressive. There are other elements in the sentence which should make us revise our view of the function of the progressive here: there is the specification "his brother", which is unnecessary if we assume the presence of a dissonant narrator (the reader already knows who Arthur is, by inference from "their father's chair" and by the specification "his brother's head", W23); and there is the expressive quasi-exclamatory structure "as *how many* times" instead of the neutral "as he had done (so) many times before". It is Waldo who is conscious of what *he is doing* here: apperceptual significance has been instilled into the action by the actant, in relation to his fraternal "duty".

---

[2] The clearest account is given by Fehr 1938:101–103; see also Banfield 1978b:428–30 and Banfield 1982:105–107/200–201 and *passim*. Banfield (200–201), like Burgess, sees the progressive as a matter of tense, not aspect. See also Bronzwaer 1970:67–69, who stresses that there is nothing *inherently* salient or figural about the progressive (in his parlance, an "expanded form" of tense): its function depends on the way it can be made to *contrast* contextually with non-progressive forms. This structural approach is perfectly reasonable.

The progressive for simple process or state need not detain us, save for the suggestion that concentrations of this aspect tend to suggest the presence of an observing consciousness:

One evening Waldo *was hanging* over the gate *watching* their father limp down Terminus Road [....] How very yellow and horrid you *are looking,* Waldo thought [....] [Dad's] shoulder *was moving* inside his coat, *fighting* for greater ease [....] They were *limping and struggling,* as if in the one body, all the way to the front veranda [....] And now, Waldo *was watching.* [W34-35]

One can sense the difference as soon as one changes to the simple aspect those verbs that can be changed: the verbs themselves involve process, but only the progressive can suggest Waldo's perception of process and his own involvement in it. Other determinants may be at work in the context, operating on selection of the processual progressive: "Towards the end, not by choice, he *was growing* his first moustache" (W79)—the context of unwillingness alone precludes "grew".

The next stage up (represented by "were limping" above) draws figural consciousness into a close emotional relation to the process immediately perceived, as in the playground-scene with Arthur's arrival: "the pale lights *were flashing* .... The fire *was shooting* in tongues", and—when Waldo shakes off Arthur's hand afterwards, and Arthur is complaining "'But when you walk fast!'"—"Arthur *was shuffling and running,* bigger than Waldo, a big shameful lump" (W45). Emotional, reactive experiencing of and *with* the processual is central here. This experiencing can, in Waldo's case, be projective, as when his imagining of a more prosperous environment arises out of, overlays, and displaces Arthur's actional-present talk of what might have been ("So they *were sitting down* to dinner in one of the brick boxes", W31). If simultaneous processuality is not formally banished by "So" here, nor is it in Arthur's section, when Dulcie solves the "riddle" of her own personality. After her direct speech, there occurs the diegetic "Then she *was laughing* for the riddle solved. She *was holding up* her full throat, the laughter rippling out of it" (A255). Arthur's perception of these gestural processes is not fully sequent ("Then") upon his mental retention of what Dulcie has just said. We are to imagine him attempting to bring Dulcie's verbal action and gestural reaction into explanatory conjunction as he perceives the latter. The binding function of the progressive can be seen in the following:

"Repetition becomes monotonous."
He *was considering* that.
"Besides," she said, "a grown man—nearly twenty-eight ...." [A256]

The sentence containing the progressive does not merely indicate continuing mental state, but is elliptical (we must supply the ending "when Mother went on to say:"); what we have here, then, is the partial overlay of reflective and perceiving consciousness. In Arthur's section, the clearest indication of this overlay comes in the emotionally tense library incident, when Waldo, like Peter with Jesus, denies his brother:

"You're drawing attention to us!"
Arthur did not understand at first.

"You will leave this place," Waldo *was commanding,* and very loudly: "*sir!*"
Indicating that he, Arthur, his brother, his flesh, his breath, was a total stranger. [A285]

Arthur's struggle to understand persists, from his registering of Waldo's exclamation to his hearing the word "*sir!*", when the penny drops. A momentary command becomes drawn out into a "process" because it is perceived as penetrating Arthur's reflections, his struggle to understand, *progressively.* The progressive can signal the actional "background" which is being mentally taken in at the same time as the process of reflection is going on: "So they *were going up* the hill again to Feinsteins' on a Saturday afternoon. How raw he had been formerly" (W131)—the second sentence, of free indirect discourse, supports the assumption that the "going" of the first sentence is being figurally experienced.

Heightened figural experiencing of stress-situations is indicated by two passages in Section 2. After the playground incident, Mr Haynes has come to complain about Arthur's punching his son; Waldo overhears the conversation:

Arthur was down with Jewel [....] While Mr Haynes *was standing* on the front veranda [....] "I warn yer, Mr Brown," Mr Haynes *was saying* [....] "I'll see when there's anything to see," said Dad. "But Arthur is the gentlest creature," Mother *was trying* to persuade. "I didn't bring along my boy's lip to show." Mr Haynes *was turning* nasty now [....] Mother *was protecting* with her tongue. [W46–47]

These progressives relate to Waldo's perceiving consciousness in different ways. "Was standing" locates Mr Haynes in respect of Waldo's temporal situating of Arthur, the reason for the visit. "Was saying" indicates Waldo's awareness of having come in in the middle of something. "Was turning" is apperceptive ("had turned" would be closer to a statement of fact, relating to Mr Haynes's words, but independently of Waldo's evaluating consciousness). "Was trying" and "was protesting" are both "overlay" progressives, where Waldo remarks his mother's gestures *after* taking in the spoken comments of his father, but realizes that her efforts are being made while his father is speaking. A second cluster of progressives signals Waldo's self-consciousness—of action and "acting"—when he assumes the role of man of the house after his father's death (W72–73).

By far the greatest number of progressives are relational. Some of the effects achieved can be delicate indeed:

Scruffy and Runt *had* started a rabbit.
"What do *you* know?"
Waldo *was worrying it* with his teeth.
"No," said Arthur.
"You were always good at figures," Waldo had to admit.
He *was yanking* at his twin's blue-veined hand. [W29]

A plainer, less responsive style might have reduced the two progressives to participles and tacked them on at the end of the previous direct speech (thus approaching analytical hypotaxis). White paragraphs them separately and signification is immediately expanded. The initial past perfect—another device for signalling belated awareness of a condition—sets up the point of reference for

Waldo's mode of reflection.[3] "Was worrying" functions not only to characterize the way in which Waldo utters his contemptuous question, but to suggest that the mental action involved is already ongoing, and simply takes this outward vocal form momentarily. "Was yanking" makes the action simultaneous with—and contradictory to the apparent tone of—Waldo's spoken admission. But there is more to it than this. The very fact that "twin" should be in the sentence draws attention to the stereotype with twinship of shared mental giftedness, which Waldo's admission reveals as false. Waldo is conscious that he is yanking at Arthur's hand, in aggressive compensation for what he has had to "admit". Similarly, the progressive in "Waldo *was striding* now" (W30) indicates not just ongoing action but also the self-conscious bonding between the import of Arthur's words, Waldo's mental reaction to them, the physical manifestation of this reaction, and his awareness of this manifestation.

The technique of separate paragraphing reinforces, elsewhere, a shift in the focus of awareness; the progressive may retain its innocuous function of marking aspectual continuity of an action or state perceived: but it usually occurs in sentences immediately following generalizing diegesis, or diegesis interrupted by direct speech:

"I'm a terrible correspondent. The girls at school are always complaining."
An elderly gentleman ... *was putting back* his watch [....] Those outside felt safe, knowing the darkness favoured them.
A lady *was bringing in* a huge tureen. [W97]

Waldo must attend to what Dulcie is saying at the same time as he perceives what is happening inside the house; he must reflect upon his security ("those" is Waldovian imperialism), and emerge from inward reflection into awareness of a process that has been going on while he is lost in thought.

But in this girl he might *be addressing* the kind of complicated human being his reading told him did not exist.
"Oh," she said, "I like to read. I've just finished *The Mill on the Floss*."
She *was looking* at him again. [W93]

Waldo has been taken out of time into inward reflection on his own relationships. Dulcie's remark takes him out of thought, or shifts the dominance-relation of introspection/ perception to that of perception/ apperception, and he realizes that Dulcie must have been looking at him before he was aware of it.

Wherever the progressive occurs, the action "progressivized" has its root aspect of objectively perceivable, ongoing process. But in many cases there is a psychological component, superadded by layout and/or by context. The progressive often typically follows direct speech. The characteristic diffidence of Mrs Brown, who always seems to be summoning up enough strength to act, is illustrated here (in all of the following quotations, new paragraphs are indicated

---

[3] Considerable use is made of the past perfect for conveying "changes of gear" or shifts in the level of figural consciousness from introspection to delayed perception of externals. See, for example, "She had got up" (W52); "she had returned to asking" (W76); "they hadn't spoken" (W76); "he had begun to hear" (W153); "then Dulcie had begun again" (W134); "had begun to knock" (W188). Arthur is not prone to this delayed-reaction syndrome.

by §): "'That's enough, I think,' said Dad. § 'Oh, Arthur,' Mother *was daring*
herself to speak, 'we understand ...'" (W40); "'Well, Mr Allwright believes
Sarsaparilla will never lose its backwaters ....' § 'Oh, dear,' Mother *was
beginning,* she seemed afraid of something" (A221). The progressive helps
indicate that what Waldo or Arthur notice are their mother's "signals", which are
issued while Mr Brown is speaking and deflect the boys' attention away from
their father's words. In the following, Arthur perceives Mrs Poulter's words, but
sees how her fidgety actions belie the engagement of her tone: "'Yes,' she said,
as though she wouldn't. § She was tweaking her cerise geranium" (A258; cf also
A288). Waldo's cognizance of the outward signs of Arthur's mental effort brings
with it awareness of the effect of Mr Brown's words *while* their father is
speaking: "Then he added ...: 'Whether she's a figure of tragedy is a matter for
consideration.' § Arthur *was grappling* with his problem" (W39). This awareness
of causality can be there while the words are being spoken: the actions of
breathing ("Walter Pugh *was breathing* hard", W126), looking ("Dulcie *was
looking* at him, obviously waiting to hear more", W153) or observing ("'What
walk?' § 'The same.' § Arthur and Waldo *were observing* each other", W210)
are foregrounded by signification.[4]

The dominant psychological situation can be that of an emergence from
reflexive consciousness and apperception into full awareness of one's own, or
someone else's, attendant action.[5] "A gentle attention prevailed, because ...
Arthur was a strong and handsome boy. Now he *was standing* astride the veranda
..." (W39)—here, Waldo is "thinking" for all of the family watching Arthur; the
"attention" that prevails recurs in the implication of awareness borne by the
progressive. Inward reflection on Arthur's impressive stance is confirmed by its
external continuity; the "Now" is not inceptive, but signals a return of Waldo's
awareness from the general to the specific. More intricate applications include
the following:

"Thank you," she said.
Oh, Lord.
"And don't remember the worst things about me." Again she *was giggling, splitting, bursting.*
[....]
"Your brother .... is he anything like you? Is he older?"

---

[4] Cf also the shift of simultaneity back to cover Arthur's helpless spoken plea: "'Give it to
me, Waldo!' § But Waldo made it unnecessary. Waldo *was tearing* the poem up" (A293). This
use of the progressive is not, of course, limited to the central narratives, occurring also in
Section 1 (eg, B11 twice/12/19/20). For example, it can confirm that Mrs Dun only becomes
aware belatedly that her thoughts have been elsewhere while Mrs Poulter has been speaking:
"'You can muck around on your own, of course,' Mrs Poulter *was saying,* 'but a friend is
what makes the difference'" (B11).

[5] For example, "And Crankshaw *looking*" (W172), where the truncation reinforces the
shock of Waldo's awareness that Crankshaw has been observing him lost in contemptuous
thoughts. Another kind of iconic representation is that of "seeping" awareness after mental
preoccupation, as in "The bell *tolling*" (W45). Most of the irruptions into self-preoccupation
come in the form of speech-act verbs: eg, "'Oh, Waldo, Waldo!' Dulcie *was* almost *crying*"
(W153; see also W26/45/78/109/111, A244–45/260/278/283).

"No," he said.
After that she *was saying* good night and *running* up some steps .... [W98]

Waldo's perception of the giggles that attend Dulcie's words represents an emergence out of the depths of his panic-stricken consciousness. Later, his perception of Dulcie saying good night is delayed—he is mentally involved in the shock of hearing Dulcie mention his brother, so that the stunned, sequential "After that" has an after-the-factness about it. There is a similar effect later: nonplussed by Dulcie's weeping, and gripped by the vision of her after the door closes, Waldo only gradually returns to his physical surroundings: "Then he and Arthur *were going away*. Arthur *was holding* him by the hand" (W140; cf W113). Or Waldo is immersed in reflections on his own state of embarrassed consciousness as the train takes him and his father "over the outskirts of Barranugli"; with no diegetic indication that the train has arrived, there is the following: "Dad *was stuffing* his book into his pocket ... and they *were getting out* at Barranugli" (W79). More thoroughly orchestrated is this last example:

Waldo could get nothing out but a bumbling, "I I I," ...
But Arthur and Dulcie *were* again *ignoring* him.
"Arthur, dear," Dulcie *was saying*, "thank you again ...."
She *was looking* into her hand.
[...]
"I shall have to make up my mind," Dulcie answered.
She *was offering* her face almost as though for a kiss ....
"For the moment," she *was saying* .... [W151]

Waldo is involved, not in the words, so much as in his own turmoil of mental intentionality. He "surfaces", becoming belatedly aware of the extent to which he has been prattling to deaf ears. *This* stunned awareness, in turn, occupies him, attenuating awareness of his surroundings. He must "surface" again, to pick up on Dulcie's words after a mental hiatus. Perception of what she is saying becomes—again belatedly—sharpened by his observation of Dulcie's attitude towards her hand, and words and gestures become inter-explanatory (in terms of the mandala-marble, which does not get brought to the forefront of Waldo's mind, because he cannot see the actual object she is holding). The same linking of words and posture occurs again. In reaction to Dulcie's "kissing" posture, Waldo forces himself into diversionary mental concentration (on her moustache)—this is broken by his perception, a split-second after the fact, that Dulcie is speaking to him.

There are three times as many relativizing, "psychological" progressives in Waldo's section as there are in Arthur's. The more radical shifts of awareness from complete introspection and self-awareness are almost exclusively the domain of Waldo. Where they do occur in Arthur's section, they correlate with generalized emotional stress. In relative terms, the progressive of figural consciousness occurs in the ratio of Waldo 0.326 : Arthur 0.260. One might, for comparison, take a modernist novel dealing largely in dialogic exchanges and with an intense psychonarrative preoccupation with the figural registration of action, reaction, expression and psychological states: D.H. Lawrence's *Women in Love,* say, where the equivalent relativized figure from a random analysis of chapters 6–11 and 18 is 0.05. Analysis of extended passages from Henry James and Conrad have yielded even lower correlations. There is, however, a close but patchy and rudimentary similarity to White's usage in the early fiction of Randolph Stow (who is in some respects an epigone of White). This must, of course, remain an ad-hoc and interim judgement: but the incidence of such progressives in *The Solid Mandala* and in White's fiction generally is strikingly high. These occurrences are not stylistic "deviance", unless from a quantitative norm (which, however, has never been calculated for any large corpus of prose fiction; in the examples discussed, an extreme of tolerance may perhaps have been reached in the aspectualizing of the verbs *keep on* and *continue*). White is merely making optimal use of the potential that already resides in the English progressive, and can, in this respect, truly be compared with such a writer as Flaubert with his magisterial handling of the *imparfait*.

II   Modality, conditionality, and free indirect discourse

SHIFTED MODALS: GENERAL

The back-shifted tenses of reported speech are encountered in narrated monologue in the indexical form of shifted modals—"will" to "would", etc., except where back-shifting is not possible, as with root and epistemic "must" or epistemic "might".[6] In *The Solid Mandala,* intentional, mentally aggressive modals can coincide with various degrees of breakdown in punctuative logic and measured syntactic patterning, all of which represents iconically Waldo's imagination working at full (emotive) tilt: eg, "He wouldn't listen .... He would do ..." (W114–15), "He would visit islands first .... He would know how to .... The Women would be waiting .... he wouldn't overlook ..." (W116), "But he would arrive .... he would go .... But now he would make it ..." (W118).

---

[6] On tenses, see esp. Bronzwaer 1970 *passim* and Coates 1983:240–41; on free indirect discourse, see esp. Banfield 1978b:428 and 1982:103–104/118/201, and Dry 1990 (for an interesting reminder that certain tense-indicating uses of *must* and *would* in nineteenth-century novels are no longer recognized as such and are "naturalized" as free indirect discourse. Cf also Leech 1971:105: "Next to direct question and exclamation forms, the clearest (sometimes the only) indicators of free indirect speech are back-shifted verbs in the Past Tense. For example, *would* in main clauses often invites construal as the back-shifted equivalent of future *will,* none of the other senses of *will* (volitional, conditional, direct future-in-the-past) being suitable to the context: *That evening he would be seeing Sylvia again*". These general pointers are sensible and useful: but Leech has chosen a poor example, as the progressive *be seeing* is the feature which effectively cuts out the other senses (apart from which, "pure" free indirect discourse would have had present-deictic "this", not "that"). "This evening he would see Sylvia again" can be construed as volitional. A fruitful ambiguity between futurity and will can be felt throughout *The Solid Mandala* (and in the Vossian discourse of *Voss,* for example), and is only one of the effects achievable by the maximal exploitation of free indirect discourse to point up the layerings of figural consciousness.

Peculiar and ingenious effects can be achieved, as in the following: "Mother would go presently .... She would walk .... She would end up .... And he would draw ..." (W168). The effect depends on prior contextualization in a punctual (rather than iterative) narrative "moment", and on a modal statement with "must" immediately before the paragraph with the *would*-modals ("So he ... squirmed on the needle-points of his buttocks. He must cling to his gift"). Waldo's inner resolution has been signalled: he intends to keep his Secret Writing to himself, and to wait out the unwelcome visitors. What the *would*-modals convey is twofold: (a) Waldo's prediction—as a mental scenario—of what his mother and he will shortly be doing; and (b) the expression of *habit,* of what he and his mother predictably do in all such (past) situations.[7] *Be going to* is a quasi-modal of epistemic prediction (eg, "She was going to be one of those ... who did not explain", W100) and root-modal intention (eg, "He wasn't going to tell her if she didn't realize", W91, or "Sergeant Foyle was not going to pass judgment", P314). Instances can thus be bivalent: "Then she would sit down to nursing the bottle. She was going to make it last" (W271); the free indirect discourse, by contextual attraction to the preceding habitual "would", expresses both Arthur's prediction of his mother's actions (this late afternoon as every afternoon) and his empathetic reconstruction of her mental intention (now as on every occasion).

Must expresses figural resolve in contexts of free indirect discourse.[8] "Had to" is formally non-modal, and lacks a centre of subjective authority (Coates 1983:55): but it functions contrastively as an index to Waldo's consciousness as soon as we register the subjective urgency of "must" in the following: "Then they were walking somewhat quicker, because Waldo *had to* defend himself .... Or rather he *must* withdraw his mind" (W62). As we get to know Waldo, we make contextual inferences that allow us (even when there is no subjective "must", as in: "Then he made his dash. He *had to* escape to somewhere", W66) to interpret his mental acts as psychological appeals to force of circumstance.

Non-perfective *might* conveying possibility is not always so unproblematical in White as *must*.[9] One instance has already been discussed in terms of narrative

---

[7] Other *would*-modals conveying simple expectation and futurity: "Soon at least they'd come out on tar" (W29), W67/73 ("would soon be buried in words")/74/106/118–19. Expectation can shade into supposition: "perhaps Dulcie Feinstein would continue in ignorance" (W95), "she would feel" (W73), "They would think" (W177), "Nobody ... would be expected to ..." (W194), "nobody would be able to accuse him" (A230), "Their limping ... together would not help" (A230), "she would see behind the words" (A248), "Her beauty would not evaporate again" (A255). Volition and resolve are the most pervasive modal shadings: "Waldo would write a play" (W40), "In fact, he wouldn't mention the return" (A248), W30/50/91/93/103/110/111/117/127/137/149–50 (a cluster of seven in a "mental scenario")/154/ 157, A254/265.

[8] Straightforward instances include: "So he must make sure of his boxful of papers" (W117), "Perhaps it was Waldo. Not everybody has a twin. He must hang on to Waldo" (A218; note the contamination with monologic immediacy from the preceding present-tense gnomic sentence), W146/ 168/183, A215/240.

[9] Examples: "Perhaps if he cut his throat he might atone for his own nature, though he doubted it" (W127); W136/142/183/187.

doubling: "His body might topple, but only his body" (W55 and A240). The free indirect discourse is employed with different contextual weightings of the modal. With Waldo (W55), there is perception of a possibility, devoutly willed into fact, but followed by disappointment that the "spirit" (Arthur's heart) shows no signs of giving up. With Arthur (A240), there is perception of a possibility subjectively and momentarily taken for fact (before Arthur catches his balance)—a clumsiness that is conceded, but then opposed by consciousness that the "spirit" (Arthur's powers of intuitive thought) shows no signs of giving up. This is one aspect of free indirect discourse not touched on by McHale (1978:278–87) in his discussion of *mono*sentential instances of "systematic equivocation, the complicating of the issue of who is speaking" (278).

AN ASPECTUAL 'NON–MODAL'

McHale (1978:265) terms the *would*–modal (discussed above) an equivalent of "the non-modal conditional", a way of getting round the lack in English of an *imparfait* (though he omits reference to the progressive as a partial equivalent). Using an open, communicative-grammar model, McHale categorizes the remaining modal indices pragmatically and semantically; there are

modal auxiliaries which refer to speculation or a supposed obligation or permission (*must, might, should, ought to, was to,* etc). These are often strongly anomalous in context, and imply a speaker whose point of view differs from the narrator's.

Whereas McHale's examples are like mine above, some of Banfield's (1982:104) complicate the issue by being perfective back-shiftings of epistemic *could* ("could have killed/been"), although she has just claimed that such occurrences are opposed to "epistemic *could*", and although such perfectives align with "past" but not with reported speech, which is claimed as the model for the deviations of free indirect discourse (Coates 1983:240). The truth is surely that perfective *must* and *should* are fundamentally polyvalent. Epistemic or inferential *must* (perfective) is essentially subjective, focusing on the speaker's attitude to the proposition made, but also does duty for the infrequent non-modal epistemic *have to* (Coates 1983:46), which is non-subjective. It is a relatively simple matter to follow McHale in evaluating force contextually when *must* is non-perfective (see above). But it is less easy to "feel" the free indirect style in perfectives such as the following, unless one relies heavily on peripheral, contextual indicators that persuade one to impute the activity to figural consciousness rather than to some disembodied consonant narrator: "Waldo held himself so rigid Arthur *must have* felt it in his spongier hand" (W31; also W173, A226/253). In the following non-perfective uses of *could,* it is the presence of lexical fillers ("of course"), propositional meaning, or impersonal "you" that chiefly determine free-indirect status, not the modal itself: "Of course Waldo could not be told about that" (A274; also W113/194); "You couldn't say she was exactly ugly" (W11; also W203); "Waldo couldn't be expected to remember every word" (W205); W143/183. The one clear case of a free-indirect *could*–perfective is the following: "He hated it. He could have thrown away the fat parcel" (W29), which is contrafactive and contextually subjective (Coates 1983:121). In point of fact, such modal structures as "could have" and "might have" are all-pervasive in the diegesis of *The Solid Mandala,* but require separate examination, as their pragmatic functions are often too distinctive for subsumption under the present heading to do them justice.

A special sub-category is represented by *could* with verbs of perception. *Can* is aspectual, substituting for the unacceptable progressive form with such verbs (Coates 1983:90–91). There is no difference in form between *could* in the past-tense, root meaning of ability and *could* in reported-speech contexts with the same meaning. Replacement by *be able to* would remove the self-evident stative (rather than dynamic and completive) nature of the full modal with verbs of perception (Coates 1983:115–17/128). Banfield (1982:201) seems not to have considered the precise nature of this phenomenon. She lumps *could* together with *should, would* and *might* as a shifted modal. Her examples, from Virginia Woolf and George Eliot, clearly signal "the representation of perception" (both "*could* see", which makes classification easy enough). But the point at issue is not that *could* is back-shifted from *can* (ie, a morphological index), but that *could* with verbs of perception is an aspectual index for perceiving (figural) consciousness in "present" or "near" time: ie, it falls under the index of progressives of consciousness. Thus "*could* feel" (W43/44/45/68/ 205; A217/219), "*could* hear" (W61 twice/73). Furthermore, Coates implies (1983:90–91) and Leech states (1971:70) that *can/could* loses its distinctive *modal* meaning with verbs of inert perception and latent cognition ("I remember/ed" and "I understand/understood" do not alter their meaning if they are put as "I can/could remember" and "I can/could understand"). With verbs of inert perception ("hear/see/feel"), *can/could* has the *added* function of denoting state—aspect, not modality ("I hear/heard" is momentary perception; "I can/could hear" is a state of perception).

It should be mentioned that the incidence of such modals is distributionally representative for the two central narratives; the modals that prevail have largely to do with Waldo's self-protective inferences and with his negative or reflexively oriented volition.

CONDITIONALS AND PREVARICATION

Very few statements with an expressed condition can be accepted at face value in Waldo's section, as the processes of rationalization involved are so devious. A possible hypothesized action without issue may be attached to a negative condition betraying prevarication. A case in point is the following: "Waldo might have leant back to continue enjoying the escape ... if his clothes tightening hadn't constrained him, together with the fear that freedom might be the equivalent of isolation" (W79). It is not Waldo's clothes that restrain him from leaning back, but the fact that his erection would show ("constrained" is thus itself duplicitous). The second half of the modal part of the sentence (expressing intention) has its correspondence in the inhibiting fear admitted in the second of the coordinate clauses ("to continue ...": "freedom might be ..."). The physical is foregrounded syntactically to distract from the unpleasant existential-emotional core of Waldo's mood. The hypothesized action may be quite improbable to us (Waldo's novel: "If it had not been for the insufferable mental climate ... he might have committed ...", W174), the reasons given for inaction equally unconvincing. The conditionals may constitute false statements: "If he had not been so importantly occupied he might have felt mortified as well" (W81)—the modal denies Waldo's "mortification", but our knowledge of him countermands the denial. "If they hadn't been knotted together by habit he might have continued resenting ..." (W204)—the modal denies his "resentment", but our knowledge of the situation countermands the denial; here, Waldo's justification for inaction by recourse to "habit" is prevaricatory, inasmuch as "habit" actually nurtures his resentment, albeit *temporarily* dulling its edge. It is, in essence, Arthur's goodness that is exploited by Waldo—the schemer granting a stay of execution. These structures of devious self-suasion can, however, suffer breaks in their defences: "If Waldo Brown had not been a superior man ..., it might have become intolerable, or perhaps had, because of that" (W60). And, very seldom, in moments of great and complex emotional stress, modal verb and expressed condition do stand, significantly, in an honest relation to one another: "If he had come closer and alone, he might have torn the rose" (W119); "If he had had to face the brown verdict ..., the same unhappiness might have risen up inside him" (W125); "Without the reminder of his wrist the boy inside him might have remained in possession" (W70–71). In another sentence—"If it hadn't been for his own visions he might have felt desperate" (W98)—this honesty might seem to obtain, but the syntactic sequencing of the clauses is prevaricatory: a mirror-image of causal sequence; it is his feelings of desperation (which the modal tries to deny) that lead Waldo to *seek* consolation in "visions".

As so often in the narrative, a course of action, mentally contemplated, is not only improbable and prevaricatory; it is also thwarted by the putative antagonist's resolute lack of notice ("Contempt might in time have transferred itself ..., but Crankshaw was not interested to wait", W172, where "contempt" is a defence-mechanism concealing Waldo's guilt about the library book). "The beige flannel circles round [the boy's] eyes ... would have turned them into targets if Waldo hadn't been the target" (W65): the innocuous modality here (= "almost looked like") is belied by the volitional nature of the modal; it is Waldo's mental aggression against the boy that is thwarted. In other cases with "would have", the possibility entertained is entirely the outcome of Waldo's self-protective desire that something be so or not so ("the Saportas would have been too stupid", W64).[10] An hypothesized action may itself be false or situationally unlikely—not within the terms of Waldo's mental world, but in terms of the "real" world as reconstituted by the reader. "Waldo might have hooted if the engine hadn't

---

[10] Also: "Nobody would have known that Waldo Brown ... could name the cars" (W115); "and if her mother had [met Arthur], she would not have connected him with ..." (W99); "He took his brother by the hand, who would have resisted if he had remembered how to resist" (W57).

beaten him to it" (W77): Waldo could only have "hooted" inwardly, not to his father's face; physical circumstance (the pathetic fallacy of the hooting train) deflates his carefully cultivated inward scorn. "Waldo might have felt magnanimous if he had not been persecuted" (W172). "Magnanimous" is prevaricatory after a paragraph in which Waldo has been mentally shredding Crankshaw and his family—this can only be the formalized posture of generous-heartedness assumed by the victor over the vanquished. The paragraph of destructive thought is itself the outcome of Waldo's feeling "persecuted", so that his reasoning—to stave off feelings of guilt at his own viciousness—is circular. The conditionals may involve paranoiac distortions of both situation and emotively generated self-image (cf "If it had not been so subtle ...", W173). Something that the modal clause factitiously suggests is desirable or pleasant can be thwarted by the intrusion of reality in the conditional ("They might have continued in this agreeable state ... if Mr Feinstein hadn't come in", W103; W96, with suppressed conditionality/111/189).

In Arthur's discourse, at least part of the sense of negative conditionals is cast in doubt by the reader's knowledge that a different interpretation of Arthur's innocent assumptions is possible. The twins are, in a tragic sense, *not* "intimate" ("If they had been less intimate ... then he might have suffered a greater shock", A291). Dulcie *is* "different" from Arthur's image of her ("If Dulcie had been different, again he might have suspected her of putting it on", A253; cf A253). Arthur cannot really "admire" his brother ("If he had not admired his brother, Arthur might have felt hurt", A268). However much Arthur may seem to be free of the taint of conditional rationalization, conditions do tend to exert a contrary pull.

I should like to consider more closely some *might have* conditionals, in order to show how contextually potentiated they are in respect of figural consciousness. Once again, even statements resembling ironic and dissonant psychonarration are actually mediations (in these examples) of Waldo's devious thought-processes. The first is contrafactive: "Waldo might have contemplated the word 'silvery', but rejected it out of respect for literature and truth" (W23); Waldo *has* contemplated this word, as "rejected" entails—he rejects his moment of weakness in considering "silver" as appropriate for the colour of Arthur's hair. "Respect for literature" is entailed in the second example, where Waldo has shifted from thinking about his protective oil*skin* to awareness of the wind on the skin of his face: "The wind might have cut the skins of the Brothers Brown if they had not been protected by their thoughts" (W25). The sense-perception of the painfully cutting wind cannot be denied by the conditional embedding: the external is at best attenuated by concentration on the inward. In moving on to self-protection by thought, the *if*-clause points up the oscillation between the two states. But not only this; there is a macrotextual point to Waldo's fraternal imperialism of reference ("the Brothers Brown"). Thought of physical unprotectedness is associated with the harm to Arthur that Waldo is planning. There are many later suggestions of Waldo's motives being concealed behind his physiognomy, and of Arthur's "innocence" about what Waldo is thinking. The conditional sentence

with its "potential" modal is only a front for Waldo's substantive thoughts; but
there is enough reality to dissolve the *irrealis*. We return to Arthur's hair in the
third example: "If Arthur had been, say, a dog, he might have touched the back
of his head. That hair" (W27). This is one of those many occasions on which
Waldo shrinks from the half-crippled positive emotions within him. The moment
passes as soon as he is brought up short by his phobia about his brother's hair.
But Waldo's state is not a simple one. He *does* think of Arthur as being like a
dog (as numerous passages reveal), so that the casual, ad-hoc conjunct "say" is
an attempt to veil this fact. The conditional sentence is conditioned by memory—
of a childhood past when Waldo could at times show affection. Now the feeling is
not immediate, but is retrieved from the past and cannot be superimposed on the
present scene: Arthur is now too much Waldo's burdensome brother, a man, and
a co-inhabitant of Waldo's failure, for the latter to be able to show affection. The
feeling is notional, and Waldo can expend affection only on objects (like his dog,
W180) that do not pose a threat to his shaky, dearly-won stability. The
conditional sentence is tragically tortuous in its acknowledgement of the ghostly
trace of a fraternal love that can no longer be demonstrated.

More tortuous still is the fourth and last example: "This head might have
flaunted an ostentation of cleanliness, if it had not been for its innocence, and the
fact that he knew Arthur was in many ways not exactly clean" (W26). "Flaunted
an ostentation" is tautologous and therefore doubly ostentatious. In setting up
"innocence" in opposition to cleanliness, Waldo is involuntarily affirming the
unassuming aura of cleanliness about Arthur's hair. But Waldo cannot abide
"innocence"—his mental slip is then corrected by an assertive appeal to general
"facts" about Arthur's uncleanliness. The accusation is weakened, as prejudiced
slanders so often are, by vagueness ("in many ways") and suggestive meiosis
("not exactly"). There is one more thing to note about this sentence—one further
determinant of its modality—which is that it encodes a scene from the past which
is only recounted (without commentary) much further along in the narrative. The
conditional sentence occurs immediately before Waldo's consideration of having
to cut Arthur's hair "every third Sunday ... on the back veranda, behind the
glass" (whence Waldo's experience of Arthur's "unclean" hair—the adjective a
euphemism for Waldo's phobic antipathy). At the Feinsteins', Arthur shows his
"innocence" (W112) by confusing a literary salon with a hairdressing salon
(though he learns, it is implied, from this mistake, W132). His "innocence", the
fact that hairdressing salons have glass frontages, and the fact that Mrs Feinstein
told how Madame Hochapfel's salon met on Sundays, have filtered into Waldo's
thoughts (W26): the obliquity of the modal sentence in its relation to the
immediate mental context matches the obliquity of memory and suppressed
evaluation.

DESIRE'S DEFEAT BY GRAMMAR

"He would have liked to. Oh yes, he would have liked to. He would have liked to *be*" (W128). This sequence expresses quite poignantly one of the main thematic strands in the narrative. My concern is not so much with the thematic import as with the fact that the modal formulation is essentially non-analytical, for all its appearance of being analytical. The "would have liked" construction is usually the closest the characters are allowed to come in thought to stepping back from their own rationalizations about *raison d'être* (which are also conveyed through modal formulae) and expressing desire: a desire which in Waldo's case is the governing dynamic of his inner life. That the discourse is inward and not auctorially analytical is indicated by various expressive features (the emotively incremental repetition; the exclamation; the typographical emphasis). More significant than the frequent resolution of the modal clause by adversatives ("He would have liked to go permanently proud and immaculate, but his twin brother dragged him back", W46; W79/94/124/131/137/201/207/68 "only"/196 "when he only had"; A272; P306/309 "if all the grass ... hadn't been ...") is the fact of grammatical inexorability, the sense of desire being frustrated by some foreordaining principle, which is enabled by the felicitous accident of the *perfective* modality. An "accident", because the mental wish—which may well have been immediately *present*—is engulfed in the logical necessity of the tense of recollective narration.[11]

PSEUDO–CONCESSIVE 'IF'

There is a conditional-concessive construction with initial *If* (actually, two constructions) which occurs in *The Solid Mandala* with greater frequency than its grammatical classification would suggest is usual. Only two sentences in the novel with an expressed condition are explicitly concessive ("*Even if* he had he would not have allowed himself", W90; W53). There are 30 conditional-concessives which begin with *if*, on the pattern of: "If she had started humbly, the music had made her proud" (W135) or "If Arthur usually got possession ..., it was because ..." (A274). Linguists classify this usage as occasional only (Quirk et al. 1972:749). Of the concessives in the novel (including modal clauses), about 94% have the "occasional" form, and of all the sentences in the novel with an expressed *if*-condition, some 38% are concessive. These figures perhaps require adjustment in view of the fact that concessives without modal clauses have been left out of the reckoning.

A total count of *if*-conditional clauses and full concessive clauses was made for the first one hundred pages of Waldo's section, with results as in the table below:

---

[11] See also, with no adversative resolution: "He would have liked to, anyway, and often the intention is acceptable" (W49); "Now he would have liked to look at her" (W91); W98/101/129; A230/ 269.

Table 5: Concessives and conditionals

		%	
if-conditionals	29	46	
even if/even though	4	6.5	}
(al)though	21	34	}54%
if-concessives	8	13.5	}
	62	**100**	

There are more concessives than there are *if*-conditionals—even more than the 54% of the above count.[12] If the concessives are taken as a closed group, informal *though*-clauses outweigh *although*-clauses by 19 to 2 (thus confirming the informal coloration of the discourse); almost 25% of all concessives have the simple *if*-form—a lower figure than the comparative figure for the modal corpus, but still significantly high.

Harry Heseltine has drawn attention to this formal feature:

one of White's most common syntactic patterns must be the conditional construction, real or hypothetical: as in *Voss:*

If the others barely listened, or were only mildly disgusted by his outburst, it was because each man was obsessed by the same prospect.

Or in *The Tree of Man:*

If Amy Parker continued to sit, it is because the rose is rooted and impervious.

Or in *Riders [in the Chariot]*:

If it had been evening, she might have done something with a fan—if she had had one.

Even in recording particular situations or events, White's prose habitually indicates possibilities beyond the present moment. [Heseltine 1963b:73–74]

These "possibilities" need clarification. The "pattern" is not the same in all three of Heseltine's examples: the first two are not conditionals at all, either "real or hypothetical", in any pragmatic sense; the *if*-clause is a rhetorical leg-in for the cleft-sentence clause of reason and has, at most, concessive force. It is a subordinated statement of fact (hence my syntactic-semantic classification "conditional-concessive"). The third sentence is a true conditional, as is indicated by the presence of the modal in the main clause and the past perfect of the *if*-clauses. But it is peculiarly doubled in its witty and bathetic bracketing of the main clause's idle surmise. There is, furthermore, no common discoursal basis for the three examples. Torn so out of context, the first could be dissonant or non-focalized narration, or focalization through an empathetic reflector-character; the second is based on a gnomic and metaphoric present-tense utterance by a dissonant psychonarrator (thus differing from gnomic sentences in *The Solid*

---

12 Concessives far outweigh conditionals if various types of abbreviated clause, exclamations and concessive-temporal clauses are admitted for comparison ("though respectfully"; "even where/when"; "much as he..."; "except that"; "Not that"; "if not/if nothing else/if anything"; the *if*-meiotic phrases discussed in ch. 5; conditional exclamations and questions). When the two main categories are again balanced out for pages 23–123 of Section 2, concessives outweigh conditionals by a ratio of 6:3.3. That is, some 65% of the total are concessives—and this leaves out of consideration all those disjuncts and conjuncts which carry concessive force ("certainly/of course/admittedly/after all/at least", for example). The mental discourse of Waldo's section is continually backtracking, constantly on the retreat; true possibilities are seldom entertained.

Mandala); the third is either consonant psychonarration or narrated monologue (the mental logic of the clause-sequencing suggests the latter). Heseltine, however, sees the prose itself as "indicating" something—are such indications independent of the characterizing constraints of the voicing? Are these "possibilities beyond the present moment" inherent in the grammatical constructions? What possibilities are there which might have to do with the "present moment"? (Heseltine's formulation invites this alternative.) If these three sentences *were* all conditional, would it not be true to say that they, like every conditional under the sun, would by definition have to do with future possibilities? The first two sentences can be naturalized, albeit with a re-shading of sense attendant on the change of form: |The others barely listened, or were mildly disgusted by this outburst; but this was because ... |; |Amy Parker continued to sit: after all, the rose is ... |. The "possibilities" of the first sentence have not been vaporized by this desecration of style: the individual obsession "by the same prospect" is still there. What "possibilities" were ever there in the second sentence? Except those *actionally* implied in Amy's posture and in the metaphysic of expectant roses? As for the third, unalterable, sentence: isn't the character entertaining future possibilities in the present moment, wishing that the future *were* the present—which we would never learn, were it not for the grammatical construction?

Apart from Heseltine, the only critic who has tackled the problem of White's conditionals in any constructive and original way has been Carolyn Bliss.[13] She regards these conditionals as "the most unmistakably Whitean sentence structures" (1986:191), though they are surely not as pervasively conspicuous as White's "*de*-structured" sentences (reserved for consideration later). Bliss's explanation (in keeping with her general thesis about White's "fortunate failure") is that the conditionals encourage "interpretative pluralism" in a fictive world that asserts the fluidity of meaning. Covertly *restricting* the range of possibilities, White overtly offers the reader more access than is compatible with the position of an "omniscient narrator", thus compelling active "partnership" (192). The trouble with this theory and its exemplification is that it upholds the principle of unresolvability to the last hermeneutic gasp, as though White's fictions were some superextended Zen koan. One example is drawn from *Voss*: "As soon as a decent interval had elapsed, Laura withdrew her hand. If Voss did not notice, it was because he was absorbed". Bliss (or "the reader") *cannot* decide "whether Voss did, in fact, notice Laura's withdrawn hand, and, if he didn't, whether the proposed explanation is supplied by the narrator or by Laura's injured feelings. (In this case, the effect of the conditional is complicated by uncertainty in point of

---

13 Delmonte (1974:37), in a negligently edited essay on *Riders in the Chariot,* simply lifts Heseltine's observation without acknowledgement; Kramer (1976:62–63) gives three examples from *A Fringe of Leaves* to show how "an illusion of depth and complexity in character" is "not conveyed by the action itself": these happen to be the conditional structures Heseltine drew attention to. None of them concerns "action", anyway (this has never been at the centre of White's fiction: rather, the interaction of mind with immanent phenomena): two concern *existents,* not action, the third reactive gesture.

view)". But there is a *hierarchy* of interpretative decisions here, which must be sorted out in order to escape the circular logic of "uncertainty of point of view". Microtextual readings are open to final decisions (even final decisions about the fruitfulness or otherwise of polysemy)—the final arbiter must be the relative snugness with which a *choice* of meaning "fits" a given context.

But I have already maintained that microcontexts alone may not suffice to resolve such problems. We need to go further than Heseltine or Bliss in formulating general principles that can deliver the (often impatient) reader of White from the ill-disciplined false democracy of "possibilities" and "pluralism". I would claim to know what *the* meaning of the *Voss*-sentence is (ie, a meaning that at least gets the reader somewhere). Let us see whether a full examination of White's non-conditional, pseudo-concessive sentences in *The Solid Mandala* can predict what my interpretation might be.

The first thing to note is that the *forms* are independent of character: ie, are not distributed in *The Solid Mandala* so as to reflect the particular modality or mental idiolect of one figural consciousness (though relative *quantities* can reflect this). What I have just stated anticipates my second point, which is that the formal mode, though chosen by the author in accordance with his own presuppositions about the mechanisms of mental logic, is not communicatively univocal. It certainly serves what might be called a neutral diegetic function, maintaining a particular tonal aura which is destroyed as soon as paraphrase is attempted. Unlike Heseltine's first two examples, however, the sentences in *The Solid Mandala* are also inextricably bound up with the psychological specificity of what is being contemplated (or reasoned) figurally: by individual characters, that is, rather than by the implied author.

The simplest case is represented by the simplest soul, Mrs Poulter. Here the discourse is unequivocally narrated monologue, so we can assume that the mental logic involved is hers: **(1)** "If she didn't have any friends without the ones she yarned with over fences, in buses, or the street, she didn't need any" (P295); **(2)** "If she cracked up like some old enamel pot it was what happens in time" (P296); **(3)** "If she and Arthur was answerable for the day in the blackberry bushes, ..., they was answerable only to the Lord God" (P300).[14] After reviewing the material appurtenances which represent for her the only comforts she has in a social milieu devoid of emotional comfort, Mrs Poulter moves from the "telly" to thought of casual "friends". The fact that this thought should occur now, in pseudo-hypothetical form, undermines the idea that her litany of home comforts is sufficient comfort. Yet, in the very moment of grammatical concession to the truth, she is defending herself against it, even before we get to the main clause with its stubborn but hollow declaration of self-sufficiency. Psychologically, we can detect disappointed desire, negated futurity; but textually, **(1)** is still a statement of fact in the subordinate clause and a rationalization only in the main

---

[14] Note the dialect coloration of ungrammaticality in **(3)**, and the figural appropriation of the gnomic present in **(2)** one verb later than formally expectable, as a true merging of the personal and the universal—quite different from the seemingly auctorial gnomic in *The Tree of Man* (cited above).

clause. In (3), Mrs Poulter *feels* "answerable" at the moment of thought, as it is not only that the imponderability of her relationship with Arthur exacts ratiocination, but also that her guilt-feelings at somehow betraying her husband demand rationalizing. In all three sentences, a social, emotional or physical fact needs explaining away. The sentence-form is not unitary in terms of semantic logic: all three statements can be paraphrastically disfigured by dropping *if* and inserting *but*, thus turning a dependence-relation into a coordination; but (2) additionally, or alternatively, involves a covert clause of reason (|She cracked up ... because it was what happens in time|).

In most of the *if*-concessive sentences, there is a sense of mental haste: of subterranean longings or emotional discomfort propelling the thinker into the quickest possible cover-up or dissipation of this emotion. This is conveyed iconically in every case (thought-sequence mirrored in syntactic sequence), sometimes in a complex way: (4) "For some reason, for the moment, he was less able to communicate with them, though if he hadn't lost the art, he would not have known exactly what he wanted to say" (A248). The cover-up is included in the *if*-clause; the sentence sounds placid enough, just as, we can assume, Arthur is able to reassure himself into placidity: but the prior heaping-up of hedging phrases betrays a deeper puzzlement and uncertainty. (5) "If there were moral reasons for his aloofness, he had not yet thought them out" (W127). This is the most devious of Waldo's concessive thoughts, where prevarication has already infected the *if*-clause. Waldo, in effect, asserts that there *are* "moral reasons" for his avoidance of social responsibility in the matter of war: his guilt about being accused of dereliction of moral duty generates the whole statement, ultimately collapsing and overpowering his truth-assertion in the very moment at which he implies that such "reasons" can in time be supplied. The main clause betrays itself, too: for behind the pretence of logical consideration ("thought ... out") lurks the fiction-making of "thought up".

The *if ... because* sentences are perhaps easier to approach, because the semantic frame is more clearly demarcated.[15] There are very few sentences with this pattern in White that are not generated out of a sense of psychological disequilibrium on the part of the thinker. The *if*-clauses, although all reducible to statements of fact, are there because the figural consciousness has registered a

---

[15] Two sentences have prepositional-gerundive causality instead of *because:* "If passion stirred in George Brown, it was for the most unassuming manifestations of nature" (W159); "If he sometimes bit his spoon ..., it was for remembering ..." (W206). Jespersen, incidentally (1940:377-78), is the only classic grammarian who has attempted to explain the specific semantic force of pseudo-concessive *if*-clauses (other grammars practically ignore this familiar construction): "What we may term pseudo-condition is found when the *if*-form is used rhetorically to point a contrast, or to show that two statements are equally true .... 'If he had done wrong, he always confessed his fault'". Jespersen continues: "Similarly the reason for a fact is given in this form", and provides three examples, one from Macaulay in the *if ... because* pattern, and another from a modern source: "If he hasn't married it is because he was crossed in love in his youth". Even though their focus of attention is syntactic patterns, Curme, Kruisinga, Zandvoort, Quirk (1972) and others offer not a single example of the *if ... because* construction.

disquieting perception or has had an apperception forced upon it. It is, however, the easiest thing in the world for a reader to skim over such sentences, to take them simply as stylistically elegant and dispassionate packagings of facts. But the very presence of a left-branching construction is a warning index to an indirection which is more than just a matter of stylistic choice (ie, "literary" syntax instead of more easily and immediately graspable coordinate or right-branching structures).[16] We have already encountered a maximum of figural prevarication and dissimulation in left-branching sentences with a modal component: and the same phenomenon is discernible in these pseudo-concessives, which (a) hold the reader in suspense until final resolution of sense, and (b) have only the narrowest grammatical platform of main-clause factuality—the tiny cleft-sentence "it was", which is flanked by subordinate and thus "suspended" clauses.

The most innocuous, most "factual" case is (6): "If George Brown threw away *Teach Yourself Norwegian* it was not because he no longer needed it" (W79), with the continuation: "He could never rely on himself to sit in the train without a book". Like most of the *if ... because* sentences, this is subliminally autodialogic, in that a character (Waldo) is not only explaining an action to himself but is also doing so because he has asked himself why the action should be so (or, rather: the question has been put to him as an inchoate twinge of emotive reaction). We should not forget that the sex-lecture episode, in which Mr Brown has been reading this book on the train, has proved an emotional débâcle for the father as well as for the son. If George Brown is sensitive enough about books to go and burn *The Brothers Karamazov,* he is sensitive enough to "throw away" the U.T.P. handbook (Waldo's verb is revealingly strong) in order to avoid being reminded of an embarrassing incident. Note that Waldo's negative self-answer is no *reason* for his father's action: he has noticed that his father has discarded the book, cannot face the possibility that *he* (Waldo) might be implicated in the act, and proceeds to explain it away reductively in order to get himself off the hook. The closest that a character gets to *admitting* disquietude is, significantly, in the dark aftermath of Waldo's death, when Arthur's defences are down yet he is so tainted by "experience" as to fabricate the most convincing of rationalizations: (7) "If he continued experiencing guilt ..., it was because he knew Waldo would have ..." (P307). Between these poles of ostensible neutrality

---

16 In Section 1, 86% of the complex sentences are loose (with trailing coordinate or dependent constituents); they are linear, sequential, lacking in tension, and generate no strong sense of climax; four-fifths are fundamentally biclausal; the remainder have parenthetical, non-dependent embedding. All this points to the presence of an iconic or mimetic principle whereby sentence structure reflects the relaxed informality of everyday speech (and thus figural rather than auctorial-narratorial consciousness). The very few sentences that are periodic (with a "literary" promotion of anticipatory constituents that are subordinate or dependent) are fundamentally biclausal—the left-branching is thus minimal, and sense-resolution unimpeded by sentence-length. The conditional, concessive, reason and time clauses all strictly match the *sequence* of the actions or mental acts narrated. The more thoroughly the discourse is subjectivized (in Section 2 and after), the more we should expect the relation between loose and periodic, right- and left-branching, informal and "literary" syntax to reflect mental and emotional patterns.

and emotive openness, figural thought moves in a measured dance of willed self-deception, in accordance with the sentential pattern.

(8) "If Waldo accompanied them voluntarily it was because he knew it to be his fate" (W44). Waldo's thought about the playground-torture scene has a slightly stunned tone: part experiencing (in keeping with Waldo's passivity as sacrificial victim), part recall of experience (in the analytical "voluntarily"). Waldo must always "know", although knowledge is the least of it in the situation he finds himself in—what he must rationalize away is his cowardice in not being able to resist his tormentors and his *not* knowing what lies in store for him. **(9)** "If he stumbled at that point it was because he had turned his right toe in" (W57-58). The observation that Arthur has stumbled is a perception which seems to belie what Waldo has just been thinking about his brother being "steadied by thoughtfulness". It is clear that Waldo doesn't want to think that Arthur's comment—"'I forget what I was taught. I only remember what I've learnt'"—could be anything but shallow. It dare not, say, be profound enough to cause Arthur (who has just been yelled at by his brother) to stumble physically because emotion arising out of awareness of the seriousness of his utterance has unbalanced him. After all, what Arthur has said undermines Waldo's whole *raison d'être* and delicate psychological equilibrium, which are based on the formal processing of other people's thoughts, not on direct experience. Hence Waldo's hurried conviction in attributing the stumbling to purely physical causes. **(10)** "If no comment was made by Dad ...—if Dad seemed unaware ..., it was because ..." (W82)—Waldo *has to* be "suddenly convinced" (at the end of an elephantine sentence representing Waldo's puzzled, resentful working-out of his father's lack of interest in his Writing)[17] that his father is a failure as a writer. **(11)** "If he sometimes bit his spoon ..., it was for remembering ..." (W206)—the clumsiness entailed in Waldo's involuntary clenching of his teeth on the spoon, in an access of horrified relief, *must* be put into rational terms by someone as intent on bodily caution, as embarrassed by the unpredictable autonomy of the *physis*, as Waldo is.

Many of the *if ... because* clauses in Arthur's section involve a drawing back, in their very articulation, from the truth of the thought being conveyed in the *if*-clause. **(12)** "If the thought didn't grow unbearable, it was because ... Waldo was in need of a kind" (A239)—the thought that Waldo will sour his relationship with Mrs Musto *has* grown "unbearable"; it is only the main-clause rationale that can console Arthur in his imminent loss, can remove the unbearable from his shoulders. **(13)** "If he was at all flustered it was because her beauty ..." (A244)—Arthur *is* flustered, and he knows it shows in his gauche behaviour; but "at all" tries to minimize the effect. **(14)** "If he no longer felt moved to take down a book, it was because ..." (P307)—the dispassionate neutrality of the *if*-clause conceals a terrible, guilty shrinking from an act which might remind him of the

---

17 After the initial *if*-clause there are, successively: (1) an appositional phrase, (2) a relative clause, (3) two reduced relative participial clauses, (4) an embedded coordinate object-clause with (5) an attached relative clause ....a hiatus of drawn mental breath, then ... (6) an *if*-clause resumption with (7) a nominal-object clause attached.

chain of causality—the Books, the Secret Reading, the depth of acquired insight, the secret poems—that has constituted a series of ultimately lethal hammer-blows to Waldo's crucial self-esteem. **(15-17)** These form a group: "If he did not add Mrs Allwright it was because she did not fit ..." (A227); "If he stood alone it was because his employer would be out ..." (A232); "If he hadn't got to know Mrs Mutton either, it was because there was nothing to know" (A286). All look as though they mediate facts, yet all turn on the secret pivot of Arthur's vulnerability. After all: Arthur himself admits that Mrs Allwright is the only person who ever disliked him—if he can be so trusting of others as to suspect nobody else, how vicious must Mrs Allwright's antipathy have been, how implacably, silently echoic that of her sister, Mrs Mutton! "If he stood alone", in context, does not state a fact. We already have precisely this fact in the previous paragraph, with Arthur hiccuping and twisting his finger in abject fear—not at the prospect of serving customers (for he is a gregarious, social being), but at being deserted by Mr Allwright and given over to the back-stabbing watchfulness of these two back-room Furies. Arthur is isolated, standing "alone", fearful of the double "retro-spect": Mrs Allwright behind his back, inside, ready to stab; Mrs Mutton "visiting behind the shop".[18]

I cannot emphasize enough just how precisely calculated such formal syntactic-semantic patterns are in the novel, how impervious to any charge of slackness or stylistic automatism. The *if ... because* construction and the less formal *if*-concessive are hallmarks of White's style—constants of his "mind-style"—and may, of course, be employed for different purposes in his other novels. Regarding the persistence of *if*-concessives in White: to draw on just two modernist (but not modern) novels for comparison, both with a high proportion of free indirect discourse but with conspicuous intermittent dissonant psychonarration as well, there are no more than about five full *if*-concessives in Conrad's *The Secret Agent*, but about 28 in James's *The Ambassadors*.[19] Of those

---

[18] Other *if ... because* sentences that can be consistently explicated syntactically in terms of figural emotion can be found at: W161 ("If he resisted toying with the idea")/206 ("If Waldo did not criticize further"); A240 ("if Arthur did not march in time")/241 ("If he was not encouraged")/274 ("If Arthur usually got possession") and, quintessentially a disguising of intention, A292-93 ("If Arthur picked up ... that old dress").

[19] I supply the following instances from Conrad and James, marked in **boldface** for discourse features—generally absent from White—which provide clear indications of the clausal logic; and marked with **boldface number/letter** to indicate *modification* of topic from clause to clause (**1a, 1b**) or *contrast* of topic from clause to clause (**1, 2**):

Conrad: "If he could not give the great and curious lady a very definite idea[1a] as to what the world was coming to, he had managed without effort to impress[1b] her" (ch. 6); "If he believed firmly that to know too much[1a] was not good for the department, the judicious holding back of knowledge[1b] was as far as his loyalty dared to go" (ch. 6); "And if Mr Verloc thought for a moment[1a] that his wife's brother looked uncommonly useless, it was **only** a dull and fleeting thought[1b]" (ch. 9).

James: "If the effort directed to this end involved ... the presence of Strether—consisted, that is, in the detention of the latter for full discourse[1]—there was **yet** an impression of minor[2] discipline involved" (ch. 2); "If Waymarsh was sombre[1] he was **also, indeed**, almost sublime[2]" (ch. 3); "If he had begun yesterday with a small grievance[1] he had **therefore** an

in Conrad, none is an *if ... because* construction. In James, there is one such construction. The "feel" of this sentence-type in White is, at first glance, very nineteenth-century—almost, indeed, as though it represented the measured, judiciously explicative voicing of one of James's sovereignly speculative narrators. But, although a general affinity of stylistic register may be confirmed by the James/White comparison in this respect, the *if ... because* construction is peculiarly White's own.

It would be unfair of me to quit this subject without making good my earlier claim to know *the* meaning of the conditional sentence from *Voss*. Context cannot be ignored, though the above analysis of sentences from *The Solid Mandala* would allow one at the outset to put forward the testable hypothesis that it is Laura who has noted (it could be with surprise, or with disappointment) that Voss is paying her no attention, and who plays down the probability that he has not noticed her withdrawing her hand (for him to be so oblivious would confirm his social gaucheness and the fact that she has been slighted) before excusing his behaviour to cover up her embarrassment and disappointment. It is clear from the prior context (consonant psychonarration with "Vossian" coloration) that Voss is both overwhelmed by the scene of leavetaking and exhilarated by the prospect of the journey. His social gestures are automatisms (punnily, "after a fashion"), and he forgets that he is still holding "Miss Trevelyan's hand" (the full name accompanies Voss's perception of the hand's gloved impersonality). There is a shift of perspective to Laura (with a shift of naming to "Laura"). Her pseudo-concessive statement allows for the fact that there is no guarantee that the "absorbed" Voss is not noticing externals (Laura's presence) with some part of his being. The left-branching syntax underplays as it generates tension. This *psychical* tension spills over into Laura's subsequent, fatalistic thought and gesture concerning Voss. Through Laura's syntactically controlled perspective, we gain a powerful impression of the effects of Voss's underlying

---

opportunity to begin to-day with its opposite[2]" (ch. 5); "He had not had the gift of making the most[1a] of what he tried, and if he had tried and tried[1a] again ... it appeared to have been that he might demonstrate what else, in default of that, *could* be made[1b]" (ch. 5; emphasis in original); "If the playhouse was not closed, his seat at least had fallen to somebody else" (ch. 5); "But if he didn't know,[1a] in so important a particular, what was good, Chad at least was now aware he didn't[1b]" (ch. 8); "The differences were there to match; if they were doubtless deep,[1] though few, they were quiet[2]" (ch. 8); "If the light, however, was not, as we have hinted, the glow of joy, the reasons for this also were perhaps discernible to Strether" (ch. 34); "If he had just thought of himself as old,[1a] Chad, at sight of him, was thinking of him as older[1b]" (ch. 35); "If there was nothing for it but to repeat,[1a] however, repetition[1b] was no mistake" (ch. 35); "and the turn his affair had, on the whole, taken was positively that, if his nerves were on the stretch, it was because he missed violence" (ch. 8).

It will be noted that the semantic patterning in the Conrad sentences is the same, whereas James's sentences exhibit more variety and more clausal complexity. Allowing for the temporary opacities occasioned by James's phrasal nesting, however, these communications are more *transparent* in their witty subtlizing than those in White.

singlemindedness. There is no *reason* to suppose that the pseudo-concessive
sentence encodes either White's or Voss's or a dissonant narrator's perspective.[20]

III   Gnomic statements: a feature–analysis

AUCTORIAL OR FIGURAL ATTRIBUTION?

The general question of gnomic, present-tense statements has already been
touched on several times. I shall therefore restrict discussion of narratological
theories to those not mentioned so far, by way of a preface to my commentary on
a classified list of gnomic sentences in *The Solid Mandala*. The usual view of
gnomic sentences is that they unmistakably reveal the presence of "the author's
voice" (eg, Lodge 1984:103), and form the chief constituent of the narrative
mode called "commentary" or "comment". Unlike report, speech and
description, comment is "ideational" because it is independent of the parameters
of time and space though reflecting on matters which arise in fictive time and
space. Comment is easily identifiable as such: it is not susceptible to "epic" back-
shifting of tense, and inhabits a "neutral time-sphere" (according to Bronzwaer
1970:51, who finds the phenomenon unproblematical enough not to discuss it).
Bonheim (1982:12/30) also regards this mode as easily identifiable: it uses
"evaluative modifiers, generalizations not imputed to one of the fictional
characters, or judgments using a fairly high level of abstraction". Comment in
fiction relates, in genre-terms, to the "essay, philosophical discourse, sermon, or
newspaper editorial", and is avoided by "writers of fiction in our age" (except for
the post-modernists), "especially in its pure forms, that is, unalloyed with the
other modes, at sentence and paragraph length and in the present tense"
(1982:31). It can be seen how problematical the category of comment might
prove to be in the case of Patrick White's fiction, especially when the mode is
understood in its broader manifestations, and in view of Bonheim's prescriptive
aesthetic aside that "too much comment spoils a work of art".

One recent monograph on White, in a survey of White's critical reception,
endorses without analytical examination of the text the view that "gnomic
utterances" or interspersed *sententiae* are conspicuously present in *Voss* and other
novels by White—utterances which, it is claimed, comment obtrusively on what is
narrated and break the narrative flow. Harry Heseltine is cited approvingly:
"again and again [White] intrudes into the text of *Voss* through direct comment,

---

[20] Similarly, there is no *reason* to accept David Martin's view (1959:55–56) that another
pseudo-concessive statement in *Voss* doesn't "tell" "plainly"—or that White's English is full of
"irrelevant" detail, representing a toiling that is "all in the mind". The statement Martin quotes
is: "The German sucked in the fringes of his moustache. He could have suffered from
indigestion, if it was not contempt". The modals relating to perception in *The Solid Mandala*,
like those in *Voss*, warn the reader that the *mind* (and here it doesn't matter whose it is) is
grappling with its own reactions to sense-impressions. The syllepsis is not "irrelevant", but
essential, as are the modal and pseudo-concessive structures, in reinforcing the visceral, even
painful, force of Voss's megalomaniacal superiority of vision. That much at least the mind—
any mind—is surely supposed to take in.

overt moral judgment, or universalizing proposition" (Heseltine 1965:400, in Stein 1983:23; see also 16). Yet the possibility is not entertained that there might be a contradiction between acceptance of this view of comment as auctorial engagement and the view of, say, Brian Kiernan, who sees "the impossibility of locating White himself in the total complex poetic drama of *Voss*" (Kiernan 1971:123–26, quoted and endorsed by Stein 1983:26). As the concept of irony does not find its way into the discussion at this point (though it does independently of the question of narration elsewhere in Stein's study), the possibility of contradiction must stand. There is no denying that "direct" comment plays a central role in *Voss*. But it remains to be seen whether the narratorial function of such "directness" is everywhere to be taken as the intrusion of an omniscient implied author of a traditional stamp, and thus as tending to "spoil a work of art". Morley quotes a gnomic sentence wherein the Moravian Brethren accept Voss's actions, "taking it for granted that even the apparently misguided acts obey some necessity in the divine scheme" (Viking, p. 45). This she sees as "another example of authorial control of point of view without actual commentary .... the internal point of view in the novel controls the reader's attitude towards Voss" (Morley 1972:130). Morley is rebuked by Stein (1983:28), who clearly believes that sentences like the one quoted represent fully White's own comment on the Brethren's motivation. I think he is wrong; but it is Morley's own fault that her point has not been taken—*she* feels that the gnomic statement is a narratorial representation of the Brethren's *own* universalizing thought-processes, but she nowhere makes this properly clear. More shoring-up is necessary, of course: one random narrative instance cannot prove the rule. But the narrational frame for the quotation from *Voss* also involves closer familiarity on our part with the exceptionally wide range of White's diegetic bridges to mimetic utterance. "Taking it for granted that", in White's scheme, is less likely to be a psychonarrational exit from the Moravians into purely auctorial sentiment than a tag prefacing a statement which is closer to *direct thought* than to anything else. And this despite our expectation of the proper status of a nominative clause after *that*.

Throughout *Voss*, unmarked direct thought occurs, either "normally" tagged (eg, "How much less destructive of the personality are thirst, fever, physical exhaustion, he thought, much less destructive than people", 23), "abnormally" tagged (eg, "Then they are committed to each other, Laura Trevelyan saw", 15), or un-tagged (eg, in a clearly psychonarrational passage relating to Laura Trevelyan, after tagged direct thought: "though of course, the young woman realized, it is always like this in houses on Sunday mornings while others are at church. It was, therefore, but a transitory comfort. *Voices, if only in whispers, must break in.* Already she herself was threatening to disintegrate into the voices of the past", 8). The universalizing tenor of these examples is essentially no different (contextually indistinguishable) from such "gnomic" statements as "Order does prevail" (8), "But the purpose and nature are never clearly revealed" (10), or even almost a whole paragraph (eg, "Such solid stone houses, which seem to encourage brooding .... but to the children of light, who march in, and throw the shutters right back", 11–12). The slightest attention to the immediate narrational and perspectival context is enough to reveal how such statements emanate from figural awareness, and are not incursions of auctorial commentary. In *Voss,* White may make serious play with certain conventions of "omniscience" (one of the most unnerving being repeated proleptic allusions, couched in the future-in-the-past modality of "would", to the ultimate fate, and fateful intertwinings, of the various members of the prospective expedition). But the "commentary" in White, though it is certainly designed to shake the reader's complacency (as Stein notes; but what aspect of White's language *doesn't* achieve this aim?), need not make the author a didactic or moralistic writer (as Stein also claims). Such an assertion, anyway, runs counter to White's express denial of any intent to sermonize (see White 1973:138–39).

It is evident that critical presuppositions play a large part in determining the presence of comment in narratives. There is, even in Cohn, a tendency to seize on superficial formal characteristics as signalling only auctorial comment, and a concomitant rationalizing away of contradictory evidence (the maximum position allowed being a "marriage" of irony between narrator and character). Bonheim's category depends upon the identification of contextual, text-pragmatic determinants which make comment *necessarily* non-figural—generalizations must not be imputed (explicitly, one assumes) to "one of the fictional characters": ie, by an unequivocal diegetic-narratorial act. On the other hand, comment for Bonheim depends for its identification on partially applicable formal considerations such as present-tense marking. Other markers include conjuncts and disjuncts such as *after all, possibly, it might be that* for "observations and connections" not expected "of a casual spectator". The connecting observer who is not "a casual spectator" need not, however, be a non-figural consciousness (Bonheim would surely not deny this possibility; but his argument does). These formal markers are not primarily evidence for the presence of narratorial comment, but are potential second-level corroborations of a classification reached by logical, deductive means. The gnomic sentences in *The Solid Mandala* are formally and contextually (text-pragmatically) non-auctorial and figural. The gnomic sentences in *Voss*, which are equally conspicuous, *seem* to operate at the opposite polarity to that of figural consciousness, but have been taken to be so because the critics have been swayed by the presence of other "auctorial" features that really do play constructively with the generic conventions of nineteenth-century narration. The *real* "contamination" operating in *Voss* is between "gnomic" narration and the main protagonists' (Voss's and Laura's) "gnomic" vision—each with its own character, its own infection of the will. Even if this hypothesis were false, these two novels would at the very least offer the possibility of a paradigmatic range or scale against which to measure that feature of White's style which critics have claimed most strongly reflects his tendency to steer his narratives by means of apodictic intrusion. If my argument for zero-degree comment in *The Solid Mandala* is valid, then there are no grounds for assuming that White the artist is *by nature* an interfering implied-auctorial presence in all his fictions.[21]

It should at this point be mentioned that current narrative theory allows for the retention of the present tense in free indirect discourse (as in reported speech) "in 'general saws', proverbs, timeless truths" (McHale 1978:252.*n*3). As an extension of this, once free indirect discourse has been established, "the present tense can be safely used to convey subjective statements, if there is an advantage in so doing. For a generalisation ..., the present tense makes the assertion seem more confident and dogmatic" (Pascal 1977:83; cf also 96). Statements of a universal nature involve different "insinuations" in the present tense from those conveyed in a free-indirect "past" tense; a shift out of the gnomic present invariably lends temporal meaning to generalizations—they lose their "claim to absolute truth" and seem to be thoughts (of characters) devised as rationalizations (Pascal 1977:49). One can, of course, always proceed on the principle adopted by Chatman, Cohn and Bonheim, and consider the possibility (for them, the probability) that a present-tense generalization is auctorial-narratorial; but one has to weigh up the effect of this on textual comprehension against the effect achieved contextually if one postulates that the generalization is figural (there is a good example of the application of such a deductive procedure to a passage from Flaubert, in Pascal 1977:101–102).

THE GNOMIC STATEMENTS IN IMMEDIATE CONTEXT

Gnomic statements characteristically co-occur in White with certain markers. Some features are narratologically formal, others contextual and related to the sense conveyed by the gnomic formulation. More than one marker may apply to a given passage. There are seven central markers.

1. The *So*-marker. The presence of a sentence beginning with *So* immediately after a gnomic statement can indicate a shift of consciousness from an inward rationalization (of the form taken by—or given by Waldo to—an inward vision) to a concentration on inward or external perception: **(1)** "Standing as she had never stood in fact, *because, although memory is the glacier in which the past is preserved, memory is also licensed to improve on life. So* he became slightly drunk with the colours he lit on entering" (W192–93). In other such sentences, a lesser degree of rationalization is apparent in the gnomic statement. The resultative force of *so* is attenuated in one dimension in the example above, and in the following:

---

[21] In a recent book-length study of White (1988), David Tacey reproves the critics for their reliance on the "embellishments" of White's "authorial commentary". But Tacey is not denying the direct, pervasive presence of such commentary; he is merely claiming that there are better (deeper) sources in the text for Jungian interpretations. Like most of White's critics, Tacey dislikes the author's "characteristic manipulation of his reader" and is relieved to find a novel like *The Eye of the Storm* which exhibits detachment. There are no indications in Tacey's study, linguistic or otherwise, about what it is precisely that he takes to be "authorial commentary".

(2) Still Dulcie hesitated ... or because she was *one of those wives who finally expect their husbands to deal with the difficult matters.* So Saporta, an ox, ... heaved and said: (W66).

(3) Take Goethe. Goethe must have worn a track .... The vanity was that men believed their thought remained theirs once turned over to the public. *All those goggle-eyed women reverent ... trailing ... and earnest young people* fingering .... *because it is ordained that great works of art .... done-by-the-public sculpture.* § So Waldo raced the traffic up the Barranugli Road (W118).

(4) But you might have thought of an escape from Dad, if you had been cleverer or brutal. *Fathers are no more than the price you have to pay for life, the ticket of admission. Life, as he began in time to see it, is the twin consciousness, jostling you, hindering you, but with which, at unexpected moments, it is possible to communicate in ways both animal and delicate.* So Waldo resented his twin's absence .... (W76).

(5) *Youth is the only permanent state of mind.* There was no stage in his life when he hadn't felt young—he insisted—except sometimes as a little boy. *If growing old is to become increasingly aware,* as a little boy his premature awareness irritated his elders to the point of slapping. *So there are, in fact, no compartments ....* § Today I am thirty, he had calculated .... (W119).

The adverbial behaves as though it were summing up, resuming, or joining logically the sentences on either side of the gnomic statement[22]—but is retained in another dimension.

In (1), the frame is free-indirect-subjective (preceding: "He need not mention names, but"; "he could see"; the self-congratulatory "designed by special cunning"; the disjunctive syntax of "Standing"; following: the expressive "How his heart contracted"). Waldo becomes "slightly drunk" because the "two selves" of his maternal ancestry are standing there in unreal transformation—"So" links this fantasy-perception to the emotional reaction entailed, with the gnomic statement between the two. The result-aspect of "So" is maintained in the direct connection between improvement on life (the gnomic sentence) and the force of Waldo's reaction. In (2), the resumptive sense of "So" links the action "Dulcie still hesitated" to Saporta's reaction, skirting the gnomic in the process; the consequence-sense of "So" is maintained in the direct connection between pragmatic husbands (gnomic clause) and the reaction Waldo would expect to follow. In (3), the whole of the paragraph (including the gnomic sentence with its expressive indices) is free indirect discourse, as is the previous paragraph. The emergence from thought into action is signalled by the single-sentence paragraph with "So". The resumptive sense connects Waldo's *continuing* hurried walking with the implied *inception* of this at "scuttled" on the previous page. The resultative sense of "So" connects the anxiety generated by Waldo's thoughts

---

[22] Cf Quirk et al. (1972:669.*n*(b)). Greenbaum (1969:70–71) classifies *so* as an "illative" conjunct indicating "that what is being said is a consequence or result of what has been said before", but also points out that *so* can be "partly continuative, partly summative", or even "virtually weakened to sequential *and*". Cf also Halliday/Hasan (1976:240–241/256–57) on "the two planes of conjunctive relations, the external and the internal" which may coexist in conjunctions (additive, adversative, temporal or causal). The narrational shading of *so* that I am analyzing seems not to have been considered by Halliday/Hasan, however, and is certainly not included in their Summary Table of Conjunctive Relations (242–43), although central to cohesion.

(gnomic present) with an increase in speed of walking and with sharpened present awareness. In (4), Waldo's resentment at Arthur's absence is resumptively linked with the pre-gnomic thought (not given in the passage above) about the consolation afforded—in contrast with Mr Brown—by Arthur's presence. But the "So" also has resultative force, linking with the immediately preceding gnomic sentence. The effect of this bi-referentiality achieved by "So" is to heighten the coherence of mental, figural logic. Besides: circumstantially there would be no reason for a non-figural narrator to draw an explicit consequence with "So" from a gnomic generalization: such generalizations are meant to be self-explanatory.

2. **Aspect and transition-marking.** The occurrence of gnomic statements immediately before sentences in the past progressive similarly indicates an emergence of figural consciousness from inward contemplation into perception of external situation. The following sentences mediate this:

(6) He took his brother by the hand .... *But twin brothers, brothers of a certain age, at times only remember what has been laid down in the beginning.* § They were walking on .... (W57).

(7) As it was, Waldo could even make a compensation out of the prospect of prolonged mutual habit. *Habit in weaker moments is soothing as sugared bread and milk.* § Arthur was now preparing to go in and make the bread and milk .... (W204).

(8) He still made a point of wearing ... his butterfly collar .... Although not of the latest, *there is a period at which anybody's style is inclined to set,* Waldo Brown liked to think *in timelessness.* § Then, every one of his bones was breaking. (W67).

Sentence (6) has the additional, internal feature of a coyness or vagueness— "brothers of a certain age"—that has no point unless figurally generated; (7) reveals rationalization, and includes a simile using a specific detail from the local context in such a way as to compromise the universality of the gnomic statement; (8) has a diegetic tag connecting the gnomic thought with the character. The following passage is also imbued with the transitional: (9) "Everybody had begun to share his agony, but that, surely, was what *tragedy is for.* § When Mother suddenly tried to throw the expression off her face ..." (W230). The discourse moves from Arthur's assumptions about the reactions of others (which we must relativize against Waldo's account), through the *argumentum-ad-hominem* conjunct "surely", to a delayed inception of the gnomic one verb too late: a bridge indicating the embedding of the truism in figural consciousness. Finally, the new paragraph with interruptive, disjunctive "When" functions in a similar fashion to *So*–sentences and progressives, signalling a move of consciousness from rationalization to external perception.

3. **Rationalization.** Many of the gnomic sentences can be regarded contextually as figural rationalizations. The gnomic statements conform to Pascal's view that the present-tense form lends strong, dogmatic status, and to his suggestion that a past-tense form would *signal* a personal rationalization. Rationalization, in White's representations of mental processes, must momentarily convince the character who is thinking (just as, at the macrostructural level, Waldo's distortions of temporal relations must not be perceived immediately by the reader, or by Waldo, for what they are). The following gnomic is a semantic joke: (10) "He had never felt guiltier, *but guilt*

will sometimes solidify; he could not have moved for a shotgun" (W61). Generalization here represents mental flight from full acknowledgement of personal guilt—a flux of emotion is, as it were, gnomically frozen, kept at arm's length by introspection. This sentence is, in effect, also a resurfacing into discourse of the gnomic thought (with free-indirect markings) expressed in the following (both contexts having Mrs Poulter, looking, and the guilt-nexus in common): **(11)** "The dust-coloured bus plunged .... *Look into a passing bus, and more often than not you will see something you would rather not* .... Mrs Poulter's face was too stupid ..." (W60). Here one last example: **(12)** "... and where he began without delay offering his services. § *Time thus spent is not life lived, but belongs in a peculiar purgatorial category of its own.* Waldo got used to it ..." (W177). The evasive rationalizing of **(12)** is not auctorial endorsement of Waldo's "peculiar purgatorial category", not even an ironically dissonant endorsement, but is Waldo's way of covering over (by recourse to vague, general justification) the humiliation of the situation he has got himself into.[23]

4. Comparisons and citations. Passage **(2)** above and the following have gnomic statements which take the form of universalizing comparisons that are self-defensive strategies, neutralizing and distancing potential antagonists by knowledgeable reduction of them to items in a predictable set:

(13) Saporta stood smiling *in the manner of those men who will never have anything of importance to say and in its absence hopefully allow good-will to ooze out of the pores of their faces.* He had despised Saporta from the beginning .... (W64).

(14) And continued smiling at him *in the way of those who know through hearsay or intuition that something is being hushed up.* § As he had to live with it, he decided to ignore her indiscretion (W162).

To this extent, the gnomic statements constitute rationalizations. The comparative-concessive structure in the middle of **(5)** above similarly rationalizes. Part of the passage is free indirect discourse with a diegetic tag: the *weakest* part of the rationalization; while the dogmatically confident phases of mental logic, borne on a wave of emotion, are in the gnomic present. The beginning of **(5)** is gnomic in another sense, too, for it is a "citation" from Waldo's own notebook-thoughts (just as many of the gnomic utterances in *Voss* are "citations" from Voss's philosophical theory). The following, too, is a "citation" after an impersonal passive tag, the whole being embedded in free indirect discourse: **(15)** "... the cleft hinted at again in the chin, which, it was said, *is the sign of a lover.* Waldo almost sneeze-laughed. Love me, Cranko, in a white hat!" (W172). One last example is similarly embedded: **(16)** "There she was, wiping and coaxing that nut, *as a woman will cuddle a baby, provided it is hers, after she has let it mess herself.* The sergeant couldn't abide a slut" (P313). This is *non*-rationalizing (truly gnomic) and sincere in effect, as befits Sergeant Foyle—a shifting of tense to free-indirect past would, as Pascal suggests, cast in doubt the sincerity of the figural thought.

---

[23] Further instances of rationalizing discourse in gnomic sentences can be found on the following pages: W113/114/158/175 /184/207/208.

5. Immediacy. This group has a gnomic present which, in contradistinction to group **4**, conveys the immediacy of present figural thought—a kind of stunned sense of the individual's cognitive will being lost in an ocean of paralyzing contingency, as in the following:

(17) ... trying to remember what his intentions could have been. But he was unable. *Intentions exist only in time.* § "Give me my spect—my glasses," he was able to order (W67).

(18) It troubled Waldo no end the night he woke to discover the worst had happened. *Sinking low is never sinking low enough.* Since he had not yet recovered his vocabulary, he could only call faeces shit (W211).

(19) ... to lose his name, if not the hateful load of his body. *Streets are full of guesses which rarely develop into questions.* Certainly in the days when the city had been celebrating ..., people had .... (P305).

Or of present figural recollection of habitual past experience which has attained a kind of comforting universal validity: **(20)** "Remembering the springy green cushions grass *can become as it collaborates with sleep,* he decided to take the train back" (P309).

6. Tagged discourse. Here, a verb of mental operation (or, in a wider sense, a diegetic tag) is found in the immediate vicinity of the gnomic statement. This is clearest in **(4), (5), (15)** and these examples:

(21) Love, he had found, *is more acceptable to some when twisted out of its true shape.* § Not that Waldo would accept much (A279).

(22) in this one instance he had listened to reason, sensed the shocking anomaly of it, and choked her off. *So that human relationships, particularly the enduring ones, or those which we are forced to endure, are confusingly marbled in appearance,* Waldo Brown realized, and noted in a notebook (W167).[24]

The following looks at first sight a good instance of auctorial-narratorial comment, in view of the verbal configuration of the gnomic passage:

(23) Arthur did not particularly notice Dulcie's greyness or her glasses, nor that Mr Saporta was setting in fat, *because friends and lovers enjoy a greater freedom than their bodies: they are at liberty to move out of them, and by special dispensation, communicate with one another through far-sighted eyes.* § It was Waldo who suffered, Arthur regretted, from his meeting ... (A279).

This would be so *if* we were to take it as a representation of articulated rather than preverbal thought. But the clincher for the presence of figural consciousness

---

[24] This is one of those statements with which Argyle (1967:64) has difficulty: the remark "exhibits a habit and sentiment that are White's. Attributed to Waldo, we despise them because there is nothing in Waldo to persuade us to do otherwise; but this is to learn to despise an aspect of White's work which elsewhere we have found valuable. [This] example of Waldo's generality is the wisdom that underpins the whole novel. If it lacks dignity, then so does *The Solid Mandala* ". Argyle has surely missed the point, apart from the fact that "dignity" is not at issue in this novel (except for Waldo's attempt to maintain it). To despise Waldo is to react at a comparatively shallow level of social decorum which is not adequate to a perception of the desperate mental straits he is in. Waldo is no klutz: he can recognize *appearances*. But this is *all* he can do; trapped in his rationalism, he can only register perceptions scribally, and can neither act for change nor *see* the compelling inner logic of relationships. White, by contrast, *can* do so as an artist, not least by the critical tension generated by irony. White and Waldo are the same, and are not.

comes in the next paragraph with its focusing (therefore linking) cleft-sentence structure and the tag-clause "Arthur regretted".[25]

7. Free indirect discourse. This group exhibits either internal free markings as in (3), (4), and (11), framing by free indirect discourse ([4] at the beginning; [5] at the end; [15] and]16]); or the expression of a mind-set which the reader has come to recognize as specific to the character whose thoughts these must be—apart from which, a process of rationalization, mental evasiveness, and/or aphorism-coining is contextually discernible, as in (4).[26]

At the level of what is traditionally regarded as the strongest indication of formal narrative dissonance—the gnomic present-tense statement—the discourse of *The Solid Mandala* exhibits the closest consonance between diegesis and figural consciousness. There are no exceptions to this pattern: the narrative is in this respect wholly "reliable".

---

[25] Many other passages involve the parenthetical framing of the gnomic within free indirect discourse. This may convey a flight into rationalization (W55–56); intrasentential slipping within free indirect discourse (W70); free-indirect coloration within the gnomic, followed by a sign that this mode of figural thought has been broken off (W208); or a flowing into the gnomic out of expressive, disjunctive free indirect discourse (W211).

[26] See further instances at: W49/55/56/69/70/136/148/194/ 208/211; A293.

8

LEXIS, RHETORIC AND FIGURATION

I   Imputations of intention

A central feature of mental action in *The Solid Mandala* (and in White's other fiction) is the imputation of intention and purpose. The presence of imputing statements in dissonant psychonarration leads the reader to conclude—in the absence of a thought-tag—that the auctorial narrator is doing the analysing. In White, even diegesis that is not formally marked for free indirect discourse can be referred to the mental processes of the characters whenever the motivation for actions or gestures is contemplated or established. Most such probings of purpose are innocuous, but may entertain possibilities of intention in the form of either/or alternatives, in keeping with the frequent alternative-formulae (such as "out of spite for Goethe, or respect for posterity", W211).[1] Personal actions may be signalled as wilfully transgressing Waldo's own code of verbal behaviour ("Deliberately he used an expression he had always found repulsive", W91) or may be marked ambiguously to show the involuntary defeat of intention ("He heard himself make it sound like a natural function", W93). Intention, purpose or reason in Waldo's discourse are seldom characterized by strongly conjunctive syntax, as in "Then they were walking somewhat quicker, because Waldo had to defend himself" (W62), where the *because*-construction is openly intention-bearing, thus reflecting Waldo's inward sense of urgency.

Intention-clauses frequently encode rationalizations and prevarications—the syntactic form they take suggesting the mental fabrication of an aura of bland self-evidence. "Waldo treated the old herringbone rather roughly, to show that what he was doing had been dictated by duty and common sense" (W23)—Waldo gives reasons of "ethical rectitude", after the fact, to conceal what he realizes is his brutal treatment of Arthur. "At the time, to correct himself partially, he said:" (W34)—here, the intention is so formulated as to play down the fact that Waldo's original denial was conscious, not accidental; the idea of "partial" correction places self-interest before love, truth and honesty. Waldo's section is saturated with such reflexive statements of intention.[2] When attached to the

---

[1] Cf W103/147/160 with W66/77/91/93/147.

[2] For example: "he arrived late to show he wasn't all that keen on coming" (W99); "not to nurse a sense of deprivation, simply out of curiosity" (W124). In "Waldo could modulate his voice, more to impress than to please" (W26), the gradation of alternatives looks "honest", but tries to conceal how un-pleasing his voice is. In "They would start to punch each other, to

behaviour of others, Waldo's conclusions about intention are, as we have already seen, frequently expressions of an exacerbated sensitivity amounting almost to paranoia.[3] There is only one comparable passage in Arthur's section, at the very end, when his benevolence is shattered by Waldo's reading-aloud of his poem: "Which Waldo exaggerated quite horribly and deliberately ... deliberately blaspheming" (A293)—but this is no distortion. The inverse of this—where Waldo realizes that he is doing the persecuting because he is trapped in circumstance—is expressed in a sentence which would bring any linguistically sensitive reader up short: "He kicked the nearest of the blue dogs—Scruffy it was—on deliberate purpose" (W117). Of course, Waldo kicks the dog on purpose, but the purposiveness is attached to the "accidental"—it could just as easily have been Runt according to the diegesis (ie, Waldo's prevaricating discourse), though Arthur's spoken words suggest that the target wasn't accidental. It is not the dog Waldo wants to get at, but Arthur: the act of brutality (directed at Arthur's dog "on ... purpose") is meant to show Arthur beyond words, but calculatedly, what Waldo feels ("deliberately"). The pleonasm is thus perfectly logical in its doubling of purpose, though it undercuts Waldo's action—makes it seem childish and petty—through its schoolboy-solecism character (subverting the jokey phrase "accidentally on purpose"). Once again, Waldo's mental "language" has let him down.

Waldo is alienated by his analytical rationality from taking human gestures as a natural part of the whole man. The uncoupling of gesture, the crippling assumption that it is part of a quotidian repertoire of artifice, may entail Waldo's fixing on appearances as a means of rationalizing his own negative emotions, as when he sees the young Poulters "lowering their eyes to avoid the glances" (W140), or when he observes Dulcie "rasping out with what was intended as punctuating laughter" (W90). It may seem as though it is merely the suspect quality of artificial gesture that Waldo seizes upon (eg, "Mother would smile to encourage him", W53).[4] But what is also being inadvertently revealed, beyond the cold analysis (which can be very acute, very funny in effect), is Waldo's profound, embarrassed self-consciousness and his own essential duplicity: it takes a thief to catch a thief. If one were constrained to view Waldo narrowly through the thematic perspective of the artist-figure (as does McCulloch 1983), then he embodies one of the perennial paradoxes of the artistic personality, and is a version of the recurrent figure of the Vivisector or murderous anatomist.

Arthur, by contrast, is invariably engaged in an act of primary recognition whenever statements of purpose and intention occur in connection with figural

---

ward off any shame, as well as for the pleasure of it" (W32), Waldo manages just in time to tack on the less disreputable motivation.

[3] For example: "the visit ... undoubtedly malicious in conception" (W187); "trying to undermine his integrity" (W190); "all those ... conspiring against him" (W197); "the reason ... could only have been to deceive" (W197); "he was waiting to trap him" (W208); various formulations with "on purpose" and "deliberately" (W61/160/168).

[4] Or: "Carefully she looked away, to show she did not understand what was being arranged" (W95); other instances include: W51/52/101/105/109/146/182

perception of gesture (eg, "which meant ... she had begun to get sick of him", A260).[5] There is no *shock* of recognition, but there is a tonality in Arthur's discourse that suggests, not a self-conscious awareness of artifice, but a full acceptance of the inevitability of what is perceived. Arthur's decodings of intention, furthermore, are openly personalized (with verbs of cognition and clear causal markers such as "because", "so as to"): they are not distanced from himself or abstracted like so many of Waldo's (with *to*–infinitives and passive constructions).[6]

II   Indeterminacy and ellipsis

At the other extreme from the imputation of intention is the inability or reluctance to probe more deeply into significances. Occlusion by design characterizes Waldo's mode of perception. It reflects his self-satisfied, superior knowingness (indeed: his desire to see himself as "sly", W179), as when he averts his face "from something" (W28), when he knows "from what he knew, that ..." (W32), or when he views the Misses Dallimore as "specialists in what is done" (W49). A double receding from knowledge is exhibited in the way in which Waldo deals with Arthur's heart-tremor ("whose mechanism had in some way threatened his continuity", W55): his genuine incomprehension of the mysterious dysfunction of the *physis* goes hand in hand with his euphemistic vagueness about the phenomenon (steering clear of the death he has on his mind).

In general, however (and this applies to the whole discourse of the novel), when a psychological process or state is beyond comprehension, or when cognition is caught unawares beyond reasoning, then indices of indeterminacy or inchoateness are what they are. We find areas of contextual underdetermination, which demand much interpretative energy for their resolution (the reader's failure to expend this cooperative energy results in White's language being

---

[5] Or: "looked the other way so as not to appear annoyed" (A242); other instances include: A221 ("recognized"), A222 ("knew"), A226 ("realized"), A228 ("knew"), A235 ("because she obviously wanted him to"), A253 ("which suggested"), A291 ("knew").

[6] This is confirmed by the two full constructions of reason in Section 1. The dominant sociolectal coloration of the first is that of Mrs Dun and Mrs Poulter: "Each of the ladies sat rather careful, because they had not known each other all that long, and [because] the situation had not been proved unbreakable" (B11). The simple yet alert social formality of "the situation" correlates with the women's simple ideology of social intercourse; this is reflected in the explicit *because*–connectors, which make the explanation for their "careful" posture less sophisticated, less of a disjunctive external commentary, than if a semi-colon had been used instead of "because". The clause-structure is disarmingly wide-eyed, operating at the simplest level of hypotaxis ("It is even arguable that a conjunction like *because*, which occurs almost exclusively in final-position clauses in colloquial language, is, for the purposes of that variety of English, nearer to a coordinator than to a subordinator"—Quirk et al. 1972:795). The other, psychonarrative sentence, which starts with suspensive subordination, does not have this open quality: "Because Mrs Poulter was growing misty with the past her friend felt it at last her duty to direct her" (B16); the local context, details of phrasing, and the structuring of reason and intention here, all suggest not Mrs Dun's simplemindedness but her calculating watchfulness.

accused of "portentousness", "vagueness" and the like). The indeterminacies often fall into patterns, such as the use of the word "something" and its lexical allies, with or without supporting modalities of indefiniteness, as the fulcrum of perceptual process. Such signals fit in with seeming-indices and with many of the backtracking alternative-formulae in the narrative.[7]

One sign of indeterminacy is the recurrence of the word "circumstances" and cognate formulae: "In the present unsettling circumstances of course she would feel she must comfort somebody afflicted like Arthur" (W73); "In the special circumstances, it did not seem improbable, and Waldo let him" (W170). These two examples are clearer than some, referring as they do to Mr Brown's and Mrs Brown's death respectively.[8] In some cases, no pat equivalent can be given for "circumstances", "things", or "situation", and closer examination of the context when an explanation does seem available reveals, often enough, further layers of implication (at W170 above, for example, where it is also Waldo's distracted reaction to his mother's death which colours his passive acceptance of Arthur's proposal to have her cremated). The very vagueness of peripheral formulations makes the reader suspect that indeterminacy is present for good reason. Another feature is the hedgings-in ("present", "temporary", "more appropriate", "special") which heighten the implication of extenuation, yet at the same time wish these "circumstances" (as stated; or those *not* stated) away. "Johnny and Norm would not have known what to answer in much easier circumstances. Now they were frightened. Waldo was frightened" (W45). Figural consciousness shrinks from articulation. The reader must tease out the implication here that Waldo's tormentors (in keeping with his passivity) are not responsible for these difficult "circumstances"—that some external force has compelled them into ritualizing acts. But the "much easier" conditions are purely hypothetical: verbal resistance from Arthur would be inconceivable in any "circumstances", even those unspecified ones where Norm and Johnny normally exercise dominion over the twins. "In more normal circumstances there were only the scars where the acne had been on the back of his neck" (W31). With great effort, the reader can grasp that the *abnormal* "circumstances" are the special ones of Waldo's mirror-gazing as an attempt to achieve union with the past. The "more normal" ones are those everyday occasions when Waldo can feel the traces of the physical (adolescent) past: traces not rendered accessible by looking in a single mirror. "In the circumstances, as he stood picking at the quince leaves, it was a minor

---

[7] "While numbers, or *something,* continued to strengthen Arthur" (W43; see also W34, also with "perhaps" and "some possible"/32 "something else"/71/85/107/118 "some hostile thing"/143/167, A237, P303); *"some* distress, of feminine origin" (W27; see W44/47, twice/73/81/158, A227); *"whatever* it was" (W73, A243); "somewhere" (W92); "somehow" (W94). Cf the alternative and/or self-correcting formulae: "saying, or gobbling" (W109); "although, or perhaps because" (W187); also W85/116/ 119/153/158/170/171/188/ 190/211,A216/218/220/223/231/238/242 "but delicacy or something"/269/ 270.

[8] Other instances: "the wounds inflicted on him by circumstances" (W81, referring to the burden of Arthur); "the temporary circumstances" (W131); "more appropriate circumstances" (W145); "in the circumstances" (B17; A285, referring to the library incident; A291, referring to the transvestite mirror-gazing scene); "the situation" (B11/21, P309).

shock to notice the hairs on his man's wrist" (W70). The phrase of contingency
takes off from "an intolerable situation" immediately prior to it (cf the reverse
pussyfooting in Arthur's discourse at A291). The "situation" of his father's lying
dead and of his retreat from this fact *is* the "circumstances" in which Waldo finds
himself emotionally. That is, the outward (external circumstance) and the inward
(psychological state) are seamlessly conjoined.

But, here and elsewhere, the phrase with "circumstances" is tonally slippery.
In every case, external reality does not impinge on pragmatic man but on the
psyche: the eye of the storm is a hard-won *linguistic* calm only. Here is
ratiocination situating acts of cognition and precognition within a temporal and
spatial frame—but what is being despatched within this frame is unspeakably,
ungraspably disruptive of emotional equilibrium. "In the circumstances" is not an
ironical counter to be played in the discourse-game: it is the last resort of the
equilibrist's shaky common sense in the face of events whose effect on
consciousness must be shut away *from* consciousness.

As a would-be artist, who wants only to write about himself, Waldo has an abnormal
awareness of circumstances. This tends to overlay the circumstances themselves, Duncan
notes, "with the colouring of the subjective and hence intensifies the schizophrenic dilemma".
[McCulloch 1983:47]

I don't know whether Duncan (1969:77) and McCulloch have based their
comments here on the specific occurrences of the word "circumstances", or on
broader macronarrative considerations: but it does seem, if "circumstance" in its
explicit occurrences has been a deciding factor, that their argument is an instance
of a synecdochic fallacy (Bonheim 1983:201). For a start, Waldo not only
doesn't get far into writing the *auto*biographical *Tiresias a Youngish Man:* he
doesn't get off the ground with a quite different project, "some vast corrosive
satire on the public services" (W171). There is no necessary correlation between
the egoism of the "would-be artist" and Waldo's awareness of circumstances.
Indeed, "awareness of circumstances" is another way of saying: painful self-
consciousness *plus* intellection upon external reality. If anything, this would
amount, not to the artist's gift of close observation, but to the crippling of the
imagination by reason (a theme White dwells on in his autobiography and in
interviews).

Most of the events or situations which are expressly designated as
"circumstances" simply impinge on Waldo as an individual, and some of them
(the deaths; the torture-episode; Arthur's presence) would tax anybody's
sensibility. "Circumstances" only *look* external to the figural consciousness in
discourse-terms. They are not overlaid with subjective coloration, but subjectivity
tries to thrust them from itself. In order to be registered at all by a
hyperconscious personality such as Waldo's, external events must be intrinsically
so ego-related that they are subjectively *within* before they can be evaded by
mental subterfuge (ie, by the discourse itself). I am not competent to judge
whether Waldo finds himself clinically in a "schizophrenic dilemma", though I
should doubt that the phrase accords with the psychological traits revealed in the
discourse.

There are two further aspects which could prove troublesome for a thesis that argues for the uniqueness or special nature of Waldo's relation to circumstance. The one is that Arthur's discourse, too, reveals that both twins classify emotionally affecting situations as "circumstances". The other is that the phrase "in the circumstances" occurs outside Waldo's and Arthur's discourse in this novel, and also pervades White's other novels.[9] This all suggests that the phrase is as much "mind-stylistic" as anything else, and—like syntactic habits—is a universal-psychological marker for the functioning of a certain *level* of consciousness rather than of a certain *type* of consciousness. Some characters— Waldo is perhaps the prime example—function compulsively at this level of awareness, which may also be steered more conspicuously by rationality. But this means only that Waldo is characterized by exacerbated self-consciousness and by the virtual attenuation of the integral personality; it does not mean he represents a recognizable and *efficient* type of the artistic personality. The novel is a study in psychical failure, spiritual disaster. One can argue, like Duncan, for some existential rupture in Waldo, some discontinuity or abyss of being; but this is caused by rationality's immune-system reaction to the exposures of self-consciousness, not by these exposures themselves.

There are very few cases of verbal ellipsis outside of "pure" narrated (interior) monologue, and these can for the most part be explained as colloquial usages appearing in diegesis which is otherwise unmarked for informality. Occurrences of the verb "realize" without an object-clause, for instance, are quite

---

[9] The telltale, *functional* presence of such phrases is ignored at the critic's peril. A stylistic dualist, Wolfe pursues his synonymist's quest for "objective" clarity as follows: "Aggravating the problem [of vagueness], White prefers to use link verbs and subjective complements instead of action verbs which would convey the same idea [*sic*]. Instead of saying 'the additional duty laid upon the mother was a source of embarrassment to the parents' [*Riders in the Chariot,* Viking, p. 107/Penguin, p. 103], he might have ended the sentence with the phrase 'embarrassed the parents'". Wolfe misses the phrase "In the circumstances" preceding the words quoted, and fails to ask himself how it is that both parents can be embarrassed by the actions of one of them. The distanced phrasing encodes Moshe Himmelfarb's embarrassment, not only at his more religious wife's ritual attention to their son, but also at her self-consciousness (a recursivity of embarrassment); and, because the occasion of embarrassment is a public ritual, consciousness of this is encoded in the "public" stereotypicality and indeterminacy of the phrasing. Something similar happens when Wolfe is confronted with the story "Dead Roses" in *The Burnt Ones:* "'Some of the women experienced a twinge on glimpsing the youthful situation which existed between the Mortlocks' [P49]. 'Which existed between' says nothing *about* the link joining the Mortlocks. Substituting 'bound' would both define the link and save a word. 'Youthful situation' causes a similar problem; it, too, lacks power and clarity .... These violations of verbal economy flaunt [*sic*] basic rules of sentence formation" (Wolfe 1983:25). Wolfe does not see that "twinge" alone suffices to explain this retreat into prosaic indeterminacy: the young Anthea's revitalizing of the ageing, aptronymically named Mortlock is in itself a doubtful achievement, as the macrocontext conveys; and the discreet formulations reveal much about the reluctance of "the elderly women" to face up to their envy at the "situation", and to the fact that it is compromised by tonality. Similar figural retreats explain all of the other phrases ("twilight/innocent situations", "something of an irrational nature", "some revelation of a personal kind/of a stunning nature") which Wolfe pillories.

normal in speech ("Oh—I didn't realize!"), but look a little strange in this novel. "For a long time after everyone realized, she persuaded herself ..." (W35): three times "realize" appears without nominal-clause resolution, with contextual reference to Arthur's peculiar behaviour or mental status (W35/53, A224). At W53, the implication is buried beneath another, that of twinship; once it refers to the fact of being in love (A253); once it is naturalized by the actional context (W34). Two occurrences of "recognize" are similarly a little odd (the first having reference to Arthur's "abnormality" and Mr Dun's cognizance of it: "a small mean face recognizing", W30; the second to Waldo's gestural behaviour towards Bill Poulter: "wondering whether Bill would recognize or not", W142). One could say that what is known well enough to the characters, or is regarded by them as somewhat delicate, tends not to be spelled out. The same applies to constructions which imply their continuation before one gets to the end, anyway. In a sentence like "... *Urn Burial* in the Everyman, which Waldo had suspected might be of interest until he found out" (W43), the resolution "[that] it wasn't [of interest]" is superfluous to what the verb of cognition itself implies. Something visible to the character is not made visible to us, for example, because the figural consciousness is focusing on an absence and on the person rather than on his clothing: "His arms, usually exposed as far as the armpits, for he had had her cut off the sleeves" (W142), which does not require the complementation "of his undershirt". Lastly, sentences which end "the morning when Waldo accused" (A230) or "Waldo had ordained" (A290) may have no explicit verb-object. This is understandable if one considers that resolution would require an analytical statement of something already familiar to a character but *yet* to be presented scenically. The effect of withholding here, of course, is to give the action expressed by the verb a hollow portentousness which inadvertently takes the mickey out of Waldo as High Priest or Grand Inquisitor.

III   Psychological verbs and predications

Seymour Chatman (1972:10–22) has studied psychological verbs in late James; "characters are, irrepressibly, thinking beings ..., and even physical acts cannot be dissociated from mental origins" (10). The conspicuously high proportion of verbs of mental action in James reflects the characters' most typical activity; such verbs are not employed narratorially to analyze the characters, and the "limited narrative point of view" or "centre of consciousness" is optimally represented by verbs of mental action impinging on or reacting to the fictive world in which such consciousnesses are located. In Patrick White as in James (even in psychonarration), readers are made both to experience with, and distance themselves critically from, the figural consciousnesses through which states, actions and events are filtered. In respect of discoursal mediation, the semantics of psychological verbs is a question of style, where means are inseparable from goals, "expression" from "content". The nature of White's use of these verbs is the primary motivation for discussing them here. In a nutshell: White's fiction constantly gives the impression that mental action is indeed being "analyzed"—but in a peculiarly direct, unelaborated, take-it-or-leave-it mode, whereby the thinking agents are, as it were, irradiated by the glare of their own processes of perception and reaction. Psychological verbs in White "feel" as though they are being used almost impatiently, as a kind of shorthand notation, by a coercive narrating intelligence. It is easy to identify this intelligence as an "intrusive narrator/author", less easy to discard this misapprehension in favour of the differentiated representation of figural consciousness.

Using Chatman as a model, and (like Chatman himself) in the full awareness that the classification of mental activity is frequently arbitrary, I have roughly analyzed psychological verbs and predications in Sections 2 and 3 of *The Solid Mandala*. Quantification has proved unavoidable, as it is the incidence of certain modes of consciousness which leads the reader to make judgements about character-psychology. Chatman sets up four chief categories:

1. **Perception** is the mental identification and organization of sense-stimuli. Late James contains relatively little pure perception—perceptual verbs shade off into apperception or the cognition of moral or psychological issues.

1.5. **Precognition** is statal, durative, a mental "focussing or dwelling upon something ... without coming to an actual cognition about it" (Chatman 1972:15): ie, knowledge. Precognition may be triggered off by perceptions, or it may be independent of a sense-environment; it relates to states of affairs and propositions, not to objects.

2. **Cognition** is momentary and time-bound, presupposing "a state of ignorance or indecision before the cognition and one of knowledge after" (16).

Both cognition and precognition (like perception) can be active or passive, **performative** or **recipient**. The precognitive in James indicates that figural thinking is tentative, nebulous, perhaps chaotic, as in the contemplation of delicate moral issues. But by far the greatest number of James's psychological verbs are cognitive and recipient: characters are "*receivers* of 'felt experience' rather than deciders and judges" (17). Performant verbs are often introduced to be negated—characters are thrust back into a state of reception. I have examined the particular sub-domain of receptive cognition (*seem, appear, be as if*) separately (ch. 6.II above)

3. **Beliefs and attitudes** are "static in the sense that cognition has already taken place" (20). In perception, there is no actual predication; in cognition proper, there is predication through mental effort or through passive reception; in belief or attitude, predications are statically existent in the mind.

Some of these categories overlap and are hard to keep apart (eg, recipient cognition and precognition); and context usually has to be examined in order to tell whether a mental action is "cool" or "warm" (emotive). Indeed, the notion of psychological "verbs" is too narrow to function as an analytical tool in isolated relation to the macronarrative. Our inferences about the characters' psychological attitudes towards the products of cognition must be taken into account. (In *The Solid Mandala*, this can lead us to corroborative indices of somatic reaction, blindness, touch; to topicalized abstractions such as "love", "control", inexpressibility, reason, "principles", "conviction", "truth", mirroring, walls, secrecy, etc). The following table—which has not been filled in where categories are too elusive for the insertion of specific verbs to have any useful exemplifying function—classifies a few common psychological verbs under Chatman's headings:

Table 6: Psychological verbs

COGNITIVE/JUDGING/VOLITION		EMOTIVE/FEELING	
PERFORMATIVE	RECIPIENT	PERFORMATIVE	RECIPIENT
1. PERCEPTION			
observe, watch, look at	feel, hear, notice, see		feel
1.5. PRECOGNITION			
wonder at, ponder, contemplate, seek, consider, think of/over, listen to, ask oneself whether	feel, be conscious/ aware of/ interested in	fear, doubt, desire	suspect
2. COGNITION			
decide that, learn that, surprised, desire to do,	recognize, realize, become aware, sense	admire, love, hate	be relieved, pleased, disgusted, shocked,
see, conclude, propose that, admire, think sth., guess	come to discover .... be as if, seem, appear		
.... avoid, conceal			
3. ATTITUDE AND BELIEF			
(always) believe, know	understand	admire, love, hate, resent, envy	be jealous

PERCEPTION

Acts of perception are usually implied via the presence of descriptive indices to sense-stimuli (colour, light, sound, etc). With verbs of performative and recipient perception, there are significant distributions. Arthur's section opens with verbs of seeing (A215/218). His seeing otherwise borders on cognition or apperception: he can "'see right into'" transparent, simple people (W29), can "see" the sound of music in advance (A232), can "look at other things" beyond the boring scripture-pages (A224), and can "see the lights of the prescribed cities" in Mrs Feinstein's verbal tour of Europe (A245). Acts of imagination, of inward vision, are involved. He records the import of facial expressions (A252/275). His absorption in situations may attenuate perception when the import of the percept is peripheral: he only "half-sees" Waldo's arrival at Dulcie's (A244), and "did not particularly notice" signs of ageing in the Saportas (A279; this last recollective, of course). On the few occasions on which he is embarrassed, his perception is reflexive ("She noticed at once, and covered herself", A279), or becomes a willed operation upon substantials, as in the proleptic mandala-reference to him walking and "looking at the stones" (W29). Here, Waldo notices that Arthur is "perceiving"; and it is typical of Waldo that his seeing is non-recipient, always calculatingly performative, mood-dependent, and frequently reflexive (at his first meeting with Dulcie, "he looked at her to see whether she admired him", etc, W92–93).

This willed observation starts off innocuously enough—in boyhood, he "enjoyed studying his twin" (W32)—but begins to take on a slightly sinister aspect the more such verbs appear. He watches his father limping home from work (W34); and the same verb rounds off the incident it opens: "And now, Waldo was watching" (W35). "Watching" in the sense of parental supervision is then topicalized, followed by Waldo's claim (true in one sense, ironically false in another) that he could "see far enough into" Arthur. The perceptual operation that apparently leads to this "in–sight" is his watching—but the result is willed inaction; he keeps from his parents, and to himself, any secret knowledge thereby gained (W35). Waldo does his nose-picking covertly, but "would watch to see his brother caught out" doing the same (W37). Where he does involuntarily perceive, the attendant reaction is usually negative ("noticed with repulsion", W138), often with a hasty verbal cover-up: "it was a minor shock to notice the hairs" (W70, the syntax playing against the "major" shock of finding his father dead). He "could not avoid staring into his brother's hair, fascinated" (W26)—the fascination comes obsessively from *within* him, thus undermining the "accidental" force of "could not avoid" and exposing "staring" as even more than performative perception. Visual perception, in sum, is for Waldo a matter of covert control and calculation; for Arthur it is open and value-free even when performative. Waldo's acts of perception have an immediate reflex on the ego;[10] Arthur's represent an opening out into the metaphysical.

If we look at verbs of feeling and touch, and make no formal distinction between perception proper, imaginative recuperation, performative sensation and recipient precognition, we find that Waldo inhabits a sensory-deprivation unit; occurrences of the relevant verbs, nominalizations and predications are in the ration of roughly 1 (Waldo) : 25 (Arthur). Waldo fears being touched physically (W73), while Arthur is happily haptic.[11] There is a willed, self-protective side to his touching, however. Although it is more obvious that it is Waldo who fears that the secrets of his nightmares may be revealed to Arthur, the latter also checks by touch to ensure that his dreams (the latently blasphemous blood-dream, offensive to Waldo's rationality) have not been overheard (A262). That this secretiveness is both a protection of Waldo and a betrayal of Arthur's

---

10 This needs to be taken together with a set of indexical details which effectively cancels out the possibility that Waldo's perceptions can bring him insight. Until Arthur arrives to save him, Waldo is practically blind to the playground blood-ritual in progress about him (W44–45); he feels the knife on his neck, but sees nothing; fear has suspended perception and fantasy-"vision" has taken over (W138). Wind and light sting or blind his eyes (W31/56); unspectacled, he cannot see (W67/73–74); his world and his thoughts are "blurred" (W83/126), he is "blinded" by Arthur's words (W196), by the Feinsteins' packing cases (W150); emotional strain makes the day "not quite in focus" (W201); in his retreat into inward "vision", the latter is almost "destroyed" by Dulcie's mundanity (W97). And there is an otherwise oblique reference by Arthur to blind people marrying blind people (A246).

11 See touch-indices at W109, A217/227/237/239/244/249/ 252/269/287.

relationship with him is immediately made clear emblematically, when "his own special" mandala (which he later discovers is Waldo's) rolls away as he reaches out "to feel for" it (A262). The theme of the breaching of secrecy, and its appearance in terms of a mirroring of the twins, comes up again in relation to touch ("If Arthur usually got possession of what Waldo did not tell, it was because he had his sense of touch", A274—again, touch as protection and disclosure). Waldo hates "the smell of his own mucus" (W26), but at the remove of imagination can "finger" the reseda silk of his decadent namesake's garment. Arthur can "smell" in imagination or through almost telepathic sensitivity the situation of others (A245/249). His aural perception is apperceptive (A268), likewise his tactile receptivity ("could feel", A217; "felt too large, too shy", A250—one of the few somatic indications of his self-consciousness). Arthur's feeling is otherwise recipient precognition, while the quasi-momentary nature of his mental actions may push precognition into recipient cognition.[12]

COGNITION AND PRECOGNITION:
KNOWLEDGE AND UNDERSTANDING

There is continual feedback in *The Solid Mandala* from beliefs and attitudes into cognitive acts of "seeing", "knowing", etc. The fundamental opposition of mind or reason and spirit or soul as located in the two brothers is thematized and averted to in the twins' attitudes towards the Greek myths. Mr Brown, the rationalist, regards the gods as convenient fictions opposed to the reality of human existence, and not as necessary illusions arising out of, and corresponding to, that reality (cf W33). Yet he unconsciously yearns for the "other truths" that his failed rationality cannot provide. At any rate, Arthur does see the reality and truth of the myths, while Waldo doesn't. Two conflicting truth-systems are set up, and the cognitive apparatus of each twin will react according to the rules of this conflict. Much play is also made in the novel with such concepts as "faith", "belief", "conscience", "principle(s)", "conviction" and "enlightenment", which can be made to occupy space on both sides of the divide separating reason from faith proper. Waldo's "conviction" (cf W55–56) is not like Arthur's, which is a form of intuitive certainty (A264), strengthened by his being and doing in the natural world (A281), before ebbing away with the loss of his shadowy fraternal counterpart (P313).

Arthur, Waldo knows, is "not impressed by reason" (W31). Waldo, Arthur knows, "knew how to think", while their mother is guided by superior principles ("Mother who knew better than anyone how things ought to be done", A229). Arthur also sees the limitations of Waldo's theoretical and derivative orientation: the close relationship with Mrs Poulter (the potentially *sensual* side of which Arthur is willing to face and even to build up out of all proportion) is something

---

[12] Recipient precognition: "could feel inside him" (A219); "something was nagging at him" (A237); "sensed" (A250); "felt he would make her see" (A265); "half sensing" (A273); "couldn't help feeling" (A282). Recipient cognition: "felt he had to call out" (A221); "felt Dad turn against him" (A230); "was relieved to feel" (A238); "could tell" (A261).

Arthur assumes Waldo "had read about but not experienced" (A268). The shaky foundation of Waldo's knowledge—his refusal of realities which would press upon any man (even an Australian) with a spark of involvement, moral or political, in humanity—is indicated in his sceptical designation of the battles and suffering of the Great War as "that hypothetical Front" (W128). His reflection in the mirror may be his sole evidence for "that intellectual ruthlessness he *knew* himself to possess" (W120); "how *convincing* an impression he made Waldo *knew* from observing himself obliquely in the plate-glass windows of shops" (W58). This shaky knowledge, backed up by decisiveness, produces a peculiarly dangerous brand of "understanding": "Waldo *understood* that those who lowered their eyes in passing were paying homage to someone of his mother's stock" (W59). This is the defensive conviction of fantasy. The passers-by are lowering their eyes because of the presence of Arthur (or because Waldo himself has a weird look about him), not because Waldo embodies his mother's family grace. It takes Waldo another two sentences to drag himself out of the mirror's embrace and face up obliquely to the fact of Arthur. (Concealed here, too, is Waldo's fantasy-encoding of his own death, with mourners filing past the open coffin; it takes Arthur's living presence to raise Waldo from his imagined tomb of posthumous homage.)

Waldo doesn't simply "know" things: he "knew, from what he knew" (W32). He responds smugly to Mrs Poulter's intimations of charitable solicitude: "Waldo *knew* how this sort of thing embarrassed his mother" (W141). "Waldo *knew* he was the only one of those present who *understood*" the reason why his mother looks embarrassed, "which made him contemptuous of other people's stupidity, and proud of his alliance with Mother" (W85). This kind of "understanding" is little more than a desperate desire to be part of a conspiracy ("knowingness", W165) of his own plotting. In his youth, he embraces theory, taking up Pelmanism, a correspondence-course method of training the mind (W58). He fantasizes about the intellectual intercourse he will enjoy with Dulcie by letter: "That was the way, according to collections of correspondence, he *knew* it to be done" (W91). Self-consciously conversationless at the Feinsteins', he desperately reassures himself: "Yet he *knew the theory* of it all" (W112). Through masturbation, he cannot transform his image of Dulcie into the "flesh which *in theory he knew* it to be" (W127). He avoids "fleshly love—while *understanding its algebra*, of course" (W183). Waldo is not very "convinced" by rationality when his own plans are at stake—he persuades himself that he is impressed by Dulcie's "rational approach" to her mother's "'matter of … conscience'", but then looks at her "to see what line he should take next" (W152). When something upsets the precarious equilibrium of his preening practicality, he doesn't "know exactly what attitude to take" (W87). He bites into Mrs Feinstein's *Mohntorte:* "As he *wasn't sure how he felt about it,* he wondered what to tell them if they asked" (W103). Waldo is capable of branding as the truth what he realizes *is* the truth—his betrayal of his father, his pity and lack of love for him—only as he is saying it (W92), and, in the next breath, can be caught unawares by another truth (his self-hatred), which he tries to pass off as flippant untruth: "He didn't believe all he said, ever" (W92). He doesn't believe all he thinks, either, as the discourse persistently reveals. But everything must be accounted for, kept within the purview of his cognition, though his efforts are constantly thwarted (as when his mother seeks refuge with his "dill" brother "suddenly quicker than Waldo could account for", W73).

Other people's relaxed tolerance towards Arthur is something Waldo cannot "believe" (W50). His own "lack of judgement" is always only "temporary" (W56). Although he "knew he was bad-tempered" (W58) and can be coolly rational about his inability to control his temper, he resents in Dulcie, whom he would prefer to typecast as illogical and emotional, the fact that she is "cool and reasonable" (W136). She is thus "unassessable" (W140); "perhaps in the end her eyes would give away their secret and all would be explained" (W103). Dulcie's eyes—so reasonable yet emotional—become his obsession; this is the closest Waldo gets to submission to the precognitive. He also feels trapped by his brother's "reasonable" explanations, prevented from continuing to believe in his irrationality (W198), until Arthur lets out the devils of *Karamazov*: "'And *you* understand!'" (W198–99). Both in childhood and in old age, Waldo as much as admits that he is tyrannized by intellection. In the sleepy schoolroom, "It was good not to have to think" (W42). The *thought* that his self-control might collapse under him "didn't bear thinking about" (W208). This burden, which weighs him down through to the next morning, can be thrust off only by means of banal, practical, diversionary activity, "to prevent himself giving room to his thoughts" (W209). In between these narrative extremes, there is the unremitting emphasis on "truth" and rationality, his failure to "understand" the real, and his escape from desperation into the comprehensibility of "his own visions" and "own imaginings" (this much Waldo himself confesses, W98). What starts off as his "wondering" about Arthur's literary ideas (W40) grows into his contrast between the comparative safety of writing at home and the necessity of facing "Arthur and his own doubts" (W106/126), and ends up as despair, horror, and the extinction of the rational.

When we turn to Arthur, we discover no labyrinth of rationalizations, no thin veneer of rationality, no "truth, illuminated by imagination", collapsing into the arid bathos of filing cabinets and calculations (W150). Even Waldo knows that his brother "certainly knew" (W32), and that "it was better not to be sure how much, or how little, his brother understood" (W33). When it comes to the solution of final problems, like the truth of the word "totality", Arthur, in turn, "would not have cared to ask an intellectual favour of Waldo's face" (A239). Truth and knowledge are effortlessly close in the grammar of Arthur's discourse. He "added Mr Allwright to what he *knew as truest*" (A227); "if he had not *known* [Dulcie] to be *genuine* ..." (A253); he "*knew* that [Mrs Poulter] was worthy of the mandala" (A267). He knows, or "had found", that "love ... is more acceptable [as a kind of truth] to some when twisted out of its *true* shape" (A279), and sings his song of "lying" lovers, with no word between twins "to express the truth" (A280). Waldo inadvertently points to the effect of Arthur's truth: in the Library, he accuses Arthur of "'making this scene to humiliate me

.... That has been your chief object in life. If you would be truthful'" (A283). But Arthur's chief object in life is surely to "be truthful" in his unconditional, protective love for Waldo and the suffering, myth-less world; and it is this truth which humiliates Waldo, and eventually helps destroy him. Thinking is not easy for Arthur, as it requires discipline and linear concentration, from which he seeks to escape into sphericity and ubiquitous immediacy.

There is a nice symmetry on this point, anticipating Waldo's mention of Arthur's "chief object in life". By the end of the War, Waldo has become the first of Arthur's "two preoccupations", but one to whom it is difficult to communicate "his discovery of the spirit" (A280). Although he carries Waldo's mandala with him (ie, thought of him), he must retreat periodically into contemplation of "his own, in which the double spiral knit and unknit so *reasonably*" (A280). Arthur's "second obsession" (the Books) parallels Waldo's first (Secret Writing); but his struggle with the *Upanishads* is often a struggle with "linear" meanings not his own, and he reflects that "Hindu smoke was [perhaps] the only true and total solution. As for the lotus, he crushed it just by thinking on it" (A281). This is the smoke Arthur has read about, and the "uncurling" smoke associated with his mother's cremation in a later episode recounted earlier (A274). The uncurling is like the descent/ascent spiral of his mandala, the knotting and unknotting of the brothers' twin-ness, and a pure object of contemplation beyond intellection. What the texts also reveals, however, is a certain bivocalism in the "true and total solution" of smoke and burning. Arthur has had to force on Waldo's attention the cruelty of the Nazi crematoria, which are only in Europe because "'we didn't think of it first'" (W174). The phrasing hints at the Final Solution, and there is a prolepsis of the cruel truth of Waldo's end, his papers cremated in the "wreathing" smoke and fire, in his attempt to escape Arthur's spiral of love. The lotus which is central to the Hindu and Buddhist philosophies Arthur has been reading about is a complex mandalic symbol of androgynous, solar/lunar unity. What Arthur crushes by attempting to employ the tools of ratiocination so dear to his brother is the unity of their double selfhood (quite apart from any consideration that Arthur has a mistaken idea of sitting in the contemplative lotus position and crushing under his sheer weight the lotus-pad he is sitting on). It is from Arthur's formal engagement with the Books, his oscillation between intuitive contemplation and active intellection, that the "revelations" proceed which lead downwards to destruction.

"Knowledge" ultimately comes to Arthur, "not through words, but by lightning" (P307); this is why he endorses his parents' view that Christianity, as mediated through words and institutions, is not "true" (A261), why he *knows* his own words to Dulcie "could not be true" (A244), why he is pleased, "though not deceived", about what Dulcie's Jewish-gnostic uncle *says* about Arthur's *zaddik*-aura (A275). Cognitive and attitudinal verbs and predications relating to reason and not-believing run in the proportion of six to one, Waldo predominating. Verbs and predications relating to knowing, understanding, truth and believing run also in the proportion of six to one, but this time with Arthur predominating.

In the case of such recipient-cognition verbs as "realize" and "discover", the ratio in Arthur's favour is as high as ten to one.[13] The appearance of these verbs in Arthur's section is so serenely innocent, so lacking in the duplicitous lexical variety and semantic shape-changing of Waldo's verbs, that the reader is perhaps inclined, once he has started to "see through" Waldo's rationalizations, to take Arthur on trust. After all, two self-deceivers in a row is a bit much to expect. But someone like Arthur who is by nature so inclined to see the good side of those he loves is quite possibly deceived by appearances—which is what sometimes happens. And someone like Arthur who is so unconsciously bent on filling with love and truth the dark void left by the departing gods is likely to wreak the blind retribution of the gods on those who are already so inwardly fragile or crippled that only a miracle of empathetic intelligence could heal them—which is what *must*, and does, happen, without Arthur ever really *knowing* what he has done.

With many of Arthur's verbs of knowing,[14] a critical reading begins to undermine any objective basis for his cognitive certainty or its rightness. The best example is the scene in Len Saporta's carpet-shop (A251), where Arthur wants to share with Saporta the "secret" of his love for Dulcie, as a protective mandalic blessing on her union with the carpet-dealer. Arthur reveals to a baffled Saporta the secret of the mandala in the carpet, which is, for Arthur, a good omen of this prospective union. Arthur may "know" that Saporta is one of the "unalterable" ones (A249), but he has mistaken stolidity for solidity, misreading the mind's construction on the face: Saporta is puzzled at Arthur's conspiratorial facial expression, and Arthur mistakes his puzzlement for Saporta's own conspiratorial gravity. One must concede to Wilkes (1969:107) the partial validity of his view that Arthur is impercipient—but he is not always so: ie, he is not a "dill"; and his peculiar kind of impercipience constitutes overriding faith in his own percipience. He *wants* others to share in his wordless understanding; this is how he would like the world to be, a merging of consciousnesses in universal love. Wilkes can see no reason for an attachment arising between Arthur and Saporta: the latter's "behaviour suggests no more than a kindly tolerance". The same *rationalistic* doubt surely arises with respect to all of Arthur's attachments. And anyway: Saporta hardly shows *kindly* tolerance. *Pace* Wilkes, it is not

---

[13] Compare the few occurrences of "realize" in Waldo's section (W31/92) with those from Arthur's section (A226/240/252 /253/264/268, twice/279/280/290). There are no instances of discovery through realization in Waldo's section; if he ever is put in the position of undergoing such pronouncedly recipient cognition, he doesn't let on. His elective role is performative; he seeks control over the already existent; not even his literary aphorisms are true discovery, as this requires humility. Arthur searches, and eventually discovers, just as he ultimately—and lethally—uncovers. Cf the incidence in Arthur's section of "discover", "find out", "learn", "get to know" (A217/220–21/222/ 223/225/233/240, P307). Exploration precedes discovery, as performative precognition. Whereas with Waldo "considering" is a pretext (empty mental idling), it is a serious matter for Arthur, as even Waldo, with a touch of authoritarian, big-brother vanity, observes: "He was obviously giving thought to what his brother was trying to impress" about the "reasonable" (W31; see also A245/256).

[14] Note especially: A217/230/231/239/243/249*/251*/252*/ 271/273*/293*/P306; in the asterisked examples, Arthur "knows" through mistaken subjective assumption.

Saporta who gives Arthur's name to his son; he is merely a barely comprehending, possibly reluctant, agent of Dulcie (almost as though Arthur and not he were the prospective father of the child). What is at issue is not the trueness of the people Arthur calls his "friends", but the trueness of Arthur's desire to love, which is not invalidated by the error-frequency of his cognitions and beliefs. Permanence and harmony can only be striven for; their greatest promise is constantly negated by flux and disorder. Arthur's certainties and attachments are no more "mistaken" in terms of "reality" than the imprinting of a greylag goose, and all the more moving for that.

As a judge of his habitual environment, Arthur is usually decisive and right.[15] The question of rightness as such may not be at issue: it is, rather, the representation of a cognition as having been brought to consciousness and then "re-cognized"—Arthur is conscious of performing correctly the cognition or apperception of a signal or sign. Something has been brought more sharply into focus than would be "normal", and he is pleased at having "seen through" a (for him) difficult piece of behaviour and intention. Fully directed at himself, however, or reflected back upon himself, are other acts of cognition or expressions of attitude such as the following: "Arthur knew how to retract what some people considered his aggressive personality" (A245; also "reckoned", A246, "recognized", A221, "knew", A291). There is no guarantee that the situation obtains as Arthur assumes it will; so that the verb is deprived of external truth-status. Knowing is tantamount to faith, and faith may not suffice. He can be overwhelmed by an involuntary state: "He realized his watery mouth was hanging open, but knowing did not help him close it" (A276). "It was inconceivable" to him that Mrs Poulter might not want to walk with him—"He knew this .... Or did he?" (A260). The roundabout structure of the negative statement, so untypical of Arthur, is a sure sign of a loss of assurance, hardly made up again by the simple verb "knew", and confirmed by the free-indirect-thought question, a rarity in Arthur's discourse. This careful implementation of straightforward "knowing" verbs explains much of the impact at the close of Section 3, especially after the "revelations" and the tearing-up of the poem, and down to Arthur's entry into the room where Waldo is lying stricken (A293–94). The past-progressive "was convincing him", implying consciousness immersed in situation, gives way to an involved, indirect *that*-sentence with the statal "was evident"—Arthur as suffering, helpless recipient. In the next sentence, the nominal participle "knowing" has control, only to be mocked—this "did not help Arthur to act". He is reduced first to recipient perception ("could smell"), then to the status of an animal, "snivelling, sniffing". Even the finding of Waldo on the bed seems volitionless. In this state of primal perception, "Arthur saw". For the first time in the narrative, there is no predication: everything that has ever been the object of his cognition is somehow involved, but the verb, so placed, actually

---

[15] "Arthur knew this meant Mr Allwright wasn't willing to tell, just as he knew Waldo was put out" (A222); "So Arthur knew he was dismissed" (A237); "Arthur waited, because he saw it was intended"; see also examples with "know" at A228/233/265.

allows no conclusions to be drawn about the *kind* of mental act involved (again, all and everything, before the cumulative verb of seeing is specified). Recipient perception and apperception confront a nominalization of that verb of negative emotive attitude that is *least* frequent in Arthur's section and *most* frequent in Waldo's: "He saw the hatred ....".

Arthur is subject to other modes of knowing and seeing than those customary in the present classification: his prefigurative and recuperative dreams, for instance (A224/260–64), which contrast with Waldo's waking or semi-conscious dreams (W174/209). There are also numerous statements that betoken a high degree of prescience in Arthur's mental makeup, or a sense that the present will be immutably there in the future, or that the intuitions of the past are, at the moment of present realization, confirming the future. Contrasted with these categories are many verbs (quite negligible in Waldo's section) of precognitive incomprehension, uncertainty, not-knowing, and inexpressibility (this last correlating well with somatic indices to Arthur's speech-difficulties). At the mildest, there is the verb "wonder" in the sense "to ask oneself" (A253/262/287). In childhood, he is "arrested" by the strange posture and factual communication of the distracted Mrs Mackenzie: "Arthur wished he knew what to say" (A221); this state remains as intriguingly inchoate to us as it is to Arthur. There is usually more going on inside him than he can account for whenever he is taxed by adults on his reactions or his silence (A216/223–24/248). The mental reaching into a blank of immediate futurity contrasts, in its frequent conditional aspect, with the certainty of the indicative aspect common in the statements of "prescience" mentioned above.[16]

Instinctual doing and thinking lie close by the group just illustrated: "Why he wrote, or for whom, he could not have told, nor would he have shown" (A290)— Arthur's writing is, nevertheless, associated with guilt, as is his surreptitious reading at Mrs Musto's; it is an activity that is compulsive and secret. "In time, he thought, he might, perhaps, just begin to understand" what is offered by books (A229); "Waldo was in need of a kind. What that need could be, Arthur was not yet certain" (A239); it is clear from the reserve of the discourse how merely provisional these states are.[17] Arthur's most intense uncertainty co-occurs with speechlessness and epiphanic urgency in the presence of the dying Mr Feinstein: "he was too confused to know exactly what he saw" (A278); but he evades the efforts of Dulcie to treat him as a divine instrument: "Whatever she intended to convey he was glad not to grasp it"—a fine gradation in potentialities between the precognitive and the cognitive, "cold" and "warm".

---

[16] "Arthur was glad to splash around with his unmanageable hands, which, he now realized, she would never notice" (A244); "He had already begun to pant for what must have happened" (A269); "Then Arthur knew he could never explain what was too big" (A278); see also A237/243/245/249/251/255/267/272. These precognitions, convictions and signs of prescience are different from narrative prolepsis or recollective subjectivity (see ch. 4.I above).

[17] Cf also: "he could not have told, but knew" (A217) A217 ("puzzled"); A227 ("did not altogether understand"); A228 ("didn't know").

Waldo, Arthur knows, "was suspicious of men" (A218). Suspicion, a precognitive act of performative emotion, is subject to considerable contextual gradation. There are about four times as many occurrences of relevant lexical items in Waldo's section as there are in Arthur's, while the gap is even wider once one has taken more delicate semantic implications into consideration. The three occurrences of the verb "suspect" in Section 3 are all robbed of factive validity (A250/253, P305). Waldo's suspicions, by contrast, are (un)healthily direct. Because "suspect" is only half-way towards conviction, it can function as a "meiotic" formula, its assumed caution concealing various emotions contextually, from disappointment and lingering hope to mild panic and physical unease.[18] It may pretend to ironic superiority ("while bees began to investigate, till she brushed them away. Angrily, Waldo suspected", W49) in a precocious child catching a glimpse behind the façade of social behaviour. Suspicion may be concealed beneath assumption: "Whether Arthur understood, or had listened at all, Waldo doubted" (W33). Waldo's convolutions of suspicion produce rationalizing projections: "You could only despise ignorant, suspicious minds. Or the simple, wide-open ones" (W144). The incubus of paranoia begins to thrust suspicion aside towards the end of Waldo's narrative, and the incidence of "suspect"-verbs falls off rapidly.

PERFORMATIVE COGNITION AND WILL

Waldo is so self-conscious, so diffident about his place in the world and panicky about the imminent disintegration of self, that he must *will* himself to act and to think. "After all", he thinks, "you can overcome anything by will" (W208). Will finds its expression in method; lecturing Arthur in old age as he fusses with his papers, he outlines his philosophy:

"A disorderly life, a disorderly mind," Waldo said. "You won't understand, Arthur, the mental handicap physical disorder can become. You don't need to. In my case an absence of method could undo the plans of a lifetime." [A287]

Waldo's firm resolutions ("plans") are often more of a "mental handicap" than physical disorder—which, in the broadest sense, he will never be able to escape; there is seldom an issue in action, unless further mental action. Decision and will in Waldo's section take many lexical forms (decide, plan, will sth., allow oneself to do sth., choose, refuse to do, force oneself to do, be determined [not] to, [mentally] propose to do, desire [to perform some mental act], *want* and modal *will* together with their negation). The ratio of such verbs is 7 (Section 2) : 1 (Section 3), all of Arthur's verbs being simply "decide", always with a potential or actual issue in verbal or other acts.[19] This can produce contrastive ironies: Arthur is blithely and briskly decisive in resolving a problem relating to a

---

[18] Cf "Waldo began to suspect parents remain unconscious of a talent in their child" (W75); "he felt lighter, but always had been, he suspected" (W213); also W23 ("mistrusted")/48/69/94/ 108/125.

[19] A220/239/248/255 ("decided to go up alone/to ask help/not to admit to Waldo .../to say"), P309 ("decided to take the train back"), A282 ("decided to tell. And decided not to").

meeting at the Feinsteins' (W107), assuming he has been invited—whereas Waldo, who thinks he has concealed the double invitation from Arthur, is doubly helpless and irresolute. Guilt leads Waldo to abdicate will and blame destiny for his actions (cf his contemplating the direction "he had not chosen", W57/60). Disturbed by thoughts of Dulcie, he "convinces" himself to reject thought of her (W98). He "wills" the train to "dislocate the vision" of his father's disturbing facial expression (W54)—the same train that intrudes on his thoughts later as he tries to compel himself to resist Mr Brown. At Mrs Musto's party, his firm "intention not to be made an exhibition of" (W89) is but a momentary regaining of control—after which he can only defend this salient by going to the other extreme and "despising" those who rendered him uncertain in the first place.

Planning and intention are associated with covert self-interest and the exercise of control. Waldo's desire to impress Dulcie conflicts with his desire to conceal his egoism from her: his discourse tries to cover over irresolution by invoking his secret will ("he had had to abandon a plan", W93–94). He covers his diffidence while courting that unknown quantity, Bill Poulter, with an elaborate texture of incipient intention, culminating (in a prelude to disastrous failure) with "Waldo made his decision" (W142–43). He pretends to respect the decorum of death and bereavement in order to conceal his own opportunism (now that Mrs Feinstein is out of the way he can perhaps implement a half-conceived plan to propose to Dulcie). But his hypocrisy exudes from every line, "decision" darting into the narration in the interstices of his protestations of concern and discretion:

it was a shock .... her death found him abominably unprepared .... he felt he didn't want to overhear .... Then he decided to listen, and perhaps turn it to practical account .... So Waldo decided to walk over ....

—and, at the end of a devious list of six minimalizing expressions:

He had, if he wanted to be truthful with himself, thought vaguely, though only vaguely, once or twice, that in the end he might decide to marry Dulcie Feinstein. Now her mother's death was helping a decision crystallize. [W148–49]

The central strand of intention in the actional-present narrative, of course, is the plan to kill his brother. It is there in the very first sentence of Section 2: he "decides" to go for a walk "at last": ie, after careful inspection of Arthur, brooding after his heart-tremor (W23). Oblique adversions to the grand plan filter in later (eg, a "hitherto evil morning ... of decisions", W56); and, looking back on failure at the end of the walk, he "had decided Arthur should die" (W205).

Waldo's somatic self-control is essentially a form of concealment, as are all of his acts of will, although what he conceals is not the "brilliant truth" (W193) he thinks lies beneath "the disguise he had chosen". Characterizations of his tone of voice invariably indicate that he is applying strategies to conceal emotions not consonant with surface intention.[20] Emotion is the great threat (he must "put his mind in order", W56; "Naturally he disguised his feelings", W127; "you could always control your impulses", W95). But his emotions continually slip the leash,

---

[20] W25 ("answered brutally", "said carefully"), W28 ("answered facetiously", "said very distinctly"), W29 ("asked more gently"); he "could modulate his voice" (W26), "could not, he hoped, have made it sound colder" (W56).

and he is left trying to present his inward reactions to himself as subject to control. He had planned, "had decided to do something about his temper" but had failed (W58). Logic collapses as self-control is both denied and linked with control of others: "he would have to control, as he had always known how to control, himself, his parents, his colleagues—and his brother" (W30). It is at this point that he "realizes" his own breathing is out of control; frightened for his own safety on the "killing" walk, he "decides" that they will turn back, but actually does so only at Arthur's behest (W69).

Willed avoidance is actionally central to the narrative. Waldo avoids or turns down invitations (what he would call controlling his colleagues), "escapes" from his father (W79), avoids Dulcie in her very presence (W89), hides from Haynes and Mrs Poulter (W188/141). He is, however, already in the throes of emotion by the time he takes evasive action, which occurs frequently (averting or turning his face away, averting or withdrawing his mind, W26/28/62, A292).[21] Where emotional attachment is of a type familiar to him, Waldo thinks he is more controlled in his willed disavowal of it (cf love and gratitude, W49/55–56). Emotional attachments which are merely notional are defamiliarized as soon as they impinge on his rationality (he "proposes" to love his dog, W180, has "the desire to exercise his generosity", W185, "decides" in his helplessness to keep a whore at a distance through words and, unable to stop her kissing him, can claim that he has "such control of himself", W184). He can speculate on the possibility of making certain decisions before concerning himself with their substance ("he would have to decide what", W50). As Arthur notices, his decisions can involve selecting a moral pretext for avoiding the unmentionable; his will has to catch up on his emotional equilibrium ("Waldo hedged ... and decided almost at once", A256). Disclaiming decisiveness about the way he feels, he is already feeling.[22]

Decision is a matter of selection. Waldo applies his will to the acquisition of "personal" attributes from without (W69/94). It is therefore not surprising that his "plans of a lifetime" centre on his Secret Writing, which is the exercise of control and the will (W82). If Waldo's Secret Writing takes the form of list-making, collection and collation, this may be not least because a useful pun is in the offing. This "putting together" (as in his schoolboy gift for "composition", W74) is like the putting—and keeping—together of the fragments of a personality, restoring order out of disorder. Why, otherwise, should Arthur see his family as "already avoiding, composing" (A267)—the latter an unusual ellipsis for "composing themselves" (showing composure, putting themselves together emotionally, "collected" as well as united against him)? In all fairness, it should be pointed out that Arthur, too, conceals, controls, and acquires. But, except where the acquisition of knowledge is a means of protecting Waldo, it is people,

---

[21] Further indices to withdrawal through the enlistment of will: W90 (with Dulcie), W65/209 (avoiding thought or "mental anguish"), W58 (refusal to listen), W126 ("deciding" that wartime "shouldn't concern them"), W69/114/161 (determination to avoid thinking of his father's death).

[22] W87 ("didn't know exactly what attitude to take"), W103 ("wasn't sure how he felt about it"), W120 (forestalls "the probable question of how he felt" about turning thirty).

whole individuals, who are collected, not dead fragments of thought on paper (A220/227/239/274). "Perhaps Arthur even had a secret life of his own", muses Waldo (W81); and indeed he does (A242), not to mention his Secret Reading. On the three (only) occasions on which Arthur consciously and explicitly exercises "control" (A269/274/279), it is over his emotions—and always for his brother's sake. Control, in Arthur's section, has another semantic shape: "protection". On the one occasion when Arthur is pushed too far—in the Library, when Waldo is hysterically trying to dismantle all that Arthur is trying to protect—he is "almost glad he couldn't control himself" in the heat of self-defense and argument (A284).

EMOTION: DEGREES OF PLEASURE AND DESIRE

The Solid Mandala is a novel which, though full of situationally determined irony and humour, is prevailingly sombre in terms of the aura given off by the mental life of its characters. There is nothing particularly positive about the emotional reactions and states referred to—which is one reason why it seems less of a breach of classificatory principles to include here, under verbs and predicates of emotion, certain cognitive and precognitive verbs ("admire", "be interested in") whose "feeling"-quotient may be low to non-existent.

Arthur is clearly the Most Happy Fella.[23] Waldo scores low on pleasure (excepting the qualified ecstasy of books and orgasm). He can be "pleased" at the pseudo-humility of his own words (W52), which is, rather, the vanity of the devious wordsmith; he can look forward to the prospect of "enjoying" his mother's company (W61)—and this he indubitably does, but in a spirit of pure narcissism. The closest to honest pleasure in the narrative is closer to relief, and is elliptically expressed: "It was good not to have to think, but sit" (W42); these childhood moments do not recur. His pleasures in adulthood are muted, preening and aestheticized, even down to the prissy syntactic embedding ("Particularly did he appreciate ... the Mitchell", W182). It is in the nature of things that Waldo's mental self-pleasuring escapes direct verb-expression or predication; ellipses and rationalizations do duty instead for his narcissism.[24] Apart from Waldo's and Arthur's "obsessions" and "preoccupations", Waldo can be variously "fascinated", "entranced" and "impressed" by any phenomenon which serves to fuel his obsessions (W26/101/152). Arthur can be "fascinated, if not actually frightened" (A226) by the unfamiliar sight of Mr Allwright praying. Things people say are ideas which Arthur "likes", which are "of the greatest interest" (A219/227), to the degree in which he creatively misunderstands them. Interest and admiration, then, are the product oif Arthur's innocence, not of his knowingness. On the other hand, his admiration for his brother and mother have less to do with pleasure than with loyalty.

---

[23] See predications with "happy", "glad", "pleased", "content" (A215/216/246/275/276), constructions with "please", "enjoy" etc (A223/227/232/240/248/258/273).

[24] W98/122–23/140/179 (predications with "superior"); cf also W120/53/81/92.

Performative precognition is applied to objectives which, in Waldo's section, are and remain impossibilities. Waldo's desires are sometimes not far from the farcical or pathetic, or are freighted with self-deception. He may "hope" and "long" for "a friend of his own sex" or "an intimate intellectual companion", but he is hopelessly mixed-up—with Bill Poulter, the surrounding diction is heterosexual, with Dulcie, platonic. Arthur's desire is initially pragmatic: he "wants" to be trusted and understood (A218), goals that are uncertainly fulfilled. Longing for the impossible surges at the end, in his dark night of the soul (P306/308). There are few indicators of relief or reassurance in either narrative. Arthur is relieved that the wrong sort of person or situation is not about to run athwart his private search for mandalic totality (A238–39/251; cf also A276). Waldo, in every case, is relieved at getting out of a potentially embarrassing situation associated with Arthur (W109/153/193/ 194/197), whereby attention is drawn away from this bald fact either by extreme obliquity or by projective misrepresentation.

EMOTION: LOVE

Arthur loves unquestioningly. Towards the close of Section 3, references to love represent an awareness in Arthur of its problematical status that is absent in the earlier phases of his narrative. It can be said that the perception of love moves from simplicity to complexity, with a parallel growth in Arthur's awareness of negative emotion (hatred, shame, guilt). In childhood, no distinction is made between Arthur's love for his mother, the sea, and the icebergs "he would have loved to see" (A218); one sentence gives way to the next, and the boundary between attachment and desire is erased. No essential distinction is made between people and things, all of which are both loved and associated with the sources of Arthur's knowledge.[25] Arthur's attitude is compromised or relativized through the perceptions of Waldo, who abhors open protestation or discussion of love (W41/111; A245). There are signs that Waldo's childhood narcissism is still balanced against moments when he can love his brother and feel an uncomplicated attraction to the world of things (W37/42). But there are also signs that budding intellectual solipsism is beginning to cloud his perception of his brother's reactions (such as to the mention of fennel in Waldo's school essay: "Arthur laughed low, loving it", W43). In late adolescence, he mockingly gives the label "love" to nationalistic solidarity (W127)—but there is a dynamism in the prose that suggests how drawn to this heady, extravert emotion one part of him is. From his middle years onwards, "love" becomes some quantity "out there": not even a simple supposition or vague feeling, but the act of will controlled (even generated, or avoided) by the intellect ("He thought he loved Dulcie", W136; "Waldo proposed to love his dog", W180, in a parody of Arthur's declaration of love for his ferret, W41). In old age, the concept of love for other

---

[25] "He loved other people's houses" and "the ladies" (A219/221); he "loved the classical façade" and "Demeter ... Athene" (A223); he "loved watching" Mrs Poulter, her hair, her jewellery (A264).

human beings must be distorted into something Waldo can choose or reject, depending on the extent to which "love" disrupts his pristine selfhood (W55–56). Incarcerated in what has become the nightmare of the present, he retreats into the past of "their Quantrell heritage", which he loves "to distraction" (W175); the nature of this love is perfectly conveyed in the competing valencies of "distraction": gushy, hysterical decadence; excess; madness. His mental image of Arthur as they walk together in old age shows his indulgent hostility, even envy, towards his twin:

Arthur loved it. He loved the service station. He loved to stare at people .... Arthur loved the Speedex Service Station because .... [W59]

This is an acidulous internarrative imitation of the anaphoric sentence-pattern at the beginning of Arthur's section, which conveys the simple directness of Arthur's childhood love of exhibitionism and of sensuous surfaces (A216).

A third instance of anaphoric patterning occurs in Mrs Poulter's subsection:

[She] loved a handsome man .... She loved, she had loved Bill .... She loved his throat ... loved where the hair began and ended. She loved him, her husband. She loved him. [P297–98]

One of the most heart-rending passages in the book (not in the above compacted form, of course), this makes up part of a paean to sexual love—the only one in the book—but one that is uttered against the background of Bill Poulter's inability to express love. The intensity of desire is unabated in the face of total deprivation—but the anaphora builds up to a point where Mrs Poulter's avowals (already compromised by a fatal adjustment of tense) have become a litany against despair and guilt. Even the denatured word "lovely" takes on an aura of grace in Mrs Poulter's discourse, and helps prepare for the critical transition from physical desire and deprivation to transcendent love and temporary maternal fulfilment. At the marriage of the Poulters, "the trees was lovely, big smooth-barked gums standing straight and cool by the river" (P297); "unlike their own lovely-fitting grooved love of the beginning" with Bill, Mrs Poulter's secret love for Arthur "could not be fitted to word or hand" (P300). And at the end, she embraces Arthur, "all the men she had ever loved", though "the positions of love did not come easy to her" (P311).

NEGATIVE EMOTION

Surprise (W92/175) is too equable an emotion to fit many of the situations Waldo finds himself in; the verb downplays the real strength of his reactions. "Thunderstruck" is just right for Arthur's reaction to finding the mandala-definition (A238). Arthur tends to be openly "amazed", especially when he notices people ageing (A247/263/289).

There are so many situational, verbal and figurative indices to fear in Waldo's section that it constitutes one of the major climatic zones in his mental and emotional landscape. What might pass unnoticed is the fact that explicit indications of fear (psychological verbs and predications) occur equally often in both Waldo's and Arthur's narratives, and that there is almost twice as much overt indication of fear in Arthur's section as in Waldo's. Waldo "dreads" death and decay (W26/71/167), the truths Arthur might confide in him (W196/207). He "fears" the treachery of eyes (W92) and Dulcie's sexual maturity (W151), is "afraid" of not impressing her (W96) and of social humiliation (W89), is "frightened" of intellectual failure (W104). Arthur, by contrast, "feared for Waldo" (A228)—but there is an element of fear *of* Waldo in Arthur's attitudes. Though he has "the shakes" and "trembles" for Waldo (A243), it is not just because his brother may be hurt by his inability to relate to the Feinsteins, but also because Waldo may have queered Arthur's pitch with the family. Because Arthur doesn't want to tarnish his self-image as loving and protective, he cannot be *afraid* to ask Waldo a favour, but "would not have cared to ask" one (A239). He is "not actually frightened" by Mr Allwright's praying posture—he retreats from admitting it (A226). Not understanding why on earth he should be left alone by Dulcie in Saporta's presence, Arthur is as close to panic ("afraid … horrified and disturbed", W275–76) as he will ever be until after the mortal climax of the book, though his "terror" at his own words and thoughts in the Library Incident runs a close second. Not *knowing*, rather than threats to his person, is what discommodes Arthur most.

Both twins suffer mentally—Waldo because of the burden of his brother, Arthur because of his relationships and because of his brother's suffering. Hurt by Dulcie's silence, Arthur (for the only time in the narrative) "did not want to think" about the matter (A253). Repeatedly, Arthur feels pity, sympathy, regret for Waldo's suffering (A269/274/279). There is no correspondence on Waldo's side.[26] This litany of suffering—where does it have its psychical origin? Not in the unavoidable fact of Arthur's existence, not in Waldo's failure with Dulcie—but deep within himself; his is the intolerable burden of the Self. By contrast, Arthur is almost impervious to hurt, as absorbent of it as he is physically "spongy".[27] If one probes deeper into Arthur's serenely simple formulae, one finds that his equilibrium is not always absolute; but his general psychological disposition makes him resilient—these are not expressions of wide-eyed innocence or ignorance. But Arthur's natural stoicism, though it may enable him to feel sympathy, does not leave room for an empathy with Waldo strong enough to forestall the final catastrophe. To ultimate consequences, Arthur is impervious to a fault.

We are moving closer now to the dead heart of the wasteland—dead, but quickened by some of the darkest, most visceral, most destructive (one is tempted to add: most evil) emotions. Quantitatively, the psychological verbs in question have the highest incidence in the book; distributionally, Arthur does not figure *at all*, only Waldo. The first group are verbs and predications of recipient negative cognition. Some few are attempts to maintain a semblance of dignity amidst wholesale emotional annihilation, as after the Pitt Street Encounter ("Waldo had

---

[26] "It was Waldo who suffered" (A279), "could not" or "could hardly bear" (W27/39/41); he must "bear" or "endure" "intolerable" situations (W56/60/70/125/167/208).

[27] "He "did not care. Or he did" (A218), "could not even care" (A223); "did not mind/care" (A228283); was "undisturbed" (A228); things "did not worry/disturb" him, "nothing could hurt" him (A225/226/228/290).

been too angry, too upset", W64, the second adjective "correcting" the distortion into implied grievance of the first). Mental verbs are avoided when Waldo re-experiences his dead father; instead, there are nominalizations, sometimes moralized ("outrage", W70). Waldo is "furious" at Arthur's proficiency at jumping through the social hoops that Waldo is too hogtied to negotiate (W113); there is the distinct sense that Waldo has been done an *injustice*, and, behind that, helpless frustration. When Dulcie tells him Arthur has given her one of his "glass marbles", Waldo is "astonished, then horrified" (W152). This predicate-gradation is only partly construable as a double-take (first puzzlement, then realization). There is something bivalent about "horrified"—such an old-maid's word for a reaction to bad taste (Arthur up to something again, compromising him), but also with a ground-swell of real *horror*, as if this symbolic pact—which Dulcie has clearly *entered into*—has opened up a dark pit of irrational forces to Waldo's staring inward gaze.

Waldo's sense of order, cleanliness and decorum is upset by Arthur's "wiping out the basin with his fingers, which annoyed Waldo considerably" (W206). One senses the blunting of the edge of hysteria, the application of restraint. The next stage up is when the disruptions of Waldo's refined and dignified microcosm are characterized in terms of blenching paralysis or bad taste, mentally or quasi-viscerally, via expressions of disgust, revulsion, being "appalled", and loathing.[28]

Reaction has shifted with "loathing" (W199) to performative mental action; and it is here that consciousness becomes raw, naked and *unequivocally active*. If until now there has been an intermittent to-and-fro of some of the seven deadly sins—pride as narcissism and solipsism; lust in the mind; sloth as intellectual inertia and spiritual stasis; anger; gluttony; covetousness as selfishness—as well as such more venial ulcerations as mendacity and Waldo's "secret vices"; if there has been a relative absence of the Platonic or natural virtues—certainly no justice or temperance; perhaps fortitude of a sort in Arthur, Mrs Poulter, Mr Brown; only a mocking shadow of wisdom or prudence in Arthur's prescience—and merely a carnivalesque representation of the theological virtues of faith, hope, and charity; if all this, then there is still a place for love, for its dark brother, and for envy, the other deadly sin. What we find, of course, is that hatred, envy and resentment combine in Waldo to produce a corrosive and self-destructive chemistry.[29]

---

[28] Predications with "appalled" (W59/87/185/193); verbs and predications with "disgust" or "distaste" (W35/50/67/154/190/ 197); repulsion and recoil (W91/127/138); "Waldo could have thrown up" (W147), "Arthur made Waldo sick" (W166). There is plenty more where this came from.

[29] At the mildest level, he is constantly "irritated" (W81/91/100/182). He "envies" or is "jealous" of his brother, of other people's language, of Haynes's virile hair, of the sexual pleasure of others, even—thinks Arthur—of his brother's relationships (W25/35/88/187/190; A268). "Resent" and "resentment" are ubiquitous (W48/71/76/125/126/133//165/185/ 186), likewise bitterness (W24/76/89/145).

At the climax of the narrative, Arthur at last "sees", in Waldo's facial expression, the "hatred" intrinsic to Waldo (A294). After fleeing the house, Arthur is beset by thoughts about hatred (P305), and there is a concentration—for the first time—of indications that he has been overwhelmed by self-consciousness and guilt, and wishes to flee his social self, "if not the *hateful* load of his body". Although there is a retreat from the openness of verbs, for the first time in the discourse centered on Arthur we find an emanation of hatred from Arthur himself. "Hateful" means both "filled with hate"—the hatred which has entered Arthur from Waldo's dying stare—and "hated": hated both by Waldo and by Arthur. Along with guilt and shame, self-hatred has entered Arthur's mental universe. No amount of weak rationalizing—and rationalizing is now made an explicit mental mode for Arthur ("Waldo had always hated people but always rather, well, as a joke") can erase the awareness that "the hatred which only finally killed" has infected "the sleep they had shared", as Waldo is "infected" with the "incurable disease" of Arthur's love.

And it is Arthur's instinct for love which is in part a search for protection. On three occasions towards the end of Section 3, potentially strong antipathy in Arthur is attenuated through meiotic discourse. When Mrs Poulter tries to force on him a dogmatic belief in Christ, "for the moment he cared less for her" (A261)—not "disliked", or worse; the negative emotion that is repressed then finds its outlet in his physical exhaustion and exacerbated nerviness. When Waldo manages to separate Arthur from Mrs Poulter, "if he had not admired his brother, Arthur might have felt hurt" (A268). When his mother seems to withdraw her love as she withdraws into her thoughts, "Arthur would have liked to admire their mother less" (A269). These are the nearest he ever gets to directing negative feeling towards others.

Waldo's unremitting hatred is sometimes disguised as acts of aggression (W95/199), as a vaguely aesthetic antipathy ("despise", W64/89/92), or as an intellectual attitude (contempt, W85/144/172). Usually, however, it is open, direct(ed), "honest". As Table 6 indicates, "hate" is both cognitively performative (a mental act) and attitudinal (a mental state). Under the specific diegetic conditions in *The Solid Mandala*, it is not always possible or desirable to view individual statements with "hate" as either one or the other. Sometimes the attitudinal aspect is central (W121/127). Sometimes the performative aspect is made lexically clear ("Suddenly he hated that strength" of his father, W165; but even here, the germ of hatred must be already within Waldo). "Waldo would have hated to touch" the sweating Dulcie (W90); hatred as phobia is pre-programmed in Waldo, but the verb is performatively directed at an anticipated contact. Of his "blackheads and pimples": "Waldo hated that. He hated his interminable pimply face" (W75)—an attitude, but narratively a performative, too, for he is standing before a particular mirror in a particular cognitive situation. He "hated" the "aggressive white" of the wellbred youngsters (W88)—an attitude, stemming from a sense of social inferiority, but also a regular, aggressive pulse of mental performance. It is not least in view of such considerations that one can speak of the action of the novel as taking place in the minds of the characters.

Because, therefore, of its bivalency in conveying both state and action, "hate" is an ideal verb for maintaining emotive continuity in a narrative of figural discourse. More specifically, it is narrationally prefigurative, joining Waldo's state in life to his state in death, his mental acts in life to his last mental act before death—a state, an act, which is the bringer of death, just as it was subliminally Waldo's mental "murdering" of others throughout his lifetime. In psychological, metapsychological and narrative terms, the weird and horrible climax of the novel has been more than adequately motivated throughout. The structured working-out of this motivation in Waldo's narrative can be examined by keeping a close eye on the contextualizations of the verb "hate".

In Waldo's narrative, several important occurrences of "hate" are associated with Arthur's hand and with the conflict between two radically dissimilar modes of thinking and coming to knowledge.

(1) In the actional-present narrative (W29), Waldo reacts to Arthur's talk about coming to knowledge about simple, "transparent" people as follows: "He hated it. He could have thrown away the fat parcel of his imbecile brother's hand". The simple directness of "He hated it" is offset by its referential indeterminacy. "Mystical" or intuitive epistemology is associated by Waldo with unreason and the non-abstract substantiality of Arthur's "imbecile" hand. "Hated" is attitudinal (against this kind of talk), performative (for the expression "more transparent"), and attitudinal-performative (for the hand as "it"). (2) Overleaf (W30), Waldo tells Arthur to hurry up; "He hated his brother". "Hated" both represents Waldo's permanent attitude and is a sudden performative reflex of his prior thought: instead of "intellectual companions", he has the burden of his brother's intuitiveness. Hatred has shifted from the synecdochic (hand) to the whole (Arthur), with the hand still present (Waldo implicitly jerking on it to hurry Arthur to his doom, as he does explicitly elsewhere). (3) In the second or recollective narrative (W42), "Arthur would catch hold of Waldo's hand, which even then Waldo hated". Good evidence for the figurally referential nature of the linkage-system is the presence of the adverbial "even then" 13 pages after its actional-present coreferent. At this childhood stage, "hate" seems narrowed to detestation of the physical and of Arthur's dependency. (4) In the actional present (W58) Waldo's hatred is directed performatively and attitudinally at Mrs Poulter, whom he sees as the pragmatic, personal philosopher responsible for Arthur's cast of thought, even before Arthur gets to talking about her views: "Waldo yanked at the oblivious hand. Mrs Poulter was one of the fifty-seven things and persons Waldo hated". The latent jokiness is thematically serious enough: these "Fifty-Seven Varieties" are for Waldo the same one thing—the disordered materiality of the world and intuitive ("oblivious") access to it. (5) People who can render Waldo "transparent" by knowing him too well threaten his secret intellectual control over disorder: "He hated almost everyone, but above all, his family. They knew too much" (W80). (6) After the return from the actional-

present walk, after Waldo has failed to lead Arthur by the hand to his doom,
Waldo asks his twin:

"Don't you care if people don't like you?"
"No," said Arthur. "Because they mostly do."
Waldo hated his brother for moments such as these. While knowing he should be thankful
for Arthur's insensitivity. [W205]

"Insensitivity" takes us back to the "oblivious hand". Waldo's question is both an
indication to Arthur of hatred, and an exasperated revelation of his own suffering
self-consciousness. To think or to know you are disliked is to experience the
cruelty of the human community. Arthur may be wrong in his assessment; but he
has "understood" in his own way and has thus fulfilled Mrs Poulter's philosophy
of calm stoicism. Hence Waldo's hatred: not just for Arthur's "insensitivity"
(which at the same time spares Waldo from exposure), but also subliminal *envy*
that Arthur does not suffer from intellectual hyperconsciousness. It is a form of
wisdom that is irrational.

(1) to (6) represent, not discrete instances of attitudinal and performative
hating, but a logical nexus with the same antinomies constantly implied. A
second strand which impinges on the one just discussed is a slightly different
working-out of the persistencies of figural consciousness.

(1) At school, "Waldo hated Johnny" Haynes (W43) for his proficiency and a
practical form of knowledge which leaves no room for outbursts of impractical
Gothic fantasy like Waldo's (it is, in part, Johnny's anti-intellectualism that
provokes him to torture Waldo). (2) When Waldo realizes that the stranger in his
garden is Johnny Haynes (W189), it is not just the bitter memory of school that
precipitates Waldo's hatred, but Haynes's anti-intellectual reference to Mr
Brown's Greek pediment. In the first flash of memory, the idiom for mutual
antipathy—"they could have cut each other's throats"—encodes retributively both
the knife-torture in the playground and the Gothic "composition" that triggered it.
But it is only after the Greek-pediment reference that Waldo's reflections open
onto memory and life generally. "So it was natural he should continue hating
Haynes". "Continue" has the same long-range figural deixis as "even then"; it
connects the "hating" with the "hated" in (1). Narrationally of note is the *cool
logic* or malevolent coldness with which this most savage of emotions is
mediated. (3) The visit itself has already been characterized proleptically as
"undoubtedly malicious in conception" (W187). When Haynes's words
benevolently contradict Waldo's suspicion and suggest that Arthur is not really
"loopy", "Waldo had never hated Johnny Haynes so intensely as now" (W190).
The visitors leave—but not before Waldo has wished the dogs on them in archaic,
bloody retribution. This invocation takes us back to *immediately before* the
prolepsis of the visit, where "Arthur's dogs" are seen as chewing up Waldo's
papers, destroying the record of the past in the present. Waldo wills the dogs to
wreak a similar vengeance, in the present, on the past. The visit is "malicious",
an act of hatred against him: he will counter in kind. (4) These dogs have already
come in at the tail-end, as it were, of a concentrated litany of hatred occasioned

by Waldo's increasing paranoia and his slipping away from rational self-control
(as exemplified in the purchase of the plastic doll for Mrs Poulter):

So he got to resent Mrs Poulter, and everyone else who made mysteries as the Peace
declined. He began to hate the faces leering and blearing at him in the streets. He hated, in
retrospect, Crankshaw and his priests. He hated his brother Arthur, although, or perhaps
because, Arthur was the thread of continuity, and might even be the core of truth.

Some years later, when they got them, he hated Arthur's dogs—though technically one of
them was his own. [W186–87]

Why this sequence of "hate"s? Obviously, the new paragraph for the dogs leads
on associatively from Arthur; the time-gap is secondary—what is topicalized is
the motivation for Waldo's hatred of them. Why should the librarian "Crankshaw
and his priests" come in here? With Waldo's meticulous sense for order, "in
retrospect" is a finely pedantic touch: the "priests" are "O'Brien" and the other
"priests in white hats" from before Waldo's resignation from the old Municipal
library (W172–73). In another way, however, "in retrospect" is a further *leurre*
or false clue: we shall find that Waldo's consciousness is superimposing points of
past time, and that the present sequence of "hate"s is chronologically sequent,
once the *previous* reference to "hate" in the *sujet* is placed in temporal context:

(5) Such was the texture of mind he had cultivated, Waldo only saw this dialogue printed black
on its transparent screen perhaps six years afterwards, and immediately realized O'Connell was
somebody to hate.

Arthur's dogs helped him to reach his conclusion. [W178]

The dialogue remembered is that between O'Connell and a colleague; Waldo
hates the fact that here is a man who doesn't like him (thinking him "nutty": ie,
lacking in reason), but who defers to the advice of the "honest" Crankshaw in
giving Waldo a chance at the new Library. It is a reluctant deference: "'No man
can afford to be honest'", O'Connell says, when trying to get rid of undesirable
employees. Waldo's reaction: "(This part alone made Waldo Brown inclined to
lose the faith he didn't have in human nature)". No wonder Waldo asks Arthur
((6) above) if he minds people disliking him. Hate is thus programmed in
Waldo's "transparent" memory, O'Connell singled out as "somebody to hate".
Waldo's "plan" to acquire a dog depends on Arthur's dog: Arthur's dog prompts
Waldo's "conclusion" of hatred:

The confirmed perfidy of Crankshaw, not to mention O'Connell, perhaps recommended the
honesty of dogs. So Waldo in turn grew sly. [W179]

The play here on "honesty" and "sly" foregrounds the connection with
O'Connell's remarks on Crankshaw. What we also have in these references to
honesty, perfidy, men and dogs, and "faith ... in human nature" is an
internarrative link with Arthur's section and its prolepsis: "even dogs are less
brutal than men" (A217). It is precisely because he has been humiliated by the
"dishonesty in other men, in Crankshaw, not to mention O'Connell" that Waldo
now humiliates the dog. Hatred for Crankshaw; hatred for the dogs (a double
hatred, ultimately, for they do not allow themselves to be humiliated). "In
retrospect", then, does not take us back to the *original* "priests" of Crankshaw
(Father O'Brien), but to those *later* "priests" with Irish names, serving their

"bishop" Crankshaw for the sake of his sense of "continuity". By the time we get to W186, Waldo's allocation of hatred has shifted its focus from agents to instigators: first O'Connell (W178), then "Crankshaw, not to mention O'Connell" (W179–80), then "Crankshaw and his priests" (W186)—which now serves to gather together a whole stretch of Waldo's private humiliations: not just the moment of an overheard conversation and the six years following, but all the years before that. Hatred and memory are so interdependent that attitude, performative cognition and the re–cognition of recollection become inextricable in the dynamic of the narrative.

The patterns of occurrence set up by psychological verbs and predications not only serve as main hinges on the swing-door opening into thematic analysis. They also nestle at the centre of vast webs of indexical and associative detail and, by their unadorned, non-analytical mode of implementation, underscore the differentiated centrality of figural consciousness in the narration. In a narrative of paradigmatic twin-ness, indivisibility and severance, it is significant that the two verbs that form the architectonic base in *The Solid Mandala* should be the extremes of the one scale—"love" and "hate". White's other fiction exhibits similar stylistic configurations of psychological agency, though the characterological fit may, of course, be different (as, for example, in the maniacally hegemonic mental operations of Ulrich Voss).

IV   Iconicity

Most of what is observable stylistically in White's language might be said to boil down to the mimicking of psyche: in fact, the presence of iconicity can be pointed out easily enough and can even (as in Edgecombe 1987 and 1989) be applied as an *omnium gatherum* to account for White's style. But the concept of iconicity, like the concept of style itself, touches uneasily on the age-old and vexed question of the relation of content to form—indeed, of whether the form/content dichotomy is a real and useful one at all (Hirsch 1975:564 has pointed out that in stylistics there is often "uncertainty whether a trait should be judged as a form or a content"). Epstein (1975:41) has been frequently attacked for his wholesale methodological assumption that formal organization(s) can mimic content. Barthes (1971:4) contends persuasively that, although there is "a certain irreducible grain of truth" in the belief that there is an opposition of content/*signifié* to form/*signifiant*, such a binary opposition cannot do justice to the nature of texts or to our interpretations of them. Discourse is layered; depending on which "codes" or semantic levels are sought out, a text can have ascribed to it several subjects or contents. The fact that any one "content" can be seen to be coded against a "style" or "form" is no argument in favour of fixed binary opposition. What is important is that the notion of close paraphrasability may be questioned by virtue of the fact that style/form (one irremovable code in a text) can be evaluated only against the several contents it generates and delimits. Of the three fundamental positions dealt with by Leech (1981) in relation to *materia* and *forma*, I would sit uneasily on the fence between *monism* (choices of expression entailing, or even generating, change of content) and *pluralism* (multiple meaning according to function: all linguistic choices are meaningful and stylistic, and are related to different ways of mediating the cognitive realities or "sense" of experience). Pluralist arguments vary greatly in detail (one need only compare Richards, Jakobson and Halliday, three of its chief exponents, or consult the valuable summary of style-theories in Bronzwaer 1970:10–40).

To speak of stylistic "choice" in hypothesizing why a statement is made in a particular form is not to presuppose that selection can be made from a number of genuine alternatives: this would be to accept the principle of *dualism*, with expression or style involving optional transformations or variants of irreducible subject-matter. Style configurations are not significant along a single axis. If we say that something could have been put differently (less "manneristically", "portentously", "jerkily", etc), we can only do so by ignoring the rhetorical situation. If cognition of an event can be stylistically marked in different ways (to mediate character-consciousness; to mediate, say, implied-auctorial consciousness of the "same" event), there is no unitary event but only various, interaugmentative or contradictory, constructions of what we term an event. Fictions present consensual, perpetually provisional models of, or propositions about, reality; some models are likely to be more salient than others at any moment of the reading experience. This needs to be kept in mind, should one decide to apply to *The Solid Mandala* the categories of iconicity or mimetic forms postulated by Epstein or Leech.

It is difficult to discuss iconicity except in terms of incidental instances of, say, iconic syntax. The most typically Whitean manifestation of iconicity is atactic sentence-structure, which has internally normative status and which will be discussed separately below (ch. 10.II). I have tested Epstein's and Leech's categories on Section 1 of the novel; here are some results, presented in fairly strict hierarchical sequence, from low-level objective iconicity to high-level subjective mimesis. At a given level of this hierarchy, there are lower and higher grades of stylistic schemata (the lowest being phonological and/or graphemic; the middle being syntax; the highest, combinations of the foregoing).

Objective mimesis of phenomena external to the consciousness of the observer occurs at the phonological level in the mimicking of Bill Poulter's probing at his tooth: "doing things with his tongue to the tooth which was always with him" (B18). Objective syntactic iconicity occurs in a long sentence (B12) whose complex "jumpy" parentheses mimic the frequency of the bus's joltings. Interruptions of direct speech mimic vocal interruption ("'What, I wonder,' she asked, 'made you,' she coughed, 'come to live down Terminus Road?'", B12). "The bus was making slow progress, on account of the pay-as-you-enter, and queues at the shelter, and kiddies who had missed the special" (B13)—this is syntactic-graphemic mimesis of "slow progress" through over-coordination (=

continuity) and reinforcing commas (= interruption). The whole compacting weight of a sentence is made to bear down rhythmically and syntactically on the "small, dry, decent friend" (B12) of the ample Mrs Poulter, who is thus represented as physically overwhelming Mrs Dun while the discourse otherwise presents this contact as "perhaps" beneficial. This example is also phonologically, graphemically and syntactically mimetic of Mrs Dun's attributes in the narrower compass of the adjectives quoted above (short words in a tight grouping, punctuatively reinforced, with "dry" alliteration).

These instances are about all there is to find in Section 1 in the way of purely objective mimesis. There is, too, little phonological play, but some high-grade co-occurrence of graphemic and syntactic mimesis, especially at the higher levels of dramatic and self-reflexive iconicity imitating (respectively) a narratorial/auctorial and figural or reflector perspective. Textual order can reflect "the order in which impressions occur in the mind" (Leech 1981:236). "When the bus jolted her back to the surface of her normally bright nature—you could always rely on the bus—she said:" (B14). The interruptive parenthesis here is a mimicking of the shift from reverie to immediate reality, its free-indirect phrasing imitating that "normally bright nature" which is Mrs Poulter's response to "normality". "Mrs Dun's teeth snapped. Shut." (B17). This mimics a transitional event phonologically (dentals and sibilants) and syntactico-graphemically (a full stop separating the verb from its complement). As the objective physical event must be unitary, the mimesis draws attention to dramatic suddenness and finality; hence it also intimates the presence of a subjective recorder of a subjective reaction. Homology (where the text-structure imitates the discourse self-reflexively, as in a digressive passage on the topic of digression) is also operative here: "snapping" is reflected in the shearing-off and isolation of the complement "Shut".

Psychological iconicity can be achieved by graphemic "choice". Such sentences as "The bus became a comfort" (B12), "She was happy again" (B13) or "Mrs Dun was entranced" (B16) suggest, via their isolation from prior but sense-related statements and via their structural brevity, that feeling is unadorned, simple, and experienced immediately for itself. Ellipsis can imitate syntactically the situational awareness of a *persona*—cf the discussion of "could not believe" above: the sentence mimics the absence of an "object of belief". A sentence can be well-formed but semantically elliptical and lacking in contextual cohesion: "Mrs Poulter decided not to bother" (B15) needs our resolution (eg, "to bother [following up Mrs Dun's unpleasant line of thinking]"). What Mrs Poulter doesn't want to face mentally and verbally is mimetically ellipted from the sentence. "'Yes?' Mrs Poulter's voice reached out" (B21)—here, the "blank" after the verb is iconic for the absence of a receptive addressee (cf "reached out [to/towards her]"; similarly: "But Mrs Dun could not oblige", B21). "'What?' she protested. § Looking stricken for the accident" (B18)—here there is graphemic-syntactic mimicking of figural subjectivity. The dependent clause, which is semantically coexistent with the speech-act verb "protested", is separately paragraphed and cut away from the main clause to mimic Mrs Dun's "stricken" concentration on the object of thought which motivated the speech-act. There is much syntactic iconicity which melds the psychological and the temporal, iconizing thought-sequence at the simple level of periodic sentence structure. Simple sequencing through coordination can mimic figural subjectivity: "The old men rose up again in Mrs Dun's mind, and she hated what she saw" (B20). Inferred linkage ("... mind; she hated ..") would make us construe "hated" as state or reaction; the overt linkage conveys the naked immediacy of her hatred; and, because coordination creates the expectation of like bases in the linked segments, the dynamism of "rose up" contaminates "hated", so that the latter verb takes on the colouring of a *willed act* (in keeping with Mrs Dun's *pre-set* attitude). Graphemic-syntactic iconicity at the psychological level can be illustrated by the following: "'Yairs,' said Mrs Dun. Then, because never let it be hinted that she did not make her contribution, she added: 'Yairs.'" (B11). The drag of the long embedded clause suggests a hesitation which counterindicates the message, and which mimicks the time-lapse between utterances; the statement is pseudo-objective, and is actually figurally subjective. All in all, most instances of iconicity in Section 1 occupy the middle ground of subjective dramatic and psychological mimesis. There is little here or in Sections 2 to 4 in the way of conspicuous play with sound and sense (White's poetic instinct is too subtle to push him in the direction of the floridities which mark the prose of a sub-sub-Joycean like J.P. Donleavy).[30]

In the novel as a whole, White shows himself to be a masterly, if sparing, deployer of the now standard formal representations of "stream of consciousness". These techniques do not, of course, constitute a *lexicon rhetoricae*, but serve exclusively the iconic mediation of psychological states. One of the more conspicuous is "psychological" aposiopesis, with sentences broken off in midstream (eg, "He hoped he wouldn't give himself a heart."— W115-16).[31] Most effects are highly specific contextually. At the Pitt Street Encounter, "Saporta put a meaty hand" (W66): the erasure of deictic adverbials ("[out]/"[under his elbow in support]") indicates homologically, even before the ensuing words and actions, that Waldo has deliberately *not* taken cognizance of, or has shaken off, Saporta's gesture of aid. The knitting together of stunned, fragmentary perceptions is conveyed by the interruptive medial placement of the (pre)cognition clause in "His fist had split, *it seemed,* Johnny Haynes's lower lip" (W45); the aesthetic, textural echo of "split" in the positioning of "it seemed" is merely a by-blow. Asyndetic structure and aspect-shifting can reflect rapid changes in consciousness: "Arthur was taking, had taken him in his arms, was

---

[30] But there are subtle phonological effects throughout, as in the following: "Then he said very distinctly, enunciating from between his original teeth, in his cold, clear, articulate voice:" (W28); "distinct" unvoiced velar and alveolar plosives (technicality is inevitable here), in conjunction with tightly measured syntax, mirror Waldo's deliberately "distinct" articulation.

[31] Further: "How dreadful if Dulcie." (W56); "It had, in fact, until Arthur. Why had Arthur?" (W56); "He wished he could remember what Mrs Feinstein's nose." (W135); "They did not suggest that Arthur." (A228).

overwhelming him with some need" (W47); or action is so reflected: "'Here, Arthur,' Waldo was beginning to say, to interrupt, to drag him off" (W109). Here, the progressive in the speech-tag is re-used deviantly for an action; and "to interrupt" itself incorporates an anaphoric reference to speech and a cataphoric reference to ensuing action. Apart from this, the to–infinitives are also ambiguously intention-laden. Hiatus can be used effectively to point up the confirmation, or defeat, of expectation. A good instance of doubling with variation to reflect the differing intensity with which a spoken utterance is registered by the brothers comes in the twice-told scene where Mrs Brown asks Arthur not to go to work on the day Mr Brown is found dead.[32]

Graphemic (punctuative) iconicity is employed to mediate the dynamics of consciousness. The comma after the initial adverbial in "Then, every one of his bones was breaking" (W67) points up the moment of shocked impact before the recovery of full sense-awareness. When Waldo comes to an exhausted, terrified halt on his headlong dash during the walk, this is tantamount to a blank in perception, or a fainting-spell, as can be detected in the progressive of re-emergence following Arthur's question to him: "Because Waldo was standing. Still" (W119). The adverb is punctuatively disembodied because Waldo is— putting consciousness of his immediate location back together bit by bit. "'No,' he said, slow"—not "he said slowly"; both the punctuation and the single-morpheme adverb mirror Waldo's halting consciousness of his own speech. There are sly spatializing games played with graphemic devices, as when Waldo reflects: "Since Dad died in 1922 she had been dependent on him. (Arthur contributed something.)" (W120). Arthur's contribution is relegated to the sidelines. Waldo's picture of the family has a different kind of relegation—this time a segregation of the conspicuous—which is achieved through the judicious use of the dash: "they used to sit on the veranda in a fairly compact, family group—Arthur a little to one side, picking his nose till Mother slapped him. (Waldo, who picked his in private, would watch to see his brother caught out.)" (W37). The family group is already being discompacted in Waldo's prevaricating consciousness with the compromising word "fairly"; and before the dash there is a further, anticipatory mark of division in the (otherwise grammatically incorrect) comma before "family". The parentheses around the last statement are there only to ensure that Waldo's secret self is separated off from the rest of the family.

Referential cohesion may be utilized for iconic effect, as in "she ... looked down to see what it was, and crushed the ... plums which were grating under her feet" (W48). Here, there is Waldo's external perception of his mother's gestures of perception, the coreferent being specified only at the end of the sentence after "it" has been identified cognitively by Mrs Brown and, through her action, by Waldo. A similar iconic postponement of coreference occurs in the following:

---

[32] "'I'd hoped you would *stay with us,*' Mother said, '*today.*' She added quickly, without looking round: 'I'm sure Waldo would appreciate it.'" (W74); "Then Mother's: 'I hoped you would *stay with us.*' § Though her voice made him interpret it as 'me'. He was afraid that, on finding himself left out, Waldo might feel hurt. § '*Today,*' said Mother. § If only today" (A270).

"They were so dry Waldo had to lick his lips" (W115), where the lips only regain nominal identity *after* "they" have been resensitized.

Uncontrolled syntax (in a sentence with "control" as its theme, W30) can reflect the undermining of resolve by emotional disequilibrium during the process of thought (cf also the sentence beginning "After all", W67). Similar, if grammatically less extreme, instances of jagged or jolting sentence-structure occur throughout Waldo's narrative. Iconicity is, in most such cases, equally classifiable as a copying of the hesitancies of actual speech, were the sentences concerned not preverbal thought.[33] Arthur's section is comparatively free from such stuttering or phrasally clotted syntax. Even the closest we get to it—when Arthur is under pressure towards the end—is less jolting in its effect than claustrophobically suspensive, when the main-clause "Once ... Waldo shouted"

---

[33] Some examples: "He was getting some satisfaction out of telling, yes, he had never put much of it into words before, but it was—the truth" (W92); "Dad, though, was not unaware, so it seemed, painfully, of some of the responsibilities he shirked" (W77); "When they were building the house—not them, the Browns, because the boys were too small, and Dad's affliction prevented him, and none of them could have, anyway, ever—but the men ..." (W36); "Afterwards, as they walked down the road called Terminus, where nobody else had begun to live or some perhaps, in the past, and given up, the Brown Brothers were alone as usual, at last, and Arthur tried ..." (W45); "It is ridiculous, he panted, to think I may pop off today, or tomorrow, why, I am good for another twenty years, taking reasonable care, keeping off salt, animal fats, potatoes, and white bread" (W119); "He had, if he wanted to be truthful with himself, thought vaguely, though only vaguely, once or twice, that in the end he might ..." (W149).

The failure to see the connection between figural subjectivity and the representational configuration of the diegesis results in such observations as the following: "A writer so prone to long sentences should also pay more attention to syntactic flow. The subject and main verb of the third complete sentence of *Riders in the Chariot* are divided by thirty words, four commas, and a colon .... White needs four commas to stumble through a ten-word declarative sentence: 'The fact was, Mordecai knew, his mother had, simply, died'. The commas detract from the simplicity and dignity of the death" (Wolfe 1983:24). The first thing to note is that the long passage referred to (Viking, p. 12/Penguin, p. 15, second-last sentence) is pointed differently in the American and English editions: the American starts a parenthesis with a colon but ends it illogically with a comma, while the editions of Eyre & Spottiswoode, Penguin and Cape use two logical, bracketing dashes (which would weaken Wolfe's general assumptions about auctorial intention). Regardless of whether the pointing is weak or strong, what has escaped Wolfe's attention is the consistency with which diegesis centering on Mary Hare is shaped syntactically to suggest rabbity nervous energy and a sequencing of intense but momentary shifts of perception. And, in the particular sentence concerned, the gap between subject ("Her hands") and main-clause predicate ("were now hung with dying ants, she observed with some distress") is an iconic gap of delayed perception, linking general somatic awareness while she examines "her surroundings for details of interest" with a change of somatic condition. The prose enacts this—as it does in the ten-word sentence from the same novel (Viking, p.123/Penguin, p.118), whose introductory "The fact was" has clearly misled Wolfe into thinking that this is an auctorial comment or corrective "declaration", when in fact it introduces a representation of Himmelfarb's own thought-processes: his stunned, halting resistance to Aunt Zipporah's and his father's angry altercation about whether his mother was suffering when she died. And, as the act of dying is not depicted, or witnessed by Himmelfarb here, to talk about the death's "simplicity and dignity" is irresponsible towards the specifics of the narrative.

(A282) is interrupted by ten adjuncts. Even in the dark night of Arthur's soul, there is no marked increase in jagged syntax to reflect mental states—at most, one sentence which punctuatively imitates an action: "And heard the sound of a glass marble, leaping, out of his control, away" (P306).

The other extreme to passages that are heavily broken by internal punctuation is represented by the "rapid smear-tactic" of withholding internal punctuation altogether (the Molly Bloom mode). Iconicity in this regard may be a mimesis of visual perception: "The cryptomerias the retinosperas the golden cypresses were running together by now" (W63). "How it soared its slow white rocket above the black cedars into taut sky returning into ball as it plummeted past the black cedars down" (W89); here there is also a "reconstitutive" breaking of a cohesion rule in the fully deictic repetition of "the black cedars", and a "spatial" redistribution of participle and the adverbial particle "down" to tighten the nexus between process and perception. This example, incidentally, is preceded by a beautiful instance of prosodized structure, and a transgression against normal phrasal collocation, to imitate the regular to-and-fro of a tennis-match: "Back and forth, forth and back went the felted fated ball". There may be a suggestion that somatic self-awareness and consciousness of the temporal envelope around action or state have been conjoined: "hurried throbbing springily" (A276), or "Their flesh was flickering quivering together" (W48); or neutral process is directly controlled by the exigencies of visual perception (as during Waldo's car-counting, W115/116). Usually, however, unpunctuated passages have all the internal syntactic disjunctions and parenthetical fragmentations characteristic of mental projections under intense emotional pressure or, less disjunctively, in recollections of experiences.[34] The first few lines of Arthur's section (A215) are classically inchoate like the fragmented childhood memory at the beginning of Joyce's *Portrait*; but closer examination reveals, also, a delayed relinquishing of this mode, with later sentences ("Sometimes in the stillness ..."; "He was so happy ...") being either underpunctuated or breathlessly segmented to show the conjunction between consciousness and action. One whole paragraph towards the end of Arthur's narrative indicates that the suspensive, heavily comma'ed phrasing already noted (A282) has been dropped, its place being taken by the even more claustrophobic absence of internal punctuation ("Now the dry woodwork ticked the rusty iron creaked ...", A291); the physical environment is pressing down more forcefully upon Arthur's resistant psyche. It should be stressed that such strategies are not the only ones employed by White for the representation of cognitive processes. Nor are the latter, or reflexively controlled action, the only recipients of manipulative syntax, rhythm and punctuation: the "external" portrayal of Mrs Musto as a busy social bee (W86) is just as effectively supported iconically by additive phrasing which "presses on" like the lady herself.

---

[34] For example: "He would do ... in a blaze of last years" (W115); intermittently at W117 *infra;* in Mrs Poulter's discourse: "it would not be a kindness to announce: ..." (P315–16); "In the days when ..." (P300).

V   Repetition, variation and parallelism

Certain words assume a leitmotivic or indexical character, encouraging the reader to reflect upon the mental relationships established between different situations. In this respect, White resolutely handles lexis in the same structurally poetic way as he handles metaphor or the sense-impression vocabulary that is traditionally classed as "imagery". The prime examples in *The Solid Mandala* are the lexemes "oblique/obliquely", which pervade Section 2.[35] The verb "hate" has the largest entry in Waldo's mental lexicon, as we have seen. Although it is never implemented in patterns of expressive repetition (ie, where acceptable cross-referential reduction would be possible; Leech 1981:247), this word can still occur at least in tandem, so as to suggest "a suppressed intensity of feeling— an imprisoned feeling, as it were, for which there is no outlet but a repeated hammering at the confining walls of language" (Leech 1969:79). The closest to a traditional expressive repetition appears in the free-indirect statement "But he would not, would not let it happen" (W127).[36] Other instances of repetition or parallelism with reflexive reference are less obvious, because spaced in the diegesis ("He wouldn't listen", W114 and W115).

Sometimes repetition at close quarters has a stop-start, resumptive effect, to convey a character's singlemindedness ("So Waldo raced the traffic"/"As Waldo raced the traffic", W128); or it indicates such a degree of mental emphasis on a fact that the reader cannot help suspecting the concealed intention ("There was nothing you could have accused her of. Nothing", W144). Separately perceived, scattered actional data ("She almost burst .... She nearly split .... was busting herself", W96) may be picked up later ("Again she was giggling, splitting, bursting", W98) with such compressed exactitude that we are made to feel the keenness of Waldo's awareness. Waldo's obsessions may be conveyed in the redundancy of spaced parallels, even when verbal variation is introduced ("the line where knowledge didn't protect", W46; "the almost visible line beyond which knowledge could not help", W47; whereby the compact obliquity of the first betrays Waldo's reluctance to touch on the topic, the phrasal elaboration of the second a bursting forth out of these confines). Similarly conveyed is Waldo's state of emotional exhaustion after the Incident ("He was too tired .... He was so tired .... He was too tired ... too weary ... too tired", W201–202). Quasi-

---

[35] "Waldo liked to look ... obliquely through" (W58); "observing himself obliquely" (W58); "one of his less oblique moments" (W61); "to glance, if only obliquely" (W62); "taking an oblique path" (W93); "carefully chosen, oblique ways" (W93); "the visit ... more oblique in execution" (W187). In Section 1, where the context is situationally determined by the tactful tactics required to establish a relationship, the salient words are "friend/friendship" (eleven occurrences) and "waited" (five occurrences; other central "transactional" recurrences include "smile" and "protect").

[36] Three repetitions of single words can, I think, be discounted as (a) contextually pointless or at least unproductive, and as (b) the result of a corrupt text: "walking hand in hand *back back* up along the Barranugli Road" (all U.K. editions, p. 69/Viking, p. 62); "filled *not not,* he hoped, with indecent impatience" (Eyre and Cape, p. 155/Penguin, p. 154/Viking, p. 146); "If *Arthur Arthur* Brown died" (only Viking, p. 109; cf all U.K. editions, p. 117).

anaphoric repetition can take on theoremic character, as though Waldo were caught up in the inexorability of what he is deducing ("Which meant .... Which meant ...", W110), or in the embarrassing obviousness of what he perceives in the gestures of others ("She began .... She began ...", W91). What is perhaps the most complex configuration of anaphoric repetitions occurs in connection with ataxis and intrasentential adverbial bonding (W71–72).[37]

Arthur's section is generally free from such repetitions and variations. At the very beginning (the infantile/childhood phase), there is an instance of building-block logic which rests on reformulations of simple sentences with the word "sick" (A215), and a recurrence of sensuous markers to underscore the functioning of Arthur's primal sense-awareness ("velvet seats .... velvet edge .... answer ... too velvety ... linings of dark red velvet", A217). One must scratch about fairly assiduously to uncover negative persistencies that are an index to emotional misgivings which never reach the surface in the discourse (as in the variation of the privative adverb "hardly ... scarcely ... 'Hardly'", A271—though even here the effect is disguised by being embedded in "logical" thought and in direct speech). Only in the "dark" phase at the end is there one conspicuous repetition, and this is a simple case of iconic re-experiencing of unbearable duration ("even after Waldo had walked him and walked him and, yes, walked him ...", P306).

VI   Capitalization

The capitalization of key words can function as an index to figural attitudes or to narratorial irony. In "She professed to Love All Flowers" (B17), the capitalization follows a quasi-reportative tag and stands almost as a quotation. In Waldo's narrative, however, the same phrase in free indirect speech is left "privileged": ie, is not subjected to Waldo's ironic interference, probably because the datum is conveyed as something new to him (W141), whereas it isn't to the narrator in Section 1, who is at pains to limn the regularities of Mrs Poulter's character-profile. One must proceed cautiously in the case of concepts that have public, rather than private, reference, as it is easy for publishers'

---

[37] Waldo has been waiting for his mother to appear after Arthur's disclosure that Mr Brown is dead, and is not only dreading that she will make him look at the corpse but, more importantly, is also expecting her to take the first step over onto his side, now that she and her son are free of the husband and father. Instead, Waldo is made to realize that the death has shut her off from him. What we get in the ensuing diegesis is a set of variations on the same theme rather than a sequence of new information. Mrs Brown's state as perceived by Waldo remains constant: the dull pain of his resentment at being excluded persists as he scans the situation again and again. Waldo's apperception of the causal nexus which is responsible for his being left, almost traumatized, on the sideline is underscored by dulled repetitions of weak nominal clauses, disjunctive relative clauses, and vaguely resumptive-resultative adverbial clauses: "*What had happened* had no connection .... *What had happened* had happened .... *So* their mother .... *Which* she had .... *Which* had now .... *So* her arms .... *So* she went ...".

editors and readers to make alterations that quickly cast a pall over confident speculations.[38]

Waldo, as a boy, is clearly fascinated by the clichés with which family acquaintances (and family-members) have categorized his mother socially. These clichés have citational function, but there is already the tension of irony pulling at them. Waldo, if not as a child then as a recollecting adult, is sneering at the criticism (siding with the cliché) in "She didn't Come Out of Herself, which was a Bad Thing in a new country" (W32); and he is sneering at the pitiful consolation offered in exchange for the condition capitalized in "For touches like that she had Married Beneath Her" (W35). Waldovian irony is present in self-distancing capitalizations such as the following: "one of the Boys" (W128); "that hypothetical Front" (W128, where the adjective is actually what tips the scales); his father's "Intellectual Enlightenment" (W145); Dulcie as "Goddess of a Thousand Breasts" (W157); Crankshaw and "Numbers of Readers" (W172). Waldo's mental citings can reflect adult curiosity about his "Writing" (W29) or can decline to endorse its importance citationally ("'Waldo's writing'", W82) before Mrs Brown's direct speech does so ("'your Writing'", W82). They can also indicate the social value placed upon "a Promising Lad" (W74) or upon passing exams "with Flying Colours" (W114).

Certain traumatic events are capitalized in Waldo's mental orthography ("the Encounter", W64; "the Incident", W202), and Dulcie at one stage cannot be summoned to mind by name, so humiliating is the memory ("the day of his ... parting from Her", W160). There is only one object that is non-citationally graced with an initial capital in Arthur's section, and that is his "second obsession", "the Books" (A280–81); the concept is lent the multiple dimensions of something both institutionally beyond (in keeping with the "Library's" status as repository) and occult, arcane, hermetic or cabbalistic (cf Mrs Poulter's lower-case attitude, B17). When Arthur as a little boy overhears Uncle Charlie saying (contextually, of Mr Brown) "'You wouldn't expect it of Him'" (A217),

---

[38] In this same passage (W141), the introit is a half-sentence of reported speech: "Mrs Poulter told Mother the War had got on Bill's nerves". The First World War is so capitalized throughout all editions (Eyre and Cape, p. 142, Penguin, p. 141, Viking, p. 133). Elsewhere, however, where there is no question of the diegesis being pure free indirect discourse, the characters are bonded to the public event through capitalization *only* in the English editions (ECP130, ECP280, EC299/P298)—"War" and "the First War" are demoted in the American edition to lower case (V122/270/292). Conversely, the American edition is consistent in printing "the Peace" (V173–74), whereas the English editions all slip up once ("The peace, he remembered ..." (ECP182 *supra*). Such editorial incursions, foul-ups, or discrepancies start to look more serious the closer we get to concepts that are potentially nameable public institutions. In several cases, the implication, conveyed through capitalization, that characters are seeing the significance of these institutions is obliterated in the American edition, which lower-cases "the Bank", "the Library", and "the Churches" (cf EC53/P52 with V46; EC107/P106 with V99; ECP160 with V152). The whole point of one statement is erased when the American edition prints "orchard" (V63) in "he would go outside ... into what they called the Orchard" (ECP70). In this example, of course, the citational nature of the designation is ensured by the naming-verb, and figural attitude is not directly the point of the capitalization. This also applies to "the Side Garden" (W47).

the "Him" indicates not so much the speaker's investment of referential significance (for which *italics* would be normal), as Arthur's perception of the suprasegmental tonality of the word, and *his* awareness that "Him" stands for a known person whom he has not yet identified.

Possibly the most revealing presence and absence of capitalization is to be found in Mrs Poulter's discourse. Pronominal substitutions for the Godhead are lower-case in strict free indirect discourse; this is supported by her contention that Christ is a "man" (P298). After the discovery of Waldo's corpse, it is "He" who releases "His hands from the nails" (P303) before becoming "her Lord and master Jesus" who "had destroyed himself that same day" (P312)—a kind of before/after identification. Proleptic of Mrs Poulter's ultimate declaration of Arthur as a "saint" replacing Christ is, finally, her thought of Arthur as "Him—Arthur" (P301), whereby the apposition is both a mundane clarification and a provisional disavowal of any higher significance.

VII   Syllepsis

Heseltine (1963b:72–73) argues for the function of style as the "linguistic embodiment" of White's belief that "the world is dual, ... composed of both spirit and matter, which, though separate, are capable of being fused the one into the other". He cites the description of a ruined house (in *Riders in the Chariot*) "stripped by bombs and human resentment" as evidence of White's dualism. The construction (explicitly identified by Lawson 1979:291) is syllepsis, where a word is made to stand zeugmatically in the same grammatical relationship to two other terms, the sequent collocations being syntactically parallel but semantically distinct. Whereas Heseltine and Lawson justifiably attribute this dualistic and recombinatory tropism (in puns as well as in syllepsis) to the author's worldview, my interest lies in the way in which such semantic play promotes psychological perspectivism at the level of fictional discourse.

Sylleptic formulations can suggest how unfamiliarity flattens the contours of what is perceived—as when two discrete external observations by Mrs Brown are yoked together to suggest that Mr Poulter is merely a qualitative pendant to his wife: "A cheerful young woman *with a high colour and the surly husband*" (W61). This represents iconically Bill Poulter's muted background presence, and contrasts with the extravert impression of his wife previously conveyed. The effect is inevitably humorous when the focus is on subsidiary characters—as, too, when Mrs Musto is discovered by Arthur after she has been weeping: "She flopped into a chair, as though she could not have stood any longer, *her ankles and emotions swelling* as they were, and sat like a half-filled bag of flour" (A235). Here is a classic, reductionist matter/spirit yoking. The secondary, speculative image of a middle-aged woman resting up because of a chronic physical ailment imputes something of the histrionically programmatic to the attitude of emotional suffering. There is, too, a blending of interrelated visual data in the one act of perception: Arthur's mind is sorting out what he sees, as with the glimpse of the girl "disappearing as fast as *her new button-boots and the crowd would allow*" (A252).

Syllepsis can topicalize the unity Arthur experiences as existing between a social ritual and the manifestations of nature enclosing it: "When *the tea came, and the rain,* ..." (A245). There is, elsewhere, perhaps the implication that Arthur has a unifying sense of perception—as when he stands in the Feinsteins' garden listening to the music Dulcie is playing: "In which music broke and scattered, or *lashed back, tail to fang, like snakes or thoughts*" (A242). The effect of the music is violent: he hears fragments, which he cannot bind together rationally, but can experience prelogically as the timeless in the temporal, as dynamic recurrence. The archetypal image is that of the Cosmic Serpent forming an endless hoop, consuming itself as thought is self-consuming.[39] There are really two abstracts yoked here; but the concrete analogy for music informs the "mental" concept, and vice versa. Mrs Poulter recounts her fantasy of bejewelled ladies, and "Arthur listened, who was *grinning with the glare and the mass of jewellery*" (A264). The physical and local (squinting in the sunlight) is yoked to what *looks like* the material but is actually "spiritual" (Arthur's smiling response to a mental picture which is conjured up by Mrs Poulter's recounted imaginings, and which is as immediate to him as light). The reciprocal informing of concepts is anticipated a few lines earlier, in a sentence which has two pairings with physical acts—the first an emotion/senses duality, the second a duality of faith and inward vision ("conviction" being for Arthur essentially emotional and precognitive, and "dreams" a species of *materia* as episteme): "He half closed his eyes, *out of pleasure, and against the sun,* and from then on all that was spoken and acted was *as inescapable as conviction and dreams*" (A264).

In Waldo's section, the rhetoric of syllepsis is more brutal—even crass; and we are often reminded, through the effect of violent straining, of Waldo's unconscious adoption of his father's jokey manner (a manner he reacts against by trying to outdo and refine it). A sentence whose opening phrase is decidedly heteroglossic (a universal cliché which for Waldo is a grand self-justification, and for White and the reader a thematic distillation of all that is wrong with this Secret Writer) rolls with even measure downwards to an equally bivalent, sylleptic close. Mind and matter remain at a sterile remove from each other, as can be seen from the mechanical way in which mind informs matter and is made substance:

His life was his book, until at some point in age and detachment it wrote itself logically into *the words with which his mind and notebooks were encrusted.* [W162]

The yoking of the abstract to the concrete suits Waldo (or his mind-set) down to the ground: it is as though the conventional structure of syllepsis (or auctorial

---

[39] The analogy is slight enough in the text, but we must remember that the centre of consciousness represented as forging it is Arthur's own: it is a prolepsis of Arthur's reading of *Psychology and Alchemy,* where Jung discusses the Ouroboros, the Androgyne, or potential before actualization, like thought. The Ouroboros is, like Arthur, associable with solar passage, and incorporates truth and cognition in one; a connection with Dulcie as lunar goddess may also be present.

manipulation of it) enables him to keep at a deviously self-protective distance from the implications of his mental processes. Occupied with fratricidal thoughts about Arthur, he overlays these with anticlerical musings and a killing analysis of his relationship to his parents; the resulting amalgam of exhilaration or guilty excitement is impinged on by *materia* in the form of the *pneuma* of the elements. The physical comments on, or unmasks, the psychological by informing it, in an extravagance of chiastic double syllepsis:

On this hitherto evil morning, *of a cold wind and disturbances, of decisions and blotting-paper clouds*, Waldo Brown's convictions helped him to breathe less obstructedly. [W56]

Consciousness that the unpleasantly physical constantly threatens to irrupt into the mental domain is never far from Waldo's discourse. Sometimes syllepsis is kept at a pitch of resentful, formally diluted generality: "Like injustice, the dust always recurred to daze" (W83). Usually, the degree to which conceptual yokings are violent is an index to the intensity with which Waldo registers situations: "He would draw the curtain of her skirt, shivering for the hour, or an offence against taste" (W168). Here, the grammatical disavowal of pure syllepsis indicates Waldo's unwillingness to face up to the sexual—if not incestuous— aspect of the mother-son relationship. He registers the complicitous and Waldo-excluding nature of a communal gesture: "all three exploded into fruit cup and understanding" (W88). The construction placed on a gestural situation may be the inverse of this, the implication being that Waldo is compelled to draw an unpleasantly physical generalization from what he initially registers specifically in abstract terms. This occurs, for example, when he overhears the Haynes woman talking about the Browns' smelly grease-trap: "At once they were laughing the possibility off, together with anything rancid" (W190). Waldo's own experience affects his interpretation of what he hears; and the tacked-together quality of the syllepsis is as coarse as the implications of what he thinks.

Waldo, being a victim of his own aspirations and self-regard, is correspondingly victimized by the Bergsonian threat of mechanical incongruity inherent in syllepsis. Sometimes we can assume that he, too, is pitifully aware of how the spirit is relativized, is dragged down, by matter—as when he continues "living on top of a clogged grease-trap, and the moment of creative explosion" (W183); aware, too, of how the spirit fails the flesh, and of how sexual failure parallels the collapse of aspiration: "But Waldo declined. And so did the Peace" (W184). Elsewhere, the narcissistic endorsement of physical externals is too smart, too sharp, not to puncture his ballooning self-image: his moustache "shone, he liked to think, with personal magnetism, as well as a dash of brilliantine" (W131). There are, however, some moments in which the zeugmatic rhetoric captures the mind as it functions at a level of unassailable seriousness. The three instances in the run-up to Arthur's mandala-dance (A264) are of this sort, as are two that occur in the preludial fantasy of the transvestite scene (W192). In one, the effect of syllepsis is almost an accident of thought, as the disjunctive structure suggests:

Mother kept what he liked to think of as a sense of moral proportion. Which he had inherited together with her eyes. [W192]

Waldo is, of course, exposed by his own thoughts as always; but the reader's analysis of the delayed effect of this should pinpoint deadly irony rather than the ridiculous. In the second instance—when Waldo retrieves from the past a mental image of the ancestral staircase, "designed by special cunning to withstand the stress of masonry and nerves" (W192)—we are in the presence of a mind-set which is violently baroque (or perhaps Gothick). The compaction of the material with the psychological is a form of Secret Thought which invites us to conjure up a picture of a neurasthenic, *fin-de-siècle* gentlewoman clutching the bannister on the half-landing. Invites us—but offers no confirmation. The trope is also Waldo's turn of mind, broad and oblique enough to allow the yoking to reverberate limitlessly.

VIII   Other (chiefly polysemic) tropes

Syllepsis is a kind of punning, a structural exploitation of polysemy. There are other instances of wordplay which repay examination, especially in the light of the characterizing discourse of *The Solid Mandala*. But first I should like to dispose of a couple of features in the verbal texture which concern the straining of the tolerances of truth-content. One feature—of Section 1 and of Waldo's narrative, but not of Arthur's—is hyperbolic utterance. Mrs Dun is, for example, variously "fascinated", "entranced" and "terrified" (B11/16/17). The narrator withholds endorsement of such excessive reactions to premisses-in-the-world which the "normal" reader would not find at all fascinating, etc; there is ironic play here with an epistemological gap. In Waldo's discourse, however, hyperbole is characterological. Sometimes it is relatively easy to translate physiological exaggeration into terms of psychological shock, as when "Waldo was deafened" by a mild remark from Arthur (W29), or when Waldo sees the builders as "paralysed with doubt" (W37). At other times, the actional context exposes the self-aggrandizing rhetoric, as when Waldo "stalked ..., knowing in what direction enlightenment lay" (W56), or when he contemplates "his momentous transfer" to the new library building (W182). Elsewhere, hyperbole is the outgrowth of Waldo's propensity for writing feverishly dramatic mental scenarios, as when he wonders, after hastily leaving Dulcie, "whether his scorn had knocked her bleeding to the steps" (W157–58) as in a "Tudor imbroglio" degeneration of Greek tragedy. Lastly, Waldo's hyperbolic mental constructs can be undercut by the knowledge we have gained, by inference, that reality is a lowlier thing than he imagines; and these constructs can, through the very phrasing, point to a diseased heart of darkness beyond the edge of hyperbole—as when coy indeterminacy and overevaluation meet in his thoughts of "family matters of an exalted nature" (W161), of "the great baroque mess of their Quantrell heritage, which Waldo loved to distraction" (W175), or of his being "pinpointed" by the nocturnal storms down Terminus Road, "accused of every atrocity" (W174). Hyperbole is less a manifestation of wit than of Waldo's emotionally distorted perspective, and fits in with a multitude of lesser excesses of emphasis in his discourse.

Also characteristic of Waldo's narrative is another type of extremism which consists in the bringing together of terms which are, on the face of it, conceptually incompatible—not so far, really, from the sylleptic yoking of dualities mentioned above. Statements of this sort need not have the formal rhetorical configuration of oxymoron, and may be too swiftly reconcilable with the reader's own world-view to offer the stiff resistance of paradox; but what is conveyed is Waldo's double vision of personal circumstances. His self-consciousness makes for a self-conscious rhetoric equally attuned to the detection of duplicity in others and to covert self-confession. He notes how Dulcie replies "with a candid reserve" (W71), or he evolves "a kind of taut joviality" to protect himself from "confidences in trains" (W127). Psychological incompatibles can be submitted to logical structuring: emotive complexity is thereby familiarized ("He could hardly bear, while exquisitely needing, the rusty creaking of his memory", W27); a negative polarity can be granted a specious validity by genetic association with a positive polarity which itself does not convince: "Waldo yearned ... to an extent where his love had become hatred" (W30); or the interdependence of contrasting terms exposes radical uncertainty: "Ridiculous, when not frightening" (W40). Other self-projections are similarly undermined, as when Waldo contemplates his jaw, "pronounced ... in its delicate way" (W67). Extreme subjectivity can generate self-control: "Waldo ... should have trembled, if resentment hadn't tempered him" (W107), or loss of control over even primary perceptions: "Waldo could not decide whether he was hearing what he heard" (W107). Paradox can convey the acuteness of sudden alienation: "So Waldo was in the position of a stranger, but one who knew too much" (W34); and the elusive near-immediacy of the past returned ("some familiar stranger", W183). Synaesthesia can be exploited to mediate emotional disarray ("He went and scorched himself with a glass of iced lemonade", W88). Waldo's quickness to detect self-defensiveness in others can lead to the erasure of a middle term which could make, say, his father's behaviour more sympathetic—as when the latter is represented as talking about Mrs Poulter, "making it sound contemptuous because [he had] a weakness for her" (W159). There is nothing strictly comparable in Arthur's narrative. The closest would be the slightly Zen quality of his listening to "the sound of silence" at the bank (A219) and the inappropriateness of "suspecting", in the following piece of free indirect discourse, to Arthur's mind-set: "Yet you could not have caught the merchant's eye without suspecting him of gentleness and honesty" (A250). It is also typical of Waldo's discourse that conventional expectation should be defeated ("The longer she lay living", W169, not "dying") and that statements should end with relativizing negations ("to lose the faith he didn't have", W177; his father's stare, "directed outward, and not", W54; his feeling "free, in fact, if not in fact", W194); and the quibbles involved in the wish "Perhaps if he saw better he would see" (W67) and in the assumption "that nothing can be only nothing" (W55) are characteristic of Waldo's tense vision.

It is, however, wordplay in the broader sense that is the most conspicuous presence in the novel as a whole. Section 1 is pervaded by lexical ambiguity, a kind of double perspective which ironizes situation at the same time as it permits the narrator or implied author to keep at a noncommittal distance. In some cases a figurative construction (of a concretive, animistic or dehumanizing metaphor) coexists alongside the contextual possibility of a literal interpretation. If "the situation had not been proved unbreakable" (B11), *breakable* suggests both "generally fragile" and "able to be terminated". If Mrs Dun is a "dry ... friend" (B12), she is both bloodless, sapless, etc and taciturn. If the women's eyes "followed the tunnel" (B14), this is both the enclosed "path" of introspection and the interior of the moving bus with tree-lined streets outside the windows. "Excitement had not been good for" the chrysanthemums (B20), whose bent petals Mrs Poulter "was attempting to repair"; the formulation is metaphorically animistic (contextually linked through symbolism with Arthur); but the "excitement" has also been Mrs Poulter's own fidgeting. If "the bus faltered" (B20), it is slowing irregularly (innocuous literal dictionary-meaning); but there is also animistic figuration, the bus anticipating empathetically Mrs Poulter's hesitation. Other, essentially non-figurative ambiguities in Section 1 can be listed schematically:

Table 7: Lexical ambiguity in Section 1

The bus became a *comfort* (B12)	consolation	physically comfortable
benefited from it more (B12)	positively affected	(negatively) the recipient
protection of their hats (B12)	social (shielding fr. life)	physical (against weather)
brightened with the leaves (B13)	emotion (grew happier)	physical (was illuminated)
surprised at the *substance* of it (B14)	quantity, extent	import, message
Mrs Dun could not *believe* (B15)	grasp a meaning	understand by nature
doing things *with his tongue* (B18)	with his tongue	by means of words
he was very *moderate* (B18)	in drinking	(*not*) in behaviour
how life ... *arranged* it (B18)	caused to be so	set out like furniture
Mrs Dun was so *shaken* (B18)	physically jolted	emotionally upset
Looking *stricken* (B18)	shocked	physically struck
She *sensed* the scabs (B19)	guessed, deduced	felt (paraphysically)
nursed her curiosity (B21)	solicitously, as of baby	"favouring" sth. painful
the other could be *involved* (B21)	caught up in a situation	psychologically complex

Outside Section 1, there is a tailoring of polysemy to fit the (inferable) verbal competence of the central characters (and, of course, to fit their individual modes of consciousness). Some polysemy encodes the sexual tenor of the context, whether crassly (the "sheer ejaculation" of words, W121; the train sniggering "smuttily", W79) or by subtle association (as between "locked in" and "connect with", W203, or Waldo—still thinking of the sex-lecture on the train—"giving himself" to the "more pneumatic" bus, W145). As a rule, however, the wordplay is not topically classifiable. Semantic manipulation tends to coarsen or obtrude when Waldo is most on the defensive (ie, on the attack) mentally: he is "superior ... to his superior" (W122), and perceives Crankshaw as dismissing "his superior subordinate" (W173). Indeed, Crankshaw's serious manner so rankles with Waldo that it can be made the object of a pun which, embedded as it is in a laboured analogy with punitive cutting, reveals the pain behind Waldo's sneer: "He had the hands of one who had felled timber, without having known the feel of an axe, except the one he used, *by law of gravity*, on those beneath him" (W171). A proleptic statement reveals that Waldo will "discover some familiar stranger approaching his less approachable self" (W183); of this stranger, Waldo later hopes that "a stroke would ... strike his visitor down" (W187)—although, regarding his identity, "Waldo racked his memory, and was racked" (W187).[40] Associationism (Waldo's antipathy to both brown and black as chthonic colours) accounts for "Brown eyes he blackballed" (W120), his abhorrence of expressive gesture, and a desire to bring Dulcie down, for "Her shoulders ... were getting above themselves" (W135).

There is a peculiar cultivation (as with syllepsis) of the common ground shared by abstract and more concrete or originary senses of words: the drift of the verb "impress" (W31/48) is in this direction; the physical is contrasted incompletely with the cognitive in "Waldo Brown, so thin, was filled not inconsiderably by knowing that nothing can only be nothing" (W53), where his self-congratulating negativism makes him swell in imagined stature as well as in imagined intellectual riches. The observation that Mrs Musto is "rich" bleeds immediately into the statement "she loved to eat rich food" (W84), the adverb of cognition in the following into the adjective of aesthetic judgement: "The uncontrolled tennis ball had plainly branded the side of her face. She was also plain" (W89). A number of paronomastic references are aimed at Mrs Musto—by association with her ubiquitous motorcar, at her mechanical urge to organize people ("Everything was *geared* to Mrs Musto's orders", W83); by association of the garden-party visitors, who outclass Waldo, with the prosperity-emblematism of the well-kept grounds ("Mrs Musto and her overcultivated garden", W91). The cavalcade of gilded youth departing from her house is summarized, with help from Tennyson, as a self-possessed élite ("the charge of the motor brigade", W96). To characterize her bad luck with men, a collocation appropriate to card-games is overlaid on a subverted proverbial catchphrase ("She had been bitten once, no, twice, ... and did not want to risk her hand again", W114).

Polysemic play may suggest the correspondence between a conspicuous object of attention and a conspicuous degree of attention to self (the peacock's tail

---

[40] Such semantic play can be taken for White's wilfulness: "Substituting manner for clarity and precision, White ... often misuses nouns as badly as he does verbs. The following sentence ascribes different meanings to the same noun: 'The son resumed relations with relations' *[Riders in the Chariot*, V123/P118]" (Wolfe 1983:139). The hyperconsciousness of the play with "relations" mediates, rather, Mordecai's awareness of the artificiality of social roles: his is an intellectually distanced commitment to action of the sort expressed.

"had eyes for Waldo only", W88), or between Waldo's mirror-gazing and his immersion in ego ("... smiled at himself in reflection", W120; "he was prepared to face it", W120). Ambiguity of reference can mark the continuity between inward reaction and its outward manifestation ("Waldo staggered", W66, and "the latter rattled", W178, both incorporating the statal passive by contextual implication), or the imperceptible shift from independent to guided motion (as in the semantic-syntactic pun on "stirred", W61, in relation to Mrs Poulter's breasts as "puddings"). Continuity of thought can be suggested by propinquity, as when Waldo seems to be generalizing about "elderly ladies" surviving "what was more a *harness* than a relationship" (W24) and later about being "saddled" with Arthur (W25). The correspondence between the outward and the inward is expressed in the idea of "their father's limp *disjointing* his thoughts" (W174); the recoil of intention upon the intender is captured in the double-edged verb "mortify" (W180). Wally Pugh's rank-and-file literary aspirations are ironized by Waldo thus: "Walter was going to ... join the ranks of the Australian poets" (W123)— >hindsight allows Waldo to consign Wally, before the narrative fact, to the "ranks" of the Australian war-dead.

Once again, Arthur's discourse is transparent by comparison. No violent emotion moves beneath the surface of the few instances of lexical ambiguity in Section 3 (the "outcome" of Arthur's lamp-cleaning is "so lucid", A290; "Glass was shattering enough", A280). There is the faintest hint that Arthur is aware of his behaviour being open to critical scrutiny ("arrested, as it were", A233; "declared himself", A226) or serving to protect him (eg, the subterranean association between the humbugs he buys and his desire to "sweeten" Mrs Allwright, A226). Glancing associations such as the adjective in "the more *fruitful* evenings seen through leaves" (A223) testify to the oneness of Arthur's experience (the "fruits" of knowledge gained from his father's readings from mythology; simple absorption of the divine presence in the natural: ie, Demeter and "her ripe apples"). Only with the radical assumption of responsibility for his dead brother do we find signs of a corresponding change in Arthur's consciousness: ie, a perception of disjunction as conveyed through polysemy ("Waldo was lying *still*, but *still* attached to Arthur at the wrist", A294; "knowledge had come to him ... by lightning. § *They,* however, were not much struck", P307).

In Section 4, finally, a subsidiary point of view such as that of Sergeant Foyle is made the vessel for semantic echoes that cut across boundaries of focalization. Of Mrs Poulter: "perhaps she was upset by his catching her out in too private a position. The train of events would have rocked many women hysterical by now" (P313); or: "But this old, at any rate, elderly biddy, was clean. Clean as beeswax" (P313). "Too private a position" takes up from the quasi-liturgical implication of "the positions of love did not come easy to her" (P311) in her obeisance to the saintly Arthur; but the phrasings also encompass the earlier references to Mrs Poulter's sexual yearnings, and bring back momentarily the voyeur-scene and the "private position" of Waldo's corpse. The revitalized metaphor of the train (drawing back from the vulgarity of "off her rocker"), and the nexus between hysteria and sexuality, link up with the sexual content and repressed hysteria of the scene with the shaking train in Waldo's section (W77). The simple reference to "beeswax" ties in with the voyeur-scene (Mrs Poulter's waxy flesh) and with Arthur's association of her with beekeeping. The openness of the narrative to poetic associations of this sort does not compel the reader to narrow interpretative strategies. It is, rather, like all the varieties of polysemy discussed here, a way of maintaining referential intensity without the sacrifice of verbal economy.

IX   Deviance and 'idiosyncrasy'

The rhetorical and figurative language of *The Solid Mandala* is as specifically motivated as the novel's syntactic structures, whose unconventionality and/or sheer pervasiveness may at first prove disturbing. What may be less easy to explain are the occasional or even unique occurrences of phrasings which one would be tempted to call solecistic. Are these signs of artistic impatience; can they be justified as appropriate to a specific text or context (as normative deviance); or are they evidence of what A.D. Hope so harshly termed "verbal sludge"? In tackling such questions, one must avoid lapsing into the pettiness and pedantry of the schoolmasterly grammarian;[41] too many of the world's finest novelists have, at least on occasion, broken the "rules" for narrower considerations of accidence or idiom to constitute valid guidelines to the effectiveness or autonomy of style in fiction.

Most of what is substandard or solecistic in *The Solid Mandala* can be taken as part of a character's idiolect. Some lexical repetitions which serve no readily apparent communicative function can be put down to slipshod editing by the publishers. Most of the remaining phrasings that seem to be in some way deviant can be thrown into a grab-bag, so scattered or occasional is their occurrence. There are, however, two features which are persistent enough to be called characteristic of White's style (or of the implied-auctorial idiolect); neither of them can be criticized on the grounds that they are solecistic. There is, first, the matter of **prepositional usage.** White persistently uses "for" where modern usage would have "because of" ("Waldo grew guilty for his own foreignness"; "shivering for the hour"; "for scenting sexual motives"; "shy for some power"; "wincing ... for their father": W105/168/173, A227/270). There is no problem of meaning here—White has availed himself of a prepositional structure that is familiar to us from such expressions as "panting for rage", "shouting for joy", "sighing for love", and even "for fear of/that". The category "under the influence of a subjective condition" has been stretched, extended—but why? A parallel can

---

[41] Least of all when the critic throwing stones is highly visible in his own glass house. One critic who castigates White for "stylistic errors" (indecisiveness, "jawbreaking" *-ly* adverbs, clichés, bad grammar, "mismanagement of relative pronouns" and "problems of punctuation"), and who presumes to improve White's prose by re-writing it, himself uses "infers" when he means "implies", "sub-literary" for "sub-literate", "flaunt" for "flout". (Cf Wolfe 1983 *passim.*)

be found in the distinction (discussed below, ch. 10) between *for* and *because*: White has avoided forms of prepositional linkage which would suggest explicit causal analysis. Meaning cleaves close to immediate psychological process, and steers clear of any possibility that figural (or auctorial) reflection upon that process might be construed by the reader. It is not a matter of White's selecting a more formal or more poetic formulation to lend dignity to a verbal representation.

The second clear case in which an apparently archaic, obsolescent or even (for some) curious or solecistic construction is used is White's placing of **relative clauses**. Here are four such sentences: "Waldo was furious, who in the end had not known ..." (W113); "Norm sniggered, who ... had been caught at it" (W44); "He took his brother by the hand, who would have ..." (W57); "Arthur listened, who was grinning ..." (A264). It is such a normal thing for postmodifiers to stand adjacent to their antecedent that grammatical descriptions of modern English do not spell it out. In all but the third example above, we would expect the relative clause to be embedded between subject and verb in the main clause. But it is immediately clear what such a scrupulous construction does to the sentence. The main-clause predicate is so brief, and the relative clause so long by comparison, that the effect would be bathetic. The balance of the sentence is maintained by the pursuit of two clear principles: the information in the relative clause is truly subordinated to the information in the main clause, and is not permitted to disturb the integrity of the latter; the guideline (or rule) "antecedent < > relative" need not be followed. In earlier English, far greater syntactic tolerances were possible; White is merely exploiting the potential of the language instead of submitting himself to narrow conventions. The effect, once again, is not that of formality for its own sake, but of the avoidance of analytical incursions into the structure of statements.

Allied to this are features which have loosely to do with **accidence**: the frequent blurring of the morphemic distinction between adjectives and adverbs, and a lack of concern for conventional prosodic considerations. In "Waldo used to walk quite prim and virginal" (W142) or "Dad replied low and distinct" (W37), it can hardly be the case that the adjectival forms are being used with no difference of meaning from –*ly* forms (as in "We had to drive slow/slowly all the way"). Reduce the sentences to |Waldo walked virginal| and |Dad replied indistinct|, and our natural resistance is unmistakable. The use of adverbial forms would have restricted description of manner to the mode of action: analytical, explicit relations of accidence would separate action from actant. The forms actually chosen generate a tension between an attraction of mode to actant and of mode to action: the effect is one of totality of characterization, where the description of the nature of an action is logically (and psychologically) inseparable from the description of the whole person. Mr Brown's mode of speech and Waldo's mode of walking are only partial manifestations of their whole being (which is "low and indistinct" or "prim and virginal" to Waldo). Discourse can make this even clearer: "'I don't know,' Arthur grumbled. § But not bad-tempered" (W29). The atactic *but*-sentence is formally conjunctive with

"grumbled" (ie, |grumbled, but not bad-temperedly|), but is at the same time a
discrete piece of free indirect discourse, a movement away from the action
perceived to the actant observed (|But he was not bad-tempered [merely because
he sounded so]|).

A more radical erasure of reference-boundaries can be found in "They shared
secrets *warmer* than appeared" (W28), where it is impossible to determine
whether the statement means |They *shared* secrets *more warmly* than appeared
[to be the case]| or |They shared *secrets* [which were] *warmer* ...|.
Psychologically, both points of reference are entailed; hence the deliberate
grammatical irresolution. On one occasion, the norm that is violated is that of
following a current-copula verb with intensive adjectival complementation (eg, "it
tasted bitter", "he looked dejected"): "'No,' she answered. § From where he was
walking, as mostly, a little behind, he thought it sounded *sulkily*" (A262). The
violation promotes cohesion, at the same time as it prevents the descriptive term
from conveying narrational commitment to analytical perception (|"——," she
answered—sulkily[, he thought]|) or internal mental analysis at a remove from
perception (|He thought it sounded sulky|). With the paragraph-division (§)
where it is, the melding of two constructions is an effective way of representing
the continuity between Arthur's immediate perception and the cognitive operation
performed (at some spatial and psychological distance, as the hesitant, chopped
sentence-structure suggests) on that perception.

Intensive complementation with comparatives is sometimes performed with
morphemic modification (inflection) when the norm requires adverbial (or lexico-
paraphrastic) modification: "the eyelids looked their nakedest" (W77); "Dad ...
grew silenter in the face of silence" (W77); "Arthur was closest to his twin when
silentest" (A230); "Even when they were silentest" (A246). Apart from the
epistemological problem thrown up by the semantic implications of silence and
(less so) nakedness—aren't these inviolably absolute states?—there is a scrupulous
avoidance of a strong signal for logical analysis (|more/most silent|) which
would compromise the immediacy of the cognitive act. In a narrative of figural
consciousness, we are perhaps conditioned to tolerate such deviations as
reflecting "informal" or even "juvenile" mental processes or sociolects—but this
hardly seems to be the point at issue here. More radically, morphemic
comparatives can occur with disyllabic adjectives which are also, at first glance,
neologistic: "The cestrum was at its scentiest at night" (W79); "he would remain
a bigger, shamblier boy" (W132). *Scenty* is listed for the first time in the *OED*
Supplement (3:1521), and is marked as "rare"; of the two quotations given, one
is Antipodean (from the New Zealand novelist David Ballantyne), but there is no
necessary correlation between lexis and geography. The word is a useful one for
avoiding wholesale commitment to the notion in *scented* that a quality has been
added rather than being intrinsic. What we reconstitute as *shambly* is, on the one
hand, quite ad hoc; it suggests a permanent locomotor characteristic of the whole
person, whereas *shambling* might suggest something narrower, on-and-off. The –
er/–*est* morphemes can be felt as tolerable with such weak –*y* endings. I suspect
that a certain interdependence has been operative here on White's lexical choice:

the more "normal" item would have obliged him to employ explicitly analytical adverbial comparatives (|most scented|, |more shambling|).[42]

There are only three instances of what is arguably imperfect syntax. One omits a preposition ("But Dad probably suffered without telling, or [by] giving expression only indirectly to his pain", W33). Two are misrelated absolute constructions ("Seated in the bus her own charity made her smile", B18; "Although weak in mathematics his gift ... persisted", W74).

Elsewhere, **collocative deviance** gives evidence of a style that is averse to spelling out what needs no spelling-out. Ellipses are not uncommon: "Mrs Feinstein began to protest by [making] noises" (W109); "Mother was standing by, in support, though [fiddling] nervous[ly] with her beads" (W36). The edge of perceptual specificity is taken off these statements by ellipsis. Semantic overdeterminations such as "flaunted an ostentation" (W26) or "on deliberate purpose" (W114) have already been explicated. There may be a retreat from the slightest hint of unwanted specificity involved in the occurrence in "normal" structures of even indefinite determiners: "no longer [a/any] question of an oeuvre" (W174); "in [a] muffled tone" (W49). Grammatical propriety may be observed, but lexical co-occurrences may be unexpected: "for more than *years*" (W79); "it was *coolly* awful to sit ..." (W83, merging perception with apperception); "and his glance *hoped* that ..." (A276, merging gesture with intentionality); "the *too* collapsible parasol" (W84, a subversion of the functional sense of the adjective by the dysfunctional). In the construction "looking ... into the elder Miss Dallimore's material" (W52) there is ellipsis of the metonymic and a redistribution of noun elements to suggest the embarrassing closeness of Arthur's scrutiny to the "material" of Miss Dallimore herself (cf |looking into the material of the elder Miss Dallimore's dress|). One adjective which resists infinitive complementation can be forced into that function by being inserted paratactically: "They were both proud *and shy* to do so" (W156; cf the undesirably analytical and *un*selfconscious smoothness of |shyly proud to do so|). Compression of discrete referents can lead to a statement's having a shadowy resemblance to normal syntax: "As it was too probable to answer" (W140)—the *idea* expressed by Arthur (that Dulcie and Mrs Brown might not like each other) is "probable": indeed, *too* probable, which itself borders on deviance; but what Dulcie does not "answer" or respond to is the *statement*, not the idea; both, however, are inextricably linked, as the syntax suggests.

A sentence may include an element that is not parsable in terms of surface structure: "Instead, she went, *it soon sounded,* to prepare and fetch food" (W101). The italicized parenthetical is not grammatically equivalent to "it seemed"; it resists reformulation as a nominal clause (*|it soon sounded that she went to prepare ...|); and the inadequacy of an adverbial clause of hypothetical

---

42 Other aspects of functionality may be involved in certain morphemic occurrences. To reject "uglily" and "oilily" as "barbarisms" is to ignore this—specifically, the homologous iconicity involved (the first adverb *is* ugly; the second *is* oily). And one should pause before laying the blame for "brittlely" on White instead of on his American publishers, whose edition is the only one with this form (V257 "brittlely"; EPC266 "brittly"). (Cf Wolfe 1983:24.)

meaning is immediately apparent (?|Instead, she went, and it soon sounded as though she was preparing ...| or ?|Instead, it soon sounded as though she had gone to prepare ...|). This last operation fails because the process of inference implied by "it soon sounded" is temporally conditioned and takes place in Waldo's consciousness. The dominant situational characteristic of the context is Waldo's intense concentration on Dulcie and his only marginal registering of actions performed by others. This example can stand for many in which conventional patternings are wrenched out of line in order that complex motivations may be represented.

In "The Feinsteins were too private an experience, then, to resist Arthur" (W106), the basic complicating structure is "too private to resist Arthur", which has an unsettlingly incomplete semantic contour. Possible resolutions include: (a) the Feinsteins would not be able to resist Arthur; (b) Waldo's mental experience of the Feinsteins would not be able to withstand an intrusion by Arthur. The disruptive presence of Arthur is inescapable, then, at two levels within the one statement: in the external, social realm and in the internal, mental realm. Arthur (Waldo is thinking) cannot be kept out of his thoughts because the proprietary nature of those thoughts fathers fatefully the reality that Waldo fears. Such compressions are not limited to Waldo's narrative. In Arthur's section, "Mother continued shocked" (A219) cannot be expanded into |Mother continued to be shocked|, because it is not just a general state that is suggested but (as the ensuing diegesis and direct speech make clear) also the specific mode of verbal action (|continued to speak [to him] in shocked tones|). What cannot be done is to "correct" the phrasing punctuatively (|Mother continued, shocked, even after ...|), as "shocked" is already old information ("it shocked Mother terribly"). "Continued" is made to do double duty.

These are not false economies, but foreground a blurring and overlaying of discrete cognitive categories that are felt to be unacceptable precisely because one percept modifies or conditions another. Hence the overloading in "as stupid as he *more than* expected" (W36), and the bi-directional pull of the word "exactly" in "Mrs Poulter's face was too stupid *exactly* to accuse Waldo" (W60). Apart from such compactions of sense, there are also countless instances of lexical and syntactic selection which reflect both the mental set of the observer and the nature of the percept or apperception, as in the stiff formality of "Sobriety descended *quite*" (W97, instead of "completely"), or "An elderly gentleman *of bald head*" (W97, instead of "with a bald head").

With the very few exceptions noted, grammatical and lexical deviations in *The Solid Mandala* need to be treated with every bit as much circumspection and tolerance as the exquisitely motivated extravagances which we have come to accept as idiolectally "normal" in the poetry of, say, Gerard Manley Hopkins, e e cummings, or John Berryman. It is not always cummings who "speaks": he also makes his personae "voice" themselves in idiom, syntax, and the disjunctions of layout, as does Berryman (with Henry and Mr Bones, for example). White's deployment of language may create effects of fierce wit which are, of course, attributable performatively to the author. But the wit (whether good or indifferent), and the deconstructive blows applied to the "rocks and sticks of words" by the hammer and hatchet of White's creative will, embody (even more than in the poets mentioned) the resistance and tension that characterize the processes of figural consciousness. The stylistic embodiment of these processes occurs also at levels of structure above those of the word, phrase, clause, or simple sentence.

COHESION AND DEIXIS

In his discussion of the connectivity of the elements of a text (its rhetorical organization of meaning), Geoffrey Leech comments:

Cohesion is an important part of what makes a text ... but it is not always an important aspect of literary style. In literary fiction it can most often be seen as a background to more significant style markers, just as the framework which makes a building hang together is rarely the most interesting part of its architecture. [Leech 1981:245]

If cohesive markers are architecturally inconspicuous as a rule, White's practice makes him a grand exception: his alert, intense approach to the handling of cross-referential elements (pronouns, articles, etc) and sentence linkage makes *The Solid Mandala* (or any other of his novels) a Centre Pompidou of foregrounded cohesion.

I   *it*–deixis

An examination of Section 1 of the novel reveals that a considerable weight of deictic responsibility falls upon the coreferential or replacive impersonal pronoun (ie, apart from its function in prop-subject and anticipatory cleft-sentence constructions: eg, "It was so important to be decent", B12; "It did not occur to her to ask ...", B17; "It was as though ...", B21). Very few instances of *it* have an explicit coreferent (let alone a specifically nominal one: compare "The *bus* became a comfort. Even when *it* jumped ...", B12, with "Her husband would have *spat* if *it* didn't normally happen indoors", B17), and even here coreferentiality is exploited. "[Mrs Poulter's] swelling forms ... seemed to invite the experimental *pin*. Often got *it*, too" (B17). The laconic *it*-reference is bifunctional. We are caught off guard, having accepted the pin-metaphor as *rounded-off* in its indication of an "abstract" psychological process. The "pin" is still quite "tangible" in the second sentence, and made even more concrete (ie, less resolvable into abstract terms) by the reduced expressiveness, which also plays on such informal idioms as "she always *got it* in the neck". In "waiting to swallow down some longed-for *communication* while half expecting *it* to choke her if she did" (B21), coreference is inconspicuous until the enclosing metaphor of swallowing and choking reattributes to pronoun and noun a high degree of pseudo-concretion. Via the "thing"-word *it*, semantic filling or near-reification is reinforced in the discourse.

The *it*-pronoun often corefers with a preceding direct-speech statement, straightforward construal by the reader being frequently hampered in some degree. It supports a necessary focalization on character-consciousness rather than on narratorial mood, and nudges the reader to make interpretative constructions of various kinds. "'Yairs,' Mrs Dun admitted, and would have made it higher if some phlegm had allowed" (B14)—"it" refers to the direct speech but not to the speech-act description in the tag. "Mrs Dun did not answer, and it seemed to give her the upper hand" (B20)—"it" refers to a "zero" speech-act; the stronger anaphoric "this" would have registered narratorial analysis emphatically, whereas "it" is light, even casual. The pronoun goes easily with the indefinite "seemed" (but not as a clausal extraposition), and makes Mrs Dun's withholding of an answer to Mrs Poulter's rhetorical, *ad-hominem* question "'But what can you do?'" seem all the more an *absence* of will. "It", together with the form of the accompanying observation, belies and therefore foregrounds the ironical assumption that Mrs Dun's muteness could be design. A long, emotive piece of direct speech is followed by: "It was long-winded for Mrs Dun" (B14). A solicitous narrator might have nominalized ("It was a long-winded statement …"). White achieves two goals with "it". The pronoun retains a substantiality—in keeping with Mrs Poulter's evaluations—which nominalization would have weakened; and the relative inexplicitness of the deixis suggests the unclassified, immediate presence of Mrs Dun's remarks in Mrs Poulter's mind. Nominalization would have taken the thoughts "outside" and subjected them to narratorial scrutiny. (It is not a question of the implied author treating the implied reader as so percipient an equal that he is signalling with "it" just how *self-evident* the coreferent is.) At the next level we encounter various shades of ellipsis and ambiguous coreferentiality. "It" unadorned (eg, "… one of the young lady typists lost her balance. It was those stiletto heels", B13) can permit the co-residence in free indirect thought of specificity (*that young lady*) and generality (*these young ladies nowadays*). Generally, these *it*-statements underdetermine, keeping the thought at arm's length from an amplifying, and thus externalizing, mode of narration (eg, "It could have been that", B19; "Mrs Poulter had hoped to avoid it", B16, where the coreferent is a speech-act but also an unarticulated complex of incidents at the level of memory and narrative structure; "And Mrs Dun could feel it", B21, where "it" is the inconspicuous fulcrum upon which psychological parallelity and psychological incompatibility uneasily balance). The effort of comprehension required leads the reader inwards into the consciousness of the characters: it is their attention rather than the narrator's which is made to fix on a situational object. In almost every cross-reference with "it", tension is generated between apparent self-evidence and actual opacity.

Ian Watt (1960:293) points to the frequent difficulty in Henry James of distinguishing between narratorial and character-awareness, taking as an example the inexplicit anaphoric reference of *it*; Chatman's discussion of James's late style turns to a large extent on the functions of this pronoun. As *it*-deixis is also central to White, it is worthwhile summarizing Chatman's findings preparatory to examining the occurrences of *it* in the rest of the novel:

1. *It*-deixis is frequently vague in James, referring to "a whole phrase or sentence or paragraph or even a more or less implicit idea" (55). Deictic pronouns replace abstractions or intangibles,

converting them grammatically "into things, entities, as substantial as any character" (56). "James' practice clearly violates the copybook rules about 'clarity' of pronominal reference, yet its effect seems brilliant'" (62).

2. Expletive *it* (a transformational, cleft-sentence construction: eg, "It was with Waymarsh he should have shared it") is just as "evocative of the sense of intangibility" as deictic *it* (55). It focuses on relationships and intangibles rather than on objects and tangibles, especially in "as if" constructions (73–75), and occurs, when introducing infinitive and *that*-clauses, in conjunction with "lively predicates" involving "abstract propositions".

3. Deictic *it*, and deixis with other pronouns, is seen by Chatman and others as a rigorous sifting-procedure: complexity, ambiguity or intangibility of coreference is meant to ensure that the reader will be sufficiently on his toes to respond alertly to James's subtlest effects.

On this last point (as I have already indicated), I think that James and White differ, in intention if not in effect. It should also be noted that deictic *it* in Chatman's examples almost always has a specific grammatical coreferent (eg, "effect", "anomaly", "destiny"), but one which may be located at some remove from the pronoun, and which may itself be a "first-level" abstraction that demands considerable interpretative exertion from the reader. Further, although Chatman stresses the "empty" or "copying" status of expletive *it*, he inevitably views the pronoun as bearing semantically functional weight in James. Bolinger (1977: ch. 4) has since demonstrated fairly conclusively that *it* is rarely just a syntax-ordering device in such constructions.

Both James and White employ *it*-deixis with coreference to prior direct speech (though James's practice is more extensive than Chatman makes it out to be: see ch. 10 below). If, however, James does not differentiate clearly between narrator and thinking character (Watt's and Chatman's view), it is generally the case in *The Solid Mandala* that *it*-deixis is purely figural. About two-thirds of White's deictic *it*-sentences corefer with direct speech. Sometimes a semantic component makes the relationship clear: it may be a verb of audition ("That made it sound worse", W94); it may be a verb, noun or periphrasis of communication ("It was more confident than a question", W66).[1]

The reader has otherwise to make do without indications of what the coreferent might be. Sometimes formal proximity or contiguity is a clue, as with phrases intervening in direct speech ("actually it was a man", W63, which is also elliptically expletive: |who was exclaiming|; "Mrs Feinstein protested against it", W138, where there is an iconic equivocation with medium and message; "he was bursting with it", A284). It is, of course, the direct-speech thoughts that are being considered by a character, though it is very seldom indeed that the act of

---

[1] Verbs of audition: "It sounded spaced out in a smile" (W67); "She pronounced it frankly" (W94) "It sounded so plain and sane" (W96); "It didn't sound convincing" (W152); "Insects in the air made it sound more fretful" (A271); "It sounded so inevitable" (A270); cf "But neither Waldo nor Mother had ears for it" (A270). Communication: "As it was too probable to answer" (W110); "She would have liked ... to keep it light, giggly, and Australian" (W131); "Waldo got it in quickly" (W153); "He said it in a tone not suited to his voice, but felt he carried it off" (W154); "It was more than advice" (W160); "It was the exact tone of his dictation" (W176); "sniggered, and it did not fit her face" (W196); "Her voice added to it" (A236); "she sighed. It was like somebody turning in bed" (A269); "because it was a difficult one to answer" (A282).

judgement is psychonarrationally mediated (eg, "It was sensible enough, he thought", A263). As a rule, a simple existential copula serves to indicate that a judgemental statement is to be taken as free indirect discourse rather than as narratorial comment. From "It was too much" (W82) we infer that Mrs Brown's inquiry about Waldo's "Writing" is taken as foolish, excessive curiosity (similarly: "It was too feeble, too foolish", W27; "It was too brutal for Waldo", W195). Sometimes a copula-statement functions as a thematic bridge between the specific direct-speech context and the broader context. Waldo mentally rationalizes turning down Wally's dinner-invitation on (apparently) threadbare grounds of tiredness: "It was true, too" (W126). Although we do not accept the "truth" of the excuse vis-à-vis Wally, we are persuaded to accept the "truth" of Waldo's obsessive love-hate attachment to the privacy of Terminus Road in the paragraph that follows. His excuse—that he is "played out" when he gets home from work—is exposed as a psychological truth concealed beneath a lie about his physical condition. Narrational bridges are more conventional in Arthur's section (eg, "It was disappointingly true", A221). More opaque is Arthur's judgement on what he has told Dulcie about not having to escape from his brother's influence: "It was too obvious" (A255). As a bridge, this points up the contrast with what Arthur sees as Dulcie's blindness to the obviousness of his argument. A copula-statement may include a nominal paraphrase of prior direct speech, as when Arthur makes what for him (in Waldo's eyes) is a surprisingly sensitive suggestion: "It was quite an idea" (W74). But the statement is isolated, in a paragraph of its own; foregrounding through layout makes us unsure about Waldo's response (irony, envy, or surprised approval?): simple opacity suggests that complexity of emotional response may be involved.

A deictic *it*-construction may at the same time be elliptical for a (cataphoric) continuation, as after Dulcie tells Arthur she has a headache: "It must have been the airless room" (A247; ie, |which had caused her headache|); Arthur's direct-speech proposal, "'I'll open the window,' said Arthur", is provided with a deictic coreferent: "But she did not seem to think it might help". The referential weight placed on *it*, the disinclination to provide *redundant* paraphrases of what is clear from the direct speech, keeps the reader close to the familiarity-horizon of figural consciousness. If, occasionally, a nominal coreferent is introduced into the same sentence as an *it*-deictic, this does not occur as it does in James, where "appositive" or "slightly un-English" or "anticipatory" deixis is quite common (from Chatman 1972:63: "It would serve, this spur to his spirit, he reflected"). "'Are you a Catholic?'" Crankshaw asks Waldo "very gently" (W172). The next paragraph begins: "If it had not been so subtle, if Waldo had not been keyed up to match his wits against Crankshaw's question, he might simply have turned ..." (W173). We are already conditioned to trace "it" back to the question; the noun "question" is not needed to clarify the pronoun appositively, but to provide an object for the parallel but psychologically distinct *if*-clause.

Subject- and object-relationships can be expressed via dynamic or causative verbs. A character reflects upon the effect of his own statement on a listener ("It appeared to convince", W72) or even himself ("It made him feel like Arthur's elder brother", W148), or the speaker's own reflexive reaction is observed ("She did honestly believe it", P312).[2] In other cases, the speaker is reacting to information supplied by another speaker ("After trying it out, he was tolerably content", A276), or a more complex inward reaction is conveyed.[3] The extreme of deictic referentiality is probably Waldo's connecting his own polite self-recrimination with the situation between himself and Dulcie: "It could have made it worse if Dulcie hadn't been so cool and reasonable" (W136). Two pages later, a similar, reduced deictic formulation is found, but with objective reference: "Dulcie, he realized, had begun to cry. Very softly. Which made it worse" (W139). It is ostensibly the softness of Dulcie's weeping that makes its effect stronger; but "it" can't be pinned down to this—it expands referentially to cover the whole *situation* of Waldo's "proposal" and its awkwardness for him.

Proximity to direct speech does not ensure that the coreferentiality of an *it*-deictic sentence is made clear in terms of psychological motivation, as witness the sequence: "But Waldo was deafened by it", "He hated it", and "Waldo was worrying it with his teeth" (W29). In each case, Waldo is undeniably upset by the direct-speech message. But the emotion is inchoate. We are forced back to the words spoken, but without fully satisfying our desire to grasp the situation, which is beyond intellection, and is represented *by grammatical reference* as being so. Whether we are constituting thought about speech or thought about thought, *it*-constructions frequently convey not just a character's inward and immediate (hence unmediated) familiarity with a momentary situation, but also his tendency to evade what he has been confronted with. The sentence "Waldo dreaded it" (W26) corefers roughly with Arthur's prediction that the gate will fall to bits, but also with the broader contextual coreferent of decay in general. Mr Haynes makes a cheery remark to Mr Brown "at last, after it had grown embarrassing" (W37). What is "it"? Nothing but the maximum possible (iconic) revelation of Waldo's shrinking embarrassment at the unspoken silence of the workmen. Otherwise unarticulated discomfiture can similarly be expressed through deictic *it*. Particularly in Waldo's section, coreferents are hard to pin down—as with the statement "It made him look over his shoulder" (W71). Is "it" the fact that Waldo's father has died? that he has hair on his wrist? that he remembers expressing his opinion on a writer? In the same stretch of narrative, the topic sentence of a paragraph begins: "It was early morning too, which made it worse" (W69). The second "it" could refer to any one of several interconnected concepts in the previous paragraph: Waldo's being the first to discover his father dead; his

---

[2] "It made Arthur giggle" (W42), "Mrs Feinstein liked it so much" (A241), "But Mrs Musto ignored it" (A236); "It made her grow thoughtful" (A241), "It made Bill laugh" (P316); cf "The importance of it made the sherry slop" (A271).

[3] "He would have liked to give it further thought" (A245), "'But,' said Waldo, ignoring the more sinister aspect of it" (W198). Arthur responds to Mrs Poulter's comforting words: "It was so much what he had hoped for" (P310); Waldo is overcome by Arthur's questioning: "It tired Waldo" (W57) or is made sceptical by Mrs Feinstein's friendly claims: "He did not believe it" (W100). Arthur reflects on a remark by Waldo about Mrs Mackenzie: "It was of the greatest interest to Arthur" (A219).

recoil from this "explosion"; the unpleasantness of the "explosion" of discovery. None is quite enough; we are compelled to construe "it" as indicating a whole complex of perception and attendant emotion.

Waldo, after hearing the Council workers talking about his brother, can barely digest what he has heard: "it" cannot be articulated diegetically, and is kept under pressure until Waldo gets a chance to talk to Arthur: "Then it all came out of Waldo, not in vomit, but in words" (W147). The gasping, barely coherent delivery of Waldo's direct speech stresses how raw and disparate the simmering mental brew of "it" has been, how strongly one part of him has needed distance from his own sexual disgust. When Waldo is "astonished, then horrified, at the strangeness of it" (W152), "it" cannot simply be taken to refer to Dulcie's words—or, better, to what she communicates to Waldo about Arthur's glass marbles; "it" is reverberant, and Waldo's reaction is also to the whole situation, including his own emotional involvement in it. The main effect is again an impression of overwhelming emotional response, but a complex response to complex stimuli that have hardly been more than apperceived.

A straightforward case of Waldo's mental shrinking from naming names—here, the guess that Wally Pugh is dead—is represented in the following by the absence of a prior coreferent and the merest hint of a deductive basis: "He knew it must have happened because she was in black" (W129). A more extreme—but grammatically resolved—instance of iconically presented precognition ("She ... looked down to see what it was", W129) was discussed earlier. Sometimes there is a combination of inexplicit ambient coreference and "expletive" ellipsis, as when Waldo empathetically feels the embarrassment of the family members confronted with the "situation" of Arthur's histrionics: "It was suddenly so grotesquely awful" (W40) and "It was suddenly too much for everybody else" (W39). In both cases a paraphrase of deictic *it* (eg, |Arthur's behaviour| or |The situation|) is possible, or a filling out of an expletive ellipsis (eg, |to have to hear Arthur going on like that|). Saporta invites Waldo for "'a bite of tea'"—"It would have stuck in Waldo's throat" (W65). "It" is exploited for its possible "tangible" coreference with "bite"; but the construction also allows for the notional continuation |to accept Saporta's invitation|, so that Waldo's inward disgust has both a local, external stimulus in the speaker's words and a more complex, reflexively generated psychological stimulus.

Similarly inexplicit but psychologically reverberant coreference is ubiquitous in Waldo's section.[4] By contrast, one seldom experiences any difficulty in

---

[4] For example: "It should have been Waldo's *mind,* Waldo knew" (W26); "Yet he knew the theory of it all" (W112). "Norm ... caught at it" (W44)—this is close to an idiomatic or colloquial use of deictic *it* to mean something sexual (like masturbation) which needs no specification "among men". "It was unusual .... It was most unusual" (W60–61)—this is a tricky bit of free indirect discourse, referring to the expression on Mrs Poulter's face, which could mistakenly be linked with Arthur's mental reaction to what his brother has so mysteriously said. "If it was immoral, then he was immoral" (W116)—the closest possible coreferent is some two paragraphs back. "Waldo liked that. It made him look rather sly" (W119)—ie, Waldo's well-shaped thought about youth, time and memory. Waldo's thoughts are the implied coreferent in "It excited Waldo" (W99), "It was all so exhilarating" (W150),

determining precise (but never lexically explicit) coreferents for deictic *it* in Arthur's section or in the free indirect discourse attributable to other characters in Section 4.[5] Only twice are there uncertainties of resolution. "It was a good beginning" (A244) could refer back to Arthur's own speech, or to the general welcome he has received from the Feinsteins. "So he had to fight against it" (A294) is fully internalized, a reflection of Arthur's desperate terror: there is no suitable grammatical coreferent, and any attempt to construe reference paraphrastically (|Waldo's hand/steel grasp/accusation/imprisoning clutch|) cannot do justice to the turmoil of Arthur's reaction, which is to both physical and mental stimuli. As in so many cases in Waldo's section, pronominal deixis is a sign here that mental objects and operations cannot be rendered analytically accessible to figural consciousness—let alone to the inquisitive reader, who is left to reconstitute emotion as best he can from the same raw material available to the characters.

By comparison with anaphorically deictic *it*-constructions, expletive or cleft-sentence *it* is a communicatively innocuous style marker, such thematic extrapositioning being a standard feature of English. Expletive *it* becomes interesting only when it is persistently associated with specific discoursal content (as is the case in Chatman's discussion of James's focusing on intangibles). In *The Solid Mandala,* the following aspects are noteworthy:

1. The *it*-construction frequently distances affective concepts from the "patient" ("It was a minor shock to notice ...", W70).[6] In other words, the statal passive (|He was slightly shocked to notice ...|) is avoided. Emotional situations are not fully internalized, but are kept grammatically at the level of impersonal ambience *at the same time as* the construction serves to front the very element which the figural consciousness would keep at arm's length.

2. There is a conspicuous correlation between expletive-*it* constructions (often, of course, the only way of presenting the information in a convincing syntactic envelope) and a context of rationalization ("It was only too bad that ...", W81).[7] There is always an appeal to impersonal ambience, nowhere more

---

"It was too long, anyway" (W91); there is a partial coreferent in the direct thought and tag of "Poor Arthur, Waldo thought, and might have been loving himself, it was so genuine" (W42), and a postponed coreferent after "It began haunting Waldo" (W174).

[5] A few examples should suffice: "Arthur was enjoying it" (= what Mr Allwright is doing with the counterfeit coin, A227); "as though suffering it in her flesh" (= Mr Allwright's hammering, A227); "It gave her so much pleasure, Arthur could only share it" (= the ritual of drinking Mrs Feinstein's lemonade, A241); "It added to the mystery" (= the fact of the "young girl inside", A241); "Somewhere it had to happen" (= Mrs Poulter breaking down in tears, P315); "It would all trickle out in time" (= the news about the fate of the twins, P315).

[6] Also: "It surprised Waldo that ..." (W103); "It came as a shock ... when ..." (W146); "In the meantime it amused him to see ..." (W146); "It was a shock to him" (W148, with anaphoric reference); "It was certainly a shock" (W150, with anaphoric reference); "It troubled Waldo no end the night he woke to discover ..." (W211); "It continually amazed Arthur Brown that ..." (A247).

[7] Also: "It was natural for Arthur to accept ..." (W81); "So it was only natural he should ..." (W189); "It was only natural to talk ..." (A262); "It always gave him some satisfaction to

evidently than when feelings of embarrassment, anxiety or panic must be pushed
down under a surface appeal to reason.[8]

3. Particularly with negations of expletive-*it* constructions, the reader is given
the feeling that Waldo (for such negations occur almost exclusively in Section 2)
is only pretending to clear the decks, to hasten in the direction of honest
disclosure. As such structures are by nature cataphoric and contrastive, we seek
clarifying resolution of the negation. Such "clarification" usually takes the form
of a plunge into prevarication, diffuseness, or evasiveness, and one realizes often
that the truth lies in the statement that is negated ("It wasn't the prospect of his
father's self-exposure which was shaking him", W77).[9]

4. By far the largest category of expletive-*it* sentences is contrastive in
function: stress is laid syntactically on the behaviour of one person ("It was the
old men who lingered", W57).[10] This kind of focusing need not, of course,
automatically be an argument in favour of the alert sifting and comparing activity
of figural consciousness; but the circumstantial evidence for this view is
convincing. One sentence towards the end of Arthur's section is explicitly and
symmetrically contrastive: "If it was Arthur who got the shock, it was Waldo
who took fright" (A292). A large number of other statements do not have this
formal double focus, but highlight the actions of one twin or the other ("It was
Arthur who lifted the weights", W26).[11] Unspoken in the instances from Waldo's
discourse is his awareness of where Arthur is superior to him, or where his own
behaviour is consciously or instinctively calculated to set him at a safe remove
from Arthur. Arthur, by contrast, is continually aware of his twin brother's
exposed sensibility: the unspoken corollary is Arthur's awareness of his own
indomitability: "It was Waldo who suffered" (A279); "It was his brother who
kicked" (A292); "It was Waldo who shrivelled up" (A292). A formal contrast
between Waldo's breathing as a sign of psychical disturbance and Arthur's as a
sign of physical disturbance is apparent in the following: "Waldo's breathing
sounded pacified at last. § It was Arthur who bit his breath the morning he got
the shock" (A292). It will be noted how many of these expletive constructions are
concentrated in the one, fairly late, passage of Arthur's narrative (A292).
Arthur's awareness of fraternal difference has, it could be argued, been
sharpened by the presence of the threat to existence represented by his heart-

---

..." (W120); "It was reasonable enough ... to suppose ..." (W129); "It was a good thing
perhaps that ..." (A267).

  [8] "It was natural ..."; "But it had to be remembered ..." (W154); "It was most important
that ..." (A273); "So it became imperative at last" (W191).

  [9] Also: "It was not the Feinsteins themselves who interested hinm particularly" (W106); "It
was not its beauty ... which interested Waldo" (W119); "It was not that he was cold, exactly"
(W152); "For it was not the dog he was humiliating" (W180).

  [10] Or: "It was Miss Dallimore ... who did the talking" (W49); "It was Mrs Poulter's smile
which released them both" (W186); "It was himself who was ... the keeper of mandalas"
(A240).

  [11] Or: "It was Arthur who decided ..." (W107); "It was Waldo who collected them ..."
(W36); "It was Waldo who disturbed the peace" (W38); "It was Waldo who was moved ..."
(W189).

tremor, and syntax is implemented to help convey this. In general, it can be said that expletive *it* in its contrastively focusing function correlates with a thematic substratum in the narrative: that of ("ingeminate") sibling rivalry.

II   Definite and demonstrative deixis

It has often been observed how much use Henry James makes of coreferential links between sentences—particularly via demonstratives (*this/that*)—as he unfolds situational complexities (see, for example, Gutwinski 1976:86–126, Leech 1981:107–108). This discoursal function of demonstrative coreferentiality is not conspicuous in *The Solid Mandala*. *This/that*-deixis generally serves to point up the emotive component in a narrative of recollection, and coreferents can often be classified as exophoric (ie, implicitly present in figural consciousness, but not presented narrationally in the immediate prior context). Complicating the study of demonstrative deixis is a situation peculiar to spoken or written reports and, by extension, to most narratives: the fundamentally contrastive deictic schemata of direct speech (in which *this/that* are deictic upgradings of *the*, and form a closed system based on proximal differentiation) are compromised, reduced or transformed, depending on pragmatic context, by the "narrative distancing" of *this* to *that,* in a kind of parallel to back-shift in verbs.

The proximal status of the immediate grammatical referent (ie, *this*-nearness) can often be sensed behind a *that*-demonstrative, especially in Waldo's section. In "—*that* dead weight on the left hand" (W115) or "*That* hair" (W27), for example, syntactic isolation suggests that the sentences are in free indirect discourse, and that coreference is to a percept in Waldo's consciousness at the moment of narrative enunciation. "That hair" picks up from the frequent earlier references to Arthur's hair, but there is only an associative immediate coreferent ("he might have touched the back of his head"). We are encouraged thus to sense an emotive component in the deixis. The text is saturated with demonstrative indices to psychological familiarity, often (as above) with a strong implication of figural distancing. "About the same period *those* Miss Dallimores called" (W49); "*That* Mrs Poulter, for example" (W144); "his mother was waiting with *that* woman" (W73)—in each case, there is a touch of Waldovian negativity. By contrast with Waldo, Sergeant Foyle regards Mrs Poulter at an unemotional distance, yet as somebody familiar: "there was *that* Mrs Poulter kneeling beside Arthur Brown" (P313). In each case, the reader is obliged to check his initial understanding of specific deictic functions against the context: the anchoring of deixis in figural consciousness demands such efforts of resolution. Representations of a character's immediate experiencing of a situation are constantly embedded in broader contexts of personal familiarity; percepts previously registered in consciousness, but not in the narrative, are deictically marked: "Here Mr

Hetherington grunted in *that* fat way" (W44); "seated on *that* beaded stool" (W85); "She laughed one of *those* laughs" (W48).[12]

An object's specific features may have been noted already in the text, but at a great narrative remove ("*that* gate", W118, with previous mention at W26-27). Such oblique coreferentiality strengthens the reader's apprehension of a character's mind working self-containedly. Here we usually find ourselves following the movement of consciousness independently of immediate actional context, as when Waldo or Arthur are involved in recalling previously un- narrated experiences ("on *that* gooseberry bush", W25; "Waldo ... making *that* scene", A283—a "scene" already narrated once: but in Waldo's section). Waldo also imagines empathetically the attitudes of others towards him. This is encoded in a straining of the limits of bivocal diegesis via demonstrative deixis ("*that* boy", W33, referring to himself through Mrs Musto's eyes; "*that* small head", W33, referring to himself as "seen" through the eyes of outsiders). When restrictive postmodification is present, *that* links the referent more intimately with the realm of mental and emotive familiarity than would the definite article ("the box ... *that* old David Jones dress box", W118; "to rent *that* small room in the city", W126; "sitting at *that* deal table", W48; "with *that* priest who wrote ...", W171-72). On the few occasions when proximal *this* occurs, it is possible to feel a difference in referential function in the two respective central narratives. In Arthur's section, *this* functions as an informal continuative deictic, in harmony with the general tendency of the diegesis to be relaxed and translucent ("Leonard Saporta was a born relative. § Arthur had met *this* Mr Saporta ..."). In Waldo's narrative, *this* is both psychologically proximal (the referent is on Waldo's mind, within his purview) and emotively reductive at the same time ("*this* Dulcie", W91; "*this* ugly girl", W158; "*this* old man", W179; "*This* obscene old man!" W196).

White's highly individual use of the definite and indefinite articles—his exploration of the potentialities of a functional grammatical system to achieve the subtlest nuances of narrative and psychological perspective—has been thoroughly investigated by Heltay (1983), in the first (and, to date, only) attempt to come to grips systematically with White's style. The articles show the sensitivity with which White transfers "his observations intact from his own fantasy to that of his readers", establishing "perspective" by differentiating between the familiar and the new, or "things perceived *anew* under fresh circumstances"; "the narrator is

---

12 White's individual handling of relative-clause constructions can often be explained in terms of a subtle interaction with strong deixis: "He gave one of *those* big laughs, which come up ... from the region of the pocket-book" (W155); "Their flesh was flickering quivering together in *that* other darkness, which resisted all demands and judgements" (W48). Here, premodification is made punctuatively disjunctive with postmodification. Avoided is the natural temptation to reduce *that/those* to a merely cataphoric dependence on the detail in the relative clause; immediacy of psychological reference takes priority over analytical relations (which would dictate zero comma after strong demonstrative premodification). At W155, there is the additional discontinuity between narrative "gave" and gnomic "come up", serving to point up the perceptual distinction between Arthur's recognition of Saporta's kind of laugh and the reflective justification (as it were) for the distributive demonstrative.

able to project simultaneously onto the scene he is describing a kind of instant X-ray picture of his characters' accompanying mental processes or inward response to it" (Heltay 1983:64). One aspect of White's style, then, has been satisfactorily explained. There is nothing essential I should care to add to Heltay's analysis, except to encourage scepticism regarding any *equality* of communicative status between narrator and character ("simultaneously"—this is, of course, the conventional "mimetic" explanation of free indirect discourse), and to offer a few illustrative comments on the use of the articles in *The Solid Mandala*. Although the novel is listed as being among those discussed in Heltay's book, it is in fact not touched on. Many of the article-based narrative effects peculiar to White happen not to occur in *The Solid Mandala*. The novel's intense focus on a narrow range of figural consciousnesses effectively prevents it from being a source of examples for the ways in which a "narrator" or "the author" manipulates perspective.

In Section 1, the definite article is used quite normally to refer to previously mentioned concretes (the ladies, bus, typists, rail, men, petals, chrysanths). As this article "tends to signal continuity on a contextual, rather than textual level" (Leech 1981:96), we also encounter its "familiarizing" use as part of the *in medias res* technique, thus implicating an implied reader who is already familiar with the narrative context (the girls, tea-break, ticket, shelters, windows, brick, gutters, seat, shovel, glass): in short, with all the physical data entailed in the section-title "In the Bus" and in the substance of the characters' experience (see also Stanzel 1982:212–15). The initial marking of such data as unique underlines the characters own propinquity to them; so that the definite article can serve as a consciousness-focalizing device like the demonstrative *those* ("those stiletto heels", B13; "those old men", B19). This also applies to otherwise pre- or postmodified nouns (such as "the tunnel which led inward", B14; "the thick green silence", B14). There are a few cases where under-determination overtaxes (and thus nullifies) the convention of privileged access (notably with "the situation" and "the circumstances", which were commented on earlier). Sections 2 to 4 offer more variety, of course, than Section 1.

In a passage in which "Mr Mackenzie produced *the* [cf |some|] humbugs … and pointed out *the* [cf |a stuffed|] fox in its place on the window-ledge of *a* landing" (W53), the definite article with these first mentions of humbugs and fox in punctual narrative can be taken on several levels. Waldo is recollecting a scene familiar to him in memory. He is also registering the actional deixis ("pointed out") of Mr Mackenzie: the statement encodes the latter's familiarity, so that recollection conveys direct experiencing grammatically at a secondary level, while the unfamiliar landing is re-experienced in memory at a primary level. Later, in a sentence of iterative narration in the actional present, it is stated of Arthur that "Ron Salter sometimes had *the* lollies for him" (W59)—here, the lack of a prior coreferent or zero determination signals Waldo's mental acknowledgement of a pattern of habitual past action.

Immediacy of figural perception may be involved, as in the actional-present narrative (W114): Waldo's reconstruction of the putative thoughts of a passerby in reaction to Arthur's mimicking voice is preceded by a linking statement of direct perception: "So that now ... *the* mother with kiddy in stroller turned round to wonder". The woman's existence, the definite article tells us, has already been noted by Waldo, probably while Arthur has been loudly "assuming" Mrs Allwright's voice. She only becomes important *now*, as a witness to Arthur's embarrassing behaviour. That she is unimportant in herself is indicated by the conspicuously generic classification of the objects which define her as a "mother": the zero-articles reduce her, along with her infant and the stroller, to a type (as in the title of a genre-painting). Definite deixis may be used to indicate Waldo's self-conscious awareness of his own familiar gestures ("Waldo smiled *the* smile which left *the* token of a dimple in his lean right cheek", W177) or the familiarity to him of psychological states that are narrated for the first time ("Waldo on hearing the name again felt *the* little twinge", W51). Narrative of figural recollection also accounts for such non-cohesive determiners as in: "On his way home ... Waldo bought *the* doll" (W184–85); or in: "Then there was *the* visit ..." (W187; this sentence-opener is followed by four adjectival phrases but no restrictive postmodification).

Very subtle effects are achieved with non-coreferential definite deixis. The ironically "jumbled" sentence of mental re-cognition, "And very soon they were approaching what could be *the* lit house" (W97), has been discussed in a different context. There are several ways of analyzing the following example: "'There!' hissed Miss Glasson, nudging, half-pointing at *the* figure in *a* raincoat at the other end" (W197). Miss Glasson's previous direct speech has prepared Waldo to see "an old bloke" and "a funny old man"; "the figure" is perhaps an adequate cohesive resolution of these prior indefinite references. What may escape the reader's attention, however, is the distance Waldo still is from "the figure", and the vagueness of Miss Glasson's pointing gesture. Waldo, however, has no difficulty in perceiving this specific "figure" among all the readers in the library. The narration behaves deviously as Waldo retreats from acknowledging the fact that it is Arthur—not just any smelly old man, albeit so contextualized in Waldo's oblique and complex mental re-experiencing—whom he sees. We learn shortly that it is only Arthur who is wearing a raincoat, so it is additionally possible to see Waldo as registering this fact ("*the* figure" because the only one in *a* raincoat). But the central implication, partly concealed by the others, is that Waldo already knows the person who is seated at such a distance that he is perceptually only a "figure". This encrypted distancing anticipates Waldo's ultimate denial of his brother at the end of the library scene. Another sort of distancing can be detected in: "The rather fine tenor voice, of which *the* parents had been proud, and Dulcie Feinstein had accompanied in the first excitement of discovery" (W26). This is the first time Waldo's parents are referred to in Section 2; a couple of lines further on, Waldo's voice is mentioned specifically in relation to "Mother" and her opinion of it. There is no communicative advantage in an omniscient narrator's resorting to this form of impersonal deixis, followed by subjective naming; but there is nothing in the prior context, either, that could explain why character-focused perspective should be mediated in this way (instead of with "his"). The definite article, in fact, expresses Waldo's self-involvement or egoism, to which even the closest of natural human relationships can only be an instrumental pendant. We learn in time that Waldo is peculiarly estranged from his parents as a referential entity; that he has driven a wedge between mother and father; and that it is only his relationship with his mother that involves a subjective, proprietary or responsive push in her direction.

This impression is reinforced, in a passage mixing free indirect discourse and consonant psychonarration, when Waldo and his father walk to the train. Not only is there a diegetic clarification of their relationship in the form of a Waldovian gnomic statement ("Fathers are no more than the price you have to pay for life", W76), but reference maintains alienation:

> So Waldo resented his twin's absence and freedom as he walked with *their* father between the throng of weeds up Terminus Road, George Brown lashing out with his gammy leg, to keep up with *the* son holding back for him.
>
> On one occasion *Dad* said, "You run on ahead, old man. I'll take my time." [W76]

The possessive "their" shares the relationship between the two brothers, as Waldo's thoughts have centered on "twin consciousness"; the status of the parent-son relationship falls short of personal allegiance (|with *his* father| or, more committedly, |with *Dad*|), which is signalled only notionally by "Dad" when Mr Brown actually speaks. That is to say, Waldo registers his father's speech as personal address, acknowledging his attempt to play the role of father but without the naming-mode implying that Waldo is reciprocating in terms of affection. Between these sentences, Waldo is represented as wholly alienated, as viewing the roles of parent and son from the outside—first by identifying his father by his "public" name (on this, see section IV below); then through the expedient implementation of the restrictive postmodification rule. The participial-relative clause resists a possessive like "his"; but the structure with the definite article would normally suggest a differentiation between *this* son and another, which cannot be the case. Waldo classifies himself as "the son" because this is what he is to his father and to any imagined onlookers. It is not a role to which Waldo readily accedes, hence the objectifying definite article. (Compare also the insistence on "*their* father", even when it is only Waldo's attitude to him that is involved: "There were times when Waldo loved their father, he really did. He would have liked to, anyway ...", W49.)

Other effects of distantiation are achievable via the article. After Waldo has removed and crumpled up the blue dress, he tries to smuggle it past Arthur, "carrying under his arm *the* ball of *some* article" (W194); ten lines further on this statement is deictically resolved ("He threw the dress behind the copper"), but the prior context of undressing has given us our clue. Waldo's mental priorities are reflected in the definite "ball", the indefinitely placed "article". He is so desirous that this (for him) conspicuous object be inconspicuous in terms of specific identity that he denies his own familiarity with the "article" (self-revealingly: of clothing) and projects onto it what he hopes will be Arthur's perspective of non-recognition. In the account of Waldo's being caught snooping round Feinsteins' (W125), at least four instances of definite deixis occur which mediate figural perspective. The implicature of two of them is clear enough ("*The* icy moment finally arrived" following "waited"; "He was not wearing *the capple,* but *a* bowler hat" determined by prior familiarity). The others are more subtle: "And then *the* footsteps began approaching"—the whole scene is narrated as immediate experience within figural recollection; the clue lies in the conjunctive-consecutive "And then". Waldo has been concentrating on peering through the slats of the blind on the window; what the definite article does is mark as familiar to his sensorium (ie, as a rupture of attention) what was unfamiliar to it *before* (on the periphery of his engrossed awareness while snooping). The fourth is laden with implications: "Waldo was transformed forcibly into *the* complete stranger". The indefinite article would be false to the situation, in which Waldo is uniquely experiencing *his* alienation; Mr Feinstein is not a stranger to *him*. As well as this, the cliché "the compleat gentleman" is evoked: not by accident, as Mr Feinstein is formally (unfamiliarly) dressed as a "gentleman". Not only his icy manner but also his outward appearance serve to distance the older man—and this impression Waldo turns back on himself. The definite article is also generic (in the sense of the collocation it echoes), so that Waldo is reduced or despecified in his subjective identity.[13]

Definite deixis is less conspicuous in Arthur's section, but often suggests that Arthur is imagining the realization of some pre-existing mental pattern ("They were *the* long-legged lovers", A246; "they would never divide ... into *the* two faces", A249). Arthur's section is suffused with a serene familiarity of reference, as though the central consciousness had everything enclosed within the compass of his understanding. Hence the ease with which we accept a first-time reference like "That night he dreamed he was licking *the* wounds" (A262), whose nearest coreferent is direct speech a page earlier including the words "Our Lord", "blood" and "crucify". The other possibility is that the non-distanced definite deixis of familiarity is particularly appropriate to representation of oneiric states. One of the most curious, telling, yet easily unremarked instances of definite deixis occurs before the one just mentioned, and is similarly related to an oneiric context: "Once Arthur dreamed *the* dream in which *a* tree was growing out of his thighs" (A260). Two planes of perspective are superimposed: the immediate-perceptual and punctual, as indicated by "Once" (in which case one would expect an indefinite article of first reference for both nouns); and the recollective, with Arthur summoning to mind an experience familiar as dream (in which case a definite article with "tree" would be a possible but unnecessary overdetermination). A third possibility is that this is one instance of a repeated dream. The blending of implications produces an uncanny result, in keeping with the novel's focus on Jungian themes and innate prescience: Arthur intuits that the

---

[13] The objective equivalent to this generic reduction is the use of the indefinite article in connection with the *physis* of someone Waldo already knows—and who has already been introduced by name—to suggest subjective alienation from unpleasant prototypical gestures: "a small mean face recognizing" and "Mr Dun ... erected a behind", W30, whereby such collocations as "erected a shed/wall" also feed into the latter clause to suggest both barriers and dehumanization.

dream has archetypal ramifications (which in fact it does). The unique (or instance of a repeated) experience is also an encounter with the known, as dreams tend to be. The joke is that we are made additionally uncertain about whether the diegesis represents direct experience (the dream-narrative trick in fiction), immediate recall in the night (narrationally implied), or long-term recall (the novel as memory-narrative) by the ensuing sentence: "In the morning of course he could barely remember". As a further, intertextual joke, the archetypal root (as it were) of Arthur's dream is familiar not only as dream but also from its textual origin. Arthur must already have encountered the pictorial substance of his dream in Jung's *Psychology and Alchemy,* Figure 135 of which is an alchemically symbolic drawing showing a reclining man's penis of spiritual creativity in the form of the Tree of Life.

In conclusion, it should be mentioned that withholding definite deixis can also mediate the state of figural consciousness. In both main narratives "*the* dogs" are constantly present, whether as Waldo's negative obsession or as Arthur's chief comfort. But when Arthur frees himself from his dead brother's clutches and flees the house, it is a change of deictic reference that most radically conveys his sudden panicky plunge into self-absorption: "Before he slammed *a* door on the shocked faces of *dogs*" (A294)—not "*the* door", not "*the* dogs". Arthur is no longer in touch with his defamiliarized surroundings.[14]

III   Character-identification as 'modal deixis'

Character-identification ("he", "his friend", "George Brown", "Waldo") is included under deixis on grounds of convenience. As with the treatment of spatial, temporal and affective dimensions, the concept of relative distance is involved, on the plane of narrative perspective, focalization, or modality: hence "modal deixis". As I have had occasion to remark already, it is normal for the reader to assume that the naming of characters in narrative is a functional index to the presence of an auctorial narrator, whereas an increase in the frequency of substitutive reference ("familiar" names in "outward" reference; personal pronouns in reflexive contexts) indicates an empathetic entry into the mind of the character being referred to.

Stanzel (1982:245) relies on the universal validity of this assumption in marking out the criteria for "personal" or figural narration. Macrotextual considerations are often dominant in Stanzel's reasoning: hence his chief example, Joyce's *Portrait,* where the "early-draft" periphrases of *Stephen Hero* are dropped, names appear seldom, and Stephen is referred to throughout by the personal pronoun. In a summary presentation of his own earlier studies on "die Personalisierung des Erzählaktes" in Joyce's *Ulysses,* Stanzel (1982:226–32 *passim*) rightly indicates the subtle way in which the consciousness of the figural

---

[14] Geoffrey Dutton (1971:39), faced with the unenviable task of summarizing and discussing all of White's works in 44 pages, inadvertently (?) refamiliarizes the deixis as: "And it was he that slammed *the* door 'on the shocked faces of *the* dogs'".

"medium" has had superimposed upon it the consciousness of the auctorial "medium" (this narrational melding resembles in part the ambiguity of focalization often encountered in free indirect discourse and is one manifestation of what Bakhtin calls "bivocality"; cf also Pascal 1977:21).

Sympathetic qualification (eg, "poor Strether" in James) and "auctorial periphrasis" (eg, "our hero") are *non*-neutral indices of auctorial presence; these are absent from *The Solid Mandala*. If "our hero" is clearly complicitous, most other forms of classificatory periphrasis are narratorially neutral. Periphrasis is employed, it is commonly assumed, as "elegant" variation—as an auctorial or narratorial means of introducing variety (a service to the implied reader as reader). But it can also be implemented (often simultaneously with the intention of reducing monotony) for ironic, analytical reasons, as in the following, where there are thematic and contextual reasons for choosing this normally *less* likely sequence: "She [Mrs Poulter] turned to investigate *her friend's* seamed and yellow cheek, but *Mrs Dun* was too discreet to cash in on anyone's approval" (B17). The term "elegant" variation implies an element of sophisticated choice, all things being equal. But White is not interested in variety for its own sake, and is also prepared to engage in "inelegant" variation. Whatever their function might be as an index to narratorial presence, White's shiftings of designation are always locally specific or situationally evaluative—usually with the aim of indicating figural reaction of some kind. This is evident if one takes one of the very few instances of persistent variation in Section 1—a category that is socially classificatory, is marked for age and sex, and crosses the dialogue/narrative interface:

the neighbours — two brothers — two twins — two retired gentlemen — the Mister Browns — the Brothers Brown — the Brothers Bloody Brown — the boys — the two boys — his sons — the two men — the retired brothers — the two old men — the old gentlemen — the old men — two grown men — two men — the gentlemen — the old men — those two old fellers — two respectable old gentlemen — those old men

White is quite capable of sovereignly ironic play with the convention of "elegant" variation: perhaps the best example is the naming texture of *Voss*, which is intentionally (intertextually) contaminated by the high-Victorian extreme of this technique. On the surface, the result can have an almost parodistic feel to it, and the reader's sense of mocking, wilful, mandarin authority is reinforced. As soon as one stops trying to brush away these annoyingly persistent flies (the hypnotic—almost *un*varied—recurrence of "the German" instead of "Voss", for example) and decides for once to test them for their *functionality*, one discovers that they constitute a most subtle metering system for psychological attitude. It is, for example, not for the sake of "elegant" variation that Mr Bonner's first private encounter with Voss (V15–20) should have "the [shabby/cloudy] German" in proximity to Bonner's view of his visitor and "Voss" whenever the latter's own thoughts and opinions are mediated independently of Bonner's evaluations; or that Mr Bonner's shape-changing ("Mr Bonner", "Edmund Bonner", "the merchant", "the draper", "the thick man", "the man whose money was involved") should (with the single exception of Voss's designation of him as "his patron") be keyed to variations in the man's own sense of social identity.

The principle of substitution (pronoun to name, or vice versa), of course, has a functional aspect at the straightforward level of text-cohesion. Pronouns replace names wherever speaker-identification is not otherwise ambiguous. Names are used obligatorily (often after untagged dialogue) in Section 1, for example, to avoid association with a different person (name or pronoun) or to individuate from a plural pronoun, irrespective of whether the immediately preceding utterance is direct speech or diegesis. To avoid the possible confusion of speakers in longer strings of dialogue, names are occasionally introduced with neutral tag-verbs. Where this signposting of dialogue is not necessary, there is character-focalized mediation of thoughts, feelings and perceptions. Although the "frame" may be clearly narratorial ("Mrs Poulter"), the pronominalizations contained therein are indices to figural consciousness, as are the accompanying external namings (eg, "Bill" for personal perspective, "Bill Poulter" for his wife's perception of his public identity) and periphrases ("her husband"). We may, of course, still speak of a blending of "media"; but it is a rough blend only, character rising to the surface.

These assertions require further elucidation; as they clash in part with Stanzel's rules of thumb, I should perhaps turn briefly to his narrative theory once more. In discussing passages from the Wandering Rocks episode of *Ulysses,* Stanzel notes that the extracts examined (various occasions on which Father Conmee encounters people on the street and talks to them) reveal ruptures in the conventions of non-figural narrative, as well as stretches of free indirect discourse in which the consciousness registering the conversation is not that of Father Conmee but that of a third person (the auctorial narrator) whose style of narrating begins to resemble that of a "reflector"-character. Stanzel's proof for the absence of internal perspective in the narration is the repeated occurrence of name and honorific instead of the personal pronoun: "Father Conmee was wonderfully well indeed"; "Father Conmee was very glad indeed to hear that"; "Father Conmee was very glad to see the wife of Mr David Sheehy M.P. looking so well". These sentences are "approximate transpositions" of what Father Conmee and Mrs Sheehy say to each other. Stanzel does not remark on the "replacement" of "her" (for direct-speech "you") by "the wife of Mr David Sheehy M.P." in a statement whose wording is otherwise parallel to spoken idiom. This, like the presence of "Father Conmee" instead of "he", would support Stanzel's view that the perspective is external—were it not for the pragmatic context, which can be identified as the verbal interaction of a parishioner with a priest in the latter's extended social (rather than narrowly pastoral) role. It is, of course, possible to imagine an observer formally (and persistently) identifying the priest in this role by so naming him (and, presumably, omitting to grant Mrs Sheehy the same degree of referential attention), and to assume that a persistent use of "he" would shift the perspective to Father Conmee's own consciousness.

But replacing the names with pronouns produces a curious effect which we would surely resist: the statements quoted above now feel as though they are *endorsing fully* the sentiments expressed (as though there were thought behind utterance, or thought *instead of* utterance). And it is also possible, if we consider the original formulations again, that Father Conmee is himself aware that he is addressing a parishioner—and not, say, an intimate friend or personal acquaintance—and that the formal naming is an index to his awareness that he is speaking phatically in the capacity indicated by the designation "Father Conmee". In this case, what is being conveyed to us in free indirect discourse (or, more precisely, free indirect speech) is the speaker's/figural narrator's pragmatic self-image as it is constantly checked against consciousness of the probable expectations of the addressee (in this case, Mrs Sheehy, who is classified by the *speaker* in terms of her socio-marital status). This consciousness of self could also be present when the priest chats jocularly and paternally with "three little schoolboys" (Stanzel 1982:230). Once again, Father Conmee is aware while speaking that he is executing a social function expected of a priest, and is aware that the boys are aware that he is a priest (he is, after all, doubtless dressed as one). Stanzel, however, takes the sentence "The boys sixeyed Father Conmee and laughed" in order to demonstrate perspectival superimposition: "sixeyed" being an index to figural consciousness, "Father Conmee" to external narration. I have no quarrel with Stanzel's conclusion that the narration is "personalized"—only with the firmness of his assumption that *nomen* instead of *pronomen* must mean non-figural orientation. There should be a system of safeguards allowing consideration of psychological and text-pragmatic determinates alongside our conventional reactions to patterns of referentiality that are linguistically determined.

I should like to test this assumption—that naming instead of pro-nominalization, and various *levels* of naming or nomination, can differentiate levels of figural subjectivity rather than being just narratorial mediation—on various deictic sequences in *The Solid Mandala,* starting with instances where Stanzel's theory is *not* involved in any way: ie, with passages in which Waldo or Arthur is represented as thinking of or (re)acting to somebody other than himself. Such instances customarily involve "elegant" variation and the disambiguating use of names to ensure the identity of actants. The Brown parents are referred to as follows in Sections 2 and 3 of the novel:

the parents	
his mother and father	
Mother and Dad	
George Brown	(Anne Quantrell)
their father	their mother
his father	his mother
the old man	
Dad	Mother

Pronominal reference ("he", "she", "they") is, of course, also present. "Mother" and "Dad" are markers of stylistic register. They indicate individual social role-relationships in such a way that the "mode of expression" is "incompatible with the narrator's voice"; passages including such namings are classifiable as free indirect discourse or, at the very least, as extremely consonant psychonarration (Banfield 1973:23–24; McHale 1978:270). Such indices to figural consciousness are the rule throughout Waldo's and Arthur's narratives, and furnish a kind of norm against which to measure deflections. Arthur's narrative, for instance, employs these family-relationship names so persistently that the very few occasions on which other forms occur are conspicuous enough to require explanation. When Arthur senses his father's embarrassment in the cow-tragedy scene (A230), it is still "Dad" whom he feels "turn against him". A couple of paragraphs on, the shift from "*Dad* didn't seem to think it would" to "For *his father* it would have been detestable" could be explained as elegant variation; but the topical context has to do with the (im)possibility of an empathetic relationship between an "afflicted" father and his "afflicted" son. Arthur's mental speculation encodes the distance at which he now perceives himself to be from "Dad". Relationships are also invoked when Arthur decides to ask for help with the word "totality" (A239). He mentally singles out "Dad, or Waldo" as possibilities at dinnertime; Waldo is discarded: "But suddenly he knew *his brother* wouldn't"; "That left *their father*". Nouns instead of names hint not only at the speculative or notional level at which Arthur mulls over the problem of appealing to authority, but also at the anticipated distancing of Waldo. The relationship is subjectively reduced, but is maintained in the sibling reference involved in "their" (instead of "his"), which is then repeated in "Why did he not propose to ask *their mother*, he wasn't sure" (distance again). The moment at which Arthur actually makes his final decision implies a shift from speculative distance to perceptual immediacy and subjective commitment: "So there was *Dad*. Cleaning his moustache of salmon".

What now occurs is an unprecedented shift to formal naming when Arthur registers Mr Brown's reactions (A239–40) to his question: "*George Brown* looked at first as though he had been hit"; "Again *George Brown* might have been recovering from a blow"; "*George Brown* recommended". Such namings do not indicate a temporary reversion to auctorial perspective: they suggest, rather, the impact on Arthur's consciousness of gestural behaviour which makes his father "unfamiliar" to him. Arthur sees him as others would see him if they were not friends or members of the family: he is bathed in the naked light of public neutrality, a mere human being like anybody else, lacking the privilege of filial trust. His apophthegmatic wisdom ("'Accuracy in the first place can only be called a virtue'"), uttered in a situation where he has already amply demonstrated his uncertainty, is an attempt to set up a façade of impersonal expertise: "George Brown recommended" implies as much. Arthur's expectations have not yet been shattered—he accepts this "public" pronouncement, although it is not to be received as a communication wholly characteristic of "Dad". The three occurrences of "George Brown" remain isolated moments of alienated perception. Arthur's father is constantly refamiliarized here as "Dad", even when he exposes his bumbling inadequacy in responding to his son's enquiry. The suggestion we are left with is of Arthur's acceptance of this inadequacy: "Then Arthur realized *Dad* would never know, any more than *Waldo*"; any less familiar a naming would have signalled distancing rejection.

Distancing and rejection are involved on the next occasion in the text when the designation "Dad" fails to occur—the morning Arthur discovers his father's corpse (A269): "the morning *their father* died"; "finding *their father* in the dark room"; "Arthur touched *George Brown's* hand"; "Not that *George Brown* had done more than withdraw from Arthur a second time"; "Excepting the morning *George Brown* died". Mr Brown has ceased to exist in a way that would allow Arthur to think of him as "Dad". Instead, the discourse refers to him in relation to both of the boys: "their father" is contiguous with diegetic reference to Waldo. The original, emotional, withdrawal (A230) was maximized by the use of "their father"; the second and final physical withdrawal takes Arthur's father irretrievably beyond filial claims, into the realm of the public and the impersonal—"George Brown" is, in Arthur's consciousness, severed from role-relationships and "exists" only in terms of the most generally valid yet most specifically personal of nominal designations. This form of naming persists in retrospective diegesis (A274), in a context of naming where "Dulcie and Leonard got married" represents the norm of familiarity: "That was already as far back as 1922, the year *George Brown* had died". This distancing is not markedly apparent in the case of Mrs Brown, for whom "Mother" is the usual form of reference: "After *Mother's* death their twin lives would not have diverged" (A274). Here the alternative of "their mother" does not offer itself, on stylistic grounds, as this occurs elsewhere only when Arthur is conscious of filial obligation to her and fraternal obligation to Waldo simultaneously (eg, A272–73), and on the sole occasion on which he comes close to expressing discontent at his mother's loss of interest in him ("Arthur would have liked to admire *their mother* less", A269).

Waldo lays so much claim to Mrs Brown's affections that the normative alternation in his narrative is between "Mother" and the proprietorial, Arthur-excluding "his mother" (eg, W28/120/145/162/ 167). "Their mother" occurs very occasionally: in diegesis centering on Waldo's ruminations about family relationships (W72/160); when Arthur's co-presence cannot be denied (W71/72/158); and once when it is clear to Waldo that Mrs Brown has distanced herself from her children (W158). Twice (in connection with a proleptic reference to her death, and with reference to her cremation) she is named a "true Quantrell" (W167/171)—an expression of Waldo's desire to restore her to "dynastic" status by removal from the nominal, stigmatic ambience of her husband. Once the narration has to be "corrected" as an imperiously indulgent mental gesture on Waldo's part to accommodate Arthur ("Some people would have considered his—*their* mother, dowdy", W120). Narrative perspective is sometimes ruffled by insertions of "Mrs Brown" into passages otherwise referring to "Mother". In such cases, we can imagine Waldo perceiving his mother playing a social or "public" role in (diegetically approximated) conversation with people outside the family circle.[15]

In Waldo's discourse, the word "Dad" cannot be regarded as more than a token acknowledgement of familiarity: ie, it is not an index to positive emotional attachment. The relationship is forever being neutralized into passively accepted consanguinity ("their father"). Proprietorial reference ("his father") occurs, not as an act of will (cf "his mother"), but solely where Waldo is unavoidably confronted with parental authority in situations excluding Arthur, and where such confrontations impinge forcefully on Waldo's emotions.[16] The ultimate in neutrality is reached in the frequent identification of Waldo's father as "George Brown". I attempted above to justify this designation as a reflex of Arthur's attitude—forbearing to mention that its occurrences have an explicit prehistory in Waldo's section.

Straight after a long passage on the twins' childhood relationship with their father (referred to as "Dad" except for one generic classification, "the heads of father and son", where Waldo is projecting the opinions of outsiders), there is the statement: "Often strangers, and always children, were fascinated by *George Brown's* boot, which was something members of the family hardly noticed" (W33–34). Now, this could easily be taken for a momentary auctorial intrusion; but contextual details undermine this assumption. Disjunctive constructions precede, implying emotive involvement; and the status of Mr Brown's limp as habitual and unnoticed is placed in question by the fact that Waldo is then represented as watching "*their father* limp down Terminus Road"—where Waldo's consciousness is (narrationally) still conditioned by the emotive distance of "George Brown", and can return to close familiarity ("As *Dad* walked his thin lips were slightly parted", W34) only in stages. Waldo has been looking at his father through the eyes of "strangers": by which token "George Brown" is not meant to be a name that these "strangers, and always children" could readily put to the limping man. "George Brown" is simply Waldo's sign for a complex process of estrangement from the Wounded Father—an estrangement whose existence Waldo can try to underplay (it is all too palpable elsewhere in the narrative), but which sharply focused as soon as Waldo suffers humiliating implication in the public curiosity devoted to his father's surgical boot. The effect is bivalent—perhaps confusingly so: both cold imaginative empathy and emotive dissociation.

---

[15] "Mrs Poulter could have been expecting Mrs Brown .... Mrs Brown was too erect and cold" (W72); "Mrs Brown once remarked she hoped the market would not let Mrs Musto down. § But somehow Mother did not altogether care for Mrs Musto" (W84); "Mrs Brown didn't actively dislike Mrs Poulter ..." (W167).

[16] "His father's was the first death Waldo ... had to face" (W69); "It wasn't the prospect of his father's self-exposure which was shaking him" (W77); Mr Brown's imposition of the moustache (W79–80); "He might even have admitted his father to their circle of enlightenment if Dad had walked in" (W85); tension at the dinnertable (W125); "his relationship with his father" (W145; cf also W161).

This kind of naming is soon topicalized, and Arthur is implicated in the act of naming: "Later on, when the twins got to refer to their father as 'George Brown', Arthur affectionately, Waldo with irony and understanding ..." (W37). The *intention* behind the appellation and the tonality of reference is not explained narratorially, but is taken as self-evident (ie, by Waldo, on behalf of himself and his brother). Here are some other sentences employing the reference to "George Brown":

1. "George Brown" as he referred to their father when he had learnt to tolerate him, clung to his principles, or illusions .... [W48]

2. Then George Brown their father, a wizened man with a limp, got up and went in to stoke the stove .... [W49]

3. George Brown, as the boys referred to him in fun, was stuck at the table where usually he sat out the darkness. [W70]

4. ... as he walked with their father ..., George Brown lashing out with his gammy leg, to keep up with the son holding back for him. [W76]

5. How he resented brown eyes, whether in Dulcie Feinstein, Arthur, or George Brown .... [W125]

6. ... this man who was also by accident his father .... Dad had retired a year or two early .... George Brown had to suffer .... After his retirement George Brown mostly sat .... If passion stirred in George Brown, it was for the most unassuming manifestations of nature. [W158–59]

7. Mrs Poulter ... used to bring dishes to George Brown. It amused Mother. [W160]

8. She knew, apparently, it would be a long time from then, because she died ten years after George Brown her husband. [W167]

9. ... his sympathies were somehow with Dad over *The Brothers Karamazov*. Which George Brown had carried to the bonfire with a pair of tongs. [W199]

A string of such references, interspersed with "Dad", occurs when Waldo and his father are seated in the train and Mr Brown is agonizing his way h his dutiful explanation of the facts of life (W77–79). Waldo is humiliated, embarrassed, scornful: his father is obviously as inadequate to the task as he is to explaining the word "totality" for Arthur. Although he is ostensibly trying to fulfil a standard paternal role, it is a role that is foreign to him, and one which Waldo refuses to acknowledge. The naming indicates both Mr Brown's estrangement from the role (in a *public* conveyance) and Waldo's resulting estrangement from his father. Examples 1–9 cannot all be said to accord with the claim that the appellation "George Brown" is used "with irony and understanding". The formulation in 1 is already a climb-down from this, and 3 a further reduction, in a sentence whose two main elements (the mode of naming; Mr Brown's physical attitude in death) clash grotesquely. Examples 2 and 4 draw us back to the very first occurrence of "George Brown" in connection with the Wounded Father; the association is ultimately with *weakness,* as it is in 5–7. It is evident from many passages in the novel that the name "Brown" is dwelt upon because it evokes mediocrity, a total lack of distinction (at least as far as Waldo is concerned). These various namings thus suggest how Waldo's consciousness keeps throwing the name "George Brown" back in its bearer's face; even when this reproof is suppressed, it is a resonating undertone, so that it can truly be said that Waldo employs the name "with irony" if not with understanding (in the sense of sympathy). The most extreme juxtaposition is to be found in **9,** which seems to violate cohesion rules—"George Brown" seems for a moment to be a different person from "Dad"—until we see how Waldo's shifts of consciousness are precisely reflected. "Dad" occurs in a context where Waldo can afford to be concessive in his alignment with his father (at W120, Waldo aligns himself so securely with his mother that he can afford to bask in the role of husband-substitute, patting his safely absent father on the head, as it were: "Since Dad died in 1922 she had been dependent on him"). The image then evoked when "George Brown" goes to destroy the book that threatens to expose the weakness of his rationalist beliefs is that of a resolute "public" Inquisitor. This "externalized" role, however, is perforce contaminated by the other connotations already set up in Waldo's consciousness by the name "George Brown", so that Waldo's endorsement of the act is subliminally undercut by pathetic negativity.

Other "modal deictic" sequences exhibit a similarly sensitive correlation with a character's shifting emotive constitution of other characters. Arthur's discourse is either neutral-to-respectful in its namings[17] or unchangingly loyal to a fixed form of reference, as in the case of "Dulcie" (no matter whether her behaviour in his presence is positive or negative—except in the mandala-dance, when he formally declares "his love for Dulcie Feinstein, and for her husband", A265). Waldo's narrative, by contrast, is characterized by sudden swings (as between "Dad" and "George Brown") and a much more prominent emotive component ("Mr Feinstein/old Feinstein/Mr Feinstein/the old boy", W104–108). Gradations in perception and familiarization are sensitively marked ("this one coming into the room/the young man/Mr Saporta/Leonard Saporta/ox-eyed Saporta/Saporta", W155–56). The quintessential instance is the handling of Dulcie Feinstein at Waldo's first (W89–98) and second-last (W157) meetings with her. At the first meeting, the designation "Dulcie" is taken over at the outset from Mrs Musto's own direct speech, even before Waldo has been introduced to her. Externalizing terms are then interspersed ("the girl Dulcie", "the girl in pink"). The initial, tentative stretch of conversation is prefaced prejudicially by a mental note on "this ugly dark girl", then conducted in subjective close-up, as it were, by means of wellnigh unrelieved pronoun reference. Waldo's self-defensive reduction of Dulcie is then signalled deictically in "this Dulcie" (W91) before her full name is "quoted" ("Dulcie Feinstein", W94) in a context juxtaposing it favourably with the name "Brown". From now on it is intermittently downhill, with the emotional stasis afforded by "she" or "Dulcie" being offset by a distancing use of her full name (W95/97–98). At the second-last meeting, where Waldo learns that Dulcie is engaged to Leonard Saporta, the prelude includes a "public" use of the full name as Waldo toys with the idea of marriage (W149). Having pumped taut his fantasies of marital bliss, Waldo registers the identity of his love-object in the

---

17 "Mr Saporta"; "Mr Feinstein"; "old Mr Feinstein"; "The woman at Barranugli/The woman/those people at Barranugli/Mr and Mrs Thompson" (A218); "Mrs Poulter/their neighbour/Mrs Poulter/the woman in the iron hut" (A256–57).

familiar form of "Dulcie" (W150–56) until the truth dawns on him: at which
stage there is a sharp reversion to "Dulcie Feinstein" (W157), an attempt to
regain superiority via reductive periphrasis ("a rather coarse little thing"), and a
lapse into projective, sarcastic distancing ("Mrs Saporta" > "This giant
incubator" > "Dulcie Feinstein Saporta", W157).

It could be expected that, because of sibling intimacy, narrative discourse
which is figurally oriented would have one brother referring to the other by his
Christian name (or, in the absence of coreferential ambiguity, as "he"). This is
often enough the case: Waldo's narrative refers to "Arthur", Arthur's to
"Waldo". Evaluative expressions requiring "the presence of some evaluating
speaker other than the narrator" (McHale 1978:269) also indicate figural or free
indirect discourse.[18] Further away from the core of personal familiarity,
however, there are role-relationship expressions ("his brother") which—leaving
aside the remote possibility that an auctorial narrator might consider the reader to
be in constant need of a reminder about consanguinity—cannot be accounted for
simply in terms of the stylistic desirability of elegant variation.

It is made formally clear in free direct thought ("My brother, Waldo would
breathe", W25) and free indirect discourse ("It was all very well to hang on to
your brother's hand", A229) that the characters thinking are represented as
themselves identifying the relationship. Elsewhere, it is the thematic and
psychological tendency of the narrative as a whole which conditions us to read
such expressions as "his brother" (eg, W24–25/39/197/201, A229/273/284–
85/290–91/292–94), "Arthur his twin brother" (W81), "his twin brother Waldo"
(A286) or "Waldo the twin" (A228) as reflecting the character's own
preoccupation with the duties and burdens of fraternity and twinship. Harder to
assimilate naturally is full-name reference (of the "George Brown" or "Anne
Quantrell" type already discussed). Arthur's narrative never has reference to
"Waldo Brown"; but there are frequent references in Waldo's narrative to
"Arthur Brown", usually in close proximity to the familiar designation "Arthur".
Sometimes occurrences are plainly quasi-citational, as when Waldo speculates
uncomfortably about what "other boys" might think of "Arthur Brown" and his
domestic activities (W36). Elsewhere, Waldo can be construed as perceiving his
brother to be the object of "public" attention (in the playground, for instance,
because of his mathematical wizardry, W42; at the Feinsteins', as the recipient of
Mrs Feinstein's "understanding", W108); or Arthur's untoward behaviour in a
situation also witnessed by others induces shocked estrangement or ironic
distancing in Waldo (the playground fight, W45; Arthur's love for Woolworths,
W55; his dribbling, or conspicuous verbal behaviour, in public places and at the
Feinsteins', W57/60/109).

The final problem to be examined is that of full-name reference ("Waldo
Brown") to the focal character. As I stated at the outset, we are conditioned by
linguistic convention to interpret such reference unquestioningly as external to the

---

[18] "Poor Arthur" (W42); "funny old Arthur" (W76); "the wretched Arthur" (W174); "poor
old Waldo" (A245); "silly old Waldo" (A249); "poor Waldo" (A290).

character—as originating in the consciousness of a dissonant or consonant (psycho)narrator. When we examine the more restricted domain of narration represented by free indirect discourse, however, we find that current narrative theory rejects the validity of this assumption. Banfield (1973:32) concedes that *nouns* are infrequent with reference to the subject of consciousness in free indirect discourse, but her examples are all drawn from first-person narratives, where referential discordance is apt to be experienced most acutely by the reader. In a later, elaborated study (Banfield 1982:70–73/206–209/311.n19) she sets out the ground-rules: nouns and proper nouns can appear in free indirect discourse but *not* in sentences of represented thought (which must employ pronouns). In "representations of perceptions (and of non-reflective conscious states in general) any appropriate [noun phrase] may refer to the SELF", "as long as the appellation or description does not present information unknown to the SELF"; "the proper name is the name the SELF knows himself by, as opposed to such descriptive phrases" as "the quaker librarian" (in *Ulysses).* This, then, can account for the coreferentiality of the Christian names with the focal figural consciousness: the frequency with which "Waldo" appears in Section 2 is not an index to an auctorial narrator's intimacy (affectionate or otherwise) with the presiding intelligence. In conventional third-person narratives, of course, with no formal markers of free indirect discourse, the latter situation could be said to obtain (the mimetic representation of a one-sided relationship of intimacy between observing psychonarrator and the character observed); but *The Solid Mandala* cannot by a long shot be termed a conventional narrative.

In my discussion of the possibility of non-focalized narration (ch. 5 above), the naming-gradient "Mr Brown" > "Waldo Brown" > "Waldo" (W183) was found to be explicable in terms of figural consciousness (Waldo's propensity to projective self-dramatization: writing himself into the Secret Writing of his life). All more "public" namings can be similarly explained, whether role-relationship markers (such as "the Brothers Brown" or "the Brown brothers"), surnames with courtesy-title ("Mr Brown"), or full and reduced forms ("Waldo Brown", "W. Brown"). To take the least usual forms first: "W. Brown of honourable service" (W115) occurs in a passage of syntactically broken interior monologue, and signals Waldo's imaginatively "retrospective" observation of self as mediated by a eulogistic obituary. Occurrences of the courtesy-title ("'Who can say,' Mr Brown said", W166; "Mr Crankshaw was several years his junior when appointed the superior of Mr Brown", W171) indicate Waldo's consciousness of his own role in a professional context—he questions Crankshaw's authority through noncommittal formality of tone and expression (though the "said"-tag works ironically against the "say" of the rhetorical question), and "Mr Brown" also encodes Waldo's reaction to being so addressed by Crankshaw when the latter questions his efficiency. At W171, details of the narration point to figural focus, quite apart from the book-end structure of the sentence, with the iconic distancing of the two names from each other, and the inside-out coreferentiality of "*his* junior" and "Mr Brown".

Nominal appositions function as figural identifications with a role—whether derived from an evaluation originally external to the thinking self ("Arthur, Waldo's big dill brother", A294; "Arthur, stupid Arthur", A234), ironically projected via exclamatory discourse ("As though her little boy Waldo would take for granted anything she might arrange for him with his big brother", W74) or, most radically, as wishful projection of a desirable self in a quasi-schizoid frame which omits personal naming ("He admired the sound of her kind strong son", W166). Instances of full naming ("Waldo Brown") in Waldo's section outnumber those in Arthur's section 8 to 3 (or, adjusted for text-length, 2.7:1.4). Some examples:

10. When Johnny found that Arthur Brown could solve mathematical problems .... [A228]

11. Nobody could remember, not even Arthur Brown himself, when he developed his head for figures. [A231]

12. This development gave Arthur Brown a satisfaction more intense than any he experienced .... [A232]

13. Arthur Brown was taken on by Mr Allwright about the time Waldo began at Barranugli High. Arthur Brown's apprenticeship was arranged quite quickly and easily .... [A232]

14. The yellow dung went plop plop. Arthur Brown would roll on his seat in time with the buggy .... [A234]

15. All this was most mysterious but rewarding to Arthur Brown. [A236]

16. It was the most exquisite fulfilment Arthur Brown had experienced yet. [A244]

17. But many of them kissed Arthur Brown. [A252]

18. Arthur Brown visited them all through the two children and several miscarriages. [A275]

19. In the First War Arthur Brown had been all fireworks and singing. [A280]

20. When the chair collapsed under Arthur Brown he wasn't hurt. It was such a joke. [A281]

In all of these cases, though in varying degrees, Arthur's awareness of self is located in an interpersonal "public" context: what is mediated by full naming is consciousness relativized and bounded by social ambience. Arthur is aware that Haynes is interested in only one aspect of his self (one externally indicated role) and views himself through Haynes's eyes (10). The context for 11 is actually provided in later sentences, where it is made clear that Arthur has to respond in this partial role to "public" interrogation about his gift. In 12, 15 and 16, the experiencing of intense emotion is concomitant with Arthur's consciousness of being located in a significant social or cultural context: the full name is an index to a simple sense of self-importance within a social role (breadmaking with Mother; playing the piano with Dulcie; conversing with Mrs Musto; cf also the formal mandala-ritual performed in Mrs Poulter's presence: "So Arthur Brown danced", A265); and it is Arthur's consciousness of himself as performing a social (not just a personal) duty that is paramount in 18. In 13, the self is caught up in the machinery of public existence, formally and impersonally acted upon: Arthur's self-image reflects the way in which he senses he is being viewed. This is also true in other ways in 14 (he is accessible to the gaze of those he passes in the trap), 17 and 19 (he is immersed in a mass of public celebrators and is aware of that "non-personal" part of himself whose presence is all the mass demands), and 20 (the insouciance of the second sentence is ironically relativized by the first, where the naming suggests that Arthur *does* think of how the other—quiet—users of the library react to the noise he makes).

This is not to say that White does not exploit the rhetoric of the text to establish a bivocal or heteroglossic perspective. A case in point is the following (where the "second voice" is that of the macronarrative and its thematic implications, rather than that of auctorial comment):

Of all these jewels or touchstones, talismans or sweethearts, Arthur Brown soon got to love the knotted one best, and for staring at it, and rubbing at it, should have seen his face inside. [A228]

Close spatial deixis ("these") is as unreliable an index to figural consciousness (McHale 1978:265–66) as is the epistemic-alethic modal "should have" (Coates 1983:82) for a logical assumption on the part of a narrator external to Arthur. Why should reference be to "Arthur Brown" at this point? The previous paragraph started off with "Arthur", and both paragraphs continue substitutively ("he/his"). We are also compelled to consider the next (single-sentence) paragraph: "Waldo the twin used to scoff at the marbles". This would normally reinforce an argument for non-focalized narration, "the twin" supplying explanatory information—though we might ask why, seeing as we already know this. The four nouns applied to the marbles, and Arthur's action, suggest a condition of magical undecidability about their status: but we do end up with something of an inside view ("got to love the knotted one best"). If we accept that "Arthur Brown" is a means of distantiation, we could imagine the other boys at school as being the observers, were it not for the core of the sentence with that reference to an inaccessible subjective attitude. Two—possibly concomitant—resolutions offer themselves for consideration. The general context is that of the "public" exchange of marbles: Arthur is aware to some extent that his favouring and withholding of these marbles is subject to public scrutiny within the context of the trading or swapping of taws. Full naming indicates his awareness, which is set off against the privacy of the significance he attaches to his marbles—he is "self-important" within the context of yet another treasured ritual (cf examples 3, 6–7 above). The "second voice" connects "Arthur Brown" contrastively with "Waldo the twin", Arthur's attachment with Waldo's scoffing, the knotted taw with "his" coiled one. It is only on later readings that the family/fraternal/twinship aspect of the naming (the sharing of the surname) reveals itself as the axis on which the fateful and ironic symbolism of the mandalas revolves.

In Waldo's case, full namings usually suggest acute self-consciousness rather than self-awareness. There are many instances of "Waldo Brown" in the first or actional-present narrative where his actions or situation vis-à-vis Arthur provoke in him a strong, *controlling* sense that there may be other people watching him/them (eg, W27/30/56/62/63/115). The full name similarly occurs when Waldo traverses public territory (W60), particularly when role-playing is involved (W83/170/177), when he senses that a disruption of equilibrium may have made him look ridiculous (W46/57/63), or when his traversal of terrain is potentially exposable as moral transgression, as in the voyeur-scene (W61). He may be entertaining an image of his public self which (he hopes) conceals a secret and private self (W74/115), or may be aware projectively of the (luckily not eventuating) possibility that he might be publicly spotted, as when he overhears the Council workmen (W147). The diegetic enunciation of Waldo's beliefs, prejudices, prevarications and lovingly groomed fragments of philosophy—whether merely thought or actually expressed by him—tends to be attributed to a "Waldo Brown" (W27/56/60/67/177) who sees himself as he would have others see him. This also extends to his consciousness of his personal appearance (W127, where he borrows the diction of adult praise) and of his role as Secret Writer (W129/173, where the style lightly hints at the biographical mode). The effect can be one of ironic subversion, as when the "public" persona entertained exposes the factitiousness of the "private" artist's emotion (W30), or when Waldo responds to Dulcie's remark about George Eliot: "'A very passionate girl, Maggie,' said Waldo Brown" (W93). A kind of stunned iciness of consciousness may be mediated, the awareness of a self threatened by imminent scrutiny from without: this Self as Voyeur is the "Waldo Brown" who crosses the road to spy on Mrs Poulter (W61). imagines Haynes and his woman copulating (W190), and peers through the window to find his father exposed in death (W70). In this last instance, the personal self has been shocked into absence; Waldo is flung centripetally away from emotional confrontation with the scene, fleeing first mentally then physically, before retreating even further behind his public persona's assertion of "facts". The threefold occurrence of "Waldo Brown" gives the last sheen of psychological polish to a masterfully mediated scene. Sometimes more complex psychological effects may be suggested, as when "Waldo Brown" realizes that Mrs Feinstein's nose reminds him of a penis (W136): the image is "forbidden", and full-name reference hints at the shrinking of consciousness from the thought of What the Others Would Think If .... The past locus which provides the experiential basis for the forbidden identification (a clergyman's penis in a public lavatory) is also evoked, both as a formulated memory and via Waldo's imaginings of his public self standing in a public place.

Arguably the cleverest effect of all is achieved in the transvestite scene (W193). Encased in his mother's blue dress, Waldo is able to deny his public identity ("It was no longer Waldo Brown") after contemptuous reference to "the pathetic respect" which he thinks "public" persons "had always paid him". The possessive "his" immediately changes to "she" for the course of an icily ecstatic paragraph, before the whole trance of abandoned Self is broken by the re-emergence of "Waldo Brown". Waldo hears a voice (not immediately identified as Arthur's): his first thought is of being caught in a compromising situation (somebody looking in on the double self at the mirror; his projection of his outward self as seen by an intruder); at the same moment of rupture, he mentally scrambles back into the garb and identity of "Waldo Brown".

In the kinds of naming discussed in this section, we are as readers obliged to reconstitute character in line with the ways in which two central consciousnesses, Waldo and Arthur, constitute themselves. Naming-gradients suggest the various degrees to which figural consciousness is able to empathize and self-dramatize. White has handed over referential authority, not to "a narrator of some kind, who impersonates the characters in the course of the relation of the history" (Docherty 1983:65–66), but to central characters who are made to impersonate the voice of conventional omniscient narrators. Ultimate generative authority, of course, rests with the author. Docherty, in an interesting chapter on "Names" in earlier and recent fiction, rightly insists that "the real author is simply the next link in the chain of impersonations"—there are "simply different degrees of accessibility to the real source or sources of authority behind the speech-acts of the characters, and behind the historical process of the reading or creation of this fiction" (1983:64). Although he does not consider the kind of radical manipulation of the rhetoric of naming practised by White, it is evident from Docherty's study that White—like those novelists who avoid using names altogether and force the reader to generate character from pronominal references—is exploring the subjectivity of characters (and readers!) rather than the moral (etc) status of strongly predetermined "selves". It is this, more than any other feature of narrative discourse and style in White, which is most subject to misconstruction by readers attuned to conventional narrative voicings (and conventional accounts of these voicings, like Stanzel's), simply because the rhetorical overlap with these voicings is complete. It is (like gnomic statements) a technique recurrent enough in White's repertoire to mislead critics into detecting express and intrusive authority on his part when no such authority is functional in the text.

SENTENCE STRUCTURE AND COHESION

I   Cohesion, conjunction, and character

Adverbial linkage of the "normal" sort between sentences is restricted in Section 1 of White's novel to temporal analysis. There are, that is, no intersentential logical connectors relating to attitude, causality, logical or thematic process and the like. Characteristic of the discourse of the novel as a whole, however, are four categories of grammatical linkage which, appearing conspicuously at the beginning of sentences, largely have to do with non-temporal relations. Two are connectors or adverbials: the conjuncts *So* and *Then*. Two are conjunctions: *For* (an adverbial, coordinating conjunction) and *Because* (a subordinating conjunction). The clauses of reason thus constitute independent but atactic constructions.[1] This is more acceptable with *for* than with *because;* the latter is felt to be normal at the head of a sentence in completive responses to questions with *Why* (cf also Quirk et al. 1972:752). As a sub-set of *So* there is also *So that*—these are classifiable together semantically, but the occurrence of the latter (a subordinating conjunction) at the head of a sentence is a sign of an atactic construction. The chances of finding cohesion between atactic constructions with *Because* or *So that* and the immediately preceding clause (= previous sentence) are much greater than in the case of sentences with *For* or *So*. Partly because of the programming of our expectations by syntax, we also customarily read *Because* and *So that* as signalling logical relations more explicitly, forcefully and specifically (*Because* signals reason more transparently than *For; So that* necessarily signals result or intention: *So* does not).

I have already demonstrated how discourse markers (mainly conjuncts and disjuncts with cohesive force) can function as indices to figural consciousness, their relative occurrence being character-specific. Reference has also been made to the figurally focused, illative conjunct *So,* which maintains cohesion after gnomic sentences. The statistical occurrence of such overt connectors cannot

---

[1] The concept of ataxis is discussed in detail in section II of this chapter. Previous narratological analysis of such sentence-initial cohesion has been limited to isolated observations on the occurrence of *So* (see note 9 below, on Heseltine 1963b) and *For*. Banfield (1978a:292; 1982:66/288.*n*1) supplies a transformation test (embedding after a reporting clause with *that*) to show that sentences beginning with *For* in *Mrs Dalloway* are attributable to Mrs Dalloway's consciousness and not to a narrator's. Banfield agrees with David Daiches' observation that the purpose of *For* in Woolf's style "is to indicate the vague, pseudo-logical connection between the different sections of a reverie" (Daiches 1960:209), but disagrees with his view that it is "the author's conjunction (not the thinker's)".

prove the presence of figural discourse; but their existence in *The Solid Mandala* (and in White's other fiction) needs to be measured against the preference in modern fiction for "inferred linkage", or simple juxtaposition, reflecting the general reliance on inference in the interpretation of fictional texts.[2]

FOR/ BECAUSE

With *For*-sentences, Arthur's narrative tends to mediate relationships (cause, including reason or motive) more formally, and with an appeal to self-evident truth; 70% of the *For*-sentences occur in Section 3 (six times more frequently than in Waldo's section). By contrast, one senses in Waldo's narrative a certain urgency about arguing for the truth of assertions: atactic *Because*-constructions foreground the provision of reasons and are stronger cohesive markers; 80% of the *Because*-sentences occur in Section 2 (twice as frequently as in Arthur's section).

Linguistic discussions of conjuncts and conjunctions focus on examples which reveal clearly the anaphoric or cataphoric relations in question: it is not difficult to analyze the content of statements to explain why a particular connector has been used. Grammatical linkage in imaginative prose is usually corroborated by lexical cohesion. For example, in the following four extracts from Conrad, the presence of the linking conjunction *For* is justified by its coreference with lexico-semantic details. In the second example, where the *For*-sentence is unequivocally non-focalized, coreference is deducible from the associative, psychological or supplementive accord between the fear of pain and tenderness of soul; in the others, lexical items are identical or paraphrastic:

Old Giorgio, coming out, did not seem to be surprised at the intelligence as much as she had *vaguely feared*. For she was full of *inexplicable fear* now—... [*Nostromo*, III.12]

She was afraid of betraying herself. She was *afraid of pain, of bodily harm* ... and witnessing violence. For her *soul was light and tender* with a pagan sincerity in its impulses. [*Nostromo*, III.13]

He had *exaggerated* the strength of their fury and the length of their arm ... *too often to have many illusions* one way or the other. For to *exaggerate* with *judgement* one must begin by *measuring with nicety*. [*The Secret Agent*, ch. 11]

Except for the fact that Mrs Verloc breathed these two would have been perfectly in accord: that accord of prudent reserve without superfluous words, and sparing of signs, which had been the foundation of their *respectable* home life. For it had been *respectable* ... [*The Secret Agent*, ch. 11]

Such tight lexical cohesion with *For*-sentences is untypical of *The Solid Mandala;* the following does, however, exemplify it: "Arthur was looking old, but seemed *the younger* for a certain strength. *Or lamplight.* For lamplight rinses the smoother, the more innocent faces, making them *even more innocent and*

---

2 The preference for inferred linkage is so pervasive in such masterpieces of stream of consciousness as *Ulysses* that the high degree of logical articulation in a novel like Beckett's *Watt* can readily be seen as a form of overdetermination reflecting the psychological and philosophical preoccupations of the eponymous character (see Leech 1981:250–53 for analysis of these novels and for a discussion of (in)explicitness).

smooth" (W208). "Lamplight" is provided with a support-system of other correspondences (also italicized here) which can be established by the reader only inferentially. *For* also stands at the boundary between distinct mediative styles: the atactic sentence is succeeded by a well-articulated gnomic statement. But for whose benefit, and by whom, is a motive established via *For?* It is surely Waldo, explaining to himself in as controlled and general a manner as possible why the lamplight should falsify his brother's appearance. The *For*–sentence doesn't represent Waldo's mental attempt, while observing Arthur, to explain what he sees; it represents, rather, Waldo's retreat from his first apperception ("a certain strength"), which he finds intolerable, into gnomic generalization. *For* signals the onset of a factitious justification imputing factitiousness: Waldo's thoughts, but not the issue of an act of perception. Hence the sudden (atactic) pouncing on the alternative explanation that offers itself.

In other apparently simple cases where the reader unquestioningly accedes to the functional presence of *For*, the scope of cohesion and the implications of the logical connection can vary considerably: "He would have liked to throw the hand off, but was afraid of disturbing Uncle Charlie's thoughts. For his fingers were thoughtful as his voice increased" (A217). The *For*–sentence "explains" not just Arthur's being "afraid" but also his tactile intuition that Charlie's "thoughts" are expressed through the fingers resting on his neck. Although the sentence-structure is serene (like Charlie's voice and the motion of his fingers), there is overdetermination through semantic parallels and contrasts. *For* helps mediate this uneasiness in Arthur's mind about the threatening strength behind Uncle Charlie's dreamy gentleness, and about his being immobilized by this almost hypnotic caress. Arthur's perceptions are inseparable from his stifled reactions to them. *For* is present here because it performs a task that inferred linkage (omission of a connector, with or without the use of cohesive punctuation such as dash or semi-colon) cannot perform: it establishes the serene inexorability of the situation.

For can mark a shift in a character's focus of perception rather than simply "motivating" a phrase—as in the following, where the italicized words serve as the fulcrum of such a shift in perception: "Her breasts two golden puddings, stirred to *gentle activity*. For Mrs Poulter was washing her armpits at the white porcelain ... basin" (W61). Here, "stirred" is the barest signal that Mrs Poulter's breasts are not moving of their own accord: the ultimate agent of their "activity" is not in Waldo's narrow field of rapt focus at this stage. A narrowing of focus can be quite abrupt, involving a shift from seemingly objective perception to mental inference: "Waldo couldn't help noticing her knees, because her skirt was drawn up higher than usual, exposing the coarse calves which filled her black stockings. For at least she *wore* mourning" (W150). *For* seems only to establish an objective and logical cohesion; but it really marks Waldo's flight into a feigned moral stance after he is jerked into awareness of his voyeuristic preoccupation. *For* is truly pseudo-logical here, just as the shift of perception is pseudo-natural. Elsewhere, a shift of focus can be signalled by a new paragraph, at the same time as continuity is ensured via *For:*

... he would have liked to counter it with something really good .... He would have to rely on a few ballads to decorate his passable voice.

For he sensed that Mrs Feinstein was about to invite him to take his turn at showing off.

"Don't you in any way perform, Waldo?" [W137]

The *For*-sentence is only pseudo-cohesive. If we took it straight, we would have to conclude that Waldo's resolve is motivated, not by Dulcie's poor performance, but by what he senses in Mrs Feinstein's behaviour before she speaks: ie, the sentence with "would have to rely" would be construed as cohering cataphorically. In fact, shift of focus to the (unreported) expression or gestures of Mrs Feinstein coincides with the confirmation of what Waldo considers is the desirability of his will to sing. Through "For he sensed", we can infer that Waldo, too, has given off strong signals; there is a subtext to the thought about the ballads, and *For* translates Waldo's projection of desire into a wish to read confirmative desire in Mrs Feinstein.

Shift of focus, with or without the subversion of *For* to reflect a duplicitous mental strategy, is seldom apparent outside Waldo's section. In Arthur's narrative, *For* signifies the motivation for assumptions or inferences that are meant to imply calm acceptance of ineluctable truths (eg, A220/230/233/234/244/275/288). "They might never have known each other. For he too was becoming a stranger, in the forbidden doorway" (A288)—here, the *For*-sentence is actually Arthur's explanation (in terms of perception of self) for the use of plural reference in the first statement. We have got used to Arthur's showing awareness of the psychological states of other people, but it is seldom that he is made self-conscious. It is more usual to infer somebody else's condition from one's own. Arthur, by contrast, has become the victim of his own empathy: inescapably so, as the *For*-construction implies.

Atactic sentences beginning with *Because* can establish simple causal relationships in both main narratives. Usually, however, the ataxis foregrounds both the rational and evaluative presentation of a causal nexus and its significance (however uneasily mediated) to the figural consciousness. Separate paragraphing at the *Because*-sentence, though it may indicate a shift in topical focus, emphasizes the subjective and emotive salience of what is being stated (thought). Compare: "His long, bony ... wrist was exposed by the retreating sleeve. Because he was growing too fast" (W74) with: "She ended awkwardly in mid-air. § Because Arthur had gone up too close to her" (W109).[3]

Even when an immediately proximate sentence, or a word or phrase in that sentence, is being glossed by the *Because*-statement, the reader is made to feel that some intermediate psychological complexity is the real referent of the clause of reason: it is the delicate motion of consciousness that is being registered. Most of the *Because*-sentences in Waldo's section are intensifications of this kind of cohesive function—providing, for example, the figural thought underlying a

---

[3] Also (no separation): "Because everything ..." (W64); "Because whatever it was ..." (W73); "Because Mr Brown ..." (W183); "Because this rather confusing oddity ..." (A228); "Because he would not have cared ..." (A239); (paragraph separation:) "Because Arthur seemed ..." (W45); "Because Crankshaw ..." (W166).

speech-act, or a focusing of Waldo's perception.[4] The statement of reason can even be redundant: eg, "Because the piano was the dominant object in the room" (W101); Waldo is aware of the obviousness of asking Dulcie if she can play the piano, and is testing the accuracy of his earlier inference that "The piano was obviously Dulcie's" (W100). The *Because*-sentence often involves a sharpening of attendant emotional awareness, rather than explaining, say, a direct-speech utterance—as with Arthur's confessional self-betrayal, uttered against Waldo's hysterical reading: "Because ... his brother's voice was convincing him of his blasphemy against life" (W293). This is the only such statement in Arthur's discourse, in the climactic phase.

Then

Then-sentences are twice as frequent in Arthur's narrative as in Waldo's. Fewer than 10% are to be found within the paragraph (eg, W39/42/62/105/140, A263/282). The great majority start off a new paragraph, whether as a consequence of an indenting rule after direct speech (38%) or as a diegetic continuation (53%). *Then* thus occurs at the peak of cohesive strength between sentences: customarily sentences on either side of a paragraph division.[5] One of the commonest of time adverbials, *then* is a temporal-boundary adjunct in the contexts being examined here (Quirk et al. 1972:482–84). Simple temporal sequence in modern narratives can easily be left to the reader's powers of inference: sentences, actions, thoughts follow on, in paratactic juxtaposition. Any move to point up sequence is motivated redundancy, usually on the part of a narrator wishing to stress sequentiality. Hence the frequent renunciation of hypotaxis in modernist and postmodern narratives which do not wish to grant primacy to narrators who promote "the illusion of an untroubled surface and an unimpeded development" (Hayman 1981:182).

It cannot be narratorially advantageous in *The Solid Mandala* to point out temporal-sequential relationships at the level of micronarrative action. Even in the few cases where pure sequence seems to be conveyed, the operation of

---

4 For example: "Because Waldo was standing. Still" (W119; causal nexus blurred); "Because fire is the only privacy ..." (W118; disjunctive, attenuated causality: cf Quirk et al. 1972:549–50/752); "Because although ke knew none of it was real, it was" (W44); "Because war was breaking ... out" (W126); "Because at his age ..." (W182); "Because Dad never went to sports" (W33, explaining an analogy derived from vicarious experience); "Because he knew this was something he could not bear to share ..." (W39, rationalizing a harsh spoken refusal); "Because people did not always realize ..." (W53, embarrassed corroboration of Arthur's spoken explanation); "Because in a crisis ..." (W74, rationalizing unexpected spoken encouragement of Arthur); "Because the storekeeper ..." (W37, Waldo rationalizing his father's discomfiting weakness of argument). Such instances are clearer, yet still oblique, in Arthur's narrative: "Because he knew he loved to exhibit himself" (A216); "Because he, not Waldo, was to blame" (A294).

5 This agrees with one of the typical cohesion patterns observed by Halliday: see Gutwinski 1976:130 on Hemingway and James.

figural awareness is involved.[6] The kind of cohesion signalled by *Then* elsewhere is almost invariably a precise mapping of mental reaction. There is never a sequencing of narrative units which are balanced or equivalent in value, intensity or significance, but rather a marking of the boundary between discrete cognitive modes:

> Ridiculous, when not frightening. Waldo would write a play, something quite different, when he had thought of one.
> Then Dad, who had brought the dining-room to light, called from inside: "What about tea, Mother?" [W40]

This example can stand for many passages where it is not even really valid to talk of an action taking place after the mental or physical activity previously represented. Formally, free indirect discourse gives way here to a separately paragraphed, elaborated initial speech-tag and direct speech. Psychologically, action is perceived (Waldo hears his father calling, after—or possibly at some temporal remove from—noticing the light go on) from within introspection. The act of (auditory) perception interrupts (or irrupts into) the flow of thought, and is retrospectively registered as perfectly sequent upon the mental activity that has been curtailed.[7]

The structural principles of altered focus, shift in subjective intensity, and contrast (between thought or speech and perception or motion) are consistently apparent, whatever the differences in analytical detail. Intense activity and/or stasis can be released or broken by motion (W49/66, A294). Tense anticipation can be followed by fulfilment or release of tension through speech or action (W44/62/138/210). Attendant gesture is central to many *Then*–sentences. "Then" suggests figural perception of significant gesture or of a change in gesture or verbal behaviour rather than mere addition.[8] Sometimes the diegesis itself implies that the observing character is trying to scan gesture for its relation to shifts in the intention underlying speech (W109/179). A concentrated act of perception may suddenly give way to a distinct but causally related state of strong or transfigured realization (W207/208, A240/259/267/278). Lastly, personal

---

[6] "It made Arthur giggle. Then Waldo might giggle too" (W42; Waldo's giggle is reactive, never initiatory); "Then there were the mysteries" (W160; ironical awareness that bathos, not "mysteries", will follow); "Then Mother's:" (A270; the atactic shorthand of Arthur's expectant investment in what his mother will reply).

[7] Free indirect discourse followed by a shift to perception of externals can be found at W190 (Waldo thinks, while observing, then is wholly engrossed in visual observation), W64 (Waldo pulls himself out of emotional introspection in order to answer Dulcie's question—a question posed two paragraphs back but, in real time, a second before; *Then* coheres both psychologically and textually), W70 (reflection on literary activity gives way to sudden immersion in visual perception), A239 (one level of thought gives way to another, and to physical gesture), A244 (desire for action, expressed abstractly in free indirect discourse, gives way to implied perception of action: ie, desire fulfilled). See also A294 ("Then Waldo ..."), P308 ("Then, on a street corner ...").

[8] Examples can be found at: W36/39/88/147/154, A239/242/254/271/276/277/283, P310. Emotional vocal reaction may be triggered off by subjectivized perception (implicit in "scenic" direct speech; explicit in free indirect discourse; W147/169/208/212).

emotion (in the form of positive anticipation) may be betrayed by perceived reality (W181/184, A253).

What lies at the basis of all these *Then*-sentences in their relation to immediate context is the dramatic pointing of the mechanics of figural consciousness. There are passages, too, where cohesive conjunction is clearly a formal foregrounding device, given the presence of, say, such adverbs as "suddenly" or "again", which would normally provide enough cohesion in themselves (W170/203, A215/238). Sequencing with *Then* provides an unambiguous frame for the subjectivizing progressive aspect (W62/67/140/208, A255), where the presence of an adverb like "suddenly" is less significant (W153, A283). Subtle perspectival overlaps (balancing a character's subjective involvement with his own speech or actions against awareness of the incursive presence of someone else) are achieved through the co-occurrence of *Then*-sequencing and the past perfect (W39/154, A288). As with other forms of grammatical cohesion, *Then*-sentences in *The Solid Mandala* issue simple signals to the reader to mark relationships—without, however, these relationships (which are not just temporal but subjective apprehensions of time, sequence and causality) being explicitly presented to him. These signals are invitations to inference—to the reconstitution of mental processes on the basis of the merest traces, in words, of their preverbal configurations.

SO

Like White's other connectives, *So* is cohesive in the way in which it performs a switching function at the transition-point between two levels, phases or states of figural consciousness.[9] Connections are not made analytically explicit, just as consciousness "knows" pre-analytically or pre-rationally that causality has made its presence felt. In White, the subjective amplitude of perception and cognition is constantly understated. Through linkage, the reader is alerted to connections, true: but he must still sift psychological clues, as though linkage were only inferred. An instructive contrast is offered by the prose of Swift, where, as Louis Milic (1967) has convincingly demonstrated, connectives (*for, but,* etc) are used irregularly—even speciously—to conjure up through hypotaxis an impression of rhetorical persuasiveness, even though the logical clarity of the argument makes such connectives wholly redundant and even misleading. Swift communicates for effect by grammatical overdetermination. In terms of grammatical cohesion, White's connectives underdetermine relations that are psychologically crucial. At

---

[9] Heseltine (1963b:73) has drawn attention to the fact that "One of the most frequently recurring of White's incomplete sentences is the result-clause introduced by the conjunction 'So'". He handles what is primarily a matter of syntax (what I term ataxis) as "oddity of structure" or "eccentric" punctuation. Be that as it may: Heseltine rightly indicates the effect of the technique in suggesting the importance of the "individual moment" in experiential continuity, though he does not say for whom it is important. Importantly, Heseltine adds that "consequences in White's world" "are less logical than emotional". Emotion does indeed predominate: but the relationship between logic and emotion is more subtle than this, as the persistence of specific connectors and atactic sentence-structure suggests.

the same time, compensation is offered by other formal means, such as the visual salience of separate paragraphing (almost 80% of the *So*-sentences in *The Solid Mandala* appear at the start of a new paragraph).

In White's novel, statements introduced by *So* tend to drag along in their wake an interlacing of a character's perceptions of his physical situation and the introspection prompted by that situation (eg, "So he sat ...", W54; "So that in the end ...", W79). *So*-sentences (and, even more strongly, atactic sentences with *So that)* are also the simplest way of suggesting the ineluctable nature of emotional reactions: the victim is ensnared in a primal logic beyond rational control (eg, "So he went away ...", W47; "So he ran ...", P305). This holds true even when an action seems only to be a reaction to physical sensation ("So he stood up", W213); and the patterned sequencing of paragraphs or sentences beginning with *So* foregrounds the sense of stunned entrapment in circumstance (W72/208).

So can encode the otherwise unexpressed mental decision, leading to action, which is prompted by the unanalyzed implications of immediately prior direct speech ("So they turned", W69; W112/129/211). In Arthur's section, the issue in action is usually more explicit (eg, "So he crawled ...", A264). This is also true of *So*-sentences linking direct speech to Arthur's interpretation of it ("So Arthur Brown realised ...", A226) or to his resolve to act ("So Arthur had to tell Mrs Poulter", A256). It is as though Arthur were conscious, whenever he encounters situations requiring rational decisions, of his sheer achievement in making the right logical step. Mental preparation for action in Waldo's case is, by contrast, more strongly influenced by hidden depths of calculation and implication (eg, "So there was nothing for it but to go", W210). *So* may indicate that a character has perceived a gesture as confirming, or about to confirm, an inference (often in free indirect discourse) made on the basis of his perception of prior behaviour (eg, "So Dad wet his lips", W34). In such cases, the function of *So* as a nexus for both anaphoric and cataphoric reference corresponds to the partial resolution of psychological tension (cf also Waldo's perception of Saporta's role in filling the tense silence created by Dulcie, W66, and Waldo's dinner-table fantasy, W31).

Cohesion is usually more complex than this. Mr Brown comments on Waldo's birth-defect, and the statement "So Waldo grew delicately in the beginning" (W32) looks like a simple confirmation of causal implications. But it is actually a covert admission of Waldo's hypochondriacal response to parental solicitude. Parataxis (the delayed revelation of the next sentence, "It was expected of him") and the polyvalency of *So* ensure that the representation of Waldo's behaviour is protected from evaluative analysis. "So he said now: 'Wait, Mother. Let me see to it'" (W72)—the initial tag here encodes the issue, in a resolve to speak, of Waldo's appraisal of (a) the tenor of what his mother has said, (b) the tone in which she speaks, and (c) his own capacity to react self-protectively in tense situations. The force of *So* is only established by hindsight, after we have read the next paragraph, with its thicket of references to self-conscious role-playing. At a first reading, we are likely to take *So* only as indicating resumption; we can take in Waldo's decision to help out his mother, but we cannot immediately see how his decision is, in effect, to dissimulate. The layering of figural motivation that is made possible by multiple coreference is also seen in Arthur's reaction to seeing Waldo in the blue dress:

> Oh he might have cried, if he hadn't laughed, through the beads and roses, at himself, in Waldo's blue dress. Bursting out of it. His breasts were itching.
> So Arthur had begun to scratch, and call. [A291]

This passage is suffused with indices to figural consciousness. Superficially, *So* links sensation ("itching") to reaction ("scratch"). Beyond this, however, is another linkage—between Arthur's uncontrollable gasp of laughter (reinforced by the equivocal "Bursting" to blend his perception of Waldo with his empathetic identification with him) and "call". Arthur calls to the dogs in order to mislead Waldo about the motivation for his laughter; this decision to conceal is too rapid for analysis—and the concealment is encoded in the sentence structure: all we have is *So,* and the chiastic distancing of motivational elements (laugh/call) from each other. (Cf the double cohesion of *So* in another situation of concealment, A238.)

Figural realization of the personal significance of perceived gesture or situation is conveyed more explicitly in Arthur's section ("So Arthur knew he was dismissed", A237) than in Waldo's ("So Waldo was in the position of a stranger", W34). *So* may link action to a mental plan of action, usually conveyed in free indirect discourse (eg, W142/183/209; A230/265). It may link action or reaction to a process of inference in free indirect discourse or to a specific perception of gesture.[10] Or introspection in free indirect discourse may, via a *So*-link, be represented as conditioning an action which has continued, as it were, throughout the introspective phase: linkage is both broadly resumptive and narrowly causal.[11] There are, of course, cases where *So*-sentences seem primarily to fulfil conventional narrative functions, such as establishing simple logical connection (eg, "So the first ...", W69; "So he learned", W75; W70/89/127/182/187/188/215; P305). But such instances are so outweighed by cohesive markers that are indubitably psychologizing in function that statements of simple logicality tend also to be attributable to figural consciousness.

There is one area where subjectivity seems, at first glance, not to be the point at issue: passages where linkage with *So* initiates a kind of restatement, and diegesis proceeds at a general (iterative) level of discourse after a specific

---

[10] "So Waldo kept quiet" (W149); "So Waldo slowed" (W119); "So at least dotty old Arthur kept quiet" (W171); "So Waldo in turn grew sly" (W179); "So towards evening ..." (W208); "So he went away" (P309); W192, A220/255/249.

[11] "So Waldo stalked" (W56); "So Waldo Brown decided ..." (W115); "So Waldo raced" (W118); "So it was only natural ..." (W189); "So when Waldo stared ..." (A224); "So Arthur had to go carefully" (A230); "So he trembled" (A243). This also applies even more subtly at P309, where the sentence "So the drowsily revolving wheels ... carried him back" not only continues on from "he decided to take the train back", but also allows Arthur's represented thoughts about Mrs Poulter in between to be located as both preliminary to the journey (= the motivation for his decision) and as expressed on the train and bus journey. Cf a similar but more radical "dissolve" or superimposition of thought and situation via *So* at A248, where Arthur thinks about the pierrot-music at the shop and on the tram.

(punctual) instance of a generally obtaining situation. The relationship between the specific and the general is thus temporally broad in scope.

1) She used to sit on the front veranda, twisting the wedding-ring on her finger. It was pleasant for all of them to be together there, particularly after the southerly had come. (2) Once when the southerly was blowing, Dad jerked his head in the direction of the wind, and said "Just about the cheapest fulfilment of anybody's expectations." (3) It was the kind of remark which appealed to Mother. For touches like that she had Married Beneath Her.

(4) So the boys were taught to wait for the southerly .... [W35]

In this example, there is (1) an iterative beginning, followed by (2) the narration of a specific scene, followed by (3) two general evaluative sentences which could be taken as Waldo's thoughts either on the spot or in retrospect. It is obvious that there is an expansion of the narrative horizon with the onset of the new paragraph: but what is the precise function of *So?* Does it mean "And in this way" or "Through such remarks of Dad's"? This would be to argue for proximal cohesion—although (3) actually interrupts the direct line of cohesion, which would be with (2). Yet proximal or semi-proximal cohesion cannot account for the total signification of (4). "Taught to wait" also relates to the second sentence of (1); it is the pleasantness of noncommittal togetherness, especially under the soothing influence of the southerly, that conditions the boys to wait for the release offered by the wind. Their father's words articulate a kind of confirmation of this, but the anecdote is filtered through Waldo's point of view so ironically and condescendingly that (2) and (3) must be regarded as an inset, loosely related to the main line of cohesion. *So* is therefore resumptive, moving the narrative forwards again on a broad causal base. A similar shift in temporal focus on a vaguely subjective basis of causal connection is found elsewhere in the novel, and can be said to be an important stylistic means of structuring the discourse.[12]

II   Ataxis and the rhythms of consciousness

GENERAL CONSIDERATIONS

As I have already indicated, many critics have drawn attention to White's broken, staccato, jerky, truncated sentences or syntax; none, to my knowledge, has analyzed, explained or justified the effects of this syntax convincingly in terms of the requirements of a given narrative; the chief effect, it seems, has been on the critics, who have reacted with aesthetic irritation or bafflement. Analysis of Section 1 of *The Solid Mandala* reveals a small number of such sentences. They may be free-standing coordinate clauses (eg, "But she did not comment"; "And Mrs Dun could feel it"; "When suddenly she seized her companion ..."). They may be complex sentences, usually biclausal ("When the

---

12 "So they moved through the landscape of boyhood" (W75); "So the lives of the brothers fused ..." (W81); "So Waldo continued remembering" (W106); "So he continued living too far" (W126); "So he got to resent Mrs Poulter" (W186); "So that before very long they were living ..." (A223); "So, it was not so much ..." (A274); cf. also: "So, they were retired" (W204), "So Arthur retired" (A286).

sight of his hands ... would rend her, and she would ..."; "But one was the
leader, she could sense"; "And Mrs Poulter lightly touched the white chrysanths
she was protecting ..."). There are free-standing subordinate clauses ("Like that
blood-pressure thing was on your arm"). There are free-standing coordinate or
subordinate clauses with subject-ellipsis ("But barely giggled"; "As if hoping to
confirm something"), and subjectless or verbless clauses ("Often got it, too";
"Creating in the bus"; "The Mr Browns, for instance"). In Section 1 there are, in
all, some 17 sentences (out of a diegetic total of 145) which are graphologically
disjunctive in this way, but formally conjunctive.

This observation needs to be considered in relation to White's mediation of
narrative information in terms of quantity (sentence-length) and complexity
(sentence-structure). In White's fiction generally, there is a tendency towards
balanced narratorial extremism. He scrupulously avoids close approximations in
lexical length between adjacent sentences; my statistical analysis of three-page
segments from various of his novels shows that this principle of sequential
contrast is set aside in no more than about 5% of the sentence groupings.
Moreover, this involves an avoidance of the mean or average at two levels of
organization. At the level of paragraphing, up to one-quarter of White's diegetic
sentences appear singly between dialogue-segments; irrespective of the presence
or absence of direct speech, up to 35% of White's diegesis appears in graphically
isolated paragraphs of no more than one or two sentences. At the sentential level,
there is a preponderance (in some novels, up to 40%) of "short" sentences (from
one to nine words), offset by "long" sentences worthy of a Conrad or a James.
Unlike the sentences of the latter writers, however, White's longer sentences do
not correlate highly with syntactic complexity; very few go any deeper than two
degrees of subordination. Quantitative complexity is thus generally offset by an
avoidance of conspicuous syntactic complexity—there is a tendency to avoid
discoursal patterns that might betray the heavy narratorial hand of the structuring
analyst. At the other end of the scale, lexical simplicity or brevity at the sentence
level is offset by a prevalence of conspicuous pseudo-coordination of the kinds
exemplified above—there is, then, a narratorial engagement in analytical
structuring, but the notion of "analysis" (to loosen again or undo) is made to
show in the sentence structure. What is at issue here are the principles governing
the syntactic organization of linear information. This is central to questions of
White's verbal style, and warrants a brief linguistic excursus at this juncture.[13]

In verbal communication, given information (theme or topic) normally
precedes new information (rheme or comment); with the latter, the principle of
end-focus is paramount. New information is characterized phonologically by
nuclear stress, syntactically by (end-)focus. Tonal and informational units (or
segments) can be indicated graphemically by punctuation marks. In a sentence
with a number of syntactic units, relations of salience are thus punctuatively
regulated. The full stop closes a sentential pattern of segmentations which, under

---

[13] The following summary has been synthesized from various sources: Strang 1968:195;
Turner 1973:70–75; Leech 1981:210–30; Halliday 1970:160–64; Ducrot/Todorov 1981:271).

normal circumstances, are semantically interactive. Thus, to break up with full stops sentences which are normally "coherent" is to emphasize the independent informational status of the segment(s) so separated. What comes just before the full stop takes end-focus. It is a technique which generates maximum salience.

In minimal, chiefly monoclausal sentences, each clause is as important as the clauses in neighbouring sentences, and it is ordering or sequence that we must rely on to determine the significance of the whole. Neither segmentation nor salience are manipulable variables in such sentences. In complex sentences, coordination is of course sequential; but the combination of segmental linkage by punctuation (inferred linkage) and by conjunction (overt linkage) smooths away segmental salience to orientate all information towards a single end-focus. Whatever the mental source in consciousness of that which is enunciated, we take this ordering of information as a sign of the presence of a relativizing consciousness. Subordination generates salience hierarchically through syntax, creating a relationship of foreground and background (subordination; dependence), treating some information as presupposed or predictable. Consider the following hierarchy of simple informative sentences:

1. John jumps. He runs. He can't walk.
   (Parataxis. Independence. Juxtaposition. Three end-foci.)
2. John jumps; he runs; he's quite an athlete.
   (Parataxis. Independence. Inferred, punctuative linkage. One end-focus.)
3. John jumps; indeed, he runs; he can't walk, though.
   (Parataxis. Independence. Punctuative and adverbial linkage = interclausal or intrasentential cohesion. One end-focus.)
4. John jumps. Indeed, he runs. Yet he can't walk.
   (Parataxis. Independence. Adverbial linkage = intersentential cohesion. One end-focus.)
5. John jumps and runs, but he can't walk.
   (Coordination. Medial status. Conjunctive and punctuative linkage = intrasentential cohesion. One end-focus.)
6. John jumps and runs, although he can't walk.
   (Hypotaxis. Dependence. Conjunctive and selectively punctuative linkage = intrasentential cohesion. Subordinated end-focus.)
7. Although John jumps and runs, he can't walk.
   (As for 6, but with subordinated theme.)

It should be clear from these seven variously processed statements that the following is difficult to place within the rough hierarchy:

8. John jumps. And (he) runs. But (he) can't walk.
   (Parataxis or graphemic disjunction. Independence. Juxtaposition. Three end-foci.)
   (Coordination or intersentential conjunction. Independence. Intersentential cohesion. One end-focus or rheme semantically; three end-foci syntactically.)

Let me re-state what is involved here. Non-finite clauses, and finite clauses (as in example 8 above) which would normally be in a dependence-relation to a preceding main clause, are isolated graphemically. Their quantum of information is thus granted a salience which pulls against our expectation that markers of coordination or subordination are there to relativize the information conveyed. Otherwise well-formed finite clauses beginning with a coordinating conjunction or a subordinator are deemed normal in modern linguistic classification, irrespective of whether they occur in speech or in writing.[14] It is thus not unusual in literary prose to encounter occasional instances of this sentence-structure, which can even become a verbal tic in such writers as Faulkner or Lawrence. In terms of sentence-connection, neither *and* nor *but* nor *when* (= *and then*) causes us any difficulty during the reading-process, "despite a tradition of prescriptive teaching against the practice" of starting sentences in this way (Quirk et al. 1972:661). All that needs to be noted at this stage is that *and* and *but* are the vaguest of connectors: two ideas have a positive or adversative connection, and it is up to the reader to find out what that connection is. "The implications of the combination vary and they depend on our presuppositions and our knowledge of the world" (Quirk et al. 1972:560). As the "world" we have knowledge of is a fictive world, these sentence conjunctions are the barest signals to us to reconstruct otherwise implicit relationships of causal and temporal sequence, contrast, commentary, concession, condition, resemblance, plain congruence, unexpectedness or affirmation. Such sentences abound in *The Solid Mandala*. In some instances, it is hard to see how else a sentence could be related to immediately preceding elements (by using adverbial conjuncts, for instance) without upsetting the delicate balance of equal focus on an "envelope" of direct speech and a single intervening diegetic sentence.[15]

The maintenance of a relentless equilibrium of significance is often central to narrativity in White's fiction. If the principle of end-focus operates most clearly at the level of the simple sentence, then several end-foci are present in more complicated structures (cf the example sentences above). As with intonation, however, closure (marked in speech by a falling tone) is important: as we read, we expect sentential climax or something like a "final end-focus" with the completion of information (or comment). Persistent parataxis generates persistent closure and a feeling that climax has not been worked for. Hypotaxis and multiple coordination mean delayed closure and the generation of climax. Simple coordination has an intermediate status, depending on semantic circumstance. It is normal to expect closure, but minimal climax can so often be felt at the clausal level that matter-of-factness and predictability are built into such coordination. Hence punctuation marking finality or closure (the full stop) in what would normally be coordinated or subordinated sentences tends to introduce climax into (or increase the independent salience of) clausal segments which would otherwise be non-final. The result is that the reader senses a tension between the significant

---

[14] In which case, speech carries a distinctive intonational superfix, and writing a sentence-break: "She promised to come ... But I don't rely on it ... Although you never know" (example from Strang 1968).

[15] Cf the straightforward instances in Section 1: "But a sadness was moistening Mrs Poulter" (B12–13); "And Mrs Poulter lightly touched ..." (B16); "When the sight of his hands ..." (B18).

(the formal granting of salience via disjunction) and the self-evident (the "entropic" effect of frequent clausal climax).

We cannot speak here of the presence of *parataxis* proper (a total absence of formal grammatical linkage, coordinative or subordinative) or of *hypotaxis* proper (formal linkage between clauses, together with punctuative continuity). It might be useful to refer to these other sentences as being *atactic* (formal markers of grammatical linkage being defeated by separative punctuation). The term *ataxis* was first used by Bernhard Fehr (1938:103–104) to characterize "Substitutionary Perception". His examples are of straightforward connectorless sentences, and he contrasts "ataxis" with "syntaxis"—but he means, in effect, parataxis, in contrast to hypotaxis, and nothing more radical. The term "ataxis" was revived by Bonheim (1982:65) with reference to "syntactic fragments" only: "the kind ... which are thought to go through one's head when one thinks", and which are thus characteristic of narrated monologue. Atactic structures in these senses would, I presume, range from well-formed, finite sentences (Fehr) to single words and extensive or extended non-finite sentences (Bonheim). Let "ataxis" cover all three categories defined here; combine the essentially psychological justification for their presence with the essentially functional explanation of their communicative impact; and it is easy enough to see why White should employ atactic sentences so pervasively in fiction whose central concern is to represent the pulse and emphases of figural consciousness.

ATAXIS IN ACTION

Because ataxis is so prevalent in *The Solid Mandala,* I can do no more than indicate, by way of brief analyses of representative passages, how subtly and precisely White orchestrates the tonal shifts in mental processes. The reader is probably most receptive to, or accommodating of, ataxis and disjunctive syntax when it is contextually and formally evident that the mode of consciousness being represented is that of wholesale introspection:

1. If it was immoral, then he was immoral. Had been, he supposed, for many years. Perhaps always. The million times he had buried Arthur. But only now, or recently, had he perfected his itinerary of islands. [W116]

In **1**, narrated monologue can be converted directly to quoted monologue (with "I"). The rational equation which is set up self-defensively by Waldo in the first sentence is "well-formed"; but this defence immediately begins to sag with the deletion of pronoun reference in the next sentence: the laconicism is an attempt to cast off the weight of guilt, and it is no longer clear whether Waldo is thinking primarily of himself (|He had been|) or is trying to keep his "vice"—thought of Arthur's death—as a moral category separate or distanced from himself (|It had been|). "He supposed" is not a psychonarrational tag, but a figural parenthesis of concession. The third sentence (which could have been conjoined to the second with a comma or dash) is separate because the realization has its own salience: guilt is pressing home, and peaks in the exclamatory hyperbole and topical explicitness of the fourth sentence. Emotion and confessional self-confrontation, however, are resisted by Waldo's pirouetting away from a near-eternity of past (fratricidal) immorality to a different kind of perfecting in fantasy; his thought turns away at "But", moving forward into a more pleasant projection of the "immoral".

2. No, he would not touch a penny of Arthur's wretched account. He would make it over to that skinny Jew boy Arthur Saporta, with brown flannel patches round his eyes. Whatever Arthur Saporta meant. Beyond the fact that he had his mother Dulcie Feinstein's eyes.

If Arthur Brown died.

But it finally seemed improbable, on that morning or ever, which meant the alternative. Waldo scuttled at the thought. He was still young enough not to believe in his own death. [W117]

The "well-formed" sentences at the start of 2 are coloured by free-indirect indices (ejaculation; projective modals; emotive epithet and deictic), the second closing with a hint at Waldo's mental picture of the boy. The boy's name itself now deflects Waldo's inward attention, as his assumption of all-absolving magnanimity—with Arthur's money!—occurs in connection with resentful recollection of how the Saportas' child was not given his name. The sentence is ambiguous: it is conjoinable with the preceding one if it is concessive in force (|No matter what|), but is disjunctive if interrogative in force (|Whatever did/could ... mean?|). The fourth sentence could be joined by a comma to the third—but that would mean losing the double suspension in Waldo's mind of the name and the boy it is applied to, and the return to further consideration of the eyes. Apart from the segmental, individually salienced chain of thoughts, there are the various continuities between these thoughts; ataxis preserves all of this. There is now a return to a focus on Arthur ("Arthur Brown" distinguishes him from "Arthur Saporta" but also maintains the connection that Waldo so resents). Why the separate paragraphing—is it an abrupt resumption and change of topic? Intensity is clearly being suggested—but motivated by the thought of Dulcie's eyes: a surge of revenge-feelings, to pay back his brother for taking Dulcie from him. The disjunctive adversative opening the next paragraph initiates another change of mental pace and modality—a settling-down, as it were, or resignation to well-formed prose.

3. so that it came as a relief ... to realize that, with such a build, in a year or two, a stroke would probably strike his visitor down.

If visitor he were. And not some busybody of an unidentified colleague. Or blackmailer in search of a prey. Or or, Waldo racked his memory, and was racked. [W187]

Ataxis in 3, from the start of the new paragraph onwards, represents the unnerving of the self: the gloatingly malevolent thoughts preceding are confident and well-formed by comparison. While still anonymous, the visitor is treated as an object, in analytically hypotactic prose. As soon as the possibility of a personal (subjective) connection enters consciousness (the first stirrings of memory), each hypothesis is considered in turn, each with its own stab of emotion, until the stutter of failed syntax at the end.

4. So Arthur decided to say the one or two necessary things, and go. He, who could not help himself, could not have helped his brother now. Arthur is the backward one. That was the way

the relationship had been arranged. Of the twins. The twin brothers. Waldo had wanted it. Waldo is the one who takes the lead. Joining them together at the hand. And because Waldo needed it that way, only the knife could sever it.

Like Mother's breast. [A256]

Arthur's thoughts in **4** include citation of outside views, in keeping with his awareness that he is closing himself out of the scene with Waldo and Dulcie. The sentences having to do with decision, action and self-justification are flowing and well-formed. Arthur's objectivity ("the relationship" deriving from the quoted statement) is continued in the two atactic or absolute sentences that follow—but the non-integration of these formulae follows not so much because the idea of "relationship" is being explained, as because Arthur is investing himself emotionally in more intense consideration of his link with Waldo. Emotion is inferable, if only because the problem raised by the terms Arthur focuses on is that of equality versus difference. Hence the reversion to "rational" syntax with "Waldo had wanted it": Arthur tries to find authority for the inequality imposed on him, but the vague referentiality and brevity of the sentence work against any sense of conviction, and citation has to provide additional, external authority. The sentence following the citation, had it been comma'ed onto the emphasized words, would have constituted Arthur's mental picture of himself and Waldo walking. Disjunction, by contrast, foregrounds the thought, persuading us to see Arthur as recognizing the emblematic implications of that picture: oneness achieved by the external (physical) imposition of superior authority. The "And"–sentence preserves loose cohesion, and moves back in the direction of the "well-formed" rationalization: or, rather, to Arthur's lucid prescience of Waldo's need. Associationism, and a turn to another (but equally emblematic) topic, accounts for the disjunctive, separately paragraphed clause of comparison in free indirect discourse.

Extreme ataxis is also tolerated by readers familiar with modernist narration when what is being represented is perception under subjective stress, rather than thought. In Waldo's terminal condition, just before the extinguishing of vital consciousness, the scenic is the last coherent element in the text—pure tag-less mimesis of speech, signifying full subjective awareness of relationship to the world:

5. He was entranced by Arthur's great marigold of a face beginning to open. Opening. Coming apart. Falling.

"Let me go! Wald! Waldo!"

As dropping. Down. Down. [W214]

The first sentence of **5** is well-formed, psychonarrational. The participial fragments represent successive phases of distorted visual perception, already cut adrift from the set of relationships established in Waldo's consciousness for the last time. After the direct speech, Waldo's effort to "connect" is erased by a falling into self. "As dropping" could mean |Arthur said, as Waldo felt himself falling/dropping down, down, into a bottomless pit|—or something equally banal. Ataxis merges subject and object—already initiated as Waldo's loss of control over visual perspective draws Arthur's face towards him at the same time as (we infer from details in Arthur's narrative) he is actually drawing his brother closer by pulling on his wrist.

The mental processes attendant upon perception are often implied by the iconic representation of action, as in the following example, which is self-explanatory:

6. "Good-evening, Mrs Poulter," Waldo said.
And then stood. Time had stuck for the two of them. [W186]

In 7 below, the clumsy, abrupt angularity of Waldo's "running ahead" (a boy's misconstruction of his father's colloquial invitation) is conveyed by ataxis, which allows for productive ambiguity of resolution:

7. On one occasion Dad said: "You run on ahead, old man. I'll take my time."
And Waldo had. Literally. Spurted up the road on twisting ankles, arms jerking, books thundering in his half-empty case. [W76]

We can reintegrate the clauses thus: | And Waldo had run ahead—literally: [he had] spurted up the road ... | —whereby the verbalization is laconically informal. Or we can view the sentence | And Waldo had literally spurted up the road ... | as having been chopped up—Waldo's self-consciousness jolting the thought (in experienced recollection) into fragments as he runs.

Simple disjunction, coupled with careful dosages of sentence-length, can convey both the nature of observed action and the quality of subjective perception:

8. "Ralph," she said, "was not worth the silver to stand 'im in."
And opening her mouth she cried out, out of the back of her throat, out of her matrimonial past.
But shut up pretty quick. As though she had realized something for the first time.
"Come to think of it," she said, "this other one—this creature—is the dead spit of Ralph!" [A237]

Mrs Musto's cry is not separable from her condemnation of Ralph: the inclusion of "And" marks both the vocal transition and Arthur's perception of the connection between words and gesture. This otherwise well-formed, near-sylleptic sentence is followed by a new paragraph, whose first sentence conveys lexically, grammatically and iconically (ie, in brevity) Arthur's perception of sudden cessation, and in terms of register (a plunge into colloquialism) Arthur's apperception of Mrs Musto dropping her mask of histrionic emotionalism. The clause of comparison is disjunctive: Arthur's effort of interpretation is not smoothly integrated into the act of perception, but is provoked by it. We can imagine a mental hiatus before the onset of reactive speculation. Moreover, it is possible by hindsight (scanning the succeeding direct speech) to see the isolated subordinate clause as cohering both anaphorically and cataphorically: encoding, through its salience, Arthur's anticipation of Mrs Musto's articulation of that "something".

Two passages are concerned with Waldo's perception of Arthur's manipulation of a mandala-marble. In the first, the physical context is Waldo's writing-area, which he would like to have entirely to himself:

9. Mother could be relied on to drop off. But Arthur stuck. Standing by the lamp, head inclined, staring into one of those glass marbles. Watching the revolutions of a glass marble on the palm of his hand.
   "If you have to stay, don't fidget, at least!" Waldo ordered. [W168]

Arthur's prescience runs counter to Waldo's desire: the second sentence shows this through the adversative and the stolid brevity of its structure. Waldo is waiting, and waiting entails temporal process and anticipation: hence the disjunction of Arthur's processual activity, which forms the focus of Waldo's negative fascination. Participial disjunction involves suspension: the actions become absolute, and it is as if Waldo were being mesmerized by the "revolutions" of the marble. The paraphrastic slide from "staring" to "watching", from "one of those glass marbles" to "a glass marble", is an additional index to Waldo's fascination with repetitive suspension. This phase is broken by the act of speech, and by Waldo's reassertion of control ("ordered"). Disjunctive syntax, conversely, had taken over before the initial sentence, which was well-formed in accordance with Waldo's confidence vis-à-vis his mother. The second passage, in which it is the public realm of the library that threatens to be the scene of Waldo's exposure by his brother, similarly has a mantle of well-formed sentences around a core of disjunctive syntax or short sentences:

10. There he sat, exposed, though, under the dismal grease-spots. Munching and mumbling over, of all things, a book. Playing with a glass marble. How it would have crashed, shattering the Public Library. But never smashed. Arthur's glass was indestructible. Only other people broke.
   Having to decide quickly what action to take Waldo pulled out an excruciatingly noisy chair and sat down exactly opposite. [W198]

The first sentence of the first paragraph presents a coherent visual scene in close focus, while the last two are terse—well-formed, yet pregnant with Waldo's obliquely expressed resentment. The next paragraph constitutes a shift from intense perception to resultant action, and the sentence-structure is correspondingly rational, logical, hypotactic, and smoothly flowing. In between, discrete foci of perception are presented: the human agent recedes, and the object of his action (book; marble) takes centre stage. Once again, there is process, waiting, expectation, tenseness; the only intermediate resolution possible is purely notional, in the free-indirect exclamation initiating the train of thought centering on the notion of threatening chaos or disorder. Even Waldo's projective inward exclamation is followed by ataxis ("But never smashed"): by the sudden realization of Arthur's solidity.

The devolution from well-formed to fragmentary sentences correlates not so much with a shift from external narratorial control to the "syntactic fragments ... which are thought to go through one's head when one thinks" (Bonheim), as with a shift from rational control on the part of a character to emotional disequilibrium or to an overlaying or colouring of rational perspective. In the following passage, the first sentence is sophisticated in structure, with accretions of subordination, an inserted conjunct, and punctuative linkage:

11. On fitting his eyes to the slanted slats he couldn't see anything of course, because of the angle; he had more or less expected that before making the attempt. And then the footsteps began approaching along the gravel. From round the side. He stood and waited. [W124]

Waldo is—or would like to be—in control of what he is doing, and is able to quell the incipient embarrassment of seeing nothing by some swift rationalizing. The second sentence, with its blocked coordination, implies that the obtrusion of an alternative focus of perception does not come as a shock: he is too involved still; can register precisely ("the footsteps") what he hears; can place it in time ("began approaching"); but has not fully shifted his attention away from the window. The full, chill shock comes in the third sentence: Waldo's aural antennae are twitching now. The closing sentence is well-formed yet brief: Waldo, in tense anticipation, has (as the full context confirms) given himself over to whatever fate might have in store for him.

Emotional stress or involvement can be signalled more conspicuously by syntax. Contextual clues usually provide the reader with enough information to prepare for such disjunctions—as, for example, when Waldo, in the transvestite scene, is disturbed by the falling lamp:

12. He kicked at the pieces. And went back.
    To the great dress. Obsessed by it. Possessed. His breath went with him, through the tunnel along which he might have been running. Whereas he was again standing. Frozen by what he was about to undertake. [W193]

The break between the paragraphs could arguably be realized in cinematic terms by a change of camera-position. Waldo's half-involvement in the fantasy-projection he has been wrenched out of is indicated by the disjunction between the kicking of the glass fragments and the move back—motion with attenuated awareness of personal agency (no pronoun reference). "Obsessed by it. Possessed" indicates through passive participles, ataxis and pronoun-suppression a total absorption of self by object. The sentence that follows is well-formed: Waldo resurfaces momentarily, long enough to be somatically aware; but the coherence of the sentence essentially reflects the recapture of self in mental motion (the tunnel-metaphor suggests this kind of enclosure, and the tenuousness of "might"). Waldo's apperception of the contrast between the rushing movement he has been lost in and his resultant immobility is conveyed by the pseudo-logical "Whereas" and its caesura; and the last, statal, iconic sentence speaks for itself. Distinct, yet comparable representations of the interrelationship between physical action and attendant emotional state are numerous;[16] and there is an interestingly atactic passage in Arthur's section which ostensibly presents Waldo's transvestite activity from the outside, but which is actually Arthur's empathetic absorption in his twin's identity ("... he might have suffered .... Or stroked his ... moustache", A291).

---

[16] See, for example: "So he went away ... submerged roses" (W47); "'This gate, Waldo' ... And the gate opened. Once again" (W26); "He regretted not being years younger .... As soon as he got back, Mother said:" (W158).

As Arthur's narrative has received less attention so far, I should like to offer as my last example a longish passage from the description of the day Mr Brown is found dead:

13. Waldo by then was running off, away from the house, into the garden. It was much as Arthur had expected.
And finding their father in the dark room. Because touch was his approach. Arthur touched George Brown's head. Before pushing his way through the house. Before bursting out on the classical-tragic veranda.
The words were shouted out of him: "Our father, our father is dead!"
Not that George Brown had done more than withdraw from Arthur a second time. Who would bear it now as before. Perhaps their afflictions, which had caused the withdrawal, helped him to.
Or Waldo's running away.
Soon Waldo was coming back along the path, and Arthur had to control his own unhappiness. [A269]

The first paragraph is brief, hence salient, to mark the high degree of attention Arthur accords to his brother's action (which is framed, via the progressive, within Arthur's sudden, inchoate intuition that something has happened). The first sentence, with its perspectival flow, indicates Arthur's clear perception of movement; there is no tension mediated in the second, which is equally well-formed and marks a calm, cognitive response to an anterior precognition. The next paragraph, however, brings a relativizing of clear perception under pressure from emotion. Cohesion with the previous sentence ("expected") is ensured by "And", but the structure with "finding" cannot be made to conjoin with the preceding one without considerable transformation. In other words, the hint of a connection reflects the melting away of thought of what has been "expected" in the face of the actual discovery ("finding"). The "Because"–sentence does not cohere with the preceding one, either, although we have become conditioned by the narration to expect such atactic sentences to be subordinated to a preceding main clause. There is coextensivity of physical action and heightened emotional state; we can postulate that Arthur locates his father "in the dark room" by touch (indeed—assuming that a pun is present—by "approaching" his father, groping through the dark to touch him). But how, then, was Waldo able to see the dead man through the window? The emotional flurrying of the surface of syntax has perhaps blinded us to the will-o'-the-wisp nature of this paragraph. As in **7**, there is also the possibility of tilting the mirror slightly to get quite a different image: of a single sentence, moving Arthur into the room and out of the house again, but a sentence hacked into fragments of intense, subjectivized perception.

The diastole of consciousness continues, with a return to coherent (passivized) action in coherent syntax (the freshly paragraphed tag and direct speech). The next paragraph reads like implied-auctorial comment—but it need not be seen thus. Arthur has been shown to be acutely aware of his relationship with his father, and as prescient about suffering. He is aware, even in his state of grief-stricken abandon (and certainly in its recall), of what this death means for him. He is trying to regain control over himself by resorting to the broader perspective of memory (a perspective that is, of course, thrust upon him). This seeking of order in abandonment is already heralded before the direct speech in the pun of "bursting out on the classical-tragic veranda", which encodes the simultaneity of both the immediately physical and vocal (Arthur's movement and utterance) and the recollectively vocal (Arthur's declamation of the cow-tragedy of loss before his father on this same "stage"). The middle sentence ("Who would ..."), with its disjunctive relative clause, hints disturbingly at a programmatic stoicism: how deep is this grief? Arthur is, in essence, "showing off", going through the motions of emotion. He must, however, be caught out by his own thoughts—which is just what happens, with the sudden realization that he has the stage to himself because of Waldo's defection. Hence the separate, afterthought paragraphing of the "Or"-sentence. Closing the sequence, the next paragraph reverts to external perception (with a subjective progressive as at the outset), and mirrors Arthur's "control" in its syntax.

Ataxis in *The Solid Mandala* and White's other fiction is not a device for implied-auctorial emphasis; nor is it the reflection of the presence of an empathetic narrator distinct from the characters; nor, finally, is it a means of differentiating one central character or figural consciousness from another. Quite simply, it is the central stylistic device for the representation of mental processes as universal mechanisms. Give or take a shade or two of difference in mentality between Waldo and Arthur, the reactions implicitly registered are those beneath the skin of circumstance, and are common to all. Table 8 (next page) reveals as much.

The relative distribution of individual grammatical markers is nowhere significantly different between the two main narratives, except at **9,** where Arthur tends more to perceive in terms of coordinate relations than does Waldo; at **10(b),** where (as already noted) Waldo rationalizes perceptual relations far more often than Arthur; and at **15,** where Arthur's narrative seems to have three times "more" atactic clusters than Waldo's—although the larger relative figure for Arthur should be compared with the absolute parity obtaining in the narratives, with due consideration of the degree to which such clusters are predetermined by the psychological situations cast up by the plot. Of particular note (in view of the earlier discussion of narrative cohesion) is the group of statistics at **16–19.** Comparatively few of the disjunctive sentence-types listed occur after direct speech with automatic indenting. The extra salience effected by separate paragraphing almost always coincides with contexts in which a greater intensity of emotive coloration is present than when such sentences occur within a paragraph. From 40% to 100% of the most straightforward of all cohesive markers in narrative (covering addition, contrast, interruption, and temporal subordination) start off new paragraphs in this novel. A calm, even cold, maintenance of formal control over logical relations ensures the surface continuity of discourse; but this continuity is simultaneously relativized by the dramatization of disjunction through graphical separation. It is nowhere more apparent than at these paragraph junctures that shifts in the direction and intensity of narrative discourse are identifiable with analogous shifts in figural consciousness.

Table 8: Distribution of disjunctive or atactic sentences

A: SENTENCES STANDING SINGLY (PARAGRAPH)
OR AMIDST "WELL-FORMED" SENTENCES

1. And + SV	W	44	.23
	A	26	.30
2. But + SV	W	82	.43
	A	39	.45
3. Conjunctive **When** + SV	W	9	.05
	A	6	.07
4. And + V	W	10	.05
	A	2	.02
5. But + V	W	11	.05
	A	1	.01
6. And + V-less phrase	W	9	.04
	A	2	.02
7. But + V-less phrase	W	4	.02
	A	1	.01
8. Or/Nor + SV/S/V	W	14/8	.07
	A	5/3	.05
9. Total with And/But	W	63/97	.33/.51
	A	37/41	.43/.48
10. Adverbial clauses			
(a) of time	W	19	.1
	A	15	.17
(b) of reason	W	21	.11
	A	5	.05
(c) of concession	W	7	.04
	A	8	.09
(d) others	W	14	.07
	A	8	.09
11. Total adverbial clauses	W	61	.32
	A	36	.42
12. Total single sentences	W	271	1.42
	A	154	1.81

B: CLUSTERS OF DISJUNCTIVE OR ATACTIC SENTENCES

13. 2 sentences	W	33	.17
	A	13	.15
14. 3 sentences	W	11	.05
	A	6	.07
15. More than 3 sentences	W	6	.03
	A	7	.08

C: SOME CONSTRUCTIONS BEGINNING PARAGRAPHS

16. And	W	36	57%
	A	19	51%
17. But	W	42	43%
	A	32	78%
18. When	W	8	89%
	A	6	100%
19. Clauses of time	W	8	42%
	A	11	73%

NOTE: The narrative sections concerning subsidiary characters have not been included, as the figures for each category are too small to allow reliable comparison. The figures for Waldo's narrative (W) are calculated against a spread of 190 pages, Arthur's (A) against a spread of 85 pages. Decimal figures represent number of occurrences per page of the relevant section. **16–19** are percentages of the occurrence of these constructions within the total for each narrative. Conjunctive **When** = "And then".

11

STYLE AT THE INTERFACE:
SPEECH-TAGS[1]

I   General formal considerations

I have occasionally mentioned speech-tags (ie, at their simplest, the "he said" bits that follow or precede direct speech) in earlier chapters—for example, with reference to "minimal or notional" auctorial presence in speech-reporting, and to "un-tagged" or purely "scenic" representations of speech (ch. 6, ch. 9); in a transferred sense, there are also "tags" indicating mental operations ("he suspected") in narrative contexts of indirect discourse (ch. 7). In most cases, however, speech-tags have not been examined in their own right, but have been regarded as of indexical value in determining the presence of other features of narrative discourse (eg, in ch. 10).

But one cannot read far into *The Solid Mandala* (or any other novel by White) without being struck by the fact that a great number of the speech-tags encountered in direct-speech contexts are ironically weighted in some way, and/or may leave an impression of being in some respect "deviant". I have picked out a few such tags from my analytical corpus for *The Solid Mandala*. Can they be grouped at all in a general way, if only to point out *what* might be unusual about them?

1 As he shouted: (A273)
2 Then Waldo punching. Waldo shouting. (A231)
3 Only Arthur grumbling: (W166)
4 Muttering still: (W211)
5 Then Mother's: (A270)
6 "——" Waldo's voice was reading very loudly, deliberately blaspheming, "——." (A293)
7 "——?" was Mrs Poulter's argument. (W166)
8 "——," he dared, "——?" (W165)
9 "——," Waldo felt himself compelled. (W123)
10 Arthur told quietly after that, but told: (W144)
11 He continued babbling, he heard: (A244)
12 When Waldo overheard: ((W193)
13 "——?" Waldo heard. (W53)
14 "——," Mother was daring herself to speak, "——." (W40)
15 "——," her sister improved on it, but faintly. (W49)
16 "——," Dulcie paused. (W152)

---

[1] A fuller version of this chapter has appeared in *REAL: The Yearbook of Research in English and American Literature* 8 [1991/92] (Tübingen: Gunter Narr, 1992).

17 "——," Arthur smiled, "——." (W115)
18 "——," Arthur yawned. (W175)
19 "——," Mrs Poulter/she[/he] coaxed. (B20/W160/[W143])
20 "——," he reassured. (W40)
21 "——," he[/Waldo] reminded. (A251/[W114])
22 "——," Arthur corrected. (W53)
23 "——," Waldo[/Crankshaw] offered. (W143/[W176])
24 "——," Mrs Poulter became of the opinion. (W167)
25 "——," Arthur was struggling, kneading with his hands, "——." (W207)
26 "——?" Waldo felt it was required of him to ask ——. (W128)
27 "——," Waldo felt he ought to say. (W151)
28 "——," he dwindled. (W63)
29 "——?" Dulcie finished laughing, and asked. (W134)
30 "——," she recovered herself and added. (W155)
31 When she was again free, she blurted: "——." (B14)
32 "——," he would grumble, and then regurgitate: "——!" (B18)
33 "——?" Waldo tried not to shout. (W113)
34 "——," Waldo did not exactly gasp. (W65)
35 "——," he didn't shout.
36 "Don't catch *me*!" Mrs Dun decided. (B20)
37 "——," he decided at last. (W23)
38 "——," Mother was trying to persuade. (W46)

There are speech-act verbs in atactic structures (1–4)—but it is the ataxis rather than the tag-position or the tag-verb that draws attention to itself. There is ellipsis of the speech-act verb (8–9) or the speech-act tag; or we find ataxis plus ellipsis of a noun-phrase equivalent of a speech-act verb (5^2). The tag subject may be synecdochically shifted from the actant to the voice (5–6), or from the actant to a noun-complement of the direct speech itself (7). We feel the lack of a personal indirect object with "tell" in 10. In 12–13, there is no speech-act tag, but a tag of audition (ie, with ellipsis of the speech-actant object [Arthur say]). In 11, there is a teasing double relationship: is "he heard" an asyndetic tag of audition, or is "He continued babbling" the initial tag and "he heard" a parenthetical comment or postposed head ("He heard [how/that] he continued babbling")? "Speak"—quintessentially speech-actional though it is—does not occur in modern true tags, but it is comma'ed-in by White in 14 as though it is both a tag and a parenthetical comment. In 15, we can accept "improved" as a highly specific speech-act verb of linguistic processing, but are put off by the prepositional-object phrase "on it" pulling away from the direct speech and referring back to the previous speaker's words—this sort of thing is "not done". We are expected to take "paused" in 16 as neither a speech act nor a pure gesture of vocal hiatus, but as a devolution from the one to the other. "Smiled" and "yawned" (17–18) do not specify the act of speech as such but the gestural accompaniment (other writers can be found using these verbs in this way)—but "smile" *could* be an interim gesture instead. Verbs like "coaxed", "reassured", "reminded", "corrected", "offered" and "was trying to persuade" (19–23, 38) feel a little bare without a personal indirect object, while "decided" (36–37) is a

---

[2] Perhaps standing for: "Then [Arthur heard] Mother's [voice saying]:" or (inferrable from the previous tag, "So Arthur said:": "Then Mother's [voice said/was saying]:"

verb of mental process, here characterizing the utterance itself. The verb phrase in **24** skips over what would have been a speech act, to focus on the hearer's and speaker's relation to the content of the direct speech. We may be puzzled by **25**, as we cannot be sure whether Arthur is "struggling" with his speech (anomalous speech-tag) or with his hands (crypto-tag of attendant gesture); actually, he is doing both. There is a density in the verb-phrase structure of **26–27** that is uncommon, while in **27** the syntactic focus on speech-act intention temporarily casts in doubt the factiveness of "say" itself. The verb in **28** does not tag the whole of the direct speech, but only its dying fall. In **29–30** there is in both sentences an iconic exploitation of normal (immediately adjacent) tag-position; the speech-act tag proper has been displaced by prior attendant gesture. "Blurted" (**31**) is defamiliarized and made more physical in the absence of "out", and "would ... regurgitate" (**32**) also denotes a more general physical act, but in its situational context serves to suggest the vocal expulsion of unpleasant, half-digested ideas while eating. In **33–34**, the negative component is an uncommon way of tailoring the modality of the speech-act verb, and the negation of the non-initial verb in **35** is not "normally" permissible.

What we have here, generally, are instances of the maximizing of contextual ironies via simply structured diegetic tags. It is not so easy to "read past" them on the way to another piece of direct speech, or to a paragraph of diegesis. Apart from this, these tags are already moving away from the standard mid-field ("said/replied/asked") in the direction of the perimeter, be this heightened physicality in the speech-act ("blurted, regurgitate") or the insinuation of pre-verbal intentionality ("coaxed, decided"). The impression should not be created that White's speech-tags are preponderantly of these types: in Section 1 of the novel, 46 of the 90 tags are "said", and a further 37 speeches are unmarked or "zero"-tagged for "scenic" representation or objective mimesis. Yet tagless dialogue, too, is never neutral conversational exchange: the pragmatic context is either *highly* innocuous (consensual small-talk) or marked by negative reactions (scepticism, suspicion, defensiveness). Although "said" occurs so frequently, White ensures that the reporting-clauses are sufficiently varied to avoid any impression of monotony or Hemingwayesque laconicism. He does this by switching from subject-verb structure to verb-subject inversion, by switching from proper noun to pronoun, by adding coordinate or subordinate clauses to one of the "said"–clauses, by interspersing more specific speech-tags, and by combining two or more of the strategies listed. This would indicate not only a high degree of sensitivity to details of form in general, but also a consciously delicate deployment of speech-tags for highly differentiated diegetic purposes; even their absence is manipulated into patterns of signification.

It might well be asked (in view of the fact that the question was not raised earlier) why the analysis of speech-tags should in any way be central to matters of style (rather than to "interpretation", should this be regarded as a discrete field of enquiry). The question is in so far legitimate as the experience of most readers of novels is probably (as I have just insinuated) that speech-tags are the bits of a narrative that have to be got over on the way to and from mimesis (or speech)

and extended diegesis. Speech-tags proper are the stepchildren of both
narratology and narrative stylistics. In fact, however, they constitute (by the
degree of specificity with which they are present, and even by their absence) *the*
crucial interface between "legitimate" narrative discourse and that whole realm of
"directly" represented speech. Without the concept of "reporting-clauses",
moreover, it would hardly have been possible to develop systematic theories of
the function of free indirect discourse. If, as I claim, White's use of speech-tags
is conspicuously individualistic and thus indicative of a particular style and
narrative method, where is one to look for theoretical and practical observations
that might help one to approach this novelist systematically?

There is no shortage of "practical observations" among the reviewers of
fiction (from whom we can expect some reflection of popular aesthetic
expectations); and occasionally novelists, too, mention the subject of speech-
tags.[3] In his *Reflections on "The Name of the Rose"*, Umberto Eco picks up
tantalizingly, but then disappointingly drops prematurely, the topic of tagging—in
the process providing yet another definitional term for the phenomenon ("turn
ancillaries"; Eco 1984:30–32). Particularly astute is Eco's stress on speech-tags
as a matter of style, and on the interpretative role of the reader.[4] Some of his
assumptions though, are not universally valid: that tagging has something to do
with "dramatism" (ushering characters onto the "floor" or stage); that tags are
"ancillary" (only in some respects are they *subservient* to direct speech); that
elaboration is automatically identifiable with auctorial intervention.[5]

---

[3] They write disapprovingly of "colorful substitutes for 'said': 'quizzed', 'gurgled',
'crooned' ..." (Lardner 1978:161), of "absurd avoidances of the words 'he said' ... which are
so typical of bad fiction" (Fisher 1985:1228), or suggest that even the "technique of dialogue"
using "I said" can be mechanistic (Brown 1986:895). The academic analysis of speech-tags is
itself amusingly satirized by the novelist David Lodge in *Small World* (a macho writer uses
only "he said" for his male characters, but "expressive verbal groups" such as "she sighed" or
"she cried passionately" for the speech of women (Lodge 1985:184). In an interview on craft,
Nadine Gordimer states: "I simply cannot stand he–said/she–said any more .... if I can't make
readers *know* who's speaking from the tone of voice, the turns of phrase, well, then I've
failed" (Gordimer 1983:108–109). Cf also the comments of the Russian Formalist, Boris
Eikhenbaum, in a 1925 essay on Leskov, *skaz* and modern prose, where Mikhail Nikolaevich
Zagoskin is cited because of his impatience with the explanatory "he said" convention and his
preference for full dramatic or scenic form (Eikhenbaum, "Leskov and Modern Prose", in
Striedter 1981:215).

[4] More astute, certainly, than a recent little survey of "some different ways of representing
speech in fiction" (Hughes 1990:252), which insinuates that the tagging of direct speech is a
colorful, often extravagant, but ultimately unnatural "ploy" providing the critic with little more
than "an absorbing pastime".

[5] Some degree of differentiation can be found in Roger Fowler's remarks on the tagging-
procedures of D.H. Lawrence (on whom more later). After listing "numerous speech-
introducing expressions" in *Sons and Lovers*, he indicates that "these comments are more than
'stage-directions' giving indications of the behaviour of the speakers"; "they add an emotional
colouring deriving from the narrator's analysis of the relationship between the characters.
They make manifest an aspect of the narrator's ideology" (Fowler 1986:119). This view is
also exemplified by Carter/Nash 1990:95–97 in an excellent brief analysis of a conversational
situation in Galsworthy. Fowler takes the standard view that "the words and phrases used to

A starting-point complementary to that of Eco might be sought in certain observations by Seymour Chatman within the context of narratological theory:

The use of such tags as "he thought" or "he said" ... is not a strong indicator of narrative mediation, for the convention of "he said" is not much more conspicuous than that of the separate paragraphs to indicate a change of speaker in dialogue or of the character's name followed by a colon in printed forms of plays. Mediation does begin to appear when the tag employs certain "interpretative" verbs—"he surmised" or "he insinuated", or the like. The minimal phrases "he said" or "he felt" present a kind of norm; they add nothing—they represent a minimal representation in the process mode. Theoretically, quoted dialogue is the minimal case; the only necessary assumption is that the author has copied the speech of the character. (Chatman 1975:237–38)

Chatman is at all times cautious about committing himself to preconceptions about auctorial intervention: hence the processual neutrality of his term "narrative mediation". It is noteworthy that Franz Stanzel regards "scenic representation" in its other sense of a reflection of events in consciousness as the domain of interior monologue. The reigning presupposition in his characterizing of true "scenic representation" (speech with diegetic accompaniment) is that a speech-tag is present, and that the conciseness of any extension of the speech-tag in the way of "stage-directions" and comment usually allows the whole to retain for the reader an immediacy *independent of* narratorial/auctorial "intrusion" *at the same time as* the minimal diegesis present is a sign of auctorial presence or of an "I"–narrator (Stanzel 1982:192–93; cf 243–44).

There is, however, nothing on the face of it to prevent such minimal diegesis from indicating the presence of a figural (ic, non-auctorial, formally non-"I") consciousness, to which can be attributed the perceptual-cognitive task—as a listener or interlocutor—of making pragmatic sense of the speech-act situations mimetically presented. The end-effect, of course, is in most cases an overlay or consonance of implied-auctorial narrative intention and figural involvement. At any rate, it cannot be said that Stanzel has applied himself to the question of "inquit-formulae" (the original German term derives from Latin rhetoric; "inquit" [*he said*], was customarily inserted into passages of direct speech to reinforce or indicate the status of the latter) and their extensions. The functional significance of speech-tags for Stanzel is clearly indicated by his reductive use of the loose analogical term "stage-directions".

Representative contemporary views of the function and status of speech-tags will generally be sought in vain in the writings of theoretical linguists. Leech/Short (1981) do not consider at all—in a book on style in prose fiction—the strategies adopted by novelists to provide diegetic adjuncts to "directly" represented speech-acts. Traugott/Pratt (1980:43–44) exhibit similar interests, yet manage also to devote a page or two to written dialogue in fiction and to the explicit discussion of "speech styles" in written narratives "as clues to a character's background or personality, for instance, or as signs of the social meaning of a situation". Their attitude towards speech-tags proper, however, is

introduce speech inevitably indicate the narrator's comments on and interpretations of the utterances of the characters" in a form of "third voice".

revealed on the one hand by their evident fascination with writers who (like William Gaddis) manage to bring off extended dialogue-passages without external, diegetic aids; and, on the other, by their impatience with tagging procedures which are redundant, in that they offer the reader the kind of information he has got already from the direct speech itself. The authors regard the whole topic as yawningly self-evident (with the notion of "cues" hinting at the assumption that such "trappings" function as "stage-directions").

Apart from Chatman, Dorrit Cohn, Ann Banfield and others concerned largely with the function of speech-tags in free indirect discourse and other forms of diegetically mediated speech, thought, and preverbal mental activity, we must rely on Peprník (1969) and Bonheim (1982) to provide us with a systematic investigation of the normative characteristics of speech-tags or "inquits" in prose fiction. Peprník's study is instructive on the historical spread of certain categories of tag-verb from the eighteenth to the twentieth century. As Bonheim claims, on the basis of statistical research, to furnish universally valid "rules", "norms" and "conventions", an investigation of White's tagging practice is obliged to take his findings as a benchmark, albeit a not entirely satisfactory one. Bonheim's concentration on the quest for classifiable concrete universals seems to be based on the assumption that the ubiquity of speech-tags as hinges between speech and narrative makes their specific functional mode self-evident. Although regarded as formally significant, they are at the same time seen as uninteresting semantically and, in terms of contextual pragmatics, as embellishable at will (ie, as a matter of "fashion" or "manner").

The most curious stance is the serenity with which Bonheim points out contraventions of the "norm" without granting the possibility of centrality to such contraventions. That is to say, there is no due account taken of the possibility that a narratology or poetics of fiction (at least of modernist fiction) has more use for a theory of deviation than for a normative theory. It could be argued that those novelists whose tagging procedures most correspond to a normative theory are those whose sensitivity to language is least evident (or evident anywhere else but in their handling of the mimesis-diegesis interface called "speech-tags"); and that, by the same token, those novelists who indulge in "abnormal" tagging are those who are most aware of the potential of language and narrative technique.

Bonheim's classification of speech-tags (1982:75) according to position with relation to "the speech to which it is attached" is a straightforward one. A tag may have **initial** position ("The same steady voice answered him. 'Yes, keep it about two points off the port bow.'"); **medial** position ("'I don't know,' the sailor said. 'I hurt bad.'"); or **final** position ("'What were you doing on the floor?' I asked."). "In modern prose the inquit tends to come in final position. Second in popularity is the medial position" (75). Bonheim's own table of tag-distribution (76–77) does not bear out this ranking. If we take the (undefined) term "modern" to start with No. 9 on his list (Conrad), we find that only Lawrence and Keith Waterhouse have more terminal (final) than medial tags, while the sample from Paul Scott is a moot point; in the other six authors, the situation is the reverse.

Of the seven authors I have analysed,[6] only Lawrence has more terminal tags than medial. In the following table, I juxtapose Bonheim's findings (1982) with my own [1984]. The figures are percentages of the four types initial (I), medial (M), terminal (T) and zero (z):

Table 9: Speech-tag distribution

	(1982)					**[1984]**			
	I	M	T	z		I	M	T	z
Eliot (1860)	15	43	22	20					
Dickens (1860)	31	37	16	15					
Hardy (1891)	3	31	19	47					
Conrad (1900)	7	43	38	12	(1904)	18	39	27	16
James					(1903)	10	45	7	38
Lawrence (1913)	1	29	6	24	(1921)	6.5	18	63	12.5
Faulkner (1929)	3	64	28	5	(1932/48)	21	41	34	4
Ellison (1947)	4	41	25	30					
Waterhouse (1959)	34	11	27	28					
Naipaul					(1961)	16	32	18	34
Stow				^	(1963)	4	35	21	40
White				^	(1966)	11	39	30	20
Scott (1975)	22	6	8	64					

Bonheim's assertion would seem to be valid, not as a general tendency set aside from all other textual considerations, but rather under one special condition: "Authors that give preference to short speeches, which is the prevailing tendency in the twentieth century, strongly prefer the medial and final positions" (79). Thus, it *might* be possible to find authors using more terminal than medial tags when their "short speeches" tend not to exceed the length of one sentence (as happens to be the case with Lawrence); but the assertion is, I repeat, not borne out by either Bonheim's or my own statistical findings.

Bonheim further observes that "the modern tendency is to let speech follow speech, if possible without interruption. An inquit in medial position is one way of allowing speech to follow on speech. The more radical tendency is to do without the inquit altogether" (75). It is overstating somewhat to say that the use of speech-tags is "a constant reminder of the narrator's presence" (75) when the

---

[6] Henry James, *The Ambassadors* (ch. 1–2, 33–34, New American Library edition, 1960); Joseph Conrad, *Nostromo* (ch. 5–6; Octopus Books omnibus edition, 1981); D.H. Lawrence, *Women in Love* (ch. 18; Penguin edition, 1960); William Faulkner, *Intruder in the Dust* (ch. 5 and 10; Penguin edition, 1960) and *Light in August* (ch. 2, Penguin edition, 1960); V.S. Naipaul, *A House for Mr Biswas* (ch. 3; Penguin edition, 1969); Randolph Stow, *Tourmaline* (ch. 8; Penguin edition, 1965). The extracts for analysis were "dissected" into their smallest analytical units (the paragraph, wherever this involved contiguous tagged or free-standing untagged direct speech). The Conrad produced 94 such units, the Lawrence 90, the Naipaul 96, and the Stow 210. The extracts from Faulkner's *Intruder in the Dust* involved 98 such "speeches". In James's *The Ambassadors*, the analysis produced 191 units, in Faulkner's *Light in August* , 86.

narratives in question are "third-person" and are otherwise in strongly focalized, figural or consonant narration. In such cases, the reader is not disposed to register tags as signalling the palpable presence of a narrator with a personality distinct from that of a character—least of all when the "reporting clauses" constitute those "minimal tags" of which Chatman writes and to which Eco refers. Norman Page, in the course of arguing for the historical and genetic connection between stage-drama and techniques of speech-representation in the novel, observes that to draw attention to "paralinguistic qualities such as stress, pitch, intonation, volume, vocal quality ... in the accompanying comments ('he muttered', ' she shrieked') ... is to throw the major burden of reconstructing a particular variety of speech upon the reader" (Page 1973:26–28). If there can be a narrator "intruding" in such cases, it is not in order to cancel the reader's constitutive role but rather to encourage him in that role. It should be noted in passing that Page quite rightly concentrates on "mimesis" rather than on the speech/diegesis interface in his study of speech in the English novel. But he briefly reviews the "constantly varying proportions" in which tag-information is supplied to avoid confusion of speakers: tag-variation, either as a "novelistic habit" (Bonheim's stance) or for "expressive" purposes; to indicate the expressive accompaniments of speech ("stage-directions" common in the theatrical Dickens, but infrequent in Jane Austen with her interest in the non-circumstantial "moral implications of a scene"). Whereas Page at least applies the term "stage-direction" to what could genuinely be conceived of as a "dramatic" stage-exit after a closing speech (1972:131–32), he seems to share Bonheim's distaste for interpolated "comment or moralizing" in dialogue-scenes. Whereas this may indeed involve intrusive narrators, scenic or behaviouristic narratives like the dialogic sections of Faulkner or Hemingway are rendered no less what they are by the presence of speech-tags. Bonheim almost suggests as much, in saying that "modern narrative", because it favours the "dramatic" stance of speech, tries to make speech-tags "as inconspicuous as possible" (76).

   Zero-tagging of direct speech, conversely, may have something to do with auctorial self-effacement, but there is no necessary correlation. Scenic, tagless presentation of dialogue—frequent in Hemingway, almost always in Ivy Compton–Burnett, Henry Green or William Gaddis—may relate to behaviouristic, narratorial withdrawal or to a strong figural presence. In other writers there is no such correlation. Bonheim's own list includes Paul Scott, with 64% zero-tags. An upper-middle-echelon novelist, Scott is not given to implied-auctorial effacement. What, too, are we to make of the samples from Henry James (38% zero-tags) and Hardy (47% zero-tags), not to speak of Jane Austen with 54%—and this in view of Bonheim's statement that "the decrease in the use of inquits in the last half century has been traced to the influence of Joyce's *Ulysses*" (76)? Joyce's influence can hardly account for the preponderance of zero-tagging in pre-Joycean authors—or for the practice of Paul Scott, or for the failure of the statistical listings to correlate comfortably. The fact of the matter is that the narrational context for this kind of zero-tagging is *not* direct speech but "the unsignalled quoted monologue" as "a hallmark for stream-of-consciousness novels" (Cohn 1978:63). The whole area lies outside the domain Bonheim is examining, and cannot have general relevance for the use of tags by "modern" novelists who are not high modernists. Nor can it account for the prevalence of minimal tagging, and the relative absence of zero-tagging, in a high-modernist novelist like Faulkner, who is, anyway, quintessentially a novelist of figural consciousness *and* one given to strong narratorial control. Lexico-semantic considerations such as these are important for the examination of White's practice—but chiefly in connection with what might be termed architectonic considerations (of which zero-tagging is the most radical instance).

Associated with zero-tagging by Bonheim is a category of "crypto-inquits", where "the description of the speaker or of his manner of speaking has been separated out" of the tag "and now often stands by itself", frequently taking the form of "a stage direction [sic], followed immediately by direct speech"; "crypto-inquits tell the reader who is about to speak or has just spoken" (83–84, 88). I shall be examining the category of crypto-tags in some detail presently.

Bonheim goes on to talk about "author-specific habits":

Henry James brought the art of the inquit to a high polish, and his inventive use of the form even attracted comment from his critics. Some authors are acrobats of the inquit, and pride themselves on the variety of ways they manage to avoid the conventional and humdrum forms. Less obvious are the inquit-habits of Conrad and Lawrence, although distinctive in different ways. [Bonheim 1982:78]

The theory of tag-usage implicit here would seem to be one of negative *choice:* unconventional applications as a studied avoidance of the conventional. Such a theory runs close to a fullblooded endorsement of form/content dualism, for which there are formal differences between writing "he said/retorted/after an instant risked" and zero-tagging or a crypto-tag, but no appreciable difference in meaning: as tags are redundant anyway, the reader's ability to construe for himself the force of a direct-speech statement can suggest that "many a new awareness of a norm allows—may indeed positively invite—a ' foregrounding' or deviation from that norm for rhetorical purposes" (89). Only on matters of specific detail does Bonheim appear to view tagging procedures as a matter of effective communication rather than of decorative or optional or idiosyncratic "rhetoric". Long speeches require initial or medial inquits to avoid the "awkwardness" of terminal positioning; or initial inquits if these are longish and "weighted heavily with embedded description" (79–80). There are topicalizing restraints operating on the parameters VS/SV/Noun/Pronoun/ SO/OS (81–85). This, however, is hardly enough. A formal classification of speech-tags will shed little light on narrative style unless parameters are included to account for the scaling of semantic specificity in speech-act verbs, to explain the communicative logic underlying apparent anomalies, and to justify formal differences by recourse to principles of cohesion, contextuality, and the structuring of direct speech itself.

II   Multiple tagging

A speech (of whatever length) attributable to one character can have more than one speech-tag. Where this occurs, the formal categories "initial", "medial" and "final" (or "terminal") can become problematical in terms of the dynamics of speech-representation.

COMPARATIVE PASSAGES

For the purpose of the present argument, I wish to take as my first test-corpus the speeches analysable out of a representative stretch of William Faulkner's *Intruder in the Dust*. About 12% of these can be formally classified in terms of the position of the tag attached to the direct speech—but various factors within the architecture of the speech as a whole render such classification fuzzy with respect to the whole speech.

In all of the speeches in the group of 12%, there is one tag that is "final" or terminal only in relation to the direct speech it is attached to. In every case, further speech-segments from the same speaker follow. These may be medially or terminally tagged, or may have internal initial tags::

1 "——," his uncle said. [——] "——," he said. "——?" [6 lines of diegesis.] "——," his uncle said. "——." (p. 114) (medial)
2 "——," his uncle said. He said: "——." But Miss Habersham was already talking. She was looking .... (p. 107) (internal initial)
3 Miss Habersham in the front seat with his uncle said "——." [——] She leaned forward to look ... at the sheriff. "—— Go on," she said. "—— Go on," she said. (p. 127) (terminal)

Complicating the dynamics are such features as crypto-tags. The second sentence in the following is a typically Faulknerian sign of imminent speech, thus making the statement before the final direct speech an initial tag, and preventing the whole from being construed as medially tagged:

4 "——," his uncle told Aleck Sander. Then his uncle looked ... watched ...."——," [1 paragraph of diegesis.] "——," she said. "——?" (p. 108)

A similar tension exists in 3 above, with another "look"–sentence, which acts as a crypto-tag for the first portion of the subsequent direct speech. The construction is thus: initial tag—initial crypto-tag—pseudo-terminal tag—terminal tag. In 5, there is an initial participial tag ("talking again") with a colon to mark cataphora; but the direct speech, which cannot be split as in the example just analysed, is also terminally tagged:

5 "——," his uncle said. "——[1 page]——" and there it was again [5 lines] talking again: "——[half a page]——," his uncle said and this time he noticed [6 lines]: "——[1 page]——" and it would have been again but this time his uncle didn't pause "——[15 lines]——:" and stopped this time waiting for her to say it and she did: (p. 220)

The re-identification of the speaker cataphorically is a specific feature of Faulkner's tagging-procedure (ie, the tag is within the segment, after separately tagged direct speech belonging to the same speaker). Note these "medial" initial tags:

6 "——," Miss Habersham said. She said "——" too. She said, "——:" already moving, meeting [1 paragraph]. She said: "——?" (p. 107; note the punctuative gradation).

Faulkner also moves away from same-line initial tagging of direct speech—only about 9% of his initial tags are so placed. More usually, the tag is attached to the end of a diegetic segment, but the direct speech is separately paragraphed below the tag. Where the diegesis is brief, the tag often flows, as it were, out of the previous speaker's direct speech:

7 "—": which ... seemed to be worse [3 lines] until his uncle came out fully dressed ... and said:
   "——?" [1 paragraph]—she said:
   "——!" so that he actually stopped .... (p. 102)
8 ... and he jerked ... the voices buzzing ... : the sheriff's:
   "——?" then L's:
   "—[1 paragraph]——." (pp. 111–12)

There are probably three interdependent reasons for this procedure. (a) Faulkner wants to avoid tags that could be construed as conventionally "auctorial"—hence the largish proportion of crypto-tags without conventional reporting-verbs (eg, **8**). (b) He wants direct speech to be set out "dramatically", to promote the impression that speech is being registered, at least at its inception, without mediation. And (c) he wants to bind all the elements of discourse (mimesis; diegetic tags; psychonarrative diegesis; narrated monologue; quoted monologue) into a pulsating flow rather than a succession of discrete entities. Figural consciousness is present all the time, its focus of attention constantly shifted by subtle angles of rotation. Faulkner's layout, meticulously nuanced punctuation, and tagging combinations (and clashes) constitute a finely balanced system designed to maximize the effectiveness of minimal diegesis. Semantically minimal, that is: 92% of the tag-verbs are *say;* the verb is omitted frequently; only about 12% of the tags have any degree of adverbial modification to amplify meaning; *say* is applied indiscriminately to both statements and questions.[7]

---

[7] The mental life referred to here is least likely to be found in first-person narratives which ostensibly lay such inner lives bare as actional and reflective testimony. The maximum potentiation of character-consciousness (at the very latest from Flaubert onwards) has resided in the ambiguating modes of third-person narrative, in which one has the systemic possibility of contrastive analysis in respect of focalization and the like. Unless the flux of consciousness can be detected in the mode of narration (as in Faulkner), minimal tagging procedures can hardly have a "consciousness-marking" function attributable to them. With novelists whose narrative style in respect of speech-tags does not demonstrate any measure of internal architectonic variety, it is wellnigh impossible to prove that a uniform diet of "she said/he said" serves a *positive* functional purpose rather than being an inert presence. For example: in the novels of Margaret Atwood, as Reingard Nischik has shown (Nischik 1991:110–13), there is no deflection whatsoever from a narrow normative range of "inquits" (with "she said" overwhelmingly on the one side and "she added/repeated/screamed" on the other). The statistical ratio for these tags which Nischik adduces for the first-person narrative of *The Handmaid's Tale* (10:1) is, unfortunately, about par for the course with the majority of novelists. Nischik's attempt to make of this "underlexicalization" an index of societal uniformity in a post-holocaust society is therefore doomed to failure: first (within the terms established by this one novel), on the evidence of normative novelistic usage; second (within the terms established by Atwood's oeuvre), on the evidence of the one writer's uniformly

In the extracts from Henry James's *The Ambassadors* taken for comparative analysis, there are various grades of multiple tagging. Here are some instances of true initial tags in non-initial position within the same speech:

9 "——," Strether smiled. To which he added with an irrelevance that was only superficial "——." (p. 12)

10 She quite concurred. "——." And she added: "——!" (p. 14)

11 She had scarcely to say it ...."Yes,——." It was not till a minute later that she added: "——!" (p. 353)

12 "——." To which, in the next breath, Miss Gostrey added "——!" (p. 361)

In **9**, the verb "smiled" is a true tag which is yet "fake", in detailing a gestural accompaniment to a speech-act. Although it is not a speech-act paraphrase, it is a widespread tag, in James .and in more recent writers. In **10** and **11**, the two pieces of initial diegesis are in that grey zone between true tags and crypto-tags. In both cases, the verbs "concurred" and "had ... to say" are separated off from the direct speech to which they cataphorically point, but the verbs are still speech-act verbs, not nominal paraphrases, say. Example **11**, however, is compromised by the grammatical self-containedness brought about by the deictic "it", which anticipates the direct speech; it is closer than "concurred" to being a crypto-tag. In all five examples, it will be noted how the "non-initial" initial tag-verb is *add,* which is reinforced by various kinds of diegetic cohesion, ranging from simple additives (**10**), through comparative-temporal constructions (**11**), to cataphoric sentential relatives (**9**). The verb *add* would be counted as redundant by the detractors of tagging—but closer examination reveals that it is not simply an addition that is being denoted by the tag, but also the various degrees of interstitial silence preceding the addition. Such taggings serve a kind of prosodic pointing function. Furthermore, in the subtlest ways, they promote the reader's impression that the speaker's intention (or some suggestion of it) has been registered by a figural interlocutor (or narrator) prior to the continuation of the speech.

Another group of Jamesian "non-initial" initial tags includes verbs which could be regarded equally well as true speech-act verbs or as generalising crypto-tag verbs referring to actional process:

12 "——." His wonderment showed at this moment as confirmed, but he presently went on. "——. Did she strike you," he asked, "as anxious?" (p. 358)

13 "——." He had thought a moment, but he went on. "——?" (p. 360)

In **12**, the first part of the diegesis is comment (taking up from "wonder" in the zero-tagged direct speech)—the speaker's registering of his companion's reaction. The tag with "went on" is followed by medially tagged direct speech with *ask—* one of those most redundant of verbs for interrogatively marked speech. The topic that is foregrounded here, however, is precisely that of the interaction between mental weighing-up of a situation and judicious interrogation. The "went on" tag attaches initially to the tactically preparatory statement, the "asked" tag to

---

innocuous tagging-procedure. Atwood's speech-tags cannot be regarded as an index to "mind style"; they escape the net drawn up by Nischik for a range of other discoursal features in the work of this Canadian writer.

the execution of the speaker's interrogative intention. We have here, too, one of those less usual divisions of the sentence-constituents in the middle of the question, the effect of which is to mediate the speaker's cautiousness or delicacy of approach. In **13**, the initial direct speech is zero-tagged; then comes an unusual application of the past perfect, conveying the speaker's own reflexive consciousness of hiatus; and "but he went on" signals not only resumption after a pause but also mental resolution to resume. In both cases, there is once again an emplacement of the tags with due consideration of intersentential cohesion.

Similar linking-initial tags can be found in even more complex arrays. In the following examples, the tag is itself elliptical, with no speech-act verb:[8]

14 "——. But it isn't," she declared, "because I'm [14 lines]——. How can I be indifferent," she asked, "to——?" And as he found himself unable immediately to say: "——?" (p. 348)
15 "—— — well," she beautifully brought out, "when ——? I've wanted to see you often when I couldn't," she pursued, "all these last weeks. ——?" Then as if the straightness of this appeal, taking him unprepared, had visibly left him wondering: "——? ——. It gives me a kind of detestation—" She pulled up short. (p. 349)

The speech is "scored" to indicate changes of tonality (both vocally tonal and mentally strategic) which the figural listener (Strether) registers in the speech of Maria Gostrey. In **15**, the "declared"-tag is actually resumptive: the first part of the direct speech is really zero-tagged, and it is only at "'But'" that Maria launches into her declaration. There is diffidence or cautious defensiveness both here and in the next tag, medially placed within a question: in both cases (as in **12** above), the tag breaks into a statement or question at points of tight constituent juncture, thus serving to undermine the tonal certainty which terminal tags would have lent to unbroken sentences. In **15**, which is textually adjacent to **14**, a change of tonality is evident. Maria is now increasingly open in her questions and statements, and the medial tags occur at phrase-boundaries which are less tight—but tension is still present. Maria's resolve and frankness at "she pursued" are surprising even to herself, so that the "forward" semantic implication of the verb is accompanied by a slight vocal hesitation hinted at via tag-placement. In both cases, the elliptical initial tags are cohesively marked by cataphoric reference ("unable ... to say" and "this appeal" connecting with the immediately preceding question) and by additive/consecutive markers ("And", "Then"). Finally, there is a terminal crypto-tag in **15** ("She pulled up short") which is not a redundant paraphrase of the interruptive dash—the tag is not telling us that Maria has broken off; it is telling us that Strether has registered this break, as the free indirect discourse that follows bears out ("Oh, but he wanted to hear"). The free indirect discourse, in turn, acts as a crypto-tag of mental intention for the speech-act question that follows. Without these two pieces of diegesis, Strether's (zero-tagged) question would look like an interruption of

---

[8] This is a diegetic condition which Bonheim does not consider in his chapter on tags. A passage from John Wyndham, however, which Bonheim cites (64) for its "stichomythic" alternation of direct and indirect speech, offers a succinct example of direct speech which is unmarked except for initial "And:"

Maria's speech. The crypto-tagging is crucial to the characterizing of the external speech-situation and the concomitant mental processes.

Other instances of multiple tagging without these "non-initial" initial tags are similarly alert to minute shifts in vocal tonality:

16 "——, as I've ... let you know I've felt," Strether said, "the most——. But you ought," he wound up, "to be easy."

The two medial tags have not been inserted so much to identify the speaker or the nature of the speech-act delimited by the verb, as to mark Strether's intense efforts to express intimate views about Maria to Maria as delicately as possible. The first tag marks a vocal pause at a parenthetical conjunct, the second Strether's mental pause, his awareness of the need to "wind up" both his speech and the immediate sentence as tactfully as he can. James's tags psychologize the speech-situation in respect of the speaker, or mediate the listener's perception of significant tonal (suprasegmental) gradations in speech, and/or his mental construction of communicative strategies.

The intercalation or juxtaposition of true tags and crypto-tags is a characteristic feature of James's "pointing" of speeches, together with tight control over cohesive reference, as in the following example, in which a large chunk of diegesis (Strether reflecting on the whole implicature of his situation vis-à-vis Maria Gostrey and Chad Newsome) is interposed:

17 "Oh, you're all right, you're all right," he almost impatiently declared; his impatience being moreover not for her pressure but for her scruple. [20 lines of consonant psychonarration] He had the advantage that his pronouncing her 'all right' gave him for an inquiry. "——?" He spoke as if [7 lines of psychonarration slipping into free indirect discourse]. (p. 347)

Here Strether reflects also on his own delivery, in the terminal crypto-tag with "He spoke". The crypto-tag with "inquiry" points forward to the question, and the embedding provides cohesion with his initial statement. Among the many effects, there are several instances of the last tag in a sequence being a crypto-tag with initial or annunciatory function—here is a cluster of these:

18 She watched him ...."——." As on this ... he protested ... she had a moment of explanation.
        "——[18 lines]——."
    Strether could only listen ... and weigh his chance. "——." He waited a moment. "——?"
    She had her own hesitation, but "you don't!" she finally exclaimed, setting him again in motion. [7 lines.] He looked at the hour ... and then ... had another pause. "——." (pp. 14–15)

Immediately apparent from an inspection of comparative passages from Conrad, Lawrence, V.S. Naipaul and Randolph Stow is the infrequency of multiple tagging. James's characters are talkative, and they often speak at length; this might be said to encourage diegetic intercalation. But the infrequency of multiple tagging in these other writers does not correlate with the length of speeches. Stow and Naipaul have the briefest speeches, tailed closely by Lawrence; Conrad's speeches, by contrast, can run to half a page. The number of multiple taggings is not significantly different from author to author; and in only one case does Conrad use more than one tag within a long speech. Conrad's additional tags are self-explanatory ("continued", "added", "pursued"), and are clearly marked for change of tone. Conrad's multiple tagging may simply mark the hesitant repetitions or resumptions within the direct speech, with medial breaking favoured:

19 "——," he pronounced slowly, as if weighing ...."——," he continued, thoughtfully. (p. 495)
20 "——[12 lines]——"—he did not say ' robbed', but added, after a pause—"exploited!" (p. 482)

In 20, there is a diegetic oddity (also encountered in White) in the use of a negated speech-tag to convey a moment of mental calculation. In 19, we run up against the problem of classification again: one speech includes a hiatus (by inference from the verb "continued"), and must be contrued as having two terminal tags, end on end. There is a good example of the same feature in Lawrence:

21 "——," cried Winifred in excitement. "——!" [——] "——!" cried the child, in rousing excitement. "——!" [4 lines of diegesis.] "——!" she cried, seeing ...."——?" she whispered excitedly, mysteriously, looking up at ...."——? ——" she chuckled wickedly to herself. (p. 270)

Here, two stopped medial tags are followed by three terminal tags end on end. Lawrence's fascinating way with redundancy and repetition is also evident here: the "empty" tag-verb "cried" occurs three times in succession, variety being supplied by a shift from name to noun to pronoun; all five verbs have postmodification, the second modification "in rousing excitement" being partly redundant and partly incremental upon the first; the third is participial, the fifth an –ly adverb, while the fourth combines these two. As a closed group, the tags are patterned sensitively enough; a sense of the essential unity of the experience being conveyed is preserved, along with the simplicity of a child's behaviour (though the persistence of simple patterning in other contexts weakens this generous assumption somewhat). Here are two further instances of Lawrence's multiple tagging:

22 "——," said Gerald, coming up and ...."——," said he. (p. 267)
23 "——. ——!" She laughed quickly, then added: "——?" (p. 268)

In 23, there is the very common "fake" tag "laughed" for a vocal gesture accompanying the speech-act, followed by a terminal-initial tag with a predictable verb, which is there partly to signal a change-down of tone (ie, not just addition, but also the cessation or diminution of a laughing tone of voice). The devices employed for text-cohesion are the simplest possible, while the medially tagged speech at the start of 22 has a terminal-initial tag attached to it additively, with an old-fashioned inversion. No resumption after a vocal pause is implied; there is no trouble here with the identity of the speaker.

Naipaul's multiple tagging requires little comment: it has none of the touch of unfathomable weirdness characteristic of Lawrence. Most noteworthy is the following:

24 "——." She laughed ...."And then," she went on, "he was [——]. Died," she repeated, and waited. (p. 94)

This is a speech broken by a crypto-tag of vocal gesture, whose logic is followed out by the ensuing medial tag ("she went on"); and the last (terminal) tag is in itself redundant ("she repeated") but necessary as a hook on which to hang a diegetic, gestural extension ("and waited"). In the only two instances of multiple tagging out of 210 speeches in Stow, a shift of perspective is indicated, and the verbs are "minimal":

25 "——," Byrne said, breaking ...."——?" he was asking, coming .... (p. 93)
26 "All right," he said, "——. Ah, but," he said, shaking ...."God, I'm——." (p. 96)

In 25, two terminal tags, both with participial modification, are placed end to end; the second tag indicates figural perception (by Kestrel) of Byrne's words as he changes his tone in switching addressees. In 26, two medial tags are placed end to end, the second (with additional participial modification) marking a jagged shift in tone of voice as the speaker ceases to dwell on the external and factual and expresses self-disgust.

WHITE'S PRACTICE

In the types of multiple tagging he employs, White seems close in spirit to Henry James. In the cold light of statistics, however, there are considerable differences. Some 16% of the speeches in James have multiple tags, in White only 5%. Half of James's multiply tagged speeches have a crypto-tag somewhere in the sequence; this is the case in under 20% of White's. (In James as a whole, there is one crypto-tag for every two tagged or zero-tagged speeches; the ratio of crypto-tags to normal tags in White is, by contrast, 1:11.)

Many of White's multiply tagged speeches have internal initial tags:

27 Mrs Poulter said: "——." She paused, then she did not ask, but said: "——. I love Bill," Mrs Poulter said. (A264)

This has a pair of initial "said"-tags, additively joined. There is also a negated tag resembling that in Conrad (20), and the following internal initial tag resolves the verb "paused". A conspicuous feature of the tagging here is its minimal variety: three *said*s in a row, constant SV patterning, and the close repeating of the proper name draw attention to themselves, inasmuch as White's procedure is usually much more highly differentiated. When the context and the content of the direct speech are examined, the reason for the gaucheness becomes clear. Mrs Poulter is herself being awkwardly declarative, and her self-consciousness shows in the hesitantly annunciatory structure. The crowning touch is the terminal tag, attached to an equally unconvincing direct-speech profession of love ("Mrs Poulter" reinforces the unconvincingness); the "public" or impersonal jars stiffly with the "personal".

Some 40% of White's internal initial tags have the verb *add*. In the following four examples, it is the syntactic aspects of the tagging that are particularly instructive:

28 "Do you think," said Arthur, "we ought ——?" but looked at Waldo, and added: "——. Yes," he said, because Waldo was looking so furious, "——." (A292)
29 "That is to say," said Dad, he could not clear his throat enough, "it means," he said, "'—— '," adding: "——." (A240)
30 "——," Mother said, "today." She added quickly, without looking round: "——." (W74)
31 "——," she said drily, "I suppose." Adding quickly, however: "——." And more meditative: "——." (W165)

In **28**, the first speech-segment is medially tagged to show mild hesitation; the second is a self-conscious declaration, correspondingly tagged and with four-square coordination with the first segment; the third segment is medially tagged at the earliest point at which it can be hinted that Arthur must take protective action in response to Waldo's look. Mr Brown in **29** is awkward and hesitant throughout. The tag-breaks fall at natural medial junctures, but the first is clotted by an asyndetic parenthetical clause indicating vocal embarrassment. The last, initial, participial tag is so compact ("adding:" again) that the colon of cataphora raises expectations high: but the annunciatory pause is followed by the most bathetic (and, for Arthur, disillusioning) of direct-speech statements. His father has, as it were, been choreographed into helplessness.

The difference between **30** and **31** is not so much one of pace (the two speech-increments in **31** coming quicker than the one in **30** because the tags are shorter) as of mode. In **30**, Mrs Brown has her wits about her, but she is in her cups in **31**, where the whole statement is marked by subsidence from a normal tag, through a participial tag which is either elliptical (= And, more meditative now, she continued:) or crypto- (her alcoholic associations have made her lurch into another topic). There is, further, something "stage-direction"-like about the tag-progression, as though Mrs Brown's drinking has made her vocal delivery more histrionic, more pronounced. In **30**, Waldo's reactions, or construction of the speech-act, are built into the tag. The medial tag ("said") is ambiguous: does Mrs Brown pause (because "today" reminds her of the presence of her dead husband)—or does Waldo register the word "today" especially, concentrating on the exceptional nature of the situation, not on the fact that it is Arthur who has been asked to stay at home? The second tag comes, implicitly, after a pause. Is Waldo registering only his mother's last-ditch mollifying tactic in granting him centrality? Or is he *anticipating* (ie, up to the colon) that his mother will go a further stage towards him and away from full commitment to Arthur? The free indirect discourse that follows makes clear how ironically Waldo sees through his mother's words. It does seem that the cataphoric tag-placing correlates not just with the speaker's behaviour but also with the (indirect) recipient's mental expectations. This latter kind or function of tagging is characteristic of White, but not, say, of James, where expectation is explicitly built into crypto-tags and other diegesis rather than into the tag-positioning and tag-structure as such.

The remaining examples in this overall group can be analysed as terminal tags followed by initial tags, with the tag-sections back to back. Items **32–37** are structurally the simplest and most concise, but are offset by various complicating factors:

32 "——?" he hedged, and decided almost at once: "——." (A256)
33 "——," said Waldo, but would not explain beyond: "——." (W175)
34 "Yes," he said, and: "Not exactly." (A237)
35 "Yes," she said, and quickly: "No." (W90)
36 "——," Waldo was commanding, and very loudly: *"sir!"* (A285)
37 "——," he murmured, then: "——," he called back. (W139)

In **32**, the tags are indices to attendant mental circumstance rather than to vocal mode: Waldo analyses his speech-act strategy as he goes. Via the modal and the negation, **33** pulls uneasily in the direction of prior mental process (the actual speech-tag, moreover, is not there—"beyond" would need completion with "saying", as "explain" has been partitioned off grammatically, as it were). The interaction between tempo, mental (re-) calculation and speech-act is nowhere clearer than in **34–36**, where the tag-verb has been ellipted away after a coordination (cf the ellipses in James, **14–15** above, where the diegesis is much more highly analytical, and is built into a new sentence). In **36**, the tag-verb is absent not just on grounds of economy (because "was commanding" is already there): what is involved is a surprise factor—Arthur is taken unawares by the alienating form of address, can register its aural impact, but is in no emotional state to "provide" an analytical tag. In **34**, precognitive rapidity explains the absence of a tag like "added"; in **35**, Waldo barely has time to register a flicker of hesitation before Dulcie expresses a change of mind.

Item **37** is also anomalous. Because of the cataphoric colon, "then:" itself functions as an elliptical tag, but the direct speech is also terminally tagged. "Then:" encodes Waldo's registration of Arthur's gestural preparation for further speech; the terminal tag registers the modality with which the speech-act is actually performed. There is a similar use of annunciatory "then:" with a true tag (this time, stopped medial) in Conrad and in Stow:

38 His tone remained light .... He waited for a while, and then:
    ——," he said, with ... desperation. (Conrad, p. 486)
39 He dragged .... Then: "——," he said. "——." He sat .... (Stow, p. 154)

In Stow, it can be supposed that Kestrel is interpreting Byrne's physical gestures (which are diegetically mediated) and that "then:" is similarly a representation of Kestrel's awareness that Byrne is about to speak.

The most straightforward taggings correlate with simple spoken messages:

40 "——," she said. Then, looking at ..., she said very softly: "——," (A261)
41 "——," Leonard Saporta replied, sweating ..., and explained with awful earnestness to Waldo: "——." (W156)
42 "——," Waldo commanded in a lower voice. "Please," he repeated, and added very loudly: "sir." (W200)
43 "——," Waldo said, and added, by inspiration, he congratulated himself afterwards: "——." (W173)

The message may even be simplistic in its declarativeness (**40**), or "simplistically" hammered home by redundancy to indicate how painfully obvious the strategy is to the listener (**41**). Item **42** is partly iconic, in that there are pauses between the bits of speech while Waldo struggles to find the right words for getting rid of Arthur. Item **43** is clotted with a Waldovian, prevaricating parenthesis; the paranoiac artificiality of Waldo's words is thus underscored by a comment clause that upsets the flow of simple coordination (and the tag, incidentally, confirms Bonheim's view that comment fits less well in tags which are not terminal).

Multiply tagged speeches make up only 6% of all the tagged speeches in *The Solid Mandala*. It is to be expected that tag-verbs suited to such speech-act contexts should be present in conspicuous numbers. 70% of all the *add*s, 60% of the *repeat*s and 27% of the *explain*s occur within this 6% of speeches—and 12% of all the *say*s. The latter would not be surprising in writers like Hemingway, Faulkner or Lawrence (who employ heavy doses of *say*-tags), were they to use multiple tagging frequently, which they don't. In White, who does employ highly differentiated tags, speeches including two or even three *said*s tend to stick out like a sore toe. Instead of explaining this as sloppiness or inconsistency, however, it is advisable to take individual speeches on their own merits, and to try and determine whether White is not perhaps deliberately flattening his tagging-*ductus*.

In some few cases, *said* is employed in array without tag-variation (always "she said") primarily because of the normative implications of delivery:

44 "Oh," she said, "——. I'm really," she said, "a very mundane individual." (W101)
45 "——," she said, sitting down on .... "——," she said, "killingly." (W101)
46 "Oh," she said. "Nothing," she said, tilting .... "That is," she said, "——." (A268)
47 "——," she said. "——. At least," she said, "nothing formal.——. Dancing," she said, "can compensate.——." (A272)

Multiple tagging with *said* correlates well in White with adjacent single-tagged speeches with *said*. The superficies of the speeches is that of innocuous delivery, or draws attention to the mechanics of speech, especially in **47**, with Mrs Brown's efforts to articulate speech while drunk: identical "empty" tags mark drunken emphases in the spoken discourse. In **44** and **45**, Dulcie is making apparently airy and casual small-talk; in **46**, Mrs Poulter is affecting nonchalance or neutrality: repeated neutral tags signal that Arthur as addressee senses from the pauses at the tags that the spoken discourse is self-conscious.

Compare the following:

48 "So this is Waldo Brown," said Mr Feinstein. "How are we doing, Waldo?" Mr Feinstein added. (W103)
49 "——!" protested her mother, breathing heavily. "——," Mrs Feinstein added, turning to .... (W102)
50 "——?" Bill responded antiphonally as he rolled his next cigarette. "——," he dared add. "——." (W143)

In **48**, Mr Feinstein's first statement is banal, and his question repeats Waldo's name redundantly, in an attempt at social heartiness. Phatic superfluity is matched by conspicuously unnecessary tagging within a very narrow compass. There is a component of figural perception here as well, in the representation of the speaker (via his "formal" surname) as playing a "public" role. This can be contrasted with **49**, where the verbs are more specific, and are modified participially. Further, Waldo sees the speaker in relation to Dulcie ("her

mother") within the dynamics of turn-taking, and only later as "Mrs Feinstein",
where the naming connects with the topic of her speech ("my husband") and with
a shift to a more formal topic. Whereas Mr Feinstein's addition is vacuous (cf the
tag "dared add" in **50**, where a significant pause is followed by a bathetic lapse
into triviality), Mrs Feinstein's acts as a semantic indication of temporal lapse
and change of topic, and as a hinge or hook for attendant gesture, the object of
which (the clock as topic of conversation; Mr Feinstein's awaited arrival) will
become significant presently.

   To indicate a change of tone or tonal stress, the tag-verb can be non-specific
("said"), so long as it is inserted in the right place:

51 "——," he said, "——. Waldo," he told her, "is just about the jealousest thing you'll find."
(W151)
52 "——," she said, "but——. Besides," she said "——." (W125)
53 "——!" she was panting. "——. I am so relieved," she said, "you are——." (W201)
54 "——," Mrs Allwright was saying, "that——. Mind you," she said, "I——." (A225)
55 "What," she said, "Arthur, I never suspected," she said, "that you were——." (A237)
56 "——," he said. "——," he reminded. "——." (A251)
57 "Oh, all that!" said Arthur Brown, spinning a cow-turd. "——. About Him," he said.
(A261)
58 "——. That," she said, sinking her mouth in the glass, "was——. But how deliciously
memorable"—working her mouth around it—"after——. Do you know, Arthur," she said,
looking at him, "——." (A272)

In **52**, the second medial tag (identical to the first) signals a heavy interconstituent
pause (with "'Besides'" unusually full-stopped) and a tonal climb down from
formal reproof. In **53**, at the end of a long speech, the tag marks a shift to
intimate solicitude. In **54**, there is heavy tonal emphasis and a change of pace at
the second tag, the repetition of the verb also underlining the factitiousness of the
spoken discourse. In **55**, the second medial tag marks a heavy stress and a tonal
curve on the word "suspected" in the direct speech. In **57**, the second, terminal
tag marks a change of tone with a change (or narrowing) of topic: the context
suggests a degree of conversational disengagement on Arthur's part, which is
supported by the neutral tagging. Both **56** and **58** also have tags where there are
shifts in topic and tone. The additional elliptical or atactic crypto-tag in **58** marks
Arthur's perception of how difficult it is for his drunken mother to pronounce the
word "memorable". Change of tone and change of topic can be determined by the
reader as he analyses the import of speech-acts. The tagging serves as a pointing
device for such analysis, rather than committing the diegesis to a narrow, fixed
interpretation. The resulting flexibility of import also makes it easier for the
narration to suggest a continual dynamic of interpretative response on the part of
the speaker or listener. The simplest functional instance of this is when the
insertion of a second tag into a speech serves to mark a change of addressee, as
in **51**—if no tag ("he told her") had been included, there would be no grounds for
assuming that Waldo is actively registering (in the diegesis) the fact that Arthur is
talking to him.

   The insertion of tags to hint at the perception of speech-act mode or change
of tone is effected primarily in the following:

59 "Well," he said carefully, "if——," and sometimes Mrs Poulter did, "—— more"—he formed his lips into a trumpet—"more transparent," he didn't shout. (W29)
60 "Waldo," he said, "——, can't I? Can't I?" he repeated. (W39)
61 "——," Mrs Feinstein said. "——. Acchhh, yes!" After this expression of pain and reverence, she put the tray down, and turned quite skittish. "——," she said, looking at her daughter, "and——." (W102)
62 "——," Dulcie warned. "——. How is Arthur, Waldo?" she asked.
   He was already mumbling off along the road. (W131)
63 "——," she said. "——. Arthur, for instance," Dulcie paused. "——.——. He brought me," she paused again, "——." (W152)

In **59**, we can assume from the free-indirect-discourse interruption and the descriptive crypto-tag about Arthur's lips that Waldo is actively following Arthur's delivery; the anticipation generated makes the anomalous (negated) terminal tag much more logical than it might otherwise seem. In **60**, both tags are superfluous. Arthur has already been identified in a crypto-tag as starting "to gulp for words", so that the medial tag constitutes a minimal spacing for a "gulp" where Arthur addresses Waldo by name. To use a "repeat"–tag where the direct speech has just shown the repetition can only be an underlining of Arthur's urgency and of Waldo's perception of this. In **61**, the first "said"–tag provides a minimal, conversational pause. The crypto-tag has a binding function in pointing anaphorically and cataphorically, and also ironizes Mrs Feinstein's speech and gestures through Waldo's sensibility. The second medial "said"–tag is there to provide a hinge for Waldo's perception of attendant gesture, which is intimately associated with the content of the sentence. In **62**, Dulcie's question is terminally tagged as a question because Waldo registers it at a spatial remove from her earlier words, and feels that it touches on a topic painful to him; the simple tag is significance-generating. In **63**, "paused" is actually a verb of speech-act cessation, but is treated as intermediate between a speech-tag and an asyndetic crypto-tag. For good reason—pauses, like smiles or laughs, need not be contrastive to a speech-act, but can instead be attendant markers. Moreover, these points of diegetically marked vocal hesitation can be said to correlate with Waldo's sharpened attention to the content of Dulcie's speech. The second tag in many such cases is not there to signal to the reader a contentual alteration, but rather to signal both the speaker's and the figural auditor's awareness that the alteration carries significance.

The main function of second and third tags can be to ensure that spaces or pauses between segments of a speech are adequately pointed (**79–80** below; **50** above), or to mark more radically broken or hesitant delivery:

64 "——, Waldo," said Mr Feinstein, taking a very strange one off the knob of a chair, "this——. Well," he said, "it——. But if I wear it—which I do," and he popped it gravely on his head, "it is——." (W104)
65 "——," Arthur continued to bellow, "——," he choked, "——." (W45)
66 "——," he said, "what," he said, "what form——." (W93)
67 "Golly," she said, "you're a kid," she said, "Arthur, at times!" (A259)
68 "——," she added. "Because——" she paused in thought, "in case——." (A246)
69 "——," Waldo said,——. "I'd take, I'd keep them," he said, "if I were you——." (W129)

70 "I am not in love, though," she said. "At least," she said, "I am afraid," but there she halted. (W154)

71 "——," Miss Dallimore continued, "——"—and here she was searching—"——." (A259)

72 "But perhaps," Miss Dallimore revived again, "perhaps in time"—she was at her marmalady brightest—"——!" (W51)

73 "——." Perhaps that was going too far. "I mean," he said, "it is——, and nothing I can say in sympathy will help," he said, "either——." (W152)

74 "——," he said, "is——," he added, "——." (W195)

75 "——," Waldo said, "and——. What I have found," he stammered, "is——." (W153)

76 "——," he admitted. "——," he stammered, "——." (W69)

77 "Well," said Waldo, getting up, "——, but," he positively insisted, "know when——." (W156)

78 "Well," he said, "it——. So very simple," he repeated. (A240)

79 "——," he said. "Yes," he agreed, trundling slower. "——. Christians," he said, "are cruel." (A261)

The gasping pauses of the terrified Mrs Poulter (**67**), the choked incoherence of Arthur (**65**) and the stuttering resumptions of Waldo (**66**) are good examples of the iconic tagging of vocal delivery. The crypto-tag in **68** marks a pause as a pause to convey Arthur's awareness of some (unarticulated) deeper motivation for Dulcie's changing the substance of her speech. In **69–70**, and implicitly or explicitly in other cases, the repeated tags mark jerky delivery in order to point up the self-consciousness with which the characters try to use language (note the simple verbs again) to express intimate concepts. In various ways, items **64–79** all have multiple tagging to suggest the emotional disequilibrium accompanying the utterance, the nervous searching for something suitable to say (**72**); social inadequacy to the task of formulating a topic (**71**); self-conscious calculation (**73**), deliberation (**74**), or awareness of the artificiality of what is articulated (**75, 77**). The tag may redundantly foreground a repetition (**78**) because the speaker, in his embarrassed inadequacy, pathetically implies as much by a change of tone. In **79**, Arthur is playing along with Mrs Poulter conversationally—but unwillingly, conscious that he is "speech-acting" until he is forced at the end into making an uncompromising declaration; the medial tagging marks the lingering caution in his manner. Iconic diegesis can play its part in self-conscious statements, whether via the specificity of a speech-act verb in a syntactically "stammering" location in the sentence (**75–76**) or via parenthetical crypto-tags in free indirect discourse which occur at the pause or tonal shift that they are commenting on (**71–73**).

It has been remarked that "while there can be no doubt that intonation is linguistically relevant (it can distinguish interrogative from declarative, after all), there must be considerable doubt as to whether tone of voice involves linguistic parameters at all" (Quirk et al. 1972: 1047). White has tackled this problem head-on, as much of his multiple tagging demonstrates, by at least ensuring that the suprasegmental component of intonation which is present at phrase-boundaries is marked by tags in ways that invite the reader to deduce shifts in tone of voice. He thereby manages to avoid heavy dosages of diegetic speech-description (except where figural mental states are involved), refines the texture of the narration, and preserves the "scenic" character of direct speech without having to commit himself to the behaviouristic, functionalistic disengagement typical of a Hemingway or a Lawrence. Faulkner chooses a path which is much narrower than White's; his tagging procedure can achieve great sensitivity of effect, but with a necessary constriction of the range of effects. James, in an earlier age, could mediate tonal shifts with hair-trigger precision, too: but his basic strategies are skewed in the direction of greater, and decelerative, analysis of speech-acts and the paraphernalia of mental action and reaction surrounding these, because of his massive implementation of grammatically discrete crypto-tags. Of the writers surveyed, it is White who achieves the greatest degree of integration between direct speech and speech-act diegesis; and it is White who is most prepared to take syntax, semantics, punctuation and tagging "norms" as far as the logic of the resources of English will allow.

III   Initial tagging

WHITE'S PRACTICE

Bonheim (1982:76–80 passim) views speech-tags in regard to their position in the manner of an architectural engineer: the load-bearing capacity of the tag is the main factor in his deliberations. This leads him to conclude that tags which are long ("heavy with embedded description of the speaker or his situation": eg, "She stopped, as if she were communing with the past, and then said shrewdly:") tend to precede the speech, while narratorial comment tends to be embedded in terminal tags. The second factor determining initial tagging, Bonheim argues, is length of speech: long speeches require initial tags.

In *The Solid Mandala*, 58% of White's speeches with initial tags consist of only one sentence, a further 14% of only two sentences. White thus uses initial tags predominantly with short speeches. The initial tags in the novel were classified into eight groups according to diegetic function. There are only two categories which overlap with Bonheim's: tags which are placed initially *primarily* because the speech that follows is long (ranging from four to nine sentences in length); and tags which are placed initially *primarily* because they involve description of the speaker or his immediate situation. These two categories together account for only about 10% of the speeches in White. If embedding and lengthiness are formally discernible in initial tags whose primary function lies elsewhere, then there are still no more than about 22% of all tags which can be explained according to Bonheim's criteria. One must take the concept of "embedded description of the speaker or his situation" narrowly—otherwise, the whole idea of the speech-act relevance of attendant diegesis is rendered meaningless. The example from Bonheim quoted above describes both the immediate circumstances prior to a speech-act (the gesture of "she stopped", with the cohesive embedding of "and then") and the modality of the speech-act itself ("shrewdly"). The most conspicuous element, however, is pseudo-descriptive at best, since "as if/though" analogies should, in Bonheim's modal scheme, count as narratorial comment. There is, at any rate, a strong admixture of description and comment, most of it relating to the speaker's situation immediately prior to a speech-act. By this token, the following kinds of tag in White would qualify within Bonheim's scheme:

1 Arthur told quietly after that, but told: "(7 sentences)" (W144)
2 His father put on his gravest expression, and said in his most prudent voice: "(3)" (W79)
3 Arthur called back then, as though he had been giving it thought: "(1)" (W113)
4 Then Waldo read aloud, not so menacingly as he would have liked, because he was, in fact, menaced: "(1)" (W212)
5 Fearing his friend, at this, if only at this point, might be in need of assistance, Arthur began to chatter on what probably sounded too high, too irrelevant a note: "(1)" (A251)
6 She wasn't laughing, so, lowering his head he read out aloud, pushing the words well forward with his lips, because he almost doubted he would be able to form them, he was so excited: "(3)" (A238)
7 Anyway, Mr Saporta had returned, and the day Arthur went to his shop, approached with the appearance of a merchant receiving a genuine customer—certainly business was pretty slack—and clapping his hands together, asked: "(1)" (A259)

Several of these tag-extensions incorporate description which is actually "narratorial comment" (3–5) or free indirect discourse (6–7). These extensions, furthermore, are often diegetically cohesive, the run-up to the speech-tag proper including anaphoric or consecutive-additive words binding the speech-situation with the prior narrative situation (eg, "after than", "anyway, ... the day"). When these cohesive signals, and the kind of non-immediate diegesis of action exhibited at the beginning of 7 above, take the upper hand, then it makes little sense to talk of the speech-tag being embedded in description of the speaker or his immediate situation. That is to say, we find linking diegesis including the circumstances or the speaker's actions prior to the speech situation, rather than diegesis which constitutes a preparation for, or accompaniment of, speech. Tags plus situational diegesis like the following do not count as elaborated tags:

8 Later on, when she was ill, and fanciful, and old, Anne Brown, born a Quantrell, said to her sons absently: "—(6)—" (W80)
9 Then, when she had gathered up her knees inside her arms, and laid her face against her shoulder, she began dreaming, as she rocked: "—(9)—" (A278)
10 Once, at the height of a storm, when the rain was coming down aslant, in slate-pencils, against the roof, the water coming through the rusty tin, in that same place, into the basin, in the scullery, and the quince-trees squeaking against, the rose-thorns scratching on, the panes, Waldo shouted: "—(1)—" (A282)

The same applies to some 23% of White's initial tags, where they are attached quite naturally to, or arise out of, the flow of the narrative.

Every multi-phrasal or multi-clausal diegetic sentence with an initial tag after it tends to be received differently from medial or terminal tags, or from terse and unadorned initial tags (what Bonheim characterizes as "an unobtrusive *I said* or ... a pungent *growled* or *snapped*" [80]—banal tags these, stereotyped even in differentiated form, but the standard, according to Bonheim, "in the modern novel"). It doesn't matter where the actual speech-tag occurs in the diegesis. The main point about initial tags is that they are cataphoric and annunciatory. The effect of anticipation can be heightened by subordinate sentence-constituents (the best example being 10 above), or even by degrees of coordination (2, 7) or heaped postmodification (3–6). The presence of strong pointing via the colon (with unelaborated tags in particular) rather than weak comma-pointing serves to "dramatize" diegesis in a manner quite the opposite in effect to coloned stage-directions in drama-texts, which exact no engagement from the reader.[9]

White is highly sensitive to the communicative quality of initial tagging; the eight-group classification I have adopted serves to explain his technique better than a formalistic categorization:

Group (1) tags signal the attitude of expectation adopted by the figural listener, the resolution of expectation, and the like. Prior diegetic or mimetic context is a critical factor in allowing the reader to conclude that the tagging serves primarily this function:

11 "Because I want to see life," Waldo answered brutally. "You don't want to deny me that?"
   Arthur said: "No."
   Waldo was punctured then. (W25)

The initial tagging with a colon can hardly be explained here as systemic variation ("'No,' said Arthur" would have done well enough, if this were the case). Nor is there a norm that calls for initial tagging after a question—nor, indeed, does this constitute even a norm internal to this novel. A clue is, of course, offered by the diegesis that follows: "punctured" itself indicates the deflating of expectation. If we concede that Bonheim's observation about short speeches taking terminal tags is correct, then White has clearly gone out of his way here to contravene this norm. If the sentence with "punctured" were absent, the initial minimal tag would still convey anticipation, and the brevity of the following direct speech a "puncturing" or anticlimactic resolution. The principle of cataphora, applied within a narrative context appropriate to it, is a strongly psychologizing principle: it is Waldo who expects some response consonant with his own present emotional pitch. Here are some examples of Group (1) tags:

12 Arthur felt the need to ask: (W81)
13 But all Arthur would say was: (W99)
14 For the man had begun to knock, and ask: (W188)
15 Only Crankshaw grumbling: (W166)
16 Muttering still: (W211)
17 Then Mother's: (A270)
18 Arthur said: (W123)
19 When she had told him, Cis said: (W129)
20 And Dulcie said: (W137)

---

[9] On the colon and cataphora, see Partridge (1964: 53–54); Quirk et al. (1972: 1065–66); Halliday/Hasan (1976: 17). Peprník (1969: 145–46, 151) regards the "formal features" of tags as "becoming more and more unsettled," along with an historical blurring of the difference between reporting verbs proper (those referring to the mode of the speech-act) and "verbs from ... new spheres" referring to attendant mental or gestural attitudes. He sees the colon as indicating "the connection with the communication of the direct speech"; the comma relaxes the boundary: the tag and the direct speech are merely parallel; the "most recent development in punctuation is the use of a full stop; between the two parts of communication there is merely a contextual interrelation." As should become clear in the discussion of White's practice and that of the comparative authors, there is more functional significance in punctuative gradation than Peprník's account allows for.

Initial tagging in this group consistently implies a listener's fearful, nervous, or simply keen anticipation of the imminent resolution of a situation through a speaker's words. The situation set up may be gestural (the figural observer has been trying to interpret the actions of another character) or vocal (the figural listener is already in the process of interpreting the discourse-signals of a fellow-interlocutor). The cataphoric, "here it comes!" effect can be almost wholly independent of anything explicitly relevant in the immediate context: ie, the initial tag may indicate a kind of coterminousness, signalling that the speech which follows immediately elicits the sharpened awareness of a figural listener. It is crucial for Waldo (**13** above) to concentrate his attention on what Arthur has to say about the Feinsteins—there is a kind of question raised in the preceding diegesis regarding whether or not the Feinsteins know Arthur, but the connection between the thoughts mediated in the diegesis and the substance of the speech is signalled entirely by the nature of the tag (see also especially **18–20** above).

Group (2) tags are performer-oriented, and signal various degrees of calculation, intentionality or self-consciousness. The annunciatory, cataphoric tags usually help indicate that the speaker is aware of his own speech-delivery, and/or that a figural listener is aware that the speaker is aware. Here is an example of the former:

21 Now when he heard his own breathing united with Arthur's, and realized how it might startle a stranger, he thought it better to advise:
   "It won't do not to remember that your heart may be starting to give trouble ...." (W31)

Or there is Waldo, recovered from the shock of almost being caught by Arthur as he stands in his mother's dress, addressing his brother after concealing the garment—he deliberately talks away from any topic related to himself, and concentrates on what Arthur has said about catching Mrs Poulter out:

22 Now at least he was free, in fact, if not in fact.
   When he returned he said: "It serves you right, Arthur. It must have embarrassed you to intrude like that on someone else's privacy." (W194)

The situational irony here is inescapable once one realizes that Arthur's talk about Mrs Poulter has itself been a pretext to deflect Waldo's attention from the thought that he might have been caught out by Arthur. An example of the second implication occurs after Mrs Feinstein, in the presence of both Arthur and Waldo, mentions that Leonard Saporta won't be visiting the house that day:

23 "Is he a relative?" Waldo asked.
   Mrs Feinstein said: "No."
   The mention of relatives set her off sighing again, and he hardly dared, though did finally enquire after the Signora Terni of Milan. (W138)

Once again there is a foregrounding followed by incommensurately brief direct speech—not that the relative length of the speech is the deciding factor. If the conventional context at this point were entirely casual, terminal tag-placement would have been in order. What comes across is some almost imperceptible hesitancy on Mrs Feinstein's part, after which she commits herself to an answer that hangs there, significance-laden. *Waldo's* perception of significant delivery, however, does not translate in the diegesis into an interpretation of the reply;

instead, he picks up on her separate vocal gesture and connects it with part of his own question. In the process, he sails right by the possibility that Saporta, though not a "relative", is all set to become one where it will hurt Waldo most. After we have read the concise comment (free indirect discourse) on Waldo's question in Arthur's section, the initial tag, colon, and minimal (non-explanatory and noncommittal) spoken answer become keenly ironic. Other performer-oriented instances include the following:

24 So he said now: (W72)
25 Sometimes adding: (W86)
26 This time Waldo said: (W126)
27 On several occasions—— Waldo tempted his mother by asking: (W145)
28 He cleared his throat before replying: (W158)
29 He continued babbling, he heard: (A244)
30 He replied, simply, sadly: (A280)
31 To call or laugh: (A291)

Group (3) tags are essentially citational, heralding a typical or habitual piece of direct speech. They are thus annunciatory in a perfectly conventional sense, and the speech itself often occurs in the middle of a piece of diegesis, as would a quotation:

32 [Paragraph of diegesis, then:]
Dad used to say in the beginning: "Arthur's so strong [two sentences]."
[Paragraphs of diegesis follow.] (W33)
33 [One-sentence paragraph of diegesis, then:]
Mrs Poulter would come and say: "When we was [5 lines of direct speech]."
[One-sentence paragraph of diegesis.] (W159)

In most such cases, the direct speech is illustrative of comment made in the preceding diegesis. Related to these are Group (4) tags, which have attached to them descriptions of, and/or comment on, the speaker and/or his immediate situation; these have already been discussed:

34 One evening Dad, after he had ..., said between pulling out the milk:
"Now this is a job for a boy like you, Waldo.——.——?" (W36)
35 When a lady approached him, ..., and fetched out a screech ...:
"You big *man*, where have you *bin*?" (A280)

In Group (5), the tags (which are customarily very short) function as a kind of jolt or jerk, whereby the given figural consciousness (Waldo or Arthur) is moved from free-indirect-discourse introspection onto the plane of the immediate perception of speech. Such tags are occasionally atactic, or may include a speech-act verb in the progressive figural consciousness:

36 There he stood, a little apart, on the white, windswept grass. With Johnny saying: "That bloke hadn't reckoned on one more murder ...." (W44)
37 Even before Waldo gave one of his looks, which, when interpreted, meant:—— so my reply, Arthur, is not shit, but shit!
As he shouted: "No, Arthur! Go, Arthur!" (A273)
38 He knew the men by sight,——, the other a stooge to his companion of the moment.
Holmes was saying: "Sawney bugger!" he laughed without mirth. "——. ——. ——?" (W146)

In Group (6) are those initial tags whose dominant function is to mark the inception of longer sections of direct speech (eg, sentence **9** above). In the small Group (7) are such constructions as the following:

39 "I'd hoped you would stay with us," Mother said, "today." She added quickly, without looking round: "I'm sure Waldo would appreciate it." (W74)

This is an example of an initial tag which (as the tag-verb "added" itself indicates) is an addition to a section of direct speech that has already been tagged; these tags are, as a rule, only mildly annunciatory, and generally need to take this position on systemic grounds. In Group (8), the tags are instances of iconic function, whereby a vocal gesture (pause for breath, etc) is marked immediately prior to speech:

40 He once gasped: "Obviously not for copulation."
Then when his panting had subsided, and he had thought it out: "Why," he said finally, "to protect us ...." (W181)

As I have already suggested, not all of these tag-functions are mutually exclusive; in particular, there is considerable double-classification possible between Groups (1) and (2), as befits a taxonomy which is situational and essentially psychological.

COMPARATIVE PASSAGES

James uses initial crypto-tags involving diegetic analysis (Strether's evaluative perception, or mental construction, of conversational dynamics). In only one case (an elliptical or verbless tag with attendant gesture) is a true initial tag furnished with a "dramatic" colon ("Her friend wondered; then with raised eyebrows: '—?'" [p. 361]), though such pointing is more frequent with internal initial tags within longer speeches, where the tags can be classified as belonging to Group (7) above:

41 "I know that too," Strether smiled. To which he added with an irrelevance that was only superficial: "I come from Woollett Massachusetts." It made her ... laugh, (p. 12)
42 "—[15 lines of direct speech]—. How can I be indifferent," she asked, "to how I appear to you?" And as he found himself unable immediately to say: "Why, if you're going, *need* you, after all?——?" (p. 348)

In no case does the context in James suggest that the initial tags have a psychological component, involve citation, entail heavy embedding, or introduce long speeches.

Conrad exhibits his own kind of sensitivity. He sometimes employs comma'ed tags, which are either semantically low-keyed or fairly minimal in terms of speech-act verbs ("said [in a soft tone]", "muttered", "murmured"), or arise out of longer pieces of diegesis (eg, "who was murmuring hastily"):

43 Decoud muttered, "Oh, yes, we must comfort our friends, the speculators."
[4-line paragraph]
Basilio, standing aside against the wall, said in a soft tone to the passing ladies, "——." (p. 483)
44 Charles Gould smiled at the round, startled eyes of the dealer in hides, who was murmuring hastily, "Just so. Just so." (p. 498)

Conrad's coloned tags (with indented direct speech) include a "histrionic" element that might well suggest figural attention to the speech heard ("ruminated ... then began afresh"; "lips ... forming the words"):

45 He ruminated his discontent for a while, then began afresh with a sidelong glance at Antonia:
"Yes, the noise outside the city wall is new,——." (p. 482)
46 [One paragraph of diegesis] In her whole figure her lips alone moved, forming the words:
"Martin, you will make me cry." (p. 488)

Lawrence uses drably minimal speech-act verbs ("said", "added", "cried"). Both his true initial tags with indenting of direct speech, and his internal initial tags, involve consecutive vocal gestures or actions. They are as lacking in specific functionality (apart from the fact that direct speech follows) as James's tags:

47 As she sketched she chuckled to herself, and cried out at times:
"Oh, darling, you're so beautiful!"
[9 lines of diegesis] and then cried, with real grief for the dog, and at the same time with a wicked exultation:
"My beautiful, why did they?" (p. 265)

The peculiar technique of intercalation employed by Faulkner in *Intruder in the Dust* has already been discussed. In the corpus from *Light in August,* there are three true initial tags with a colon, all minimal (eg, 48 below); in another case (49), the tag is comma'ed and preceded by a subordinate clause:

48 [One paragraph of diegesis] Byron said to Mooney: "I am surprised at that.——." (pp. 30–31)
49 (One paragraph of diegesis] When the foreman came in, one said: "Well, I see you have lost one of your apprentice firemen." (p. 33)

The use of the colon itself is more important to Faulkner as a cohesive device than the initial placement of his minimal tags (though there are stretches in other novels by Faulkner where strings of present-tense initial tags occur, to suggest the inexorable, subdued, reflex dramatism of dialogue). There is even a case of a medial tag followed by a cataphoric colon instead of the expected full stop:

50 None of them had ever seen him before. "Except that's a pretty risky look for a man to wear on his face in public," one said: "He might forget and——." (p. 26)

Naipaul's practice is almost as featureless as Lawrence's, except for the fact that, like Conrad, he uses both commas and colons, invariably with tags employing the minimal *said*. The comma is functional: a cool, undramatic continuation is effected between the two or three phrasal or clausal components of initial diegesis (participial or coordinate embedding of gesture in the main) and the direct speech:

51 Mrs Tulsi looked as though——. Chewing, she—— and said, "——?" (p. 90)
52 [5 lines of diegesis] Lightly, smiling——, he asked Mrs Tulsi, "——?" (p. 101)

In the one instance here where a colon is used, it comes after a minimal tag, and the context suggests that the tag could be analysed into one of the groups used for White, as a psychological component of fulfilled anticipation (the bridging of an awkward silence) is involved:

53 Mrs Tulsi chewed and said nothing.
   Seth said: "I know Ajodha. You want me to go and see him?" (p. 90)

Apart from a mild admixture of initial crypto-tags of attendant gesture, there is nothing particularly noteworthy about Naipaul's tagging practice.

    Randolph Stow is a more interesting case, since much in *Tourmaline* and his other earlier novels suggests that he has worked his way out from under the shadow of White, possesses a not dissimilar artistic personality, or (as Sharrad argues) resembles White and Koch in his abreaction against an earlier and drab conventional narrative modality. The overall mixture of tags differs from that in all the other writers, including White. Whereas Stow favours terse speeches, like Lawrence, he is much more given to zero-tags, for example—but the zero-tagging occurs in passages of dialogue that are low in tension, whereas White uses zero-tagging almost invariably at points of great psychological tension and figural wariness. Stow's initial tags are almost as infrequent as Lawrence's, but their cataphoric relation to the minimal direct speech following them is intense and deliberately effected. There is one internal initial tag, which is sensitively pointed after the medial tag to suggest a conscious pause by the speaker rather than smooth additive continuation (**54**). There is some light embedding of attendant gesture (eg, **55** below), and a use of that milder form of ataxis characteristic of White ("And ...", "But ..."). Adverbial postmodification also resembles White's in its foregrounding internal punctuation (cf **56** below with **30** above):

54 "I don't mind," I said; adding: "He's an interesting boy." (p. 87)
55 And Byrne, on the slate paving of the yard, kept muttering: "'S all right, Deb, 's all right." (p. 94)
56 She said, indifferently: "I can't imagine anything else." (p. 87)

Stow's tags, finally, fit easily into the two categories set up for White (Groups (1) and (2)) that signal psychological involvement. The respective conversational and diegetic contexts reveal and confirm these functional classifications. Nevertheless, even in passages of equivalent length to those drawn on for comparison, White's practice is far more finely differentiated and sensitive than that of the other novelists.

IV   Intrasentential tagging

Much can be said about the functions of medial tags that would be relevant to the poetics of the mimesis/diegesis interface. There is, for example, the fact that such tags, by definition, constitute a diegetic interruption of what would otherwise be pure mimetic flow, whereas true initial and terminal tags essentially leave direct speech alone for its "actual" duration. The perceptibility of "telling" thus differs according to tag-position. Given a baseline of minimal (non-modified) tagging, the reader will tend not to pay much attention to terminal tags: it is the speech itself that commands his concentration, and he is keyed to moving on to the next speech–turn. Although Bonheim claims that it is modern practice for a tag "to be ... pushed into the left margin to get it out of the way, as in a dramatic text" (76), it can be argued that such a practice does not really get initial tags "out of the way" in the sense of making them narrationally inconspicuous. Tags tend to interact with the adjacent diegetic context, and can, as I have endeavoured to show, be made functionally most conspicuous indeed. But it still holds true that exostatic (initial and terminal) tags, unless they are deliberately potentiated by additional diegesis or punctuation, are less noticeable than endostatic tags (ie, tags of any positional variety which occur in the midst of a passage of direct speech). Although all speech-tags are, as reporting-clauses, grammatically classifiable as "comment clauses", it is endostatic tags which are most like true comments in the speech-pragmatic sense. We notice *while* someone is represented as speaking that the speech is being diegetically edited. The discussion of multiple tagging above, moreover, suggests that internal tagging can fulfil other, contrastive or systemic tasks than signalling narratorial presence or serving as hooks on which to hang descriptions: it can signal shifts of time, topic or pace, for example.

In order, however, to determine what stylistic constants might obtain with regard to medial tags, and to establish gradients of deviance or individuality, it is necessary to examine such tags as a closed system. Medial tags can be divided into two classes: **stopped,** and **intrasentential.** Stopped tags are followed by a period. More precisely, an anaphoric relationship is established between (a) a piece of direct speech which would be complete in the absence of a tag, and (b) a piece of diegesis (conventionally based on a speech-tag) which refers back to that speech. Furthermore, (c) a second piece of direct speech must follow, as a rule syntactically independent of the first. If (c) does not occur, the tagging is, of course, terminal. This medial structure is present in Bonheim's normative example ("'I don't know,'—— said. ' I hurt bad'").

The other—intrasentential—class of medial tags involves the invasion of the structure of a direct-speech sentence. Whereas medial tags as a whole constitute the largest positional type in modern narrative, intrasentential tags are generally much less frequent than stopped tags. Conrad's and Naipaul's stopped tags are twice as frequent as intrasentential ones; 80–90% of Lawrence's, Faulkner's and Stow's medial tags are stopped. White is an exception, in that the distribution is almost exactly fifty-fifty. James stands alone at the other extreme from Lawrence and company: only 22% of his medial tags are stopped (but we have to remember that he uses crypto-tags; due regard for these stopped-tag equivalents, however, still does not bring the figure for James up above about 32%).

Stopped medial tags in White are generally attached to sentences of direct speech which are short and simple in terms of their constituents ("'Come along,' Waldo ordered. 'It's only old'", W56). With longer speeches, one has to fall back on explanations that account for the tag in terms of major informational units marked by tonal shift ("'I bought the pen-knife, didn't I, Mum?' Arthur said. 'Last time. With my share of the draft'" W50). In the latter example, it would theoretically have been possible to place the tag elsewhere. As soon as one starts moving the tag around experimentally, however, one realizes how much influence placement has on the tonal information (and thus on the meaning) that the reader deduces from a printed representation of speech. Where spoken sentences are longer, especially in terms of the number of main constituents and phrase-boundaries analysed out of them, an intrasentential tag may have to be inserted if a tag is to be used at all. There seem to be six syntactic situations—often marked in a zero-tagged sentence by internal punctuation—in which the occurrence of an intrasentential tag is felt by the reader to be natural, "acceptable" (readers can, of course, be persuaded to accept anything, so that my use of the adjective is artificially demarcational), or unexceptional. I list these situations here, with sample-sentences from White:

(1)   Interjections before the tag:

1 "Yes," said Arthur, "but——." (W24)
2 "Why," said Miss Dallimore, "——." (W52)
3 "Now," she said, taking——, "——." (A259)
4 "Ah," said Mr Allwright, "——." (A222)

(2)   Vocatives, imperatives, appositives before the tag:

5 "This gate, Waldo," Arthur was saying gently, "will——." (W26)
6 "Tell me," she said, more sympathetic, or inquisitive, "what——?" (A238)
7 "Your brother," she said, "is he——?" (W98)

(3)   At clause-juncture:

(3a) Coordinate clause after the tag:

8 "Perhaps if we hang around she'll come out," said Arthur, "and then we can——." (W27)
9 "If you read the paper," he coaxed, "and I see you do take the *Herald,* you——." (W143; parenthetical)

(3b) One clause subordinate:

10 "Even as a little girl," said Mother, "Mollie was the soul of kindness." (W50)
11 "Most," said Mother, "considering Mollie is not the best of correspondents." (W50)
12 "When the money has been saved up," said Mother, "you shall both——." (A231)

(4)   Adverbials, especially disjuncts and conjuncts, before the tag:

13 "In any case," she said, "——." (W51)
14 "Come to think of it," she said, "——." (A237)
15 "Besides," she said, "——." (A256)

(5)   Repetition or resumption of initial segment:

16 "Our father," he bellowed, "our father is *dead!*" (W71)
17 "His head," Mrs Musto explained, "his *business* head was——." (A236)

(6)   Pause indicated or implied in the tag or tag-supplement:

18 "The main thing," said Dad, sucking his sparrow-coloured moustache, "is to——." (W77)
19 "You," she said, clearing her throat, because——, "wouldn't mind——." (W95)
20 "—— before reaching these to-some-extent," Mr Feinstein cleared his throat, "enlightened shores." (W104)
21 "This nude lady," he explained, and winked, "represents Reason——." (W105)

Category (6) is an exception to the rule that punctuation would normally mark phrase-juncture: the placing of the tag is, in effect, explained by additional diegesis (participial clauses for attendant gesture; in **21**, a coordinate clause to signal gestural punctuation of a significant tonal curve at the end of the deictic phrase "This nude lady"); or a crypto-tag represents a vocally punctuated pause.

In many sentences classifiable under Category (3), clause-juncture need not be indicated punctuatively; what is decisive for acceptability is our knowledge that clause-juncture in speech is suprasegmentally conspicuous. It is this fact which explains why certain classes of subordination should be felt as less "acceptable". Before nominal and restrictive-relative clauses, there is no sharp melodic change, and with good reason—referential unity with the main clause is essential, and is ensured by tonal continuity. This, however, should not persuade us to the easy assumption that writers introduce medial tags at points of syntactic but not tonal juncture merely because the existence of a notional gap is convenient for the tagging of longer sentences. Take a simple instance, where one of the Dallimore sisters has been crawling to Mrs Brown about how delightful it has been for them "'to make the acquaintance of the Honourable Mrs Thourault's cousin'". Arthur is fascinated by the name and by the non-Australian honorific, and mimicks Miss Dallimore's words, thereby disconcerting her:

22 "The only pity is," said the persevering Miss Dallimore, "that Mr Brown should still be at the Bank." (W51)

The adjective "persevering" happens to give the game away in this tag: the norm of neutral tonal continuity is not guaranteed in a conversational context where resistance is offered to natural delivery. Miss Dallimore has been spooked by Arthur, and has to assert herself above what, she anticipates, may be further disruption: so she tries to pretend that there has been no disturbance of the conversational register she has adopted—not, however, by proceeding with tonal equanimity and obeying the norm for this kind of sentence but, paradoxically and with situationally ironic effect for the reader, by forcing insistently against the norm to ensure that she still has the say. The invisible effect (invisible, or silent, in print) is that Miss Dallimore makes "is" into a fall-rise tonal nucleus to show that her utterance up to now is non-final.[10] In 23, the tag-position highlights what must be a rise-fall nucleus of surprise on "suspected"; similarly on "coincidence" in 24:

23 "What," she said, "Arthur, I never suspected," she said, "that you were another one for books." (A237)
24 "It is a most curious coincidence," Miss Dallimore said, and her sister Dorothy supported her in muffled tone, "that we should be paying this visit——." (W49)

Other points of juncture in nominal sentences marked by tags can similarly be construed (after due consideration of the conversational context) as being marked for significant tonal deflection from the norm. This also applies to relative sentences (eg, 30–33 below), which normally "have the main stress on the last

---

[10] There is a summary of stress, rhythm and intonation in Quirk et al. (1972), the chief tonal nuclei and pitch changes being treated in II.12–14: 1044–46, II.17: 1048. More than one interpretation is doubtless possible, but I imagine "is" here to have a high pitch-onset on the vowel, followed by a fall, followed by a rise of non-finality including the sibilant. With tempo, "as with height and range or with tone of voice ..., we can easily slip beyond the normal bounds of linguistic description" (Quirk et al. 1972: 1049).

stressable item in the postmodification" (Quirk et al. 1972: 1041). In the White examples, the melodic or pitch pattern of the part of the sentence before the tag has been shifted away from the norm under emotionally triggered situational pressure on rhetorical configuration. The remaining examples below fall into rough groupings according to formal, syntactic analysis. The break, ·at its simplest, can come before a nominal clause (25–27); 34–47 have prepositional adjuncts or *to*-infinitives in a dependent relation to adjectives or nouns; 48–58 split the subject off from the predicate; 59–61 split *wh*-words and conjunctions off from the remainder of the sentence:

25 "You realize," he said, "this is to bear out a theory I expounded." (W108)

26 "I can never remember," she complained, "whether I have paid the rates." (W162)

27 "Don't tell me," said Mrs Poulter, as prim as Waldo, "that you don't believe in Our Lord Jesus Christ?" (A261)

28 "She seemed to think," Maria answered, "that he might have gone away with *you*." (James, p. 358)

29 "And you may imagine," he continued, his tone passing into light banter, "that Montero—— ." (Conrad, p. 485)

30 "It was all because of the old essay," Arthur was keeping on, "that Johnny Haynes thought was silly." (W46)

31 "That is not a word," said Dad, "I ever want to hear in my house." (W80)

32 "The letter," Arthur said, "which you left lying on the dressing-table." (W107)

33 "Oh, I think it's a thing," he said, "that you must——." (James, p. 12)

34 "It's nothing," he said, "but exercise." (W63)

35 "People die," he said, "usually in one of two ways." (W69)

36 "That depends," she said, "on a lot of things." (A259)

37 "What I really want to do," he said, "is write." (W93)

38 "I mentioned them," said Mother, "only this morning." (W52)

39 "It's that long," she said, "since I got a letter." (A258)

40 "I'm really," she said, "a very mundane individual." (W101)

41 "Perhaps," she added, "I shall—for I'm staying over." (James, p. 7)

42 "The failure to enjoy," Miss Gostrey explained, "is what I mean." (James, p. 13)

43 "But it isn't," she declared, "because I'm afraid——." (James, p. 348)

44 "But you ought," he wound up, "to be easy." (James, p. 349)

45 "But I'd be terrified," the other said, "of rams." (W88)

46 "I would have been interested," he grumbled, "to take a look at old Waldo." (W190)

47 "That's cheerful," he laughed, "for your benefactor!" (James, p. 353)

48 "But the house," he said, "looked dead." (W130)

49 "I think Dulcie," said Arthur, "will probably grow a moustache." (W80)

50 "*God,*" he said, and the spit spattered on Waldo's face, "is a kind of sort of *rock* crystal." (W87)

51 "And you," she said to Arthur, "musn't be upset, because Mr Brown isn't really hurt." (W67)

52 "Our only disappointment," Miss Dallimore confessed, "was that Lord Tolfree——." (W51)

53 "Tennyson," he said, "is, I suppose, everybody's property. Tennyson," he added, "wrote so much he must have——." (W195)

54 "Waldo," he told her, "is just about the jealousest thing you'll find." (W151)

55 "That," Mr Saporta agreed, "is a very fine Turkish rug." (A250)

56 "Christians," he said, "are cruel." (A261)

57 "The man," she said, thoughtfully, and very calm before this outburst, "was——." (Conrad, p. 486)

58 "We Occidentals," said Martin Decoud, using the usual term——, "have been——."
(Conrad, p. 487)
59 "What," he asked, "is the meaning of 'totality'?" (A240)
60 "Why," Waldo asked, "do you have to listen to that stupid, babbling cow?" (W144)
61 "Why," asked Arthur, "should we keep what hurts?" (A293)

The main function of such tags is not to shock the reader by unmotivated audacity; nor is it to *annotate* the specific tonal configuration of the direct speech—it is the task of descriptive diegesis to attempt this, where the danger is always that of suggesting analogies which do not quite match up to the subtlety of the tonality, or which even try do the reader's thinking for him. Indeed: intrasentential tagging at unusual junctures serves to point out to the reader that he shouldn't be reading smoothly through speech, but should be re-examining context against speech in the awareness that the narrator is nudging him and/or that a reflector-character or focalized figural consciousness has picked up on something in the inflection or tone of a speaker which, though inchoate as yet, and unanalysed, has still been felt. It is this kind of subtle—and unobtrusive—marking for a particular tonal "presence" that White's prose shares with that of James and Conrad. The passages from Lawrence, Faulkner, Naipaul and Stow contain *no* "less acceptable" intrasentential tags, whereas the percentages of total speech-tags for James, Conrad and White are 38%, 22% and 24% respectively.

Sometimes it is the word immediately before the tag that is given exceptional tonal "stress" (to use the term loosely). This may be indicated graphically (eg, **50** above), but usually is not (eg, **36**, **39–40**, **49**, **54–55**). The context may imply a reason for the specific highlighting, be it a change of addressee (**51**) or a coincidence of vocal emphasis and physical punctuation (as with Waldo's surge of negative emotion on "nothing" as he jerks at Arthur's hand, **34**). Words are, however, usually "leaned on" in more subtle ways. Waldo's prevarication (**53**) leads him to try and gain thinking-time by attacking the topic-word "Tennyson" with enough heavy deliberation to make it sound as though he is being serious and honest rather than evasive. In **35**, Waldo approaches the unpleasant topic "die" gingerly and with enough annunciatory tonal lift to give him time to think up a classification permitting him to wriggle out from under Arthur's contemplation of his earlier attack of hysteria. In **52**, there is a semantic and tonal convergence between the noun "disappointment" and the tag-verb "confessed". In **38**, the pronoun-referent is not being stressed or in any other analysable way treated unusually; the sentence is closer to being an "acceptable" Group (4) one, with adverbial modification of the verb after the tag. What Mrs Brown is doing is spacing her speech, starting with a neutral statement of fact but signalling in advance the reproof to her husband's memory that is indicated in "only this morning". These pauses may be truly annunciatory; the diegesis that follows Waldo's declaration in **37** justifies the isolation of the words "is write" after the tag. The tonal configuration—especially the onset or attack—of single words before the tag may involve sudden resolution (eg, Arthur taking the bull interrogatively by the horns in **59**), or a checking of strong emotion (eg, **60**).

Hesitation at the prospect of saying something potentially hurtful or upsetting may be implied (**56**, **61**), or a momentary groping for the right expression (**48**). These suggestions certainly do not exhaust the potential range of tonal emphasis, prosody and context-specific *melos* within speech. White appears to be hypersensitive to such potentialities of meaning, as his tagging for vocal "presence" is much more varied and much less amenable to snap analysis than that of his predecessors James and Conrad. Nominal and relative constructions apart, the more radical syntactic breaks are comparatively few and far between in the latter two. In Conrad (**57–58**), the direct speech preceding the tag ends with a thoughtful, pre-formulatory pause before an apodictic closure of the sentence (**57** even categorizes the tone as thoughtful in the tag-modification). James's practice, too, is relatively transparent. In **47**, the tag itself indicates that it coincides with a vocal break; "enjoy" in **42** is clearly stressed; in **41**, "perhaps" (which is not disjunctive in this kind of structure) is semantically hesitant, and we can assume that the speaker does hesitate. In **43–44**, there is a degree of congruence between the specific speech-act verbs and the interpretation of the unusual tag-placement as indicating the slightest of tonal pauses before a cautious commitment to frank admission. The kind of sensitivity in social intercourse that is adumbrated is quintessentially Jamesian, and is to some extent consonant with the *Zeitgeist* as mediated through a particular social class.

I should not wish to suggest that White's technique is a—perhaps the ultimate—refinement of a principle of narrative mediation which is early modern(ist) or even a fossil remnant of a nineteenth-century "fashion". This would be facile. (By contrast, it is not facile to compare White's vision and narrative compass with those of the great French and Russian novelists of last century—the comparison stands up well to scrutiny and has often enough been made; but not, so far as I can determine, on grounds of specific stylistic or discoursal features.) Like White's tagging practice elsewhere, the intrasentential pointing exploits the natural resources of the language: it is deviation from the bland norms of fiction, perhaps, but not the quirky abuse of syntax. Nor is White's tagging automatic, in the sense of being reflexively systemic or decorative. "Less acceptable" intrasentential tags can be found in novels by writers who (like Patricia Highsmith, for example) are fascinating manipulators of the vagaries of human psychology but often woefully inept manhandlers of narrative devices. Highsmith is a "contemporary" writer, operating on the shadowline between crime-fiction and the mainstream novel. High Modernists may also exhibit such tagging procedures, and reveal sensitivity—Virginia Woolf, for instance, in the watershed phase before the full implementation of modernist narration. There is a sense of "presence" and of narrative rhythm in Woolf, as in White; and none in Highsmith.[11]

---

[11] Cf Highsmith, *Edith's Diary:* "'I don't know,' Edith said with difficulty, 'if you expect me to fight'" (102); "'I'm gonna make shur-r,' Norm said, 'he breaks a knee'" (109)—both with minimal tags, object-clause constructions, and vocal hiatus indicated (in a tag-modifier; in the direct speech itself). These are the only instances of "radical" intrasentential tagging in the first half of the novel. There are five in the first half of Woolf's *Jacob's Room,* all with *said*

V   On the gradability of true tags

White's true speech-tags can occasionally pull one up short—much more often than in the case of James, say, for all the latter's technical refinement. It may be a matter of semantic specificity (as with the unusual verbs of vocalization applied to Arthur's utterances). These tags are easy enough to get used to. Although such verbs as *gobble/gollop* obey normal structuring rules, the reader may find himself checking nevertheless to see whether they really do behave like *say/shout*. This, however, is merely because sememes infrequently encountered in such contexts are usually checked against syntax in this way. But one tends to experience various degrees of difficulty in coping with what feels like a stretching of syntactic tolerances, rather than of semantic resources; or suspicion arises that semantic and syntactic habits may not be quite in line with one another.

Are there persuasive linguistic explanations for these various degrees of felt deviance from comfortable norms? Bonheim and Peprník are of little assistance here; Bonheim observes:

The inquit is also subject to fashions .... nineteenth century novelists show a preference for highly differentiated final inquits like *retorted Jerry* (Dickens) or *she breathed* and *I after an instant risked* (Henry James). In modern popular literature the differentiated inquits are used to steer the sympathy of the reader *(he sneered, she bravely countered)*, who needs to be constantly posted as to how he is to view what the characters say and do. [Bonheim 1982:78]

Bonheim sets up no guidelines to help us decide whether he is right in calling his handful of tags "highly differentiated". I take him to mean that the tags are not "conventional" *verba dicendi* like *said, asked* or *replied,* but are semantically more specific. This specificity, then, we are expected to take as a nineteenth-century "fashion". In my lexical research, tag-verbs were collated for White and the other novelists listed in the above table. Conrad uses *retort*—is he modern or premodern? White uses *breathe* three times—does this make him recidivist? James does happen to have the most "differentiated" verbs (among them *break out, bring out, challenge, concede, concur, confess, intervene, prevaricate,*

+ noun-subject tags: "'Our friend Masham,' said Timothy Durrant, 'would rather not be seen in our company'" (47); "'His sister,' said Timmy, 'is a very pretty girl'" (47); "'I rather think,' said Jacob, taking his pipe from his mouth, 'it is in Virgil'" (60); "'We think,' said two of the dancers, breaking off from the rest, and bowing profoundly before him, 'that you are the most beautiful man we have ever seen'" (71); "'Now let us talk,' said Jacob, as he walked down Haverstock Hill between four and five o'clock in the morning of November the sixth arm-in-arm with Timothy Durrant, 'about something sensible'" (71). Woolf uses these tags to give salience to speech; the last-quoted also constitutes a narrative subsection in itself. The first two imply cautiously measured declaration; the participial modification in the next two indicates vocal hiatus. In the fifth, the speaker is taking his time, measuring out his invitation against a background of physical movement—tipsy movement, as the broader context suggests: so that we can conclude that the speech of these two young men is correspondingly influenced by alcohol or at least by post-party languor; the *uninterrupted flow* of the circumstantial detail in the adverbial clause, too, is consonant with light-headed figural perception.

pursue, re-echo, return, wind up). But is Conrad's technique significantly plainer if he employs such verbs as *agree, answer, begin, comment, correct, interject, interrupt, plead, suggest* and *whisper*? V.S. Naipaul and Randolph Stow are contemporary novelists. How "undifferentiated" is their tagging procedure if it includes *admit, burst out, demand, echo, gasp, lie, object, offer, weep* and *whisper*? Faulkner is obsessively attached to *say*—but how less "highly differentiated" in his prose than *breathe* are such verbs as *hiss* or *sigh* or *wail*? How are we to distinguish between tags that are, in terms of notional grammatical connectivity, "true" *(retort* to characterize the mode of the speech-act; *breathe* to characterize its delivery) and those that are anomalous or elliptical *(risk* for *risked saying)*? And, finally, is it really the case that "highly differentiated inquits" are found in "final" position? If we stick with James, and with the assortment of verbs listed above, we find that only twice out of 17 occurrences do these tags appear in terminal position. The situation is no different with the other writers mentioned.

Bonheim sets things up so that one cannot help but infer that "good" modern novelists are only doing right by steering clear of "differentiated" diegesis. We are, essentially, back with the modernist theory of the self-effacing narrator. This is clear from the second category of "differentiated inquits" presented—where the implication is that only "popular" writers (second- and third-rate talents? or writers of Gothics?—it is unclear what is meant) treat their readers as undiscerning dolts. The examples given, however, in no way prove that it is the sympathy of the reader that is being manipulated. *Sneer* and *counter* are no more exclusively part of the repertoire of "popular" writers than any other speech-act verbs; what is lost by replacing them with *say* is simple an indication of the specific pragmatic nature of the speech-act. Without the context of a particular piece of direct speech, we have no way of telling whether the tag is fully redundant or genuinely informative. The only evaluative word in Bonheim's quotation above is "bravely", which could be attached with equal ease to "undifferentiated" tags like *say* or *ask,* and to "differentiated" tags like *retort*. And it is not the specific tag but the macrocontextual pattern of diegetic "behaviour" which enables us to determine whether a writer is being unnecessarily helpful or manipulative, projective of his own construction of a speaker's behaviour or of a witnessing character's construction, serious or ironical or sentimental. What Bonheim may have in mind is the archly self-conscious and sophomoric employment of highly specific tags where the speech they are attached to is too banal or bathetic to bear the weight of such conspicuous subtlizing. Any number of schoolchildren intoxicated with the magical potency of an ever-widening lexicon have over-used tags in this way. But this is no automatic case against highly specific diegesis in (otherwise) high-quality fiction. Conversely, no amount of stylistic and narrative sophistication in Lawrence's novels can remove the all too frequent impression that he doesn't give a hang for tagging strategies; viewed with a critical eye, his tags are a colossal monument to grimly insensitive monotony and redundancy.

Perhaps help is forthcoming from another quarter, in Ann Banfield's transformational-generative exploration of the syntactic predeterminants of free indirect discourse. She does, after all, present her own version of tag-types according to their position. In discussing the "special linguistic forms for reporting the act of utterance itself", Banfield calls speech-tags "verbs of communication" (Banfield 1982:23–24), which are characterized, "not just semantically, but also syntactically, by [their] ability to take an indirect object referring to the addressee/hearer". Initial tags are called "introductory clauses", medial and terminal tags "parentheticals", which follow the direct speech or are "interpolated at certain points within it" (1982:42). "In derived structure, the parenthetical may occur at any point within the quoted clause, as long as the elements to the right of the parenthetical form a phrasal constituent" (1982:284.n18). Partee (1973b:416–17) essentially argues that we cannot test the validity of the initial-tag/speech relation by applying a subordination-transformation with *that* to produce indirect speech. Instead, we have to conceive of two independent sentences which are coreferential, with a notional cataphoric proform pointing from the sentence with the verb of communication to the direct-speech communication: eg, from "She said, 'I'm tired'" we get "She said *this/the following:* 'I'm tired'" rather than "She said (that) she was tired". In order to account for parentheticals, Partee (1973a,b *passim),* Emonds (1976:54) and Banfield (1982) contort themselves into various transformational-generative postures, ending up with some sort of consensus based on the notion that the reporting-clause refers back, with coreferential terms such as *so/thus/like this* (but not simple *this)* being suppressed or understood. Medial and terminal tags, it is argued, cannot be derived from initial tags, since certain types of positionally restricted tag-verbs reject the insertion of the deep-structure demonstrative object *this.* What is absent from these theories is a deviation factor allowing for the psychological or text-pragmatic convincingness of diegetic procedures which play productively with normative syntax.

All in all, transformational-generative deep-structure studies such as Banfield's fail to account for the acceptability- or familiarity-gradient of tag-verbs. The irreducible assumption remains that true tags involve a syntactic relation to direct speech. Indeed: in terms of historical semantics, we do not need to pose any deep-structure reference with *this* (or *so,* or *thus),* as the conjunction *that* was itself originally demonstrative-deictic in force (cf German *daz > das > dasz > daß).* I do not think that readers of narrative scan tag/speech interfaces by subliminal reference to the kind of deep structure cited by Partee and Banfield. It is more likely—given the baseline assumption that both direct and indirect speech are representations and not actual, primary speech-phenomena—that a convertibility relationship exists of the type suggested in Quirk et al. (1972:778–85 *passim)* The speech-tag for direct speech functions like a main-clause disjunct or conjunct, so that there is at one level no difference between the comment clause in "At that time, *I believe,* labour was cheap" and the tag-clause in "'It's time we went,' *I said".* Notionally, however, the subordination of the speaker's words through *that* (with or without nominal supplementation, ellipsis-filling, or bridging paraphrase) in indirect speech is paralleled in direct speech, which functions as the direct object of the "reporting" verb. "'I am your friend,' he said" = "*What* he said was *'I am your friend'*" or "*'I am your friend,'* was *what* he said".

The tag-verbs in *The Solid Mandala* and in the comparative chapters from other writers can be broken down into groups according to the underlying complementation. Expressive components of the direct speech may allow minimally adjusted transcription or compel wholesale paraphrase. Verbs found only in White and not in the comparative passages have been italicized:

1a   *that*

add, admit, *advise,* agree, announce, answer, command, comment, *complain,* concede, concur, confess, *confirm,* continue, *decide,* declare, demand, explain, *insist, maintain, mention,* object, observe, *order,* plead, *promise,* pronounce, protest, *recommend,* remark, *remember,* repeat, reply, *respond,* retort, return, say, suggest, *warn;* cf also: *become of the opinion*

1b   (vocal mode)

babble, bellow, blare, blather, blubber, blurt (out), call (back/out), *chant,* chuckle, cry, *ejaculate,* exclaim, gasp, *giggle, glumph, gobble, gollop, grumble,* hiss, moan, *mumble,* murmur, mutter, *pant, roar, scream, shout,* shriek, sigh, *snigger, snivel, stammer, trumpet,* wail, *whimper,* whisper

2   *whether*

ask, en/*inquire, wonder*

3   *the fact that*

apologise (for), *harp* (on), *muse* (on)

4   Object + *that*

inform, persuade, plead (with), promise, *reassure, remind, tell*

5   Object + *to*–Infinitive

advise, *appeal* (to), challenge, *coax, command, invite, order,* plead (with), *persuade,* promise, *recommend, remind, warn*

6   *to say that*

dare, go on, interrupt, intervene, *struggle;* cf also: *feel compelled*

7   *by saying that*

begin, correct (+ Reflexive or Object), (re-)echo, *finish,* go on, *hedge,* interject, interrupt, intervene, *keep on,* lie, prevaricate, *persist,* resume, wind up; cf: *quote* (+ Object), *pursue* (+ *the topic*)

8   *the remark that*

bring out, *offer, throw in*

9   *with the remark that*

break out, burst out, *fetch out*

10   , *saying that*

chatter, ramble on, *pause* (or: *and said that*)

11   *to* Object, *saying that*

speak, talk

12   recast as: Subject *said*, + *–ing*-Participle transform + , *that*

breathe (or: breathily), *choke, dream* (or: dreamily), *eruct, gulp, hiccup,* laugh (or: laughingly), smile (or: smilingly), *start, stutter,* weep, *yawn*

13   recast as: Subject *said*, + paraphrase + , *that*

click (with a clicking sound), *dwindle* (his voice dwindling), *flute* (in a fluting tone), *low* (in a lowing voice), *rattle* (in a rattled/rattling voice)

14   not convertible when direct speech is a quotation

read, read aloud, read out, sing

15   Object *say(ing) that*

hear, overhear

16   Object *of –ing*-Participle

accuse

It is probable that writers employ tag-verbs by analogy with, or by semantic extension of, "acceptable" tag-verbs which allow monotransitive or ditransitive complementation of some kind, either directly or prepositionally. In Category **1** above, it is not a decisive factor in tagging whether a verb is transitive or intransitive, so long as a transactional relationship can be established. *Retort* is anomalous in this regard, as it is restricted entirely to tag-position with direct speech and to *that*–constructions (*"He retorted a cutting remark"; "He retorted *me/*to me"). This transaction can relate to the communication itself *(add),* to the communication and to another actant *(say/admit),* to another communication or its utterer *(answer/interrupt* in Groups **6–7** above), and so forth. Dictionaries and grammars do not confirm the possibility of a *that*–construction with *plead,* or with most of the vocal-mode verbs. These are simply marked, generally, as transitive or intransitive. Vocal-mode verbs in Group (**1b**) that are not marked for transitivity, or which (like *glumph, gollop* and *blurt* without *out)* do not appear in the dictionaries, can be understood as behaving like verbs that are so marked, and/or like verbs which are explicitly marked for tag-function (eg, *answer, ask, continue, grumble, reply, say, whimper).* Dictionaries sometimes define vocal gesture as being concomitant with speech (see definitions for *gasp, breathe, break out* in *Longman* 1978) if not with direct speech. Sometimes transitivity is indicated, but restricted to non-verbal sign-function ("She laughed her disrespect/smiled a greeting/giggled her amusement"). But it is easy to see how the notion of sign-function can be extended into tag-function. Partee, for example, in discussing "indirect quotations" with *that*–clauses, maintains that verbs of communication like *say* can report *non*-verbatim propositional content, while communicative verbs of manner like *giggle* introduce "near-quotes" or sententials conveying both form and content (Partee 1973a:325–37). In most instances from Group (**6**) onwards, a verb of saying can be construed elliptically. In the tag as given, the speech-act is foregrounded or overdetermined in terms of processual relations (eg, *begin),* contentual modality (eg, *hedge),* non-actant audition (eg, *hear),* or vocal and tonal modality (eg, *choke, low).*

Within any group, there are tag-verbs which sound perfectly normal, others that do not. It is not, however, syntactic or semantic deviance that accounts for the relative strangeness of the latter, but simply the fact of unfamiliarity itself. Verbs that have seldom been found in tag-position have merely been activated in accordance with their latent semantic-syntactic disposition. In the last analysis, then, it cannot be said that White (or any other creative deployer of tag-verbs) is "ungrammatical" or solecistic in his narrative practice. It should also be remembered that the semantic specificity and range of a writer's tags can make themselves felt at either end of the scale of frequency. White may seem to use a wide range of uncommon tag-verbs—far more uncommon than the verbs used by his nearest "rival", James; but *say* still represents 60% of all White's tag-verbs, twice the percentage found in James and Conrad. Yet, whereas White's uncommon tag-verbs tend to make us forget how undifferentiated his tagging can be when it is felt necessary, the fact that Faulkner uses *say* in 95% of all his tags is enough to make his employment of this "common" verb a most uncommon thing indeed.

VI   Crypto–tags

Crypto-tags are customarily recognizable as such by the fact that they are not attached to direct speech and do not involve a speech-act verb. They do, however, have a diegetic relation to direct speech. Some formal cohesion between diegesis and mimesis may be effected punctuatively, as when an initial tag is followed by an annunciatory colon (Conrad: "her lips alone moved, forming the words:" p. 486; Faulkner: "the sheriff's voice was mild, almost gentle even:" *Intruder* p. 113); but coloned initial tags can more often be construed as elliptical true tags (James: "Her friend wondered; then with raised eyebrows:" p. 361). It comes as a slight shock to find Faulkner placing a crypto-tag in the same relation to direct speech as a true tag ("' ——,' Mooney's tone was quite pleasant, easy" *Light* p. 36), in order to narrow asyndetically the gap between speech-representation and its mediated analysis. I mentioned earlier Bonheim's view of the function of crypto-tags as identifying a speaker before or after he has spoken. When James's tags are examined, however, it becomes apparent that the psychonarrative diegesis (which ranges from consonance to the dissonance indicated by the epithet "poor" in "' ——,' said poor Strether, looking grave", p. 15, or the elegant variation of "our friend——missed the thread" in a four-line crypto-tag preceding direct speech, p. 23) is mainly structured with other functions in mind. The crypto-tags convey Strether's active mental engagement in deciphering the intentions of other speakers while they are speaking, and in formulating and reflecting upon his own vocal, gestural or inward responses and strategies. How can we account otherwise for a crypto-tag like 11 below, which clearly describes immediately prior speech but does not identify the speaker?

There is very little referential distance between crypto-tags and adjacent direct speech in White; and there is a great variety of approaches to tagging, far wider than is the case with the resourceful James. Simple nominal-appositive tags (eg, **1**, with an elided recurrence; also **61** above) are infrequent; distance is narrowed via citational structuring (**2**) or by a blurring of the distinction between vocal gesture and speech (**3**; also **35** above):

1 When they were seated Mrs Musto would give her usual command: "Wind 'er up, Stubbens'—and to the objects of her kindness, as Stubbens wound and wound: "Hold yer ribs, boys,——!" (W84)
2 He would make a remark such as: "——." (A234)
3 "' Sometimes when it is early or late,'" Waldo's voice came bursting, gurgling, wavering like water escaping from the bath, "' I have thought——.'" (W43)

Common to James and White is the use of cohesive *it* as the fulcrum of the tag, with inexplicit coreference to the direct speech (and, implicitly, with its preformulatory mental content). In James, the structure is straightforward: either object-cohesive (**4–8** below) or subject-cohesive (**9**)—compare the use of *it* in diegesis mediating reaction (**10–12**):

4 "' Mr. Lewis Lambert Strether'"—she sounded it almost as freely as if a stranger were in question. (James, p. 12)
5 "—— it's how you see me"—she caught her breath with it—"and it's——." (James, p. 351)
6 "But think of me, think of me——!" She exhaled it into air. (James, p. 352)
7 She had scarcely to say it—"Yes, she has been here——." (James, . 356)
8 "She can't really help"—he had taken it up—"being aware?" (James, p. 361)
9 "——. I was dog-tired when I sailed." It had the oddest sound of cheerfulness. (James, p. 21)
10 "I come from Woollett Massachusetts." It made her for some reason—the irrelevance or whatever—laugh. (James, p. 12)
11 "Yet wasn't your little Chad just your miracle?"
Strether admitted it. "Of course I moved among miracles——." (James, p. 360)
12 "Are you so sorry for her as that?"
It made her think a moment—made her even speak with a smile. (James, p. 361)

In White, there is an almost tactile emphasis on the conversion of thought into speech (**13–15**) or on the effort to overcome physical impediments to speech (**16–17**). The grammatical structure with coreferential *it* may suggest the disengagement of the speaker from the utterance, its factitiousness (**18**) or its mere expediency (**19**). In **20**, a clever effect is achieved through complementation of the speech-act verb by *it:* Mrs Feinstein is made to utter what she is protesting against:

13 Then,——, he came up with something which was on his mind, and spat it out, wet: "——." (W87)
14 Then it all came out of Waldo, not in vomit, but in words. "——!" (W147)
15 "——," he was bursting with it, "——." (A284)
16 "——"—working her mouth around it—"——." (A272)
17 "——?" With difficulty he forced it out, through his stuffed mouth, past his fatty lips. (A234)
18 "——." § He said it in a tone not suited to his voice,——. (W154)
19 "——!" Waldo got it in quickly, so that she would understand,——. (W153)
20 "Old, old." Mrs Feinstein protested against it. "Very aged." (W138)

Ellipsis may be involved, either to make the perception of speech "disembodied" yet immediate (**21**), or to suggest that the hearer has inferred the nature of the speaker from the voice (**22**—Waldo is thus represented as psychologically distanced from his speaking brother), or to connect the unattributed speech heard with the speaker, of whose presence Arthur becomes belatedly aware (**23**). Ellipses, and the multifunctionality of *it* in English, generate complex diegetic implications, as can be seen by comparing the two crypto-tags in **24**: both are contextually interconnected. The coordinate clause is made to do double referential duty—Mrs Brown looks at Arthur without having half her attention elsewhere as before, and she speaks "only for him" this time, instead of half-speaking to the sun. Referentiality is maintained intensely with the utmost economy of means:

21 Again it was: how do you like it? what do you make of it? (A217)
22 "——"—actually it was a man—"——." (W63)
23 "——!" It was the young lady, that Miss Glasson. (A281)
24 But mother ignored him, or at least half. She half-spoke to the setting sun.
　　"——," she said.
　　Then she looked at him again, and this time it was only for him.
　　"——." (A216)

In **25** below, *it* functions as head of a clause that is elliptical ("... to say") yet is treated as a true tag: White operates frequently in this twilight zone between conventional true tags and fully disjunctive crypto-tags. In **27–29**, it is impossible—because of the punctuation of the direct speech—to determine whether the terminal diegesis is a representation of a listener's thoughts about the speaker and the speech during the process of audition, or after it. In **28**, the progressive aspect and the "normal" verb of vocal gesture suggest that Waldo has his attention shifted to Arthur and his embarrassing mode of speech while Mr Feinstein is finishing his own speech; so we tend to take this as a true tag. There is a tag of audition in **27**, a possible ellipsis of a (redundant) speech-verb [speaking/saying], and an objective separation of voice from actant (as there is in the even more effective example **26**). Item **29**, in the death-scene, is perhaps the apotheosis of White's play with syntax and meaning. If we take it as a true tag we can paraphrase it as: "Waldo gasped ' ——!' in order to hear his own voice" (ie, again: for it is slipping away from him as he loses control). If we take it as a crypto-tag, we can paraphrase it thus: "When he heard his own voice, Waldo gasped". In both cases, "gasped" means the sharp drawing-in of breath in order that Waldo may speak loudly enough to hear himself speaking. But it also connotes the expression of terminal emotion during and/or after delivery of his accusation. The tag (true and crypto-) conveys iconically the breakdown of mind and body.

25 "——," it suddenly occurred to Dad. (W38)
26 The words were shouted out of him: "——!" (A269)
27 "——?" Waldo heard his cracked voice. (W102)
28 "——?" Arthur was gibbering with hope and pleasure. (W108)
29 "——" Waldo gasped to hear his own voice. (W213)

The punctuative character of physical gesture is generally clear: the tapping (**30**), the wry mouth (**31**) or Mrs Brown's expression (**32**) all function annunciatorily. Bill's axe-blow is a terminal punctuating of his spoken refusal

(33), the Silkworm's shudder an underlining of her spoken disgust (34); likewise Mrs Feinstein's smile (35). But, in the last-cited as in 36, one can also take the visible gesture as an accompaniment to speech. Vocal gesture (laughter, sighing, etc) can serve to herald a range of mood in speech (37–38), can link and/or accompany speech (39–40), or can reinforce the termination of speech (41–42):

30 But one of the juniors would come tapping on his desk: § "Mr Crankshaw, Mr Brown." (W172)
31 "——!" Then, making an ugly mouth: "——." (W166)
32 "——?" Then Mother looked shy, for her. "——." (W50)
33 "Nah." Bill swung the axe, and split the knottiest chunk of wood. "Never ever have the time." (W143)
34 "——!" The Silkworm shuddered inside her cocoon. "——." (W198)
35 "——." Mrs Feinstein smiled for the sick, though it could have been she enjoyed the sickness. "——." (W138)
36 "——." § As Mrs Allwright elaborated, she very discreetly lowered her eyes. (A227)
37 So Arthur had begun to scratch, and call. § "——?" (A291)
38 Waldo laughed. § "——." (A292)
39 "——." Mrs Feinstein sighed. "——." (W112)
40 "——!" The old boy laughed. "——!" (W108)
41 "——!" A man spat. (A252)
42 "——," but there she halted. (W154)

With the stopped medial crypto-tag in 43 below, there may be uncertainty about whether additional gesture is involved, or an evaluative paraphrase of a direct-speech exclamation. In some crypto-tags of vocal or physical gesture, aspect may suggest that the action or attitude is attendant on speech (progressive in 44–46; past perfect in 47) *or* that the hearer perceives gesture separately from speech: the tags are therefore bivocal. So is 48, where the speech-act verb in the progressive suggests that it is Waldo's reflexive analysis of the direct speech. But the normative, "narratorial" character of diegesis is an essential background presence as well, in order that the reader can grasp how the crypto-tag as a whole, with its redundancy and lack of specificity (we know already that this is what Waldo must be doing), works against the norm to convey Waldo's egoism and emotional alienation. Other interpretative tags also play with norms: given White's practice elsewhere, 49 could just as easily have been a bound tag—it has been made a crypto-tag, however, precisely because Arthur's justification follows his impulsive question and is disjunct from it.

43 "Oh!" She made a little unhappy sound. "——." (W94)
44 "——!" Dulcie was almost crying. "——!" (W153)
45 "——." Arthur was swaying in his chair. "——." (W200)
46 "——!" Arthur was enjoying it. (A227)
47 "——!" Waldo had begun to cry. "——!" (A282)
48 "——." He was telling the receiver of a man who died. (W72)
49 "——?" It seemed reasonable enough to inquire. (A261)

Other crypto-tags are paraphrastic of adjacent speech or of the hiatus between speech-segments (with a progressive of process and figural apperception: 50–55), sometimes in a manner that requires from the reader a decision about whether to take the crypto-tag as referring specifically to the direct speech following (and generally indented: **56–57**).

50 "——." Mr Haynes was turning nasty now. "——." (W46)
51 "——." Arthur was shaping his defence. "——." (W213)
52 "——," Mother was daring herself to speak, "——." (W40)
53 "——," he was bursting with it, "——." (A284)
54 "——"—Dulcie was busting herself—"——." (W97)
55 "——"—here she was searching—"——." (W51)
56 Waldo exploded finally. § "——." (A267)
57 But she continued creating. § "——!" (A289)

A classic case of a grammatically self-contained, paraphastic crypto-tag that is subverted into use as a true tag can be found in **58** below, while the medial crypto-tag in **59** might have been designed specifically for deep-structure enthusiasts of anaphoric proforms; the structure is, of course, parodistic for oracular delivery. White's customary sensitivity to the potential afforded by intrasentential pauses is illustrated by the way in which various degrees of structural self-sufficiency in medial crypto-tags precisely mirror the vocal pauses (or mental flashes of perception themselves). There may be a perfect, "naturalistic" fit between abrupt vocal gesture and hyphenated tag (**60–62**). Smoother transitions bordering on accompaniment, where speech shades into gesture, are marked by commas (eg, **63–64**), and mental—usually Waldovian and ironizing—comment is similarly paced (**53** above, and **65**, versus **66–67**). It is perhaps worth noting that, on the occasions on which crypto-tags most conspicuously resemble true tags—but for the fact that they are "packed" with their own internal object, thus preventing a natural fit (**25** above, **58**, **68** below)— they occur medially with speeches that follow on from general, descriptive narrative.

58 "——," Walter Pugh returned to the subject on a later occasion, "——?" (W126)
59 "——." So Crankshaw uttered. "——." (W177)
60 "——"—Waldo caught himself—"——." (W115)
61 "——"—Waldo snorted—"——." (W210)
62 "——"—he formed his lips into a trumpet—"——." (W29)
63 "——," this time Miss Glasson only half-giggled, "——." (W197)
64 "——," she paused in thought, "——." (A246)
65 "——," and sometimes Mrs Poulter did, "——." (W29)
66 "——"—he could be so reasonable—"——." (W82)
67 "——"—she was at her marmalady brightest—"——." (W51)
68 "——," Mr Feinstein referred to his children, "——." (A277)

It is particularly noticeable in **71** that the crypto-tag is being used to mediate this change in topical direction: it jars especially, but is explicable as representing Arthur's belated mental identification, from in the midst of Mr Feinstein's slurred speech, of who exactly is being referred to as "' they'". That is to say: tag-structures and tag-position are iconically determined, rather than being diegetic evidence of a "helpful" narrator.

VII   A note on tag–modification

To summarize Bonheim again on the "weighting" of tags with the "static modes" of description and comment (1982:79–80): the more extensive the modification applied to a tag, the more likely it is that it will come in initial position; long terminal tags are "hard to compose"; and the "modern" tendency in all positions is to have unelaborated tags, or to do without them altogether.

I have taken as a test-case the "neutral" tag-verb *say,* in order to determine what kinds of modification have been applied to it by White and by the authors represented in the comparative passages. Modifications and additions to tags can be organized into groups, in order of roughly ascending length and/or phrasal complexity. The simplest level is that of adverbial postmodification; also included here are cases in which the tag-verb (if initial) occurs in a sentence-initial coordinate main clause. The next level up is represented by participial clauses and other "absolute" constructions; there is, as a rule, punctuative isolation of the speech-act verb and its nuclear clause from modifiers. There may also be one or more adverbials present. The third level covers descriptive diegesis which is contained (before or after the tag-clause) in an additive coordinate clause, or where the tag-clause itself is in a participial (hence additive) relation to an immediately preceding sentence. The fourth level involves the full-clausal modification of the tag-clause proper (its verb or its subject). These are rough-and-ready groupings, and do not always correlate with physical length.

Initial tags: none of the writers except Faulkner and White is significant for his use of *said* in initial position. 60% of Faulkner's tags are unadorned, 38% of White's. Almost all of Faulkner's remaining initial tags (33%) have simple adverbial modification; 25% of White's are adverbial. The second-largest of three fairly equal groupings in White is accounted for by clausal modification (levels three and four together). Faulkner would count as "modern" in Bonheim's system; those authors who are not represented here would be so, too—except for James, whose initial crypto-tags could be taken as "weighted" substitutes for true *say*-tags. White establishes his own norms, internal to a given novel (so far as we can yet tell). It can, however, be said that he confirms the observation that initial tags can be weighted easily.

Medial tags: 96% of Faulkner's are unadorned; there follow, in descending order: Naipaul (80%); James (73%); White (71%); and Stow (61%). Conrad and Lawrence (with long and short speeches respectively) do not figure significantly in their use of medial *said.* Faulkner automatically drops out; of the others, three prefer simple adverbial modification as the next stage up (James: 28%; Stow: 22%; Naipaul: 14%). White, once again, stands alone, by virtue of the fact that the remaining 29% of his medial, modified tags are evenly distributed for simple-adverbial (11%), participial (10%) and clausal (8%) modification.

Terminal tags: 92% of Faulkner's are unadorned. Four of the other authors are grouped around the half-way mark for unelaborated tags (White: 54%; Stow: 50%; Lawrence: 49%; Naipaul: 45%). Conrad is the exception here: half of his tags have simple adverbial modification, the other half participial. Faulkner, as in the case of his initial and medial tags, makes up most of the balance with simple adverbial postmodifiers (7%). Lawrence and Stow evenly split the balance between adverbials and participles (exactly 27% each, 26% each, and 22% each respectively). Again, it is White who shows the most differentiation: 13% adverbial; 20% participial; 13% clausal.

In none of these writers (at least so far as the test-corpus is concerned) does phrasal or clausal complication play a significant diegetic role in any tag-position—except for White. As far as tag-verbs *other than "said"* are concerned, the following percentages (on the left) indicate their incidence in the total number of occurrences of tag-verbs; the percentage of the total that are modified is given on the right: The numbers of verbs are not large enough to yield significant figures on positional distribution of modification; but the modification of *say*–tags is generally in line with that of other tag-verbs. But whereas a percentage-deflection between the two groups is noticeable in the comparative writers (a gap of up to 28% between *say*–tag modifications and those with tags apart from *say*), the statistics for White are uncannily symmetrical. Faulkner is exceptional in shifting to more complex modification once he gets away from the verb *say*.

Table 10: Modification of tags other than "say"

James	82%	25%
Conrad	65%	65%
Lawrence	49%	51%
White	44%	45%
Naipaul	34%	53%
Stow	31%	54%
Faulkner	4%	0%

More instructive are differences in style and function (and I am taking all verbs together here). Tag-modification in the James passages serves largely to promote cohesion or contrast between consecutive speeches, and to mark Strether's perception of the handling of subject-matter in speech. Modern readers may be struck by the medial positioning of some of the simple adverbs ("she beautifully brought out", "she sadly confessed", "he goodhumouredly said", "he almost impatiently declared"), but there is nothing unusual about the modifiers otherwise. Most of the interest lies in the particularity of the tag-verbs themselves, and in the interwoven crypto-tags. Conrad's modifications serve exclusively to mark very clearly and succinctly characteristics of vocal delivery and tone. Lawrence gives equal attention to vocal delivery and to attendant or sequent action. I find many of his modifications vaguely annoying: they tend to be vacuously general ("in a bright manner", "in a rather frightened voice") or clumsy ("being purposely fatuous", "with emphasis, chuckling", "with nonchalance").

The general absence of postmodification from Faulkner's tags means that any additions that do occur tend to draw attention to themselves ("Brown said, in a merry, loud voice cropped with teeth", "she says behind her fading smile, with the grave astonishment of a child" *Light,* pp. 36, 39); and it is evident that the narrative is organized to make the most of such occurrences. The topic of Brown's teeth is reverted to, for instance; and the long double adverbial describing the girl's appearance and tone of voice occurs in the first tag after a change from past- to present-tense narration, to indicate Byron's alert "scanning" of her. The same applies to *Intruder in the Dust,* where postmodifications are more frequent ("he said mildly, almost innattentively:", "saying at last in a musing baffled voice:", "his uncle said, not quite turning [...] he said briskly, turning the door loose now", pp. 106, 109, 213). We are attuned to noting closely any indication of vocal mode or attendant gesture—apart from which, there are occasional features which reveal the continuity of Faulkner's narrative style from novel to novel, such as the use of the classificatory definite article to promote cohesion and suggest the degree of alert attention which the auditor brings to bear on speech-persistencies ("saying in the plaintive heavily-sighing voice:", p. 210; "his uncle said in the harsh voice:", p. 212; and one of those long, suspensive accretions of detail so familiar elsewhere in Faulkner: "and then went on in the mild sighing reluctant voice which was already answering his uncle's thoughts even before his uncle could speak it:", p. 212).

There is nothing distinctive about Naipaul's modifications. They range from the workmanlike to the pedestrian: ie, accord with Bonheim's "norm" of "modern" unobtrusiveness. Simple *-ly* adverbs predominate, with a quick-sketch lack of nuance ("desperatcly", "helplessly", "happily", "softly", "lightly"). Stow, like Naipaul and Lawrence, has nothing particularly interesting lexically about his modifications—but the finely nuanced pointing of syntactic juncture is a communicative subsystem which Stow clearly lays great store by. In the first-person section of the novel extract, two simple coordinations—one conjunctive, the other participial, both leading out of a tag into a further segment of direct speech—are marked by a semi-colon pause:

"Yes," she said; or hotly affirmed. "——." (p. 87)
"——," I said; adding: "——." (p. 87)

The first semi-colon precedes a radical specification of neutral "said", as though the figural narrator has done a double-take, picking up belatedly the tonal import of the speech. The second, as with White's and James's medial tags, marks a pause (for thought) before continuation of the speech. Similar pointings after the return to third-person narration mark the psychonarrator's empathetic or iconic registering of the neutrality of tonal delivery when compared with the speech-content: "he said; but without any particular discourtesy, or even interest", p. 89; substitution of a comma or a dash would destroy this effect). Compare "' ——,' he said; remote, pontifical." (p. 90) with the commas in "' ——,' he said, with cold conviction" (p. 90) or "He repeated it, in a dead voice:" (p. 90), where the modifications are "closer-in" to the speech-act verb, imputing to it a stronger background of intent. In "' ——,' Kestrel said again; and stood up" (p. 95), the semi-colon underscores the measured pause implicit between the termination of speech and the action of getting up. The next two examples are instructive:

"There's no denying it," he said (with a certain embarrassment), "you're——." (p. 89)
"——," she said. With great pain. (p. 89)

In the first, the tone and/or facial expression suggested by the modification are marked as covert yet discernible, via the graphic device of bracketing, while the stasis in the second isolates and concentrates the emotive content of the phrasal modifier.

White's modifications were examined according to the tags to which they are attached. Initial-tag modifications range from the very short or even elliptical to the very long and packed:

(coordinating:) Then Mother's: (A270)
(coordinating:) Muttering still: (W211)
(subordinating:) As he shouted: (A273)
(adverbial:) Only Crankshaw grumbling: (W166)
(participial:) Fearing his friend, at this,—— might be in need of assistance, Arthur began to chatter on—— too irrelevant a note: (A251)
(subordinating:) Once, at the height of a storm, when the rain was coming down aslant [3 more lines], Waldo shouted: (A282)

Medial-tag modifications are generally fully biclausal (ie, above the level of simple adverbials; participles and coordinate verbs usually have complementation or postmodification), but they are seldom longer than this. The same applies to terminal-tag position, except for coordinate verbs, which tend to stand unelaborated as sufficient diegetic marking of speech for attendant or sequent action or gesture.

The range of semantic references is, at the very least, that represented by the classification of James's crypto-tags: ie, centred not simply on the speech-acts but also on attendant vocal or physical gesture, on figural thoughts about the specific speech-situation or about the broader actional situation; and so forth. There is no conspicuous patterning in the stylistic detail of the modifications. Enough examples from White have been discussed in previous sections to illustrate how varied the detail is. Even at the level of simple adverbials, where one could expect an abundance of –ly forms (as witness the comparative saturation of the extract from Naipaul), there are no more than about 30 of these standing alone after the verb in the whole of Sections 2 and 3 of *The Solid Mandala,* and I have traced only three instances of the same –ly adverb being used more than once in the book. This fairly banal example is still cogent enough to suggest just how alert White is to the filigree-work of verbal fashioning that is essential to the mediation of his fiction. And this scrupulousness about, and sovereign control over, his materials is not merely some reflex disinclination to repeat himself. White has simply proceeded on the assumption (hard to fault) that there is no place for unmotivated redundancy, for flaccidity of muscle or thinness of blood, in narration, least of all when what is at stake is the delicate representation of the mental life of characters.

The diegetic interface of tagging-procedures should be incorporated into the inventory of standard scanning procedures for narrative style. Bonheim and countless others may, of course, be right—for a given writer, the findings may indeed reinforce the stock view that tags are an unnecessary or, at best, irritatingly dysfunctional, "decorative" or badly executed phenomenon. The limited text-corpus on which I have drawn has provided some indication of how colourless the tagging-interface can be (Naipaul, for instance). It is also indubitably true that there can be a minimal functional role for a simple "he said/she said" routine in narratives that are otherwise perfectly gripping and well-formed at the diegetic level, and unfailingly interesting and colourful at the mimetic level of direct speech. A quintessential contemporary example is the crime fiction of Elmore Leonard: here, no reader will notice the speech-tags at all, let alone sense an absence of elaboration.

With a writer like Faulkner, however, the narrative theorist (and the common reader) passes over the relentless surface primitivism of the speech-tags at his peril. The "simple" mode has been intensified to the level of the exceptional, for purposes that have intimately to do with the transportation of the reflexivity of character or narratorial consciousness.

This would also be true to some extent of Joseph Conrad's or Henry James's procedure—but cognizance must also be taken of the extent to which the diegetic coloration of speech-tags in James, in Randolph Stow and—most conspicuously of all—in Patrick White serves to reinforce a perspectivization (of speaker or auditor) that merges the sensibility of narrator and character, as in James, produces intermittent irruptions of this blend in otherwise quasi-"scenic" tagging, as in Stow, or erases the role of "external" narrator completely in favour of the inner voice of character-consciousness, as in White. It is perhaps a fruitful paradox that the Russian practitioners of *skaz*, such as Leskov, Zoshchenko, Gogol (intermittently) and Dostoevsky (quintessentially) should have striven to fulfil the intention stated by Zagoskin—see Eikhenbaum 1925 (fn, 4 above)—and distanced themselves from the interface of tagging procedures in favour of "marked", originally "oral" modes of narrative "speech" which constitute the Asiatic Mode of what is better known (or, since Bakhtin, is a distinctive counterpart to) free indirect discourse. Patrick White, by steering resolutely in the opposite direction, and utilizing transgressively the whole arsenal of tagging procedures, can be said to be the apotheosis of the high-modernist mode of narration. Like Faulkner, but at the opposite extreme of Faulkner's extreme economy in the midst of boundless flux, White developed his own inimitable brand of *skaz* based on that diegetic principle of mediation which the Russians shunned. Any "dramatism" to be found in White's tagging technique serves the reactive modality of mind, not the easy option of providing "stage-directions" (despite White's love of drama, and his proficiency in that medium).

Because this is so, one must allow oneself to be productively irritated by White's always justifiable "deviations" from—and front-on exploitation of—a narrative procedure whose normative mode of application is not necessarily the Real Right Thing merely because most writers stick to it. The best writers are arguably those who excel in as many areas of narrative competence as possible, and who are confident enough in their awareness of narrative traditions to row against the current. Patrick White was such a writer. This small linguistically oriented window onto his narrative techniques may possibly nourish a conviction that he has done at least one technique to death by pulling out all the stops. But his is surely but one approach to exploiting the natural resources of the English language. In an age of metafictionality and postmodern malaise, there must be a writer lurking somewhere who is willing—if only parodically—to put up some opposition both to the purely scenic-behaviouristic mode and to normative minimalism. But it would have to be a pretty alert writer with a profound investment in the mental life of his or her characters.

12

INDEXICAL DETAIL

White, in a letter to Geoffrey Dutton, indicated that writing for the theatre had encouraged "a quite different style" in *The Solid Mandala*; it involved "simplifying and abbreviating to save his theme from coming to grief 'in a lush labyrinth of poetic prose ... I have tried to develop more of a throw-away technique'" (Marr 1991:453). This clarification of technique, however, reduced the surface density, but not the underlying density of implication, which is arguably more difficult to retrieve than in the earlier novels; the difference of style is not a matter of kind, but of degree. White loved "the accumulation of down-to-earth detail. All my novels are accumulations of detail. I am a bit of a bower-bird" (White 1973:139). It is the compulsion to surface accumulation that White has curbed.

In the foregoing discussions of lexis, rhetoric and figuration, the features chosen for examination individually clarify discrete moments and broad sweeps of textual meaning ("content"), but are additionally noteworthy because they form "behavioural" consistencies in expressive, stylistic terms. To move beyond paradigmatic consideration of narrational intentionality and verb-implementation, indeterminacy, ellipsis and other polysemic tropes, iconicity, and structural-semantic patternings is to enter territory where individual tropological functions have a higher value than anything that can be produced in the way of generalizations about "style". Take, for example, metaphor. A stylistic analysis of a passage or a work will almost invariably include consideration of metaphors. Finding them is no great problem, and their analysis can clarify theme; but, in terms of style, a particular writer's "metaphoricity" can be extremely difficult to analyze linguistically or philosophically (on these points, see especially Bloomfield 1975:286–88). The semantic foregrounding of metaphor can constitute the writer's rule-book for an individual work of literature; and, as metaphor is the essential analogical condition of our knowledge of the world, analysis of metaphor explains the world of a work, rather than characterizing an author's "figurativeness" as such.

There is a special problem involved in any attempt to take, say, the metaphors of the "bower-bird" White and examine them as a closed stylistic system. White's intuitive, rather than analytical, propensity resists the hierarchization of tropes. In terms of the way he organizes language, an examination of metaphor alone—or its epistemological polarity, metonymy; or simile; or "imagery"—is a loss-making venture, as White's instinct is to weave into the nest of signification any "device" he has to hand. He does this with discriminating indiscriminateness, and the resulting prose texture is eclectic, catholic. This constitutes a complex stylistic "feature" at the macrotextual level. The best way to approach it, I would suggest, is to think in terms of the "function" of "indexical detail". By "function" I mean the expressive, stylistic and structural relation to narrative discourse, action and theme of a wide variety of signifiers. It has long been customary to use the term "imagery" for the kinds of features indicated here. This term can be used when there is little doubt that colour-words, say, are meant to be retrievable by the reader through superimposing an attribute upon a mental construct of some object "narrated" in the text. With White, it should not be used to cover metaphor or simile. There are neither cogent philosophical nor convincing psychological grounds for using the terms "image" and "imagery" in this way (see Furbank 1970)—all the more so as White has himself frequently endorsed the close connection between his secret desire to be a painter and the "primary-image" texture of his prose. Indexical detail is essentially unrestricted by classifications such as imagery, metaphor, simile. It may consist of these; of symbols; of analogies; of cultural or intertextual allusions; of words used literally for descriptive or other purposes. It may arise out of any kind of mental act "performed" (or narrated as performed) by any agent within a fictional narrative. The chief feature of such details is that, though they each function autonomously—or even autotelically—within the text, they are productive of general conceptual or thematic categories by virtue of the implied author's exercise of his stylistic prerogative. He has chosen to make details cohere or contrast in significant patterns, so that the sum is greater than its parts. He has chosen to strive for the closest possible fit between the represented, fictive world and his characters' perceptions and apperception of that world.

This method cannot be effectively applied without discursive analysis—but can show what is typical about the function of indexical style in determining *how* meaning is conveyed non-analytically by a novelist. It is not concerned in the first instance with quantitative analysis ("the relative frequency of water to machine images is, at best, rudimentary or peripheral ... though the way imagery is used is certainly a matter of style"; Martin/Ohmann 1959:192). An investigation of indexical detail can lay the ghost of the commonly held view that White's "metaphorical habit" is "florid" (Walsh 1977:85), inasmuch as Walsh states that in *The Solid Mandala* "the language is more abstinent, the metaphorical habit less florid, the manner altogether trimmer and sharper" than in, say, *Riders in the Chariot*. To pick up on my earlier discussion of "mannerism", I would suggest that the term "florid" is ill-chosen, in its suggestion that White's style is overrich in details or flourishes for their own sake. Nothing in White's fiction is there for its own sake or for embellishment, but is indispensable *as* the discoursal import of a novel. Critics who impute "floridity" to White's style downgrade it while simultaneously availing themselves of "what" it conveys (or, more likely, bypassing it for some "surface message") in order to get to somewhere else. The way to get somewhere else with White is to watch your readerly step all the way.

I Elemental and natural indices

ARIDITY, BRITTLENESS, RIGIDITY, AND THE KINESIS OF REACTION

Waldo's spirit and self, along with their metonymic extensions (eg, gait, oilskin, face, voice, vocal tone, smile, lips, throat, posture, feelings, his papers, his hands), are indexed persistently as thin, stiff, brittle, dry, tight, rigid, cracked, a "drought". The fourth corner of Arthur's mandala-dance summarizes this characterological pattern. A dynamic of attraction and repulsion is set up within Waldo relating to the moist and the fluid, the irrational and the sexual; the lexis turns persistently on such verbs as "shiver", "shudder", "shrivel", "shrink up", "cringe", "tremble". There are also subtle parallels in the reactions of son and father.

THE WATERY ELEMENT AND THE VEGETATIVE

Water is for Waldo the destructive element, associated with emotion and sexuality; when he succumbs to these instincts, it is a dam bursting ("trickle", "gush", "grew watery"). Dulcie and her metonymic extensions (eyes, hair, emotions, music, laughter) are indexed via such words as "overflowing", "watery", "brimming", "swimming", "flowed", "overflowing", "spattering", "rippling", "outflowing". Arthur notices a change in her *soma* to dryness, which is in keeping with her self-professed (lunar) changeability. The elective affinity between Dulcie and Arthur is intimated via lexical indices attached to him ("flooded", "flood", "watered", "splash") or to both of them (long-legged waterfowl). Dulcie, the vessel for Arthur's lovingkindness, is continually associated with hydrangeas (*hydros*, "water" and *aggo*, "vessel"), themselves metonymized (Dulcie's dress, her music), and functioning as a negative index in Waldo's memories and as a backdrop of vegetable moribundity whenever Waldo transgresses on Dulcie's home territory. Mrs Poulter is intermittently associated with water, but at a remove of comic contiguity via the analogy of her houseboat-like house; these analogies occur only in Waldo's section, thus linking up with his fear of the watery element. The surroundings of her house ("sea") and the dripping blackberry grove ("bay") of her epiphanic walk with Arthur are also associated with water. There is otherwise a pattern of aquatic inundation by decaying yet vital yellow grass, and a shift to "gothic arches" of grass to indicate a primeval Australian encroachment of irrationality on arid, classical-rationalist pretensions.

LIGHT: ILLUMINATION AND INTELLECT

Light, the medium of perception, is not exempt in Waldo's section from the yellow-green coloration lent to the grass. This light is sickly and jaundiced, but can be subjectively transformed on the right occasions into golden or yellow light. Light is almost always a positive phenomenon in Arthur's section, though both brothers experience at the end of their lives the choking-off of light by the encroaching, decaying vegetation around the house. Arthur's section also treats light as the illumination of love and truth, sincerity and knowledge. Waldo resists illumination, which involves relinquishing the rational self, and reduces the rational "enlightenment" of Mr Feinstein via grotesque light-imagery.

SOLAR INDICES: CREATION AND DESTRUCTION

Just as the indices of water, dryness and light cross the discourse boundaries of the various narrative sections but are differently evaluative according to the particular focal consciousness involved, so too is the imagery of fire, which is closely associated with Arthur. Both Waldo and Mrs Poulter repeatedly register the transfiguring aura of Arthur's hair (reddish, carrot, orange, "flaming", "alight", "a fire", a "harsh blaze"). There is a recurrent cohabitation of harsh light or fire with a serenity that disturbs Waldo by seeming to contradict the threat of passion, but which really makes Arthur a balanced totality of inward and outward. Other characters within Arthur's Apollonian radius occasionally exhibit kindred traces: Mr Allwright; Dulcie (the "flashes" of her "gunpowdery flesh", the "smouldering of rings", her beauty "aglow"); Mrs Poulter (her fiery wheel-tree, her skin smelling of "struck flint"). Arthur's song to celebrate the Peace also celebrates the fire of love.

Among the more explicit analogues of Arthur's mandalas is the sun itself as a red, orange or gold disc. Arthur kindles into the "flames of argument" and blows "like a flame, or spirit of enlightenment" in the cauterizing illumination of the *zaddikim*. Fire is the symbol of the cleansing process involved in evil's self-destruction—a case in point is the narrative nexus of references to the actual burning of objects (Waldo's "bonfire" of destructive release from the past of the Browns' furniture, as a precondition for the celebratory "blaze" of his imagined creativity; Mr Brown's exorcism of *Karamazov* by fire; Waldo's burning of his papers as the playing-out of the physical death or self-destruction that almost immediately follows). The sun-disc or fire-image returns climactically when Waldo, at the last moment of vision, sees Arthur's "great marigold of a face".

The combination of characterological arrays of indices, character-relationships and intertextualities supports a complex subtext of alchemical and mythological affinities centered on Arthur as solar force. He is juxtaposed as an Apollonian presence against the darker, Dionysiac blood-ritual of the playground torture-scene. He is visually emblematic of Apollo as the sun-god with a flaming disc of hair. He is the alchemical, Apollonian King as solar principle alongside his lunar sister Artemis (the changeable Dulcie, whom Arthur treats with brotherly lovingkindness, yet also desires with a pure desire). Their union is by proxy, but is somatically foreshadowed in Arthur's quasi-hermaphroditism, which corresponds to the post-Apollonian phase of unity in alchemical illustrations. Apollo and Arthur share the same traits and interests (moderation, prescience; the spirit of spontaneous poetry and music; the philosophical quest; mysterious control over mathematics; beauty in youth; a unique affinity with the elements of air, earth and water). White had read Jung on alchemical psychology, and Arthur is made to do the same; critics have identified Jung's *Psychology and Alchemy* behind a conspicuous passage relating to the "hermaphroditic Adam", but have missed Arthur's reading of the Hermetic *Tractatus aureus*, via Jung's *Integration of Personality*, on the conjunction of Venus and the solar light of love (A229). A complex herbal-alchemical symbology is worked out in the text, conjoining Arthur as solar, Christ-like "Golden Flower" (Greek *khrysanthemon*) or "new King" with the "Marian" Mrs Poulter and her chrysanthemums. By the same token, Arthur is a Holy Fool, "dill", scapegoat or *pharmakos*; he is homeopathically both solar life-/love-giver and destroyer (the Golden Flower or marigold or dill as *pharmakos* being both an alchemical remedy and a toxin). "Dill in the engravings looked like fennel" (A225); both dill and fennel have a sun-like form and promote clear vision, and are an alchemical symbol or *pharmakos athanasias* of "eternal life" (with which concept Arthur is associated). Waldo has read the *Prometheus Bound* of pseudo-Aeschylus (W38), the story of which proleptically rehearses the character-relationships in the novel and underscores the psychical interdependence of the brothers. Knowledge as fiery embers is brought from Olympus in the narthex or fennel stem by Prometheus. Via this link, Arthur can be seen as an overlay of Apollonian and Promethean characteristics, and, via linkings with Athene (Mrs Brown and Mrs Poulter) and Hephaestos (parodically present in Mr Allwright), as embodying the useful arts and positive connection with the social community. The main function of "mythic" traits in satellite characters is to provide points of transactional reference to the various traits of Arthur and Waldo themselves.

AERIAL INDICES: VITALITY, DISORDER, AND IRRATIONAL RELEASE

The central elemental indices of fire, sun and light, of moisture and aridity, with their admixtures of the vegetative, the chthonic and the kinetic (fluidity, rigidity, shivering), would be incomplete without consideration of complementary references. It is largely in contexts of a threat to the stability invested by Waldo in rationality that wind, the movement of air, and storms have significance. Arthur is in effortless communion with "the gusty light of boyhood", but Waldo's ordered thoughts are upset by the wind (W27/31/56/57/112/168/174/211), whereas Dulcie's emancipation from self-consciousness is encoded in an extended aerial metaphor (W136). Both Arthur and Waldo have the emblem of their father's rationalist sterility thrown in their faces by the wind (W161, A286). Apart from isolated aerial metaphors for the turmoil of elemental emotion (A283) or the motion of free spirits (A220), wind-indices occur only at the end of Arthur's section, when old age starts to stimulate the long-forgotten distant past.

LUNAR INDICES: FERTILITY AND FLUCTUATION

Moon-indices are mediated on several distinct verbal levels ranging from innocuous, seemingly incidental descriptive lexemes to full-blown symbolism. Dulcie's personality and metonymic extensions (eg, eyes) are associated with the moon, in her aspect of changeability and (for Waldo) unpredictability. By somatic association with Dulcie's eyes, Arthur is also represented as unpredictable. Dulcie's lunar presence hovers over the brothers' fluid embrace in "yellow fluctuating light" at Waldo's last emotional collapse. It is Arthur's narrative that brings the aspect of psychological changeability to the surface (A249/254–55, where the solid blue mandala Arthur gives to Dulcie is connotative of nocturnal moisture and lunar plenitude). Dulcie's mention of a bottle of scent with a pierrot sitting on the moon (W97) links up with Arthur's transcendent, alchemical capturing of her volatility. The alchemical shading of the language in Waldo's narrative is, conversely, associated with negative, destructive carnality (Waldo's penile pen "bottling the essence" of Dulcie's playing of the—lunar—Moonlight Sonata, W135; his imagination trying to capture the carnal "essence" of the perfumed Haynes woman in the garden, W189; Dulcie's elusiveness and Waldo's jerky tumescence connected with his dream of her "paper moon", W134). Arthur and his pierrot-song affiliate him, as the Clown of Love, with the lunar Dulcie.

The intrusion of Arthur between Waldo and Dulcie is proleptically evident in the fragment from Tennyson's "Fatima" (W121–22/130), in which almost all of the major elemental indices of the novel are present (moon; the sun as fire, synthaesthetically conveyed in terms of liquid motion; the wind; dryness).[1] The poem is a mediation of swooning, quasi-sexual ecstasy, paralleled by Waldo's reaction to reading it. In macrotextual terms, the "dry brain" likened to a morning moon is not transformed positively by lunar conjunction as Tennyson would perhaps have it: the moist, gravid moon of night has been annihilated by, or is merged with, the dazzle of the morning sun. Arthur as the fiery sun is as present here as he is during the Encounter-scene. Tennyson's poem also feeds into the metaphor in the scene where Waldo, masturbating, spies on the Haynes woman (the elusive moon of carnality is doubly evoked: by association with the pierrot-bottle; then, via "silver wire", with Tennyson's poem of swooning desire).[2]

Arthur's symbolic dance celebrates the moon in his own, preludial corner of the mandalic square (A263); there is a gradual movement in his corner from the sublunary world of sleep and dream-secrets, through the lunar and the arctic, to the solar or tropic. At the *centre* of Section 3, Arthur "danced the disc of the orange sun above icebergs, which was in a sense his beginning, and should perhaps be his end". It is indeed his *beginning*: on the first page of his narrative,

---

[1] There is much more intertextual relevance in Tennyson's poem confirming the thematic function of these indices in the novel. Indeed, the poem encapsulates the particular interaction between Arthur and Waldo as psychological types, encodes the ambiguity of Waldo's sexuality, and—unremarked in the critical literature on White—presents a germinally-proleptic, clandestine summary of the death-scene terminating each of the central narratives of the novel. See section IX below.

[2] Waldo's obsession with venereal disease corrodes his narrative (W77–78/116/121/122), right down to his "infection", not by the blood of venereal love, but by the "unnatural blood" of Arthur's poem and lovingkindness (W212). The "silver wire" relates also to the mercury (or quicksilver) treatment for syphilis (in early recipes combined with—sarsaparilla!).

he reaches for "the gold disc of the sun" (A215), then dreams of "moons" of sky-blue ice splintering from icebergs into "glass balls which he gathered in his protected hands" (A218). "Protected" is later transformed, as are the glass balls, into his role as "protective" guardian of his mandalas. At the *end*, in a momentary trance-state, the oneiric icebergs are invisible, the "orange disc" of the sun static (P314–15); the whole lunar, psychically fluid side of his identity is temporarily attenuated, in disequilibrium. He will be whole again only when he can dream the roundness of sun *and* moon.

Jungian-alchemical indices—via the mythic-alchemical aspects of Hermes, Mercury, hermaphroditism and Hermetic philosophy—are central enrichments of the novel's narrative and figurational correspondences. In a bi-elemental alchemy, the creation of the One depends on the Sun (male, fixed and sulphurous) and the Moon (female and volatile—hence "bottled cestrum", "essence"). Together—even in alchemical "battle"—they are "brother and sister", each opposing principle containing its opposite. Hence the sequent occurrence in Arthur's dance of moon and sun; hence the femaleness in Arthur, the maleness in Dulcie, the femaleness in Waldo—to summarize the three potential planes of union (within self, with the sexual Other, with the twin brother). The alchemical processes of, say, the fourteenth-century *Aurora consurgens* can be transferred to the interpersonal and perceptual levels of the novel. Arthur, the solar King, is confirmed in his spiritual identity by his interaction with a quasi-mother (Mrs Poulter) and a quasi-sister (Dulcie), both lunar, "fluctuating" Isis-personalities. Waldo is entranced by the white rose (W119)—alchemically, the Arthurian "Red King" appears out of the lunar womb of the "White Rose"—but turns away from its "only apparent" solidity. Though cold and dry, Waldo is neither solar nor lunar, but is the equivalent of the Paracelsian darkness, inertness and fixity of the natural body, quickened and inflamed by the mercurial spirit and the sulphurous soul. Without Waldo's presence and resistance, no alchemical or spiritual marriage (Arthur and Dulcie/Mrs Poulter) is possible that will reflect the wholeness of human nature. To the extent, however, that Waldo's resistance implies repression of alchemical opposites (eg, his repressed bisexuality), then he, too, is open to self-union and fraternal union. The narrative denies the possibility of such fulfilment: the "Great Work" is not completed by Waldo's self-consumption (like his papers) to psychical ash. But Waldo's decay within the decaying house releases Arthur into a state of inner conflict in which *he* must undergo "putrefaction" in the darkness of Sydney before he can begin again the climb towards regeneration.

The patterning of Arthur's behaviour allows, too, a shift from alchemical particularities to more comprehensive mythological ones. If we consider the assimilative philosophy joining mythology to alchemy and metapsychology (Hermeticism and its Gnostic admixture), it is instructive to remember that this philosophy centred on an androgynous first God who, like Arthur, passes on goodness and wisdom and is thus made both immortal and mortal. Hermeticism, like Arthur, searches for true understanding (*gnosis*) that can allow the soul to escape its bondage to matter. With a regression to myth: Hermes and Apollo are conjoint, and the Hermetic catalogue applies indexically to Arthur (brotherly interest in childbirth; proficiency in music; love of animals; "mandalic" divination and the gift of perception; Hermes, like Arthur, is an *angelus*, "angel" or messenger, purveying gossip, summoning and soothing the dying; Arthur, like Hermes/Mercury, is the "god" of commerce and merchandise).

Even in the mandala-dance, the realms of the lunar and the solar, of sleep and transcendental consciousness, are merged via the "bottled-essence" presence of the cestrum or night jasmine, with its phallically tubular yellow flowers. Of the belladonna family, the cestrum stands in Waldo's narrative for the languor of sexual self-possession as he drifts on the sea of unconsciousness (W79). In Arthur's narrative, its yellow colour and tropical provenance argue for its function as a solar, Golden Flower representing the sun's presence in the lunar night (as, zeugmatically, the moon of Tennyson's "Fatima" is overcome by solar light), "anaesthetizing" and stabilizing the fluctuations of lunar multiplicity. A notable allusive reworking of the Tennyson poem occurs when Arthur finds "most dazzling" the appearance of Mrs Musto in the late morning, her exotic costume "shimmering with moonlight" (A238). If Dulcie as a lunar figure can be contiguously related to fertility and generation, so too can Mrs Musto, though the operation of contiguity is rather the reverse. She is primarily a Demeter/Ceres figure within the highly selective, frequently comic system of mythological correlations in the novel. She is associated with crops, corn, flour and its whiteness, and food generally, and is the patroness of the life and growth of "youngsters" and of the civilizing process. The initiatory aspect of the Eleusinian Mysteries associated with Demeter is expressed in the language applied to the "elect" "initiates" at her tennis-party (W87–90); to lend an iconographical touch to the portrait: she rides, not in a motor-car, but in a "chariot". After Arthur discovers the mandala-definition in Mrs Musto's encyclopedia (A238), the indexical description of her shifts from Demeter as goddess of fertility to lunar detail (moonlight, evanescence, volatility, water)—a shift in Arthur's psychological perception which moves her from the social realm of his fondness for Demeter (A223) to the inner circle of his lunar companions. Demeter has been associated with Io, the moon-goddess and rain-bringer, emblematically syncretized with Isis, whose ceremonial worship also flows into that of Diana, Athene, and Artemis. Dulcie, Mrs Poulter and Mrs Musto are thus all typifiable under the rubrics of lunar nature and the mediation of generation, even though Mrs Musto and Mrs Poulter are childless. All three stand under Arthur's solar influence, and all three are merely suffered by Waldo in a psychological pattern of attraction, repulsion and exploitation. There is a selective emphasis on different characteristics among the three women, Demeter prevailing here, Diana/Artemis there, Io elsewhere.[3] Arthur loves both Demeter and Mrs Poulter

---

[3] The distinction between Dulcie and Mrs Poulter as Io–figures is substantiated by narrative detail, while their common basis is mediated more obliquely. It is told that Io as maiden or new moon is a white cow; as nymph, mature woman or harvest moon, she changes her colour (or phase) to red—mythographically altered to "violet" by analogy with Greek *ion*, "violet flower". Dulcie, lunar deity of the maiden-phase, is associated before her marriage with the

for their ripe and russet apples (A223/281; cf Wilkes 1969:104), the symbol of fertility, love, immortality and totality—though he has confused the apple with Demeter's true attribute, the pomegranate, many-seeded symbol of multiplicity and the emblem, too, of the inconstant Mrs Allwright/Hera, whom Arthur dislikes for her "plots, and tempers" (A227). Hera was the guardian of women; Mrs Allwright declares the animus of "ladies" towards "bold behaviour in little boys" (A226). It is Hera's servant Argos who watches over Io; this and her cow-goddess association with the Minotaur lies behind Arthur's joking with her about "bull's-eyes" (A226). If Arthur has confused apples with pomegranates, he has confirmed one of his chief functions within the metapsychological realm of the novel: that of encompassing and reconciling the One and the Many (cf Beatson 1976:18). His manual activities link him (as the One) to the Many of his female consorts (music with Dulcie; milking and butter-making with Mrs Poulter as cow-goddess; his breadmaking, pale complexion and the impasto of his song with Mrs Musto; his bringing of flour to Mrs Poulter and her surrogate child as à fertility-link between Mrs Musto and Mrs Poulter).

II   Indices to sexuality and sensuality

THE PHALLIC: SUBLIMATION, MUSIC, AND OTHER CORRELATIVES

Unequivocal sexual suggestiveness is restricted to Waldo's section. Despite Arthur's interest in "erotological works" (W196), the diction and implications of "sexual" passages in Arthur's section arc "clean" (the anticipation of revelation at Mrs Musto's, A237; his transcendent "entry" into Dulcie's flower-like face, A275; the semen-like metaphor for guilt in his mandala-dance for Waldo, A266). The innocence of Arthur's interest in sexual characteristics is clear (A256/257/279). Waldo's obsession with the sexual is, by contrast, reflexive, projective, transformative, sublimative. There are indices to his sexual fear, and to his reification of sexuality (W79/191). His diction encodes penile erection (W79/135–36/185) and masturbation (W77/127: the zeppelin/189/79: the cestrum/135: his Sunday "abuse"). Indices to tumescence and detumescence abound (zeppelin and cestrum; W184/197/134). The language of sexual explosion is metonymically transposed in other ways as well, especially in Waldo's preoccupation with books, his papers, and abstract ideas (most notably in his

---

colour white (A244/265/281). Mrs Poulter, though young, has for Arthur the aura of ripe maturity, and is associated with harvest indices (including the pig of Demeter) and the spectral domain of violet (mauve, puce and purple: W60/186/210; A289). Waldo associates Mrs Poulter with cattle (W140/144); Arthur's cow-tragedy enacts proleptically the death of Mrs Poulter's child (ie, its prior death is narrated later). Dulcie is hardly bovine (apart from her eyes), but she is accompanied by "the ox her husband" (W64), "ox-eyed" Saporta (W155), who, like Arthur, is identified with the sun (A276). Io was watched over by the ox-herd Argos, the "all-seeing" (an epithet applied to Zeus, Apollo, and the sun). Arthur, with his omniprescient vision, enters into a mystic marriage with Dulcie (cf the sacred marriage of Zeus and Io, which also applies to Arthur's other "bride", Mrs Poulter), thereby serving as Saporta's eyes until he can take over the earthly task of supporting Dulcie/Io.

comic "raping" of his paper-filled desk and dress-box). The most grotesque metonymic shifts, however, are surreal outgrowths of Waldo's repressions. He is hypersensitive to all manifestations of music, especially its "organs of reproduction" (Dulcie's piano is upright, with "ivory skin" which she lashes sado-masochistically, as it stands amidst the engorged labial upholstery of the room; W101/135/151/157; Waldo's own—spent—vocal organ is silkily penile and virile, W26/72–73/128/137; Dulcie's throat and neck are seen, in Waldo's ambivalent desire, as congesting like a penis, W64/136).[4] In the music-scene, Waldo's submerged associations of Jewishness with sexual uncleanliness and (cultural) potency come together in a vision of Mrs Feinstein's nose as a penis (W136, with variations at W64/100/108/112/132). There is throughout the novel the association of the voice with the passion and sensuality of music, and its "cello music" is for Waldo part of the "mature" ancestral mystery of Europe (W66/100/138). Waldo's reaction to music is to hurt, or to see the production of music as a masochistic torment (A265–66); music for Arthur is a source of exquisite pain. The knife-metaphor used elsewhere for Waldo's urge to separate himself from his twin and others, is applied in Arthur's section to indicate the surgery of harmony (A240–41). The twins' distinctive attitudes towards boyhood piano-practice (Waldo tune-deaf, mediocre, methodically rational; Arthur bucking against the straitjacket of "angular scales", straining towards the more concrete and the more mathematically and transcendently abstract) reflect exactly their psychology.

THE SEXES BOUND IN ONE

The narrative conditions us early to accept how lopsidedly Waldo regards the (im)balance of male and female traits within the human personality. Loss of self-control can pitch his voice into the feminine end of the spectrum, but, in his drive for confirmation of his intellectual stature, he scarcely realizes how his repressed female aspect plays its role (cf the Encounter, W66–68; his battle with Crankshaw, W166/176; his relationships with Dulcie, Bill Poulter and Len Saporta, W91/142/144/156). Waldo's attitude towards Arthur is unequivocal: he is a "big fat helpless female" (W32, A230), a designation Arthur is not prepared to dispute; on one occasion a stranger even brands him an hermaphrodite (A252). Apart from somatic indices to breasts (A265/281/291), there are intertextual conditionings indicative of Arthur's hermaphroditism as suggesting wholeness and integration of self (see especially Beatson 1976:95–96). Arthur is early

---

[4] Differently weighted is a passage involving Waldo's embarrassing intrusion into Dulcie's house: "Since his arrival, her throat was permanently raised, to whatever he might do to it" (W156). It is an image of sacrifice—as though Dulcie were offering her throat to her lover's knife—but it is also erotic, as though she were offering it to be kissed. The notion of exposure here, and, additionally, of sudden self-exposure through language, can be found in a recurrence of similar indices involving characters "holding up" or "raising" their long, muscular, flushed, or full throats (W38–39/59, A255). Not limited to the perception of one character only, this somatic index can also be found in White's other fiction, and thus constitutes a feature of authorial mind-style.

attracted to the myth of Tiresias (A223-24), which expression Waldo and his father resist. The name "Tiresias" means "he who delights in signs", which is precisely what Arthur is forever doing. One remarkable intranarrative doubling connects a complaint by Mr Brown in the Tiresias-myth scene that Arthur never speaks (ie, thinks; A223) with Waldo's complaint that his brother never thinks (A282). In the earlier scene, a subordinated observation concerns Tiresias changing into a woman; in the later scene, Arthur intelligently and disingenuously contrasts this with "the hermaphroditic Adam who carries his wife about with him inside" (A283). Waldo is horrified, and Arthur must comfort him when he erupts into hysterical sobbing. Arthur has absorbed the Jungian texts in the Library, and is aware that the Jungian "veiled bride" of the male *animus* within his body can be accommodated as Waldo to his two other Eve-brides; further, in an awareness of his solar status, he senses that his brother is the "shadow following him in the sun" (A285). Twinned to Arthur's psycho-mythological Tiresias is Waldo's, derived in equal measure from the Greek myths (via Arthur), Tennyson and T.S. Eliot. Waldo as intellectual aspirant to literary creativity conveniently restricts Tiresias to his sequentially first role as precocious intellect (ironically, Waldo, who is characterized by blindness, is slapped "as a little boy" for "his premature awareness", W119). Prophecy, blindness as seeing, and transsexuality don't get a word in, so that Waldo has effectively neutralized the potentiality of the myth in his unfinished fragment (W173-74/211-12), and the mythic notion of a seven-fold life has been perverted into a regression to childhood, then into a muted admission that old age has impaired his primary (and only) tools, and finally (via the shock of Arthur's poem) into a crushing awareness of old age. If the exhaustive indices to hirsuteness in Waldo and Dulcie and to smoothness in Arthur constitute overt challenges to sexual nature and sexual roles,[5] then references to Arthur's hair,

---

[5] There is more to the index of hirsuteness than this. If one takes those two narrative moments of crisis where Waldo is aware of his mature hairiness (W70) and Arthur's smoothness (W213), one notices that they are not discoursally "naturalized", but remain defamiliarized and foregrounded until fitted into larger indexical patterns. Genesis 27:11 states: "Behold, Esau my brother is an hairy man, and I am a smooth man". One recollects that Jacob and Esau were not just brothers, but were also twins. Once one concedes the possibility of an intertextual thread here, then the thread becomes a skein. The theme of Jewish dynastic history is inserted into the novel via this biblical story (the connection being ironically present in a comment by Mrs Brown about being "'all Jews'", W167). George Brown is a failed Isaac, ineffectually passing on the "Abrahamic covenant" (cf W145-46). Esau's resolve to kill Jacob after the death of Isaac becomes actuality in *The Solid Mandala*. The apparent denial of the expected pattern—where it would have been "logical" to have Waldo as the first-born, red-headed Esau, instead of the younger (W26) Jacob—makes sense in terms of the psychology of twin consciousness. In Rebecca's prophecy, the "two manner of people" within her are contrastively weak and strong, and the elder shall serve the younger—which Arthur does, though it is Waldo who sees his service to Arthur as a duty and ultimately unbearable handicap, and who resolves to "break his yoke from off thy neck". The Esau in Waldo-Jacob seeks the Jacob in Arthur-Esau, but Jacob must escape: the only Jacob left is the Jacob of Waldo's self, and so he destroys himself, while reaching out to destroy his twin. The question of dominance and subservience, revealed in the prophecy to Rebecca and rendered self-

apart from being a solar index, chart a shift within him towards increased femininity.

III   Union, vision, the Other and the Self

UNION

By way of prelude to this section, which is concerned with indices of seeing, blindness and mirroring, I should mention references that stress the subjective sense of oneness or unity between the twins or between one brother and another character. This zone of unity serves as a field of reference against which to gauge indices of psychical conflict, sexual division, intellectual alienation and emotional self-preoccupation. In boyhood, oneness is consensual (W24/81) and tacit (A230), though Arthur must struggle with "their double image, their never quite united figure" (A266). For Waldo, it is the vital spirit of night-time breathing that brings   them   closest   together   and   alienates   him   from   Arthur (W30/33/39/41/76/197). Arthur, unlike Waldo, has other affinities, and can feel united with his dog or with Dulcie (W181, A275). Waldo accepts union only at times of emotional stress when rationality cannot provide lasting certainty (W48/208–209); on two occasions, this close fraternal union is preceded by Waldo's narcissistic mirror-gazing (W33, A229). The central narrative feature is that Waldo avoids physical contact, while Arthur seeks and receives it.

---

fulfilling by manipulation of the blind Isaac (Genesis 27:1–30; there are parallel blindness-indices in George Brown: eg, W41/54/77/82), is shifted in the novel away from the biblical domain of the nuclear-family origins of nation-state conflicts (eg, the residual trace in Mr Brown's changing patriarchal, parodically "covenantal" endorsement of his sons), into the domain of personality-conflict, though the folk-*topos* of the quarrel for precedence in the womb is preserved (eg, explicitly at W26/148; via big/little brother indices, at W42/71/73–74, A270; on numerous occasions via the twins' holding of hands). The matrimonial fulfilment of Jacob's covenant in Laban's family is functionally split by White into Arthur's dual foci of nurture (Mrs Poulter) and culture (the Feinsteins and the Saportas). Even Esau's association with the Edomites (consistently hostile to the Jews) is reflected in Waldo's persistent anti-semitism. The incorporation of the biblical story into the conceptual weave of the novel avoids oversimplifying binary oppositions or antinomies in favour of the more truthful, flexible and complex symmetry of quaternity. If we simplify by making Arthur and Waldo white and black, the biblical inter-text (whose correspondences are more detailed than the above sketch might reveal) must remain inaccessible. Only by grasping the twins' *double duality* does White's syncretion of cultural codes and inter-texts make perfect sense. (It is also our acknowledgement of double duality that can save us elsewhere from the error of applying an Apollonian/Dionysiac frame to the twins which works only one way in terms of psychology or artistic personality.) The novel's indexical grid matches a *particular* biblical one; cf the heuristic matching of text with cultural inter-text—Abraham and Isaac, or Cain and Abel—which results in a *general* overlap, but an unsatisfactory one that does not potentiate either the action or the verbal expression of the novel.

MIRRORS

Some of the mirror-sequences have already been discussed in connection with narrative sequencing. Arthur immerses himself in the world of *Alice Through the Looking Glass*; but, whereas he gazes into the indirect mirror of books to *find* not just his own identity (the Tweedledum and Tweedledee of twin-ness) but also the means of saving his twin's identity (*The Brothers Karamazov*), Waldo seeks confirmation of what he thinks he already "knows"—which has nothing to do with Arthur but is, rather, proof of Waldo's apartness. The mirror that reflects is Waldo's instrument for mental reflection of the Self—indeed, Waldo's discourse employs just such stereotyped terms ("he must withdraw his mind from his mind's mirror", W62)—but with no obedience to the dictum *nosce teipsum*.[6] The mirror presents him with images of personal vanity, or is an avenue out of the present into the past. Arthur comes to take his brother's mirror-gazing as a Red Alert. That Waldo seeks confirmation is indicated in the "refractions" of his own sentiments that he seeks (W183), the association with the past in the *doppelgänger*-suggestion of the re-encounter with Haynes (W183). Normal adolescent mirror-gazing can involve the avoidance of truth (W75); objective truth (despite the ostensible basis of his whole rational existence) as told by the mirror is the last thing he desires; instead, his defence against self-hatred and the fear of quitting boyhood is to attack the face *in* the glass.

Arthur's gnomic well-song (W134) is connected with Waldo's narcissism, and with Arthur's own quest for identity. The plate-glass mirrors of shop-windows have a differentiating narrative function: Waldo's discourse betrays his mental imperialism, the surreptitiousness of his "speculation", and his dissimulation (W55/58). Arthur does not seek his reflection in mirrors until he notices his age at the end (A290). It is immediately after this that Arthur sees Waldo in their mother's dress before the mirror. After Waldo's death, Arthur glimpses his reflection again (P307), in an incident carefully structured to "reflect" earlier ones. It is retrospection that the mirror has forced on Arthur here—in the direction of truths that he has previously tried, without "malice", to force on Waldo. Arthur's guilty desire to reveal "himself glistening in a sphere of glass" evokes his dream of mandalic wholeness, recalls the old alchemical image of the homunculus in its alchemical sphere, and is ultimately resolved at the very end in his union with Mrs Poulter, as they are "reflected in each other's eyes" (P312). The integrative mandala asserts itself here over the potentially self-divisive Waldovian mirror.

EYES AND VISION

The theme of mirroring is contiguous, in the case of Waldo, with two interrelated metonymies of seeing: Waldo's spectacles, and Waldo's eyes. Waldo is short-sighted, and "blind" without his glasses—but he is also "blind" *with* his glasses

---

6 Apart from the title of White's autobiography, which centres on reflexive scrutiny, there are open indications of a Waldovian, reluctant fascination with mirrored identity and the past (cf especially *Flaws:* 1/3/33/46/154).

on: his rationality cannot triumph over the solipsism that governs his mode of perception, and cannot cope with manifestations of emotion. He *needs* his spectacles in order to "see" in the mirror what is no longer there except in memory (W31/120)—the young self he connects with the "ice-blue ancestral stare" of his mother's side of the family; the force of his narcissistic will *creates* an image in the mirror that can counteract the blenching horror of true recollection (W192). Waldo's relation to the present is as transformative and displacive as his relation to the past: he tends to "naturalize" the artificial (W70), without involvement *in* reality. There is, then, an inversion of the normal qualitative hierarchical relation of reality to art. The rimless glass of Waldo's spectacles is like an "emanation" of his eyes, falsifying them, making them colder and paler (W63/120); the metonymy and instrument of his intellectual rationalization, eyes and spectacles are one. Because he cannot understand the emotional bond between Arthur and their mother as he comforts her after Mr Brown's death (W73), Waldo is forced out of the disturbing present into "mirroring" and an image of himself as a child. But Waldo cannot see Arthur's "blurry" face—the sun and Arthur's towering solar presence blind his glasses, incapacitating his intellect. Acting out his exclusion, he blinds himself to what he cannot "see" by taking off his glasses (W74). Two fantasies—Waldo's dream of Dulcie's child perpetuating his "memory" in name; his dream of power through regression to the "Memory" of a feminized ancestral past—are both shattered, in each case entailing a symbolic breaking of his aid to sight (his pince-nez after the Encounter, W64/67/171; the mirror *qua* "situation" in the transvestite scene, W193—Waldo's vision shatters as though it were his glasses, returning him to the "blindness" of present awareness).

Arthur's lack of a specular interest correlates with a receptive attitude towards the eyes of his friends (A279). He is drawn to Mr Allwright, in a kind of elective affinity with his long-sightedness (W37, A222). He is excited to discover that he and Dulcie have the same colour eyes (A254), but notes that she is not always clear-sighted (A248), as does Waldo (W64/95), who is less upset by her when her eyes "shine with certainty" (W151). Waldo "blackballs" and fears the accusing intrusiveness of brown eyes (W120/125/136/163); a strong cultural prejudice underlies his preference for (Germanic, intellectual) blue over (Southern, passionate) brown. Dark eyes are obsessively associated with insentient animals; his father's "black" eyes fill him so with horror that he can even neutralize them by claiming they are brown (W41). Contrasting with this fear of eyes engulfing him in emotionality is the fear Waldo harbours that these same eyes will exclude him: their promise of intuitive, transcendental vision casting his self-same rationality into question (W54, where Mr Brown in the bank realizes the failure of reason; A231, where Arthur exercises his mathematical gift; even the twins' dogs, which encode Tiresian blindness, have mandalic eyes, and are loyal only to Arthur, W23/178–79).

The beauty of all such indices is that they are not primarily symbolic, but are perfectly realistic, and naturalistically explicable, percepts which nevertheless correlate consistently with the perceiving figural consciousness. Even the most "mimetic", direct expressions of a character's world-view are made relevant to thematic, indexical detail. Typically for this novel and its contrastive structuring, Waldo seldom expresses himself directly in metaphoric or symbolic terms: and his indirect discourse is expressively derivative from his reading, from "jokey" habits of mind, and from psychological domains that are under intense, distorting pressure. Arthur, who tends to see the world intuitively in terms of symbolic correspondences, reveals rather than conceals these correspondences in direct discourse: and his spoken observations tend to creep uncheckably into Waldo's indirect discourse.[7]

IV   Architectonic metaphor: Hindrance and stasis

WALLS AND TRANSPARENCY

When Arthur reminds Waldo that the words he is working away at (hiding his papers with "his hand as a wall", W195) are a Tennyson poem, Waldo watches "the wall of his hand ... grow transparent and unstable". Waldo erects barriers, watching out for the traps of burrowing brown eyes, evading the flux of the elements and of present time. But he cannot prevent for long the manifold encroachments on the static and seemingly solid house of the ego. The exposure of his papers to others' eyes means the erasure of a factitious self; hence Waldo's horror of transparency and his frenetic investment in secrecy. His protective hand is there over his writing (W81) when he speculates that Arthur, too, might have secrets of a simple sort. Waldo holes up in the "fortress" of his dining-room (W190) behind his "barricade of words" (W183), or behind "those merciful walls, his eyelids" (W68). His mother's genteel English voice erects an enviable "barrier" against the "adulterated tradition" of Australia (W72), and the glossier houses of Sarsaparilla exhibit for Waldo desirable "ramparts" (W118) which are yet envied for marking Waldo's own exclusion.

There are other protective walls apart from Waldo's. Arthur's mandala-dance is a structure created for the protection of others through love, no matter that "the walls of his circular fortress shuddered" (A266)—they shudder because it is the beat of his own man-child's heart within his fortress body. Institutionalized

---

[7] In the actional present, Arthur says he can "'see right into ... the part that matters'" in simple, "'transparent'" people (W29). In recollection, Waldo notes how their parents "could not see far enough into" Arthur, but Waldo could (W35); yet Waldo sees only his assumptions—that Arthur is mentally defective—and not "the part that matters". Arthur's visionary centre is something Waldo never gets used to, not least when Arthur looks "almost inside" him in the morning (W39). Nor can Waldo escape this everyday visionary perception—in the actional present, Arthur is at Waldo once more, this time about "'getting much farther in'" when he is "'really ill'" (W57); "'Words are not what make you see'". This idea of entry into the transparent entails commitment to onself and to others. In later years, Waldo's discourse turns this idea on its head: "If any, his religion had become a cultivation of personal detachment, of complete transparency—he was not prepared to think emptiness—of mind" (W177). His perversion of "religion" for faithless, self-protective rationalism is eventually corrected through the reflections of Sergeant Foyle at the end, with his notion of commitment as "old people rising transparent and hopeful ... after the sacrament" (P313).

religion is a "wall" which he keeps on "coming up against" (A262), as is the "castle" of the Jewish religion in the Saportas' house at the end, whose ramparts he cannot storm to share in the sacrament of lovingkindness (P309). Simple Christian charity is withheld by Mrs Dun, opaque and distant behind her closed glass door (P303). And Waldo is not strong enough to scale the "wall" of Dulcie's back as she plays Beethoven (W136). Waldo's paranoiac vigilance as an alert hunter "stalking" intellectual truth (W54/83), finally, is conveyed in the metaphor of snares and traps against, or of, everything from sentiment (W23/175/208) to the rank vitality of Arthur's dogs, "chewing up ... the sheets of thoughts which escaped from his mind" (W187).

KNOTS AND LABYRINTHS

There is an almost inexhaustible variety of metaphors and indications of knotting, intertwining, labyrinths. Waldo is "'born with his innards twisted'" (W32), and the dog he chooses has a belly "swollen by the knots of worms probably inside it" (W180–81). In a state of exacerbated short-sightedness, solipsism, and reduction of the external world to abstraction (W83), Waldo's mind is "a choked labyrinth without a saving thread". The Daedalian metaphor is inverted and explored further: Waldo hides at "the most secret, virgin heart of all the labyrinth" while the stallion/minotaur figure of Haynes clops around the house (W189), thinking of Arthur with his "buffalo mind ... lumbering into other people's thoughts". But he guesses that Arthur might be "the thread of continuity, and ... core of truth" (W186–87), as he moves through the "mysterious maze of numbers" (W42). Arthur is indeed the Ariadne's thread, Theseus following his "threads of thought" (A287), and also´a lumbering, Minotaurian part of the core of destructive truth at the heart of Waldo's dark labyrinth.

The twins' lives are "knotted" inside the house, as they are "knotted together by habit" (W204, A282). Waldo's Writing, as an illness and "a more esoteric form of cat's-cradle" (W29), cannot weave artistic order out of his psychical disorder, whereas Arthur can bring calm and order to Mrs Brown's deranged last days by playing cat's-cradle with her (A273, W170). The mandala which Arthur reserves for Waldo is "flawed or knotted" (A228), its knot "so tortuously inwoven [that] it would dissolve, if only temporarily, in light" (A272–73); like Waldo, it is so pale as to be colourless. Arthur, as the absent "core of truth", can become present at the heart of Waldo's labyrinth only by striking the whole knotted mass of his psyche with the uniting light of love. But Waldo rejects Arthur's gift; what can the knotted mandala do for him? To "untie" the knot is to treat it as though it were tied by reason and untiable by rationality. Impossible: the knot can only be dissolved by emotion, by the love of Waldo's other half. Yet this same knot *is* the knot of their twin lives, *and* the "choked" labyrinth at Waldo's centre. The love that destroys the knot (love in the guise of truth) destroys Waldo.

The problem of the mandala-marble is, finally, worked out in conceptual, narrative, actional and symbolic terms without any further deployment of textural

detail. Beyond it, there are other indices to inextricability, ranging from the
"twisted ropes of dark music" with which Waldo "strangles" Dulcie (A265–66)
to Bill Poulter mocking Waldo's ethereal intellectuality by splitting the "knottiest
chunk of wood ... the knots split apparently by light" (W143). George Brown's
asthma is a "tangle" of breath, and Mr Feinstein, once a bright puppet of
"enlightenment", becomes an old bedridden man, "whose strings had tangled and
trussed him" (A277). Knots of emotion are associated with Mrs Poulter
(A266/289, P302), whose bearing of a still-born child is enacted in Arthur's cow-
tragedy, the calf's head "twisting in his guts" (A230).

STRUCTURE AND TEXTURE: FRAGMENTATION, SOLIDIFICATION

Other structural and textural metaphors in Waldo's section accentuate the notion
that he is confronted by a frustrating disorder in existence which is never openly
termed "chaos" but, rather, is imposed upon by Waldo's intellection as he tries to
naturalize what he cannot grasp. Art-metaphors (eg, "impasto") recur. The
"confusingly marbled" appearance of human relationships (W167) is matched by
what he sees as his romanticized fragments of mistaken perception about Dulcie,
now merged "into the mosaic of truth". Waldo's "mosaic" is a rationalist's
fallacy, whereas the "fragments" he rejects arc the closest he will get to the truth
of necessary illusion (cf also the shattering of his life into a more realistic "fresh
mosaic" by Johnny Haynes, W189). Arthur threatens to "shatter" Waldo's mental
constructs of people (W106), while anyone can "damage the crystal core" of his
delicately illusory self. The very discourse is self-damagingly fabricated: a
"crystal" that is transparent in terms of intellectual lucidity and purity can also
condemn him to being exposed and destroyed by Arthur's own brand of higher
idealism. Waldo's entrapment in rigidity, stasis and solidification has already
been noted in relationship to his extreme self-consciousness: somatic and
psychical rigidity, environmental enclosure, self-enclosure, the "roughcast of
life" and his corroded, creaking, encrusted memory and mind. The way in which
imperfect, disordered reality presses in on his idealizing desire and intellectual
perfectionism is signalled when Dulcie starts struggling to play the Moonlight
Sonata (W135). The language becomes defensively punny, the tone schizoid ("lay
... on" as a painting-metaphor and an idiom for exaggeration, recalling his
negative "impasto"-metaphor for Arthur's song and Mr Brown's burden of guilt,
W134/146, and the "fleshy slab of hostility" for palpable atmosphere in the
Encounter-scene, W67).

   In Arthur's section, negative solidification is related to the old house and the
natural climate pressing upon Waldo (congealment, basalt storm-clouds, rain as
fragments of shale, A282; "clotting" smells and "solid" days, A286). This
contrasts with Waldo's positive evaluation of the frozen past (clothing "set ... in
timelessness", W67; his mother in her pre-Brownian form "carved out of stone",
W167, or, punningly after George Brown's entombment, facelifted into the
aristocratic eminence of the old "grave structure of her face", W161). But he
sees his family as "set" around him (W203), Dulcie's sexual maturity as "the

concrete of womanhood" (W130), the hands of his father first knotted in doubt then turned "to stone" (W159). Intuitively responsive to music, Arthur "sees" it as "splotches of sound", as part of primal disorder; in its fluid abstraction, he cannot "mould" it as he "kneads" his dough (A232), his extemporizing discords aspiring rather to the condition of water (W110). Arthur is sensitive to the reduction of his "wives" to stasis (in metaphors of statues and ivory), and attempts to restore them (A252/254/266/278).

Metaphors of ice are frequent. With Waldo, ice (often in connection with mirrors and with glass) has to do with pathological self-division: a retreat from self-in-the-present, and confrontation, then identification, with a fictive self frozen in the ice (and reflecting glass) of memory. The terrifying fluidity of time, which removes Waldo from the security of childhood and maternal-ancestral power, is elementally transformed into icy fixity and stasis (or, at most, attenuated into glacial slowness). The sudden incursion of the excluded Other shatters the glass, splinters and melts this fictive stasis, and Waldo is painfully in the world of motion and disorder again. With Arthur, ice (often in connection with mandalic indices and crystal transparency) has to do with self-integration: a reaching for the union of separated complementarities within the cosmic, universal present. It is no accident that Arthur's icebergs are contained within oceanic fluidity and motion, and are in the process of dissolution, under solar influence, towards the unitary wholeness of lunar orbs and glass balls. Unlike Arthur, Waldo becomes the hard, cold, fragile and static element which is the subjective correlative of his psychical self-projection: his illusion, if shattered, means his destruction. Arthur encourages his mandalas to catch the sunlight, warming them with soothing friction; Waldo's hatred in rejection turns the knotted mandala into an "icy" marble in Arthur's palm.

The blue dress Waldo dons is both icily rigid and fluid (W118/191–92/212, A286/291). Long before the mirror-incident, Waldo has an "icy vision of the blue woman" (W163), and his mother's dress is of "blue, reverberating ice" (W192). Waldo's mixing of memories—of his mother's blue dresses with another, ancestral family member recollected from his English childhood—is itself an act of coagulation or rigidification, a denial of sequentiality, and his self-estrangement before the mirror is connected, via the slats of a "nacreous" fan, with the "icy moment" when he peers through the blind-slats into the Feinsteins' home (W124). The Feinsteins' European dresses, with their "trickling" beads, echo the elegance of the Quantrell heirloom. The submerged associationism of such indexical detail promotes the reader's active engagement in the reconstitution of character-consciousness and obsession.

THE WOUNDED FATHER

A form of hindrance or drag on mobility which is oppressively present in the narrative is George Brown's crippled leg or foot, a focus of attention in the community, by Waldo's account, if not in the family (W33–34). His emotional crippling is heralded by his limping approach (W34), and Waldo measures his own superiority against this defect (W49). The image of Mrs Brown's inactive arms after her death is a telling parallel crippling. Arthur and "twin consciousness" are Waldo's "jostling ... hindering" "club foot" (W47/76). His "lopsided" father (W126) is omnipresent, crippling the son's own gait and thoughts (W76/174). Arthur's muted perception of his wounded father is intuitively understanding (A221/230/269); he sees his father as blameless, his true "affliction" being his crippled rationality, just as Mr Brown (when Arthur acts out the afflicted cow, A230) may be viewing his son's mental and histrionic "affliction". Mrs Brown, resenting the weakness of strong men, "could not forgive them their strong legs" (A272); with tactful understanding, Arthur can see his mother's fierce defensiveness of her husband, with his kindly, inoffensive disposition. The father's goodness "is often identical with impotence", his wound with "ineffectiveness", which the son inherits (Beatson 1976:117–18). If Mr Brown's withered leg encodes the atrophy of rational enlightenment, Mr Feinstein, of a similar intellectual disposition, also ends up disillusioned, and with a "withered arm" (A277).

V   Time and memory

The density and persistence with which references to time and memory occur in non-metaphoric form enable the metaphoric, more oblique episodes to be read precisely and unequivocally.[8] There is, first, the early topicalizing of memory as a painful necessity (W26–27), and Waldo's memory of Arthur as a recognition of both change and persistence (W26). Waldo ostensibly rejects the past as worthless, but foists this view on others (W60). He is tortured by the illusion of motion and change seemingly presented by the passing of traffic on "the same stretch of infinity" (W60); the present for him is the mundane flux of the interior world. Waldo's hedgings about the past, and his oscillatory cause-and-effect rationalization of the present, have sandwiched between them Arthur's blithe recollections of death in the recent past. These polarities—Waldo's intellection on past and present; Arthur's direct recall—are in continual alternation.

Waldo is "set", "immoveable" in past's "timelessness" (W67), unable to think back to what his future-directed intentions could have been; his abstract diction both points to Waldo's intellectual struggle to regain control, and foregrounds the theme of time. "Disinclined" to remember death (W69), incapable of remembering faces (W163), he yet views himself as being "all memory and brutal knowledge" (W78). He regards memories as exercisable power, mocking his father's value-free memorizing of Ibsen and crushing his mild views on sex

---

[8] These include Waldo's obsessive harking back to boyhood, either as structured narrative recollection (W31–32 *et sqq.*, W75); or in the narrative-present injection of boyhood emotion into an older man's gestures and reactions (W56/172); or in past/present recall of the already narrated past (W64, matching W31); or within past-narrative contexts where he is suddenly isolated, or rendered uncertain, in his manhood (W70–71/143); or when he is forced into childhood by the unbearableness of an experienced past or narrative-present incident (W73–74; W119/211).

under the weight of his own coarser sexual memories. Contradictorily, "time and memory" work against "the form of youth" (W119): the "form" is memory's frozen image, untouchable by time unless present awareness of age prevents one from seeing oneself as young in the present. Importantly for Waldo, the mental is indestructible, unlike the physical, which exists in time; this is his way out of the dilemma of time and change.

In his alienation from experience, Waldo vicariously appropriates memories from a past that is not his own (W163–64; cf W192–94). This is his "peculiar vice" or "Folly", and involves vicarious sensuality (such as infuses the mirror-gazing scene); he "invests" himself in the sensually decadent accoutrements of the "ancestral" Waldo, falsifying a past moment never "experienced" (W165); this other Waldo's bibliophile "vices", via the *tertium comparationis* of the "Special Case" segregation of pornographic books, are linked with Waldo Brown's own "dry orgasm" in the Library.[9] Waldo's attempts to ward off time frequently involve immense doses of irrational "logic". There is security in timelessness so long as it is not the suspended time of present consciousness, which for Waldo is temporal limbo or "purgatory" (W177), a painful self-entrapment in "*mean* time" (W112). Moments from the now-past personal present are recalled only when Waldo is able to revenge himself for hurt by further sublimation or prevarication. Recall is, by nature, a mental act. More often, however, such moments are forced upon his present awareness: the water boils over although (and because) he has his hand pressed down firmly on the pot-lid. People and events he doesn't want to remember because of past humiliations can trigger off unlocalizable torment ("racked", W187). The force of involuntary, almost tactile memory can (after his masturbation) even "take a hand" (W189). Unlike Dulcie (W157), Waldo can never grow out of the past, which has grown into him painfully, like a cancer.

Arthur, by contrast, neither forces himself to recall, nor is he the victim of memory's ambuscades; instead, he is as naturally "in time", past and present, as a vibrating quartz crystal. There is, of course, his gradual, at first innocent but then increasingly painful, perception of ageing (A247/263/279/289–90, P307). But his oneness with the exhilarating present is neither hermetic stasis nor a trigger for painful recollection, but a vitalizing, whipping wind (A287). Whatever Arthur registers in the present seems to Waldo to be *projectively*, not passively, experienced (W108). Whatever occurs in dreams, conversely, is barely remembered (A260); their symbolism has already invested Arthur's waking life. There is much contrastive play with the concept of "permanence" in the two

---

[9] An autobiographical inter-text is also being drawn on here. The "Gothick Folly" and locked-up "vices" of the ancestral house at Tallboys are modelled on Turret House at Felpham, where the White family spent the summer of 1926. It had been built by the poet William Haley, who was for three years the opportunistic host to William Blake. Haley chained his mad wife to a summerhouse or "Gothick folly". As a child, White was caught perusing Beardsley's erotic illustrations to *Lady Windermere's Fan*—upon which the book was locked away in "the kind of glass-faced bookcase containing the books which one never read" (*Flaws:*3/7).

central narratives (eg, W152, A228, P306). Time is immanent within Arthur, its dimensions united. That human, social, substantial domain of *told* time (which, as Waldo must discover, cannot be controlled by reason) is derived by Arthur from a version of its ultimate cosmic source, which is the motion of the sun: "Taking Mr Saporta by the wrist—the latter no longer wore the little gun-metal wristlet watch, but *a large golden disc which showed practically everything*—Arthur confirmed that it was time for him to leave" (A276; my emphases). Arthur requires only "confirmation" of what he already knows—and, in a fine, covert emblem of absence, he himself *wears no watch*. For late-twentieth-century man, this fact must border on heresy or horror: we surely feel as exposed without our time-markers as we should feel without our seat-belts. Arthur's freedom from all except a confirming glance at the "sun" is an index to our captivity.

VI   The ethical and spiritual dimension

BLOOD AND SUFFERING

Waldo's section is governed by the cruelties his self-consciousness inflicts upon him. Whereas Arthur clearly recalls the "brutal" cynicism of Uncle Charlie (A217), Mrs Brown's confirmation that the faces on her side of the family "'were too cruel'" (W163) remains unevaluated by Waldo; in his mirror-fantasies, the ice-blue ancestral stare is associated with power and authority, not with cruelty. Waldo sees his "charity" in cleaning up after Arthur as almost a mortification of the flesh, "an unjust and unnecessary torment", and dealing with his father is also "painful"; but he denies that the sadistic present of the doll for Mrs Poulter is "a bludgeon" (W186). Arthur's well-meaning concern for him is reduced by Waldo to a "sadistic" act (W68), while Waldo can also feel a "victim" of the *absence* of solicitude (W80). Recollections of youth can fascinate, despite the "flaws ... like splinters in the flesh" (W74); earlier, when reminded by Arthur that his thoughts will "'fester'" if he doesn't reveal the flaw that is so "'awful'" about Mrs Poulter (W28), Waldo retorts facetiously that "'It's splinters that fester'". We learn later that his own sexual "flaw" (spying on Mrs Poulter's flesh) has been transferred by guilt to the victim. To "escape" guilt, Waldo must try to be "cleverer or brutal" (W76). When guilt by exposure floods in, the disclosure of truth (as with Arthur's discovery of the Tennyson poem, W195) can be "too brutal for Waldo".

The notion of mortification (ie, ascetic emotional pain bordering on crucifixion), like those of torture and the "brutal", is woven into the discourse in several variations (eg, W81/89//135/180/195).[10] Two more oblique references to cruelty near the beginning of Waldo's and Arthur's sections are germinally proleptic and broadly implicative. Waldo thinks of "his crueller moments as a man" and of Mrs Brown probing "their common wounds" (W54)—a heralding of

---

10 Metaphors for self-cruelty include Waldo squirming on the "needle-points of his buttocks" (W168) and lying on "the knife-edge of his body" (W174); for the meting out of suffering, there is the phantasmagoric "sharp blades" shooting out from his knee-caps (W133) and the hyperbole of knocking Dulcie "bleeding to the steps" (W158).

their union against George Brown. Arthur recalls that the complexity of human beings makes them more brutal than the brutes (A217). Waldo's discourse is inturned, devious, itself cruel, revealing a tortuous complexity of feeling. Arthur's discourse is innocent; instead of a personal nexus, we find a clear yet paradoxical, generic hierarchy of brutality, observed from the outside. Even this Olympian externality, however, is ambiguous: for, although Waldo's psychical brutality is self-destructive, and worse than the natural brutality of the dismembering dogs, Arthur too must "find out" that he counts among the brutal men.

Arthur admits inadvertent cruelty in himself (A288); but, in exhorting Waldo to discard the hurtful past by identifying the blue dress he has found, he denies that this is "an act of malice", despite acknowledging that Waldo continues "to suffer from the brutality of their revelation" (A293) of Waldo's bisexuality and Arthur's literary creativity. Ethically, their lives' dilemma of consequence encapsulated here—to leave hurtful truths unuttered (the teleological) or to reveal all truths under the rule of "rightness" and obligation (the stoic or deontic)—is narratively unresolved, perhaps unresolvable. In terms of human psychology, however, the dilemma of consequence is eclipsed by the goal of reconciling polar identities.[11] Elsewhere, Arthur is percipient at detecting cruelty in others, though it may be the "brutality" of disguised true feelings (A268). He sees how Waldo brutalizes tired words and ideas in a mock-crucifixion on the paper of "old, bent, over-used, aluminium skewers", yet can also see Waldo himself as a dry paper bird, "pinned and persecuted", crucified by his own nature (A266).

In regard to blood-indices, the narrative is sanguinary rather than sanguine. Arthur, unlike Waldo, can accept both the realities and the transcendent aspects of blood-rituals. Because of his Gothick blood-essay (a fantasy which misses both categories), Waldo is made a "fool" of in the playground; denying the reality of myth, he still succumbs to the Dionysiac blood-ritual, yet fails to acknowledge Arthur's subtextual suggestion that Waldo's role is that of the ritual "fool" or *pharmakos*. The "imbroglio" or revenge-tragedy of home life is downplayed (blindly) as "a mere bucket of blood" (W175). Waldo blocks off the blood of passion projectively (seeing Dulcie as "staunching" her mother's grieving voice, W138), whereas Arthur, "bleeding", submits ecstatically to music (A240). Verbal conflict is seen by Arthur as bloody dismemberment (A283), whose wounds he can bear. Arthur's poem of blood and suffering, however, is a final wound that Waldo suffers and cannot bear ("He was bleeding ... While Arthur's drop of unnatural blood continued to glitter", W212). Waldo denies the blood-ritual of living, but Arthur can see that his brother's mirror-ritual is a kind of

---

11 *The Solid Mandala* is not an ethical treatise: it circumvents ethics by marrying psychology to personal religion. This is why it runs athwart the evidence of the text to claim that Arthur's "impercipience ... is indeed one of the issues of the novel. For all his protectiveness, Arthur remains unaware, until it is too late, that his effect on his twin is lethal" (Wilkes 1969a:107). It will always be too late, and Arthur is not impercipient. "At the realistic level Patrick White does not seem interested in the fact that there is a case against Arthur for destroying his brother" (Byatt 1967:76)—but the "realistic" complexities of human psychology cast ethical cases out of this particular court.

voodoo blood-sacrifice, too, with Waldo as a comical sacrificial chicken, his ancestral family standing again as witnesses in "the darkened box" of the twilight of the gods, "waiting to see, not only what might offer itself for killing, but how their own blood would run" (A291). Absorbing the theatricalness of the scene, Arthur recalls here, too, the opera-box where he experienced the "crimson flood" of music (A217); paronomastically present as well is the tragic theory of catharsis. In Section 2, however, Waldo's veins are filled with ice, his ritual that of deathly stasis.

RELIGION, CHRIST, AND *KARAMAZOV*

It is significant, in view of Arthur's poem with its reference to the bleeding of "all Marys", that he becomes Mrs Poulter's "man-child" substitute for Christ, thus providing her with the child she has lost, making her into a grieving Marian figure in a *pietà,* and redeeming her from the butchery of "normal" life (P298–99), from the armageddon-vision of suffering after she discovers Waldo's mutilated corpse.[12] Her womb now incapable of bleeding, she is revitalized by sharing in Arthur's suffering and his Love (P300). A provisional rebirth through the redemptive power of myth has been achieved, its narrative beginnings residing in Arthur's dance for "all interminably bleeding breeding cows" and the yellow cow's stillborn calf (A230, W40). With Arthur the man-child's return to Sarsaparilla, the extremes of human time are united for once in the one object of love (P311–12/313). The doll/baby index culminates here in Mrs Poulter's image of hospital miscarriage (P299), which is associated with universal human violence, with the refusal of Waldo's plastic doll to stay buried, and with Mollie Thourault's Japanese paper doll, itself torn up by Mrs Brown (W164) and connected by Waldo with the Asian Campaign of World War Two and men "tearing one another to pieces in a changed ritual" (W173). Waldo's doll parodies his preference for the synthetic over the real (W185, A288–89), just as he lies passively in Arthur's arms, a "plastic doll", "intolerably lustreless" at the end, unresponsive to his brother's love (W212). The notions of misbirth (encoded in Waldo's face, W120), doll-like artificiality, and ritual dismemberment combine in Waldo's shredding of Arthur's brain-child/birth-poem (W212, A293), in his "unmentionable", dismembered flesh-as-writing (W199) burnt on the fire (W212–13), then—reduced to the "old soft perished rubber" of his uncreating member—in the dogs' dismemberment (P302). The rendering of this "god" by "dog" proves regenerative in the sense of Arthur's purification, through suffering, from the *mysterium iniquitatis* of his brother. Jungian, alchemical analogies for this are locatable in, for example, Waldo's notebook annotations ("Death is the last of the chemical actions", W70), just as the "sowing and scattering of seed" (W213) when he burns his papers is both destruction and symbolic regeneration (1 Corinthians 15:36ff.).

---

[12] The media-images of Asian wars; the recall of past atrocities in images of Auschwitz and Belsen, in an echo of the death-camps alluded to by Arthur (W173-74); the image of rape, held at bay earlier; and the "bleeding wombs of almost all women" (P302).

The central analogical index, however, is that of Christ as redeemer of suffering and as risen King. This is only one strain among many, and Arthur is not a Christ-figure in any formal spiritual sense. The Christ-palimpsest tentatively underlies both Waldo and Arthur: first, through transfer of the indices of love, suffering, bleeding and stigmatic skewering from individual psychology (diegetic) to the philosophical content of direct speech (mimetic); second, through a double, partial centering of the peak of narrative action on Easter. The "Last Supper" of Maundy Thursday is prefigured on the Wednesday in Arthur's talk of love and the separately consumed Eucharist of bread-and-milk (W204–208). The transition to the actual last midday meal opens into the Thursday morning with Waldo's reluctant submission to Arthur's cosmic Eucharist or communion, "all the bread and milk in the world" (W208). The actional-present narrative is "suspended" after the last walk by mental analepses stressing physical and psychological descent (W211): of bloody meat to dry extract; of the substance of love to abstraction; Waldo's "sinking low" in his own faeces; his fear of descent into sleep; the sinking of words beyond conscious recall. The actual dénouement is an alchemical, double self-consumption of burning and seizure. Arthur flees, himself descending guilt-stricken into the darkness of "grief or terror", bereft of his humanity, divesting himself of his individual physical identity (P305). He is "free" to walk the streets of Sydney "unmolested", as the returned Christ incarnate was free to move through the streets of the "southern city" of Seville on the day following the Grand Inquisitor's *auto-da-fé* in *The Brothers Karamazov* (II.v.5). Preparing himself "for putrefaction" (P306), Arthur lies in the street, and the rough colloquial language of the urinating drunks nearby is a carnivalesque of Christian or Easter references (Friday, christen, bloody day, God, bastard, dead body). Losing Waldo's mandala in the "darkness", the (immortal) Arthur is "reduced to nothing" before locating the last mandala of his self (P306–307). He lumbers in suspension through the darkness of a whole week towards the Holy Saturday that isn't, before undergoing an attenuation of the Crucifixion on the Jewish Sabbath, hanging on "a rope of creepers" outside the Saportas' house, then "practically built ... into the network of steel vines" (P308–309). Next morning, "a resistance leaving him", and purified by the sunlight, Arthur returns to Mrs Poulter, who accepts him "as token of everlasting life" (P309–12). For her, the institutionalized, divine icon of Christ ("canvas") is de-crucified (P303) in her psychological movement towards a replacive affirmation of spirituality *in* the world (thus conforming with the notion of a "pre-Christian" Christ as "an autonomous psychological fact" in the process of human individuation—Jung 1971:427–28).

How is this concentration of detail on Christ prepared for earlier in the narrative, in view of criticism of the novel for the unconvincingness of the Christian theme (Kiernan:1980:98, who sees this theme as first turning up quite unexpectedly in Arthur's mandala-dance)? After an early mention of the Crucifixion (W58), indices to cruelty go underground in Waldo's narrative until the incident in the Library when Arthur expresses his bafflement at the Grand Inquisitor of *The Brothers Karamazov* and Waldo denies his brother (W200). In

Section 3, there is Arthur's naive vision of the praying Mr Allwright's "incarnation" (A227), his stiff discussions with Mrs Poulter about cruelty, the Church and Christ (A260–61), and his bracketing tree-dreams (first, of the phallic Jungian *arbor vitae* of the protective Self, A260; then its disruptive transformation into the Tree of Christ and stigmatic images, A262; cf A293). Only now comes the mandala-dance, Arthur's attempt to fulfil his dream's desire for "perfect satisfaction". As he dances the Crucifixion and the stigmata, the "silent hole" of his open mouth, signifying universal suffering, is a paronomastic reflection of that earlier quest-motif when his father tautologically explains "totality" as "'a whole ... Spelt with a *w*'" and Arthur leaves, his lips "half-open to release an interpretation he had not yet succeeded in perfecting" (A240). In the dance, his lips are no longer half-open, but have released their "interpretation": the silent, mandalic (w)hole.

In *The Brothers Karamazov*, Arthur can see no clear-cut allegiances: "'Who was the Grand Inquisitor?'" (A283). Manfred Mackenzie (1969:248) states that the unknown Grand Inquisitor is Arthur himself, as "the getter of pain" responsible for Waldo's death (A294). But Waldo, too, surely assumes the role of Grand Inquisitor, grilling Arthur for the "blasphemy" of his poem, and attempting even in death to "bring [him] to trial" (A293–94). The actual *auto-da-fé* is Waldo's against himself, in burning his papers; and, as a further complication, his arraignment of Arthur is itself "deliberate blaspheming" (A298). Waldo's paranoia at the Library has him invent a title, "*Inquisitions of a Living Mind*" (W175), and he sees the Grand Inquisitor everywhere (in Crankshaw, W172–73, or in the telephone, W162). It is Waldo, as Inquisitor, who opposes whatever Christ stands for. But this is indeed the most problematical focus in the novel—It is no wonder that so many critics have sidled away from the Dostoevsky novel actually discussed (and which White was reading for the third time during the writing of *The Solid Mandala*), into considerations of *The Idiot* or *The Double*. Waldo has no problem with the novel; he is glad his father conducted his own little *auto-da-fé* on the book, out of fear of the suffering depicted and of Ivan's solidarity with the silent smiling Christ. The difficulty Arthur has with Ivan's poem on the Grand Inquisitor is the same all readers experience if they try to read the chapter on its own, or only in conjunction with the preceding disquisition on infant suffering. Dostoevsky's characters harbour such massive antinomies, and the novel is such a complex web of interfructuating parables and theses, that the Grand Inquisitor and Ivan's double-edged rhetoric can only be even part-way resolved by consideration of the whole work. It is not hard to see how such partial beings as White's characters would be plunged into unease or panic by Dostoevsky's complexities and his demand for the acceptance of opposites. And this is the clue to the presence of *Karamazov* in White's novel. The various reactions to its entwined polarities, and our own difficulties in reconciling novel to novel, are White's hint that there is more to his characters than resides in their skeins of interrelationship. The Dostoevsky novel is a means of escaping momentarily from the snares of signification set up by a narrative whose figural discourse conveys, necessarily, fairly narrow psychological obsessions. If *Karamazov* defeats us, too, then only to force us beyond the quasi-heuristic analogy between (say) Arthur and Christ. It does *The Solid Mandala* a disservice to call it a study in sainthood, and to speculate on White's own brand of non-denominationalism (cf Mackenzie 1969:251), or to claim that the novel's vision is mystical, orthodox Christianity (Morley 1972:206). Closer to a fair judgement is Byatt (1967:76): the subject "is the *artist's* search for meaning in a demythologized world .... Dostoevsky believed in Christ. Patrick White believes in man and sees man, finally, as an artist".[13]

A great deal of the diction of *The Solid Mandala* is (like White's other fiction) "religious" in flavour, but is placed in contexts which undermine any dogmatic interpretation. Its basis is biblical; some expressions are indubitably Christian; many terms could be gnostic, mystical, even Roman Catholic; the Old-Testament, Jewish tradition is just as strongly invoked; and there is a general substratum of language drawing on the ancient mystery religions and on mythology. Shimmering ironies are set up when the psychological pressures of figural consciousness provoke the use of terms which have also been secularized, are equally applicable to areas of doctrine antithetical to "faith" and to the numinous, or cause a character so much trouble that language itself becomes part of the psychical conflict and its ultimate resolution.[14]

LOVE AND PROTECTION, FAITH, SHAME AND GUILT

The essential indexical markers of the theme of love, which is central to the novel, are to be found in the dynamics of psychological verbs (examined separately). Although "protect" and "protection" are likewise ubiquitous in terms of the psychological action of the narrative, these concepts are not in themselves subject to verbal figuration, but can be encoded in other indices such as the architectonic metaphors mentioned earlier. For Mr Brown, Mr Feinstein and Waldo, religion (or faith) is inimical to reason (or knowledge). There is in Section 2 a constant double voicing present whenever the word "faith" (or its equivocal near-equivalent, "belief") enters the discourse; Waldo is either unaware, or cynically hypersensitive to the fact, that he employs the lexicon of theology   whenever   he   expresses   his   philosophy   of   reason (W58/153/161/177/182), and, though trapped in the self, can still make free with

---

[13] See also Beatson (1976:2) on White's eclectic religious sensibility. There is ample autobiographical evidence for White's aversion to social rationality, organized religion, and specifically Christian redemption (eg, *Flaws:* 68/74/153/251–52; White 1973: 136–39) and, on the other hand, for his belief in a spiritual, non-religious, even mystical investment in human relationships and self-understanding (*Flaws:* 102/146/148/244/252) and tolerance for different cultural belief-systems (*Flaws:* 102/145). His self-redeeming interest in the Jewish-Australian cultural tradition and in intuition connect with his rejection of social religion unless it is *workable* (*Flaws:* 77/140; White 1973:138–39). See also Marr (1991:281–84/357–58/451–52).

[14] One example is the way in which Waldo the non-believer persistently—and inadvertently?—takes the Lord's name in vain (W59/77/127/190, A290).

the notion of free will (W77/168). Arthur has little to say about faith—he is too busy doing and being, trying, taking the leap—except negatively of the "faith in faith" of organized and quack religion (A286). Mrs Feinstein, and Mrs Brown in her senile decline, entrust themselves to the "faith" of spiritualism, Mrs Feinstein's *planchette*—a shortcut from subconscious to conscious—even having a mandalic circular scheme.

The grip of shame, embarrassment and guilt is omnipresent in Section 2. If these sentiments are less a recognition of Waldo's breaches of a moral order than a form of panic at threatened unmaskings of his secret self, Arthur's guilt and shame relate to the harm he imagines his behaviour would do to others in shattering their safe illusions. At the end, Arthur's turmoil of thought (P307) is a complex transcending of the conventional psychological and moral senses attached to "shame" and "guilt"; it is much the same with Mrs Poulter. Both are voluntary scapegoats for the world (however suburban and constricted her "sphere of life" might be).

VII   Colour and light imagery

I classify colour indices as imagery in the flinching awareness of White's contempt for "this awful symbol business .... Colours, like symbols, are made too much of by those indefatigable unravellers. Can't we use a colour because it *is*, or because we happen to like it?" (White 1973:140). If we do indefatigably unravel, there is not much evidence to delight statistical positivists, either. Where—knowing Waldo's subjective disposition—we might expect "dark" terms to dominate, we find this is not so. Although his aversion to orange hues is pronounced, again the incidence in Section 2 is much lower than in Arthur's. But colour-responses can also be positive; so that the statistics cancel out, except with "yellow-green" hues, which are absent from Arthur's section.

The green gloom or sickly greeny-yellow light of Terminus Road paralyses or blurs Waldo's thoughts; the "glare of yellow grass" filters out understanding. Only when Waldo acts as a sexual voyeur are these ambiguous or negative colours stripped of the danger that otherwise lies in the incursion of the solar light of reality—when this light is at its whitest (W44/208), Waldo is least protected. He is most at home in "exhausted" and artificial light, while the shadowless light of Australia mocks his attempts to "pour light on obscurity", and "jaundices", "invests" and pigments his would-be rationalist father yellow, lemon or citron. This is reminiscent of the way in which the alchemical yellow or *citrinitas*, though often "coinciding" with the "dawn" preceding wisdom, metapsychologically signifies the thwarted appearance of the sun—murky light meaning insufficient understanding (Jung 1971:431). Both Waldo and George Brown are "sicklied o'er with the pale cast of thought".

Waldo's retreat from the "warm" domain of the spectrum is foreordained in his physiognomy, which is spectrally indeterminate. He has "nondescript" hair, contrasting with Arthur's "warm" solar hair and with the "dark" chthonic or earthy hair of Dulcie and Mrs Poulter; in old age, his hair is dirty-grey, unlike the innocent/wise white or venerably "silver" of Arthur's (even Arthur's dog has the "whiter muzzle" of the two pets). His voice is "light-coloured", contrasting with the dark "'cello tones" of Mrs Feinstein's voice and the "dark" colours of Saporta's. Waldo's preoccupation with blue (the blue dress, the "nacreous" fan, his family's blue eyes, even his "blue serge" suit) is essentially a retreat from warmth. Not only is the dress ice-blue; the eyes, too, are ice-blue or cold and pale.

The chthonic or warm earth colours, primary or in admixture, may safely connote sexuality for Waldo when he is a voyeur (the brown skin of the Haynes woman and the tropical girls). Brown complexions, however, usually constitute a vague threat, or are associated by Waldo with the lower reaches of intellect. Mrs Poulter's image of her own brownish skin in youth, betokening health and sexuality, is a foil to Waldo's external view. Anything that signals the starting of blood in the flesh unnerves Waldo.[15] And, everywhere and quintessentially, there is the soft, liquid earthiness of those unfailingly brown, eternally threatening eyes, and the alien, vaguely unsettling "Jewishness" of the "beige" or "brown flannel" rings round the eyes of the Saporta children.

In Arthur's and Mrs Poulter's sections, chthonic and solar colours are not negativized. There are metonymic extensions of Mrs Poulter's mauveness (her russet apples, watermelon cardigan, and cerise geraniums). There is the rich, mythic connotation of blood which carries through Arthur's section from the red velvet seats and music of the beginning, and which flows symbolically into his crimson and green spiralled marble (ascent and descent; the red of the sun and the green of the vegetative; the blood of earth and life). For Arthur, Dulcie's violet dress is a violet dress, Saporta's "greyish-yellow skin" just that: no Waldovian subjective aura surrounds such colours. But in contexts where Waldo's presence is implicated, negatively weighted colours appear for the first time in Arthur's narrative (the yellow grass and thin light; Mrs Poulter's purple, stressed complexion). The comfortingly chthonic darkness of the bedroom and the god-forsaken theatre becomes in the dénouement the purgatorial, half-way-house darkness of the doubting spirit; like Waldo's permanent half-light, the light that cautiously announces Arthur's false dawnings during this crisis is "sleazy", before the burning onslaught of the sun heralds his resurrection.

Waldo's inability to come to terms with the rich central-European ambiguity of Mrs Feinstein is indicated in the trouble he has classifying her complexion (as grey, skin-, or flesh-coloured). Her skin as "nondescript" as his and his father's "hair-coloured hair", she is indescribable; confronted with the thinginess of the world, Waldo is as incapable of sensibly encompassing individuality without tautology as his father is in the face of Arthur's "totality".

---

[15] Mrs Poulter's mauve complexion (W60/188); the contused, beery faces of middleaged "purple" men making sexual assignations, as in an early Berlin painting by George Grosz (W78); the reddened, penile skin of women's necks (W64/161); Arthur's pink scalp and ruddy skin (W26/32); Dulcie's pink dress perhaps, by transference (W89/94–95); even the "purple" horseflesh (W179).

Colours and light-effects, then, generally appear in the novel because they *are*, or because characters "like" or "dislike" them. But emotional reaction to colour is already subjugation to the "symbolic". Not even White could have denied that his magnificently sensitive handling of painterly texture and tonal coloration has been attenuated in this novel to the tyrannical narrowness of figural consciousness. Apart from which, the setting is more circumscribed here than in most of his fiction. In *The Solid Mandala,* two tendencies are noticeable. Some colours (chiefly white, yellow and grey) are applied, occasionally with additional shading, to a wide range of objects. Sometimes tthese modifications are thematically and psychologically significant.[16] Elsewhere, instead of modification there is variation within an associative colour-field. The range of epithets applied to Arthur's hair, for instance (orange, carrot, fiery, flaming, alight, afire, blaze, red, chestnut), betokens (a) its ever-changing oneness as a "solar symbol", (b) the slight alterations in the emotional state of the perceiver, and (c) White's determination to vary the terms so that a perfect marriage is forged between the conspicuousness of natural percepts and the subordinate status of apperceptions that have a symbolic component.

VIII   Other aspects of metaphor and simile

Animal metaphors abound, but almost entirely in Waldo's section, to convey his fearful animus against the animal and the instinctual in human behaviour, and (in its spatial fixing) privacy. The effect is, of course, to dehumanize, even when the threat mediated is the disarming *appeal* of the animal (as in the string of metaphors identifying Dulcie's eyes with those of a dog). One metaphor has a biographical genesis: Eb Honeysett's gift to Arthur of a ferret called Scratch which "never came up out of the burrow" after looking over its shoulder, and which, to Waldo's embarrassment, Arthur promises to "love dearly" (W41). This resurfaces when Waldo is thinking of how much he resents brown eyes, "like soft brown animals burrowing in" (W125). In a shift from metonymy to metaphor, the brown-eyed ones have become the instinctually burrowing ones invading the secret realm of Waldo as Underground Man. "Normal" dead metaphor can be enlisted, as in Waldo's retreat into "the darker warren of the stacks" (W129). Momentarily sorry for his awkwardly affectionate father, Waldo, in a sentimentalization of the animal-element to something rabbit-like, recalls "the brown burrowing but never arriving eyes, and the twitch of a moustache on your skin" (W136). Memory of George Brown's Baptist forebears moves the metaphor away from the burrow or warren; the rodent is domestic but more horrible, the colour abyssal: "the little black rats of eyes gnawing" at the lace of the Quantrell heritage (W163). The ferret-element surfaces fully in Waldo's late

---

[16] For instance: the butter-yellow of Arthur's cow (W36/40) is balanced against the buttermilk "white sweat" of Arthur's butter (W36), permitting a glorious metonymic association of the butter with the "white sweat" of Arthur's skin much later, as he sits raincoated in the hot Library (W197).

middle age; after the preceding metaphoric deflections, the central notion of search and threatened exposure is re-metonymized on the original biographical basis, with Waldo at Terminus Road trying to ignore "Arthur's burrowing through the long grass in search of that vicious ferret, the other truth" of love (W195). The metaphor is echoed subterraneously, after the Tennyson unmasking and after Arthur has been revealed at the Library as a reader of *The Brothers Karamazov*, when Waldo turns into the Grand Inquisitor: "'And *you* understand!'" he said to Arthur *viciously*" (W199, latter emphasis mine). The very last discovery, of Arthur's poem, is made by Waldo, but it is also an uncovering of Waldo himself: by his own inquisitorial search, "not ferreting, but ferreted" (W212), he brings upon himself the truth of his own failure. This "other truth", then, is what binds and ultimately splits the twins, in an opposition of love and hatred.

Other animalizing statements cut across both narratives, this possibility being afforded by Arthur's own somatic awareness. Waldo remarks Arthur's thick nostrils, "awful muzzle" or animal "snout" (W40/47/178), Arthur his own nostrils "dilated, with pure animal conviction" (A237). Arthur has a lumberingly disruptive "buffalo mind" (W191) which—in the more agile metaphor of an animal of prey—can yet "pounce" on Waldo's thoughts (W209), while Arthur himself knows that others resent the "fleshy lumbering round their thoughts" of his mind (A281). The bovine/taurine aspect arises naturally out of Arthur's cow-tragedy, where he bellows and lows (W40), as at the death of Mr Brown (W71); the verb "bellow" is applied to Waldo only when he loses physical self-control, reduced to the animal (W211). Whereas Arthur is enchanted by Mrs Poulter's sun-warmed hair, "like some kind of sleepy animal" (A264), Waldo is repelled by Dulcie's "frizzy, animal hair" (W103) and resents the animality of other human intruders, who are a "herd of human beasts", cattle, oxen, clopping stallions or bulls (W64/140/144/155/189).

Arthur is repeatedly associated with dogs, usually via similes (W27/31/33/62/63/178). In Arthur's section, the only explicit canine reference is oneiric (A262). His devotion to the dogs (as I have already intimated) is no more incidental than the fact that Waldo's corpse must undergo a Zagreus/Dionysos-like rending by these self-same dogs, in an earthly inversion (dog for god) of divine retribution, or that the faithful, loving, doglike Arthur should be the unwitting agent of his twin's self-destruction. In the dark despair of his flight from Waldo's corpse, Arthur is reduced to the animal (P305) and, after his return, becomes one with the dogs when they are shot by the police (P311/313), while the pets' withholding of affection from Waldo is foreshadowed in his designation of his state as one of "runtish misery" (W47).

Mechanistic metaphors are frequently applied to mental processes, but without this involving reductionism—they reveal, rather, White's view of a "cool" functioning of mental reflexivity, and are therefore consonant with the slightly disembodied, distanced feel of the discourse as a whole (in this and other novels). Arthur's "mind's eye", Waldo's mind and Holmes's face are a cinematic screen (A260, W163/147). Arthur's archaic mental storage system, at ease in handling miscellaneous substantials, is a pinboard bearing a Jungian message (A281). Mrs Brown's memory is an album, then a gallery, of *tableaux vivants* (W164). Finally, in keeping with Waldo's job as Library cataloguer and his retention of resentments, his "texture of mind" is characterized as a microfilm-reader, the "dialogue printed on its black transparent screen" for later retrieval (W178).

There is a peculiar figuration of physical detachability and reification found in conjunction with facial expressions and human relationships (cf also section **IV** above). Arthur "takes leave of" his face, or is "absent without leave" (W81, A242). Mrs Feinstein "sticks on" a smile (W108; cf W104/109), others "withdraw" or "throw off" a facial expression (A230, W93). Mr Allwright's smile evasively "slides around" Arthur's marble, Dulcie's "suddenly closed face" opens (A234/244). Waldo resentfully makes great play with the mechanical gestures of Len Saporta, who works "only by consent of hinges" (W156)—a curious wild branching from the vehicle here, "consent" serving to humanize it. As a counterfoil to this, there is Arthur's view of his brother as "rigid as a closed cupboard" which only Arthur can jerk open (A243). Speaking "tunes up" the asthmatic repetitiveness of Mr Brown's cough (W61) like an old engine. Arthur's "awkward fingers would become steel tentacles reaching out for the solution of his problem" (A231), which anticipates Waldo's attempt to solve his own problem at death by dragging Arthur down with him: "the fingers of this dead man were determined, in their steel circlets, to bring him to trial" (A294)— whereby the robotic hands have become handcuffs, thus fulfilling in reverse what Waldo had always feared, "the brown verdict of Arthur's eyes" (W125). Waldo's cruel defensiveness and self-cruelty are reinforced by the metaphors of blade and knife-edge mentioned above (section **VI.1**), and by punning references to the axe of authority and retribution (W171/188), while other indices to cutting involve Waldo's *nausée* at the damp substantiality of existence, as when Mrs Feinstein cuts the *Mohntorte* "as if it had been flesh" (W102).

I should like, in conclusion, to note how Waldo's exacerbated self-consciousness is exposed to the choric intrusion of banal externals, such as the spidery, bellowing, raucous, smuttily sniggering train (W54/77/79) and the groaning, remonstrating springs of Dulcie's dusty sofa (W154–56). Such moments, though painful for Waldo, are fine examples of grotesque comedy. There are also occurrences of aestheticizing metaphor which may be projections of Waldo's tortured consciousness (eg, the "painted phlox", W113), but which seem more often to be evidence of White's own transforming eye (the "enamelled" peacock, swamp-hen, and blackberries, W88, A246/263).

IX   Onomastic and intertextual signification

White once edgily confirmed that the names of his characters are "sometimes symbolically expressive" (White 1973:141). Some names are "obviously" symbolic, whether because of the "speaking" nature of their composition, as in Himmelfarb or Godbold; because of a mythological parallel, as in Hare; or because of geographical and ethnic typicality, as in Dubbo (all from *Riders in the Chariot*). Others are derived from people White knew (Waldo; or Holstius in *The Aunt's Story*—though White's associationism here makes the latter an extremely oblique signification). There may be no conscious parabolic intention at all; so one must be careful. Name-giving is a preeminently auctorial prerogative, and escapes the generative impulses of figural consciousness in *The Solid Mandala*. Yet, even for the characters, the state of bearing a name may be bound up with questions of identity. Mr Brown jokes about the "colour" of the family name, and incorporates his Christian name into an interjection (W38). Mrs Poulter and Mrs Dun concern themselves with the names of the Browns, father and sons (B17), and O'Connell the librarian expresses disbelief about the names "Waldo" and "Brown" (W177). As adolescents, Waldo and Dulcie exchange views on their names (W94), and Arthur creates a song around the sound of the name "Thourault" (W51).

Place-names: The suburb of Sarsaparilla (the setting in several earlier works by White) is named after a plant with prickly, angular stems, which—as the Spanish provenance of the name attests—thrives in tropical or semi-arid climates (cf, in *The Tree of Man:* "There is nothing else in the bush, except the little sarsaparilla vine, of which the purple theme emerges from the darker undertones", Penguin, p. 479). Betty Watson argues that the suburb is named "after a purplish Australian softdrink" extracted from an Australian "native plant", and that the primary colours involved indicate positive values (Watson 1971:159). But the chief cultural association of the Mexican–American tonic called sarsaparilla is surely the Wild-West one: it was the drink favoured in frontier saloons by bland, teetotaller heroes, much to the scorn of the redeye-drinking villains. It is as improbable that a suburb would be named after it (or after the soft-drink for which it is a flavouring agent) as it would be to call a municipality "Seven–Up". At the forefront is hardly colour, but rather the prickly, bristling yet ultimately bland and artificial character of plant-cum-drink, as a reflection of suburban mentality, perhaps with a hint of the semi-arid provenance and of the bitterness beneath the social surface, by virtue of the fact that the chief modern use of sarsaparilla extract is to mask the unpleasant taste of medicines. The one truly ugly name is that which carries within it this particular sememe (Barranugli, which "infects" Sarsaparilla by geographical and typological propinquity). Other names, too, are perfectly good pseudo-Aboriginal before anything else. "Numburra" (W142/160) can be analyzed as "a stony sleeping-place". "Mungindribble" (W142) involves the notion of "water-hole", but also exploits the fact that early transcriptions often left native names looking vaguely European (cf Ironmongie, Mumblebone). Both are isolated boroughs, numbed, like their inhabitants, by dust, heat and distance. There is not much water around, barely a dribble except "in good seasons" (A296–97), where Bill Poulter comes from; and he brings his spiritual drought with him when he takes his young bride south. The names of the suburban bungalows are a litany of unimaginative borrowing, wishful thinking, and bad French (W58), and an especial pleasure is given by those urban and suburban place-names that are show-stoppers in their sheer vacancy, dull fatalism, or absence of specification (eg, Permanent Avenue, W128; Terminus Road; Plant Street, W57). It matters little that some of these are (like the personal name Barron Field, with its delightful evocation of a barren talent unproductive in a waste land) *objets trouvés*, like Neutral Bay (W196) or Bent Street, where Waldo is accosted by the drunken whore: the location alone reflects Waldo's sense of a "bent" or twisted presence of lust, without his relief that Arthur is "not present to pervert an already dubious situation" (W184).[17]

William Walsh maintains that White's names in this novel "stand for" ugliness (Walsh 1977:88); but many don't even begin to connote ugliness. Sociological and aesthetic impressionism can account for White's names as little as for Dickens's; what must be kept in mind is the way names interact with context. Wally Pugh's name is "infected" by the contemptuous way in which Waldo sees his earnest, fat and shiny colleague, so that the expression of distaste applied to the books in the Library ("Pffeugh", W121) flows into the surname. "Wally" may be "ugly" on the principle that short forms are vulgar, but such short forms might elsewhere carry different connotations: unassumingness, say, as with Cis/Cissie and Ern/Ernie Baker. It is, incidentally, interesting to see how the discourse shifts among "Walter", "Wally" and "Wal", depending on the kind of inward distance Waldo is keeping from Pugh (W122–23). Mrs Mutton, "more a monument than a woman" (A242–43/286), bears a name which is as depersonalized and as "Australian" as the country's sheep. Socially functional, in terms of Waldo's antipathy to Irish Catholics, is the name O'Connell. The Thourault and Quantrell connection represents a pseudo-Norman–Frenchifying of Thorold and Cantrell; the "aristocratic" touch is secured, as it is by the vaguely libertarian aura of "Tolfree". A link between Waldo's subliminal yearning for the Germanic and the aristocratic, and Arthur's appreciation of goodness, nineteenth-century England and colonial Australia, can be detected in Granny's first name, Adelaide (A217). Like her name, she is both "noble" and "kind" , and is called after the German Queen Dowager of England, as is the South Australian city (the short form being "Ada", as in Ada Avenue). The Dallimores have a speaking name: social snobs, they pay their visits, dallying more when they sense a chance for advancement. The names Dun and Poulter also have "speaking" significance (colourlessness, smallness, blunt angularity and finality in the one; the plump softness and "mauve" coloration of the pigeon in the other).

---

[17] At the corner of Bent Street and Macquarie Street (W177), incidentally,are the Sydney Municipal and Mitchell Libraries so closely associated with the twins' activities.

Mrs Musto bears the vaguely Italianate name of her caddish, philandering, runaway husband, so is in one respect not responsible for it. If it is a "sharpish", Mediterranean name, all the better, then, for the contrast it makes with the name of Ralph's replacement, Stubbens: stubby, blunt, with only a patina of well-manicured "class" to mark the fact that he is just as nasty to her as her husband was. There is a kind of automatic, distracted, willed pleasure ("must" + "gusto") in Mrs Musto's social behaviour, while her conviviality has a touch of the Bacchic in it (*mosto,* Spanish and Italian for new wine). Waldo views Crankshaw's features through a Dickensian distorting-lens (W171–72); his oversized, "jutting forehead" and generally skewed proportions connect him with the sense borne by his name (crooked copse or promontory). Hardwick, the wheeler-dealer land-developer, has a a name evoking astute mercantile "Englishness" befitting someone concerned to sell an estate made posh by its Anglo–Welsh title, Anglesey; but if there's a crooked "angle" or two in this title, there's a "tough core" of business-sense in Hardwick's name (W115). Miss Glasson, in her every word and gesture, is as transparent to Waldo as glass (W183/194/196). Mr Allwright's name carries with it, like that of Mr Bonner in *Voss* (though this character is made to belie his name), the clearest aptronymic sense of moral uprightness; in a half-circle turn, it even fits his wife as a comment on her unremitting righteousness. Mr Allwright is not only the soul of goodness and unalterable solidity: his name carries more with it than, say, Fielding's Allworthy, in suggesting both his profession (a chandler or "wright" of all kinds of foods) and his practicality as a maker (A227). Len Saporta's speaking name ("lean/lend" + "support[er]") is contextually clear enough.

Dulcie's name has little to do with her voice, which is never "dulcet" (cf Watson 1971:163). It may at its best moments have "a touch of velvet" (W131) or be "rich and gliding" (W102), and may contain "'cello notes" (W66/138); but all this is associated with a "darkness" of tone. Her voice is also giggly, practical, high, breathy, rasping, loud and shocking, or "suddenly metallic" (W90/92/96–98/139/155, A277). Dulcie's own view of her name is probably closest: she thinks it doesn't fit her at all, neither in terms of character nor of physiognomy (W94); rejecting the attribute "sweet" here, she also rejects the attribute "kind" in Arthur's section (A255). Her task is essentially that of overcoming her "wobbly" nature and learning to live up to her name. As for the surname Feinstein, it is *ekht jidish* and an adequate bearer of cultural implications, quite apart from its subversion of the autobiographically relevant name "Diamant". Its bipartite nature correlates with the particular interests which the twins bring to bear on the family. For Waldo, the focus would be on *fein:* he sees in them a cultural jewel of refinement in the desert of Australia. For Arthur, the focus would be on *stein:* the family members are separately mandalic and talismanic.

The name Waldo was an act of revenge against an "actual Waldo", "a rather nasty, thin character" with whom one of White's lovers had dallied at Cambridge (Marr 1991:449). Given White's command of German, however, there is indubitably a semantic bonus in the name, as it reflects both Waldo's fascination for all that is Germanic and also his will to order and control (deriving as it does from Old High German *waltan,* "wield, rule, control", whence also derives "Walter", as embodied in the weakened, companionate counterpart whom Waldo mentally "kills off"—Wally Pugh).[18] Thelma Herring has suggested that Arthur may derive his name from the hero of *The Faerie Queene,* and that the name is otherwise so innocuous as to make Arthur representative of the common man (Herring 1968:216–17, endorsed by Morley 1972:19). White has denied any Spenserian connection while confirming the evocation of the "common man" (White 1973:141). But there may be other intertextual possibilities. White's Arthur could be associated with Tennyson's King Arthur in the *Idylls of the King.* Given the presence in the novel of the Tennysonian; and the fact that the Brown family's cultural and psychological roots are in a nineteenth century whose popular spirit was Tennysonian (Stan Parker's mother, in *The Tree of Man,* owns a copy of Tennyson which takes on the aura and status of the family bible), rather

---

[18] There is an intertextual possibility connected with Waldo which could now only be confirmed or refuted by documentary enquiry. Either via his correspondence with Ben Huebsch, his editor at Viking Press, or via the acclaim awarded Otto Preminger's film version at its London premiere in war-time London, White may have been attracted to Vera Caspary's novel *Laura* (1942), which was issued in Britain in 1944 by White's own publisher, Eyre and Spottiswoode. The *raison d'être* of the villain of this novel, Waldo Lydecker, is similarly control over language, the products of art, and the lives of others. Central to both novels are the thematically productive divergent attitudes which the two chief male characters have towards a female character with whom they are emotionally involved. There are narrational parallels, too: Waldo Lydecker's initial narrative is rooted in selection and suppression, and is replaced later by the different "truth" of an inquisitorial police officer, whose unassuming, imaginative empathy with Laura exposes Waldo's grotesque, obsessive subterfuges. There is a wide range of characterological similarities between the Waldos. Lydecker, too, has pale eyes and an eye-defect requiring him to wear spectacles; he is contemptuous of vulgar speech and is sarcastically destructive in his use of language; he is strongly attracted to a woman with an unattainably impeccable background and self-contained personality; he does all in his power to bar another male from access to his would-be "possession"; he is a role-playing narcissist, who delights in mirror-gazing and writes an essay on "Distortion and Refraction" (Caspary's book is replete with *film-noir* mirror-references). Both Waldos have a guilt-complex about "world conditions" and human suffering. Lydecker's first-person narration is self-reflexively indeterminate; he actually ends up, in hospital, talking "always about himself, always in the third person", and his "final legacy" is a sheet of paper with a third-person summary of his relationship with Laura (*Laura,* pp. 236–37). One is reminded of the inverse effect, in *The Solid Mandala,* of the personalizing of third-person narration in Waldo's section. Like Waldo Brown, "born without the capacity for loving", Lydecker "had always insisted on the gestures of courtship" (192–93). Whereas Waldo Brown shrinks from Dulcie's masculinity, Lydecker accepts Laura's: "'the elements are so mixed in us'" (72). He also has Arthurian attributes (eg, a histrionic gift, epicene corpulence, and self-identification with a woman's femininity). Most notably, however, Lydecker is a collector like Waldo Brown. Further, he makes an admission about his own nature that would fit the other Waldo: "the lame, the halt, and the blind have more malice in their souls, therefore more acumen. Cherishing secret hurt, they probe for the pains and weaknesses of others" (20); and Lydecker's own "malice" destroys not Laura but himself. Neither Waldo confronts honestly the emptiness of his own talent. Lydecker: "I wrote smoothly but said nothing. I have sometimes suspected this flaw in my talent, but have never faced myself with the admission of failure" (21).

than in the changed Edwardian sensibility of "Swinburne's ... secret orgasms" (*The Twyborn Affair*, p. 150); given, too, the not inconsiderable datum that one of Waldo's school prizes was *The Idylls* (a book he has "actually read", W80–81, much as White actually read Tennyson at school: Marr 1991:87), as well as the possibility that White is reworking the Tennysonianism of some of his own early poetry—given all this, I would gravitate towards the inclusiveness of Tennyson's Arthur as an analogue or genetic template for White's.

Tennyson's intertextual presence is apical: the poem presents itself as an "angle of entry", the two extrapolated sides of the apex ultimately exhausting themselves in the remaining two punctual extremes of a triangle. This triangle of ever-increasing saturation in Tennyson (for examination of the *Idylls* can lead to the uncovering of further intertextual affinities in both Tennyson's other poetry and his personal life) is overlaid by the triangle of White's novel. The further one gets from the indexical correspondences between Tennyson's poem and White's novel (at the apex), the broader and more generally significant the analogies (actional, structural, symbolic, mythic, psychological, cultural) between primary text and inter-text—until a stage is reached where the input of data for comparison (in either direction) is no longer matched by an output of confirmative correspondences. So that the triangle's base is never reached (except in such doublings as formal and traditional parody).

As a narrative frame for Arthurian exploits, the *Idylls* are characterized by defeat and disaster, and the poem is as obliquely tragic—the end contained in the beginning—as *The Solid Mandala*; both poem and novel are doom-laden and shot through with the presence of suspended time. The schematic simplicity of the poem is absent from the novel, which in Waldo's section has some of the complexity of fragmented remembrance and stress on memory characteristic, respectively, of Eliot's "Gerontion" and *The Waste Land*. But both works are deeply concerned with the conflict between Sense and Soul, both are imbued with a teleological pattern which is mysticized and charged by the nature of the discourse employed. Most importantly, both works can be said to exhibit what Tennyson called "a parabolic drift" (like *The Waste Land*) resisting simple allegorical or symbolic reduction. In both, there is a process of "social" disintegration embodied in specific character-types: the *Idylls* present a universal decline from a programmatically established ideal, whereas the false ideal of rational enlightenment is never attained in *The Solid Mandala*, and the true ideal of human wholeness is shattered indefinitely by psychical dissolution. The *Idylls*, it has been claimed, anticipate Jungian psychology (particularly in the *anima* or image of the unconscious; Stevenson 1948:135–36, Ricks 1972:267)—which is perhaps an irony of double intertextuality if we recall the Jungian scheme of *The Solid Mandala*.

The poem's psychological and modal relevance to the novel seems persuasive, notwithstanding contemporary objections that Tennyson's Arthur was a figure in a charade, a prig, a "wittol" (see Ricks 1972:267–76). Arthur and his faithful fool, Dagonet, can hear the silent music of Camelot's civilized values, despite the contention of Tristram that his brother must be a fool to ignore the chaotic (Dionysiac) forces that overwhelm even the highest application of true reason. Both the *Idylls* and *The Solid Mandala* abound with unifying images of music, reflecting the attempts of both Arthurs to create (Apollonian) harmony out of discord. Tristram is reminiscent of Waldo, with his constant harping on his brother's mental deficiency.[19] Both Arthurs represent man's higher nature (Soul, or Love), striving to sustain harmony but assailed by the antagonism of the nether self (Sense, or even Intellect). King Arthur is "Ideal manhood closed in real man" ("To the Queen", 1.38), thus parallelling Spenser's Arthur, even to the notion that the "ideal" is a necessary illusion, which must be striven for in states of doubt, despair, and acknowledgement of the persistence of evil. Tennyson apparently meant his Arthur to be a partial analogue to Christ; White's Arthur is explicitly made so. Both Arthurs have their three brides, and the necessary companionship of women who are "mundane". More importantly, King Arthur is in one dimension a "solar hero", the poem being made to follow the seasons (with persistent verbal indices of sun, light, and flame), from innocence to suspicion, confidence to cynicism, stability to nihilism. At the close of the *Idylls*, with the dissolution of the mandalic wholeness of the Round Table, King Arthur has a mind "clouded with doubt", like Arthur Brown after his brother's death. There is nevertheless at the heart of both poem and novel the Arthurian sense of personal immortality and the conviction that visionary truth can be sought by man in the flesh and in directed human action.

The evil powers of Tennyson's wasteland—false philosophies of rationalism, exaggerated ascetic withdrawal, inaction, crimes of sense and malice (cf especially Priestley 1949:250–55)—come from the Germanic north (as embodied particularly in Tristram, and echoed in White's Waldo). Like White, Tennyson is concerned to explore consciousness; the Knights of the Round Table are not allegorical representations of *moral* qualities, but of subjective, ever-changing states of mind. Like Waldo's literary projects, Tristram's rationalist pursuit of the "ideal" of the Holy Grail is delusory, leading only into a wasteland of disorder and disintegration.

I wish to narrow the focus of discussion once more—to Tennyson's "Fatima"—before widening it again into consideration of much broader (Nietzschean) implications. Two commentators (Herring 1966:73; Mackenzie 1969:248) have identified Waldo's library-poem as "Fatima"; Mackenzie senses "a good White mordancy" in the specific choice. What might have appealed to White from the outset is the fact that the poem is based on a fragment of Sappho (*Fragment 2,* "He seems to me equal to the gods") which treats of unsatisfied, homosexual physical desire, though it could equally well have been a legitimate

---

[19] Cf Waldo's designations for Arthur (W29/46/58/75/81/95/171). Arthur, like Tennyson's Arthur, is aware of what others think of him: his discourse cites similarly Waldovian epithets with conscious self-reference (A224–25/228/294). King Arthur is not fooled by threats of chaos, and is aware of the difficulty of his task. Arthur Brown, in his own transformative way, accepts Waldo's epithets, even at the climactic moment (W208) when his Apollonian offer of uniting Love is construed by Waldo as madness, as a denial of that shallow order of reason that Waldo hopes will keep him from Dionysiac chaos.

projection of heterosexual frustration.[20] The point, for White's putative interest, would lie in the indeterminacy—the boundaries of sexual identity in *The Solid Mandala* are blurred, though it was not until *The Twyborn Affair* that the enigma of bisexuality became the central theme and structural dynamic of White's fiction. Tennyson's first version of his poem (1832) bore no title, and was thus enticing in its sexual ambiguity for whomever chose to take the phrase "my narrow frame" as somatically male. The orientalizing title, "Fatima", was added in 1842, along with the second stanza of the final version, which dwells on the "burning drouth" (l. 13) of a woman's frustrated waiting for her lover.

Love is personified in "Fatima" as a solar force which is both generative and destructive; love vivifies (making the speaker throb) yet also parches, bringing disequilibrium to the "constant mind" (which becomes the "dry brain" in stanza 4), withering the lover and whirling her like dry "leaves in roaring wind". Already, this first stanza confirms the figuration of the lines quoted in *The Solid Mandala*. Even clearer is the presence of indices relating to Waldo which I have already enumerated: withering; shuddering; dry leaves; being at the mercy of the wind. One can add to these the idea of blindness (the speaker strains her sight against the noonday sun, then is "blind"), which is reinforced by "dazzled" in stanza 4 and by the drooping soul of stanza 6, "blinded with ... the shining eye" of the lover-Sun. There is, too, the notion of the lover-Sun's *vital* influence, in the word "throbbing", which also permeates the diction of *The Solid Mandala* in contexts of sexual desire or transcendental yearning. Waldo's aridity, unlike that of the persona in "Fatima", comes from within; and he is impervious, or resistant, to the lover-Sun's generative influence. Unlike Waldo, the speaker in "Fatima" surrenders to the natural elements, caressed by the "sweet gales" that precede the sun, her heart bursting "into blossom at his sight" (ll. 10–11/22–25/34–35). The night, in the poem, is only an irksome way-station before the eastern dawn (ll. 8–9), whereas for Waldo the dim light of interiors and the dark of late evening are his *locus amoenus* (though he is afraid to sleep).

The ambiguous death of Waldo has a parallel in the closing lines of "Fatima" (ll. 39–42):

> I *will* possess him or will die.
> I will grow round him in his place,
> Grow, live, die looking on his face,
> Die, dying clasp'd in his embrace.

There is perhaps a syncretistic reworking of transformation-myths (eg, Clytie changed into the constant heliotrope) in these lines. Be that as it may, at the moment Waldo dies, "entranced by Arthur's great marigold of a face" (W214), Arthur goes "crumbly as one thing for love and now the death of it" (A294), and we are left in the dark about whether Arthur has tried to clasp his brother in his despairing, loving embrace. Undeniable, however, is the fact that Waldo "grows

---

[20] Cf Ricks 1969:382-84, Turner 1976:59. For all the use Catullus made of her as a model, there is no evidence for Sappho's having been lesbian. (Cf also White himself, *Flaws:*183.) Some of her poem-fragments express emotion towards girls in her intellectual circle, ranging from sororal attachment to deep passion, but she was probably bisexual at most.

round" Arthur, clutching his wrist in death. Waldo's *will* is implemented: he does "possess" his brother at the end, *and* dies (as something later dies in Arthur, too, through the loss of his brother).

The presence of "Fatima" in *The Solid Mandala*, as well as constituting an actional and psychical analogue, signifies the art-object which, once espoused by Waldo, leads to the reality of death, in a species of intertextual predetermination. Apart from this, it is a metonym for a deeper involvement by White in a dialogue with Tennyson as a writer equally concerned with the sharp bifurcations and shadowy intercalations of human personality. Both writers see the "living will" of subjective vitalism as pitted against the dark, chaotic, Dionysiac forces of "over-consciousness" (Brashear 1969:12–14); so much is also clear from *The Idylls of the King*. Waldo's chief psychical and actional instrument is the will—the desire to control himself and others. His "reason" has little to do with the quest for "enlightenment", despite the ubiquity of the concept in his discourse. True reason in the novel is not Cartesian (the formula *cogito, ergo sum* in Waldo's case would be an index to the pain of self-consciousness rather than to the promise of enlightened order between subject and object), but Platonic. It is Arthur's vision which is societal, optimistic, trusting of things, yet humanistically rooted in enlightenment (illumination) and Platonic love.

The polarity of Dionysiac and Apollonian forces in Tennyson's poetry is independently confirmed later in the arguments of Nietzsche. Similar confirmation of this polarity is manifest in the complementarity of psychical and social forces operating within or between characters in White's novels (so that one could posit an intertextual triangle: Tennyson—Nietzsche—White). *The Solid Mandala* is the quintessential dramatization of these forces, traceable to the acknowledged bivalency within White's private and artistic personality (if not within us all). On a broader scale, *The Solid Mandala* and White's last two novels transform the partial tracks and traces of monstrous or monumental personalities in the earlier fiction, re-shaping them into broader avenues of ingress into the novelist's own interior life. They thus constitute a peculiar form of analytical autobiography. The Nietzschean vector which provides clarification in respect of *The Solid Mandala* in particular can be located in *The Birth of Tragedy* (which itself is one of the novel's embedded intertexts).

In *The Birth of Tragedy*, Nietzsche sees two conflicting forces operating within human consciousness. The Dionysiac is a death-longing or desire for self-annihilation, dragging consciousness into chaos, disintegrating the ego, which is buffeted by the irrational indifference of nature and is ultimately imprisoned in the stagnation of the darkly chthonic. We have seen the indexical underpinnings for this force in the novel. Man's will is not (as Waldo would believe) a system of control (like reason), a holding sway over the Dionysiac, but is itself a Dionysiac force. Thomas Carlyle can be quoted in Nietzsche's support:

This is he whom business-people call Systematic and Theorizer and Word-monger; his vital intellectual force lies dormant or extinct, his whole force is mechanical, conscious: of such a one it is foreseen that, when once confronted with the infinite complexities of the real world, his little compact theorem of the world will be found wanting. [Carlyle 1831:6]

This gets pretty close to describing Waldo, and one of the two principal modalities in Tennyson's poetry. There is more in Carlyle's "Characteristics" (esp. pp. 5–9, 15–16) to confirm the antinomies revealed in White's novel: the healthy understanding, argues Carlyle, is intuitive, not logical; "self-contemplation ... is infallibly the symptom of disease"; "unconsciousness" is the evidence of "wholeness"; consciousness produces "the barrenest of all mortals ... the Sentimentalist ... a perpetual lesson of despair, and type of bedrid valetudinarian impotence" who can only talk of virtue and duty in the abstract; the decline of religion, mystery and myth coincides with the rise of soulless logic; and, in fine:

Unconsciousness belongs to pure unmixed life; Consciousness to a diseased mixture and conflict of life and death: Unconsciousness is the sign of creation; Consciousness, at best, that of manufacture. [Carlyle 1831:16]

By contrast with the Dionysiac of the "Systematic and Theoriser", the Apollonian resides in the all-out effort to seek and maintain the integrity of the ego and the identity of the self. In Nietzsche's terms, Arthur strives for original Oneness, the redemption of the *principium individuationis* through illusion, showing us how "there is need for a whole world of torment in order for the individual to produce the redemptive vision" (Nietzsche, quoted in Brashear 1969:43–44).

Waldo, himself tormented and given to irruptions of cruelty, refuses to take cognizance of the "whole world of torment" which Arthur seeks to comprehend. Waldo's self-delusions and self-aggrandisement are not to be identified with the integrative function of Apollonian illusion. There are indications in the novel that Arthur is aware of the difference between delusion and necessary illusion (an awareness impossible within the delusional discourse of Waldo's section). As with White himself, the connection between illusion, theatre, exhibitionism and art is evident in Arthur's childhood (A216), including his making of promises "he would have to break"—an Apollonian illusion-making that does not conceal the self but preserves it as well as avoiding hurt to others. The quest for necessary illusion is linked, too, with myth through art. Even in the Wagnerian twilight of the gods, Arthur seeks the substantiality of mythic illusion whose truth his father later tries to deny: "Who and where were the gods?" (A217). To the kids in the schoolroom, Arthur gives "the performance they expected of him" (A231). Absorbed in contemplation of his mandala-marble, with "the golden disc" of the sun "spinning closer in the sky", he sits within "the empty theatre of the distance spread around him", his concentrated tranquillity making "the circle of the distant mountains ... close around him" like a contracting amphitheatre (A233). Occupied in "working out his own needs and relationships", he wishes that "the curtain on his mystery hadn't stuck halfway up" (A239). Flustered by Dulcie's beauty, he knows that his diversionary talk about Mr Feinstein's *capple* (ie, about rationality) is only "a performance", a necessary illusion (A244). Upset by Waldo's accident in Pitt Street, Arthur is compelled to a double illusion in the hospital. He has to appease the bossy ward-sister (the embodiment of rational social order in a context of personal chaos) by acting calm, and has to calm down his brother by acting more upset than he really is (ie, the possible loss of Waldo is less a source of grief for Waldo's sake than for Arthur's, since Waldo's demise would mean the dissolution of Arthur's identity: "he couldn't afford to let him die"). Arthur's quest for identity-preserving enlightenment takes place in a parabolic realm of illusion, "his mind venturing through the darkened theatre in which the gods had died in the beginning" (A290). Coming across Waldo standing at the mirror in their mother's dress, Arthur so identifies with him (experiencing "already some such translation in himself of his brother's personality") that he sees himself standing there, and takes Waldo's will-driven, delusional descent into the Dionysiac realm of under-consciousness for healing, empathetic, ritual illusion (A291)—this is the closest adumbration in the novel of what Nietzsche meant by "the birth of tragedy".

Waldo registers, but cannot interpret, the fact that "Arthur would assume the voices of those who were addressing him" (W114) in his Apollonian urge to identify himself, through illusion, with the societal One. Dulcie admits to a desire to "show off brilliantly in public", but confesses that she is too "mundane" to succeed (W101)—in keeping with her lunar nature, the Apollonian is pulled down by the Dionysiac. Waldo is "entranced" by her mentioning that a cousin "'can impersonate people ... killingly'" (W101), but only because such illusion-making appeals to him as a means of concealing the disintegrating self through defensive damage to others. Waldo is uneasy about other people's motives instead of giving himself up to the possibilities of illusion. For him, Dulcie seems to be rehearsing a dialogue from a "dark rôle he had expected on the first occasion, when she hadn't played it" (W101); he wonders "whether Dulcie would affect surprise" at his marriage-proposal (W150). He projects his own dis–ease onto those around him and is blind to the need for illusion. As Arthur reflects,

Instead of Waldo's afternoon, it would become Waldo's tragedy, because he wouldn't know how to act. Only Arthur and Dulcie in the end would know the parts they and others must act out. [A245]

Waldo's tragedy is, essentially, his self-imposed isolation from beneficial, social involvement with other people, his inability to share his horror of the Dionysiac void of consciousness with anyone but (on occasion) his twin. The word "act", too, is nicely equivocal: just as Waldo's disintegrating personality cannot be healed by relinquishment to the necessary illusion of social roles (he is much too burdened by self-consciousness to "act" these roles), so is he incapacitated by consciousness, incapable of positive action in his chthonic imprisonment. There is, revealingly, no double "birth of tragedy" in the family circle on the Greek veranda (W38–41, A230). Only Arthur, with his Apollonian drive, is capable of spontaneously giving birth to a calf and to the whole illusion of tragedy. Waldo, the "Systematic ... Word-monger, ... his whole force mechanical", gets his idea of tragedy from a book and, "never easily carried away", must filter his preconception through the ordering, iron will of the written word. He is incapable of spontaneous birth from within. The same dark absence of the Apollonian turns up elsewhere: it is Arthur, not Waldo, who responds to the "actual" tragedy of their father's death by enacting "brass despair" (W71, A269); Waldo's question to Dulcie about acting out "'great tragic parts'" (W93) is spontaneous, but only in the sense that "he had never thought it in his life" and is dissimulating to impress, to conceal his true self from Dulcie.

Central, I think, to an understanding of the twins and of the subtextual presence of Tennyson in the novel is Nietzsche's notion of the replacement of the purely Apollonian resistance to chaos with Socratic, "theoretical man", who escapes the truth of Dionysiac disorder by pursuing objective ideas, scientific optimism, prim virtue and detachment.[21] Tennyson tends to distrust theoretical man, who is also identifiable with Waldo—against whose investment in a brittle, false rationality White places Arthur's higher, Apollonian objectivity. What Arthur at the same time embodies, of course, is a higher, ecstatic subjectivity opposed to Waldo's irrational, subterranean emotionalism. Nietzsche's evolutionary re-classification does not alter the antithetical basis of White's character-pairing, but only enriches this pairing in its complex valencies (like the Jacob–and–Esau nexus) by introducing a zeugmatic pattern of *levels* of antithesis. The constant feature (in both Tennyson and White) is the presence of Nietzsche's "Dionysian beast" (Brashear 1969:50–51).

In rounding off this excursus on intertextual affinities between characterological and actional indices in *The Solid Mandala* and the metamythic psychology of Nietzsche, I must perforce mention that the surface movement of the narrative might easily tempt the reader to locate the Apollonian in Waldo and the Dionysiac in Arthur, if one were to take, say, the measuredly geometric "artistic" strivings of Waldo and the unshackled, extravert, wordless dancing and histrionicism of Arthur at face value. But Arthur's mandala-dance describes (or *inscribes*, the body writing kinetically upon the earth) total, *geometric* form. He does not *need* words to give form to the instinctual—Dionysiac ecstasy (disorder) is under his Apollonian control. To identify Waldo as an Apollonian artist and Arthur as a Dionysiac force is to set up a false equation. Although Nietzsche states that myth (Apollo and Dionysos) disappeared when Greek tragedy "died" under the onslaught of Socratic, theoretical man, it must be emphasized that White's attempt at reviving tragedy by reintroducing myth into the artistic representation of a secular world is not based on a purely Nietzschean characterization of the Apollonian and the Dionysiac, but allows for a truly *pre-*Socratic, polysemous interpretation of myth. In White's fiction, there are no simple binary polarities.

Superficially, Arthur (like most of White's illuminated ones) is a Dionysiac figure: but it is significant that all of the detail of *disjecta membra* in the book is indexed to Waldo. The symbolic operation of the Dionysiac dismembering leads in myth to a rebirth out of destruction; in conflict with the vainly equilibrizing tendencies of the Socratic, the Dionysiac forces within Waldo tear him apart. Arthur, who cannot exist without him, re-enacts this death within himself and is reborn on the other side of reason, but still with his old, now chastened, urge to

---

21 In my alignment of the Dionysiac/Apollonian/Socratic nexus with Tennyson, Nietzsche and Carlyle, I am indebted to the extended comparative analysis of William Brashear (1969:12–51 *passim*), which also provided the stimulus for my application of these intertextualities to White.

Apollonian order. It is true that Waldo rejects the Dionysiac spirit: but this means neither that he is potentially Apollonian in the broader mythic connotations of that god, nor that he is wholly impervious to the emotional and orgiastic extremes of the Dionysiac. Nor does it mean that Waldo's rejection of the Dionysiac can be narrowly identified with a rejection of his brother: his antipathies are much more broadly directed than that, and it is significant that the peaks in Waldovian negativity coincide with his unwilling recognition that Arthur has given at least some degree of (Apollonian) aesthetic form to the spontaneous surge of primal (Dionysiac) creativity, or (as in the Library Incident) has devoted himself to a programme of Apollonian self-enlightenment. The standard aesthetic indices to the Apollonian and Dionysiac personalities cannot be made to apply coherently to Waldo and Arthur. It is Waldo who described Arthur as ugly—but this cannot make him an exemplar of the Dionysiac inchoate, of spiritual beauty without form. Waldo himself is hardly beautiful, and can also concede that his brother is handsome. What supervenes to thwart any narrow allegorical scheme is the central fact (central to all of White's fiction) that our *physis* continually obtrudes to remind us of our humanity: nobody is exempt. Beatson (1976) repeatedly and persuasively points this out; it is an idea that is consonant with a Jungian, anti-Cartesian world-view—the body calls constantly to the mind, recalling it to oneness.

Nietzsche argues that Dionysiac art affects the Apollonian talent by inciting us to an intuition of universality and to a translation of Dionysiac wisdom into Apollonian artifice. Does Arthur, whose artistic expression seems formless, thus require the completive agency of Waldo's Apollonianism? This would be to assume that aesthetic expression entails technical perfection, and that the shapelessness of Arthur's art somehow disqualifies him from any indwelling Apollonian capacity. But is it not Waldo's obsession with technical perfection that cripples his urge to enactment? Do we not respond to the *truth* of Arthur's rough hewings of music, word, image and motion—and are these not an enactment of a terrible beauty whose goal is ultimately social, inclusive, Apollonian?

Nietzsche's thumbnail sketch of Apollo runs as follows:

the god of all plastic powers and the soothsaying god. He who is etymologically the "lucent" one, the god of light, reigns also over the fair illusion of our inner world of fantasy .... But the image of Apollo must incorporate that thin line which the dream image may not cross, under the penalty of becoming pathological, of imposing itself on us as crass reality: a discreet limitation, a freedom from all extravagant urges, the sapient tranquillity of the plastic god. His eye must be sunlike, in keeping with his origin. Even at those moments when he is angry and ill-tempered there lies upon him the consecration of fair illusion .... Apollo himself may be regarded as the marvellous divine image of the *principium individuationis*, whose looks and postures radiate the full delight, wisdom and beauty of "illusion". [Nietzsche 1956:21–22]

The evidence for an Apollonian Arthur stares one in the face in such a passage. Waldo's final role in life is Socratic, and characterized by inadequacy. If there are Waldovian indices that momentarily persuade us to see Waldo as an ironized embodiment of the Apollonian, then the problem we come up against is the question of the ultimate intentionality of psychologized discourse. The illusion Waldo is under is not "fair" or "consecrated". He is unable to provide a "dream image" but (according to the novel) is "incapable of sleep for dreaming". He embodies "discreet limitation" but is not rewarded by tranquillity or controlled temper, and cannot cope with Arthur's "extravagant urges". All this is psychologically true—except that Waldo is in no way a "god of light" in any Apollonian sense as mediated by the indexical detail of the novel. It is also true that Arthur is as free from "extravagant urges" as a character in the process of synthesis can be. Arthur does possess "sapient tranquillity", is indeed the soothsayer, the "lucent" one, the distiller of dream images, the keeper both of "fair illusion" and of reality. It is no accident that his anger (as when he runs to Waldo's defence in the playground) subdues his beholders: the indexical detail is (as we have seen) explicitly solar, suggesting his divinity and the impossibility for Waldo of determining whether his brother is "fair illusion" (myth) or "crass reality".

The central, incontrovertible emphasis is on the Socratic element in Waldo's character.[22] It is in the interests of all the narrative specificity of *The Solid Mandala* to show Arthur as embodying the incomplete synthesis of the Dionysiac with the Apollonian The Dionysiac urge does not overpower the Apollonian. There is nothing of the Apollonian in Waldo's nature or behaviour: incarcerated as he is in the prison-house of will and reason, he re-sists the Dionysiac manifestations of the mythic in the social and natural world about him, represses or distorts the Dionysiac which is latent within his psyche, and is thus incapable of releasing himself into the world. Where the refusal to face the *terribilità* of one's essence is so extreme, there is no substance which can be aesthetically shaped by Apollonian agency. By the same token, we should thank the gods that White himself had the iron strength of personality to direct his own Apollonian gaze so unremittingly on his own Dionysiac depths, stifle the Socratic tendencies of his quotidian personality, and unite all in the *terribilità* of his art.

Onomastic implications have thus opened out into broader, but equally specific, considerations of intertextual potentiation—whereby any over-enthusiastic determination of "sources" and "influences" should be checked by the reminder that White has been in no way subservient to the conceptual systems, or expression, of prior texts; nor is his novel a carefully woven tapestry of parodic or ironic intertextualities. We should, however, remain aware of the possible "cultural texts" underlying White's representations of parallelism and antinomy. The most persistent "cultural" presences are those of myth and religion. If we poke inquisitively at the polysemous, shimmering plurality of these indexical patternings, however, we find that the narrative encodes "references" to actual

---

[22] This is, in psychological terms, discerningly analysed by Ann McCulloch (1983) in the course of an examination of "White's allegiance to Nietzsche" in *The Solid Mandala*. In all other respects, McCulloch's interpretation runs counter to mine.

and fictive literary texts which seem not to have exhausted their referential potential in being bits of data among many others within the characters' domain of consciousness and action, or even within an auctorially imposed naming system. What look like ice-floes in the potentially vast, but selectively mediated, personal identity and oceanic consciousness of the characters are also—or "really"—the tips of manifold icebergs floating in the oceanic consciousness (and subconscious?) of the author. Concealed inter-texts can be retrieved by following up conspicuously "extra-textual" citations.[23] And there are inter-texts, conspicuous in the narrative simply because they occur (as titles: *The Golden Bough*; *The Brothers Karamazov*; *Tiresias a Youngish Man*; as silent predications, by contiguity, on an author's name—Barron Field; Mary McCarthy; Clare Booth Luce—or on a participant existent: Demeter; Athene; Hera), which become "inconspicuous" once the reader gets on with his or her reading.

---

[23] One example: what Waldo takes to be Crankshaw's "obscure reference" to a "mistake" made in his "report on damage" to Frazer's *Golden Bough* "years ago" (W172) is "obscure" enough to be textually foregrounded, and to prompt resolution by the reader. My resolution of the enigma (im)planted by White is the following. Waldo, probably in the course of his accessioning-activity at the Municipal, steeped himself in the poetry of T.S. Eliot. The title of Waldo's *Tiresias*-novel triggers consideration of intertextual affinities—not simply with Waldo as a Prufrock, but more centrally with Waldo as a Gerontion–figure (both of Eliot's poems being accessible to Waldo in *Ara Vos Prec*, 1920). In *The Solid Mandala* as in "Gerontion", we have "the apparently disorganized flow of reminiscence in the mind of a single character", a blind and sterile old man, a sufferer from spiritual failure and the lost power to love (Smith 1956:57), who retreats into inertia, evading the excitation of impotent flesh through the exercise of memory "in a wilderness of mirrors". Gerontion is essentially identical with Tiresias, the blind seer of Eliot's *The Waste Land*, which Waldo will have read in 1923–24. The Prufrock/Gerontion element is thought up by the prematurely aged Waldo after his father's death, "A Youngish Man" constituting a wilful inversion typical of Waldo's cognitive dissonance. Eliot's preoccupations in *The Waste Land*—universalism, pessimism, élitism, scepticism, and an individualist-impersonal ethic and aesthetic—accord well with Waldo's fundamental attitudes, not to speak of the technique of "collation" employed in the poem. Eliot, the persona of Gerontion, and Waldo have this in common, as does the Fisher King in *The Waste Land*, "shoring up fragments against his ruin" by time. Further, both "Gerontion" and *The Waste Land* have anthropological, fertility-myth underpinnings deriving from Frazer's study of myth in *The Golden Bough*. Waldo will have been referred to this massive work by Eliot's notes to *The Waste Land*; a rationalist like his father, he would be drawn to a "scientific" explanation of myth such as Frazer's, while at the same time reacting with fascinated repulsion to the chthonic atavisms detailed there. One such detail leaves its intertextual trace—its origin in the full 1911 third edition of Frazer, and in reduced form in the 1922 abridgement—when Waldo, retreating from Dulcie after she rejects his marriage-proposal, has a vision of her as she stands at the top of the steps: "Mrs Saporta, increasing, bulging, the Goddess of a Thousand Breasts" (W157). Waldo has got this from Frazer's disquisitions on the Aventine/Ephesian moon-goddess of fertility, Diana or Artemis, with their references to a "many-breasted idol", a "great many-breasted goddess of fertility", and a "goddess with a multitude of protruding breasts"—a rank iconic hyperbole for sexuality and maternal fecundity which Waldo's mind distils and re-generates in disgusted contempt. Moreover: Waldo's suspicion of Crankshaw's suspicion could be less paranoid than usual; the damage Waldo reports could have been done to *The Golden Bough* by Waldo himself.

The assumption that such intertexts or "factual" metonymies are only locally significant is, however, usually mistaken. We should not "naturalize" White's narratives too far, and assume that realistic referentiality is always operative in the interstices of poetic texture, thus apparently confirming our tendency to expect "prose" significance whenever detail is not foregrounded. In handing his narrative over to the play of figural consciousness, White withdraws from intratextual auctorial commentary. White is nonetheless present in submarine guise, inviting us with insistent impassivity to realize that indexical patterns construable without the aid of external literary reference will gain an additional brilliance and coherence once we see that these patterns are informed by the *detail* in prior texts.[24] These texts are seldom explicitly signalled; this would involve an intrusion into, or arch artificializing of, figural consciousness. Auctorial viewpoint is thus transported via a subtle, modernist intertextuality which (unlike Eliot's) avoids intratextual allusion or citational structure.

---

[24] These texts can have various derivations. At Dulcie's, Arthur wins favour by his spirited pierrot-song with its parodic intimation of the Well of Narcissus; at a four-page remove, Waldo's defence against such aesthetic insufficiency is his notion of "something really good" that would shame Dulcie: *Der Jüngling an der Quelle*, a song by Schubert whose title likewise evokes a relationship to water. The song is a setting (1815) of a deceptively simple four-liner by Johann Gaudenz Freiherr von Salis-Seewis, in which a love-sick youth addresses a gently purling spring and the undulating, whispering poplars surrounding it; these slumbrous sounds, rather than offering him relief from thought of Elisa (in Schubert: Louise), his standoffish beloved, only make things worse for him by sighing her name. What we find here is an inter-text for Waldo's personality. The personal emotion imposed upon nature through the pathetic fallacy defeats the speaker's will to forget, while the word used to characterize the beloved ("spröd") can, within the same semantic field, be shifted onto Waldo himself (*spröd* involving as it does the notions of coyness, dryness, aridity and cold reserve). The narrative persecutes Waldo with ironic parallels mocking his aestheticized erotic desire (note, too, that the dry leaves in Arthur's earlier song "twitter—And titter!").

A second, equally "submerged" or holographic inter-text is the mandalic Panderma carpet which Arthur excitedly discovers as Saporta turns his "first quality Oriental rugs" "as though they had been the pages of a book" (A250). The carpet is a "page" in an inter-text which, like Mr Feinstein's Torah, contains different knowledge for different readers. The Panderma rug is a degenerate imitation of the Anatolian Ghiordes prayer-rug made for the use of devout Muslim Turks and Arabs; their religious function and symbolic design were encapsulated in the double-temple pattern at the centre, which evoked marriage and thus made the object a suitable part of a maiden's dowry. Saporta, solid and practical, ignores the carpet's spiritual identity, whereas Arthur's mandalic consciousness intuitively seizes upon its symbolism of union. The carpet can thus be seen as connected centrally to Arthur's implementation of his blue mandala in effecting the marriage-union of Dulcie and Saporta. Another "Byzantine" link might be forged: there is a further degenerate form of the Ghiordes carpet apart from the Panderma rug, and that is the Smyrna carpet, with a mandalic, quadriradial, floral design. Not only did the hedonistically decadent ancestral Waldo live in Turkey—he also died at Smyrna, the mandalic centre of three great faiths: Islam, Christianity, and Judaism. The linking figure in the carpet is that of spiritual degeneracy versus functioning faith.

13

BROADER PERSPECTIVES

I   The persistence of style–features:
The Twyborn Affair

One task of future criticism needs to be the macroscopic investigation of White's work to determine the precise extent to which the style-features and modes of narrative discourse accounted for here constitute fundamental continuities, and the extent to which significant discontinuities arise. I have attempted a first, sampling expansion of enquiry by examining White's second-last novel, *The Twyborn Affair,* for stylistic and discoursal persistencies. This kind of sampling cannot, of course, be regarded as a network of such indices, and the present method suffers from being divorced from a general discussion of the novel. The rest of White's fiction would also have to be submitted to analysis in order to secure confirmation and maximal differentiation.

The first striking characteristic is the recurrence in *The Twyborn Affair* of detail already present in *The Solid Mandala.* There is mostly a persistence of lexical collocation or close concordance at the semantic level. The basal persistency, however, may not appear to be a style-feature in the narrower sense, but rather a continuity of thought, theme, philosophical stance—a continuity independent of thematic or symbolic paraphrase. Such persistencies can only support the hypothesis that stylistic and discoursal features recur because they form necessary elements of signification within a greater whole which extends beyond the confines of individual novels or stories. In this first list, which I present without further commentary, recurrences range from single lexical items to topical or notional features of the action. In some cases, I include parallels to *The Solid Mandala* from novels other than *The Twyborn Affair.* These parallels were encountered by chance; nevertheless, they show how White's other novels might confirm the author's verbal preoccupations. Deliberately excluded are broader patterns of indexical detail involving "imagery" and metaphoricity; this is a huge, almost untapped field of its own.

An initial miscellany is made up of lexical, phrasal, and grammatical recurrences. There are idiolectal, intransitive uses of colloquial and intransitive verbs such as *gollop (Twyborn Affair = TA,* p. 276; *Solid Mandala = SM,* p. W47), and syntactic-iconic peculiarities like "Mother continued shocked" *(SM* A219; cf "continued listless", *Riders in the Chariot = RITC,* pp. 259/463) or "Saporta put a meaty hand" *(SM* W66; cf "put his hand", *Eye of the Storm = EOS,* p. 99). Obliquities and wordplay recur:

... ill-health, poverty, any phenomenon which threatens personal continuity *(TA* 402). Cf: Arthur ... whose mechanism had in some way threatened his continuity *(SM* W55).
... the direction she had chosen, or which, perhaps, had been chosen for them *(TA* 226). Cf: ... the direction Waldo knew now he had not chosen: it had chosen him *(SM* W57).
the positions of love *(Vivisector* = *Viv* 349; *SM* P311).
... one who put his faith in reason *(TA* 156). Cf: ... damage temporarily his faith in reason *(SM* W58).

Here are some other, sometimes faintly metaphoric, lexical favourites:

Mrs Golson was racked. What should she do? *(TA* 68). Cf: Waldo racked his memory, and was racked *(SM* W187).

Mrs Golson finally exploded *(TA* 110). Cf: Waldo exploded finally *(SM* A267).

Would he accuse her from the carpet ...? Joanie could not have borne to be accused again .... *(TA* 108; cf also *TA* 363). Cf: Mrs Poulter's face was too stupid exactly to accuse Waldo *(SM* W60); He stood accused of every atrocity *(SM* W174).

"home", as opposed to Joanie's "Home", where the shops were *(TA* 59). Cf: "They come out from Home" *(SM* B15).

a certain ginger colonel ... the colonel's opulent crotch *(TA* 141). Cf: opulent crutches of purple men *(SM* W78).

the bottoms erected between himself and the shambles ... *(TA* 168). Cf: Mr Dun, who had finished looking, erected a behind *(SM* W30).

he wondered whether Eadie realised *(TA* 173); Perhaps Don Prowse realised *(TA* 186). Cf: realised (oblique euphemism, *SM passim)*.

Mrs Golson did not altogether believe *(TA* 111). Cf: Mrs Dun could not believe *(SM* B15 and elsewhere).

the felted balls flying back and forth *(TA* 29); the thud of the felted ball *(TA* 79). Cf: forth and back went the felted fated ball *(SM* W89).

There is a large number of actional and notional recurrences, including the interest of certain characters in Christian Science *(TA* 24/365; cf *SM* A286, *RITC* 244, *Flaws* 241), the ubiquitous hydrangeas *(TA* 62; cf *SM* W66/105/ 112/120/139, *Flaws)*, asthma *(TA* 34/108/ 115; *SM* W35; *Flaws* 140; Marr 1991 *passim)*, herb manuals *(TA* 114; cf *SM* A225), and dressing up as the Primrose Pompadour *(TA* 269; cf *SM* A216). The aptronymic significance of the bird-eyed, cackling Mrs Tyrell's name is an echo of Mrs Poulter, "a pigeon-coloured woman" *(TA* 180–81; *SM* B17); in both novels, women of this caste have an interest in funerals and "the layun out" *(TA* 200; *SM* W169). Further:

At this point we reached the gate, which will fall off its hinges if nothing is done about it *(TA* 31); "The gate'll fall down if they don't do something about it," he declared like any practical Australian male *(TA* 57); *"Qui sait?"* Mrs Golson gasped back as she pushed against the collapsing gate, which finally fell *(TA* 115). Cf: "This gate, Waldo," Arthur was saying gently, "will fall to bits any day now" *(SM* W26); "... pushing at the gate which had not yet fallen down *(SM* W204).

Unlike Maud, who scarcely ever dreamed, or if she did, was spared remembering, Kitty once found herself taking part in a dream involving a clamorous plane-tree, its foliage replaced by the faces of girls *(TA* 309). Cf: Once Arthur dreamed the dream in which a tree was growing out of his thighs. It was the face of Dulcie Feinstein lost amongst the leaves of the higher branches .... In the morning of course he could barely remember *(SM* A260; cf Marr 1991:151).

that old coat and skirt which will last for ever *(TA* 61). Cf: ... inexhaustible tweed. (It was that good English stuff, from amongst the things discarded ..., some of which were lasting for ever) *(SM* W23).

the spider-moustache which descended and withdrew as on the night when the shutters blew open, never before, never again till now *(TA* 156). [Cf the one (moustachioed) kiss from Waldo's father] *(SM* W34)

... iron bedstead ... brass knobs *(TA* 188); brass balls jingling *(TA* 243). Cf: the iron bedstead ... the jingle of brass balls and dislocated iron *(SM* W62; W175).

"I'm so grateful, my dear, that you should have offered me your friendship." But immediately started wondering whether it had indeed been offered *(TA* 87). Cf: Mrs Dun wondered whether she had been wise ... to accept Mrs Poulter's friendship *(SM* B21; cf B11).

Love is over-rated. Not affection—affection is to love what the minutiae are to living *(TA* 76–77; *Flaws: passim*). Cf: It was almost the only gratitude he felt he owed his parents—not love, which is too demanding in the end, affection perhaps, which is more often than not love watered down with pity *(SM* W55–56).

She derived visible consolation from her own charitable act *(TA* 118). Cf: ... her own charity made her smile with faint pleasure *(SM* B18).

"Oh, people are cruel! One only asks for trust—certainty .... That's why one keeps dogs, I suppose" *(TA* 167). Cf: [The twins bought the dogs] "so that we could have something additional—reliable—to love. Because we didn't have faith in each other" *(SM* A284); even dogs are less brutal than men, because they are less complicated *(SM* A217).

women were probably honester than men *(TA* 223); "True friendship .... if there is anything wholly true—certainly in friendship—comes, I'd say, from the woman in a man and the man in a woman" *(TA* 360; almost verbatim in *Flaws)*. Cf this pervasive theme in *The Solid Mandala,* and in *Flaws* and Marr 1991: *passim.*

"Oh, the Australian emptiness!" *(TA* 63); the shadowless Australian light *(TA* 173; cf White 1958, White 1969). Cf: "... reared in the light in an empty country .... There aren't any shadows in Australia" *(SM* W160).

Many recurrences have a predominantly metaphoric expression, such as furniture "straining at its buttons" *(TA* 232) or "straining to hold the stuffing down" *(SM* W100), and the phrase "the embroidery of life" *(TA* 175; *SM* A258). Most centre on the nature of *physis* and the mechanisms of mind:

[the mind's] dark screen *(EOS* 98). Cf: [the mind's/memory's] black transparent screen *(SM* W178).

"Remembering is a kind of disease I suffer from" *(TA* 158; *Flaws* and Marr 1991: *passim)*. Cf: He could hardly bear, while exquisitely needing, the rusty creaking of his memory *(SM* W27).

[eyes as] brown ferrets *(TA* 148). Cf: [brown eyes] like soft brown animals burrowing in *(SM* W125); The brown burrowing eyes *(SM* W136); "that vicious ferret, the other truth" *(SM* W195).

holding with Gothic hand against his chest the book *(TA* 135). Cf: Then his gothic shoulders would arch more acutely, and his already inactive hands turn to stone *(SM* W159).

The ruddy skin of this clumsy but touching girl is peppered with little moles that suggest that somebody once let off a shotgun at her. She even smells of gunpowder *(TA* 24). Cf: flashes of gunpowdery flesh *(SM* W157); [Mrs Poulter's skin] smelling ever so faintly of struck flint *(SM* A287); he could almost smell their gunpowder flesh *(Viv* 124).

Eadie's ... the eyes of an old, troubled dog. The soft white-kid face *(TA* 422). Cf: Catching sight of that interminable face in shrivelled kid *(SM* P307).

inside their encrustation of rings *(TA* 55). Cf: their mail of rings *(SM* W163; cf *SM* P308).

Swinburne's ... secret orgasms *(TA* 150). Cf: A throbbing of books ... an orgasm in dry places, a delicious guilt of the intellect *(SM* W122).

[when writing a letter:] waited for what comes shooting out, finally, like milk, or sperm *(TA* 241). Cf: Waldo wished he could have conceived a poem .... If it would only come shooting out with the urgency of shit and music *(SM* W111).

There are in *The Twyborn Affair* the same idiolectal handlings of grammatical features—here are two of the relative-clause types familiar from other novels: "each other's high-lit teeth, of which Angie's were only very slightly buckled" (134); "Prowse would be a different matter again, who now came stamping into the house" (236). There is the same causal implementation of the preposition *for* (eg, "Ursula could only ... laugh for the extravagant answer she had just received", 345; see also 146/256/364/403). There are the same modal/adverbial restraints on action ("The woman could not laugh enough", 114; cf *SM* W108), the same oblique cementings of abstract to concrete (eg, "Madame Sasso parried necessity like an expert, then appeared to remember", 125; "... declined food, with incredulous chins", 102). There are the characteristic tropes: subversions of cliché (eg, "tossed ... on what seemed the dilemma's only possible horn", 81); paronomastic expressions which revitalize dead metaphor to lend an ironic, often slightly distanced muting to experienced action:

trousers he had worn on and off over the past twenty years (74);
Mrs Corbould rose to the occasion (126; standing up);
entered the past through the present (284; sodomy);
extricating himself from ... a trap, a sticky one at that (221; after copulation);
lay it on thick (310; exaggerated cosmetics);
though she detected in his laughter a slight edge which was meant to cut (369);

—and synaesthetic complexes (eg, "drawing from the warped keys the same skeins of passionate colours", 100).

In the following brief passage taken at random from the text of *The Twyborn Affair* (16–17), there are various features worthy of comment:

"Only change the wheel," he muttered, somewhat disconsolately it sounded.
If she had sounded stern, it was that Joan Golson had never felt so much her own mistress. In her naughtiness, she made haste to get away before her servant should offer advice, or turn into a nanny or a husband and exercise some form of restraint. But he did not murmur, and as she escaped up the hill, she was conscious of her foolishness in thinking she might be of importance to him, to anybody, except as a source of rewards (to Curly perhaps, though he, too, expected rewards) least of all to the charmed couple at the villa for whom she was risking, if not her neck, her ankles, to catch sight of once again. So she hurried, and panted, and several times ricked an ankle on the stones, in her rush to humiliate herself perhaps in their eyes as an eternally superfluous character. But did arrive.

These few lines are, one might suppose, relatively innocuous from a discoursal and stylistic angle; yet they still serve as a good example of White's skill at rendering the texture of action and consciousness. I shall take the style-features as they occur in sequence:

1. "it sounded" is included non-parenthetically within the tag-extension (Mrs Golson's perspective).

2. "If ... it was that"—the ubiquitous concessive-explanatory conditional (Mrs Golson comparing her own behaviour with her husband's).

3. "Joan Golson" follows on from the "figural" pronoun and indicates reversion to personal-name role-identity, whereas "Mrs Golson" (before this passage) had conveyed consciousness of the mistress–servant relationship.

4. The word "naughtiness" projects a "bad-child" role-awareness, with mental undercutting of the preceding, prevaricating mental assertion.

5. "was conscious" is a characteristic borderline index of mental operation for *self*-consciousness (the most consonant form of psychonarration, like minimal thought-tagging generally).

6. "to him, *to anybody,* ..." is an asyndetic parenthesis, and counts as a corrective after-thought of consciousness.

7. The connection between "anybody" and "Curly" is already provided deictically at another level of consciousness in *"a* husband ... restraint".

8. Typical of this novel only is the retreat from phrase-juncture marking (with a comma) after a closing parenthesis.

9. "if not her neck, her ankles"—an hyperbole is here paronomastically refreshed ("to risk one's neck") to produce a quasi-syllepsis (concessive structure linking an abstract or pseudo-concrete to a concrete). The construction, within the sentence, is asyndetic, and the sequence of phrase-junctures is iconic for Mrs Golson's stumbling, and for her attendantly jolted thought.

10. "So" triggers or indexes resumption of full external awareness, and the lexis and phrase-linkage (short words, comma'ed addition) suggest iconically the nature of the motion figurally perceived.

11. "several times ricked an ankle" is *ben trovato,* all the more so as "to rick an ankle" is a perfectly everyday expression; White has not only picked up on the phonological propinquity *risk/rick* (so that the "risk" she fears becomes reality), but also encourages us to imagine Joanie Golson's helplessly uncontrolled gait ("*an* ankle", not "*her* ankle"—she is no longer aware which one, because both are repeatedly subjected to pain).

12. "in her rush to humiliate herself"—White conjoins polysemically in "rush" Mrs Golson's humiliating (because unladylike) physical flight and the mental precipitation this makes her think of.

13. The discourse-marker "perhaps" is awkwardly placed (being attracted to "in their eyes"), with no formal marking of parenthetical status. The "intention" imagined by Mrs Golson is thereby checked mentally.

14. The atactic closing sentence signifies and enacts the character's sudden awareness of completion (arrival). The *do*-proform coheres loosely with the preceding, resistance-filled statements, conveying emotional relief.

Most of these points can serve as springboards for consideration of other instances of the phenomenon noted, or of other phenomena which belong to the stylistic and discoursal sub-systems concerned.

1. SPEECH–TAGS. Although "he muttered" is itself unexceptional, its periphery has clearly undergone Whitean treatment. The broad area of tagging-procedure has the same configuration as in *The Solid Mandala*. Intrasentential tags and crypto-tags can break and mark the tonal juncture of direct speech. In the following, corrective epanorthosis is inserted:

"I've never gathered," she gasped, no, her corset wheezed, "your husband's profession—that is," she said, "if he had one before he retired." (88)

Other comma'ed crypto-tags include (from the same page): "her head was still bent above her operations" (intrasentential); "Madame Vatatzes seemed to gnash her strong white teeth" (initial-terminal). See also "But paused" (intersentential, stopped medial, atactic crypto-tag, 134); "Kitty sounded most vehement" (306); "giggled" (134), "mumbled" (148). There is the characteristic stretching of semantic-syntactic tolerances ("Mrs Golson contributed, and added,", 101; "'Oh,' she withdrew into her chair", 153; "before venturing breathlessly to hope,", 104; "Mrs Golson told,", 366). Serious play may be made with tagging-redundancy ("'My dear, I quite forgot,' she remembered", 89), or with nineteenth-century nominal-copula tagging conventions ("was Mildred's breathless suggestion", 150). A long initial tag, with much phrasal left-branching, may serve to indicate psychological preparation for a speech-act (151). Initial speech-tags in this novel are "de-psychologized" or de-intensified, a comma being used instead of an annunciatory colon as is the practice in White's other novels, in keeping with a renewed emphasis on the automatism of social conversation.

   2. MODALITY, ETC. There are structures already familiar from the other novels which convey pseudo-concessive/conditional mental shifts:

If Prowse didn't reply, it was because she was leading him out of the room. (290)
If he was less dishonest than the regulars, it was because his unconscious reasons for disguising the truth were usually pure. (416)
If the river appeared at first sight hostile, it was through the transience of its coursing waters .... (179)
If Prowse's confidence touched Eddie, it could have been in the light of his own contemplated defections .... (187)

Main-clause completion is often non-causal ("If she thought better of the hand-play, she continued to feel extraordinarily daring", 82; see also 81/170/210/221/305/337/363). Typical, too, are if–constructions of forestalled desire or shifted perception and introspective cognition with perfective might–modals (eg, "She might have replied if, in her memory, she had not still been driving up the rutted road beyond St Mayeul", 15; "He might have enjoyed that more if he hadn't felt moved to ask:", 270; see also 88/91/113/116/136–37/150/191/223/256/264–65/276/290/321 twice/399). Defeated desire is encoded in analogous constructions (eg, "She would have liked to let off a firework in his face, but as she did not have one at hand, she replied dully,", 112; see also 114–15/292), as is change of perceptual awareness through external agency (eg, "If it hadn't been for the baby's scream, silence would have descended on a landscape ...", 277; see also 169).

   The do–proform is infrequent, but is applied effectively (eg, "He did look at her at last", 368; "Spring did take over at last", 247—with "the climate", its nearest, barely explicit coreferent, six pages earlier, 241).

   3. NAMING–GRADIENTS. As in *The Solid Mandala,* naming-gradients convey the character's degree of self-awareness when the predication is self-referential, and the perceiving character's appraisal of the person observed when predications are externally oriented. On page 93, for example, naming is

informal ("Joanie") when Joan Golson is propinquitous to her husband, then formal ("Mrs Golson") for her appearance in public when her consciousness of self is relativized towards an environment lacking intimacy; finally, pronominal reference replaces naming for phases of inward reflection. In a scene in which she must act as self-conscious hostess to Eudoxia and Angelos Vatatzes (101), the naming is formal ("Mrs Golson"), then neutral ("Joan Golson") in a paragraph of introspection leading away from free indirect discourse ("Poor Curly!"); "Joanie" or "to her" would have taken her too far away from half-awareness of her "formal" role.

The reflector- or focalizer-figure can be the main protagonist, Eddie Twyborn (285), the object of perception Don Prowse, who is giving orders to the men and is thus perceived in his (assumed) public role. For this role, he has adjusted his appearance, so is perceived thus: "Mr Prowse shaved regularly now"; when Eddie looks at Prowse's shaven skin, personal (and interpersonal) reaction is encoded: "Don would lower his eyes on finding himself scrutinized" (ie, by Eddie, whom he has sodomized, and who has thereby been forced into seeing him "on first-name terms"). That the scrutiny is performed in an ambience where it is detectable is suggested by full naming of the focalizer ("Eddie Twyborn", not "Eddie", which would suggest no psychological tension and would have shifted focalization to Prowse; pronoun-reference is systemically impossible here). There is a further remove of actant-(self)identification in this passage: the observing consciousness is twice referred to as "the jackeroo". This is a role-identification by Eddie which accords with his assumptions about the way he is being perceived by the other station-workers and/or by Don Prowse in his administrative role (cf "that boy" in *The Solid Mandala)*.

Such impersonal role-identification can occur in passages of free indirect discourse ("mother and son", 153; "the defendant", 156; neither of these is in character-external focalization). The whole novel turns on the enigma of sexual identity, and there is "genetic" parallelism in the names (Eudoxia—Eddie—Eadith; Edward; Eadie)—so that the full name or Christian name is often foregrounded (sometimes for covert polysemous riddling: "Doxy"; sometimes as a pet-expression encrypting the implosion of identities: "'E.'" as Angelos's form of address to Eudoxia). In Part Three especially, where it is in the interests of the narrative that the reader be persuaded to "believe" suspensively that Eadith Trist is psychologically a woman, there is a great increase in the frequency of pronominal reference (often anaphorically: eg, 311).

4. PUNCTUATION. Parentheses often take this form:

... at the ramshackle gate, Curly cap in hand, wearing the smile he usually adopted for foreigners (because you couldn't accept that the Greek's wife had anything Australian) Joanie adjusting the gossamer ... (111)

The effect of ")" without a comma is to make the bracket do double duty. As this is linguistically "illogical" (and "irregular"; hence the disapproval of Wolfe 1983:215: "parentheses will make him forget rules of punctuation"), we are persuaded to infer that there is a representation here of "mental flow" across such boundaries. Parenthetical statements are made less susceptible to being construed as implied-auctorial in origin (it is well known now that classic stream of consciousness foregrounds discoursal/mental fluidity by underdetermining formal phrase markings). *The Twyborn Affair* has a highly conspicuous amount of formally parenthetical diegesis with punctuative de-emphasis at phrase-junctures (see also 17/21/73/90/100/118 for other examples). The parenthetical technique in general—apart from the above examples, parentheses usually occur at the end of a paragraph or in the form of a separate paragraph—is foregrounded, not for the conventional purpose of auctorial comment, but to convey the sense of the casually speculative consciousness functioning at more than one level of self-evaluativeness. Even in respect of punctuation, however, there are differences: Part Three *always* signals close of parentheses *and* comma-juncture where phrasal constituents are clearly discrete (eg, 323/377), whereas the other sections obey the principle of erasure analysed above. This difference reflects the (narratively) crucial need for Eadith Trist to exercise precise control over self and its social extension.

Relative-clause pointing , as elsewhere in White, is deviant, with its customary mixture of an initial reluctance to separate individual yet closely associated percepts, and occasional punctuative concession to division at the end of parentheses (in the following examples, the "missing" comma is marked by ˆ):

Mrs Edmonds ˆ who was waiting on them ˆ smiled ... (216)
... brick ˆ which might have been reduced to a sullen ruby, seemed ... (319)
While Thatcher ˆ who took the dogs for walks, ... stank ... (151)
He stood mopping his high forehead ˆ on which sweat was glistening. (101) .

5. MEIOSIS AND INDETERMINACY. The phrasal *if*-construction is frequent in *The Twyborn Affair* (and in the other fiction) as a discourse-marker (eg, "—if not melting", 111; "if not with moths, with mutton chops", 198; "if not in time, in experience", 281), as are other downtoners and figurally meiotic formulae (eg, "(or) at least", 13/18/112/133/149/ 229/305; "not to say", as in "fascinated, not to say awed", 135, 188; "meekly enough", 92). Subjective markers of figural, indeterminate perception and cognition are also frequent (eg, "perhaps", 89/133/230/306; "as though", 89; *seem/appear*-indices, 81/85; perfective *must/could be,* 85/180). These are standard Whitean techniques for projecting the process of evaluation in figural consciousness; but the author can also introduce the careful syntax of a parodically Jamesian style to convey Mrs Golson's self-consciousness (82–83), and "the bright colours of retrospect" can be conveyed in a ten-line sentence of straightforward phrasal sequencing (222).

A step up from phrasal qualification and simple juxtaposition is represented by the frequent patternings of indeterminacy or bifurcation:

... snorted ... either in surprise, or out of contempt. (227)
Some of their progress ... humiliating ... some of it comforting. (227)
dreaming, or thinking. (272)
an animal acquiescence ... on the other hand ... a less passive drizzle. (280)
brave or proud enough. (305)
the book he had been, or intended, reading. (135)

6. SYLLEPSIS. The dualism suggested above is found in its fully developed form in sylleptic or quasi-sylleptic constructions:

all pallor and resentment (188)
numbed by exhaustion and the situation (188)
chattering with cold, black mutton, and retrospect (188)
... his eyes to smart from the wind, and a little from humiliation (193)
For Sunday afternoon and the land which was hers, she was shabbily dressed (224)
She had bound her head for the journey, and perhaps country abandonment, in a chiffon scarf (270)
a mystery of silence and the wood-smoke of stale hyacinth perfume (226)
glancing in and out of the Winterbotham mirrors and between the bars of the hired music (264)
the menace invariably concealed in landscape and time (17)
had decamped to their beds with hot-water bottles ... and indigestion (125)
fluctuating ... in ... the mottled glass, as well as in his own mind (171–72)
in the luminous dark and his half-asleep he saw ... (172)

7. *SO (THAT)*–SENTENCES. This cohesive device is as frequently employed as in *The Solid Mandala* for conveying figural apperception of sub-causal continuity (eg, 92/100/106/111/ 113/121/127/164/180/193/263).

8. ATAXIS. Ataxis of figural consciousness forms the skeletal structure of the whole narrative, though the density of occurrence is not so great as in other novels by White. Figural consciousness is less strongly and persistently reactive and caught up in emotional extremity than in, say, Waldo's narrative in *The Solid Mandala*: there is more of a feeling of the foreordained, of the calm security with which sexual roles are fulfilled, in *The Twyborn Affair*. The tensest occurrences of ataxis in Eddie Twyborn's section coincide with his encounters with his father and mother. Otherwise, the most harried and nervous ataxis accompanies the appearances, in Part One, of Joanie Golson, cut loose from her Australian roots, set adrift on the Riviera, succumbing to her fascination with the Vatatzes couple. As in other novels, ataxis may be grammatically "light", but frequently with paragraphic isolation (marked by §):

§ After which they both fell silent. § Till Mrs Golson asked, ... (81)
§ When suddenly ... (81)
§ But they were off again (85)
$ For Madame Vatatzes seemed ... (87)
§ While Joanie Golson had crimped her face ... (87; cf 63/104/151)
§ But seemed .... And smiled ... (100; cf 87/111/147)

It may be used to convey retrospective thought-fragments (92/211), and may be "heavy":

§ Hypocritically. When I ... (63)
$ She must restrain herself. But didn't (66, with free-indirect modal)
§ Gulping. Biting. ... Which ... (85)
§ Before writing, ... (127)
§ Yet hesitated before beginning ... (127)

Cf also Eddie's fall from a horse (202), the activity in the bordello (326–27), and similar syntactic scoring of physical and mental process (eg, 106/113/116/ 134/236/264/284/310).

OTHER OBSERVATIONS

Free indirect discourse and other indices to figural consciousness are a constant presence throughout the novel. These may be contextually inferable, rather than formal, features, where the reader is forced to determine a consonance of voicing and perspective—direct, unadorned declaratives with psychological verbs to iconicize an immediate surge of emotion, whereby the effect is often ironically bivocal (eg, "Mrs Golson loved her", 86); hyperboles for the subjective exacerbation of simple negative emotion (eg, "cowering ... Mrs Golson quailed ... the terror in her bones", 88; "entrails", 100; "his nose looked alarming", 100); quotation-marks placed around locutions which figural consciousnesses wish to dissociate themselves from (eg, 153), Landscape metaphor can be made to encode snatches of talk and visual impressions recollected by a character half-mesmerized by a night-drive home after a party:

Then they were driving down the moonlit *clefts,* between the stereoscopic *buttocks* of hills, amongst the lazy *tatting* of *antique* trees. (268)

There is a fine example of slipping between free indirect discourse and consonant psychonarration, including the free-indirect use of full naming for role-consciousness (89–91), another with free-indirect *ought/might* (92); see also 153 *(infra)*, 155ff and 236 (with shifting between "you" and "he"). There are, too, conspicuously "conservative" or Woolfian forms of free indirect discourse which are applied to the mental discourse of conservatively libidinous Joan Golson (eg, free indirect discourse with reported-speech markings and a question mark, 81; cf also 121).

Generally, however, psychologized discourse employs the more radical cohesion-features developed specifically by White. There are, of course, many conventional proximal deictics (eg, "*This* afternoon, Mrs Golson felt ...", 83; "*here* it was", 98), but most deixis is based on extremes of modulation. One good example of subjective gradation (96–98): "the terrace table, its marble permanently stained" > "the terrace table" > "Angelos now crying, his head on *a* stained table" > "*this* hateful marble table"; cf also "*this* rather angular, flat-chested young woman" (125) or "*that* voracious smile" (149). Deixis may serve an oneiric function, as when Eddie Twyborn dozes off, thinking (or dreaming) of "*this* great eagle" (136–37). There is no prior coreferent for either the deictic or the bird mentioned (ie, as far as Eddie's "closed" narrative is concerned), and we have to infer from oblique reference to the Byzantine *aquila*–symbol in young Eudoxia's prior narrative that Eddie Twyborn is dreaming of his/her aged lover Angelos (further: Eddie wakes from his dream of grief "like a limp puppy", and later explicitly remembers Angelos for the first time as "like some old mangy, cancerous dog", 151).

Subjectively familiar article-deixis ("to rummage in her bag ... to take out *the* shagreen engagement book", 87) alternates with subjective obliquity of reference to the known ("calm except for the action of *a* furtive heart", 89; "as gilt-edged as *a* love she had always hoped for", 89; cf "*a* husband" above). Self-alienating or projective deixis is common ("Passing a wall-mirror in the hall he saw reflected ... *this figure* in *the* plaited hat", 94—tension between estrangement from the human image, identification with the object that produces the estrangement; "the Judge was informing *a* visitor" and "*a* soldier son", 157—Eddie experiencing his father's impersonal connection with him; "*this* jackeroo of theirs", 264; "It made Ursula glance at *this* grotesque creature", 359—where Eadith's following direct speech endorses her registration of what she experiences as Ursula's impression of her). Indeterminate *it*-deixis for cohesion of subjective reaction and speech or thought is frequent (eg, 151/152/254; sometimes with subversion of stock collocations for sexual guilt: eg, "caught her at it", 102; or with the tonality of cynical familiarity: eg, "Two young women were at it by the rail", 133).

As in all his novels (eg, *The Tree of Man*, p. 259, *Riders in the Chariot*, pp. 468/472/486, *The Vivisector*, p. 278, *The Solid Mandala, passim*), subjectively oblique cognizance of unspecified but (implicitly) sharply registered ambient conditions is conveyed by the cohesive expression "in the circumstances" and its elaborations (eg, 11/99/120/147–48/157/361/392/402) or "the situation" and its variants (eg, 101/109/147–48/168/223/240). White's conjectural modals and modals of externally apperceived potentiality are always markers of the characters' mental processes ("She might have regretted their coming", 263; "The younger woman spoke with a huskiness which might have masked the sulks", 84; cf also "could have", 78; 101). Elsewhere, the modality is reflexive, and is frequently cut loose from aspectuality (eg, perfective *might:* 17/102/186; non-perfective *might:* 101/102/115/224). Aspectuality is, of course, typically erased with certain free-indirect-discourse modals of subjective resolve (eg, "She must restrain herself", 66; 120). Apart from modals, aspectuality (continuous present; perfective) plays its usual prominent role in the conveying of planes of subjective awareness, and occurrences of the gnomic present are signs of figural consciousness, whether or not they are embedded in formal free indirect discourse.[1]

I have a few more observations to make on general features of narrative in *The Twyborn Affair,* but with reference to particular passages in the text. White

---

[1] Continuous-form aspectuality: "She was looking at her watch", 16; "Madame Vatatzes was following ...", 82; "the violinist was snatching ...", 85; "Her eyes were appealing to him", 152; "She was sitting forward .... She was looking ...", 153; "They were driving .... They were arriving", 270; "Curly Golson was getting out", 93—which is completed by an atactic "When" speech-tag for decision after delayed perception). The perfective aspect: "Madame Vatatzes had found what she was looking for", 86; "She had lapsed into a mystery of silence", 226; "While Miss Clitheroe had begun a recitative", 47—breaking atactically into formal free indirect discourse). Clear instances of gnomic-present embedding: "you can feel most foreign where you think you understand the language and don't" (89–90); "No! There are wounds enough without the diaries; the wax effigies of lovers are stuck with countless pins" (94); "Wives are more matter-of-fact" (118). Compare especially, among many others: "Reason is the most unstable craft, as Mrs Golson was learning" (71); "Today she suspected that fate is symmetrical" (88); "Before the two women could go to her, to initiate her into the formal grief it is usual for widows to indulge in" (126). (See also 157—on Eddie's hairbrushes; 164—figural, for stereotyped activity; 133/146/211/226/249/291–92/311.)

has provided an intertextuality which responds ironically to those critics who have mistakenly condemned him for auctorial intrusion. When Joan Golson goes to the English lending-library on the Riviera to exchange her "Hall Caine" for an Edith Wharton "long coveted but never secured" (45), White incorporates into the diegesis narrative markers for the discourse-style of light romance, with all the trappings of a firm relationship between auctorial voice and reader (or, perhaps, narratee): quotation marks around adjectives; reports of what characters did not think or say (cf Rimmon–Kenan 1983:98 on degrees of narratorial perceptibility): "Far too much had happened today; little did she know that more was to happen" (46); or (together with an auctorially evaluative epithet): "She did not know, poor thing, that others ... had experienced the same terror" (46).

I don't think this irruption of an alien narrative technique is fortuitous, and believe it to be intimately bound up with the implications offered by the two writers Mrs Golson has read or would like to read. The book she gives back is likely to be the latest novel by Sir Hall Caine, an enormously popular writer of conscientiously but crudely plotted and technically conventional late-Victorian novels featuring a sentimental, moralistic tone and sharp, melodramatic conflicts between shallowly sketched, romantic characters. This is the style that bleeds into *The Twyborn Affair* at this moment, the style Joan Golson leaves behind. It would be tempting, but unproductive, to assume that her reading-tastes are homogeneous, and that the kind of Edith Wharton she will be looking for is that of certain of the short stories, where the conduct of the sexes foreshadows the soap-opera conventions of later years and different cultural circumstances. But this side of Wharton is marginal, subsidiary, negligible. White is, rather, pointing Joanie off in a quite different direction from Caine: away from the manipulative narrativity and melodrama which many critics have professed to detect in White, and towards the work of a truly kindred soul.[2] The mention of Wharton is counter-assertive, an indicator of what White thought was a true affinity with the narrative personality of his own work.

The parodistic light-romance convention of "little did she know" does not find discreet transformation into the more elevated Proustian form of prolepsis, which is much less frequent in *The Twyborn Affair* than in White's other novels: the threefold *historia* of bisexuality is structured on the revelations of analepsis. There is one advance mention, very oblique, to Eddie Twyborn's future stay (evidently already planned by him) with the Lushingtons ("their son remarked, to take an interest in a world which was shortly to include himself", 170), which is then oneirically confirmed in a sexual image (172). But the mocking of conventions of "knowing" is continued elsewhere. A longish stretch of zero-tagged dialogue (and *The Twyborn Affair* has more longish passages of untagged, fully "scenic" dialogue than the other novels: eg, 57) between Joanie and Curly Golson is "prepared" by the initial sentence of the narrative subsection: "The

---

[2] Aside from the pleasure of onomastic correspondence (another Edith in the book), White incorporates Wharton into the novel because she had a château at Hyères, which was frequented by rich Australians and which forms part of the basis for the St Mayeul of *The Twyborn Affair* (cf Marr 1991:566–67).

Golsons did not investigate each other, unless surreptitiously, till the following morning" (56). The next half-page shuttles between alternate external views of the other partner, culminating (after Joanie's perception: "His lips looked quite revolting under the blandishment of fat ham") in a situationally undercutting sentence which has Curly identifying his wife in her "publicly" uxorial role: "Mrs Golson's pout had a chocolate stain in one corner; she could not know about that, only the dob of chocolate on the bosom of her négligée, with which she was now trying to deal". The dallying with "knowing"-conventions also occurs in the scene with the kiosk-owner M. Pelletier, where there is parodistic inconsistency, as in cheap romantic fiction (italicized French words for local colour; "the narrow strip of grit referred to in Les Sailles as *plage"* versus "this village which the more ambitious inhabitants liked to call a 'town'", 72–73). Compare also: "Joan Golson was not at first aware of music" (17), "Mrs Golson did not even pause to wonder at her own courage" (89), or "He could not have accounted for it, or not immediately" (91)—which, of course, tips back into figural reflection and is therefore a trick. There is play with Joanie's assumptions in free indirect discourse ("He could not understand that so much ... depended on it", 93), which are then auctorially deflated ("What she could not have understood was that Ange despised her"). I mentioned earlier that it is "conventional" free indirect discourse that is associated with Joanie Golson; she, and she alone, is made the victim of Jamesian epithets ("the unfortunate Mrs Golson", 81; "poor Joanie was thoroughly flabbergasted", 88). This technique, exercised so lavishly and conspicuously on a Jamesian "reflector"-character, serves to highlight the absolute interiority in the representation of the sovereignly aware central character(s), Eudoxia/Eddie/Eadith, and also serves (because of the status of the sexual secret of the narrative) to make her a *blinded* reflector of pure surface (which, of course, is otherwise inaccessible to us).

Unusual in White is the excursion into "first-person" narrative in Part One, in the form of Eudoxia Vatatzes' journal, which allows a further refinement of the techniques of quoted and interior monologue at one (intradiegetic) remove from immediate thought. Interesting in the first entry (22–32) are the subjective fluctuations of tense, and the first of several transpositions of recollected interpersonal experience into the purely "mimetic" or scenic form of play-dialogue with stage-directions: perhaps another joke by White (this time intratextual), in response to those critics who have complained that his urge to interpret is at war with his dramatic gift (see also 122–24 and, as Eddie Twyborn, 143–46).

The most remarkable instances of oblique character-identification (at the opposite extreme from Eudoxia's journal on the one hand, and the objectivity of play-dialogue on the other) occur in a passage where "they", then "she" and "him", then "the old man" and "his companion"/"the young woman" are on board a train after what is cryptically referred to as "the haste of departure" (116ff). Only the direct-speech vocative "'E!'" and, eventually, two Greek names in conversation give us a hint that these two are the Vatatzes couple. There is a later mention of Byzantium and "the Australian hetaira" (120); then the "young

woman" mentions "'a lady ... who was a subscriber at Miss Clitheroe's library at
St Mayeul'" (120)—the latter is clearly Joan Golson. But only on the last page of
the section do we learn (in French) that these two people are Eudoxia and the
now ailing Angelos (121). Even more unnervingly, there is a first-ever reference
to *"the* widow" (118): we search for prior descriptive identification, but find
none. What we do notice, however, is that reference is not now to "the old man"
but to "the old fellow"; further references to "the widow" follow, and the
diegesis becomes more speculative in respect of what is perceived. Suddenly we
realize that the controlling perspective up to the widow's departure from the
train, and from the middle of page 117 onwards, has been that of the widow
herself, and that this woman has been encoded amidst the earlier Vatatzes–
perspective in this sentence:

in one instance, gobbets of truffled *pâté de foie* conveyed by fingers as refined as the bread on
which the stuff lay, the flesh dimpling with a diamond or two, the bosom on which the crumbs
tumbled as black as the inlay of truffle itself. [underlining my emphasis]

Why is it that, before this, Eudoxia's focal perspective is so distantly identified as
"the young woman"? Because (for a start) "she" is not a young "woman" but a
man, and is projecting (or the discourse is projecting) her anonymous and sexual
status as perceived by the other passengers. The thematic essence of concealment
has found its way into the narrative discourse itself.

The play with the fictive is most noticeable in the appearance of M. Pelletier,
who is principally "there"—inserted without introductory preliminaries into a
subsection (71–76)—in order to provide a reflector-position for Eudoxia's solitary
morning swim, and for the reappearance of Madame Réboa, last heard of as the
"dreadful mother of the weeping ulcer" (26), whose daughter, the defecting maid
Joséphine, may (speculates Eudoxia) be "something of a whore" (60). It turns out
that Pelletier has had a relationship with Violette Réboa, "inspired by lust"; and
an unattributable parenthesis reports his wife's emphatic denial that Joséphine is
the product of this union. An earlier parenthesis blends in a temporally parallel
description of Joan Golson—clear auctorial manipulation, and a further signal that
the kind of "intrusive" discourse associated with Joan can also jokingly include
her even when she is absent from the scene narrated. Pelletier's as yet unclarified
function is teasingly topicalized in references to his *"raison d'être"* (itself a
language-joke mocking "local colour"), and in the perspectival play of: "It was
natural enough at this hour of morning that Monsieur Pelletier should see himself
and his iron kiosk of salt-eroded shutters as the focal point of all existence". This
is set off against: "There was no real reason why Monsieur Pelletier should
exist" (71). If we have begun to suspect (on a second reading) that the *raison
d'être* of M. Pelletier is his narrative function, this is then undercut psychonarrationally, making it clear that these have been his thoughts: "At times, at
dawn in particular, outside his kiosk, this was what he suspected". Upon which,
the Golson–parenthesis gives way to open manipulation:

Monsieur Pelletier and Mrs Golson had not met at any point; they would not want to meet;
they did not credit each other with existence.

It was only in the figure now clambering down over rocks, that the two might have agreed to converge. (72)

After some masterly seascape-description (and the depiction of natural setting—often with a transforming shift to the lexis of the visual arts—is one of the most deeply satisfying proofs in this novel of White's continued supremacy as a conveyor of tactile, visual and kinetic values), the scene begins to concentrate on "the equivocal nature" of what is seen.

"The stranger ... a man or a woman" is an indeterminacy replaced ultimately by willed conviction (74), and Pelletier, having decided that the figure is a woman's, masturbates. This act is obliquely foregrounded by a narratorially distanced, collusive, gnomic comment, drawing in the reader as narratee ("so hopeful yet so suicidal, as indeed we all are, in our sea of dreams", 74), which subverts the idea of the wet dream. Mocking auctorial perceptibility is evident in the sentence: "Strangely, it did not occur to Aristide Pelletier that the emotions the swimmer aroused in him might have been occasioned by lust" (76). "What could have remained a sordid ejaculation" is expanded to encompass all desire; and M. Pelletier quits the narrative forever, having served his purpose, hurrying to save the coffee "boiling over in a series of expostulatory ejaculations" (76). The "figure" in the water, Madame Réboa tells him, is the mad Englishwoman, wife/woman (as the conversation is in French, the relationship is suitably indefinite) of the mad Greek; she is thus at last identifiable by us as Eudoxia. At the end, however, this "figure" remains "the anonymous being" whom Pelletier "had forgotten". The marvellous feature of the episode is that we are so drawn into the enigma of the swimmer's (sexual) identity, then so deflected from considering this "equivocality" by the erasing presence of M. Pelletier's own sexuality, that only much later do we realize that Eudoxia Vatatzes *is* a man, and not a woman.

II   Style, discourse and critical performance

Examination of *The Solid Mandala* and *The Twyborn Affair* has shown how closely the reader must attend to the characteristic detail and patterning of style-features in gauging the shifting vectors of the narrative discourse. The closing comments on *The Twyborn Affair* have also indicated, paradoxically, that it is only against the assumption of psychologized narrative that we can properly judge the efficacy and intentionality of those few occasions on which White overtly manipulates the conventions of auctorial omniscience. After the discussion of narrative wholes, I now wish in this section to regress by considering fragments—namely, by discussing the views of individual passages in *The Tree of Man* and *Riders in the Chariot* that have been offered by other critics. These may be more extensive interpretations or perilously brief judgements. I shall argue that these critical evaluations are based on fundamental misperceptions of White's language as it functions in its situational context, and shall conclude by discussing briefly the degree to which parodies of White reflect perception or misperception.

THE TREE OF MAN

At least three critics have commented on a particular sentence towards the end of *The Tree of Man*. Their comments on what they find to be White's auctorial intrusiveness and "telling" are instructive. Here is the whole passage, with the paragraphs numbered for reference:

(1) After he had gone and the tracts were flapping and plapping in the undergrowth, and the black dog had smelled one with the tip of his dry nose, the old man continued to stare at the jewel of spittle. A great tenderness of understanding rose in his chest. Even the most obscure, the most sickening incidents of his life were clear. In that light. How long will they leave me like this, he wondered, in peace and understanding?

(2) But his wife had to come presently.

(3) "Stan," she said, approaching, he knew it was she, crunching over the grass with her bad leg, "you will not believe when I tell you," she said, "I was scratching round the shack, in the weed, where the rosebush was that we moved to the house, the old white rose, and what did I find, Stan, but the little silver nutmeg grater that Mrs Erbey gave me on our wedding day. Look."

(4) "Ah," he said.

(5) What was this irrelevant thing? He had forgotten.

(6) Branches of shadow were drifting across his face, interfering with his sight. The scent of violets was a cold blur.

(7) "When we always accused that fellow who was selling the magnetical water," Amy Parker said.

(8) Her face was quite pleased. She was herself bad enough to expect the worst in others. Yet sometimes, if seldom, man is exonerated.

(9) "Of course," she said, "it is all discoloured, and quite useless. Though we never did use it," she said.

(10) She was going away, but came back, and took his hands as if they had been inanimate objects, and looked into his face, and said, "Is there anything you want, Stan?"

(11) "No," he said.

(12) What could she have given him?

(13) She herself began to suspect this. She went away, wandering through the garden in search of an occupation.

(14) Exquisitely cold blue shadows began to fall through the shiny leaves of the trees. Some boulders that had been let lie in the garden all those years, either because they were too heavy to move or, more likely, because nobody had thought about them, assumed enormous proportions in the heavy bronze light. There was, on the one hand, a loosing and dissolving of shapes, on the other, a looming of mineral splendours.

(15) Stan Parker began to go then. To walk. Though his hip was stiff.

(16) I believe in this leaf, he laughed, stabbing at it with his stick.

(17) The winter dog's dusty plume of tail dragged after the old man, who walked slowly, looking at the incredible objects of the earth, or at the intangible blaze of sunlight. It was in his eyes now.

(18) When he had reached the side of the house on which the shrubby, gnarled honeysuckle had grown too big, and had reached over, and was scratching the side of the house, his wife was standing on the step.

(19) "What is it, Stan?" she asked.

(20) Her face was afraid.

(21) I believe, he said, in the cracks in the path. On which ants were massing, struggling up over an escarpment. But struggling. Like the painful sun in the icy sky. Whirling and whirling. But struggling. But joyful. So much so, he was trembling. The sky was blurred now. As he stood waiting for the flesh to be loosened on him, he prayed for greater clarity, and it became obvious as a hand. It was clear that One, and no other figure, is the answer to all sums.

(22) "Stan," cried his wife, because she really was afraid that she had been left behind.

(23) They clung together for a minute on the broken concrete path, their two souls wrestling together. She would have dragged him back if she could, to share her further sentence, which she could not contemplate for that moment, except in terms of solitary confinement. So she was holding him with all the strength of her body and her will. But he was escaping from her.

(24) "Ahhhhhh," she cried when he was lying on the path.

(25) Looking at him.

(26) He could not tell her she would not find it in his face. She was already too far.

(27) "It is all right," he said.

(28) She was holding his head and looking into it some minutes after there was anything left to see. [Penguin, pp. 476–78]

In response to this scene, Lyndon Harries states that "only through the intervention of the author, rather than from any assertion natural to the character he has created", is Stan Parker "able to see the unity of all created things":

White does not ascribe to Stan the crucial words: "One, and no other figure, is the answer to all sums". It is another Delphic utterance, and it is White's, not Parker's. Of him the author writes earlier in the book: "He did not feel the necessity to translate his own life into brave words. His life as lived was enough". And so at the end of the book the author speaks for him, and thereby has typical recourse to verbal expansion of meaning beyond what the characters or the events permit. On this point, at least, one feels that Parker would have rejected his author as readily as he appears to reject God. [Harries 1978:462–63]

About the sentence which Harries quotes (at the end of paragraph 21 above), Walter Havighurst has this to say:

In portraying this limited man Mr. White commits just one sentimentality. In the hour of his death—an old man amid the withered autumn grass—a great understanding comes to him, which for a moment he was able to share with his wife .... This mystical awareness comes as an unlikely crown to Stan Parker's groping life. [Havighurst 1955:12]

Leonie Kramer takes the sentence concerned as "White's assertion at this point", an assertion which "shows up a weakness" in the conveying of Stan's "dying revelation". "The only way in which White can make his point about wholeness and oneness is by stating it himself"—without, however, validating it "in terms of Stan's actual experience" (Kramer 1974:270).

It should be pointed out right away that the reader has already learned that Stan will die. There are two relevant prolepses: one retrospectively, in the form of a message about Stan's death, received by his daughter Thelma; one in the form of a framing preliminary adverbial ("The day Stan Parker died"), which establishes the course of events on that day. Moreover, there is an analepsis to an earlier day, when Stan has a stroke and falls to the ground in the garden; the result of this is that he must support himself with a stick. All these details about physical circumstance are important for the way we read the scene in which the sentence concerned is embedded.

The crucial questions are: whether this "experience" of Stan's is "mystical" in narrative terms; whether it, too, might not be an "actual experience"; and whether the sentence concerned is really an auctorial utterance speaking for the "inarticulate" Stan Parker. As an old man, Stan has for some time now been preoccupied with the approach of death. An earlier scene, where he is almost killed when his rifle goes off, is preceded by a visit to a performance of *Hamlet,* where he finds thematized his wife Amy's adultery and the dramatic inevitability of death. As in the present scene, there is a subsidence or implosion of awareness into the self, and a shrinking, and altering of the real proportions, of visual data. In both episodes, Stan's perception is at one point fixed on the movement of ants (see above, para. 21)—not, as in Stephen Crane's *The Red Badge of Courage,* as a naturalistic metaphor reducing soldiers' movements on the battlefield to a kind of deterministic Brownian motion, but as a correlative of reduced yet intensified psychological (ie, not philosophical) perception. It is true that the earlier passage quoted by Harries is psychonarrative—but it is impossible to tell from "He did not feel" whether focalization is dissonant (the negation representing a "telling" of a behavioural fact not accessible to an unreflecting Stan) or consonant (the negation representing Stan's own awareness of "brave words" as a translation— for *others*—of the self as the sum of personal experience). Stan is, at any rate, represented there as moving within a social ambience, in which (we can infer) his awareness includes registering the social actions of others as verbal articulation of self. At the end, however, Stan's experience is personal, private, immediate, psychological, and *physical*. An examination of the whole passage from which Harries tears his *part*-sentence reveals that Stan not only has a stroke, but is in the throes of having one. Throughout (including the two sequential lead-in scenes with the bible-literature man and with Amy and the rediscovered nutmeg grater), there is a covert foregrounding of (a) thought and its articulation (in speech and in interiorized "speech") and of (b) the coming-together of disparate domains of experience (or, more cautiously, of the epistemologically accessible and the ontologically entertainable; and of the concrete and the abstract—the latter being the red light we need to concentrate on).

Let us stick to the paragraphs (18–21) culminating in the gnomic sentence, before examining the surrounding diegesis that informs it. "When he had reached" imputes intention to Stan's actions; the relating of the honeysuckle to the house-wall has an inconsequentiality about it: a percept casually framed in time and memory. The sentence is suspended—by the initial array of subordinations, by the embedding, by the re-use of "reached" with "over", by the asyndetic progressive "was scratching". The latter, too, withholds motive at the same time as it ambiguates intention. With the verb, we normally expect the instrument of the human hand to be involved, but the repetition of "the side of the house" allies the "gnarled honeysuckle" with the (gnarled) body of Stan, scratching against the house involuntarily as he collapses against it, his fingers finding their way to the wall for support, feebly, in his phase of sensory beclouding. Stan · only now notices his wife. Her direct-speech question is redundantly tagged because he is dully aware that his ambiguous posture has occasioned it (if he were sharply aware of what she said, White's direct speech would be typically "scenic" or untagged), just as his awareness of her facial expression is conveyed by separate paragraphing. Stan does not *say* anything (there are no quotation-marks); nor need he articulate his "belief" inwardly. The sentence is radically equivocal. The "tag" splits the sentence, leaving an inchoate yet affirmative "I believe" (the surge of self, or consciousness) on one side, and a perceptual localization of Stan *in* "the cracks in the path" on the other; it is to this that his narrowed vision momentarily pulls his whole self down. The next, atactic, sentence, with its magnification of a crack to an "escarpment", justifies this narrowing in the form of a percept, not a philosophically humanizing metaphor. The continued ataxis indicates Stan's efforts to keep control of his failing, transformed perception and *physis,* as indexed in the transference implied in "painful" and "blurred". "Struggling" is projected outwards from self onto what is strugglingly perceived (the narrow focus on the ants); and there is a momentary return to the centre of self in "joyful", which relates indiscriminately to ants, sun, and Stan.

White overlays apparently religious diction on Stan's psychophysical experience, as such diction has traditionally been the channel for mediating not only the "spiritual" but also the most intense inscapes of self and all inflowing otherness. What is produced is a kind of cold or dispassionate irony, which has nothing to do with the auctorial translation of "mystical awareness" but a great deal to do with the radical indeterminacy of psychological states. "He was trembling" is linked to "joyful", as though this were an anchorite's bliss. It is not; Stan's trembling is part of the neural-somatic experience of the oncoming stroke. Certainly, he is in a state of heightened consciousness, but it is no more mystical than would be expected in such a physical state. The "intangible blaze of sunlight" was "in his eyes" before (para. 17; pure passive reception, without the implied quotidian awareness of "had blinded him"); then "the painful sun in the icy sky"; then a "blurred" sky. The "clarity" Stan "prays" for is not metaphysical; the sky is blurred which was icy (in winter, not autumn), the sun now banished from view. The feeling that his flesh will "loosen" is entailed by the trembling: the onset of physical dissolution (not the saint's transfigurative disincarnation, but the terminal floating free from *physis)* is indexed by "prayed", which does not have to do with formal, inward articulation but with the struggle of Stan's will against the attenuation of his links with his immediate surroundings.

From the blur of the sky, his perception shifts suddenly downwards to signs of self "at hand". Represented is Stan's experience of personal "eschatology": the compression of time and consciousness into a momentary radiation of concentrated clarity. "I know it like the back of my hand" is creatively subverted via the reduction of an *as ... as* comparative (not *"as* obvious as a hand" but "obvious *in the form of* a hand"). Stan's vision has shrunk to the confines of "a hand", against the wall before him—not sought out, but simply the only object within his purview; not recognized as his own hand, hence all the more powerful an index to his loss of somatic awareness (one's extremities are normally the very least that one can see of one's physical self). The normally complex intercalations of consciousness have been reduced to this simplicity (for us, perhaps, this epitome of his working life)—which is at the same time the onset of the centrifugal flight of consciousness. Stan is, as it were, a black hole into which everything peripheral to him flows. This is not meant in the sense of a conscious operation upon his immediate (or extended) environment, or of a philosophical moment of insight drawing all together. No—it is the experience of *materia* that is already stored in Stan's mind which neets in this moment of simplicity. Why is this gnomic-present sentence (whose preterite beginning attaches it firmly to Stan's mind) so dogmatic in its body, so simplistic in its close? "Sums" is both a reduction of arithmetic to Stan's untutored experiential level *and* an opening-out of the arithmetical into the summary or summarizing or epitomizing sense of *summa*. White has represented here a stock situation of the *ars moriendi* of modern man, but without its moral dimension: the last moment of (apparently) transfigured realization, which is probably inchoate in its preverbal form, but has been seen as a parallel to the transfigurative "insights" we sometimes think we bear back with us into waking reality from the last moment of dreaming. It is no accident that the timeless, gnomic *present* occurs in the last clause.

There has previously been a concentration on the identity between awareness of the self in isolation and the world with which the self interacts—hence Stan's production of the gob of spittle for the evangelist, to show that all the "articulation" on paper and in words about what God is cannot equal Stan's own wordless "articulation" (through the mouth) of God in physical terms he can relate to himself. The gesture may show "perversity", to get rid of an unwelcome visitor; but it is a reduction of the cosmic All to the private One, in utter simplicity. We shouldn't discount the possibility that the weight of sheer experience can bring an old man to a state approaching wisdom: so that an abstract like "illuminated" need not be taken as a superimposition on him of something portentous or cheaply won. Compare (just before the passage quoted above):

> "Don't you believe in God, perhaps?" asked the evangelist, who had begun to look around him and to feel the necessity for some further stimulus of confession. "I can show you books," he yawned.
> Then the old man, who had been cornered long enough, saw, through perversity perhaps, but with his own eyes. He was illuminated.
> He pointed with his stick at the gob of spittle.
> "That is God," he said.
> As it lay glittering intensely and personally on the ground.
> The young man frowned rather. You met all kinds. [Penguin, p. 476]

The gatherings-in of perceptual experience that ensue are the mind's instinctual response to an oncoming change of physical state. Stan is lost within himself—not even Amy's presence can stir him out of self. There is ambiguity in the "branches of shadow ... interfering with his sight" (6), "the scent of violets" a synaesthetic "cold blur" (6)—is Stan's sensorium receiving normal perceptions, or are these perceptions inward in source, signs of physical disarrangement? The aspectuality of "She was going away, but came back" (10) and the additive quality of the coordinate syntax reflect Stan's delayed perception. There is a good deal of poetic continuity in these pages: the evangelist has promised "great glories" "by a putting out of the hand" (the awkward deixis with *a/the* reflecting Stan's attitudinal distance from the gesture); Stan puts out his own hand, clenching his stick, to point at *his* kind of glory; Amy takes "his hands as if they had become inanimate objects" (10)—which is what his hand does become to his perception (21), defamiliarized like the "inanimate objects" of the boulders ("There was, on the one *hand,* a loosing and dissolving of shapes ...", 14, before the "loosening" of his flesh, 21). Removal of self by locomotion ("She was going away", "She went away") tips over, in Stan's case, into an equivocal, near-involuntary removal of self—"began to *go* then", in the sense of quitting the garden and in the sense of a slipping away from full consciousness. Hence the *addition* of the foregrounded, explanatory, atactic "To walk" (15), as Stan instinctively sets out for the *refugium* of the house with the onset of the change of state first signalled by the "tenderness ... in his chest" (1). In such a context, the interiorized laugh and expression of belief are as little performative as the "stabbing" with his stick, which is only part of Stan's lurching, stiff-hipped passage, overlaid by the ambiguous intimations brought by the aura preceding the full impact of his stroke.

The diction associated with Stan is, as I have said, "religious" and, typically for White, replete with *pseudo*-cognitive abstracts that are transpositions of indeterminate mental states relating to concretes. The language associated with Amy—in keeping with the complex emotional state induced in her by awareness of her past infidelity to Stan, by her yearning to possess the Other, and by her sense of Stan's recession into self—is "moral" ("bad", "exonerated", "suspect", "sentence", "solitary confinement", "escape"). When she runs up to Stan, the perspective shifts to her, the expressions "clung together" and "their two souls wrestling together" being projections of her will, not an auctorial endorsement of dual consciousness (cf Havighurst: "which ... he was able to share with his wife"). Stan is not "wrestling" with anything but his own dissolution; he is collapsing in her arms. White steps in *only* where neither consciousness is operative on sense-data. If Stan actually utters the reassuring words attributed to him (27), what precedes (26) is radically bivocal. Amy is seeking reassurance that Stan has not "escaped"; but the lack of a prior coreferent for "it" allows us to see this as Stan's perception of something not only unspecified but also now unspecifiable. Subjectively, it is Stan, too, who is "already too far" (note the withdrawal from the specificity of "too far *away*" or "too far *gone*", which opens the text out into vistas of indeterminacy), just as his wife is fading from his vision. We cannot take his inability to "tell" as an inability to speak (though this would be normal with someone who has suffered a stroke—on the previous occasion, there is no sign that he can speak), as he is represented as speaking. It is, however, tempting to take Stan's words as a massively delusionary construct in Amy's mind, a projection of her will that Stan be still alive—all the more so as the progressive "She was holding his head" is double-edged, allowing the reader to posit simple persistence after the point where there is nothing "left to see" (no sign of life), *and* to posit that Amy "sees" Stan talking to her while she is holding his head (it is not his *face* she is looking into), "some minutes after" death.

The narration is highly complex throughout, intensely duplicitous, and geared wholly to the mediation of an "actual experience" which at no stage requires interpretation in terms of mystical transcendence, of the communion of souls, or of the superaddition of auctorial utterance to compensate for a character's inarticulacy. The view that characters who are "inarticulate" must be spoken for has a great deal to do with the expectation that White's narratives do mediate "character" in the "moral" sense rather than the psychological. What follows from this expectation is a quasi-fundamentalist reliance on the direct referentiality of religious and moral diction: ie, characters are connected with the spiritual/metaphysical and the social, rather than states of consciousness being seen in their relation to *materia*.

The critics' obsession with White as "intrusive narrator" resurfaces in other comments on *The Tree of Man:* eg, White "is unable to let the dialogue alone to do its work. Think of that superb scene in *The Tree of Man* [155–56] when Stan Parker and Ossie Peabody are bargaining over a calf, almost wrecked by the intrusiveness of the narrator" (Green 1973a:402). The dialogue, however perfectly realized in its demotic cadences, is less than the half of it. Dorothy Green wants to reduce the novel to the scenic, and to pure realism: to turn White into some Henry Lawson of the dialogic. The point of the bargaining is that it is a ritual, of whose significance the participants are keenly aware; buyer and seller must be gauged in terms of their personality in order for a transaction to take place. It is the interstices of *figural* analysis of situation and character which determine the course of the dialogic strategy. There are countless indices to self-imaging and free indirect discourse on the two pages to which Green takes exception. I see no narratorial intrusiveness, no wrecking of effect. Quite the contrary: the passages of diegesis are intrinsic to the effect, determining as they do the space, the silence, the deliberation and private reflection, between conversational exchanges. And these exchanges, significantly, are marked by prosaically minimal tagging ("he said/was saying") to indicate the every-day nature of the transaction, or by "scenic" zero-tagging to indicate areas of transactional alertness. There are, it is true, statements about the nature of the characters that seem to extend beyond the perceptions of the moment—but even these are then tied into present feeling. The characters bring their whole history with them into the actional-present moment.

That misprisions of White's narrative discourse are legion can be easily (perhaps even cheaply) illustrated by the way in which A.K. Thomson tries to *defend* the style of *The Tree of Man* against its detractors. He singles out sentence (2) in the following passage, where Thelma's brother Ray is visiting her and her mother, Amy Parker:

(1) When the wood moved in the grate Thelma glowed. (2) She was, after all, pretty, or feverish, holding her neck high, which was too thin certainly, as she sat gathering crumbs with correct fingers.

(3) The mother listened to all those far-off things, eating her comfortable scone, and would have liked to feel comfortable. (4) Do the children take over perhaps?

(5) Ray looked out of the window. (6) He was struggling with a sense of injustice and the cake in his throat. (7) Long whips of vicious rain began to lash the gooseberry bushes, which had never done well in that district, though they continued to try them.

(8) "What'll you do then?" he asked, not yet decided what form his insult, or self-defence, should take. (9) "In your beige dress?"

(10) "Why," she said, flushing, "I shall pass the necessary exams [....] (11) And make something of my life," she added smoothly, taking out her handkerchief, which she had not yet used, and which had been folded into a perfect oblong, to stay in her belt. [Penguin, p. 245]

Thomson observes:

The style [of *The Tree of Man*] has been criticized as being jerky, staccato .... In its context this is an effective and dramatic piece of description. The "gathering crumbs with correct fingers" is a vivid touch indicative of Thelma Parker's character, especially when taken in conjunction with "holding her neck high" and the subtle humour of "which was too thin". [Thomson 1966:23]

The terms of presentation here ("vivid touch", "character", "humour") indicate that Thomson views the "description" as auctorially directed character-depiction; there is no indication of how the "style" is achieved. It may not be clear from this one page that the focalization and voicing not only shift from character to character (3–4 are focalized on Amy, with figural estimation of role-status via "the mother", personal deixis with "all these", figural modality, and quoted monologue in 4; 5–7 are focalized on Ray, the syllepsis compressing a moment of psychical pain, the emotional conditioning the physical), but also concentrates periodically on one character, from the outside, via the consciousness of another. The sentence in question (2) is perspectivally controlled by Ray. Thelma's flesh glows in the firelight: "She was, after all, pretty" is Ray's revised, concessive evaluation (immediately relativized by the perceptual uncertainty expressed by "or feverish"). Two pages back, when he enters the house after a brooding, resentful walk, his subjective vision makes him see his sister differently. Where Thelma had ignored him before, now she lavishes words (about herself!) on him. There is a subjective turn: whereas she had been poised before (despite having grown "thin and ugly"), he now perceives her as edgy and unsettled, without this actually having to be articulated analytically or even reaching Ray's consciousness. The syntax does this for us/him, along with the selection of gestural detail. Sentence (2) is broken so often first because Ray is interpolating concessions and reservations ("which was too thin certainly"—itself awkwardly modified as Ray catches himself overlaying benevolence with criticism), and second because his sister is nervous and self-conscious about talking to her glowering brother, whose personal history (with its self-destructive and rebellious plunge downwards into criminality and low life) contrasts with her own (with its self-preserving and conformist striving upwards into gentility). The self-consciousness becomes clear later, when "feverish" is exposed as "flushing" (10), and where Thelma's effort at poised control is belied by the fidgety sentence with the handkerchief (11). And if we do not accept the suggestion that she gathers crumbs because she is nervous, not because (as Ray would have it) she is "correct", there is a passage for comparison much later in the novel, which I shall keep to the minimum for fear of being led into further corners of White's style (the disturbing bifunctionality in the syntax of the first sentence, for example; or the emphatic "did" of figural concession and cohesion):

Then we are not to escape the Bourkes, decided Thelma Forsdyke. She looked appropriately sad.

She did genuinely become sad in the dark room, though it was for herself, that she was burying. The scents of little girls' flowers on sparrows' graves brought the tears to her eyes. Or nightlights beneath which she was suffocating, before a mother, with those simple, primary features that faces wear in the beginning, gave her breath back. Thelma Forsdyke sat crumbling cake, the big yellow one that had been made too hastily, it had holes. There were many bits of herself that she would have broken off and discarded, if it had been possible that these would not still add up. [344]

In his further discussion of the topic of White's style, Thomson isolates an interesting passage but does not manage to come properly to terms with it:

More often the staccato or broken or jerky pieces are simply fairly normal prose punctuated in an individual way. By punctuating in the normal fashion the prose is perfectly normal. But White uses punctuation in a rhetorical rather than a syntactic way and he has a perfect right to do this. By his kind of punctuation he makes us look at certain words.

If there had been neighbours, it would have been a comfort to see the smoke occur regularly in the matchbox-chimney. But there were no neighbours. Only sometimes, if you listened on the stiller days, you might hear the sound of an axe, like the throb of your own heart, in the blue distance. Only very distant. Or more distantly, a cock. Or imagination. It was too far. [17]

That extract gains immensely set in its context of silence.

For a start, this is not "staccato or broken or jerky" but *measured;* it is not the punctuation but the syntax that is at issue; and it is not a matter of rhetorical emphasis for our sake (writer to reader) but a matter of psychological representation, as in all of White's ataxis. We may well "look at certain words"— but we are always forced back to the *whole*. Thomson's closing comment above ignores the nature of the whole while ostensibly pointing to it. If we took away the "context of silence" (which is actually a diegetic piece within the extract: "If you listened on the stiller days"), there would be no diminution of effect in the ever more rarified spacings of the sentences: the ataxis, the disposition of sentence-length, the free-indirect "you" and the indeterminacies ("Only sometimes", "might hear", "Or") all work powerfully together to enact the alert straining of Stan Parker's perception.

Elsewhere, Thomson is able to interpret the function of style as the opposite of what it actually is:

Here is a staccato passage where the movement is used to convey the impression of the urgency of the work and the hurry because Stan is young, and the work is all before him:

> Never far from the dog the man would be at work. With axe, or scythe, or hammer. Or he would be on his knees, pressing into the earth the young plants he had raised under wet bags. All along the morning stood the ears of young cabbages. Those that the rabbits did not nibble off. In the clear morning of the early years the cabbages stood out for the woman more distinctly than other things, when they were not melting, in a tenderness of light. [31]

There is no urgency or hurry expressed here. As a bivocalized perspective (a neutral-narratorial shell, with the actants functionally reduced to their primary epic role; then psychonarrationally Amy's focus, as determined by the tenor of the preceding paragraph), the passage reveals a cinematic, measured sequence of discrete actional images—easily destroyed, were the first three sentences linked "normally" together. Each datum has its very own significance, and the processsual sum is that of order and measure—even the incursion of disorder ("Those that the rabbits did not nibble off") being subsumed under this measuredness (and linked via the cabbage-plant metaphor to rabbits' ears). It is noteworthy that Thomson's idea of using the macrocontext to justify style is realized by seizing on essentially social (or, in the broadest sense, moral) aspects of abstractable theme. This is how he gets from the young cabbage-plants and "those early years" to "the hurry because Stan is young"; he does not think of considering the interdependency of action, consciousness and perception within a given context.

The nature of the intensity of represented experience in White is wrestled with sensitively by Rodney Mather, who takes as his exemplifying text part of a sentence relating to the death of Stan Parker's father:

> To stay put was, in fact, just what the young man Stanley Parker himself desired; but where, and how? In the streets of towns the open windows, on the dusty roads the rooted trees, filled him with the melancholy longing for permanence. But not yet. It was a struggle between two desires. As the little boy, holding the musical horseshoes for his father, blowing the bellows, or scraping up the grey parings of hoof and the shapely yellow mounds of manure, he had already experienced the unhappiness of these desires. Ah, here, the sun said, and the persistent flies, is the peace of permanence; all these shapes are known, act opens out of act, the days are continuous. It was hard certainly in the light of that steady fire not to interpret all fire. Besides, he had an affection for his belching and hairy father, and quite sincerely cried when the blacksmith finally died of the rum bottle and a stroke. [14]

Mather sets up a theorem of experiential mediation, using D.H. Lawrence as his preferred model:

In [Lawrence's] writing we witness someone [the character] experiencing meaning; in White we receive "meaning" (aesthetic meaning), by witnessing experience in a detached, spectatorly way [....] The reader's experience is not identical with the boy's. Part of the meaning, the wit, of the writing resides in that rum-bottle, which isn't detachingly grotesque for the boy, who "quite sincerely cried", but for the reader. [Mather 1970:40]

Because of the presentational frame of an epic narrative, White of necessity exercises his selective, analytical authority more noticeably than in any other of his novels; yet there is the same subtle interweaving of levels of focalization and voicing. What looks here like purely narratorial life-summary is actually the flow of psychonarrational (and partly figural) anamnesis (with the typical self-imaging naming-gradients: eg, "the young man Stanley Parker" as the first, stiffly self-conscious labelling of adolescence, and the shift back to "the little boy" taken over from the—observed—public categorization of the townspeople). Mather mentions "the wit". If we take the conjunction (causal) of bottle and stroke as a syllepsis, then we are likely to seek an authority external to the experiencing boy or the recollecting man in order to account for it. Equally, however, we should then read "quite sincerely cried" as auctorially ironical: there is no reason why we should limit "wit" to one expression and not include another.

In point of fact, although these reactions are legitimate first responses, they are subjected to correction by the macrotext. The conjunction of bottle and stroke is *not* sylleptic: an indivisible causality links them, and there is no radical semantic subversion involved in linking both concretes to the verb "died" (where we should not ignore the processual implication of "finally"—the habit culminating in the "act"). The generic article ("the bottle") is normal in White for reference to ailments and their aetiology, and the convention is comfortably colloquial, thus easily accommodated to Stan's mind-set. If our cultural code differs from Stan's, it is up to us to make up the difference. More problematical is the clause that Mather finds equally acceptable in terms of character and reader. Stan is under strong inner compulsion, as the whole context is out to reveal, but is held back from "motion" by obligation to his Daedalian father. The "two desires" are self-oriented, distinct from whatever it is he feels for his father. The same relational abstract clangs in the text here as in *The Solid Mandala* and in other novels by White (see this chapter, section I)—not "love" but "affection", and not even that: *"an* affection". The whole statement is tacked on ("Besides") to a psychonarrational sequence devolving through gnomic, nature-pathetic free direct speech to something close to free indirect discourse ("It was hard certainly …").

The sincerity of Stan's crying is not in doubt. What is at issue, though, is the extent of his loss, and the degree to which the response is triggered by a *depth* of affection. What we have is a measure of detachment on the part of the character (betrayed by the discourse protesting too much). We are spectators, certainly; but we are only so because Stan is himself "outside". Part of the pervasive aura of the narration of *The Tree of Man* can be directly associated with the infusion into the diegesis of Stan's own detached, near-stolid or rooted consciousness, which melts so easily into the impassivity of the natural landscape that he shapes and with which he is identifiable even in the title. Where Stan "parks" himself ("Parker" being another aptronymic, then, for momentary rest, just as "Stan" evokes the stasis of "stand"), Amy, with her greed for love *(aimer/aimée)* is going to be *his* choice. The ductus of the sentence Mather discusses is ultimately referable to the further action, which reveals that affection and obligation do not hold Stan to his mother, that he must cut loose in order to return, never in order to stay. To rephrase Mather: we receive experience, or the representation of a character's mental concourse with experience, when we read White. Meaning is not gratuitously aestheticized.

RIDERS IN THE CHARIOT

This novel is fuelled by tremendous moral energy; it is a settling of open accounts, ranging from White's experiences in Germany in the 1930s, through the working-out of his fascination with Jewish culture and the cataclysm of the Holocaust, to the filtering of his own sense of being displaced in Australia through witnessing the difficulties which European refugees suffered in their efforts to gain acceptance in the Antipodes. Nevertheless, it is a novel which explores the workings of human consciousness, even in its social manifestations, rather than one which thematizes moral categories.

Brian McFarlane quotes from the gas-chamber episode with the Lady from Czernowitz. He is swayed wholly by a sense of moral outrage that is levelled against the narrative voice instead of against the action represented. He focuses his attention on one particular brief passage, which I present here in the context of several sequent excerpts:

(1) "I shall pray for us!" he called after her. "For all of us!"

(2) His hands dangling uselessly in the vacant air.

(3) Nor did she hear his man's voice attempting to grapple with a situation which might have tested the prophets themselves, for she was borne away, in a wind, and stuffed inside the bathhouse, in case her hysteria should inspire those who were obedient, duller, or of colder blood. The last Himmelfarb saw of his companion, at that stage, was the black and disordered bundle of her tearing clothes.

(4) For the men were also pressed back, by ropes of arms, and in certain cases, by naked steel. It seemed as though the sexes would never again meet, at the prospect of which some of the women screamed, and one young man, remembering tender intimacies, rasped, and ranted, until almost choked by his own tongue.

[....]

(5) Now Himmelfarb, who had been pressed inside the door of the men's bath-house, gave himself into the hands of God. His own were on his necktie. Most of his companions, on whom the virtue of discipline had been impressed by the country of their birth or election, were instinctively doing as they had been asked. One big fat fellow had entered so far into the spirit of the dream that his shirt was half-way over his head. Himmelfarb himself was still only watching the dreadful dream-motions.

(6) "Into your hands, O Lord," his lips were committing him afresh.

(7) When something happened.

(8) A guard came pushing through the mass of bodies, one of the big, healthy, biddable blond children, choosing here and there with a kind of lazy, lingering discrimination.

(9) "You will remain dressed," he ordered Himmelfarb, "and report with me outside for camp-duties."

[....]

(9) Then they began to notice that a number of other individuals, all obviously of slave status, dressed in miscellaneous garments, were assembled in a kind of informal formation.

(10) One of them spoke to his neighbour, who happened to be Himmelfarb.

(11) "The women will soon be going in," the stranger informed, in faltering, faulty German. "The women usually go in first."

(12) It was doubtful to what race the man belonged. He could have been a darker Slav, a Pole perhaps, or of Mediterranean stock, but there was no mistaking the evidence of inferior blood.

[....]

(13) But just then the door of the women's bath-house burst open, by terrible misadventure, and there, for ever to haunt, staggered the Lady from Czernowitz.

(14) How the hands of the old, helpless, and furthermore intellectual Jew, her friend, went out to her.

(15) "God show us!" shrieked the Lady from Czernowitz: "Just this once! At least!"

(16) In that long, leathern voice.

(17) She stood there for an instant in the doorway, and might have fallen if allowed to remain longer. Her scalp was grey stubble where the reddish hair had been. Her one dug hung down beside the ancient scar which represented the second. Her belly sloped away from the hillock of her navel. Her thighs were particularly poor. But it was her voice which lingered. Stripped. Calling to him from out of the dark of history, ageless, ageless, and interminable.

(18) The man her counterpart, brought to his knees by sudden weakness, tearing them furiously, willingly, on the pebbles, calling to her across the same gulf, shouted through the stiff slot of his mouth:

[....]

(19 And he felt himself falling, falling, the human part of him. As his cheek encountered the stones, the funnels of a thousand mouths were directed upon him, and poured out over his body a substance he failed to identify. [Penguin, pp. 182–84]

McFarlane seizes upon the closing sequence:

Whatever that last, pretentious sentence means ["Calling to him ..."], it cannot erase the contemptuous usage of the sub-human "dug" or the chilling callousness of "her thighs were particularly poor". A movement towards pity in White is almost always subverted by his obsessive need to underline the physical horror of the flesh. [McFarlane 1977:37]

In no way can it be said that the perspective and tonality here are attributable to White. Nor is it possible to speak of a narratorial voice identifiable socially by its *ductus*. Nor is the controlling perspective throughout that of Himmelfarb; the most that we can infer is that he sees the woman reappear again after she disappears in "the black and disordered bundle of her tearing clothes" (3). The whole scene is a narrative tour de force, and is almost indiscussible unless one is prepared to deal with the psycho-ethical implications forced on one as reader by the action.

One function of the death-camps was to process human material: the ideology of the processors being that the notion of the "human" was superfluous, and, consequently, that moral categories like "human dignity" could be disregarded as inapplicable, except as a subterfuge for enticing the "verminous" to their systematic extinction. As this was an industrial operation, notions of selection or quality-control were applicable. How does this operate within the discourse? For a start, individual perspectives are minimized or disallowed. The overriding perspective is that of an observer such as might, at a historical remove, be viewing the impersonal intimacies of these processes on documentary war-crimes film. The discourse does represent "dreadful dream-motion" of "the mass of bodies" (5, 8). There is a serene swaying between calm abstractions or phlegmatic indices of horror on the one hand, and grotesque humour on the other. Much of the diction is highly circumspect: "grapple with a situation" (3); "in case her hysteria should inspire ..." (3); "in certain cases" (4); "at the prospect of which ..." (4); "a number of other individuals" (9); "by terrible misadventure" (13); "helpless, and furthermore intellectual" (14); "Certainly ..."; "It could have been, then, that .... Or he could, simply, ..."; "appalled [without object] by its comparative emptiness" (these phrases in sentences not quoted above).

The "humour" consists partly in the way language is brought up against the intransigence of "situation" and "circumstance". "A situation which might have tested the prophets themselves" (3) invests a casual expression with new significance. Himmelfarb gives himself "into the hands of God"—this is relativized, rendered existentially absurd, by "His own were on his necktie" (5). The casual phrase "entering into the spirit of things" is subverted into ghastly indignity (5). *Dignitas* is toppled by exposure to "the system", humanity stripped. The guard chooses "with a kind of lazy, lingering discrimination" (8). "A kind of informal formation" (9) is taken up again in the cropped tag "the stranger informed" (11). Above all, the diction is contaminated by the perspective of the *Herrenvolk,* in such words as "discrimination", "equal", the vicious irony of "individuals", the movement of the neutral remark about "race" towards the expression "the evidence of inferior blood" (12).

This brings us to the sentence McFarlane singles out, "Her thighs were particularly poor" (17)—this is the diction of camp-physicians exercising quality-control, checking the goods. And if "dug" is "sub-human", it is the ambience and the ideology infecting the narrated action that make it so. The victims (if we choose to press for the possibility that the perception is Himmelfarb's), too, have been brought subjectively to this level, where physical humanity and sex are reduced to the elemental. It is the huge gap between matter and spirit that is represented here, not "the physical horror of the flesh". The discourse, no matter how hard it prods in the direction of reductive irony, is so structured as to make evident the full force of indomitable human dignity as expressed in the Lady's voice and in Himmelfarb's responses. This is why ataxis takes over at "But" (17) and then more radically at "stripped" and "Calling"—for a crucial moment, figural consciousness (Himmelfarb's) breaks emotively through the deadened impassivity of the narration, preparing for Himmelfarb's act of commitment in the iconic, emotively ruptured syntax of the paragraph following (18). Whoever finds the "Calling"-sentence "pretentious" has failed to read it in its local and wider context. It has been long prepared for—the "dark of history" is traceable back to "prophets"; "ageless, ageless" is an epizeuxis of extreme excitation echoing Old-Testament lyricism and the plaint of the Jews. Locally, the disjunction between *materia* and voice is compensated for by transposition. The Lady was a "bundle of ... tearing clothes" before her reappearance naked; her body is then a desert landscape with its "ancient scar" and "hillock"; now it is her voice that is "stripped", "ageless" instead of "ancient", "interminable" instead of "long, leathern". The motif of stripping to essentials continues—in the diegesis with "tearing", in the Lady's last words—before Himmelfarb, at the moment he loses consciousness, is re-clothed in manna.

After Himmelfarb, the intellectual Jew, is newly arrived in Australia from the horror of the Nazi death-camps, he goes to take up his first job "in the neighbouring town of Barranugli" (which barren and ugly place recurs, of course, in *The Solid Mandala)*. The scene is full of sharply observed social satire at the expense of the denizens of this commercial-industrial establishment, and it is the tonality which has exercised some critics of the passage:

(1) "Very well thought of," continued the official voice. "Have any trouble with your English, well, there is Mr Rosetree on the spot. You will not find another place anywhere around that's made for you personally."

(2) Himmelfarb agreed the position could be most suitable, and allowed himself to be directed. To abandon self is, after all, to accept the course that offers.

(3) So he presented himself at Brighta Bicycle Lamps, which functioned in a shed, on the outskirts of the town, beside a green river.

(4) Here, on arriving for his interview, he was told to sit, and was ignored for an appropriate length of time, because it was necessary that the expanding business should impress, and as the applicant was stationed right at the centre of Mr Rosetree's universe, impress it did. For, through one door, Himmelfarb could watch two ladies, so upright, so superior, so united in purpose, one plump and the other thin, dashing off the Rosetree correspondence with a minimum of touch, and through another door he could look down into the infernal pit in which the Brighta Lamps were cut out and put together with an excessive casualness and the maximum of noise. [....] Ladies sat at their assembly trays, and repeated with dainty skill the single act they would be called upon to perform. Or eased their plastic teeth. Or shifted gum. Or patted the metal clips with which their heads were stuck for Friday night. There were girls, too, their studied eyebrows sulking over what they had to suffer. And gentlemen in singlets, who stood with their hands on their hips [....]

(5) Bending down in the centre of the floor was a dark-skinned individual, Himmelfarb observed, whose temporary position made his vertebrae protrude in knobs, and who, when straightened up, appeared to be composed of bones, veins, and thin strips of elastic muscle, the whole dominated by the oblivious expression of the dark face. The blackfellow, or half-caste, he could have been, resumed possession of his broom, and pushed it ahead of him as he walked backwards and forwards between the benches. Some of the women lowered their eyes as he passed, others smiled knowingly, though not exactly at him. But the black man, involved in some incident of the inner life, ignored even the mechanical gestures of his own sweeping. But swept, and swept. As oil reveals secret lights, so did the skin stretched on the framework of his naked ribs. As he continued sweeping. It was an occupation to be endured, so his heavy hand and the rather arrogant Adam's-apple seemed to imply.

(6) Himmelfarb began to realize that the plumper of the two typists was trying to attract his attention. While remaining seated in the office, she was, it seemed, calling to him.

(7) "Mr Rosetree," she was saying, "is free now, to see you."

(8) Both the typewriters were still. The thinner of the two ladies was smiling at the keys of hers, as she hitched up the ribbon of a private garment which had fallen in a loop over her white, pulled, permanently goosey biceps.

(9) Fascinated by all he saw, the applicant had failed to move.

(10) "Mr Rosetree," repeated the plumper lady louder, the way one did for foreigners, "is disengaged. Mr Himmelferp," she added, and would have liked to laugh.

(11) Her companion did snicker, but quickly began to rearrange her daintily-embroidered personal towel, which was hanging over the back of a chair.

(12) "If you will pass this way," almost shouted the plump goddess, perspiring on her foam rubber.

(13) She feared the situation was making her conspicuous.

(14) "Thank you," Himmelfarb replied, and smiled at the hand which indicated doors.

(15) She did not rise, of course, having reduced her obligations at the salary received. But let her hand fall.

(16) Himmelfarb went into Mr Rosetree's sanctum.

(17) "Good-day, Mr Himmelfarb," Mr Rosetree said: "Make yourself comfortable," he invited, without troubling to consider whether that might be possible. [200-201]

William Walsh faults the "contemptuous", "pinched and negative" tone which he attributes to White, and comments (of paragraph 4 above): "The feeling here is not so much indignation as disgust—the lips seem to writhe at the 'ladies' and 'gentlemen'—and not so much deserved as self-indulgently released" (Walsh 1977:61). He then moves on (to the passage beginning at paragraph 12 above) to comment on style rather than tone:

the dislocations of syntax which White can use, for example at the beginning of *Voss,* with the most effective originality, sometimes, particularly in these disdainful scenes, becomes nearly mechanical. For example, it seems pointless to use so portentous an idiom to describe the movements of a typist in Mr Rosetree's office .... There is a certain dimming of critical alertness at these points, which seems to betray too personal an engagement of the author with the material in hand and too little control of his personal impulses. [Walsh 1977:62]

Geoffrey Dutton criticizes these same passages for the "sarcasm of referring to certain common types as 'gentlemen'" (Dutton 1971:32). Brian Kiernan appears at first glance to justify and correct the "morality" of the narrative tone:

With ironic gentility, White bestows on the ladies of the office the recognition of their gentility which they crave, and acknowledges the gentlemen's swagger of independence and refusal to be identified with their work roles. [Kiernan 1980:72]

But, like Walsh and Dutton, he still fails to see that the whole section is contaminated by Himmelfarb's perceptions. To say that the descriptive pitch of the narration, and the metaphoricity of the mechanical, the foregrounding of human gesture, is Dickensian would be perhaps to fall into the hands of Kiernan, who seeks a mellow (if grotesque) good humour that can align White with liberal Australianism. There are, rather, pervasive signs of something approaching the style and narrative placement of Kafka *(Amerika,* parts of *The Trial).* The perspective is continental-European, with an uneasy tension between acceptance and rejection of the defamiliarized (and alienating) mechanical.

The use of "ladies" and "gentlemen" represents the civilized European Himmelfarb's mental classifications: workers have human dignity too. Much of the detail, of course, is supplied from White's cultural code (Himmelfarb probably does not know that the women's "metal clips" are "for Friday night", or would not reflect that a typist's behaviour is conditioned by how much she earns); but most is decidedly bivocal. The *disjunction* between the courtesy epithets and the human context of mechanical labour is perspectivally split according to our constitution of our reading. We read more objectivity in Himmelfarb's perceptions (a German professor whose closest experience of factory-life is being at the receiving end in the death-camps), and more social criticism in White's disposition of detail and his attaching of Himmelfarb's inferences to human action. The reader who sees contempt or disdain in the accumulation of physical detail is overreacting to an objectively ugly scene which does not, however, provide us with more than the superficies, the latency, of what is to explode in due course as the blind ritual of Himmelfarb's mock-crucifixion.

There is a gradual intensification of focus. The sentence with "the applicant" (paragraph 4) can be read as dissonant focalization, but the long sentences that follow represent Himmelfarb's own plunge into perception of "the infernal pit", and the atactic "Or"–sentences the alighting of his awareness on discrete gestures. In the next long paragraph (5), where we have Himmelfarb's first sight of Alf Dubbo, there are traces of figural conjecture overlaid upon an Australian sociolect ("blackfellow") in the deployment of definite and indefinite articles and descriptive naming, in "not exactly" and in "he could have been"; and there is a resumption of figural perception after evaluative introspection in the iconic ataxis of "But swept, and swept" and "As he continued sweeping". In the passage that Walsh complains about, the "idiom", far from being "portentous" (it only seems so because Walsh does not understand why the "idiom" is as it is), registers the figural recipient's percepts. The inversion of the first tag ("almost shouted") indicates—bivocally, to be sure—Himmelfarb's/White's detection of the disparity between the grossness and loudness of the typist and the borrowed (or role-imposed) gentility of her words. The sentence beginning "She feared" (with its typically meiotic mental indicator "the situation") is inserted psychonarrationally because Himmelfarb's quiet, observant presence has unnerved her—he is fixed on her and her words, not on the indicating hand, which is mentioned only later, after Himmelfarb has switched focus to it. The "of course" (15) is Himmelfarb's rationalizing of her ungracious behaviour, but also (along with the latter part of the sentence) White's own inside information on her motivation. The defeating of Himmelfarb's expectation that he will be led into the "sanctum" is expressed in the atactic truncation which Walsh complains about. By now, Himmelfarb is learning, and can work out for himself the disparity between Rosetree's courtesy-formula and the actual physical situation. Before this whole scene, when the "official voice" (1) offers its optimistic assurances, Himmelfarb's enforced passivity allows him to lean on a gnomic generalization for support (2): the present-tense suspension, and the abstractions, convey the absence of specific context, which is soon enough provided.

The crucifixion-episode in *Riders in the Chariot* is worth quoting *in extenso,* because Kiernan's comments on part of it do show the critic working towards a more differentiated view of the function of the narrative discourse:

(1) If some of the spectators suffered the wounds to remain open, it was due probably to an unhealthy state of conscience, which could have been waiting since childhood to break out. For those few, the drops trembled and lived. How they longed to dip their handkerchiefs, unseen.

(2) Others had to titter for a burlesque, while turning aside their faces in an attempt to disguise what they suspected might be blasphemy.

(3) Blue was laughing, and swallowing his excessive spittle. He stood looking up, with his throat distended on his now rather convulsive torso: a decadence of statuary.

(4) He called up out of the depths:

"Howyadoin up there, eh? 'Ad enough, eh? Bugger me if the cow don't go for it!"

(5) The Jew appeared, in fact, to have been removed from them, while the archtormentor himself might have been asking for respite from torments which he had always suffered, and which, in certain circumstances, were eased, he seemed to remember. So the marble body was contorted into the changing forms of wax at the foot of the tree.

(6) The Jew hung. If he had not been such a contemptible object, he might have excited pity. Hoisted high at the wrists, the weight of the body threatened to cut them through. The arms strained to maintain that uneasy contact between heaven and earth. Through the torn shirt the skin was stretched transparent on the ribs. The head lolled even more heavily than in life. Those who had remained in touch with reality or tradition might have taken him for dead. But the eyes were visionary rather than fixed. The contemplative mouth dwelled on some breathless word spoken by the mind.

(7) Because he was as solitary in the crowd as the man they had crucified, it was again the abo who saw most. All that he had ever suffered, all that he had ever failed to understand, rose to the surface in Dubbo. Instinct and the white man's teaching no longer trampled on each other. As he watched, the colour flowed through the veins of the cold, childhood Christ, at last the nails entered wherever it was acknowledged they should. So he took the cup in his own yellow hands, from those of Mr Calderon, and would have offered it to such celebrants as he was now able to recognize in the crowd. So he understood the concept of the blood, which was sometimes the sick, brown stain on his own pillow, sometimes the clear crimson of redemption. He was blinded now. Choking now. Physically feebler for the revelation that knowledge would never cut the cords which bound the Saviour to the tree. Not that it was asked. Nothing was asked. So he began also to understand acceptance. How he could at last have conveyed it, in its cloak of purple, on the blue tree, the green lips of detached, contemplative suffering.

(8) And love in its many kinds began to trouble him as he looked. He saw the old man, the clergyman, searching the boy's body for the lost image of youth on the bedstead at Numburra, and Mrs Spice whirling to her putrefaction in the never-ending dance of the potato-sacks, and Hannah the prostitute curled together with her white capon, Norman Fussell, in their sterile, yet not imperfect, fleshly egg. Many anonymous faces, too, offered without expecting or frowning. There was the blandest experience of love: the milky light of morning poured out unadulterated over his naked shoulders. And the paints as they swirled, and as he swathed them on a bare board, sometimes as tenuously as mist, sometimes moulding them with his fingers like bastions of stone. Perhaps this, his own contribution to love, was least explicable, if most comprehensive, and comprehensible.

(9) Now the Jew stirred on the lump of an ugly tree trunk on which they had stuck him.

(10) The crowd pressed forward to see and hear, jostling the stick of an abo half-caste who did not exist for any member of it.

(11) The Jew had raised his head. He looked out from under those rather heavy, intolerable lids.

(12) From the beginning Himmelfarb had known that he possessed the strength, but did pray for some sign. Through all the cursing, and trampling, and laughter, and hoisting, and aching, and distortion, he had continued to expect. Until now, possibly, it would be given. So, he raised his head. And was conscious of a stillness and clarity, which was the stillness and clarity of pure water, at the centre of which his God was reflected.

(13) The people watched the man they had fastened to the tree. That he did not proceed to speak his thoughts was most unnatural, not to say frustrating. The strain became enormous. If they had seen how to go about it, they would have licked the silence from his lips, as a substitute for words.

(14) Then a young girl of thin mouth and smoothed hair began to run at, and struggle with the backs of the bystanders, who would not let her through. Hysteria would see to it. The scarlet thread of lips was drawn tight on some demon that she would on no account give up. [412–13]

Referring to paragraph 12 above, Kiernan notes the "deliberate ironic reservation"; crucial moments like this are ambiguous, White's intention undeterminable. "The use of the indirect third person—the intermittent filtering, in this case, of Himmelfarb's consciousness through the narrative voice—has obviously confused interpretations" (Kiernan 1980:81). In other words, Kiernan means that the character's perceptions are endorsed by the "narrator", at the same time as the author is ironically distanced from the perception of the character he is rendering. The trouble is, there is not much point in White (or, as Kiernan more aptly puts it, the "narrative voice") observing "deliberate ironic reservation" at this juncture—the investment in figural consciousness is, rather, complete here. It resides in the indeterminate experiential deictic "From the beginning"; in the gap between "it" and its coreferent, "some sign"; in the inward concession of the proform "did pray"; in the experiential iconicity of the sequentially coordinated activity-nouns; in the opening-out of the uncomplemented transitive "expect"; in "possibly" and the free-indirect modal "would be given"; in the iconic punctuation between the mental resolve of "so" and the action following the momentary pause; in the further, resultative, ataxis of discrete apperception at "And"; in the "re-defining" of "stillness and clarity"—even in the infolding indirection of the analogy transformed by syntax into metaphor at the word "reflected".

Most of the remainder of the extract is controlled perspectivally by the perceptions of Alf Dubbo, whose painter's vision translates what he sees. He has been a silent witness in previous pages, and is so again here, although diegetic indication of this comes late, in one of the few "narratorial" statements after paragraph (3): "Because he was as solitary ..." (7). But even this cannot be identified with either White or the crowd exclusively, although the vocality of the anonymising "the man" and the generic reductiveness of "the abo" make the evaluating perspective that of the mass. A similar mixture can be found as a mark of juncture after Dubbo's perspective: "The crowd pressed forward ... who did not exist for any member of it" (10); this is a cinematic long-shot, with narratorial perspective, though countless details outside these pages also allow Dubbo himself to hold this projective view of his own anonymity. It is, after all, the role which racism has forced him into that compels him here to inactivity.

"Jostling the stick of an abo half-caste" (10) employs the idiom of the crowd, but the identification cannot be theirs, as he does not "exist" for them. Dubbo is a "stick" in outside perspective, and somatically a "stick" within his own consciousness, with the designation *"an* abo half-caste" being his voicing of the identity forced upon him, his reconstitution of the unheeding white world's distance from him as an individual. The sentence is bivocal, but on both sides figurally. In 11, the split in perception between painter's discriminating eye and the subjectively typologizing gaze of racism is conveyed in the radically ambiguous deixis and evaluation of "those rather heavy, intolerable lids".

As I have said, art-diction predominates elsewhere ("torso" and "statuary", 3; "the marble body", 5; the careful description of the hanging Jew, like a genre-painting, 6; the Grecoesque colours detailed in Dubbo's free-indirect exclamatory sentence on "conveying" the crucifixion, 7; the series of images from his memory, with the Boschian emblem of the egg, 8). The discourse is characterized by figural ataxis and cohesive "So" (from the point where "understanding" takes over, 7), and by marks of indeterminacy ("offered" as an absolute participle, or as an objectless transitive, 8; the whole equivocating movement of the sentence with "Perhaps this", 8). In the sentence beginning "Now the Jew stirred" (9), ugly, untransfigured reality breaks into Dubbo's vision. The indeterminacies in paragraph 5 ("appeared, in fact"; "might have been asking"; the Whitean "in certain circumstances"; "seemed to remember"; the broken and hesitant embedding-structure as a whole) shift away from a purely figural representation of Blue's apperception, but the sentence is again bivocal. "The archtormentor", with its mythic or generic connotations, melts into Dubbo's genericizing view; the statement is prevented by being narratorial by "seemed to remember", and we are left with an impression of the profound but unplumbable disquiet experienced by Blue himself—a disquiet touching on his own experience of suffering (as recounted elsewhere), and held at bay by consciousness, as the discoursal style reveals.

This undercutting of vulgar-demotic mimesis (in direct speech) is typical of White: a critique of social action is represented in psychological terms, seldom in moral ones. One stage further removed from this are such passages as those framing the stretches of diegesis already discussed. Here, the social mass is represented as being in a state of indeterminate consciousness, with no concordance between action or perception and motivation or cognition. The discourse becomes heavily conditional or conditional-concessive ("If some ...", 1; "If they had seen ...", 13), qualified ("probably" and "could have been", 1; "suspected might be", 2; "not to say frustrating", 18). Other indices of White's style reinforce this reining-in of explicit causality ("to titter *for* a burlesque", 2; the distribution—"some of the spectators ... those few ... others ..."—familiar to us from Waldo's section of *The Solid Mandala).* What we have here and elsewhere is what looks like an ironic downplaying of Gothic excesses (and the potential excesses are there in the blood-indices) but a style which actually constitutes a representation of various strata of figural consciousness and perception, even down to the banal affective inadequacy of "The strain became enormous" (13). There is a distancing of self from the unreality of the proceedings, at the same time as the actants commit themselves, dream-like, to the reality of their participation. The strong discoursal *control* that is everywhere apparent is a holding fast to the ungraspability of quotidian horror. Hence the dispassionate *ductus* with which the young girl's "hysteria" is treated (13). Kiernan is right in suggesting that crises in White's narratives are ambiguous; but it is not *White's* "deliberate ... reservation", and his intentions are indeed determinable.

Sometimes it is a critic's positive response that manages to miss the point of the narrative style—as with Thomson's reaction to *The Tree of Man,* and as when John Colmer praises the incident in *Riders in the Chariot* where Miss Hare and Mrs Godbold ministrate to Himmelfarb after his crucifixion, the passage concerned being the following:

(1) But Miss Hare would only moan, not from pain, it seemed, but because she had again succeeded in closing the circle of her happiness. Yet she must have been suffering, for those of the children who had advanced closest saw that the red down was singed close along her chops, and the skin shiny from the basting it had got.

(2) Horrid though her appearance was, all those around her remained rooted in respect. Although the great wicker hat had gone askew, its spokes burnt black, not even Mrs Godbold dared suggest the wearer should remove it. Miss Hare had never been seen without, unless by Mrs Godbold herself, who had nursed her years before in sickness. Nobody else cared to speculate on what might be hidden underneath.

(3) Then Miss Hare sat up, as straight as her fubsy body would allow.

(4) "His feet," she said, "are cold."

(5) For she had stuck her hand under the blanket.

(6) "So very, very cold." Miss Hare's slow words followed her fingers, ending in a shiver.

(7) "Yes." Mrs Godbold could not evade it. "But you shall warm them."

(8) Miss Hare cheered up then, as everybody saw. She sat and chafed her spirits back. Or gradually lulled lower, until her face rested on the forms of feet, printing them on her cheek.

(9) All this time the man's face was breathing gently on the pillow, but the air could have been rarified.

(10) "Gracie will go for Dr Herborn," Mrs Godbold had at last decided.

(11) But Himmelfarb opened his eyes. He said:

(12) "No. No. Not now. Thank you. For the moment I have not the strength to submit to any doctor."

(13) And smiled with the least possible irony, to absolve whoever it had been for conceiving a superfluous idea.

(14) He was as content by now as he would ever have allowed himself to be in life. Children and chairs conversed with him intimately. Thanks to the texture of their skin, the language of animals was no longer a mystery, as, of course, the Baal Shem had always insisted.

(15) So he breathed more gently, and resumed his journey.

(16) So Miss Hare was translated. Her animal body became the least part of her, as breathing thoughts turned to being.

(17) The night rose and fell, to which the dying fire gave its last touch of purple through the frame of vines and window. [432]

Colmer comments:

In resonant[,] moving sentences that recapitulate key ideas and images of the novel and through syntax and rhythms that echo the biblical faith in the working out of divine providence, the novelist celebrates the wordless communion of the mad woman and dying Jew, their movement through the world of material existence, their translation into the world of pure being. [Colmer 1978c:30]

If the "syntax and rhythms" "echo the biblical faith" (and I doubt that the notion of "divine providence" is ever really what is worked out in White's fiction), then so does most of White's syntax (and "rhythms", whatever Colmer means by this). The light ataxis that is evident here ("For", "Or", "But", "And smiled") is ubiquitous in White's fiction. Two sentences (15–16) begin with "So", consecutively but with a paragraph-break; Colmer quotes the passage without setting these sentences out separately: how sensitive is he to style? Does "the novelist" celebrate, or do the characters? Whose adverbial is "of course" (14)? The pushing of tropism to its limits is a characteristic of William Schermbrucker's "novel of vision", and is evident here—in the syllepsis of the conversing children and chairs; in the indirection of the correlation between skin, "the language of animals", the pseudo-religious metaphor of "translated", and the "animal body" of Miss Hare; in "breathing thoughts turned to being", which is developed in the subjectivizing of "the night rose and fell" (a kind of pathetic fallacy linking Miss Hare's nocturnal vigil with her sense of Himmelfarb's breathing as she rests her face on his body).

The accepting quality of the discourse is an index to the consciousness of the characters, notwithstanding the mind-stylistic presence of White in the ataxis, in the disposition of speech-tags (4, 10) and crypto-tags (6–7), in the use of "it" with direct speech as coreferent (7), in the displaced relative "to which" (17). The diction and conjectural indices of paragraph (1) are, again, not those of a "celebrating" novelist, but assume the perspective of the onlookers ("it seemed", "must have been"; the modal hesitancy in "but the air could have been rarified" complicated by the tension between a physical and a spiritual or "religious" perspective in "rarified"; the demotic or affective weighting of "her chops", "the basting it had got", "horrid", "fubsy"; the temporary eclipse of the "recognizing" designation "Miss Hare" by "the wearer" because of the obtrusion of her conspicuous hat). This is informed by noncommittal abstractions of privileged, narratorial origin ("she had again succeeded in closing the circle of her happiness"). Perspectival control can be exercised through judiciously placed perfective aspect, as when the magical suspension of "the man's" gentle breathing, and the implication of an empathetic hush on the part of the observers, are cut through by Mrs Godbold's practical decision—"had ... decided" (10) encodes the delayed deflection of the observers' attention from Himmelfarb. There are characteristic meldings of concrete and abstract ("chafed her spirits back", as an oblique indication of what Miss Hare is doing to Himmelfarb's feet under the blanket, and of her desire for caritative fulfilment), immediately equivocated into a seemingly alternative but actually paraphrastically extended statement of the same fundamental gesture ("Or gradually lolled lower ...", 8).

Colmer remarks elsewhere that "the gap between authentically realized experience and apocalyptic implication is often wide in this novel. The elements of contrivance in the willed visionary encounters ... shows through in the affirmatory prose" (1978c:20). One could easily play the devil's advocate and make these words apply to the very passage Colmer so praises. But to do so would be to ignore the fact that the sense of "contrivance" emanates from the reader's inability to accept that affirmation is enacted by characters who never fit the conventional role-image of the visionary. In the scene quoted, as elsewhere, the near-comic ordinariness of these extraordinarily empathetic characters is a challenge to the reader. The self-evident status of what they enact (its status for *them)* is preserved in all its integrity. White does not explode or inflate what his characters experience, does not "affirm" in their stead. The language constantly preserves the particular level of figural consciousness appropriate to their experience.

But readers persist in bringing to the text their own extrinsic expectations of decorum, and continue to fault White for incongruity. John Colmer, again, complains of an episode in *Riders in the Chariot* (484–86) where Mrs Chalmers–Robinson "pays tribute" to Ruth Godbold's "saintly nature": it "is created in White's most brittle and mannered style, so that what should [sic] appear the unforced tribute to a genuine saint seems unreal and strained" (Colmer 1978c:35). The narrative situation is the after-lunch conversation of Mrs Chalmers–Robinson, Mrs Colquhoun and the Jewish Mrs Wolfson, all well-to-do women past their prime. The talk touches on the outrageous events at Barranugli with "'the Jew they crucified'"; the women hastily avoid entertaining any notion of "miracles" and are relieved that a spilt coffee distracts them into half-erotic contemplation of the young Italian waiter who comes to sponge Mrs Chalmers–Robinson's lap. By association with an earlier mention of Sarsaparilla, this lady recalls the maid she once had, who left her service to go there and live. The contextual irony is that the maid is now Mrs Godbold, whom the reader, but not these ladies, can connect with the death of Himmelfarb.

There is, for a start, nothing more "mannered" in the style here than is consonant with the manner of these socializing ladies. We could talk of the presence of the satirist's vision or scalpel, but to do so would merely be to talk about ultimate *auctoritas,* not about the status and function of the narrative voicing, which is, once again, not identifiable with an individualized narrator or with any *one* of the three women. There are, instead, constant tiny shifts from one figural perspective to the next—almost imperceptibly, because the strained social consensus or homogeneity and strident, cash-corsetted femininity of the group are the point of the action represented. Imputations of intention ("her smile conveying disbelief", "insisted in a voice ...", with the Whitean modal "might have been"), the slight drawings-back and meiotic formulations ("with some disgust", "almost shouting", "not to say hysterics") are as much figural indices as the progressives ("was repeating", "was … shouting", "was sponging"), perfectives ("had begun again", "had gone off") and free-indirect voicings ("Did she know!", "The old thing") and epistemic adverbials ("fortunately", "perhaps").

The manner is that of a hyperconsciousness of externals. By the time we get down to Mrs Chalmers–Robinson's "tribute" (which starts out from the colloquial sense of "saint" to indicate domestic virtue, before Ruth's erstwhile mistress finds herself sliding down into unaccustomed depths of personal appraisal), it should have been amply clear that there is no possibility of this social context allowing anything that is *not* "unreal and strained" in terms of the characters' own perception. Hence the insertion of such evaluative (figural) adverbials as "without any shame at all", and the metaphoric translation of the act of confessional (self-)exposure into the eruption of a volcano. The reductionism is only part of the effect of the whole, and must be seen against the background of physical decline and decay, the implication that these old women are battling against the tide of time as they sit in "the dark plain" and "obscure purgatory" of the afternoon restaurant. What the impermanence of self, the uncertainty of their life-journey ("where she should go next") is offset by is the unfathomableness of the permanence they long for. Although the rock of Mrs Godbold's saintliness (which Mrs Colquhoun takes to be the *eros* associated with the Italian waiter) seems to be topicalized in such a way as to render it "unreal", it is indisputable that the theme has touched the women as powerfully as the exigencies of reality allow. To mistake the tonality achieved for a tonality that is undesirable or incongruous is to allow irrelevancies of the reader's own mind-set to infect the narrative.

Such irrelevancies can cloud the critical gaze at other critical junctures in White's narratives. The clouding occurs at precisely those moments in the reading experience when confrontation with the epiphanic should go most closely in hand with an alert appreciation of stylistic and discoursal texture. In all of the example-passages from *Riders in the Chariot* that have been discussed so far, there have been interpersonal encounters that involve representations of social surfaces; and upon these surfaces is focused the hard light of figural consciousness. The same phenomenon is at work in the following encounter between two of the illuminates of the novel, who are being observed by the evil geniuses of the narrative (this will be the last—necessarily—long quotation):

(1) The two ladies stood in the shelter of a blackberry bush to observe the house in which the foreign Jew was living. The small brown house was suitably, obscenely poor. The other side of the fence, from which previous owners had pulled pickets at random to stoke winter fires, mops of weeds were threatening to shake their cotton heads. Of course there were the willows. Nobody could have denied the existence of those, only their value was doubtful

because they had cost nothing. The willows poured round the shabby little house, serene cascades of green, or lapped peacefully at its wooden edges. Many a passer-by might have chosen to plunge in, and drown, in those consoling depths, but the two observers were longing for something that would rend their souls—a foetus, or a mutilated corpse. Instead, they had to make do with the sight of guttering that promised to fall off soon, and windows which if glitteringly clean, ignored the common decencies of lace or net.

(2) "Not even a geranium," said Mrs Flack, with bitter satisfaction.

(3) Then, if you please, the door opened, and out came, not the Jew, that would have been electric enough, but a woman, a woman. It was a thickish, middle-aged woman, in shapeless sort of faded dress. Some no-account woman.

(4) It was Mrs Jolley who realized first. She was often quite quick, although it was Mrs Flack who excelled in psychic powers.

(5) "Why," Mrs Jolley said now, "what do you know! It is that Mrs Godbold!"

(6) Mrs Flack was stunned, but managed:

(7) "I always thought how Mrs Godbold was deep, but how deep, I did not calculate."

(8) "It is wonderful," said Mrs Jolley, "to what lengths a woman will go."

(9) For the owner himself had emerged. The Jew. The two ladies clutched each other by the gloves. They had never seen anything so yellow or so strange. Strange? Why, dreadful, dreadful! Now the whirlwinds were rising in honest breasts, that honest corsets were striving to contain. The phlegm had come in Mrs Flack's mouth, causing her to swallow quickly down.

(10) Mrs Jolley, as she had already confessed, had noticed the man on one or two previous occasions as she came and went between Xanadu and Sarsaparilla, but had failed to observe such disgraceful dilapidation of appearance, such irregularities of stubble, such a top-heavy, bulbous head, such a truly fearful nose. In the circumstances, she felt she should apologize to her somewhat delicate companion.

(11) But the latter was craning now.

(12) "He is big," she remarked, between her moist teeth.

(13) "He is not small," Mrs Jolley agreed, as they stood supporting each other on wish-bone legs.

(14) "Who would ever of thought," Mrs Flack just articulated, "that Mrs Godbold."

(15) Mrs Godbold and the man were standing together on the steps of the veranda, she on the lower, he above, so that she was forced to look up, exposing her face to his and to the evening light.

(16) It was obvious that the woman's flat, and ordinarily uncommunicative face had been opened by some experience of a private nature, or perhaps it was just the light, gilding surfaces, dissolving the film of discouragement and doubt which life leaves behind, loosening the formal braids of hair, furnishing an aureole, which, if not supernatural—reason would not submit to that—provided an agreeable background to motes and gnats. Indeed, the Jew himself began to acquire a certain mineral splendour as he stood talking, even laughing with his friend, in that envelope, or womb of light. Whether the two had been strengthened by some event of importance, or were weakened by their present total disregard for defences, their audience was made to know, but could not, could not tell. Mrs Jolley and Mrs Flack could only crane and swallow, beside the blackberry bush, beneath their hats, and hope that something disgraceful might occur.

(17) "What is that, Mrs Jolley?" Mrs Flack asked at last.

(18) But Mrs Jolley did not hear. Her breath was roaring through her mouth.

(19) For the Jew had begun to show Mrs Godbold something. Whatever it was—it could have been a parcel, or a bird, only that was improbable, a white bird—their attention was all upon it.

(20) "I believe he has cut his hand," Mrs Jolley decided. "She has bandaged up his hand. Well, that is one way!"

(21) Mrs Flack sucked incredulous teeth. She was quite exhausted by now.

(22) Then, as people will toss up the ball of friendship, into the last light, at the moment of departure, and it will hang there briefly, lovely and luminous to see, so did the Jew and Mrs Godbold. There hung the golden sphere. The laughter climbed up quickly, out of their exposed throats, and clashed together by consent; the light splintered against their teeth. How private, and mysterious, and beautiful it was, even the intruders suspected, and were deterred momentarily from hating.

(23) When they were again fully clothed in their right minds, Mrs Jolley said to her companion:

(24) "Do you suppose she comes to him often?"

(25) "I would not know," replied Mrs Flack, though it was obvious she did.

(26) "Tsst!" she added, quick as snakes.

(27) Mrs Godbold had begun to turn.

(28) "See you at church!" hissed Mrs Jolley.

(29) ""See you at church!" repeated Mrs Flack.

(30) Their eyes flickered for a moment over the Christ who would rise to the surface of Sunday morning.

(31) Then they drew apart. [214-16]

Of paragraph (22) above, Al Alvarez has the following appreciative words to say:

even though the behaviour of those outside the still centre of beatitude is less a comedy of manners than a stylised, roaring farce, this in itself can become a strength .... I can think of very little as subtle and concentrated as this that is being written in either form, prose or poetry. [Alvarez 1961:656]

Of exactly the same paragraph, Rodney Mather writes:

The golden sphere is interposed by White's artistic act between us and the experience talked about. It is not seen by the Jew and Mrs Godbold, and only "glimpsed" (metaphorically) by Mrs Flack and Mrs Jolley. It is an imported, factitious metaphor, essentially part of the reading experience. The vantage-point it creates supports that "quick as snakes", which is emphatically not experienced by Mrs Flack and Mrs Jolley .... The point here is that writing that seeks to render the texture of experience can, by generating image-structures, become a way out ... life for art's sake. [Mather 1970:41]

It is a strange metatextual demand to make of a metaphor, that it be "seen" by fictional characters—and, of a simile, that it be similarly "experienced". But let us turn briefly to the macrocontext. In these pages there is—must be—a narrator who provides analysis that goes beyond the articulable preverbal awareness of the observing characters. It is, however, surprising just how little such diegesis there is. The sentence "Many a passer-by" (1) is externally and hypothetically focalized, down to (especially) "rend their souls"—where the anticipated horrors can be regarded as part of the mental lexicon of the ladies (as, in *The Solid Mandala,* of Mrs Dun and, with a different weighting, of Mrs Poulter). There is the lexical choice of "electric" (3); there is the ranking in the sentence "It was Mrs Jolley who realized first" (4); there is the somatic focus of "honest corsets" (9), the communality of "wish-bone legs" (13).

Up to this point, however, the remaining diegesis is accessible to figural consciousness, even the metaphorizings (for the subjectively threatening "mops of weeds", compare the threatening grass at the Browns' and the wet "mops" of phlox at the Feinsteins'). Evaluations are generated by the psychology of *Schadenfreude* ("suitably, obscenely poor"; the sullen reluctance to acknowledge the vital presence of the willows; the sight the women must "make do with"; the triumphantly erased concession of "if glitteringly clean"). There is some free indirect discourse ("Then, if you please ... a woman, a woman .... Some no-account woman"; the ataxis in "For the owner", etc.; "Strange? ... dreadful!"), but the mode is never overworked, overextended, overly present here, or anywhere in White. The naming is figurally role-referential ("The two ladies"— compare the later, narratorially external "the two observers", and the much later, figural, ethically weighted "the intruders") or figurally classificatory ("the foreign Jew" for the ladies' initial mind-set, "a/some woman"; "the owner" contextualized against their registration of the house and the woman; "the man" contextualized against their registration of the woman plus the prospect of sexual intrigue). What Mrs Jolley "had failed to observe" she now observes with a vengeance, the emotive colouring of "such disgraceful dilapidation" (as the human extension of the house to its "owner") being a discreetly latinate and abstract beginning to a catalogue which comes right out with it at the anti-semitic, Anglo-Saxon close: "such a truly fearful nose". Then comes a retreat into mental discretion with the ubiquitous handhold of "In the circumstances". And, throughout, there has been the customary differentiation of White's speech-tags,

The long paragraph (16) detailing the communion of Himmelfarb and Mrs Godbold against the evening light blends narratorial and figural perspectives. What is witnessed must be depicted for the reader so that he, too, can be "made to know, but could not, could not tell" (the epizeuxis conveying the characters' frantic efforts to "tell" or interpret). The kinetic metaphor of the opening face is thus undercut by the inchoateness of "some experience of a private nature"—the indeterminacy of which mediates both the privacy and the observers' awareness that they need to acknowledge this to conceal their intrusion. There is a conjectural drawing-back with "perhaps", which yet involves another positive move towards the confident metaphor of light dissolving both emotions and Mrs Godbold's hair. This forward movement towards the epiphanic ("aureole") is again checked—this time, clearly, by the ladies' rationality—hence the elusive syncretism here of analytical abstracts and free-indirect modality—and demoted to "an agreeable background". A seed, however, has already been sown via the inconspicuous gnomic subordination "which life leaves behind". This is not an auctorial comment, but a projection into the scene of the ladies' own awareness of the "discouragement and doubt" in their own lives (which—though this is nowhere stated—shapes their malevolence as much as Blue's familial discouragements shape his; evil is not absolute in White). The metaphors of the next sentence are, of course, imperialistic (narratorial) representations of the ladies' preverbal apperception. The experience is not wholly accessible ("a certain ..."; the alternative formulation) and the action is resisted ("talking, *even* laughing"). The conjectural "whether"–structure of the sentence following keeps figural speculation at the forefront, but obliquely so (the talk about "some event of importance" imitating the earlier phrase; the reference to "defences", incidentally, occurs in *The Solid Mandala,* where Waldo is conscious of eavesdropping on his parents). Conjectural thought-processes are conveyed later in the free-indirect parenthesis "—it could have been ...". And we are approaching the metaphor maligned by Mather.

It is no criticism of the narrative/narration that "the golden sphere" is "only 'glimpsed'" by the onlookers. This glimpse, however, is epiphanically true. Not only that: as is commonly the case with Whitean epiphany, the "metaphors" involved—the classification is inadequate—have their feet on the ground, as it were. We should not forget the prior, generative *Ur-Gestalt* of the round faces/heads, on high, against the evening light, the esemplastic extension of this into the "aureole" of light on the (rounded crown) of hair, the Buberian implication of dancing circularity in the reference to the "motes and gnats", the psychological extension of social communion into the bridging metaphors of "that envelope, or womb of light". Mrs Jolley and Mrs Flack "see" the wholeness of perfect friendship, whose roundedness is "defence" enough against the gaze probing from without. And the light that splinters against teeth (breaking against the laughter of fortressed friendship) is the light of the evening again.

It cannot be disputed that these evil ladies, too, know the experience of friendship "at the moment of departure" (despite Mrs Jolley's probings of Mrs Flack's weak points, they stay and stick together); they also have their departure overleaf, and the experience of friendship is independent of morality. But what they witness is the intercourse of amity between people *they* would not expect (or wish) to share close bonds. Note that the preliminary metaphor of the "ball of friendship" is embedded diffusely, via a narrowing from the general ("people") to the particular. And the deictic "There" brings the experience wholly within the subjective purview of the ladies. Then comes an extension, again towards light as substance (synaesthesia), in the direction of the radical, alogical tropes so typical of White's narratives at moments of transfigured character-perception. The closing sentence of the paragraph is a narrational *leurre*, leading Mather off snuffling down a false trail. The figurally exclamatory free indirect discourse ("How private ... it was") cannot be expunged by the syntactic redirection of the sentence into a nominalization. "Even the intruders suspected" suggests that Himmelfarb and Mrs Godbold, too, must only "suspect" the quality of their encounter, which is nonsense after the evidence supplied by the interpretation of prior gesture ("by consent"). The ladies, aware that they are intruding on an unfathomable moment, must expect the actants on the veranda to know more than *they* do; it is in the nature of intrusion that this should be so. What is happening narrationally is that the ladies are already drawing back from the overwhelming experience—hence the whiplash downturn of the last clause, whose privative structure ("deterred momentarily") permits an iconic *return* to the initial situation of malevolence. Now they *are* "hating" again, re-clothing themselves, no longer out of their minds (a form of vicarious *ek-stasis*): compare "reason would not submit to that".

What follows is a conjunction of church/Christ and serpent-indices ("'Tsst!'", "hissed", "flickered"), including the colloquial "quick as snakes". This has an intertextual relevance, of course, within the pattern of malevolence—but is it true that the "image-structure" itself, at this point, is an evasion, a fabrication, not a representation of something figurally experienced? The conversation is conducted according to conventions of complicitous amicability. The participants are aware of the significance of what they say, and Mrs Flack *knows* that they have been in the position of eavesdroppers (what *we* might choose to think of as snakes in the grass or, in terms of the macrocontextual indices, envious serpents in a willow-girt Eden); she *knows* this is exciting, *knows* she must reinforce their complicity of attentiveness to Mrs Godbold, who (the aspectuality of "had begun" tells us) has started to go inside while they have been whispering. Of course Mrs Flack is self-importantly aware of how she uses Mrs Godbold's movement to reinforce their friendship. That the expression "quick as snakes" is bivocal (with Mrs Flack's demotic consciousness encoded, along with her awareness of her histrionic surreptitiousness) is quite a different matter from claiming that it is not "experienced" and only part of the "reading experience" (what isn't, anyway?).

THE ART OF DESCENDING: WHITE-PARODIES

There are no good published parodies of White—certainly nothing remotely approaching the quality of Max Beerbohm's parody of Henry James, and not even up to the indifferent level reached by A.L. Rowse's attempt to imitate the same author's style (both parodies are discussed at length in Chatman 1972:113–35). The second of two parodies of White attempted by Peter Hastings (1961) is doomed to failure by virtue of the fact that it is obliged to follow the present-tense and generic-contextual conventions of the book review; apart from which, it is far too short to encompass the most salient style-features of its model, *Voss*. Hastings has, anyway, essentially cannibalized actions and descriptive moments from his more extended parody of the same novel (1960), which likewise misses the mark.

Parodies are expected to be exaggeration; but one must be careful about what one exaggerates. It is, for example, a mistake to hammer away with too many instances of the one descriptive detail; the impression of accumulation given in a parody of modest length is not characteristic of the original—so the parody is not true to the judgement of the author of the original. Even on matters of content, Hastings is not careful enough in presenting, say, "Moss", who is reduced in terms of descriptive detail to repetition of the words "triumphantly" or "brutal", whereas the characteristic Whitean treatment of Voss is to provide a broad range of evaluations which clash fruitfully with one another—as witness the occurrences of the word "distressed", which would have offset the monolithic impression made by Hastings' parody. Too much is on the surface, and of the surface, that was characteristically oblique in the novel. To reduce Voss to a heel-clicking, bespectacled Von Stroheim is not to parody the fictional figure but to replace him with a prefabricated or stock parody-figure. This also applies to the representation of Moss's mangled teutonic English, which is not subtly exaggerated but is at the juvenile comic-book level (eg, "'You would not think without food I can so long go'"—cf *Voss* 27: "'Only recently I have eaten'", which is almost the sole instance in the novel of unequivocal language-interference). Sometimes it is neutral actional features that are incorporated ("Moess" rhyming with "worse", in imitation of Mrs Bonner's "bad poem" on "Voss" and "loss", 25), or there is a—legitimately parodistic—reduction of Laura's "ESP" fever to the effects of Moss as witch-doctor hexing "Lucy" with a voodoo doll.

Some phrases are characteristic of White ("But in time she would understand"; "Laughter welled against his uvula, gathered pressure, and burst briefly out"; "the glittering man"). Others are lifted almost whole from the text ("splintered upon the rock of my will"; "Something had made this young woman lugubrious"—where "lugubrious" is Hastings' metatextual criticism of the style, and where the deictic is, of course, a style feature). White's "grey voice" and "very red voice" *(Voss* 12/60) turns up as "a white voice", "her red voice", "a white, matter-of-fact voice". Some of White's meiotic techniques have been detected (the use of "perhaps", or "unexpected but not unpleasant sound"), and his evasive structures (eg, "Whether from deliberate rudeness or fatigue or mere indifference it would not be possible for a stranger to tell"—cf *Voss* 9). Characteristic of the affective, nineteenth-century diction of the novel, but not of White's other novels, are adverbial intensifiers; Hastings picks this up and pounds the feature into the dust (eg, "blushed most fearfully", "a most fearful wen", "most horribly"), along with subjectively hyperbolic adverbs ("[most] terribly", "tremendously"). But neither parody convinces, and it is easy enough to see why: Hastings has concentrated on incidentals (frequently, it seems, without understanding why they were there in the original), and has failed to build his parodies on a framework of stylistic essentials.

Of the features most characteristic of *Voss* (and, with one exception, of most of his other novels), the following are absent from Hastings' parodies: the *do*-proform (eg, "but she did always hesitate at first", *Voss* 7); the subjective progressive (eg, "Miss Trevelyan was saying", 15); deictic "it" referring to prior speech (eg, "It had begun to come more easily to him", 12); the gnomic present (eg, the famous "Order does prevail", 12); *So*-linkages (eg, "So the light began to flow in the high room", 12). Apart from sentences beginning with "And/But" plus verb or "And/But" plus phrasal completion (Hastings: "But did not"; "And sat brooding terribly"; "And about Rosa"; "But whispering"), there is no employment of radical ataxis apart from "As he ..." (Hastings 1960:col.2). Atactic structures have not been used at all to suggest psychological processes: they just sit there awkwardly on the page, pointless gestures. With one exception ("Mr Tatlock not so much answered as conceded"), no parodistic advantage has been taken of the rich variety of "deviant" tagging procedures so characteristic of White's novels. The same applies to the great range of applications of free indirect discourse. Granted: there are two instances ("She would not be vanquished by any man. Not by her father. Not even by God"; "Was it imagination or was this woman still daring to challenge his will?"); but there is not the characteristic variety, flexibility and textual saturation to be found in *Voss,* let alone the highly specialized use of modal verbs, or any appreciation of White's use of the articles.

Victor Niris's parody (1957), which draws chiefly on *Riders in the Chariot*, is much shorter than Hastings' first one. The parodistic effect is somewhat attenuated by the uncharacteristic content of direct speech and by too great an incidence of adjectival premodifiers. Niris is better on psychologized discourse (a wider variety of ataxis, but wilfully inserted; free direct discourse; adverbial modifiers such as "of course", "at least", "perhaps"; free-indirect questions; single-sentence paragraphs; the "you"–form). With two exceptions ("Miss Quenby ventured", and a split before a *that*–clause in direct speech), Niris neglects tagging, for all the frequency of direct speech. He throws in one conjectural modal in a disjunctive clause ("The oracle laughed richly, it could have been a woman or a man"), a sylleptic construction ("His eyes glittered with sullenness and sun"), synaesthesia ("The red laughter of a row of soup cans denied nothing", which also includes an oblique negation). White's connotative use of adjectives is well-captured ("a crimson presence", "nubile silver wheels", "the permissive air"), as is the religious diction ("the sanctum"—a straight pinch from the office-scene; "altars of frozen glass"; "votive bread"), which Niris even builds into direct speech ("'Those who *elect* to take the econ. size will be *saving* fifteen cents'"). There are also isolated attempts at onomatopoeia and sociolectal verbs (eg, "fancied"). Above all, the mundane setting that was stipulated in the competition (a scene at the Sarsaparilla Supermarket) encouraged maximum conjunction between the prosaic and the transcendental (talk of arrowroot biscuits leads to: "They stared at each other, sharing a common mystery"; there is the elevated direct speech of the "oracle", "her olive eyes glistening with vitality and malice"). Again, however, none of the central style-features listed above occurs, except ataxis.

These two parodies at least serve to confirm the fact that conspicuous disjunction of syntax is parodiable without much understanding of the function of ataxis in White; that parody underscores the stylistic centrality of the technique; and that more subtle discoursal features which are not thrust in the reader's face but which are detectable only through attentive reading do not turn up in parodies: with the result that the parodies feel "empty" (or vacuous) and off-beam, precisely because the rough surface is there without either the fine texture or the informing structure that give the style its full body.

In this extension of enquiry beyond *The Solid Mandala*, I have sought to indicate, by schematic analysis, how key style-features recur in a later novel by White (*The Twyborn Affair*). The detailed organization of White's style needs to be kept in mind when gauging the intentional pitch of his narrative discourse; to show this, I went back to earlier novels of the major phase to demonstrate what can be learnt from juxtaposing new readings against the interpretative conclusions of earlier readers. Finally, this procedure was turned inside out, as it were, by examining briefly what the process of parody can tell us in respect of White's discourse and style (parody being a potentially useful kind of re-creative, metacritical reading of texts in the form of paraphrastic transposition). In moving towards a general conclusion, I now want to go beyond the novels themselves and consider White's place in the world of modernist discourse and style that he has helped to shape.

III   Discourse again

Matters of style as discussed above have been viewed as inextricably linked with "point of view", focalization, voicing, etc. The link between these various areas is one of representational functionality. This question of function thus always arises in connection with narrative discourse as a style-system or level of style. The central problematical complaint about White's discoursal style is not that of ambiguity or indeterminacy of "point of view", or that of confusing shifts of perspective—such complaints can be settled by reeducating White's critics to recognize the narrational principles of slipping and free indirect discourse (as a fulcrum or nodal reference). The big problem (shown to be non-existent in *The Solid Mandala,* but possibly present in other novels with different concerns) is that of the intrusive author, whether in the general diegetic guise of the narrator or in the more specific manifestation of aphoristic or gnomic content. I grant figural consciousness more of a functional role in White's novels than Stanzel, say, would probably deem healthy; and I have, for convenience of discussion, viewed stretches of White's diegesis as taking the specific mediative form of consonant psychonarration. In regard to the latter, however, I am sceptical about the presence of a narrator with a specific *Gestalt.* And because my experience of reading White's novels has never brought me even remotely close to a subjective impression that an implied author or extradiegetic narrator is intruding or obtruding (although I recognize such presences in Fielding, Jane Austen or Thackeray), I am still a little puzzled about the critics' perennial complaint about White's obtrusiveness, "conscious manipulation", and the like.

I am not out to perpetrate the "fallacy of the abolished author" in the Barthesian sense (Watts 1983:26–28 has applied enough common sense to dissuade me from denying the author his auctorial immanence). Nor do I wish, on the other hand, to support the speech-act argument that, because every sentence is performative, all discourses have speakers (and therefore narrators, even if only fictive narrators), or the generic argument that it is convenient to assume narrators for all fictions "since it makes them a universal characteristic of fiction, thus separating it from drama" (Kuiper/Small 1986:497). Nor, again, am I prepared to follow Banfield (eg, 1973:34–35) all the way in making all texts narrator-less which do not have "the first-person pronoun" in diegesis or any "linguistic signs of the speaker". If "a third person narrator can play no part at all in a story he is telling" (Kuiper/Small 1986:502), then we are going to have problems with identifying the narrational instance in a psychologically and actionally self-reflexive narrative like *The Solid Mandala*. As a working hypothesis, I should like to take over Nomi Tamir's functional approach:

I do not claim that in nonpersonal discourses the narrator does not "exist". I simply suggest that in describing certain discourses we can talk about *"degree zero of the narrator"*, which means that even if there "is" a narrator, he does not fulfill any function in the narration and is therefore *negligible*.... Even if every narration does imply a potential speaker (or narrator), this potentiality is not always realized. A personal narrator, who is not only a "voice" but an individual, a distinct figure, is a full realization of the speaker-potentiality. In other cases this potentiality is left formant, never realized. [Tamir 1976:421]

One tricky loophole clause may still cause headaches: "A narrative with local realization of the potential speaker (the so-called 'intrusions of the author') will occupy a ... position near the nonpersonal pole". As regards White, examination of contextual function explains the "intrusive author" in White as a subjective delusion, as functionally "negligible", as explicable in other ways, and as a very occasional, parodistic manipulation of genre-conventions.

One can move further in this direction. Shari Benstock has made a study of Joyce's *Ulysses*, with findings that have implications for the status of narration and style in White. She rejects the conventional view that "the shifting viewpoint and increasingly embellished styles" of *Ulysses* are "products of a narrator's disposition towards his subject", including his wit and wordplay (Benstock 1980:260–61). The traditional view has a disembodied, objective narratorial viewpoint taking on a distinctive, "well-spoken" perspective distorted by the inherent colloquialism of the characters' speech. Beyond this figural, idiolectal distortion, a second or "vivid" narrator inserts a related, more hieratic (or poetic) variety of character-idiolect. Neither narrator is personalized, but both have "presence". Benstock argues that psychological motivation behind a narratorial voice is determinable only in first-person narrative (as in the Cyclops episode). In the body of *Ulysses*, there is no "pellucidly objective reporter" or authoritative "omniscient" author "hidden behind an effaced narrator". "Style is not superimposed on the text but arises from its subject" (261). In terms of free indirect discourse, "changes in point of view and tone reflect a shift in fictional contexts .... in the absence of a present speaker (the 'I'), a narrative void is created which is then filled by the subject—by character, setting, event—and narration becomes the end product of various subjects (or contexts) vying against each other for entrance into the narrative line" (261).

Analyzing the opening pages of Joyce's novel, Benstock discusses the contextual implications of various evaluative lexemes (among them the famed "stately, plump"). The "naturalistic third-person context to which the reader clings" is put in doubt by the sentences' having their source in character-perception (which may produce competing character-lexicons that function simultaneously). "This narrative doubling is a consistent feature of *Ulysses*, apparent in narration and internal monologue alike, and is achieved by a juxtaposition of contextual subjects, not by the division of narrative labors between 'speakers'" (263); it "undermines the *appearance* of objectivity" (264).

It is commonly assumed that a narrator supplies comic-ironic indicators of tone in descriptions of character-action. Benstock argues, conversely, that "probable cause" can be offered for evaluations as being "self-reflexive comment" on a character's action, arising from a non-logical area of consciousness. In "impersonal" narration, we cannot assume that a narrator is both objective *and* committed to selecting ironically evaluative terms, even though we as readers may indeed detect irony (264—65). Blandly descriptive sentences may suggest the absence of a character's thought/speech patterns, "but this does not conversely suggest the presence of a narrator's objectivity". Such narrative spaces are "filled by lexical and syntactic 'impersonality', implying ... merely inattention on the part of the subject". Benstock continues:

[free indirect discourse translates sense-data into verbal forms, levels of consciousness implying that] the most conscious thoughts tend always to be the more prosaic, specific, logical, and directly respondent to external stimuli; subliminal consciousness records reactions to experience in a disjointed and assimilative form only because it is further removed from the parataxic logicity of surface thought; it feels rather than reasons; it orders experience along associational rather than analytical modes, by correspondence and synaesthesia: *the terms in which this level of thought is rendered evoke the subject in a vocabulary that may not necessarily belong to the character's speaking or writing idiom.* [Benstock 1980:266—67; her emphasis]

The dislocations of Joyce's more "poetic", hieratic prose are a "stylized presentation", with its "vocabulary" being putatively accessible to a character, but not necessarily its *ductus*. What this prose conveys are "visceral responses that lie outside the 'thinking' functions of consciousness" (267—68); it is not the mind that orders this prose but the emotions.

I would endorse Benstock's view (and that of Iser 1976:320—21) that the reader, defeated in his expectation of narratorial guidance in *Ulysses*, creates his own series of narrator-guides (for Iser, the "implied author") in response to the foregrounding of style. In one respect, Benstock has it easier with Joyce than readers do with White: in Joyce, third-person narration is either much more clearly subjugated quantitatively to quoted monologue (towards the beginning) or to free indirect discourse or narrated monologue (from the middle of the novel onwards), and is saturated with idiolectal markings, regulated and differentiated quite cleanly in accordance with the specific narrative models Joyce has chosen to parody. In White, quoted monologue (or stream of consciousness) is rare—and even where the journal-narrative of *The Twyborn Affair* has first-person voicing, the constant shifting of tense from past to present is effected within a diegetic frame that resembles conventional "narratorial" narrative just as much as does White's "third-person" narrative. Formal disruption of the latter by slipping into discrete stretches of quoted monologue or narrated monologue is much less a felt presence in White's narratives than is the constant infusion into consonant psychonarration of "alogical" syntax and the affective and mental markers of free indirect discourse. Instead of pure, "conventional" free indirect discourse or pure consonant psychonarration, we experience a mode which is so shaped as to render impossible the functional or ventriloquial identification of a narrator with a character (we are in the character, and lose awareness of the act of narrating), or the narration seems to have all the lineaments of dissonant or intrusive psychonarration, and even auctorial comment. What we do *not* have is the "dual voice" of free indirect discourse (Pascal 1977). Instead, there is a radical duality of mutually exclusive possibilities (more like the model of bivocality or heteroglossia postulated by Bakhtin, with the "auctorial" potentiality of the text being recoverable only as an abstracted metalevel of meaning which depends crucially on the amount of thematic significance from our understanding of *the whole text* that we allow to flow back into our sequential, processual reading). As readers, we cannot be persuaded to responses that entail an impossible schizophrenia in which both states of consciousness are experienced simultaneously.

If the mental events occasioned in us by reading a text are accounted for "objectively" by our assuming "isomorphic relations [of predominance or deviation] between linguistic configurations and reader's responses" (Kintgen 1977:9—10), then this is how a "style" becomes associated with "certain linguistic characteristics" of White's fictions. If a reader's private, subjective reconstitution of White's meaning is different from mine because of his differing experiential status as an *archilecteur,* then there are good reasons why he should (like Wolfe 1983, for instance) posit the presence of an obtrusive or omniscient auctorial voice or a non-figural narrator, and find fault, incongruity and inconsistency in precisely those style features which I regard as the functional *sine qua non* and irremovable essence of White's style and narrative discourse. Constrictively conditioning presuppositions about White's modes of narration and stylistic persistencies cannot be conjured out of existence by apodictic fiat. Given the validity of Stanzel's view of modal predominances and of Genette's view of temporary infractions of dominant focalization,[3] my appeal can only be for an experimental, pragmatic assumption by the reader of an alternative set of expectations, the provisional acceptance of a different mode of entering White's texts. Apart from which, Benstock's so emphatically italicized assertion above that character-consciousness can be represented in language without consonance of style was stated decades ago by Faulkner, whose views on narration I am inclined to respect. My view is that the "objectivity" (and much of the irony) sensed in White's narratives is not a function of a patrician, auctorial, archly manipulative, smartly (or bleakly) self-conscious and manneristically automatic perspective and style, but is the consequence of the author's application of his own epistemology to the reactive and interactive relationship between fictional actants and fictive world. The representation of character has been replaced by the representation and verbal reenactment of consciousness.

---

[3] And in full cognizance of the fact that the very term "focalization" has come under critical scrutiny since Genette first introduced it (see, for instance: Genette himself, 1988:72–78; Chatman 1986; Nünning 1988).

IV   White's fellow-illuminates and the novel of consciousness

White's novels not explorations of character? This may sound strange, in view of the conspicuous strain of social satire in White's fiction (or what we reconstitute as a satiric or ironic tonality), the almost obsessively negative exploration of social gesture and petrified social codes. And it is not a harping on one tone, either: there are quite distinct organ-stop blends of satire and irony in his novels. This alone could serve to differentiate the checked discriminations of *The Tree of Man* or *Voss* from the fiercer eruptions in *Riders in the Chariot* or *The Vivisector,* the renewed, cool awareness of historical and generic ironies in *The Eye of the Storm* and *A Fringe of Leaves* from the controlled frenzy with which White indulges his savage eye through that last upward arc of self-revelation in *The Twyborn Affair, Memoirs of Many in One,* and *Three Uneasy Pieces.* But it is evident from the responses of a myriad critics and readers that this stratum of White's narratives is as often faulted as it is praised, in terms that rest exclusively on equating the effects of representation with the assumed intentionality (personal attitudes and values) of the author. White, apparently, is cold, unsympathetic, gratuitously cruel; he does not *love* his characters (or, at least, reveals an unconscionable personal animus against his more negative creations, indifference towards the others); has no *fun* in writing, is irremediably stern; has an inexplicable (and, no doubt, embarrassing) fixation on humankind as caught with its pants down—excremental reductionism. All of these responses arise from the expectation that White's narratives perform the traditional task of representing character, and that he attempts to do this by collusion with the reader via clear signallings of his ultimate authoritative presence. (The trouble being—so the argument would go—that he does not seduce us, but talks down to us or tries to persuade us by hieratic, gnomic, obtrusive rhetorical assertion in order to get us to admit his illuminates or elected characters into the social web he has re-created.)

Let us consider this question of "character". John Bayley has summarized our attitudes towards characters in fiction as follows. Consensus, our expectant perception of precisely defined behaviour limited by a character's interaction with his society, is the spirit fuelling our responses to the novel of character. Most criticism of the novel is a process of predominantly moral "placing" of character in social contexts which are almost invariably "retrospective" (non-contemporary; hence F.R. Leavis's refusal to touch anything after Lawrence). Characters are there to be "used" by the reader for amusement "or for exemplary purposes" within "an ideal society for which the great novelist has a sure instinct" (Bayley 1974:227–29). With the contemporary removal of the concept of a supreme and cohesive social order, narrative "objectivity" becomes a quality that we resist, and we are unnerved by the replacement of a concentration on character with a concentration on consciousness:

When this harmony is jarred or destroyed by the author, and our sense of collusion compromised or removed, the justification of a *character* disappears: all that remains is the isolation, the malevolence, and the sheer bad faith of the author's consciousness .... We are ultimately repelled by these brilliantly drawn characters [in Lawrence and Dostoevsky] because they destroy our sense of social justification; they exemplify and give expression to nothing but their authors' desire for *self*-justification. Their objectivity is a fraud, for we have not been consulted, as it were, in their creation, and the social contract, of which ourselves and the author form a microcosmic part, has been violated by it. [Bayley 1974:230]

For Bayley, it is the love–hate relationship of, and with, bourgeois society that makes the novel of character, and our collusion with the author, possible. Committed or countercultural novelists fail, according to Bayley, by renouncing collusion, by "using" character to convey "an exemplary picture of contemporary reality" that is entirely dependent on the author's vision, not the reader's. The novelist may resume the direct authorial role of commentator to mediate moral values by manipulating character and reestablishing the/a social order (eg, Saul Bellow). An individual conception of political man can be imposed in such schematic and exclusive terms that the reader may find it hard to accept the represented world as one of social plenitude (eg, Heinrich Böll). Graham Greene's particular brand of existential Catholicism is (as George Orwell felt in the Forties) forced through in such a way that the reader feels marooned in an ocean of spiritual crisis, without the possibility of understanding character-psychology as adequately motivated by social setting. These authors constitute a kind of intermediate grouping, an attempt to snatch society from dissolution by idiosyncratic main force.

It is, however, Dostoevsky, Bayley argues, who paved the way for the contemporary novel of consciousness that requires *no* collusion between author and reader with regard to the social order, raises no expectation that we shall find characters as moral entities conducting their lives in accordance with the constraints of a recognizable and coherent social order:

the old character contract can only be filled today by the solitary consciousness which does not attempt to compound its solipsism [by the exercise of moral virtue] but accepts the amorality which is its logical consequence. This is the only consciousness which can set up a new kind of contract with us .... [Dostoevsky's] genius in colluding with the reader is due partly to the fact that all his characters ... are really one person, himself; partly to the fact that all are involved in dream, in a dramatic relation to their own self-awareness. There can be no deadening formula in Dostoevsky because there is no social reality for consciousness to manipulate and hence to be trapped by .... In Dostoevsky the contract [of the hated and the hater] is dissolved: its partners become one flesh. And this may be the condition to which the novel ultimately aspires, not to take over the world but to unify it into *Geist,* one indivisible solution of consciousness. [Bayley 1974:234–35]

In his autobiography, White seldom mentions the novelists he has read; even more seldom does he offer the reader hints as to his response to imaginative literature. What we find instead is an unwaveringly frank expression of distaste for the factitiousness of modern society, an emphasis on the need for individual relationships, individual solutions to problems of existence, and a quite non-egocentric willingness to supply information about his private existence and familial genesis, without any regard for "social" proprieties. Considering this accessibility of the personal and the relative inaccessibility of the artistically genetic, those occasions on which authors are actually mentioned resonate with significance. It was after his first novel was published, and in the midst of his soldiering during the Second World War, that White experienced his "discovery" of Dostoevsky's *The Possessed (Flaws:* 74), a discovery that is placed in "a certain moment", for which the book "had been waiting", and one which is aligned with his rediscovery of Dickens (misunderstood and detested in childhood) amidst the atrocities of Europe: "I saw Dickens as the pulse, the intact jugular vein of a life which must continue, regardless of the destructive forces Dickens himself recognized" *(Flaws:* 96)—and it is not the restoration of the social order that White is on about here, but something irreducible and invincible in the human psyche.

Dostoevsky must have been a shaping influence on White's mature fiction. If the obsession with heightened states of consciousness is a central point of contact, then so is the ultimate reference of individual fictive consciousnesses to the psychic identity of their creator, without the ego of the latter commanding the focus of narration as a felt presence. So is the pain of self-awareness, the implication of self in a world of dream, which is a world beyond the confines of socially constituted time. The intense involvement of both writers in the darkened and the illuminated sides of individual human existence is characterized by a sinking of the mind into the abyssal depths of physicality. This physicality defines man's feeling that he lives, not any awareness of social embedding; it both relativizes and defines the upward flight of consciousness towards an ecstatic emotionality that is yet checked by the ironic heteroglossia and bifurcated vision which Bakhtin detected in Dostoevsky. Consciousness is not amoral, but pre-moral. Hence the cold passion of the discourse of both writers; pressures on consciousness which seem to have their source in the moral conditioning of character are actually the working-out of a psychomachia. This battle is for individual wholeness, and the impingement of the perceived world upon fragmentary selves is what produces the motion towards wholeness in White's illuminates (the matter-of-*fact* equability with which they accept the marvellousness of the tangible world and the incessant extraordinary conjunctions between individual consciousnesses—everything that leaves so many of White's critics fumbling uneasily with the shreds of their rational and social systems and resenting the *fact*itiousness of the visionary). It is also what produces the fissures and cracks and shifting, heaving tectonic forces of White's syntax, metaphor, tonality, narrative perspective, and serene yokings of violently contrasting dualities.

To the extent that White's novels offer a critique of vulgar materialism—to the extent that they are still in any way "social" novels—they are offering a critique of petty social cruelties which arise both out of the backlash of tortured self-consciousness (Waldo; Mrs Flack and Mrs Jolley) and out of the wilful abdication of self-consciousness (which produces anaesthesia, the inurement of self to committed relationships with other individuals). The grotesquerie and low-demotic exploration of social mores in White are indebted to the lessons of Dickens. Behind the satire of both writers, their reductions of human beings to mechanical complexes of gesture, lies the possibility of understanding (this is how consciousness makes us behave) but not of forgiveness (there have been no individual transgressions to forgive, no possibility of an appeal to social morality or to the order of religious ethics). So that here, too, we are returned to consciousness: the difference being that Dickens still had confidence in the possibility of social order, and was sure enough of his compact with the reader that he could exploit the rhetoric of representation to luxuriate in sentiment.

In order to grasp the extremes of bathos and sublimity, blindness and insight, in White's fictions, we must follow the implicit injunction to see them as necessary parts of a whole. We cannot do this by falling back on artificial social constructs—all of White's central characters simply walk past and away from these—which are external to cognition and emotion; and we cannot do so by reverting to conventional assumptions about auctorial presence. Only by seeking the constant or weaving motion of figural consciousness in the narrative, and by accepting this as the governing presence from which any deflections towards conventional rhetoric must be judged, is it possible to grasp the rough, implacable subtlety of White's style and discourse.

Except in the earliest novels, this centering in human consciousness has little to do, technically, with the stream of consciousness tradition or with the "psychological novel" as based in that tradition. Adrian Mitchell takes the easiest possible way out in reducing White's individuality to a matter of genetic synthesis in respect of all his works: "His technique and his themes reflect the eclectic interests of the post-Lawrence, Joyce and Woolf era. His own distinctive narrative manner is forged from characteristic features of their style" (Mitchell 1981:146). I have yet to find elsewhere even isolated comments on White's style that confidently assume the existence of direct lines of transformation, naming names. The overwhelming consensus of puzzlement at White's style is sufficient denial of the validity of Mitchell's claim, which is essentially a continuation of A.D. Hope's suspicions about the subjective density of the "psychological novel" vis-à-vis the virtues of "the customary realistic novel" (Mitchell 1981:123). John Colmer, by way of amplifying his (justified) view that White "has created a new kind of novel", also makes vague gestures in the direction of the modernist tradition: White "has combined the amplitude of great nineteenth-century fiction with a sophistication of technique that owes something to the expressionism of James Joyce and Virginia Woolf" (Colmer 1978c:2). Where Mitchell points to White's "concentration on the individual's perception of self rather than of life", Colmer itemizes "fluidity of movement from one centre of consciousness to another", psychological rather than clock-time, and harmony sought "through the exercise of memory" (Colmer 1978c:2, 1982:193). These are indeed Whitean characteristics—but why attach them to Joyce and Woolf, when they are also true of Proust, say, and of at least certain "great nineteenth-century novelists" (Flaubert, Dostoevsky)? Colmer further asserts that "White's novels are closely related to the stream of consciousness novel, especially a work like Virginia Woolf's *Mrs Dalloway*" (1978c:2); any sober comparison of White's mature novels with Woolf's will show that they are light-years apart in terms of what matters—the characteristic particularities of style, figuration, narrative discourse.

Except as a means of proving White's difference, name-dropping reference to modernist influences in the mature work must continue to be a critical cul-de-sac, an academic reflex. Peter Beatson's epitaph on White, precisely by avoiding too close an identification, goes about as far as one can safely go in terms of specific allegiances: "He was the Last Great Modernist", translating the vision of Woolf, Joyce, Lawrence, Conrad et al. "into the evolving prose of the second half of the century" and injecting it "into the hitherto flat antipodean literary tradition" (Beatson 1991:233).

The only attempt ever made to examine the relationship between the characteristic thought and expression of White and those of another novelist is that of Rodney Mather (1970) in his comparative discussion of White and Lawrence. Lawrentian connections (and contrasts) are set up by other critics, and not only with regard to the early fiction. Associations with Joyce, Woolf and T.S. Eliot fall away fairly rapidly (although Joyce is still detected in *The Tree of Man*, *The Vivisector* and the short fiction—see Green 1956, *TLS* 1970, Myers 1978:3). Henry James, too, is not infrequently connected with White, as is William Faulkner.[4] Aside from *Happy Valley* (whose re-publication White doggedly resisted), there would appear to be no cogent grounds for either condemning or accounting for the nature and quality of White's style by reference to his illustrious forebears. So many different critics either have quite different notions about which novelist White resembles most—*The Living and the Dead*, for instance, is influenced by Lawrence (eg, Donaldson 1962, *TLS* 1961:889 and 1962) or is "not at all Lawrentian" (Ricks 1962)—or lump together such large numbers of modernist novelists when claiming that White resembles them all. This is symptomatic of something unwholesome in the mental processes of the critics, not in the linguistic processes of White's novels. It is a much less demanding—or, at least, less exhausting—critical game to exercise one's powers of generalization and discrimination upon the categories of thought supposedly detectable in fictions (and such categories include almost anything from social criticism to metaphysics, from character or symbolism to theme or structure) than it is to determine precisely the expressive basis, in language, of one's assumptions.

White's style is so radically individual that it is resisted by those who have been attracted to the categories of thought *because* their significance resides in the style. The persistent recursion to talk of influences, and to that inadequate terminus "stream of consciousness", is in line with a critical reflex which

---

[4] James is evoked for the style of White's short stories (Myers 1978:28), for a similar treatment of abstracts (Steiner 1974:111), for tone (TLS 1973), for psychological sensitivity (Stern 1948:5). Faulkner's "complexity" of prose can be detected in *The Vivisector* (Rosenthal 1970:538), while White's earlier books reveal a tendency towards Faulkner's "densely clotted, inexorable slow march" (*TLS* 1973). Carolyn Bliss (1987:32) has quoted White as saying in a 1972 interview that he stopped reading Faulkner after a critic claimed that Faulkner had influenced him. Bliss herself draws many suggestive parallels between the two writers—more at the level of plot and theme, but also in terms of "the intricacies of motive and moral [sic] consciousness".

categorizes thought-structures in fiction so as to domesticate them within the realm of the pre-existent. It is indeed possible to perform this task successfully if a writer's style is so effaced as to influence "meaning" in no intrinsic and conspicuous way (as in the case of Graham Greene or V.S. Naipaul; this is not to say that there aren't styles which are so "effaced" as to foreground particular aspects of meaning: eg, Vonnegut's or Brautigan's). If, however, "style" refuses to go away (as with Nabokov, James, Faulkner, or White) when stared at balefully, it tends to stimulate unease in critics, who resist entertaining the idea that their neat taxonomies of significance might be compromised by a "language" they have been unable to account for. The contours of Faulkner's style have, over the years, come to be accepted as intrinsic to the signification of his fictions; and its individual lineaments of rhetoric and sentence-structure have been accommodated to conventional stylistic categories. Nabokov's ultra-literate, protean play with pre-existing styles can be recognized as the finest exemplification of parodistic discourse since Joyce; but not even his most local semantic transformations (eg, his delight in punning) lead him to step off that grand, high, silver wire between base expropriation and radical deformation. White does not perform this kind of Nabokovian high-wire act, and he is not so obsessively centred and selective in his modes of re-formation as Faulkner. Nabokov and Faulkner have been assimilated into criticism, their "message" acknowledged as being determined by the "medium". White has seldom been so blessed, the "medium" being banished to some outland beyond sympathetic scrutiny, or summarily classified as "central" before being shunted off onto some siding where it can threaten the critic's concentration no more. Meanwhile, the "symbol-hunting" so detested by White goes on apace.

Lest, then, I should myself be accused of going against what I have just been saying and aligning myself with the influence-hunters, I hasten to emphasize the potential value of *heuristic* rather than genetic associations between White and other modernist writers. To the duo of forefathers (Dostoevsky and Dickens) mentioned earlier, I would add two others to make up the heuristic quaternity pre-echoing White's style and vision: James, and Faulkner. It is possible to make instead a pentangle of affinities by including Flaubert for his doctrine of style, his transcendence of the categories of realism and naturalism, his recognition of psychological frailty and his attempts to enact the rescue of the individual from the asphyxiating, formulaic pressures of bourgeois society. If style-criticism is to be effective, it must be able in some considerable measure to account for continuities and discontinuities of style-features in terms of the exigencies of discourse as fictive representation; and there is also the reverse vector to consider: from narration to style. A high degree of coextensivity can be postulated between the kind of epistemic modality that is deducible from a particular complex of mutually informing style-features and the pattern of fictive action established within a writer's oeuvre. It is in this area that comparative stylistic analysis is likely to throw most light on the detailed functioning and *raison d'être* of White's narrative style. I have found considerable value in Seymour Chatman's investigation of James's late style; it is there that the epistemological and referential foundations of narrative discourse are most clearly revealed. Apart from my own work on tagging-procedures, modal markers and strategies of text-cohesion, there are of course other more mundane topics that would repay comparative investigation—the sentence-structure of White, for instance (patterns of lexical modification, left- and right-branching preferences, etc; cf Short 1946 on James); or further examination of the connection between punctuation and point of view (cf Menikoff 1970 on James).

It is, however, Faulkner who would furnish the most productive areas of comparison, notwithstanding the fact that the structure of his sentences, the specific persistencies of discoursal, lexical and cohesive markers, and the deployment of narrative perspective would, on the face of it, seem to provide few points of contact (despite legitimate subjective assertions of affinity in terms of the massive, ineluctable flow of narrative). Hemingway I would leave out of the present complex equation (White disliked his style; see Marr 1991:150–51). If Harry Levin's excellent essay on the style proves anything, it is that Hemingway's deceptive simplicity of language is not the same sort of simplicity (of non-scenic obliquity) often found in White. For all the American's deployment of free indirect discourse (Levin 1951:162), the technique concentrates essentially on the impact of external sensation on consciousness, whereas White's more complex narrating mode (and recoverable ideology) explores retrospection and introspection: the former a feeding off the self, the latter a kind of extramission, in which consciousness, forever evading the present moment, moves out anticipatorily to encounter sensation. The very disposition of syntax, although in both cases it can encode the equation of "emotion with bodily sensation" (Levin 1951:162), is opposingly structured in the two writers, and has a different relation to time. In Hemingway, there is a quasi-behaviouristic "exaltation of the instant" which pervades his prose (Levin 1951:160, with reference to a suggestion by Magny), whereas awareness and epiphany in White are heavily relativized.

I do not wish to end with a disquisition on the style of Faulkner; criticism has come to terms with that style and the vision that informs it. It is helpful, however, to consider the advantages that might be gained by an extension of comparative study beyond the point reached by Schermbrucker (1973), and in terms more faithful to White than those in which Mather (1970) compares him with Lawrence. The fundamental lines of affinity between Faulkner and White can be summarized as the following three, inextricably intertwined, aspects: a preoccupation with subjective temporality; a difficult, foregrounded style, without which the fictions would crumble to dust in the mind; and a problematical relationship between auctorial authority and the narrational presences experienced by the reader.

The question of the *evaluation* of Faulkner's style has always been tricky; false premises are, or were, a ghostly presence as they are in the case of White. The normative negativity of some earlier judgements is inescapable, even in appreciative reviewers ("overelaborate ... baroque and involuted ... sentences"— Aiken 1939:137). Summative analyses of the style can claim stylistic inadequacy and promptly steer in another direction: "No other contemporary American novelist of comparative stature has been as frequently or as severely criticized for his style as has William Faulkner .... However, an enumeration of his faults in style would leave still unsaid the most important things about his style" (Beck 1941:142). Or normative criteria may be thrown out of court in favour of pragmatism: "The language, the 'metaphysical' style of the writer, perhaps decadent, is indefensible from the point of view of correctness or of clarity, but it is marvelously proper for showing the unity of an interior and a qualitative world" (Mayoux 1952:171). In White, too, one should neither condemn nor bypass stylistic "abnormality", but hold it at the centre of scrutiny. In both writers, difficulty is the condition of the rewritten contract or non-social compact established between author and reader. Tonal and perspectival shifts, ambiguity and irresolution, are designed "to make facile interpretation impossible"; Faulkner's is a presentative art designed "to free the emotional life from the 'trammel' of critical thinking" (Slatoff:195, 193—by which this "thinking" may be regarded as a negative burden both outside the text, on the author/reader axis, and within it, on the axis of representation). We are touching here, of course, on the difficult topic of narrative perspective.

Claude–Edmonde Magny is in some respects a forerunner of Wolfgang Iser: she posits a "Witness" interposed between author and reader—a "Mediator" who identifies with the characters, and with whom we identify: our identification transforms us into the individual characters. Faulkner's emotion is objectified outside himself; his difficulty and obscurity force us to discriminate, to become "the authors of what we read" (Magny 1948:73–74). Another slant is offered by Warren Beck: the "very tentativeness" of characters' hypotheses, with "Faulkner's persuasive subjectivity" injecting "abstractions", "creates for the reader the clouded enigmatic perspective of reality itself" (Beck 1941:152). Another French view is that "there is an interchange of subjective awareness among the [fictional] participants that enables us to go directly to the scene and to forget the author" (Mayoux 1952:157).

It can be seen that the question of the narrating moment is as complicated in Faulkner as it is in White, and it is to such questions that many studies of the novel are addressed (eg, Ulich 1972). However, examinations of perspective and narrative structure in Faulkner customarily refer detailed analysis of rhetoric and style to the nature of the represented world or to the author's ultimate authority for this as represented world-view (eg, Swink 1972). An exception to this is the magisterial study by Weber (1969), which has as its main axis of investigation the relationship between narrative style and character-psychology, without unnecessary complication through extensive consideration of auctorial presence (a critical focus which is, of course, facilitated by the very nature of *The Sound and the Fury*). Style-studies such as that of F.C. Riedel (1957) are, by contrast, too objectively categorial and normative to provide more than a partial taxonomic basis for the attempts of others to provide a functional justification of syntax and lexis in terms of figural psychology. A lexico-semantic approach such as Florence Leaver's (1958) is useful chiefly for the connections it makes with the thematic preoccupations of Faulkner's fiction—but we must ourselves undertake the task of working back from this perspective to understand the determination of lexis by character-psychology rather than by auctorial world-view. It is critics such as Robert Zoellner (1959) and Dorothy Hale (1989) who get closest to justifying style-features functionally in terms both of auctorial world-view and of character-consciousness, and this with proper regard for the sense-constitutive burden placed upon the reader. All of the features Zoellner isolates—"syntactical ambiguity, time alternation, delayed modification, suspension and enclosure, and dramatic periodicity" (Zoellner 1959:490)—are seen as relevant to the modality of consciousness, as a resistance to "the reader's ingrained tendency to break up experience into convenient, logically divided parcels" (491); and such features might profitably be compared with similar taxonomies established for White's prose.

Beneath the research on Faulkner's style done since the Fifties lies the groundwork of predominantly French critics. Given the centrality in White of the processes of memory and "mythic" time or Hypnos, such commentaries on Faulkner have relevance, since a main preoccupation of these French critics has been the relationship between time and human consciousness.

> The past is not so much an evocation as it is a constant pressure upon the present .... Consciousness, therefore, is mostly memory. But ... memory is so much part of what actually exists that it ... does not know itself as anything but the sense of reality .... The past is not the temporal past, that which no longer is and can only be remembered. It is something here and now .... since Faulkner [unlike Proust] refuses chronological time, he has nothing to analyze, subjective reality absorbs everything and becomes fate. [Pouillon 1946:80–82]

Jean–Jacques Mayoux relates Pouillon's observations more specifically to narrative context: "Faulkner does not intellectually abstract the scene, but absorbs it into a *moment* keyed to a peculiar emotional note and quality" (Mayoux 1952:158). The imagination of Faulkner's characters "never acts, even though in face of the 'real', except by the acts and rhythms of memory" (168); Faulkner "is an idealist, for whom as for Berkeley *esse est percipi,* for whom all takes place in the consciousness and between consciousnesses" (172).

The tyranny of memory and the relativizing of present to past is not so extreme a phenomenon in White, where it is but the chief index to the function of figural consciousness generally. Sartre (1947:231–32) criticizes what he sees as Faulkner's negation of full humanity in the absence of futurity. Psychologically, however, this is not so (though it may be true to say that the fundamental distinction between Proust and Faulkner—whom Sartre takes to be kindred, not contrasting, souls—is that only the former, by virtue of the narratorial accession to analysis, enables proleptic or narrative futurity to be encoded in the text). Mayoux is acute on the question of proximate futurity in Faulkner, a presence which aligns the latter with White:

> the relation between consciousness and body is curiously strained .... at the point where they join the characters suffer a double anguish .... there is a *sensation of imminence* .... interior time ... accumulates irresistibly .... in some way the consciousness goes one way, the body another. [Mayoux 1952:161–62]

We are reminded here of the charge of "portentousness" laid against White, and of the various possibilities of dispelling this misconception by indicating the functionality of indeterminacy and ataxis in terms of figural consciousness; so that, if what Conrad Aiken has claimed about Faulkner is true ("the whole elaborate method of deliberately withheld meaning, of progressive and partial and delayed disclosure"; Aiken 1939:138), it is figural consciousness which is responsible for the withholding (and provision) of analytical meaning in White's fiction, and it is ataxis that encodes both reaction and anticipation.

There are numerous other specifica of Faulkner's style which might be brought into fruitful relation with those of White. It is clear that the "musing speculation, sometimes proceeding to the statement of alternative suggestions" which is typical of Faulkner (Beck 1941:151), is more often attributable to the narratorial level of signification than to the figural, whereas in White it is exclusively the domain of the latter. In both writers, the world is matter charged with meaning, yet also a kind of dream, and in both "concrete details are united to abstractions" (Mayoux 1952:171–72). In both, life is represented as conflict and tension, a condition of consciousness which tries "to move simultaneously and intensely towards both order and chaos" (Slatoff 1957:196). If the outcome of this in Faulkner is that the "moment to moment presentation of experience involves a juxtaposition of elements which do not seem to fit together" (Slatoff 1957:174), with both physical and psychological conditions being characterized by the oxymoronic conjunction of "motion and immobility", then White's narration and style are also characterized by compound dualities. There is seldom an impression of swift action, for example, even though, as in Faulkner, there is "something like *a language of the body,* suggested in traits, gestures, manners" rather than a classification of whole individuals as "physical classes or types ... such as one finds in D.H. Lawrence" (Mayoux 1952:160). This, too, suggests the sifting action of figural perception rather than the synthesizing action of analytical intelligence. If Faulkner's central trope is oxymoron, White's is syllepsis; in this distinction reside the affinity and the room for difference between the respective styles, world-views, and implicit theories of mental process.

In summary, I would class Patrick White among the great novelists of consciousness, as Arthur F. Kinney (1978) classes Faulkner. In order to appreciate the style and narrative discourse of either writer, we must heed Kinney's observation that Faulkner's "style and vision", as properties of the author, are determinable and justifiable only through concentrated examination of "narrative consciousness" in the sense of the represented mentality of the characters, even down to images and metaphors, which are but "synecdoches for the narrative consciousnesses which they help to define" (Kinney 1978:91). In both Faulkner and White, style *is* vision—in the immediate sense of a representation of figural consciousness or mental vision; in the mediate sense of revealing the author's attitudes towards the fictively represented world. And we should never forget the compact which these novelists forge between their texts and the reader: the crucial centrality of indeterminacy in style, narration and constituted figural consciousness exposes the delusory nature, the merely phantasmic "presence", of "auctorial omniscience". Neither Faulkner nor White needs to rely on the mandarin suasion of his own voice, just as neither structures his narratives around any single, fully coherent, narrative consciousness: they rely instead "on the reader's own *constitutive consciousness,* his ability to select what terms he will accept, his means of combining them, and, just as importantly, what he will reject" (Kinney 1978:9). If we choose to disregard the persistently phenomenological shape of their novels, as complex poetic constructs whose fragmentations demand active constitution as wholes which can never be complete or saturated like logical systems, we have failed the author and failed ourselves. It cannot be said, after an examination of White's style, that he has failed his readers.

BIBLIOGRAPHY OF WORKS CITED

NOTE: For abbreviations of White's works, see title-entries under White below

ADAMS, Richard P. 1968. *Faulkner: Myth and Motion*. Princeton NJ: Princeton UP.

AIKEN, Conrad. 1939. "William Faulkner: The Novel as Form." *Atlantic Monthly* 164 (November): 650–54. Cited from HOFFMAN/VICKERY 1960: 135–42.

ALVAREZ, A. 1961. "Chariots of Light" (*RITC*) *New Statesman* 62 (3 Nov.): 653.

ARGYLE, Barry. 1967. *Patrick White*. Writers and Critics series. Edinburgh: Oliver & Boyd.

AUROUSSEAU, Marcel. 1962. *"Odi profanum vulgus*: Patrick White's *Riders in the Chariot."* *Meanjin* 21.2: 29–31.

AVANT, John Alfred. 1975. "The Oeuvre of Patrick White." *New Republic* (22 Mar.): 23–24.

BAIL, Murray. 1977. "Questionnaire on Fiction." *Australian Literary Studies* 8.2: 188–91.

BAILEY, Paul. 1973. "King Lear Down Under." (*EOS*) *Observer* (9 Sept.): 37.

BAKER, Sidney J. 1958. (in "National Goldmine": a parody of a passage from *Voss* in the style of A.D. Hope.) *Nation* (Sydney; 8 Nov.): 26.

BAKHTIN, Mikhail. 1981. *The Dialogic Imagination: Four Essays*, ed. Michael Holquist, tr. Caryl Emerson & Michael Holquist. Austin: U of Texas P.

BALLIETT, Whitney. 1961. "Mrs. Jolley and Mrs. Flack." (*RITC*) *New Yorker* 37.43 (9 Dec.): 246–47.

BALLY, Charles. 1912. "Le Style indirect libre en français moderne." *Germanisch-Romanische Monatsschrift* 4: 549–56, 597–606.

BANFIELD, Ann. 1973. "Narrative Style and the Grammar of Direct and Indirect Speech." *Foundations of Language* 10: 1–39.

——. 1978a. "The Formal Coherence of Represented Speech and Thought." *PTL: A Journal for Descriptive Poetics and Theory of Literature* 3: 289–314.

——. 1978b. "Where Epistemology, Style, and Grammar Meet Literary History: The Development of Represented Speech and Thought." *New Literary History* 9 (Spring): 415–54.

——. 1982. *Unspeakable Sentences: Narration and Representation in the Language of Fiction*. London: Routledge & Kegan Paul.

BARNARD, Marjorie. 1956. "The Four Novels of Patrick White." *Meanjin* 15.2: 156–70.

BARNES, John. 1966. "New Tracks to Travel: The Stories of White, Porter and Cowan." *Meanjin* 25.2: 154–70.

BARTHES, Roland. 1971. "De l'oeuvre au texte." *Revue d'esthétique* 3. Cited from BARTHES 1977 (as "From Work to Text"): 155–78.

——. 1971. "Style and Its Image," in CHATMAN 1971: 3–10.

——. 1974. *S/Z*, tr. Richard Miller. New York: Hill & Wang.

——. 1977. "Introduction to the Structural Analysis of Narrative," tr. Stephen Heath (from "Introduction à l'analyse structurale des récits," *Communications* 8, 1966). Cited from BARTHES, *Image-Music-Text* sel. & tr. Stephen Heath. London & Glasgow: Fontana.

BASSO, Hamilton. 1948. (Review of *AS*) *New Yorker* 23.2 (10 Jan.): 73.

BAYLEY, John. 1974. "Character and Consciousness." *New Literary History* 5.2: 225-35.

BEATSON, Peter. 1976. *The Eye in the Mandala: Patrick White: A Vision of Man and God.* London: Paul Elek.

———. 1987. "White and Gray: Image Patterns in Patrick White's *Memoirs of Many in One.*" *Landfall* 41.1 (no. 161, Mar.): 59-76.

———. 1991. "A Personal Farewell to Patrick White." *Landfall* 45.2 (no. 179, June): 227-35.

BECK, Warren. 1941. "William Faulkner's Style." *American Prefaces* 4 (Spring): 195-211. Cited from HOFFMAN/VICKERY 1960: 142-56.

BEER, Patricia. 1976. "Magwitch Land." (*FOL*) *Listener* 96 (30 Sept.): 409-10.

BELLETTE, A.F. 1974. (Review of *EOS*) *Ariel* 5.3: 128-30.

BENSTOCK, Shari. 1980. "Who Killed Cock Robin? The Sources of Free Indirect Style in *Ulysses.*" *Style* 14.3: 259-73.

BERGER, John. 1970. "A View of the Artist as Lucifer." (*Viv*) *Times* (London; 22 Oct.): 8.

BERGONZI, Bernard. 1961. "Knight of the Will." *Spectator* 207 (3 Nov.r): 628.

BESTON, John B. 1982. "Patrick White: *Flaws in the Glass*: A Self-Portrait." *World Literature Written in English* 21.1: 83-86.

BINNS, Frederic W. 1961. (Review of *RITC*) *Library Journal* 86.17 (1 Oct.): 3304.

BLAMIRES, David. 1980. "Patrick White: *The Twyborn Affair.*" *Critical Quarterly* 22.1: 77-85.

BLISS, Carolyn. 1986. *Patrick White's Fiction: The Paradox of Fortunate Failure.* London: Macmillan.

———. 1987. "Matilda on Main Street: Naturalizing Australian Literature for American Readers." *Antipodes* 1.1 (Mar.): 27-34.

BLOOMFIELD, Morton W. 1976. "Stylistics and the Theory of Literature." *New Literary History* 7.2 (Winter): 271-311.

BOATWRIGHT, Taliaferro. 1955. "The Rich Stuff of Life in a Fine Australian Novel." (*The Tree of Man.*) *New York Herald Tribune Book Review* 32.1 (14 Aug., Section 6): 1.

BOLINGER, Dwight. 1977. *Meaning and Form.* English Language series 11. London: Longman.

BONHEIM, Helmut. 1982. *The Narrative Modes: Techniques of the Short Story.* Cambridge: D.S. Brewer.

———. 1983. "The Critical Fallacies." *Literatur in Wissenschaft und Unterricht* 16.3: 193-205.

BOOTH, Wayne C. 1961. *The Rhetoric of Fiction.* Chicago: U of Chicago P.

———. 1974. *A Rhetoric of Irony.* Chicago: U of Chicago P.

BRADY, Veronica. 1974. "The Artist and the Savage God: Patrick White's *The Vivisector.*" *Meanjin* 33.1: 136-45.

———. 1977. "*A Fringe of Leaves*: Civilization by the Skin of Our Teeth." *Southerly* 37: 123-40.

BRASHEAR, William R. 1969. *The Living Will: A Study of Tennyson and Nineteenth-Century Subjectivism.* Studies in English Literature 52. The Hague: Mouton.

BRISSENDEN, R.F. 1959. "Patrick White." *Meanjin* 18.4: 410-25.

———. 1969. *Patrick White.* Writers and Their Work. London: Longmans.

———. 1974. "*The Vivisector,*" in RAMSON 1974: 311-24.

BRONZWAER, W.J.M. 1970. *Tense in the Novel: An Investigation of Some Potentialities of Linguistic Criticism.* Groningen: Wolters-Noordhoff.

BROOKS, Cleanth & Robert Penn WARREN. 1959. *Understanding Fiction*. 2nd ed. Englewood Cliffs NJ: Prentice-Hall.

BROWN, Craig. 1986. "The psalmist's voice." *Times Literary Supplement* (15 Aug.): 895.

BUCKLEY, Vincent. 1958. "Patrick White and His Epic." *Twentieth Century* 12: 239–52. Cited from JOHNSTON 1962: 187–97.

——. 1964. "The Novels of Patrick White," in Geoffrey DUTTON, ed. *The Literature of Australia* (Ringwood, Victoria: Penguin): 413–26.

BURGESS, Anthony. 1966. "Twelve Hundred Pages and Four Marbles." (*SM*) *Listener* 75 (2 June): 804.

BURGESS, O.N. 1961. "Patrick White, His Critics and Laura Trevelyan." (*V*) *Australian Quarterly* 33.4: 49–57.

BURNS, David R. 1975. *The Directions of Australian Fiction 1920–1974*. (esp. ch. 11–13: 157–206.) Melbourne: Cassell.

BYATT, A.S. 1967. "The Battle between Real People and Images." (*SM*) *Encounter* 28.2: 71–78.

CAMPBELL, Ross. 1958. "Foggy Weather Over Leichardt." (*V*) *Daily Telegraph* (Sydney; 15 Feb.): 18.

CANTRELL, Leon. 1976, ed. *Bards, Bohemians and Bookmen: Essays in Australian Literature*. St Lucia: U of Queensland P.

CARLYLE, Thomas. 1831. "Characteristics," in *The Works of Thomas Carlyle, in Thirty Volumes*, vol. 28 (London: Chapman & Hall, 1896–99): 1–43.

CARTER, Ronald & Walter NASH. 1990. *Seeing Through Language: A Guise to Styles of English Writing*. Oxford: Basil Blackwell.

CASPARY, Vera. 1942. *Laura*. Garden City NY: Sun Dial Press.

CHATMAN, Seymour. 1971, ed. *Literary Style: A Symposium*. New York: Oxford UP.

——. 1972. *The Later Style of Henry James*. Language and Style series 11. Oxford: Basil Blackwell.

——. 1975. "The Structure of Narrative Transmission," in FOWLER 1975: 213–57.

——. 1978. *Story and Discourse: Narrative Structure in Fiction and Film*. Ithaca NY: Cornell UP.

——. 1986. "Characters and Narrators: Filter, Center, Slant, and Interest-Focus." *Poetics Today* 7.2: 189–204.

CHATMAN, Seymour & Samuel R. LEVIN. 1967, eds. *Essays on the Language of Literature*. Boston MA: Houghton Mifflin.

COATES, Jennifer. 1983. *The Semantics of the Modal Auxiliaries*. London & Canberra: Croom Helm.

COE, Richard N. 1970. "The Artist and the Grocer: Patrick White's *The Vivisector*." *Meanjin* 29.4: 526–29.

COHN, Dorrit. 1978. *Transparent Minds: Narrative Modes for Presenting Consciousness in Fiction*. Princeton NJ: Princeton UP.

——. 1981. "The Encirclement of Narrative: On Franz Stanzel's *Theorie des Erzählens*." *Poetics Today* 2.2: 157–82.

COLMER, John. 1978a. "Duality in Patrick White," in SHEPHERD/SINGH 1978: 70–76.

——. 1978b. "Appendix: Two Critical Positions (I)," in SHEPHERD/SINGH 1978: 135–36.

——. 1978c. *"Riders in the Chariot": Patrick White*. Studies in Australian Literature. Melbourne: Edward Arnold.

——. 1982. "The Quest Motif in Patrick White." *Review of National Literatures* 11: 192–210.

——. 1984. *Patrick White*. Contemporary Writers series. London: Methuen.

CONRAD, Joseph. 1904/1907. *Nostromo/The Secret Agent*, in *Lord Jim, The Nigger of the "Narcissus", Typhoon, Nostromo, The Secret Agent*. London: Octopus/Book Club Associates, 1981.

COOPER, J.C. 1978. *An Illustrated Encyclopaedia of Traditional Symbols*. London: Thames & Hudson.

COOPERMAN, Stanley S. 1955. "An Epic of Australia." (*TOM*) *Nation* 181.19 (5 Nov.): 404–405.

CORE, George. 1974. "A Terrible Majesty: The Novels of Patrick White." *Rollins Critic* 11.1: 1–16.

——. 1977. "Poetically the Most Accurate Man Alive." (*FOL*) *Virginia Quarterly Review* 53: 766–72.

CORKE, Hilary. 1957. "New Novels." (*V*) *Listener* 58 (26 Dec.): 1082.

COTTER, Michael. 1978. "The Function of Imagery in Patrick White's Novels," in SHEPHERD/SINGH 1978: 17–27.

CROWCROFT, Jean. 1974. "Patrick White: A Reply to Dorothy Green." *Overland* 59 (Spring): 49–53.

CURME, George O. & Hans KURATH. 1931. *A Grammar of the English Language*, vol.3: *Syntax*. Boston MA: D.C. Heath.

CURTIUS, Ernst Robert. 1973. *European Literature and the Latin Middle Ages*, tr. Willard R. Trask (*Europäische Literatur und lateinisches Mittelalter*, 1st ed. 1948; tr. New York: Harper & Row, 1953). New ed. Bollingen Series 36. Princeton NJ: Princeton UP.

DAICHES, David. 1960. *The Novel and the Modern World*. 2nd rev. ed. Phoenix Books. Chicago: U of Chicago P.

DANIEL, John. 1964. "Chronicling the Commercial Realities." (*The Burnt Ones*.) *The Guardian* (2 Oct.): 17.

DAVIS, L.J. 1970. "Prose is not Painting." (*Viv.*) *Book World* (2 Aug.): 2.

DEAL, Borden. 1957. "Search for Man and God." (*V*) *Saturday Review* 40.33 (17 August): 17.

DELMONTE, Rodolfo. 1974. "Various Types of Ambiguity in Patrick White's *Riders in the Chariot*." *LinQ* (Townsville) 3.3–4: 37–52.

DE MOTT, Benjamin. 1980. "The Perils of Protean Man." (*TA*) *New York Times Book Review* (27 April): 3, 32.

DILLON, George L. & Frederick KIRCHHOFF. 1976. "On the Form and Function of Free Indirect Style." *PTL: A Journal for Descriptive Poetics and Theory of Literature* 1: 431–40.

DINNAGE, Rosemary. 1980. "Her Life as a Man." (*TA*) *New York Review of Books* (17 April): 25.

DOCHERTY, Thomas. 1983. *Reading (Absent) Character: Towards a Theory of Characterization in Fiction*. Oxford: Clarendon P.

DOCKER, John. 1973. "Patrick White and Romanticism: *The Vivisector*." *Southerly* 33.1: 44–61.

——. 1974. *Australian Cultural Elites: Intellectual Traditions in Sydney and Melbourne*. ("Patrick White's Australian Literary Context": 59–76.) Sydney: Angus & Robertson.

DONALDSON, Ian. 1962. "Going Away." (*The Living and the Dead*.) *Guardian* (7 Dec.): 9.

DRIESEN, Cynthia vanden. 1978. "Patrick White and the 'Unprofessed Factor': The Challenge Before the Contemporary Religious Writer," in SHEPHERD/SINGH 1978: 77–68.

DRY, Helen Aristar. 1990. "Language Change and 'Naturalization' in Free Indirect Discourse." *Journal of Literary Semantics* 19.3 (Oct.): 135–49.

DUCHÊNE, Anne. 1966. "A Likely Story." (*SM*) *Guardian* (20 May): 7.

DUCROT, Oswald & Tzvetan TODOROV. 1981. *Encyclopedic Dictionary of the Sciences of Language*, tr. Catherine Porter (*Dictionnaire encyclopédique des sciences du langage*, 2nd ed., Paris 1973). Oxford: Basil Blackwell.

DUNCAN, R.A. 1969. "Existential Sensibility in the Novels of Patrick White." MA thesis, Melbourne: Monash University.

DURIX, Jean–Pierre. 1979. "Natural Elements in Patrick White's *Voss*." *World Literature Written in English* 18.2: 345–52.

DUTTON, Geoffrey. 1971. *Patrick White*. Australian Writers and Their Work. 4th rev. ed. Melbourne: Oxford UP.

ECO, Umberto. 1984. *Reflections on "The Name of the Rose"*, tr. William Weaver (*Postille a Il nome della rosa*, 1983). New York: Harcourt Brace Jovanovich.

EDGAR, Suzanne. 1977. "A Woman's Life and Love: A Reply to Leonie Kramer." (*FOL*) *Quadrant* (Oct.): 69–71.

EDGECOMBE, Rodney. 1987. "Patrick White's Style—Again." *Antipodes* 1.2 (Nov.): 83–87.

———. 1989. *Vision and Style in Patrick White: A Study of Five Novels*. Tuscaloosa: U of Alabama P.

EHRLICH, Susan. 1987. "Aspect, Foregrounding and Point of View." *Text: An interdisciplinary journal for the study of discourse* 7.4: 363–76.

EIKHENBAUM, Boris. 1925. "Leskov und die moderne Prosa (Leskov and Modern Prose)," in STRIEDTER 1981; 209–43.

ELKIN, A.P. 1979. *The Australian Aborigines*. 6th rev. ed. Sydney: Angus & Robertson.

EMONDS, Joseph. 1976. *A Transformational Approach to English Syntax: Root, Structure-Preserving and Local Transformations*. New York: Academic P.

EPSTEIN, E.L. 1975. "The Self-Reflexive Artefact: The Function of Mimesis in an Approach to a Theory of Value for Literature," in FOWLER 1975: 40–78.

FAULKNER, William. 1932. *Light in August*. Harmondsworth: Penguin, 1960.

———. 1948. *Intruder in the Dust*. Harmondsworth: Penguin, 1960.

FEHR, Bernhard. 1938. "Substitutionary Narration and Description: A Chapter in Stylistics." *English Studies: A Journal of English Letters and Philology* 20: 97–107.

FISHER, Emma. 1985. ". . . and before." *Times Literary Supplement* (1 Nov.): 1228.

FOWLER/GOWERS. 1965. *A Dictionary of Modern English Usage*, by H.W. Fowler. 2nd ed. rev. Sir Ernest Gowers. Oxford: Clarendon P.

FOWLER, Roger. 1975, ed. *Style and Structure in Literature: Essays in The New Stylistics*. Oxford: Basil Blackwell.

———. 1986. *Linguistic Criticism*. Oxford: Oxford UP.

FRANK, Joseph. 1945. "Spatial Form in Modern Literature." *Sewanee Review* 53.2. Cited from FRANK, *The Widening Gyre: Crisis and Mastery in Modern Literature*. Bloomington: Indiana UP.

FRAZER, Sir James. 1922/1957. *The Golden Bough: A Study in Myth and Religion*. Abridged ed. in one vol. St Martin's Library. London: Macmillan.

FREEMAN, Donald C. 1970, ed. *Linguistics and Literary Style*. New York: Holt, Rinehart & Winston.

FRIEDMAN, Norman. 1955. "Point of View in Fiction: The Development of a Critical Concept." (*PMLA* 70; also in FRIEDMAN, *Form and Meaning in Fiction*, Athens GA: 1975.) Cited from STEVICK 1967: 108–37.

FULLER, John. 1961. "New Novels." (*RITC*) *Listener* 66 (9 Nov.): 783.

FURBANK, P.N. 1970. *Reflections on the Word "Image"*. London: Secker & Warburg.

GANNETT, Lewis. 1957. "Proud, Lonely Man in Wild Australia: Patrick White's Symbolic Novel of a Wanderer's Heart." (*V*) *New York Herald Tribune* (18 Aug.; Book Review Section): 5.

GENETTE, Gérard. 1980. *Narrative Discourse*, tr. Jane E. Lewin ("Discours du récit," in *Figures III*, Paris: Seuil, 1972), foreword Jonathan Culler. Oxford: Basil Blackwell.

——. 1988. *Narrative Discourse Revisited*, tr. Jane E. Lewin (*Nouveau discours du récit*, Paris: Seuil, 1983). Ithaca NY: Cornell UP.

GEORGE, Daniel. 1961. "A Morality Play Down Under." (*RITC*) *Daily Telegraph* (27 Oct.): 21.

GHOSE, Zulfikar. 1979. "The One Comprehensive Vision." *Texas Studies in Language and Literature* 21.2: 260–79. Also in GHOSE, *The Fiction of Reality* (London: Macmillan, 1983): 76–103.

GINGELL-BECKMAN, Susan. 1982. "Seven Black Swans: The Symbolic Logic of Patrick White's *The Eye of the Storm*." *World Literature Written in English* 21.2: 315–25.

GORDIMER, Nadine. 1983. "The Art of Fiction LXXVII," intv. Janaika HURWITZ. *Paris Review* 25 (no. 88): 82–127.

GRAVES, Robert. 1960. *The Greek Myths*. 2 vols., rev. ed. Harmondsworth: Penguin.

GREEN, Dorothy. 1973a. "Queen Lear or Cleopatra Rediviva? Patrick White's *Eye of the Storm*." *Meanjin* 32.4: 395–405.

——. 1973b. "Patrick White's Nobel Prize." *Overland* 57 (Summer): 23–25.

——. 1974. "*Voss*: Stubborn Music," in RAMSON 1974: 284–310.

GREEN, H.M. 1962. *A History of Australian Literature, Pure and Applied*. 2 vols., corrected 1st ed. Sydney: Angus & Robertson.

GREEN, Peter. 1956. "Oh, For the Wide Open Spaces!" (*TOM*) *Daily Telegraph* (4 May): 8.

GREENBAUM, Sidney. 1969. *Studies in English Adverbial Usage*. Longmans' Linguistics Library. London: Longmans.

GREIMAS, A(lgirdas)–J(ulien). 1966. *Sémantique structurale*. Paris: Larousse.

GRENE, David & Richard LATTIMORE. 1960, eds. *Greek Tragedies*, Vol. 1. Phoenix Books. Chicago: U of Chicago P.

GUTWINSKI, Waldemar. 1976. *Cohesion in Literary Texts: A Study of Some Grammatical and Lexical Features of English Discourse*. Janua Linguarum, Series Minor 204. The Hague: Mouton.

GZELL, Sylvia. 1964. "Themes and Imagery in *Voss* and *Riders in the Chariot*." *Australian Literary Studies* 1.3: 180–95. Cited from SEMMLER 1967: 252–67.

HADGRAFT, Cecil. 1977. "The Theme of Revelation in Patrick White's Novels." *Southerly* 37: 34–36.

HALE, Dorothy J. 1989. "*As I Lay Dying*'s Heterogeneous Discourse." *Novel* (Fall): 5–23.

HALLIDAY, M.A.K. 1970. "Language Structure and Language Function," in John LYONS, ed. *New Horizons in Linguistics*. Harmondsworth: Penguin.

——. 1971. "Linguistic Function and Literary Style: An Inquiry into the Language of William Golding's *The Inheritors*," in CHATMAN 1971: 330–68.

HALLIDAY, M.A.K. & Ruqaiya HASAN. 1976. *Cohesion in English*. English Language series 9. London: Longman.

HANSSON, Karin. 1984. *The Warped Universe: A Study of Imagery and Structure in Seven Novels by Patrick White*. Lund Studies in English. Malmö: Liber.

HARRIES, Lyndon. 1978. "The Peculiar Gifts of Patrick White." *Contemporary Literature* 19.4: 459–71.

HARRIS, Max. 1971. "Parody Competition: Judges' Report" (see NIRIS 1971).

HASSALL, A.J. 1987. "The Making of a Colonial Myth: The Mrs. Fraser Story in Patrick White's *A Fringe of Leaves* and André Brink's *An Instant in the Wind*." *Ariel* 18.3 (July): 3–28.

HASTINGS, Peter. 1960. "Moss: With Apologies to Mr. Patrick White, to Whose Unique Talents Australia is Not Yet Accustomed." (Parody.) *Observer* (Sydney; 14 May): 10–11.

———. 1961. "But Did Not." ("The UnRed Page"; parody, in the style of White, of Xavier Herbert's *Soldier's Wives*.) *Bulletin* (Sydney; 16 Dec.): 24.

HAVIGHURST, Walter. 1948. "Pioneer Down Under." (*TOM*) *Saturday Review* 38.33 (13 Aug.): 11–12.

HAYMAN, David. 1981. "Surface Disturbances/Grave Disorders." *TriQuarterly* 52 (Fall): 182–96.

HELTAY, Hilary. 1973. "The Novels of Patrick White" (tr. John B. Beston from "Patrick Whites Romanwerk," *Akzente* 19.6 (1972): 518–39). *Southerly* 33.2 (June 1973): 92–104. (1973 omits pp. 532–37 of 1972, on German translations of the novels.)

———. 1975, tr. & afterword. *Patrick White: "Down at the Dump"/"Drunten auf der Müllkippe"*. Universal–Bibliothek 9808. Stuttgart: Reclam.

———. 1983. *The Articles and the Novelist: Reference Conventions and Reader Manipulation in Patrick White's Creation of Fictional Worlds*. Studies and Texts in English 4. Tübingen: Gunter Narr.

HERD, Jean. 1977. *Brodie's Notes on Patrick White's "The Tree of Man"*. Sydney: Pan Books.

HERRING, Thelma. 1965. "Odyssey of a Spinster: A Study of *The Aunt's Story*." *Southerly* 25.1: 6–22. Cited from WILKES 1970: 3–20.

———. 1966. "Self and Shadow: The Quest for Totality in *The Solid Mandala*." *Southerly* 26.3: 180–189. Cited from WILKES 1970: 72–82.

———. 1971. "Patrick White's *The Vivisector*." *Southerly* 31.1: 3–16.

HESELTINE, Harry P. 1962. (Review of *RITC*) *Books Abroad* 36 (Winter): 82.

———. 1963a. ("Writer and Reader"; comment on *LAD*) *Southerly* 23.3: 211–13.

———. 1963b. "Patrick White's Style." *Quadrant* 7.3: 61–74.

———. 1965. (Introduction to a study-edition of *Voss*, with an appendix on "Issues and Problems": 381–409.) Heritage of Literature series. London: Longmans, Green.

———. 1982. "The Uncertain Self: Notes on the Development of Australian Literary Form." *Review of National Literatures* 11: 85–113.

HIGHSMITH, Patricia. 1977. *Edith's Diary*. London: Heinemann.

HIRSCH, E.D. 1975. "Stylistics and Synonymity." *Critical Inquiry* 1.3: 559–79.

HOFFMAN, Frederick J. & Olga W. VICKERY. 1960, eds. *William Faulkner: Three Decades of Criticism*. New York & Burlingame: Harcourt, Brace & World.

HOLLOWAY, John. 1975. "Narrative Structure and Text Structure: Isherwood's *A Meeting by the River*, and Muriel Spark's *The Prime of Miss Jean Brodie*." *Critical Inquiry* 1.3: 581–604.

——. 1983. "Patrick White," in Boris FORD, ed. *The New Pelican Guide to English Literature*, vol.8: *The Present*. Harmondsworth: Penguin: 147–63.

HOPE, A.D. 1956. "The Bunyip Stages a Comeback." (*TOM*) *Sydney Morning Herald* (16 June): 15. Cited from augmented reprint in HOPE, *Native Companions* (Sydney: Angus & Robertson): 75–79.

——. 1963. *Australian Literature 1950–1962*. Melbourne: Melbourne UP: 12–13.

HOPE, Francis. 1964. "Poor Unfortunates." (*BO*) *New Statesman* 68 (9 Oct.): 547.

HOUGH, Graham. 1958. "New Novels." (*V*) *Encounter* 10.2: 86–87.

——. 1970. "Narrative and Dialogue in Jane Austen." *Critical Quarterly* 12.3: 201–29.

HUGHES, John C. 1990. "He Snorted Grimly." *Times Literary Supplement* (9 Mar.): 252.

HUGHES, Ted. 1964. "Patrick White's *Voss*." *Listener* 71 (6 Feb.): 229–30.

ISER, Wolfgang. 1976. *Der Akt des Lesens: Theorie ästhetischer Wirkung*. UTB series 636. Munich: Wilhelm Fink.

——. *Walter Pater: The Aesthetic Moment*, tr. David Henry Wilson (*Walter Pater: Die Autonomie des Ästhetischen*, Tübingen 1960). Cambridge: Cambridge UP.

JAMES, Henry. 1903. *The Ambassadors*. New York: New American Library, 1960.

JESPERSEN, Otto. 1940. *A Modern English Grammar on Historical Principles*, Part V: *Syntax*. 7 vols., vol.4. Copenhagen: Munksgaard.

JOHNSON, Manly. 1976. "Patrick White: The Eye of the Language." (*EOS*) *World Literature Written in English* 15.2: 339–58.

——. 1978. "Patrick White's *A Fringe of Leaves*," in SHEPHERD/SINGH 1978: 87–98.

——. 1981. "*Twyborn*: The Abbess, the Bulbul, and the Bawdy House." *Modern Fiction Studies* 27.1: 159–68.

JOHNSTON, Graeme. 1962, ed. *Australian Literary Criticism*. Melbourne: Oxford UP.

JUNG, Carl Gustav. 1971. *The Portable Jung*, tr. R.F.C. Hull, ed. & intro. Joseph Campbell. New York: Viking.

KEENEY, Willard. 1967. "Ripeness is All: Late, Late Romanticism and Other Recent Fiction." (*SM*) *Southern Review* (Louisiana) New Series 3.4: 1054–54.

KIERNAN, Brian. 1971. *Images of Society and Nature: Seven Essays on Australian Novels*. (White: esp. pp. 95–147.) Melbourne: Oxford UP.

——. 1974. "Patrick White: The Novelist and the Modern World," in Don ANDERSON & Stephen KNIGHT, eds., *Cunning Exiles: Studies of Modern Prose Writers* (Sydney: Angus & Robertson): 81–103.

——. 1976. "The Novels of Patrick White," in Geoffrey DUTTON, ed., *The Literature of Australia* (rev. ed. Ringwood, Victoria: Penguin): 461–84.

——. 1980. *Patrick White*. London: Macmillan.

KILLHAM, John. 1960, ed. *Critical Essays on the Poetry of Tennyson*. London: Routledge & Kegan Paul.

KIM, Martha V. 1989. "Critic limits White study to five novels ..." *Antipodes* 3.2 (Winter): 152–53.

KING, Francis. 1966. "Hello Twins." (*SM*) *Sunday Telegraph* (London; 15 May): 12.

——. 1973. "Ritual of a Deathbed." (*EOS*) *Sunday Telegraph* (London; 9 Sept.): 17.

KINNEY, Arthur F. 1978. *Faulkner's Narrative Poetics: Style as Vision*. Amherst: U of Massachusetts P.

KINTGEN, Eugene R. 1977. "Reader Response and Stylistics." *Style* 10.1: 1-18.

KLOSSOWSKI DE ROLA, Stanislas. 1973. *Alchemy: The Secret Art*. London: Thames & Hudson.

KOCH-EMMERY, Erwin. 1973. "Theme and Language in Patrick White's Novels," in Gero BAUER et al., eds., *Festschrift Prof. Dr. Herbert Koziol*. Wiener Beiträge zur Englischen Philologie 75. Vienna & Stuttgart: 136-46.

KRAMER, Leonie. 1973. "Patrick White's *Götterdämmerung*." (*RITC*) *Quadrant* (June): 8-19.

——. 1974. "*The Tree of Man*: An Essay in Scepticism," in RAMSON 1974: 269-83.

——. 1976. "A Woman's Life and Love." (*FOL*) *Quadrant* (November): 62-63.

——. 1981, ed. *The Oxford History of Australian Literature*. Melbourne: Oxford UP.

KRUISINGA, E. & P.A. ERADES. 1967. *An English Grammar* (= *A Handbook of Present-Day English*), Part II: *English Accidence and Syntax*. 9th ed. Groningen: Noordhoff.

KUIPER, Koenraad & Vernon SMALL. 1986. "Constraints on Fictions: With an Analysis of M.K. Joseph's *A Soldier's Tale*." *Poetics Today* 7.3: 495-526.

LÄMMERT, Eberhard. 1955. *Bauformen des Erzählens*. 3rd impression, 1968. Stuttgart: Metzler.

LAMPRECHT, Adolf. 1971. *Grammatik der englischen Sprache*. Berlin: Volk und Wissen.

LARDNER, Susan. 1978. (Review of Tom McHale, *The Lady from Boston*.) *New Yorker* (24 April): 161.

LAWRENCE, D.H. 1921. *Women in Love*. Harmondsworth: Penguin, 1960.

LAWSON, Alan. 1973a. "Unmerciful Dingoes? The Critical Reception of Patrick White." *Meanjin* 32.4: 379-92.

——. 1973b. "White for White's Sake: Studies of Patrick White's Novels." *Meanjin* 32.3: 343-49.

——. 1979. "Meaning and Experience: A Review-Essay on Some Recurrent Problems in Patrick White Criticism." *Texas Studies in Language and Literature* 21.2: 280-95.

LEAVER, Florence. 1958. "Faulkner: The Word as Principle and Power." *South Atlantic Quarterly* 57 (Autumn): 464-76. Cited from HOFFMAN/VICKERY 1960: 199-209.

LEECH, Geoffrey N. 1969. *A Linguistic Guide to English Poetry*. Longmans English Language series. London: Longmans.

——. 1971. *Meaning and the English Verb*. London: Longman.

LEECH, Geoffrey N., with Michael H. SHORT. 1981. *Style in Fiction: A Linguistic Introduction to English Fictional Prose*. London: Longman.

LERNER, Laurence D. 1965/1975. "Style," in PREMINGER et al.: 814-17.

——. 1983, ed. *Reconstructing Literature*. Oxford: Basil Blackwell.

LEVIN, Bernard. 1979. "Those Barren Leaves." (*TA*) *Sunday Times* (16 Dec.): 44.

LEVIN, Harry. 1951. "Observations on the Style of Ernest Hemingway." *Kenyon Review* 13.4: 581-609. Cited from LEVIN, *Contexts of Criticism* (New York: Atheneum, 1963): 140-67.

LODGE, David. 1981. "Self-Portrait of an Australian Misanthrope." (*Flaws*) *Sunday Times* (1 Nov.): 43.

——. 1984. "Mimesis and Diegesis in Modern Fiction," in Anthony MORTIMER, ed. *Contemporary Approaches to Narrative*. Swiss Papers in English Language and Literature 1. Tübingen: Gunter Narr: 89-108.

——. 1984. *Small World*. Harmondsworth: Penguin, 1985.

LONGMAN. 1978. *Dictionary of Contemporary English*. London: Longman.

LUTWACK, Leonard. 1960. "Mixed and Uniform Prose Styles in the Novel." *Journal of Aesthetics and Art Criticism* 18. Cited from STEVICK 1967: 208-19.

LYON, George W. 1990. "The Ordinary Bread of Words: The Dissonant Unity of *Voss*." *Australian and New Zealand Studies in Canada*: 4 (Fall): 15-26.

MCAULEY, James. 1958. "*Voss* and the Novel." *Quadrant* 2.4: 4-5.

———. 1962. "*Riders in the Chariot*." *Quadrant* 6.2: 79-81.

———. 1965. "The Gothic Splendours: Patrick White's *Voss*." *Southerly* 25.1: 34-44.

MCCABE, Bernard. 1966. "Message in Marbles." (*SM*) *Saturday Review* 49.7 (12 Feb.): 36

MCCULLOCH, Ann. 1983. *A Tragic Vision: The Novels of Patrick White*. Scholars' Library. St Lucia: U of Queensland P.

MCFARLANE, Brian. 1977. "Inhumanity in the Australian Novel: *Riders in the Chariot*." *The Critical Review* (Melbourne) 19: 24-41.

MCHALE, Brian. 1978. "Free Indirect Discourse: A Survey of Recent Accounts." *PTL: A Journal for Descriptive Poetics and Theory of Literature* 3: 249-87.

———. 1981. "Islands in the Stream of Consciousness: Dorrit Cohn's *Transparent Minds*." *Poetics Today* 2.2: 183-91.

MACKENZIE, Manfred. 1966. "*The Tree of Man*: A Generic Approach," in John COLMER, ed. *Approaches to the Novel* (Adelaide: Rigby): 90-102.

———. 1969. "The Consciousness of 'Twin Consciousness': Patrick White's *The Solid Mandala*." *Novel* 2.3: 241-54.

———. 1977. "'Dark Birds of Light': *The Eye of the Storm* as Swansong." *Southern Review* (Adelaide) 10: 270-84.

MCLAREN, John. 1963. "The Image of Reality in Our Writing." (*TOM*) *Overland* 27-28: 43-47. Cited from SEMMLER 1967: 235-44.

———. 1966. "Patrick White's Use of Imagery." *Australian Literary Studies* 2.3: 217-20. Cited from SEMMLER 1967: 268-72.

———. 1970. "Search for Truth." (*Viv*) *Overland* 46 (Summer): 37-38.

MCLEOD, A.L. 1974. "Patrick White: Nobel Prize for Literature 1973." *Books Abroad* 48.3: 439-45.

MAGNY, Claude-Edmonde. 1948. "Faulkner or Theological Inversion," tr. & abridged Jacqueline Merriam ("Faulkner ou l'inversion théologique," in MAGNY, *L'Age du roman américain*, Paris: Seuil: 196-243). Cited from WARREN 1960: 66-78.

MARR, David. 1991. *Patrick White: A Life*. London: Jonathan Cape.

MARTIN, David. 1959. "Among the Bones." *Meanjin* 18.1: 52-58.

MARTIN, Harold C. & Richard M. OHMANN. 1959. "A Selective Bibliography," in MARTIN, ed. *Style in Prose Fiction*. English Institute Essays 1958. New York: Columbia UP.

MATHER, Rodney. 1963. "*Voss*." *Critical Review* (Melbourne) 6: 93-101.

———. 1970. "Patrick White and Lawrence: A Contrast." *Critical Review* (Melbourne) 13: 34-50.

MAYOUX, Jean-Jacques. 1952. "The Creation of the Real in William Faulkner," tr. Frederick J. Hoffman ("La Création du réel chez William Faulkner," *Etudes Anglaises* 5: 25-39). Cited from HOFFMAN/VICKERY 1960: 156-73.

MENIKOFF, Barry. 1970. "Punctuation and Point of View in the Late Style of Henry James." *Style* 4: 29-48.

MILIC, Louis T. 1967. "Connectives in Swift's Prose Style," in MILIC, *A Quantitative Approach to the Style of Jonathan Swift* (The Hague: Mouton: 122-36). Cited from FREEMAN 1970: 243-57.

———. 1971. "Rhetorical Choice and Stylistic Option: The Conscious and Unconscious Poles," in CHATMAN 1971: 77-94.

MILLER, Karl. 1966. "Magic Marbles." (*SM*) *New Statesman* 71 (27 May): 780.

MITCHELL, Adrian. 1978. "Eventually, White's Language: Words, and More Than Words," in SHEPHERD/SINGH 1978: 5-16.

———. 1981. "Fiction," in KRAMER 1981: (White) 146-54.

MITCHELL, Julian. 1962. "Fiction of the Week: An Illumination of the Thirties." (*LAD*) *Sunday Times* (11 Nov.): 32.

MORLEY, Patricia. 1972. *The Mystery of Unity: Theme and Technique in the Novels of Patrick White*. Montreal: McGill-Queen's UP.

MOSLEY, Nicholas. 1979. "Seeing It Whole." (*TA*) *Listener* 102 (29 Nov.): 761-62.

MUIR, Edwin. 1939. "New Novels." (*HV*) *Listener* 21 (2 Mar.): 489.

———. 1941. "New Novels." (*LAD*) *Listener* 26 (31 July): 175.

MYERS, David A. 1978. *The Peacocks and the Bourgeoisie: Ironic Vision in Patrick White's Shorter Prose Fiction*. Adelaide: Adelaide U Union P.

NAIPAUL, V.S. 1961. *A House for Mr Biswas*. Harmondsworth: Penguin, 1969.

———. 1964. "Australia Deserta." (*BO*) *Spectator* 213 (16 Oct.): 513.

NELSON, Lowry. 1965/1974. "Mannerism," in PREMINGER et al.: 473.

NEW YORKER. 1957. "Briefly Noted (Fiction)." (Note on *V*) 33.33 (5 Oct.): 185-86.

NIETZSCHE, Friedrich. 1956. *The Birth of Tragedy*, tr. Francis Golffing. Garden City NY: Doubleday Anchor.

NIRIS, Victor. 1971. (First winning entry in Parody Competition No. 1: "a scene at the Sarsaparilla Supermarket in the manner of Mr Patrick White.") *Australian* (23 January): 22.

NISCHIK, Reingard. 1991. *Mentalstilistik: Ein Beitrag zur Stiltheorie und Narrativik, dargestellt am Erzählwerk Margaret Atwoods*. Tübingen: Gunter Narr.

NÜNNING, Ansgar. 1990. "'Point of view' oder 'focalization'? Über einige Grundlagen und Kategorien konkurrierender Modelle der erzählerischen Vermittlung." *Literatur in Wissenschaft und Unterricht* 23.3: 249-68.

NYE, Robert. 1979. "Coasting Along Together." (*TA*) *Guardian* (27 Sept.): 10.

O'BRIEN, Kate. 1939. "Fiction." (*HV*) *Spectator* 162 (17 Feb.): 276.

OLIVER, H.J. 1958. "Patrick White's Significant Journey." (*V*) *Southerly* 19.1: 46-49.

OLIVERIUSOVÁ, Eva. 1971. "Patrick White's Australian Novels." *Philologica Pragensis* 14: 190-217.

OSBORNE, Charles. 1963. (Review of *LAD* and *TOM*) *London Magazine* New Series 2.11: 85-86.

———. 1964. "Australian Attitudes." (*BO*) *Observer* (4 Oct.): 28.

PAGE, Norman. 1972. *The Language of Jane Austen*. Language and Style 13. Oxford: Basil Blackwell.

———. 1973. *Speech in the English Novel*. English Language series 8. London: Longman.

PARTEE, Barbara Hall. 1973a. "The Semantics of Belief-Sentences," in K.J.J. HINTIKKA, J. MORAVCSIK & P. SUPPES, eds. *Approaches to Natural Language* (Dordrecht: Reidel): 309-36.

———. 1973b. "The Syntax and Semantics of Quotation," in Paul KIPARSKY & Stephen R. ANDERSON, eds. *A Festschrift for Morris Halle* (New York: Holt, Rinehart & Winston): 410-18.

PARTRIDGE, Eric. 1964. *You Have a Point There: A Guide to Punctuation.* 2nd ed. London: Hamish Hamilton.

PASCAL, Roy. 1977. *The Dual Voice: Free Indirect Speech and its Functioning in the Nineteenth-Century European Novel.* Manchester & Totowa NJ: Manchester UP & Rowman & Littlefield.

PEPRNÍK, Jaroslav. 1969. "Reporting Phrases in English Prose." *Brno Studies in English* 8 (Festschrift for Josef Vachek, ed. Jan Firbas & Josef Hladký): 145-51.

PHILLIPS, A.A. 1965. "Patrick White and the Algebraic Symbol." *Meanjin* 24.4: 455-61.

———. 1966. "*The Solid Mandala*: Patrick White's New Novel." *Meanjin* 25.1: 31-33.

PILLING, John. 1978. "Four Books on Patrick White." *Journal of Commonwealth Literature* 12.3: 89-92.

POTTER, Nancy A.J. 1964. "Patrick White's Minor Saints." 5.4: 9-19.

POUILLON, Jean. 1946. "Time and Destiny in Faulkner," tr. Jacqueline Merriam ("Temps et destinée chez Faulkner," in POUILLON, *Temps et roman*, Paris: Gallimard: 238-60). Cited from WARREN 1966: 79-86.

PREMINGER, Alex, Frank J. WARNKE & O.B. HARDISON. 1965/1974. *Princeton Encyclopedia of Poetry and Poetics.* Enlarged ed. Princeton NJ: Princeton UP.

PRESCOTT, Orville. 1957. "Books of the Times." (*V*) *Times* (19 Aug.): 17.

PRIESTLEY, F.E.L. 1949. "Tennyson's *Idylls* - A Fresh View." *University of Toronto Quarterly* 19: 35-49. Cited from KILLHAM 1960.

PRINGLE, John Douglas. 1961. "Artist and Chariot." (*RITC*) *London Magazine* New Series 1.8: 68-72.

QUIRK, Randolph, Sidney GREENBAUM, Geoffrey LEECH & Jan SVARTVIK. 1972. *A Grammar of Contemporary English.* London: Longman.

RAMSEY, S.A. 1980. "*The Twyborn Affair*: 'the beginning in an end' or 'the end of a beginning'?" *Ariel* 11.4: 87-95.

RAMSON, W.S. 1974, ed. *The Australian Experience: Critical Essays on Australian Novels.* Canberra: Australian National UP.

RATCLIFFE, Michael. 1966. "Out of This World." (*SM*) *Sunday Times* (15 May): 31.

———. 1973. "Fiction." (*eos*) *Times* (6 Sept.): 12.

RICKS, Christopher. 1962. "Noises." (*LAD*) *New Statesman* 64 (9 Nov.): 674-75.

———. 1969, ed. *The Poems of Tennyson.* Annotated English Poets. London: Longman.

———. 1972. *Tennyson.* Masters of World Literature. London: Macmillan.

———. 1974. "Gigantist." (*EOS*) *New York Review of Books* (4 Apr.): 19-20.

RICOEUR, Paul. 1978. "The Metaphorical Process as Cognition, Imagination, and Feeling." *Critical Inquiry* 5.1: 143-59.

RIEDEL, F.C. 1957. "Faulkner as Stylist." *South Atlantic Quarterly* 56: 462-79.

RIEMER, A.P. 1974. "The Eye of the Needle: Patrick White's Recent Novels." *Southerly* 34.2: 248-66.

RIFFATERRE, Michael. 1959. "Criteria for Style Analysis." *Word: Journal of the Linguistic Circle of New York* 15.1: 154-74. Cited from CHATMAN/LEVIN 1967: 412-30.

——. 1971. ("Criteria"), tr. Daniel Delas, in RIFFATERRE, *Essais de stylistique structurale* (Paris: Flammarion). Cited from WARNING 1975: 163-95. ("Kriterien für die Stilanalyse," from RIFFATERRE, *Strukturale Stilistik*, tr. Wilhelm Bolle (Munich: List, 1973): 29-59, 284-92.) Includes useful addenda by the author to his original article of 1959.

——. 1980. "Syllepsis." *Critical Inquiry* 6.4: 625-38.

RIMMON, Shlomith. 1976. "A Comprehensive Theory of Narrative: Genette's *Figures III* and the Structuralist Study of Fiction." *PTL: A Journal for Descriptive Poetics and Theory of Literature* 1: 33-62.

RIMMON-KENAN, Shlomith. 1983. *Narrative Fiction: Contemporary Poetics.* New Accents series. London: Macmillan.

RODERICK, Colin. 1962. "*Riders in the Chariot*: An Exposition." *Southerly* 22.2: 62-77.

ROMBERG, Bertil. 1962. *Studies in the Narrative Technique of the First-Person Novel.* Lund: Håkan Ohlssons Boktryckeri.

ROSENTHAL, T.G. 1970. "Portrait of an Artist." (*Viv*) *New Statesman* 80 (23 Oct.): 536-38.

ROSS, Bruce A. Clunies. 1981. "Some Developments in Short Fiction, 1969-1980." *Australian Literary Studies* 10.2: 165-80.

ROSS, Robert. 1977. "Patrick White's *A Fringe of Leaves*." *World Literature Written in English* 16.2: 324-25.

RUNDALL, Jeremy. 1964. "Characters Sapped by the Sun." (*BO*) *Sunday Times* (4 Oct.): 49.

RUTHROF, Horst. 1981. *The Reader's Construction of Narrative.* London: Routledge & Kegan Paul.

SALOMON, Louis B. 1940. "Newcomer From Australia." (*HV*) *Nation* 151.10 (7 Sept.): 198.

——. 1941. "As Though to Breathe Were Life." (*LAD*) *Nation* 152.10 (8 March): 276.

SARTRE, Jean-Paul. 1947. "Time in Faulkner: *The Sound and the Fury*," tr. Martine Darmon ("A propos de *Le Bruit et la Fureur*—La temporalité chez Faulkner," in Sartre, *Situations I*, Paris: Gallimard: 70-81; originally in *La Nouvelle Revue Française* 52-53 (1939)). Cited from HOFFMAN/VICKERY 1960: 225-32.

SCHEICK, William J. 1979. "The Gothic Graces and Rainbow Aesthetic of Patrick White's Fiction: An Introduction." *Texas Studies in Language and Literature* 21.2: 130-46.

SCHERMBRUCKER, William Gerald. 1973. "Strange Textures of Vision: A Study of the Significance of Mannered Fictional Techniques in Six Related Novels of D.H. Lawrence, William Faulkner, and Patrick White, Together with a Theoretical Introduction on 'The Novel of Vision'." Unpublished doctoral dissertation, University of British Columbia.

SCOTT, J.D. 1966. "Symbol of Totality." (*SM*) *New York Times Book Review* (13 Feb.): 49.

SCRUTTON, Mary. 1956. "New Novels." (*TOM*) *New Statesman* 51 (28 April): 460.

SEMMLER, Clement. 1967, ed. *Twentieth Century Australian Literary Criticism.* Melbourne: Oxford UP.

SEYMOUR-SMITH, Martin. 1990. (Obituary notice on White.) *Sunday Times* (7 Oct.).

SHARRAD, Paul. 1984. "*Pour mieux sauter*: Christopher Koch's Novels in Relation to White, Stow and the Quest for a Post-Colonial Fiction." *World Literature Written in English* 23.1: 208-23.

SHEARMAN, John. 1967. *Mannerism.* Style and Civlization series. Harmondsworth: Penguin.

SHEPHERD, Ron & Kirpal SINGH. 1978, eds. *Patrick White: A Critical Symposium*, intro. John Barnes. Adelaide: Centre for Research in the New Literatures in English.

SHKLOVSKY, Viktor. 1916. "Die Kunst als Verfahren," in STRIEDTER 1981: 3-35.

SHORT, R.W. 1946. "The Sentence Structure of Henry James." *American Literature* 18: 71-88.

SHRIBER, Michael. 1969. "Cognitive Apparatus in *Daisy Miller, The Ambassadors* and Two Works by Howells: A Comparative Study of the Epistemology of Henry James." *Language and Style* 2: 207-25.

SHRUBB, Peter. 1968. "Patrick White: Chaos Accepted." (V) *Quadrant* 12.3: 7-19.

SLATOFF, Walter J. 1957. "The Edge of Order: The Pattern of Faulkner's Rhetoric." *Twentieth Century Literature* 3 (Oct.): 107-27. Cited from HOFFMAN/VICKERY 1960: 173-98.

SMITH, Derek. 1975. "Patrick White's Poetical Motivation: Imagery and Colour in *Voss*." Mimeographed. *A.L.S. Working Papers* (Adelaide University School of English Language and Literature) 1.2: 68-77.

SMITH, Grover. 1960. *T.S. Eliot's Poetry and Plays: A Study in Sources and Meaning*. Rev. ed. Phoenix Books. Chicago: U of Chicago P.

SMITH, Terry. 1972. "A Portrait of the Artist in Patrick White's *The Vivisector*." *Meanjin* 31.2: 167-77.

SONTAG, Susan. 1965. "On Style," in SONTAG, *Against Interpretation*. Cited from SONTAG, *A Susan Sontag Reader*, intro. Elizabeth Hardwick (Harmondsworth: Penguin, 1983): 137-55.

SOUTHRON, Jane Spence. 1940. "A Novel of Life in New South Wales." (HV) *New York Times Book Review* (26 May): 7.

SPINUCCI, Pietro. 1979. "Patrick White in Italy." Mimeographed. *Australian Literature Bulletin* (Venice) 2.1: 40-48.

SPITZER, Leo. 1948. *Linguistics and Literary History*. Princeton NJ: Princeton UP.

STANZEL, Franz K. 1982. *Theorie des Erzählens*. 2nd rev. ed. UTB series 904. Göttingen: Vandenhoeck & Ruprecht.

STEIN, Thomas M. 1983. *Patrick White: "Voss"*. Text und Geschichte 4, UTB series 1155. Munich: Wilhelm Fink.

STEINER, George. 1974. "Carnal Knowledge." (EOS) *New Yorker* 50.12 (24 Mar.): 109-113.

STERN, James. 1948. "Spinster Aunt From Down Under." (AS) *New York Times Book Review* (11 Jan.): 5, 33.

———. 1958. "Patrick White: The Country of the Mind." (V) *London Magazine* 5.6: 49-56.

STERNBERG, Meir. 1978. *Expositional Modes and Temporal Ordering in Fiction*. Baltimore MD: Johns Hopkins UP.

STEVENSON, Lionel. 1948. "The 'High-born maiden' Symbol in Tennyson." *PMLA* 67. Cited from KILLHAM 1960.

STEVICK, Philip. 1962, ed. *The Theory of the Novel*. New York: Free Press & Collier-Macmillan.

STEWART, Douglas. 1956. "*The Tree of Man*." *Bulletin* (Sydney) 77 (18 July): 2, 35.

STILWELL, Robert L. 1964. "A Dangerous Spark of Life." (BO) *Saturday Review* 47.44 (31 Oct.): 54.

STOW, Randolph. 1963. *Tourmaline*. Harmondsworth: Penguin, 1965.

ST. PIERRE, Paul M. 1978. "Coterminous Beginnings," in SHEPHERD/ SINGH 1978: 99-107.

STRANG, Barbara M.H. 1968. *Modern English Structure*. 2nd ed. London: Edward Arnold.

STRIEDTER, Jurij. 1981, ed. *Russischer Formalismus: Texte zur allgemeinen Literaturtheorie und zur Theorie der Prosa*. 1st ed. 1969; 3rd impr. UTB series 40. Munich: Wilhelm Fink.

SWINK, Helen. 1972. "William Faulkner: The Novelist as Oral Narrator." *Georgia Review* 26: 183-209.

SYMONS, Julian. 1970. "An Artist Worthy of His Art." (*Viv*) *Sunday Times* (25 Oct.): 32.

TACEY, David. 1976. "The Secret of the Black Rose: Spiritual Alchemy in Patrick White's *The Aunt's Story*." Mimeographed. *A.L.S. Working Papers* (Adelaide University School of English Language and Literature) 2.2: 36-78.

———. 1988. *Patrick White: Fiction and the Unconscious*. Melbourne: Oxford UP.

TAMIR, Nomi. 1976. "Personal Narrative and its Linguistic Foundation." *PTL: A Journal for Descriptive Poetics and Theory of Literature* 1: 403-29.

TANNER, Tony. 1966. (Review of *SM*) *London Magazine* New Series 6.3: 112-17.

TAUBMAN, Robert. 1979. "He or She." (*TA*) *London Review of Books* 1.2 (8 Nov.): 10.

THOMSON, A.K. 1966. "Patrick White's *The Tree of Man*." *Meanjin* 25.1: 21-30.

THE TIMES (London). 1939. "New Novels: The Lovable in Fiction." (*HV*) 10 March: 22.

———. 1956. "New Fiction." (*TOM*) 3 May: 13.

———. 1957. "New Fiction." (*V*) 5 December: 13.

———. 1958. "New Fiction." (*AS*) 18 December: 13.

———. 1962. "New Fiction." (*LAD*) 8 November: 15.

———. 1964. "New Fiction." (*BO*) 8 October: 15.

———. 1966. "New Fiction." (*SM*) 19 May: 18.

TLS: TIMES LITERARY SUPPLEMENT. 1941. "Novels of the Week: Poetry or Plot?" (*LAD*) 5 July: 321.

———. 1945. "The New Australian Vision: Promise of a New Literature." (*HV*) 31 March: 150.

———. 1948. "Small-Town Talk." (*AS*) 2 October: 553.

———. 1956. (Review of *TOM*) 8 June: 341.

———. 1957. "Through Barriers of Time and Place." (*V*) 13 December: 753.

———. 1961. "Attempting the Infinite." (esp. *RITC*) 15 December: 889-91.

———. 1962. "The Two Ways." (*LAD*) 16 November: 869.

———. 1964. "Sparks From a Burning Wheel." (*BO*) 22 October: 953.

———. 1966. "Reading the Marbles." (*SM*) 9 June: 509.

———. 1970. "Painter and Decorator." (*Viv*) 23 October: 1213.

———. 1973. "High Wind in Australia." (*EOS*) 21 September: 1072.

TODOROV, Tzvetan. 1971. "The Place of Style in the Structure of the Text," in CHATMAN 1971: 29-44.

TOUT-SMITH, Geoffrey. 1979. "Nightmare Uncertainties." (*TA*) *Overland* 78: 65-67.

TRAUGOTT, Elizabeth Closs & Mary Louise PRATT. 1980. *Linguistics for Students of Literature*. New York: Harcourt Brace Jovanovich.

TURNER, G.W. 1973. *Stylistics*. Harmondsworth: Penguin.

TURNER, Ian. 1958. "The Parable of *Voss*." *Overland* 12 (June): 36-37.

TURNER, Paul. 1976. *Tennyson*. London: Routledge & Kegan Paul.

ULICH, Michaela. 1972. *Perspektive und Erzählstruktur in William Faulkners Romanen von "The Sound and the Fury" bis "Intruder in the Dust"*. Heidelberg: Carl Winter.

USPENSKY, Boris. 1975. *Poetik der Komposition: Struktur des künstlerischen Textes und Typologie der Kompositionsform*, tr. Georg Mayer (*Poetika kompozitsij*, Moscow 1970), ed. Karl Eimermacher. Edition suhrkamp 678. Frankfurt am Main: Suhrkamp.

VOLPE, Edmond L. 1964. *A Reader's Guide to William Faulkner*. London: Thames & Hudson.

WALL, Stephen. 1970. "Hero of Art." (*Viv*)*Observer* (25 Oct.): 34.

WALSH, William. 1969. "Patrick White's Vision of Human Incompleteness." *Journal of Commonwealth Literature* 7 (July): 127-32. Cited from WALSH, ed. *Readings in Commonwealth Literature* (Oxford: Oxford UP, 1973): 420-25.

———. 1973. "Mortal Coils." (*EOS*) *New Statesman* (7 Sept.): 320.

———. 1974. "Fiction as Metaphor: The Novels of Patrick White." *Sewanee Review* 82: 197-211.

———. 1976. *Patrick White: "Voss"*. Studies in English Literature 62. London: Edward Arnold.

———. 1977. *Patrick White's Fiction*. Totowa NJ: Rowman & Littlefield.

WALTERS, Margaret. 1963. "Patrick White." *New Left Review* 8.1: 37-50.

WARDLE, Irving. 1966. "New Novels: Back to Sarsaparilla." (*SM*) *Observer* (15 May): 26.

WARNING, Rainer. 1975, ed. *Rezeptionsästhetik: Theorie und Praxis*. UTB series 303. Munich: Wilhelm Fink.

WARREN, Robert Penn. 1966, ed. *Faulkner: A Collection of Critical Essays*. Twentieth Century Views. Englewood Cliffs NJ: Prentice-Hall.

WATSON, Betty L. 1971. "Patrick White, Some Lines of Development: *The Living and the Dead* and *The Solid Mandala*." *Australian Literary Studies* 5.2: 158-67.

WATT, Ian. 1960. "The First Paragraph of *The Ambassadors*: An Explication." *Essays in Criticism* 10: 250-74. Cited from Tony TANNER, ed. *Henry James: Modern Judgements* (London: Macmillan: 1968): 283-303.

WATTS, Cedric. 1983. "Bottom's Children: The Fallacies of Structuralist, Poststructuralist and Deconstructionist Literary Theory," in LERNER 1983: 20-35.

WEBER, Robert Wilhelm. 1969. *Die Aussage der Form: Zur Textur und Struktur des Bewußtseinsromans, dargestellt an W(illiam) Faulkners "The Sound and the Fury"*. Heidelberg: Carl Winter.

WHALEY, Susan. 1983. "Food for Thought in Patrick White's Fiction." *World Literature Written in English* 22.2: 197-212.

WHITE, Patrick. (Editions consulted or cited = *.)

———. 1939. *Happy Valley*. London: *George G. Harrap. (*HV*)

———. 1941. *The Living and the Dead*. New York: Viking Press. Harmondsworth: *Penguin, 1968. (*LAD*)

———. 1948. *The Aunt's Story*. London: Routledge & Kegan Paul. London: Eyre & Spottiswoode, 1958. Harmondsworth: *Penguin, 1963. (*AS*)

———. 1955. *The Tree of Man*. New York: Viking Press. London: Eyre & Spottiswoode, 1956. Harmondsworth: *Penguin, 1961. London: Cape, 1976. (*TOM*)

———. 1957. *Voss*. New York: *Viking Press. London: *Eyre & Spottiswoode, 1957. Harmondsworth: *Penguin, 1960. (*V*)

———. 1958. "The Prodigal Son." *Australian Letters* 1.3: 39-40. Cited from Geoffrey DUTTON & Max HARRIS, eds., *The Vital Decade* (Melbourne: Sun, 1968): 156-58.

——. 1961. *Riders in the Chariot*. New York: *Viking Press. London: Eyre & Spottiswoode, 1961. Harmondsworth: *Penguin, 1964. (*RITC*)

——. 1964. *The Burnt Ones*. London: Eyre & Spottiswoode. Harmondsworth: *Penguin, 1968. (*BO*)

——. 1966. *The Solid Mandala*. London: *Eyre & Spottiswoode. New York: *Viking, 1966. Harmondsworth: *Penguin, 1969. London: *Jonathan Cape, 1976. (*SM*)

——. 1969. (Interview in:) Craig MCGREGOR, ed. *In the Making* (Melbourne: Thomas Nelson, 1969): 218-22.

——. 1970. *The Vivisector*. New York: *Viking Press. Harmondsworth: *Penguin, 1973. (*Viv*)

——. 1973. *The Eye of the Storm*. London: *Jonathan Cape. (*EOS*)

——. 1973. "A Conversation with Patrick White," intv. Thelma HERRING & G.A. WILKES. *Southerly* 33.2: 132-43.

——. 1976. *A Fringe of Leaves*. London: *Jonathan Cape. (*FOL*)

——. 1979. *The Twyborn Affair*. London: *Jonathan Cape. (*TA*)

——. 1981. *Flaws in the Glass: A Self-Portrait*. London: *Jonathan Cape. (*Flaws*)

——. 1982. (Interview with Michael BILLINGTON, including comments by Margaret Jones and Peter Porter.) Personal transcript. *Meridian*, BBC World Service.

——. 1986. *Memoirs of Many in One, by Alex Xenophon Demirjian Gray*. London: *Jonathan Cape.

——. 1988. *Three Uneasy Pieces* (1987). London: *Jonathan Cape.

WILKES, G.A. 1969a. "An Approach to Patrick White's *Solid Mandala*." *Southerly* 29.2: 97-100.

——. 1969b. *Australian Literature: A Conspectus*. Sydney: Angus & Robertson: 87-96.

——. 1970, ed. *Ten Essays on Patrick White: Selected from "Southerly" (1964-67)*. Sydney: Angus & Robertson.

WILSON, Angus. 1961. "The Lives of the Saints of Sarsaparilla." (*RITC*) *Observer* (29 Oct.): 30.

WILSON, Richard B.J. 1976. "The Rhetoric of Patrick White's 'Down at the Dump'," in CANTRELL 1976: 281-88.

WIMSATT, W.K., Jr. 1941. *The Prose Style of Samuel Johnson*. Yale Studies in English 94. New Haven CT: Yale UP. Cited from CHATMAN/LEVIN 1967: 362-73.

WOLFE, Peter. 1983 (for 1984). *Laden Choirs: The Fiction of Patrick White*. Lexington: UP of Kentucky.

WOOLF, Virginia. 1922. *Jacob's Room*. Harmondsworth: Penguin Books, 1965.

WYNDHAM, Francis. 1957. "New Novels." (*V*) *Spectator* 199 (13 Dec.): 844.

YAFFE, James. 1958. "Three Foreign Novels." (*V*) *Yale Review* 47.3: 463-44.

ZANDVOORT, R.W. 1972. *A Handbook of English Grammar*. 6th rev. ed. London: Longman.

ZOELLNER, Robert H. 1959. "Faulkner's Prose Style in *Absalom, Absalom!*" *American Literature* 30: 486-502.

INDEX

Note: The Index lists only terms relating to style, narrative discourse, language and interpretation which are mentioned, defined and discussed in the present study; as many such terms recur often in the course of the detailed discussion of text-passages, these occurrences are listed selectively, not exhaustively. Apart from White's own works, references to specific comparative texts are generally subsumed without specification under the names of the authors. Also included in the Index are most references (in main text and notes) to the secondary literature cited.